WEST ACADEMIC PUBLISHING'S EMERITUS ADVISORY BOARD

CORPORATE INCOME TAX ACCOUNTING

Christopher H. Hanna
Alan D. Feld Endowed Professor of Law
Southern Methodist University
Dedman School of Law

Paul H. Yong
Vice President, Chief Tax Counsel, Sempra Energy Corporation
Professor of Practice, University of San Diego School of Law
Director of Graduate Tax Programs, University of San Diego School of Law

Mark P. Thomas
Principal
PricewaterhouseCoopers LLP

HORNBOOK SERIES®

WEST ACADEMIC PUBLISHING

860 Blue Gentian Road, Suite 350
Eagan, MN 55121
1-877-888-1330

Printed in the United States of America

ISBN: 978-1-68561-274-0

To our late friend, Cym H. Lowell

Summary of Contents

Table of Contents

CORPORATE INCOME TAX ACCOUNTING

Chapter 1

Introduction

Table of Sections

§ 1.01 Traditional Domain of Financial Accounting—Tax Overlap

Accounting for income taxes has become a critically important issue for both financial accounting and income taxation in recent years.[1] However, there is nothing new about the need to account for income taxes for purposes of presenting, or to opine upon, the financial accounts of corporations or other business entities. The process of accounting for tax matters has been a traditional aspect of the responsibilities of finance and taxation officers of business entities, particularly publicly traded corporations, for as long as anyone writing this text can remember.

The nature of the process has long been familiar. In essence, there are a number of parties in this process: (i) business entities, (ii) tax administrations, (iii) financial accounting standards organizations, (iv) auditors of the business entities, and (v) tax strategists seeking to achieve overall tax/accounting results for business entities—perhaps a low effective tax rate. Each party has its own interests. Until very recently, the relationships among these parties were designed in a way that there was room for significant arbitrage at the intersection of the tax and financial accounting worlds. Recent events have changed this configuration. Nonetheless, we will begin with the traditional situation.

[1] Traditional Posture of Entities and Tax Administrations

The traditional posture of entities and tax administrations, whether the U.S. Internal Revenue Service (referred to as the IRS or the Service), state or local tax agencies, or foreign tax agencies, follows.

---

[1] We note that the principal focus of this publication is on corporate income tax accounting with respect to U.S. federal income taxes on the basis of U.S. generally accepted accounting principles (GAAP). Similar issues exist with respect to state and local income taxes. In addition, the concepts discussed will also have application for purposes of a U.S. company accounting for foreign income taxes, consumption taxes, value-added taxes and other taxes.

[a] Entities: Effective Tax Rate Minimization

From the standpoint of a business entity, an important element of taxation and financial accounting concerns its effective tax rate. In the intensely competitive world that we live in, tax is, from the standpoint of most business entities, simply a cost of doing business which, like all costs, must be minimized in order to avoid allowing a competitor to obtain a competitive advantage due to a lower effective tax rate (i.e., a lower cost structure.) In addition, an entity reporting a high effective tax rate relative to its competitors may find itself the target of an acquisition in which the acquirer believes it can lower the target entity's effective tax rate. The effective tax rate is, in turn, important for a variety of purposes for the entity. First, and foremost, is the impact on reported earnings per share (EPS) which, in many cases, drives the market value of the entity. The financial markets will carefully analyze the entity's effective tax rate in situations where there are significant variations from the expected effective tax rate. Of greatest concern to financial analysts is the determination of whether an unusually high or low effective tax rate will be sustained in the future or is it simply the result of a one-time event. Analysis of the effective tax rate then becomes a quality of earnings issue, and sophisticated analysis will value an entity based on a normalized effective tax rate rather than a one-time aberration.

A second element is the use of cash required to pay the tax liability. Frequently, there will be a substantial variance between the current year's tax expense and the cash tax liability. These deviations can arise as a result of a number of situations. For example, the accrual of an unfunded liability, such as future warranty expense, product liability or retiree medical expense, will lead to a cash tax liability in excess of the income tax expense reflected in the effective tax rate for financial accounting.

A third element is financial certainty. Establishment of a reserve for financial accounting with respect to potential uncertainties of reported tax positions will be reflected in an increased income tax expense.

[b] Tax Administrations: Tax Base Defense

From the standpoint of each tax administration, the overall objective is to ensure that the appropriate tax liabilities of entities in its jurisdiction are being paid. In essence, the critical concern of tax administrations is to make sure that their tax base is defended. After all, it is the tax base that provides the financial wherewithal for the provision of health and safety, transportation and all of the other public services of the pertinent jurisdiction.

Accordingly, the tax administrations are responsible for protecting their tax base, as well as assuring equity between entities in terms of satisfaction of their respective obligations. In this regard, tax administrations have a vital interest in auditing tax returns to assure that reasonable levels of compliance are being enforced.

In February 2013, the Organisation for Economic Co-operation and Development (OECD) initiated a tax base defense project named Base Erosion and Profit Shifting (BEPS) to look at whether, and if so why, the then-current tax rules allow for the allocation of profits to countries different from those where the actual business activities take place. In July 2013, the OECD released its action plan for the BEPS project. On October 5, 2015, the OECD presented its final package of measures to provide "governments with solutions for closing the gaps in existing international tax rules that allow corporate profits to 'disappear' or be artificially shifted to low/no tax environments, where little or no economic activity takes place." In mid-2017, several of the BEPS actions were incorporated in a multilateral instrument (MLI) currently (October 1, 2022) signed by 100 jurisdictions (but not the United States) intended to amend the thousands of treaties among signatory countries. The MLI entered into force on July 1, 2018.

In early 2019, the OECD began work on BEPS 2.0—a two-pillar framework for taxing multinationals. The BEPS 2.0 project began as an outgrowth of Article One of the first BEPS project (referred to as BEPS 1.0), which dealt with taxing the digital economy. The first pillar of BEPS 2.0 involves revisions to existing profit allocation and nexus rules to redistribute taxing rights to market jurisdictions. The second pillar involves the development of new global anti-base erosion rules to ensure that all business income is subject to at least a minimum level of taxation (currently set at 15 percent). As of October 1, 2022, the OECD's work on BEPS 2.0 was ongoing with countries considering adopting the second pillar (global minimum tax of 15 percent) in their domestic legislation.

These developments, as well as tax reform in the United States and around the world, are evolving and will be pertinent to many of the topics addressed in this book.

[2] Financial Accounting Principles

A for-profit entity's income is generally subject to federal, state and local income taxes each year. As a result, an entity must compute its income for tax purposes in accordance with the applicable tax statutes and regulations. The resulting income figure is referred to as taxable income. An entity must also compute its income for financial accounting purposes each year in accordance with generally accepted accounting principles (GAAP). The resulting income figure is referred to as pretax financial income or pretax book income (PTBI). In almost all cases, an entity's taxable income will differ from its pretax financial income. This difference primarily reflects the different objectives behind the tax rules and the accounting rules.

The differences between taxable income and pretax financial income give rise to tax differences. Some of these differences are permanent differences and others are temporary differences (previously referred to as timing differences). In accounting for such differences in the financial statements, a number of approaches were considered by the Financial Accounting Standards Board (FASB). The approach that has been adopted by FASB to account for income taxes is a comprehensive approach in which income tax expense includes the tax effects of all transactions entering into the determination of pretax financial income for the period. In other words, the current accounting period will reflect all income taxes arising from the current pretax financial income, regardless of when the taxes are paid.

FASB issued SFAS No. 109, *Accounting for Income Taxes* (later codified in FASB ASC 740), in February 1992. The purpose of FASB ASC 740 is to address financial accounting and reporting for income taxes that are currently payable and for the tax consequences of: (a) revenues, expenses, gains or losses that are included in taxable income in either an earlier or later year than the year in which they are recognized in pretax financial income, (b) other events that create differences between the tax bases of assets and liabilities and their amounts for financial reporting, and (c) net operating loss or tax credit carrybacks for refunds of taxes paid in prior years and carryforwards to reduce taxes payable in future years. FASB recognized that some aspects of accounting for income taxes, such as judging whether a valuation allowance is needed for deferred tax assets, may be complex but felt that the complexity is the unavoidable result of the need for an informed decision about the effect of income taxes on an entity's financial position and results of operations.

FASB ASC 740 applies to federal, state and local income taxes as well as foreign income taxes. In addition, it applies to an entity's domestic and foreign operations that are consolidated, combined, or accounted for by the equity method, in preparing financial statements in accordance with GAAP.

[3] Accounting for Tax Positions

In preparing the financial statements, finance officers apply the appropriate principles from GAAP. When accounting for income tax expense, current taxes payable (or receivable), and deferred taxes, it is necessary to begin with the expected treatment on the entity's tax return(s), which would normally be filed within a few months following the release of the financial statements. One aspect of income tax return preparation in the traditional context was determination of the position that was to be taken by the entity in reporting its tax liability. In this regard, the entity may have undertaken a transaction during the year. The entity would determine that the transaction should be treated as having no recognized gain or loss for tax purposes. On the other hand, it would recognize that the taxing administration may take a different position. The entity might believe that it had a reasonable basis to take the position on its tax return, and would prevail in the event of a controversy with the tax administration over the issue. As a result, it reports its income tax liability consistent with this position.

When determining the financial results of the entity, the finance officer undertakes to compute the income tax expense of the period, by applying appropriate GAAP principles. To the extent that there will be differences between the income tax return presentation of the results and the treatment of such items for financial statement presentation purposes, the entity will establish a reserve or provision against earnings for the potential liability. When filing the tax return(s) for the period, differences between the tax and financial accounting treatment of specific matters will be reported on an appropriate schedule (a Schedule M-1 or M-3 in the case of U.S. federal income tax returns) along with other permanent and temporary differences.

This situation is illustrated in Illustration 1-1:

ILLUSTRATION 1-1: USCo is a U.S.-based multinational enterprise (MNE) operating a worldwide manufacturing, distribution and servicing business relating to unique products (Unique Products). In Year A, USCo acquired a competitor, TargetCo, in a transaction that was intended to be a tax-free reorganization for U.S. income tax purposes. USCo obtained an opinion from an external tax advisor that there was a reasonable basis to believe that the transaction was a tax-free reorganization. USCo filed its U.S. income tax return for Year A on the basis that the transaction was a tax-free reorganization.

In preparing the financial statements for USCo for the same period, the finance officers of USCo believed that there was a risk that the tax authority (in this case, the IRS) could determine that the transaction was taxable. If such a position were to be sustained, the resultant tax would, when paid in a subsequent period when the matter is finally determined, have a material impact upon the financial results of USCo's operations. While the likelihood that the IRS could prevail in the matter was uncertain, the USCo finance officers determined that the financial statement income of USCo should be reduced by an appropriate amount to reflect this potential liability. Prior to the implementation of FIN 48 (FASB ASC 740–10), such a provision was colloquially referred to as a tax reserve or tax cushion. In this situation, the finance officers determined that an appropriate cushion would be determined as 30 percent of the potential tax, interest and penalty exposure. The figure of 30 percent was derived by assuming that the external advisor's opinion established a 60 percent likelihood of success, meaning that there was a 40 percent chance of ultimately not prevailing on the issue and by reflecting the benefit of increased deductions for depreciation and amortization in the event the transaction is ultimately held to be taxable (i.e., cost basis rather than carryover basis for tax purposes). The cushion for the transaction was one of many such provisions established by USCo for its Year A results.

These are the traditional elements of financial accounting for tax positions. In recent years, such principles have undergone significant evolution, perhaps fairly described as a revolution, in this arcane world of the intersection of financial accounting and taxation.

§ 1.02 Legislative, Regulatory and Financial Accounting Developments

[1] Response to Corporate Scandals and Tax Shelters

The traditional principles began changing as the financial institutions and professional bodies reacted to the financial scandals of the late 1990s and early years of the twenty-first century. In 2002, the U.S. Congress reacted to the financial scandals of Enron, WorldCom, Tyco and others by enacting the Sarbanes-Oxley Act (SOX). SOX Section 404 requires a company to establish that it has controls in place to ensure accurate financial reporting. It also requires the entity's auditor to attest to the company's internal control over financial reporting. Because matters of taxation are a significant potential exposure for all entities, an obvious source of concern for entities is whether effective controls are in place to deal with such exposures.

At about the same time as SOX was enacted, the U.S. Congress, the U.S. Securities and Exchange Commission (SEC) and the U.S. Treasury (Treasury) were all appropriately concerned about the independence of auditors. The death of Arthur Andersen LLP, shocking revelations of apparent complicity with the financial shenanigans in the financial scandals, as well as the perceived inability of the public to trust the accounting firms or profession to police itself, led to the establishment of the Public Company Accounting Oversight Board (the PCAOB). As a result of SOX and PCAOB directives, many companies stopped using their auditor for tax services.

A further element of the financial scandals of the late 1990s and early 2000s related to the proliferation of tax shelters, promoted by accounting firms, financial firms, law firms and other promoters. This led to litigation by the IRS under the phalanx of anti-tax shelter provisions in the Internal Revenue Code, seeking to impose liability, penalties and sanctions on perceived promoters. There was also litigation by taxpayers as the IRS succeeded in shutting down many of the most egregious tax shelter schemes.

While the legal and accounting professions were, appropriately, aghast at the activities of their members that were otherwise perceived to be in good standing, there was little progress in the way of appropriate upgrading of ethical obligations of professional members. On the other hand, the Treasury undertook a review of the ethical standards of practice before the Treasury, resulting in the restatement of Circular 230. There are now much stricter requirements for opinions relating to tax shelters, as well as any opinion depending upon the level of opinion being provided. Circular 230 is applicable to lawyers, accountants and others practicing before the Treasury, which includes the IRS. While the new requirements are still being digested, it is inevitable that they will have an impact on all forms of tax advice, including the nature of opinions rendered by external consultants to companies.

A traditional means of achieving confidentiality in the structuring of tax reporting positions of companies has been utilization of attorneys, whose communications have traditionally been protected by the attorney-client privilege and related doctrines. The evolutions summarized above have also had an impact on the extent to which there is attorney-client privilege relating to advice concerning tax and financial accounting matters.

[2] Accounting for Uncertain Income Tax Positions

In June 2006, the FASB interpretation on accounting for uncertain tax positions was released as FIN 48 (FASB Interpretation No. 48). This was another of the seemingly continuous flow of efforts to ameliorate the consequences to investors of the corporate scandals of the past. The scandals included tax shelters, auditing firms' selling of tax shelters, and the subjectivity that various players employed in booking tax reserves. These elements presented tremendous opportunities for companies to manage earnings. Quite a few companies engaged in tax shelters to hype earnings, achieve a higher stock price (as with the round-tripping of sales to hype earnings), and convince Wall Street that the projected lower effective tax rates would be ongoing (because management intended to continue the tax shelter process, encouraged by the auditing firms that benefitted from the process and accepted management's assertions).

The reason for releasing FIN 48 was to provide specific guidance on how to address accounting for uncertain tax positions. FIN 48 (later codified in FASB ASC 740–10) was an interpretation of SFAS No. 109 (later codified in FASB ASC 740), which addressed many issues concerning accounting for income taxes, but contained no specific guidance on accounting for uncertain tax positions.

In principle, the validity of a tax position is a matter of tax law. It is not controversial to recognize the benefit of a tax position in an entity's financial statements when the degree of confidence is high that that tax position will be sustained upon examination by a taxing authority. However, in some cases, the law is subject to varied interpretations, and whether a tax position will be sustained may be uncertain. Diverse accounting practices had developed resulting in inconsistency in the criteria used to recognize, derecognize, and measure benefits related to accounting for income taxes. This diversity in practice resulted in non-comparability in reporting income tax expense, current taxes payable (or receivable), deferred taxes, and tax reserves (or cushions).

FASB ASC 740–10 (FIN 48) prescribes financial statement guidelines for recognizing and measuring tax positions taken or expected to be taken in a tax return. Evaluation of a tax position in accordance with FASB ASC 740–10 is a two-step process.

The first step is recognition: The entity must determine whether it is more likely than not that a tax position will be sustained upon examination, including resolution of any related appeals or litigation processes, based on the technical merits of the position. In evaluating whether a tax position meets this recognition threshold, the entity should presume that the position will be examined by the appropriate taxing authority that has full knowledge of all relevant information.

The second step is measurement: A tax position that meets the more-likely-than-not recognition threshold is measured to determine the amount of benefit to recognize in the financial statements. The tax position is measured at the largest amount of benefit that has a greater than 50 percent likelihood of being realized upon settlement.

In general, differences between tax positions taken in a tax return and amounts recognized in the financial statements will result in one of the following:

1. An increase in a liability for income taxes payable or a reduction of an income tax (refund) receivable;
2. A reduction in a deferred tax asset or an increase in a deferred tax liability; or
3. Both 1. and 2.

FASB ASC 740–10 also provides guidance on derecognition, classification, interest and penalties, disclosure, and transition rules.

At the very least, it is fair to say that financial accounting for uncertain tax positions has become transparent as a practical matter. This transparency has, in turn, changed the nature of how tax opinions are rendered and received. It has also changed the nature of the tax authority examination and audit procedures, in light of the vast range of information that the IRS knows has been prepared.

The IRS created the Schedule UTP (Form 1120), Uncertain Tax Position Statement, for corporations to report uncertain tax positions. The first year Schedule UTP was required to be filed was 2010, and it was required only for corporations with assets equaling or exceeding $100 million. For 2012, the asset threshold for filing Schedule UTP was decreased from $100 million to $50 million. The asset threshold decreased to $10 million beginning in 2014, where it has remained.

§ 1.03 U.S. and Global Tax Evolutions

A wave of potential tax reforms around the world could impact many of the subjects in *Corporate Income Tax Accounting*. Broadly stated, the overall focus of these reforms is to generate activity in each jurisdiction (which inevitably may be a zero-sum matter with other jurisdictions) and to protect the domestic tax base from competition by other jurisdictions.

[1] U.S. Considerations

U.S. tax reform finally occurred in 2017 with the Tax Cuts and Jobs Act (TCJA). The headline from a corporate standpoint was the reduction of the maximum corporate tax rate from 35 percent to a single 21 percent rate beginning in 2018. In the international context, the TCJA (i) embraces a hybrid territorial/worldwide tax system with the U.S. becoming the first country to annually tax the active foreign business earnings of foreign subsidiaries (the global intangible low-taxed income or GILTI regime), (ii) seeks to protect the U.S. tax base from cross-border erosion (the base erosion and anti-abuse tax or BEAT regime), and (iii) enacts an incentive for economic investment in the U.S. (the foreign-derived intangible income or FDII regime) at a globally attractive effective tax rate of 13.125 percent.

The TCJA reflects the U.S. response to some of the issues framed by the G-20/OECD BEPS project. Similar to other countries, including that of the United Kingdom (UK), India, and Australia (and, potentially, the European Union), the U.S. Congress addressed the issues of principal importance from the U.S.'s tax base enhancement and protection standpoints.

There are a variety of provisions relating to cross-border activity (outbound from and inbound to the U.S.) that will have a substantial impact on transactional flows and the future effective tax rate (ETR) of all MNEs with activities in the U.S., as explained below.

In view of the dramatic changes in the TCJA, as well as the range of international taxation considerations under way, MNEs may want to consider approaching their home country tax authorities seeking a global tax agreement (perhaps in exchange for commitments about maintaining or expanding economic activity in the home country).

[2] The OECD, UN, EU, and Specific Country Considerations

A process similar to the U.S. reforms is underway throughout the world. The so-called BEPS 2.0 process is noted above in this chapter. It provides another stark illustration of the nature of the international taxation challenges that could be on the horizon. In fact, elements of TCJA, such as GILTI and BEAT, were the inspiration for BEPS 2.0.

While the BEPS 2.0 process could be seen as a unifying international evolution, it is still merely a beginning. The multilateral instrument that grew out of BEPS 1.0 has been signed by 100 jurisdictions (but not the United States), many of which made reservations and opt-outs that will severely complicate the actual resolution of country-specific adjustments. In addition, many countries have adopted unilateral regimes (such as the diverted profits tax (DPT)) in the U.K. and Australia, the equalization levy in India, and digital services taxes (DSTs) in various countries, such as France and the U.K.

The United Nations (UN) has undertaken to frame issues that are of importance to its member countries, many of which are not OECD members. Indeed, there is a tug of war between the OECD and the UN over treaty policy that is of particular concern to the principal source countries. The essential issue is that the source countries insist on taxing income based on the source of the underlying economic activity, not on the residence of the parent company. Residency has been the fundamental basis of OECD and U.S. tax policy since modern treaty policies were formulated following World War I, in which the model was imperial (such as the UK) and colonial (such as India) countries. Over time, the economic relationship of these groups has changed. Evolving areas of departure include taxation of technical service payments and dispute resolution.

Another element of the dialogue between the UN and the OECD, as well as the business community, concerns the appropriate tax burden that should be borne by MNEs in specific countries and the use of tax havens. There are material framework differences between the UN and OECD Models. The OECD Model was primarily developed with the interests of industrialized or residence countries in mind, while the UN Model aimed to create a model for developing or source countries. Accordingly, the UN Model adapted the OECD Model provisions relating to the allocation of income between residence and source countries to expand the rights of source countries (including the definitions of *permanent establishment, passive income, capital gains, and other income*). It is this distinction that has led to much of the controversy relating to the expansion of permanent establishment concepts in recent years, which is found in the OECD Model treaty commentary, as well as in the proposals of tax administrations around the world. The interaction between the OECD, the UN, and these countries will have important ramifications on the development of base international taxation principles, especially with respect to the paradigm of source versus residence taxation. This, in turn, will have a significant effect on the evolution of treaty negotiation and dispute resolution, all of which could impact the financial accounting considerations of MNE groups.

As if these evolutions did not provide a sufficient range of issues to be considered in terms of assessing the actual or potential tax burden of MNE groups for financial accounting purposes, the EU has also launched its own initiatives, which are often not in harmony with the work of the OECD or the UN. Presently, the most startling illustrations are the so-called state aid investigations of whether state aid received by an MNE qualifies as an illegal subsidy and the proposed taxation of digital or electronic commerce. Needless to say, the pendency of such an investigation, or finalization of a new digital regime on local or global bases with respect to any given group, would require financial accounting treatment consideration.

[3] Comment

In sum, there are material evolutions in tax policy underway throughout the world. These evolutions have a variety of pertinent impacts on MNE financial accounting policies and consequences. In the case of existing planning structures (such as in Illustration 1.1), the enactment of new rules could pose material issues with respect to existing transactional structures. In the likely event that such structures are adjusted to reflect the evolving considerations, any such change is likely to pose its own set of issues in the countries that are impacted (such as in Illustration 1.2).

The treatment may depend, in part, on the nature of the opinion received from internal or external advisors. It will also depend on the process of negotiating with the financial auditor. As the group prepares for examination by pertinent tax authorities, there will be other considerations to be considered. In the event that a tax authority challenges some or all of such elements, there will be potential attorney-client privilege issues. Finally, if the issues are put to bed via ruling, advance pricing agreement, or otherwise, then the situation could seem to be simplified.

We will note issues related to these potential changes in the respective chapters.

§ 1.04 Illustration

Throughout the text, illustrations are utilized to clarify the issues being discussed. The following illustration is intended to put into context some of the matters to be discussed in a number of the following chapters. Needless to say, the illustration is structured to facilitate discussion of the many issues that bear upon the intersection between financial accounting and taxation.

ILLUSTRATION 1-2: The situation is the same as in Illustration 1-1, where USCo is a U.S.-based MNE operating a worldwide manufacturing, distribution and servicing business relating to Unique Products. USCo provides to customers: (1) hardware, (2) software, and (3) installation services (which are provided with intangible property developed by USCo).

USCo invests heavily in research and development (technology intangibles), as well as in brand and image advertising (marketing intangibles). These intangibles contribute a significant part of USCo's profitability.

The Unique Products and associated services are provided on a similar basis in every commercially significant market of the world, with adaptations to the unique circumstances of specific markets. USCo has established wholly-owned subsidiaries in all foreign countries in which there is significant potential market for its goods and services. The function of the foreign affiliates is to provide resale of hardware and software, as well as installation services (the Foreign Installation Affiliates or FIAs).

The historic transfer pricing arrangement was that USCo sold the hardware and software to FIAs, using a resale price methodology designed to produce an arm's-length rate of return in each of the FIAs. In some cases, the FIAs have been highly profitable, in others, losses have been incurred.

Effective on January 1, Year A, USCo restructured its global business model (the Restructuring). It formed an international technology company to be responsible for developing product and marketing intangibles for Unique Products in markets excluding the United States and Canada (Int'lCo). Int'lCo was formed in a country having a low effective tax rate (FoRCntry). FoRCntry has a treaty with the United States following the U.S. Model Tax Treaty.

There were three steps in the Restructuring. First, USCo and Int'lCo entered into a cost sharing arrangement, pursuant to which Int'lCo made a buy-in payment for the arm's-length value of the existing intangibles, acquiring the right to develop them further, and agreeing to bear an appropriate portion of future research and development costs.

Second, USCo entered into a supply agreement pursuant to which it agreed to supply hardware and software to Int'lCo using the comparable profits method (CPM), with a profit level indicator of return on capital employed (ROCE). The ROCE was nine percent.

Third, USCo terminated its distribution agreements with the Foreign Installation Affiliates. Int'lCo then entered installation services agreements with each of the FIAs, which provided that the FIAs would provide installation services for Int'lCo. The transfer pricing methodology under the Agreement is the cost-plus method with a mark-up of five percent.

In connection with the Restructuring, USCo, the FIAs and Int'lCo received transfer pricing studies from pertinent offices of Global Audit & Co. Each study provided a range of transfer prices for the three elements of the Restructuring, as well as noting the pertinent documentation requirements in each country. The conclusion of each study was as follows:

"Global Audit & Co. hopes that this study will be helpful in the transfer pricing work of USCo and its affiliates."

There is no other documentation, or opinions or other support for the U.S. and other country tax results of the transactions relating to the Restructuring. Global Audit & Co. advised that these transfer pricing studies were all that was needed to be prepared for U.S. and pertinent other country purposes.

In Illustration 1-2, a number of general tax and financial accounting issues are raised along with the specific issues involving transfer pricing. For example, for financial accounting purposes, USCo will consolidate Int'lCo and the Foreign Installation Affiliates (FIAs). For U.S. tax purposes, however, USCo is not permitted to file a consolidated tax return including Int'lCo and FIAs. In addition, for U.S. tax purposes, USCo must determine whether part of its income is FDII, whether it is subject to the BEAT, and whether the income of its foreign subsidiaries is GILTI or subpart F income. For financial accounting purposes, USCo must evaluate whether the earnings of its foreign subsidiaries are permanently reinvested so as to avoid recording a deferred tax liability and therefore a charge to earnings. These are just a few of the many tax and financial accounting issues that are raised in Illustration 1-2.

In addition to some of the general tax and financial accounting issues, a host of specific transfer pricing issues are also raised in Illustration 1-2. For example, the Restructuring involved three elements: (i) USCo and Int'l Co entering into a cost sharing arrangement; (ii) USCo entering into a supply agreement pursuant to which it agreed to supply hardware and software to Int'lCo using the CPM method; and (iii) USCo terminating its distribution agreements with the FIAs, and Int'lCo entering into installation services agreements with each of the FIAs, with a transfer pricing methodology of cost plus with a mark-up of five percent. The net effect of the Restructuring, after a three-year period, was that Int'lCo was earning the bulk of the operating income of the global group.

Beyond the initial reporting of the transactions making up the Restructuring, there will inevitably be a range of further considerations that must be considered. For example, in the situation of Illustration 1-2, there will likely be transfer pricing exposure in the countries in which the FIAs conduct business, which could lead to examination issues in the U.S. and the foreign countries, as well as potential correlative adjustments once such cases are resolved. These uncertain tax positions will need to be addressed. Moreover, Illustration 1-2 presents numerous SOX issues.

§ 1.05 Earnings Management

Shareholders value companies with high and consistent recurring pretax book income or "book earnings" or simply "earnings." To achieve this goal, companies may engage in "earnings management." This section will touch on tax-themed earnings management.

A company's utilization of its charitable foundation appears to be one of the few remaining techniques for earnings smoothing. A company may use its charitable foundation so as to vary its cash charitable contributions as a function of operating results while maintaining level support to its community and charitable constituents. This technique enables charitable and community beneficiaries to rely on level or increasing annual contributions to establish long-term programs.

Charitable contributions for financial accounting purposes are recorded on a pay-as-you-go basis. Generally, the treatment of charitable contributions for tax purposes follows the financial accounting treatment. There are cases, however, in which a permanent or temporary difference will be created because of variations between the tax and financial accounting treatment of the contribution. For example, certain charitable contributions destined for use outside the United States may not be deductible for tax purposes and consequently could result in a permanent difference between taxable income and pretax financial income.[2] However, there are various techniques available to corporations to obtain a tax deduction for charitable contributions utilized outside the United States. Further, in many instances, it may be possible to obtain a deduction in the country where the contribution is directed, or even if a local deduction is not available, the contribution will reduce the amount of available cash that will eventually be subject to a dividend withholding tax.

IRC Section 170 provides that a corporate taxpayer is not allowed to deduct charitable contributions in excess of ten percent of taxable income in any taxable year.[3] Any excess contributions may be carried forward for five years.[4] The charitable contribution giving rise to the carryforward will generate a deferred tax asset. In some situations, the ten percent limit on deductibility may be avoided by treating the charitable contribution as an ordinary and necessary business expense under IRC Section 162.

Corporations may deduct a charitable contribution during the taxable year when such contribution is authorized, on or before the end of the taxable year, provided the contribution is made, in the case of a calendar-year corporation, on or before April 15 of the following year.[5] Book and tax are aligned in terms of the year to accrue a deferred tax asset. The deferred tax asset is accrued in the same year that the charitable contribution is accrued for financial accounting.

Several provisions in the Internal Revenue Code permit a tax deduction in excess of the original cost of the contributed property.[6] These additional tax deductions create permanent differences. There are several organizations whose mission is to assist corporations in locating suitable donees who meet the requirements of these provisions.

The financial impact of contributions to company foundations that are earmarked for distribution to the ultimate charitable donees in future years should be carefully considered. Funds held by the charitable foundation awaiting distribution are subject to stringent investment criteria and, generally, are invested in short-term debt instruments. On the other hand, funds retained by the company are generally expected to generate returns that equal or exceed the company's weighted average cost of capital. Consequently, the earnings "penalty" resulting from the restricted investment policy of the foundation can easily outweigh the benefits of accelerating a tax deduction for the contribution. On the other hand, prefunding a charitable contribution with intangible property that is substantially appreciated results in significant tax savings that exceed

---

[2] IRC Section 170(c)(2).

[3] IRC Section 170(b)(2).

[4] IRC Section 170(d)(2).

[5] IRC Section 170(a)(2).

[6] *See, e.g.*, IRC Section 170(e)(1) (capital gain property), IRC Section 170(e)(3) (inventory), IRC Section 170(e)(4) (contributions of scientific property used for research), and IRC Section 170(e)(6) (contributions of computer technology and equipment for educational purposes).

the earnings "penalty." In this regard, it should be noted that IRC Section 170(e)(1)(B) may require distributions by the foundation within the next taxable year in order to avoid income tax on the appreciation while obtaining a charitable deduction for the full value of the property.

The indefinite reinvestment doctrine (also referred to as the indefinite reversal doctrine – FASB ASC 740-30-25-17) may also be used for earnings smoothing. FASB ASC 740–30 provides that the undistributed earnings of foreign subsidiaries should be accounted for as a temporary (or timing) difference except to the extent that some or all of the undistributed earnings meet the indefinite reinvestment doctrine (representation that the earnings of the foreign subsidiary are permanently reinvested). The indefinite reinvestment doctrine can be applied on an entity-by-entity, year-by-year, or quarter-by-quarter basis. Further, it appears that the doctrine can be applied to a specific amount of earnings of a specific foreign subsidiary.[7]

A third method of earnings management or smoothing is changing a book accounting method. In a number of situations, a company may use one of several accounting methods for GAAP with usually one being preferred. A company may usually change its method to a preferred method, but once the company adopts the preferred method, it cannot go back to a lesser method.[8] It is preferable to adopt accounting changes during the first interim period of the fiscal year.[9] To illustrate, IRC Section 48 provides investment tax credits equal to 30 percent of the qualifying investment. However, the tax basis in the investment is reduced by 50 percent of the credit allowed. A company may use the "flow-through method" or "deferral method" in accounting for the investment tax credits and basis difference.[10] Under the flow-through method, the investment tax credit is a current tax benefit (reduction in income tax expense) but with an offsetting non-current tax expense (deferred tax liability) due to the excess, if any, of the book basis over the tax basis in the property. Under the deferral method, the investment tax credit is treated as a reduction in the book basis. As a result, the book basis is lower than the tax basis. There are two approaches in handling this basis difference: (a) adjustment to book basis, and (b) reduction to current period tax expense.[11] The first approach under the deferral method is sometimes referred to as the "gross-up method" while the second approach under the deferral method is referred to as the "income method." FASB ASC 740–10–45–27 indicates that the gross-up method may be preferable in many cases. Both deferral method approaches result in lower current year earnings than the flow-through method.

For a new investment, the company will have higher current year earnings under the flow-through method but it will have higher earnings during the remaining life of the investment under the deferral method. For an existing investment, switching from the flow-through method to the deferral method will result in higher earnings during the remaining book life of the investment. It should be noted that the cumulative earnings are the same regardless of the method employed so the difference is the amount of

---

[7] *See* Martin A. Sullivan, *Economic Analysis: Apple's High Effective Tax Rate Obscures Foreign Tax Benefits*, 132 Tax Notes 459 (2011) (Apple's total foreign accumulated earnings at the end of 2010 was $30.8 billion but its indefinitely reinvested earnings was only $12.3 billion; the difference of $18.5 billion is considered earnings not indefinitely reinvested resulting in U.S. tax expense of about $5 billion).

[8] FASB ASC 250–10–45–2.

[9] FASB ASC 250–10–45–16.

[10] FASB ASC 740–10–25–46.

[11] FASB ASC 740–10–45–27.

earnings to be recorded during the remaining book life of the investment. When an accounting method is changed, the company must recalculate prior periods' earnings as if the company was always on the new method.[12] The cumulative effect of the accounting change is presented in the current period financials as a change in the beginning assets and liabilities accounts, the opening retained earnings, other impacted accounts, and other qualitative disclosures.[13]

The deferral method results in a lower book basis so there is less book depreciation on the investment over the remaining book life of the investment. This lower book depreciation effectively shifts earnings from prior years to the current year and future years, thereby resulting in higher current and future year earnings. When new accounting methods are used, to the extent the company can choose to adopt the method early or adopt it as late as permissible, that also introduces opportunities to manage earnings.

There are a number of tax accounting principles that are fairly broad in both their application and the ability to change their application. For instance, a change in assertion of the indefinite reinvestment doctrine will impact earnings.[14] While such a change could result in heightened scrutiny by the company's auditor and the SEC, there is considerable latitude in how the doctrine is applied. Another example is the valuation allowance on deferred tax assets, both in terms of the amount and period the valuation allowance is accrued, as well as the amount and period the valuation allowance is reduced.[15]

The investment public is demanding greater transparency in financial disclosures, and the SEC has generally agreed with such demands.[16] Furthermore, analysts that follow companies within the same sector have mastered dissecting a company's reported earnings to determine earnings that are one-time events, timing events, and recurring. The highest value earnings component is recurring earnings, while one-time events and timing events are the least valuable. This brings into question the value of certain types of earnings. There is a view that companies value a low effective tax rate over low cash taxes. The evidence does not fully support this preference. Companies evaluate investments on both their return on investment (ROI) and the pro forma earnings impact. Many companies set a threshold ROI and generally will not make an investment with a low ROI even with good pro forma earnings. The investment must exceed the company's cost of capital as adjusted for the project's risk. In addition to exceeding the ROI hurdle rate, the company will look at the pro forma earnings to see whether it is dilutive or accretive to earnings. Typically, there is a strong correlation between ROI and earnings—i.e., high ROI means accretive earnings and vice versa. However, a company will sometimes make an investment that does not meet the ROI rate and dilutes earnings. These are strategic investments, like the retail industries' loss leaders. Many investments in renewable energy projects (e.g., solar, wind) are based on ROI because the stand-alone-project earnings are modest. Investment tax credits and bonus

---

12 United States Government Accountability Office (GAO), GAO–16–363, *Corporate Income Tax: Most Large Profitable U.S. Corporations Paid Tax but Effective Tax Rates Differed Significantly from the Statutory Rate*, published March 17, 2016, publicly released by GAO on April 13, 2016.

13 FASB ASC 250–10–45–1 includes a list of disclosures.

14 FASB ASC 740–10–25–3. *See* Section 2.16; Section 4.04[c].

15 FASB ASC 740–10–30–16. *See* Section 2.09.

16 *See* Nicola M. White and Andrew Romanas, *Gensler Backs Accounting Plan for More Corporate Tax Disclosure*, BNA Daily Tax Report (Sept. 15, 2022).

depreciation provide cash tax savings upfront which increases ROI. Tax equity investors are attracted to renewable projects due to their strong ROI. In fact, this is what has created a growing tax equity market in the renewable energy sector. A low effective tax rate is desirable, but a high ROI is more desirable.

Earnings management has become a cat-and-mouse game where opportunities, which investors, regulators, and auditors consider "loopholes," are plugged but new leaks quickly appear. This is mostly self-inflicted. As a result of increasing complexity in the tax laws of many taxing jurisdictions, more frequent changes in tax laws, and great uncertainty in the interpretation of such tax laws, along with the same happening in the financial statement accounting of income taxes, accounting for income taxes has become more subjective thereby resulting in differing results even among similarly situated companies, as reflected throughout this book. The subjectivity and inconsistency are a constant area of concern for analysts, investors, and regulators who desire transparency and consistent application of the rules.

§ 1.06 Overview of Publication

The seminal issues addressed in this text are the intersection of:

Financial accounting theory and pronouncements, which address the recording of revenues and expenses to provide an accurate picture of the financial results of business activity;

Tax theory and law, which addresses the same from the standpoint of paying taxes to the taxing authority, complicated by the many competing theories of recognition, economic and social policy ramifications;

The inevitable effort of entities to find the ambiguities in items 1. and 2. that can be exploited to their advantage, ultimately from an effective tax rate and earnings per share standpoint;

The reaction of professional bodies and Congress to such exploitation when it becomes a danger to the taxing authority or financial markets; and

The recording of routine and non-routine matters for financial accounting and tax purposes in light of all of the above.

This publication is not intended to be an exhaustive treatise solely on financial accounting or solely on corporate income taxation. Rather, the purpose of this text is to discuss and explain the pertinent elements of the intersection of financial accounting and corporate income taxation. Our goal is to: (i) articulate the reality of financial accounting and tax compliance in light of the new landscape entities face on such matters today; and (ii) set out a means by which entities can structure their tax planning and financial reporting in a manner to efficiently meet all applicable requirements.

As we have prepared this text, we have become duly impressed by the magnitude of the task facing finance, accounting and tax executives, consultants, analysts and commentators in trying to bring light to the complicated intersection caused by the FASB rules on accounting for income taxes, the FASB rules on accounting for uncertain income tax positions, SOX and all of the related financial accounting, substantive tax and tax accounting rules that will need to be digested and understood in specific situations.

We recognize that there may be sharp discourse on the various issues raised by specific situations at this intersection, which is predictable where there is so much uncertainty and areas of potential disagreement. We look forward to this discourse. Future editions of this publication will address the inevitable evolution of these concepts as entities and tax administrations work toward achieving a greater degree of transparency with respect to the financial presentation of taxation matters.

Chapter 2

Accounting for Income Taxes

Table of Sections

§ 2.01 Purpose

An entity is required to compute its income for financial accounting purposes each year in accordance with generally accepted accounting principles (GAAP). The resulting income figure is referred to as pretax financial income or pretax book income (PTBI).[1] In addition, an entity's income is generally subject to taxation by federal, most state and several local taxing authorities. As a result, an entity must also compute its income for tax purposes in accordance with the applicable tax statutes and regulations of these various jurisdictions. The resulting income figure is referred to as taxable income.[2] In

[1] "Pretax financial income" is sometimes referred to as pre-tax book income (PTBI), income before taxes (or earnings before taxes), income for financial reporting purposes or income for book purposes. *See* Donald E. Kieso, et al., *Intermediate Accounting* 1054 (16th ed. 2016). Some private companies utilize financial reporting alternatives to GAAP generally referred to as "other comprehensive basis of accounting" or OCBOA. Auditing Standards Board, Statement on Auditing Standards (SAS), Special Reports No. 62 (April 1989).

[2] IRC Sections 11 and 63(a).

almost all cases, an entity's taxable income will differ from its pretax financial income. In fact, the determinations of taxable income for these various jurisdictions almost always differ from each other and also from pretax financial income. These differences primarily reflect the different objectives behind the various taxing authorities and the accounting rules.[3]

The tax rules are designed to provide equitable and efficient determination of tax liability and subsequent collection of revenue and also to provide incentives for entities and individuals to engage in a particular activity based upon the priorities and revenue needs of the various taxing authorities.[4] The financial accounting rules are designed to paint a picture of the entity's operations that is consistent in its measurement on both an annual basis and across entities such that creditors, shareholders, management and any other properly interested persons can evaluate the absolute and relative performance of the entity. The Financial Accounting Standards Board (FASB) has written:

> The objective of general purpose financial reporting is to provide financial information about the reporting entity that is useful to existing and potential investors, lenders, and other creditors in making decisions about providing resources to the entity. Those decisions involve buying, selling, or holding equity and debt instruments and providing or settling loans and other forms of credit.[5]

While the rules for determining pretax financial income are fairly rigorous and based upon underlying economic assumptions and principles, the various taxing authorities have promulgated laws and regulations that do not necessarily follow rules grounded on the economic theories of financial reporting but rather may be based on political, social, or economic objectives. In addition, the difference between an entity's taxable income and its pretax financial income may be due to tax-planning strategies engaged in by the entity, resulting in lower taxable income relative to pretax financial income.[6]

§ 2.02 Tax Differences—Permanent and Temporary

The differences between taxable income and pretax financial income give rise to tax differences. Some of these differences are permanent differences and others are temporary differences (sometimes referred to as timing differences).

[1] Permanent Differences

Some differences between pretax financial income and taxable income are permanent. Permanent differences are items that (i) enter into pretax financial income

[3] *See Thor Power Tool Co. v. Commissioner*, 439 U.S. 522 (1979) ("The primary goal of financial accounting is to provide useful information to management, shareholders, creditors and others properly interested; the major responsibility of the accountant is to protect these parties from being misled. The primary goal of the income tax system, in contrast, is the equitable collection of revenue; the major responsibility of the Internal Revenue Service is to protect the public fisc.").

[4] *See, e.g.*, Michelle Hanlon, *What Can We Infer about a Firm's Taxable Income from Its Financial Statements?* 56 Nat'l Tax J. 831, 833 (2003); Myron S. Scholes, et al., *Taxes and Business Strategy* Appendix 2.2 (3rd ed. 2004); Gil B. Manzon, Jr. & George A. Plesko, *The Relation Between Financial and Tax Reporting Measures of Income*, 55 Tax L. Rev. 175, 180 (2002).

[5] FASB, Statement of Financial Accounting Concepts No. 8 (CON 8), *Conceptual Framework for Financial Reporting*, Chapter 1, "The Objective of General Purpose Financial Reporting" (Sept. 2010; Amended Dec. 2021).

[6] *See* Hanlon, supra note 4, at 833.

but *never* into taxable income; or (ii) enter into taxable income but *never* into pretax financial income. As a result, these items create a difference between pretax financial income and taxable income that will not reverse over time, i.e., a permanent difference. FASB has not defined permanent differences in *Accounting for Income Taxes* (FASB ASC 740); however, FASB has written:

> Some events do not have tax consequences. Certain revenues are exempt from taxation and certain expenses are not deductible. In some tax jurisdictions, for example, interest earned on certain municipal obligations is not taxable and fines are not deductible.[7]

FASB appears to be describing permanent differences as events that do not have tax consequences, with the two broad categories being revenues exempt from taxation and expenses that are not deductible. Permanent difference items arise primarily because of a variety of tax provisions enacted by Congress to achieve certain purposes, such as political, social and economic objectives.[8] As noted by FASB, these tax provisions generally include exclusions of certain revenues from taxable income and limit (or disallow) certain expenses as a deduction in computing taxable income.

> **ILLUSTRATION 2-1:** A corporation owns state and local (municipal) bonds. It receives $50,000 of interest on the bonds. Under the tax code, interest on state and local bonds is excluded from gross income and therefore never enters into the computation of taxable income.[9] However, such interest enters into the computation of pretax financial income. As a result, a difference of $50,000 is created between taxable income and pretax financial income. This difference is permanent—it will not reverse over time.

> **ILLUSTRATION 2-2:** A publicly held corporation pays its chief executive officer a salary of $1.4 million. The salary payment of $1.4 million is an expense on the corporation's income statement; however, for tax purposes, the corporation may only deduct $1 million as a result of the limitation for certain excessive employee remuneration under IRC Section 162(m).[10] The $400,000 difference between the $1.4 million expense on the income statement and the $1 million deduction on the tax return is a permanent difference, which enters into the computation of pretax financial income but never into taxable income.

Some other common examples of items of permanent difference that enter into the computation of pretax financial income but not taxable income include: expenses incurred in generating tax-exempt income,[11] the 50 percent limitation on deduction of meals and disallowance of deduction for entertainment,[12] fines and penalties resulting

---

[7] FASB ASC 740–10–10–1. FASB has utilized the term "permanent difference" by writing "nontaxable or nondeductible differences between financial statements and tax returns (sometimes referred to as permanent differences)." FIN 48, *Accounting for Uncertainty in Income Taxes*, paragraph B11 (June 2006). The APB defined a permanent difference as "[d]ifferences between taxable income and pretax accounting income arising from transactions that, under applicable tax laws and regulations, will not be offset by corresponding differences or 'turn around' in other periods." Accounting Principles Board Opinion (APB) 11, *Accounting for Income Taxes*, paragraph 13.f. (1967).

[8] Kieso, supra note 1, at 1066.

[9] IRC Section 103(a).

[10] IRC Section 162(m).

[11] IRC Section 265.

[12] IRC Section 274(a) and (n).

from a violation of law,[13] proceeds from life insurance carried by the entity on key employees,[14] and premiums paid for life insurance carried by the entity on its key employees.[15]

Some permanent difference items enter into the computation of taxable income but not pretax financial income. One common example of an item of permanent difference that enters into the computation of taxable income but not pretax financial income is percentage depletion of natural resources in excess of their cost.[16] Another example is the dividends-received deduction for corporate recipients of dividends, as indicated in Illustration 2-3:[17]

> **ILLUSTRATION 2-3:** A corporation owns two percent of the stock of XYZ Corporation. During the year, the corporation receives $100,000 of dividends from XYZ Corporation. The corporation includes the $100,000 of dividends in its pretax financial income and its taxable income. For tax purposes, the corporation is entitled to a 50 percent dividends-received deduction in computing its taxable income.[18] In computing its pretax financial income, however, the corporation simply includes the entire amount of the dividend resulting in a permanent difference of $50,000 between taxable income and pretax financial income (equal to the amount of the dividends-received deduction).

Permanent differences can be interpreted in one of two ways.[19] The broad interpretation of permanent differences includes any book-tax difference that is not temporary. A narrower interpretation of the term permanent difference includes only book-tax difference items that are not temporary but that also appear in the effective tax rate reconciliation in the financial statements. For example, prior to 2018, the expensing of stock options created an item that would be treated as a permanent difference under a broad interpretation of the term (i.e., a book-tax difference that was not temporary) but would not be treated as a permanent difference item under the narrower interpretation (i.e., it did not appear in the effective tax rate reconciliation).[20]

Public companies that must report certain financial statements with the Securities and Exchange Commission (SEC) must file Form 10-K pursuant to the Securities Exchange Act of 1934. In the notes to the financial statements, the company discloses its effective tax rate.[21] The effective tax rate shows the percentage (or dollars) of taxes

---

[13] IRC Section 162(f).

[14] IRC Section 101(a)(1).

[15] IRC Section 264(a)(1).

[16] IRC Section 613.

[17] IRC Sections 243–246A.

[18] IRC Section 243.

[19] *See* Lillian F. Mills and George A. Plesko, *Bridging the Reporting Gap: A Proposal for More Informative Reconciling of Book and Tax Income*, 56 Nat'l Tax J. 865, 873 fn. 9 (2003).

[20] In March 2016, FASB issued Accounting Standards Update (ASU) 2016–09, *Compensation-Stock Compensation: Improvements to Employee Share-Based Payment Accounting,* which affirmed its decision to require entities to recognize all excess tax benefits and all tax deficiencies as income tax expense or benefit in the income statement. The Board also affirmed its decision to remove the requirement to delay recognition of an excess tax benefit until the tax benefit is realized. For public business entities, the amendments in ASU are effective for annual periods beginning after December 15, 2016. For all other entities, the amendments are effective for annual periods beginning after December 15, 2017. *See* Section 7.19.

[21] FASB ASC 740–10–50–12. The reconciliation may be accomplished utilizing percentages or dollar amounts or both. The estimated amount and nature of each significant reconciling item should be disclosed.

paid based on pretax financial income from continuing operations. Permanent differences, under a narrow interpretation of the term, will affect a company's effective tax rate and its earnings per share. For example, a company that receives interest income on state and local bonds (as in Illustration 2-1) will include the revenue in pretax financial income but not taxable income with the effect of reducing the company's effective tax rate and increasing its earnings per share. In contrast, if a company pays a fine that is not deductible for tax purposes but is an expense for purposes of computing pretax financial income, the company's effective tax rate will increase as a result of paying the fine and its earnings per share will be reduced.

ILLUSTRATION 2-4: A corporation has pretax financial income of $200,000 for 2022 and 2023. In 2022, it pays a non-deductible fine of $10,000, and in 2023, it receives $20,000 of interest on state and local bonds.

	2022	2023
Pretax financial income	$200,000	$200,000
Permanent differences:		
Non-taxable revenue	$ 0	$20,000
Non-deductible expense	$10,000	$ 0
Taxable income	$210,000	$180,000
Statutory tax rate	21%	21%
Total tax expense	$44,100	$37,800
Effective tax rate	22.05%	18.9%

The permanent differences impact the effective tax rate. The $10,000 non-deductible fine in 2022 increased taxable income (relative to pretax financial income) thereby increasing current tax expense and total tax expense. Increasing the total tax expense raised the effective tax rate to 22.05 percent, which is higher than the statutory tax rate of 21 percent in 2022. The $20,000 interest on state and local bonds decreased taxable income (relative to pretax financial income) thereby decreasing current tax expense and total tax expense. Decreasing the total tax expense lowered the effective tax rate to 18.9 percent, which is lower than the statutory tax rate of 21 percent in 2023.

[2] Temporary Differences

Temporary differences occur when the time of including items of revenue and expense in pretax financial income differs from the time of including such items in taxable income. Generally, temporary differences will occur in one period and reverse out in one or more subsequent periods. Some temporary differences reduce income taxes that would otherwise be currently payable, while other temporary differences increase income taxes that would otherwise be currently payable. It is important to understand that because of the relationship between the income statement and the tax return, any

---

Id. Rule 4–08(h) of SEC Regulation S-X requires disclosure of reconciling items that are five percent (or more) of the amount computed by multiplying pretax income by the statutory tax rate (currently, 21 percent), i.e., any item that increases or decreases the tax rate by 1.05 percent or more. 17 CFR § 210.4–08—General notes to financial statements.

time there is a difference between the income statement and the tax return with respect to reported revenues and expenses, there will be an offsetting difference between financial reporting basis ("book basis")[22] and tax basis for the related assets or liabilities.

An example of a temporary difference, which reduces income taxes that would otherwise be currently payable, is the use of different methods of depreciation. Many entities use accelerated depreciation for tax purposes and straight-line depreciation for financial reporting purposes. As a result, in the early years of a depreciable asset, the depreciation deduction for tax purposes will be greater than the depreciation expense for accounting purposes. In later years, the difference will reverse out resulting in greater depreciation expense each year for accounting purposes than the depreciation deduction for tax purposes. While the total depreciation expense equals the total depreciation deduction over the depreciable life of the asset, there is a temporary difference each year between the book basis of the asset and its tax basis that will be eliminated at the end of the asset's depreciable life. Some other common examples of temporary differences include gains from installment sales of property[23] and advance payments for services to be rendered in the future.[24]

FASB ASC 740 deals exclusively with temporary differences (and net operating losses and tax credit carryforwards) and not permanent differences. Permanent differences are accounted for as part of the income statement. In addition, permanent differences affect the entity's effective tax rate and its earnings per share.[25]

ILLUSTRATION 2-5: Same facts as Illustration 2-4 (corporation has pretax financial income of $200,000 for 2022 and 2023. In 2022, it pays a non-deductible fine of $10,000, and in 2023, it receives $20,000 of interest on state and local bonds). The corporation also makes an installment sale of property in 2022, recognizing the entire gain of $16,000 for book purposes in 2022 but not recognizing the gain for tax purposes until 2023. As a result, a temporary difference (between pretax financial income and taxable income) of $16,000 is created in 2022, which reverses in 2023.

	2022	2023
Pretax financial income	$200,000	$200,000
Permanent differences:		
Non-taxable revenue	$ 0	$20,000

---

[22] Throughout this chapter, the term "book basis" will be used to mean financial reporting basis. Book basis is sometimes referred to as book value, reported amounts, assigned amounts and carrying value. Book basis, as used in this chapter, should not be confused with the term book basis used in the partnership tax regulations under IRC Section 704.

[23] For tax law, *see* IRC Section 453. For financial accounting, *see* FASB ASC 606–10–05–3; FASB ASC 606–10–05–4; FASB ASC 606–10–25–23; "Omnibus Opinion," APB 10, paragraph 12 (1966).

[24] For tax law, *see, e.g.*, IRC Section 451(c); *Automobile Club of Michigan v. Commissioner*, 353 U.S. 180 (1957); *American Automobile Association v. United States*, 367 U.S. 687 (1961); *Schlude v. Commissioner*, 372 U.S. 128 (1963). *But see, e.g.*, IRC Sections 455 and 456; *Artnell v. Commissioner*, 400 F.2d 981 (7th Cir., 1968); *Tampa Bay Devil Rays, Ltd. v. Commissioner*, 84 T.C. M. 394 (2002). For financial accounting, *see* FASB ASC 606–10–25–8; FASB ASC 740-10-25-20(c); CON 6, *Elements of Financial Statements*, paragraph 197 (1985) (treating the unearned revenue as a liability until the services have been provided).

[25] Permanent differences are not defined in Topic 740. One interpretation is that permanent differences include any book-tax difference that is not temporary. A narrower use of the term permanent difference would include only book-tax difference items that appear in the effective tax rate reconciliation.

Non-deductible expense	$10,000	$ 0
Temporary differences	($16,000)	$16,000
Taxable income	$194,000	$196,000
Statutory tax rate	21%	21%
Total tax expense:	$44,100	$37,800
Current tax expense	$40,740	$41,160
Deferred tax expense	$3,360	($3,360)
Effective tax rate	22.05%	18.9%

As demonstrated in Illustration 2-4, permanent differences impact the effective tax rate. Temporary differences, however, do not impact the effective tax rate. Rather, they create a deferred tax expense/benefit, which enters into the computation of total tax expense.

In comparing Illustration 2-5 with Illustration 2-4, the only difference between the two illustrations is a temporary difference of $16,000 in the former illustration (due to the installment sale of property). However, temporary differences do not impact the effective tax rate. Consequently, the effective tax rates in both Illustration 2-5 and Illustration 2-4 for 2022 and 2023 are 22.05 percent and 18.9 percent, respectively.

§ 2.03 Various Methods in Accounting for Income Taxes

In accounting for income taxes on the financial statements, a number of approaches have been considered by FASB (and earlier by the Accounting Principles Board) with respect to deferred taxes. Generally, three approaches have been considered over the years: (1) nonrecognition of deferred taxes, (2) partial recognition of deferred taxes, and (3) comprehensive recognition of deferred taxes.

[1] Nonrecognition of Deferred Taxes

The simplest approach is to have the income tax expense for financial reporting equal the amount of taxes payable for the year as determined by the tax return. So, for example, if the tax return showed taxes payable of $250,000, then the financial statement would simply show income tax expense of $250,000. Any deferred taxes are simply ignored. This approach has been referred to as the "no allocation" or "flow-through" approach.[26] A number of reasons have been advanced to support the nonrecognition of deferred taxes approach, including (a) the tax return determines the legal liability for income taxes, (b) estimates about the entity's future performance would be purely speculative, and (c) the two other approaches (partial recognition of deferred taxes and comprehensive recognition of deferred taxes) are too complex.[27]

Although the nonrecognition of deferred taxes approach achieves simplicity, it ignores known future tax consequences. For example, if an entity makes an installment sale of property, under the tax laws, it may report the gain under the installment method.[28] Assume the gain is $50,000 for tax and financial reporting purposes and only

---

[26] *See* Joanne M. Flood, *Wiley GAAP 2014* 754 (2014).

[27] *Id.*

[28] IRC Section 453. In fact, the installment method for reporting gain from an installment sale is mandatory unless the entity elects out of installment method treatment. IRC Section 453(d).

$10,000 of the gain is included in taxable income for the current year, the remaining $40,000 of gain is included in taxable income in future years as payments are received from the purchaser of the property. Using a tax rate of 21 percent, the entity will owe $8,400 ($40,000 gain times 21 percent) in taxes in the future when it includes the remaining $40,000 of gain in taxable income. In the example, the tax law is only affecting when the gain will be included in taxable income and not whether it will be included in taxable income.

For financial reporting purposes, the entire installment sale is recognized at the time of sale, i.e., the gain is included in pretax financial income and a receivable is set up for the payments to be received from the purchaser.[29] Recognition of the sale and the gain on the sale on an accrual basis for the financial statements requires that the tax consequences of the gain on the sale also be recognized on the financial statements. To do otherwise would result in inconsistent accounting—the sale and the gain would be accounted for on an accrual basis and the related tax consequences accounted for on a cash basis.

[2] Partial Recognition of Deferred Taxes

A second approach to accounting for income taxes is a partial recognition of deferred taxes. This is a middle ground approach, recognizing deferred taxes in certain cases but not others. Under this approach, income tax expense for financial reporting equals the amount of taxes payable for the year as determined by the tax return. In addition, specific, nonrecurring material differences between taxable income and pretax financial income are recognized as deferred taxes if the difference is reasonably expected to be paid as income tax (or recovered as a reduction of income taxes) within a relatively short period of time.

To illustrate, if an entity makes an isolated installment sale of property and defers including in taxable income part or all of the gain, the difference between taxable income and pretax financial income as to the gain from the installment sale would be recognized on the financial statements as a deferred tax liability. In contrast, depreciation differences resulting from accelerated depreciation for tax purposes would, as a general rule, not be recognized as a deferred tax liability.[30] The reasoning is that the aggregate amount of depreciation differences may become larger each year as a result of, for example, expansion of the entity's activities. In other words, the aggregate amount of temporary differences for depreciation keeps getting larger each year because new originating temporary differences (i.e., acquiring new depreciable assets) more than offset reversing temporary differences (i.e., depreciation in the later years of an asset). As a result, the cumulative amount of temporary differences will not reverse, no future tax payment will rise, and therefore a deferred tax liability should not be recorded.

While it may be true that the aggregate amount of temporary differences due to depreciation may increase over time, the deferred tax consequences of a depreciation difference for a *particular* depreciable asset ordinarily will reverse in future years. More specifically, the depreciation difference will reverse out in future years, thereby (a) increasing taxable income and taxes payable if the entity earns net taxable income for that year, (b) reducing a tax loss and a net operating loss carryback refund if the entity incurs a tax loss that is carried back to offset taxable income of an earlier year, or (c)

[29] FASB ASC 606–10–05–3; FASB ASC 606–10–05–4; FASB ASC 606–10–25–23.

[30] SFAS No. 109, paragraph 205.

reducing a net operating loss carryforward, thereby increasing taxes payable if taxable income is earned during the carryforward period. It is possible that no tax burden will take place if, in situation (c), the entity does not pay taxes during the entire carryforward period of the net operating loss.

[3] Comprehensive Recognition of Deferred Taxes

A third approach to accounting for income taxes is a comprehensive approach in which income tax expense includes the tax effects of all transactions entering into the determination of pretax financial income for the period. In other words, the current accounting period will reflect all income taxes arising from the current pretax financial income, regardless of when the taxes are paid. The comprehensive approach has been adopted by both FASB (in SFAS No. 109 in 1992) and previously the Accounting Principles Board (in APB 11, *Accounting for Income Taxes* in 1967). There are several methods for implementing a comprehensive approach to accounting for income taxes.

[a] Net of Tax Method

One comprehensive approach is the net of tax method to accounting for income taxes. Under this approach, the effects of taxability and deductibility on assets and liabilities are accounted for as reductions of the book bases of those assets and liabilities. This method recognizes that taxability of revenues and deductibility of expenses are relevant factors in the valuation of assets and liabilities. For example, the book basis of accounts receivable from installment sales shown on the financial statements is reduced by the amount of tax that will be paid on the cash receipts in the future years (when the receivables are collected).

[b] Asset and Liability Method

A second comprehensive approach is the asset and liability method. Under this comprehensive approach, the differences between income tax expense and income taxes payable in the periods in which the temporary differences originate are either liabilities for taxes payable in the future or assets for prepaid taxes. In other words, the temporary differences result in deferred tax liabilities or deferred tax assets. Deferred tax liabilities and deferred tax assets are liabilities and assets for purposes of the financial statements.

§ 2.04 Overview of Accounting for Income Taxes

The purpose of Topic 740, *Income Taxes*, of the FASB Codification, is to address financial accounting and reporting for income taxes that are currently payable and also for the tax consequences of: (a) revenues, expenses, gains or losses that are included in taxable income in a different year (whether earlier or later) than the year in which they are recognized in pretax financial income, (b) other events that create differences between the tax bases and book bases of assets and liabilities, (c) net operating loss or tax credit carrybacks for refunds of taxes paid in prior years and (d) net operating loss or tax credit carryforwards reducing taxes payable in future years.[31] In issuing SFAS No. 109, a predecessor of Topic 740, FASB was guided by the principle of promulgating standards only when the expected benefits of the resulting information exceed the perceived costs.[32]

---

31 FASB ASC 740–10–05–1.

32 SFAS No. 109, paragraph 68.

FASB ASC 740 applies to domestic and foreign entities, both public and non-public, in preparing financial statements in accordance with U.S. generally accepted accounting principles. This includes not-for-profit entities that have activities that are subject to income taxes.[33] FASB ASC 740 applies to federal, state and local (including franchise) income taxes as well as foreign income taxes.[34] In addition, it applies to an entity's domestic and foreign operations that are consolidated, combined, or accounted for by the equity method.[35] FASB ASC 740 does not apply to (a) a franchise tax to the extent it is based on capital or non-income based amount and no portion of the tax is based on income,[36] or (b) a withholding tax for the benefit of the recipients of a dividend.[37]

FASB had two primary objectives in accounting for income taxes. The first objective was to recognize the amount of taxes payable or refundable for the *current* year.[38] The second objective was to recognize deferred tax liabilities and deferred tax assets for the *future* tax consequences of events that have been currently recognized in either the entity's financial statements or on its tax returns.[39] The second objective, recognition of deferred taxes, might be more specifically stated as recognizing the *expected* future tax consequences of events that have been currently recognized in the financial statements or tax returns. Because the second objective is based on expected future tax consequences, FASB adopted a number of assumptions or conventions in achieving the second objective, which can only be accomplished through estimates and approximations.[40]

In drafting SFAS No. 109, which has been codified in FASB ASC 740, FASB had to address four basic accounting issues with respect to recognizing the effects of income taxes in the financial statements for a particular period.[41] The first issue was whether the effects of income taxes recognized in the financial statements should include the amount of taxes currently payable plus: (a) nonrecognition of deferred taxes (i.e., only the amount of taxes payable for the period as determined by the tax return), (b) partial recognition of deferred taxes, (c) comprehensive recognition of deferred taxes, or (d) comprehensive recognition of deferred taxes plus the future tax benefit of net operating losses and tax credit carryforwards.[42] FASB adopted the approach in part (d)—that is, the effects of income taxes in the financial statements should include the amount of taxes currently payable plus comprehensive recognition of deferred taxes (i.e., recognition of temporary differences) plus the future tax benefit of net operating losses and tax credit

---

[33] FASB ASC 740–10–15–2.

[34] FASB ASC 740–10–15–3.

[35] *Id.* As to limited liability companies, *see* FASB ASC 272–10-60.

[36] FASB ASC 740–10–15–4(a). If a franchise tax is partially based on income, then deferred tax assets and liabilities are recognized and accounted for under FASB ASC 740. FASB ASC 740–10–55–26; FASB ASC 740–10–55–139 to FASB ASC 740–10–55–144 (example 17 illustrating application of FASB ASC 740 to a franchise tax).

[37] FASB ASC 740–10–15–4(b). In classifying a tax imposed on an entity based on dividends distributed by the entity as a withholding tax for the benefit of recipients (and not an income tax), two conditions must be met. First, the entity must pay the tax only if a dividend is distributed to shareholders. Second, the shareholders receiving the dividend are entitled to a tax credit at least equal to the tax paid by the entity, with the credit being realized either as a refund or as a reduction of taxes otherwise due.

[38] FASB ASC 740–10–10–1.

[39] *Id.*

[40] FASB ASC 740–10–10–2.

[41] SFAS No. 109, paragraph 62.

[42] *Id.*

carryforwards.[43] In other words, FASB concluded that the financial statements should reflect the current and deferred tax consequences of *all* events that have been recognized in either the financial statements or the tax returns.[44]

The second issue addressed by FASB was how to recognize the tax effects of temporary differences. A number of approaches were considered, including: (a) the "asset and liability approach" in which tax assets or liabilities are recovered or settled in the future, (b) the "net-of-tax approach" involving reductions in related assets or liabilities, (c) the "deferred approach" resulting in deferred tax charges or deferred tax credits, or (d) a combination of the above three approaches.[45] Previously, in APB 11, the APB had adopted the "deferred approach" in which deferred tax credits and charges in the statement of financial position represented the cumulative effect of interperiod tax allocation.[46]

FASB rejected the "deferred approach" and adopted the "asset and liability approach" in SFAS No. 109 (now codified in FASB ASC 740), meaning that deferred taxes would be an asset or liability on the financial statements.[47] FASB's reasoning was that the asset and liability approach was more consistent with the definitions in FASB Statement of Financial Accounting Concepts (CON) 6, *Elements of Financial Statements*, which defines assets as *probable* future economic benefits and liabilities as *probable* future sacrifices of economic benefits.[48] FASB also believed that the asset and liability approach produces the most useful and understandable information; yet it is no more complex than any other approach to accounting for income taxes.[49] As a result of adopting comprehensive recognition of temporary differences (and recognizing the future tax benefit of net operating losses and tax credit carryforwards) under the asset and liability approach, FASB concluded that not only should a *current* tax liability or asset be recognized for taxes payable or refundable for the current year but a *deferred* tax liability or asset should be recognized for the deferred tax consequences of temporary differences (and net operating losses and tax credit carryforwards).[50]

A third issue FASB had to address was whether the measurement of the tax effects of temporary differences should be: (a) the incremental effect in the current year, (b) the incremental effect in future years, or, (c) if the incremental effect in future years, whether that effect should be discounted to present day.[51] FASB believed that a deferred tax liability or asset should be measured as the incremental effect on *future* cash flows for income taxes that will result from temporary differences and carryforwards but should not be discounted to present day.[52] FASB recognized that predictions would be needed to determine the incremental future effect and, as a result, made some simplifying assumptions.[53] For example, the enacted tax rate(s) expected to apply to taxable income in future years is used to measure the total deferred tax liability for

---

[43] SFAS No. 109, paragraph 63.

[44] *Id.*

[45] SFAS No. 109, paragraphs 62 and 64.

[46] SFAS No. 109, paragraph 207.

[47] SFAS No. 109, paragraph 63.

[48] *Id. See* CON 6, paragraphs 25–26 (defining "assets") and paragraphs 35–36 (defining "liabilities").

[49] SFAS No. 109, paragraph 63.

[50] SFAS No. 109, paragraph 64.

[51] SFAS No. 109, paragraph 62.

[52] SFAS No. 109, paragraphs 65 and 66.c.

[53] *Id.*

taxable temporary differences and the total deferred tax asset for deductible temporary differences (and net operating losses and tax credit carryforwards).[54] In addition, the total deferred tax asset is reduced by a valuation allowance if it is more likely than not that some or all of the deferred tax asset will not be realized.[55]

The fourth issue FASB had to address involved complexity.[56] FASB acknowledged the complexity involved in the calculation of accounting for income taxes but also believed that much of the complexities involved applying the tax laws to business transactions.[57] In measuring current and deferred tax liabilities and assets, the enacted tax law is used and the effects of future changes in tax laws or rates are not anticipated.[58] FASB concluded that complexities in the tax law do not justify different accounting for income taxes depending on an entity's size or ownership.[59] As a result, SFAS No. 109 (FASB ASC 740) applies both to publicly held and non-publicly held entities.

In July, 2013, FASB issued Accounting Standard Update (ASU) No. 2013–11, "Presentation of an Unrecognized Tax Benefit When a Net Operating Loss Carryforward, a Similar Tax Loss, or a Tax Credit Carryforward Exists." This ASU provides guidance on the financial statement presentation of an unrecognized tax benefit when a net operating loss carryforward, a similar tax loss, or a tax credit carryforward exists. The provisions of ASU No. 2013–11 are codified in FASB ASC 740–10–45–10A and FASB ASC 740–10–45–10B.

ASU No. 2013–11 requires an entity to present an unrecognized tax benefit, or a portion of an unrecognized tax benefit, as a reduction to a deferred tax asset for a net operating loss carryforward, a similar tax loss, or a tax credit carryforward. Deferred tax assets are discussed in Sections 2.08 and 2.09.

However, if a net operating loss carryforward, a similar tax loss, or a tax credit carryforward is not available at the reporting date under the tax law of the applicable jurisdiction to settle any additional income taxes that would result from the disallowance of a tax position, then an entity is required to present the unrecognized tax benefit in the financial statements as a liability instead of combined with deferred tax assets.

Similarly, if the tax law of the applicable jurisdiction does not require the entity to use, and the entity does not intend to use, the deferred tax asset for such purposes, then, in that case as well, the entity is required to present the unrecognized tax benefit in the financial statements as a liability instead of combined with deferred tax assets.

Before FASB issued this guidance, there was diversity among companies in their presentation of unrecognized tax benefits. Some companies presented their unrecognized tax benefits in a manner similar to the method set forth in ASU 2013–11, while others did not.

The approach adopted in ASU No. 2013–11 is commonly referred to as "netting," where the deferred tax asset, such as a net operating loss carryforward, is reduced in the event that taxable income is increased by an unrecognized tax benefit.

---

[54] SFAS No. 109, paragraph 66.a.

[55] SFAS No. 109, paragraph 66.b.

[56] SFAS No. 109, paragraph 62.

[57] SFAS No. 109, paragraph 67.

[58] *Id.*

[59] *Id.*

§ 2.05 Basic Principles of Accounting for Income Taxes

FASB has provided two basic requirements in accounting for income taxes and two basic requirements in measuring current and deferred income taxes.[60] First, a tax liability or asset is recognized (based on the provisions of FASB ASC 740–10) for the estimated taxes payable (or refundable) for current and prior years' tax returns.[61] Second, a deferred tax liability or asset is recognized for the estimated future tax effects attributable to temporary differences and net operating losses and tax credit carryforwards.[62] Third, the measurement of current and deferred tax liabilities and assets is based on provisions of the enacted tax law.[63] As a result, the effects of future changes in tax laws or rates are not anticipated.[64] Finally, the measurement of deferred tax assets is reduced by the amount of any tax benefits that, based on available evidence, are not expected to be realized.[65] More specifically, a deferred tax asset is reduced by a valuation allowance if it is more likely than not that part or all of the deferred tax asset will not be realized. Each of these four basic principles will be discussed in greater detail below.

§ 2.06 Exceptions to Accounting for Income Taxes

FASB has provided some exceptions to the application of the two basic requirements in accounting for income taxes.[66] This generally means that if a transaction falls within one of these exceptions, the entity does not recognize a deferred tax liability or asset for its temporary differences with respect to that particular transaction. In all other cases, an entity must record a deferred tax liability or asset for its temporary differences (i.e., differences between the book basis and tax basis of its assets and liabilities).

In the first exception, an entity will not recognize a deferred tax liability for the excess of the book basis over the tax basis of an investment in a foreign subsidiary or a foreign corporate joint venture that is essentially permanent in duration.[67] This exception is a holdover from APB 23, *Accounting for Income Taxes—Special Areas*, and many practitioners still refer to it as the APB 23 exception to the recording of a deferred tax liability.[68]

In the second exception, FASB has provided special rules for the pattern of recognition of after-tax income for leveraged leases and the allocation of the purchase price in a purchase business combination to acquired leveraged leases as required by FASB ASC 840–30.[69] Generally, a leveraged lease is a type of direct financing lease

---

[60] FASB ASC 740–10–25–2; FASB ASC 740–10–30–2.

[61] FASB ASC 740–10–25–2.

[62] *Id.*

[63] FASB ASC 740–10–30–2.

[64] *Id.*

[65] *Id.*

[66] FASB ASC 740–10–25–3.

[67] FASB ASC 740–10–25–3(a).

[68] *See* discussion of Investment in a Foreign Subsidiary or Foreign Corporate Joint Venture at Section 2.16 and Section 4.04[2][c].

[69] FASB ASC 740–10–25–3(c). FASB has created Topic 842, *Leases*, which superseded guidance provided in Topic 840, effective for fiscal years beginning after December 15, 2018, for a public business entity, a not-for-profit entity that has issued, or is a conduit bond obligor for, securities that are traded, listed, or quoted on an exchange or an over-the-counter market, and an employee benefit plan that files financial statements with the SEC. It is effective for all other entities for fiscal years after December 15, 2020, and

involving three parties: lessee, lessor, and a long-term creditor. The long-term creditor provides financing on a non-recourse basis and in an amount sufficient to provide the lessor with substantial leverage (i.e., generally more than 50 percent of the purchase price).[70] For tax purposes, the lessor is the owner of the property. The lessor's net investment in the leased property decreases in the early years and increases in the later years until it is eliminated.

In the third exception, FASB prohibits recognition of a deferred tax liability related to goodwill for which amortization is not deductible for tax purposes.[71] Since 1993, under U.S. income tax laws, purchased (as opposed to self-created) goodwill is amortizable for tax purposes over a 15-year time period.[72] As a result, purchased goodwill under U.S. income tax laws may result in a temporary difference that will require the recording of a deferred tax liability as the goodwill is amortized for tax purposes (i.e., the tax basis of goodwill decreases below its book basis).

In the fourth exception, FASB prohibited recognition of a deferred tax asset for the intra-entity difference between the tax basis of the assets in the buyer's tax jurisdiction and their cost as reported in the consolidated financial statements.[73] Generally, an intercompany transfer of assets between tax jurisdictions is a taxable event, and the buyer obtains a new tax basis for the assets. The buyer's new tax base will be deductible on the buyer's tax return when the buyer sells or consumes the assets. The taxes paid by the seller are deferred, and the seller does not recognize a deferred tax asset for the tax bases difference between the two different tax jurisdictions. FASB has considered eliminating this exception.[74]

On October 24, 2016, FASB issued guidance requiring an entity to recognize the income tax consequences of an intra-entity asset transfer, other than an intra-entity asset transfer of inventory, when the transfer occurs.[75] For intra-entity asset transfers of inventory, FASB decided to retain current GAAP, which requires an entity to recognize the income tax consequences when the inventory has been sold to an outside party.

In the fifth and final exception, FASB prohibits recognition of a deferred tax liability or asset for differences related to assets and liabilities that, under FASB ASC 830–10, are remeasured from the local currency into the functional currency using historical exchange rates and that result from (1) changes in exchange rates or (2) indexing for tax purposes.[76] FASB has also considered eliminating this exception but has not yet implemented its decision.[77]

---

interim periods within fiscal years beginning after December 15, 2021. FASB Accounting Standards Update, No. 2016–02, *Leases (Topic 842)* (Feb. 2016); FASB Accounting Standards Update, 2019–10, Financial Instruments—Credit Losses (Topic 326), Derivatives and Hedging (Topic 815), and Leases (Topic 842) (Nov. 2019).

[70] FASB ASC 840–10–25–43(c); FASB ASC 842-10-20 Glossary.

[71] FASB ASC 740–10–25–3(d). A deferred tax liability or asset is recognized for temporary differences related to intangible assets other than non-tax amortizable goodwill.

[72] IRC Section 197.

[73] FASB ASC 740–10–25–3(e).

[74] FASB, *Intercompany Transfers and Foreign Currency*, Board Memorandum (Dec. 1, 2004).

[75] FASB, Accounting Standards Update No. 2016–16, *Income Taxes (Topic 740): Intra-Entity Transfers of Assets Other Than Inventory* (Oct. 2016); FASB ASC 740–10–25–3(e).

[76] FASB ASC 7401–10–25–3(f); FASB ASC 830–740–25–10.

[77] FASB, *Intercompany Transfers and Foreign Currency*, Board Memorandum (Dec. 1, 2004).

FASB has been clear that the only exceptions to the application of the basic requirements in accounting for income taxes are the ones described above.

§ 2.07 Temporary Differences

[1] In General

An entity's income taxes that are currently payable for a particular year typically include the tax consequences of most events that are recognized in the financial statements for that year.[78] However, because the tax laws and financial accounting standards differ in their recognition and measurement of assets, liabilities, equity, revenues, income, deductions, expenses, gains and losses, differences may arise between (a) the amount of taxable income and financial income for a particular year and (b) the tax bases and book bases of assets and liabilities.[79] These differences are referred to as temporary differences because an assumption inherent in an entity's statement of financial position is that the book bases of assets and liabilities will be recovered and settled, respectively.[80] Therefore, a difference between the tax basis and book basis of an asset or liability will result in taxable or deductible amounts in some future year(s) when the book basis of the asset is recovered and the book basis of the liability is settled.[81]

In thoroughly understanding FASB's definition of temporary differences, it is important to understand the relationship between the income statement and the tax return, and between the statement of financial position and the tax bases in assets and liabilities. Any temporary difference (as opposed to a permanent difference) between the income statement and the tax return will result in an offsetting temporary difference between the book bases of assets and liabilities and the tax bases of the related assets and liabilities. Illustration 2-6 demonstrates this basic principle.

ILLUSTRATION 2-6: An entity purchases equipment for $100,000 (and places it in service) on January 1, 2017. It uses accelerated depreciation for tax purposes (200 percent declining balance with the half-year convention) and straight-line depreciation for financial accounting purposes, in both cases, over a five-year recovery period/useful life. The following table shows the depreciation expense, depreciation deduction, book basis of the equipment and tax basis of the equipment each year.

Year	(a) Depreciation Expense (Accounting)	(b) Depreciation Deduction (Tax)	(c) Difference ((a) – (b))	(d) Book Basis	(e) Tax Basis	(f) Difference ((d) – (e))
2017	$20,000	$20,000	0	$80,000	$80,000	0
2018	$20,000	$32,000	($12,000)	$60,000	$48,000	$12,000
2019	$20,000	$19,200	$800	$40,000	$28,800	$11,200
2020	$20,000	$11,520	$8,480	$20,000	$17,280	$2,720

[78] FASB ASC 740–10–25.

[79] FASB ASC 740–10–25–19.

[80] FASB ASC 740–10–25–20. An asset is recovered generally by depreciation, amortization, sale or other disposition. A liability is settled by amortization, payment or other satisfaction.

[81] *Id.*

2021	$20,000	$11,520	$8,480	0	$5,760	($5,760)
2022	0	$5,760	($5,760)	0	0	0

In 2018, the entity has $12,000 *more* of depreciation deduction (tax) than depreciation expense (book) with respect to the equipment. As a result, the tax basis of the equipment is $12,000 lower than the book basis of the equipment creating a temporary difference of $12,000.

In 2019, the entity has $800 *less* of depreciation deduction than depreciation expense with respect to the equipment, thereby creating a difference in 2019 of $800 between taxable income and pretax financial income (i.e., taxable income will be $800 more than pretax financial income). In addition, in 2019, the tax basis of the equipment is $11,200 lower than the book basis of the equipment creating a temporary difference between tax basis and book basis, composed of the $12,000 difference in 2018 and the ($800) difference in 2019.

By 2022, when the equipment is fully depreciated, the total depreciation deduction of $100,000 will equal the total depreciation expense of $100,000, and the tax basis in the equipment of zero will equal its book basis of zero. As a result, the differences in depreciation deduction and depreciation expense are merely temporary as are the differences between the tax basis and the book basis in the equipment.

The FASB staff has also made it clear that temporary differences are differences between the book basis and tax basis of assets and liabilities. Any tax-to-tax difference is not a temporary difference and does not give rise to a deferred tax.[82] For example, the excess of an entity's tax basis in the stock of an acquired company over the tax basis of the net assets of the acquired company is a tax-to-tax difference.[83] A deferred tax asset would not be permitted for such an excess because a tax-to-tax difference is not a temporary difference.

[2] Different Types of Temporary Differences

FASB ASC 740 applies to temporary differences, formerly referred to as timing differences under APB 11. A temporary difference is defined as "a difference between the tax basis of an asset or liability computed pursuant to the requirements in FASB ASC 740–10 for tax positions, and its reported amount in the financial statements [book basis] that will result in taxable or deductible amounts in future years when the reported amount of the asset or liability is recovered or settled, respectively."[84] Based on this definition, the term "temporary difference" encompasses more than just timing differences.

---

[82] FASB Task Force, EITF Topic No. D–31, *Temporary Differences Related to LIFO Inventory and Tax-to-Tax Differences* (March 16, 1993); FASB ASC 740–10–25–31; FASB ASC 740–10–55–53. In SFAS No. 96, FASB required recognition of a tax benefit for certain tax-to-tax differences. SFAS No. 96, paragraph 72. SFAS No. 96 was superseded by SFAS No. 109 (FASB ASC 740).

[83] FASB Task Force, EITF Topic No. D–31, *Temporary Differences Related to LIFO Inventory and Tax-to-Tax Differences* (March 16, 1993); FASB ASC 740–10–25–31.

[84] FASB ASC 740–10–20 Glossary.

There are two types of temporary differences.[85] A *taxable* temporary difference is a temporary difference that results in taxable amounts in future years when the related asset or liability is recovered or settled.[86] A taxable temporary difference occurs when the book basis of an asset is greater than its tax basis or the book basis of a liability is less than its tax basis. For example, revenues or gains that are taxable *after* they are recognized in pretax financial income are common types of taxable temporary differences.[87] Expenses or losses that are deductible *before* they are recognized in pretax financial income are also common types of taxable temporary differences.[88]

A *deductible* temporary difference is a temporary difference that results in a deductible amount in future years (or an exclusion from taxable income in future years) when the related asset or liability is recovered or settled.[89] A deductible temporary difference occurs when the book basis of an asset is lower than its tax basis or the book basis of a liability is greater than its tax basis. For example, revenues or gains that are taxable *before* they are recognized in pretax financial income are common types of deductible temporary differences.[90] Expenses or losses that are deductible *after* they are recognized in pretax financial income are also common types of deductible temporary differences.[91]

Figure 2-1 provides the four general categories of temporary differences with brief examples:

FIGURE 2-1

Categories of Temporary Differences

Categories of Temporary Differences	Explanation of Category	Examples[92]
Taxable Temporary Difference	Revenues or gains that are taxable *after* included in financial income	1. gain reported under installment method for tax purposes but immediately recognized for financial accounting
		2. gain on involuntary conversion deferred for tax purposes but immediately recognized for financial accounting
Taxable Temporary Difference	Expenses or losses that are deductible *before* recognized in financial income	1. accelerated depreciation for tax purposes but straight-

85 FASB ASC 740–10–25–23.

86 FASB ASC 740–10–20 Glossary.

87 FASB ASC 740–10–25–20(a).

88 FASB ASC 740–10–25–20(d).

89 FASB ASC 740–10–20 Glossary.

90 FASB ASC 740–10–25–20(c).

91 FASB ASC 740–10–25–20(b).

92 This list is partially adopted from Kieso, supra note 1, at 1065.

			line depreciation for financial accounting
		2.	prepaid expenses immediately deducted for tax purposes but expensed over time for financial accounting
Deductible Temporary Difference	Revenues or gains that are taxable *before* included in financial income	1.	advance payments for services to be rendered in the future immediately included in income for tax purposes but deferred over time for financial accounting
		2.	advance payments for goods to be delivered in the future immediately included in income for tax purposes but deferred for financial accounting
Deductible Temporary Difference	Expenses or losses that are deductible *after* recognized in financial income	1.	product warranty expense established as part of a reserve for financial accounting but not deducted for tax purposes until the all events test (including economic performance) is met
		2.	bad debt expense established as part of a reserve for financial accounting but not deducted for tax purposes until specifically charged off

Some temporary differences are not timing differences.[93] Generally, a timing difference occurs when an item of revenue or expense for financial accounting purposes differs from the corresponding item of income or deduction for tax purposes in a given year with the difference reversing in a future year(s). One common example of a timing difference involves the use of straight-line depreciation for financial accounting purposes and accelerated depreciation for tax purposes. In the early years of the depreciable asset,

[93] FASB ASC 740–10–25–20; FASB ASC 740–10–25–21.

accelerated depreciation each year will be greater than straight-line depreciation. But this will reverse in the later years of the depreciable asset so that over the depreciable life of the asset, total depreciation deductions will equal total depreciation expense. Consequently, the differences between the amounts of depreciation deduction and depreciation expense each year are merely timing differences.

If, however, a depreciable property's tax basis is different than its book basis when the property is placed in service, then the total amount of depreciation deductions and the total amount of depreciation expense over the depreciable life of the property will not be equal. As a result, the differences between the amounts of depreciation deduction and depreciation expense each year are not merely timing differences. They are, in a sense, permanent differences. However, these differences are still considered temporary differences under FASB ASC 740 because a difference between the tax basis of an asset (or liability) and its book basis will result in taxable or deductible amounts in some future year(s) when the reported amounts of assets are recovered (and the reported amounts of liabilities are settled). Therefore, a deferred tax liability or asset will be recognized for the temporary difference.

FIGURE 2-2

Categories of Temporary Differences That Are Not Timing Differences[94]

Categories of Temporary Differences	Explanation of Category
Taxable Temporary Difference	Reduction in the tax basis of depreciable assets because of tax credits[95]
Deductible Temporary Difference	Reduction in the book basis of an asset due to the deferral method of accounting for the investment tax credit[96]
Deductible Temporary Difference	Increase in the tax basis of assets because of indexing when the local currency is the functional currency[97]
Taxable or Deductible Temporary Difference	Business combination in which there are differences between the book basis and tax bases of the assets and liabilities[98]
Taxable or Deductible Temporary Difference	Intra-entity transfers of assets other than inventory in which there are differences between the book bases and the tax bases of the assets[99]

---

94 FASB ASC 740–10–25–20.

95 FASB ASC 740–10–25–20(e).

96 FASB ASC 740–10–25–20(f).

97 FASB ASC 740–10–25–20(g). *See* FASB Task Force, EITF Issue No. 93–9, *Application of FASB Statement No. 109 in Foreign Financial Statements Restated for General Price-Level Changes* (Sept. 23, 1993) (FASB ASC 830–740–30–1) (compute temporary differences between the indexed tax basis of an asset or liability and its restated for inflation book basis; the deferred tax expense (or benefit) is calculated as the difference between the deferred tax assets and liabilities at the end of the current year less the deferred tax asset and liabilities at the end of the prior year adjusted for inflation).

98 FASB ASC 740–10–25–20(h).

99 FASB ASC 740–10–25–20(i).

Illustration 2-7 and Illustration 2-8 demonstrate temporary differences that are not timing differences.

ILLUSTRATION 2-7: A corporation purchases a building on January 1, 2017, for $200,000. From January to June 2017, it incurs $240,000 of qualified rehabilitation expenditures with respect to the building. On July 1, 2017, the corporation places the building in service.

In 2017, the corporation will have a tax credit of $24,000, which is equal to ten percent of the qualified rehabilitation expenditures. The tax credit will reduce the corporation's basis in the building to $416,000 ($200,000 cost plus $240,000 qualified rehabilitation expenditures less $24,000 tax credit). Therefore, for purposes of computing the corporation's depreciation deductions, the basis will be $416,000. The corporation will depreciate the building for tax purposes using the straight-line method, mid-month convention and an applicable recovery period of either 27.5 years (residential rental property) or 39 years (non-residential real property).

For financial accounting purposes, the book basis of the building is $440,000. The book basis is not reduced by the tax credit of $24,000. The corporation will depreciate the building for book purposes using the straight-line method over the building's estimated useful life, which may be from 25 to 40 years. Because the tax basis in the building differs from its book basis, a taxable temporary difference is created and a deferred tax liability will be recognized. The 10 percent credit for qualified rehabilitation expenditures was repealed as part of the Tax Cuts and Jobs Act.

ILLUSTRATION 2-8:[100]

An entity acquires the stock of another corporation for $250. The principal asset of the acquired corporation is a marketable equity security with a readily determinable fair market value of $200 and a tax basis of $500. The tax rate is 35 percent. The acquired corporation has no operations and so the acquisition is accounted for as an asset purchase and not as a business combination. The acquired financial asset should be recorded at fair market value, and a deferred tax asset should be recorded for $105 ($500 tax basis minus $200 book basis times 35 percent). But no immediate income statement recognition is permitted (FASB ASC 740–10–25–51). As a result, the excess of the fair market value of the financial asset (i.e., book basis) and the deferred tax asset recorded over the cash purchase price should be recorded as a deferred credit of $55 ($200 book basis plus $105 deferred tax asset minus $250 cash paid).

Some differences between the book basis and tax basis of an asset or liability may not result in taxable or deductible amounts in future years when the related asset or liability is recovered or settled and therefore may not be temporary differences (in which a deferred tax liability or asset is recognized).[101] Illustration 2-9 gives an example of a difference between book basis and tax basis that may or may not be a temporary difference.[102]

---

[100] FASB ASC 740–10–55–189; FASB ASC 740–10–55–190; FASB ASC 740–10–55–191.

[101] FASB ASC 740–10–05–9; FASB ASC 740–10–25–30.

[102] *Id.*

ILLUSTRATION 2-9: A corporation purchases a $1 million whole life insurance policy on one of its corporate executives with the corporation the beneficiary on the policy. The corporation pays a premium of $10,000 per year. Part of the premium is for life insurance protection and part of the premium is for the cash reserve (i.e., cash surrender value). For financial accounting purposes, the corporation will expense the portion of the premium for life insurance protection of the corporate executive and will also set up an asset for the cash reserve portion of the premium. For tax purposes, however, no portion of the premium is deductible with the result that the entire premium payment is capitalized as part of the basis in the life insurance policy.[103] Consequently, a difference arises between the book basis and the tax basis of the life insurance policy.

If the corporate executive later dies and the corporation receives $1 million when the cash surrender value is $300,000, the corporation will record a gain of $700,000 for financial accounting purposes. For tax purposes, however, the entire $1 million is excluded from gross income.[104] As a result, the excess of the cash surrender value over the premiums paid becomes a permanent difference.

If, however, the corporation surrenders the policy for its cash surrender value, any difference between the cash surrender value and its book basis is gain (or loss) for purposes of financial accounting. For tax purposes, the difference between the cash surrender value and the corporation's basis in the policy is gross income (or a deduction) to the corporation.[105] As a result, the excess of cash surrender value over the premiums paid becomes a temporary difference.

FASB has noted that if the cash surrender value is expected to be recovered by surrendering the policy, then the excess is a temporary difference. If the entity expects to hold the policy until the corporate executive's death, then the excess is not a temporary difference.[106]

Some temporary differences are deferred taxable income or tax deductions and have a tax basis (i.e., balance on the income tax balance sheet) but cannot be identified with a particular asset or liability on the financial statements.[107] For example, organization costs that are immediately expensed for financial accounting purposes will not appear on the financial statements but may have a tax basis.[108] Under the tax laws, organization costs are generally deducted up to $5,000 with any excess being deducted ratably over 180 months.[109] In this instance, there is no related, identifiable asset or liability for financial reporting (because the organization costs were expensed), but there is a temporary difference that results from an event that has been recognized in the financial

[103] IRC Section 264(a)(2).

[104] IRC Section 101(a)(1).

[105] IRC Section 61(a). A corporation's basis in the life insurance policy is the aggregate of premiums paid. IRC Section 72(e)(5).

[106] FASB ASC 740–10–25–30.

[107] FASB ASC 740–10–05–10; FASB ASC 740–10–25–24.

[108] FASB ASC 740–10–25–25. AICPA, *Reporting on the Costs of Start-up Activities*, SOP No. 98–5 (1998) (expense start-up costs as incurred); FASB ASC 720–15–25-1.

[109] IRC Section 195 (active trade or business), IRC Section 248 (corporation), and IRC Section 709 (partnership). The $5,000 immediate deduction is phased out, dollar for dollar, by the amount of organization costs in excess of $50,000.

statements.[110] One way of viewing this is that a tax basis exists for organization costs (assuming they exceed $5,000 and therefore are not immediately deducted in full) with a zero book basis, thereby creating a deductible temporary difference. Based on provisions in the tax law, the temporary difference will result in a taxable or deductible amount in future years.[111] In the example of organization costs, a deductible amount will result in future years as the organization costs are amortized for tax purposes.

Another example of a temporary difference that cannot be identified with a particular asset or liability on the financial statements is a long-term contract accounted for under the percentage of completion method for financial reporting and the completed contract method for tax purposes.[112] The temporary difference is deferred income for tax purposes that becomes taxable when the contract is completed.[113]

Tax-to-tax differences are not temporary differences.[114] As a result, a deferred tax liability (or asset) is not recognized for tax-to-tax differences.[115] An example of a tax-to-tax difference would be the difference between a parent entity's basis in the stock of an acquired entity and the tax basis of the assets of the acquired entity.[116]

[3] Examples of Temporary Differences

ILLUSTRATION 2-10: An entity sold equipment (which has a book basis and tax basis of $20,000) on July 1, 2020, for $50,000, realizing a book and tax gain of $30,000. The purchaser paid the entire purchase price two years later on July 1, 2022. Assume under the tax laws, the entity reports $10,000 of gain at the time of sale (due to depreciation recapture) and reported the remaining $20,000 of gain in 2022 when the purchase price was received from the purchaser.[117] Under GAAP, at the time of sale, the entity created a receivable of $50,000 and reported the entire gain of $30,000 in financial income.[118] The entity's book basis of the receivable is $50,000 and its tax basis in the receivable is $30,000. A taxable temporary difference arose because the book basis of the receivable exceeded its tax basis. The amount of the taxable temporary difference was $20,000, the excess of the book basis of the receivable over its tax basis.

ILLUSTRATION 2-11: An entity purchases equipment in 2017 for $100,000. Assume under the tax laws, the depreciation deduction for 2017 is $20,000. Under GAAP, assume the depreciation expense for 2017 is $10,000. At the end of 2017, the book basis of the equipment is $90,000 ($100,000 cost less $10,000 of book depreciation) and the tax basis in the equipment is $80,000 ($100,000 cost basis less $20,000 of tax depreciation). A taxable temporary difference

[110] FASB ASC 740–10–25–26.

[111] *Id.*

[112] FASB ASC 740–10–25–25. Congress has recently required that taxable income from all long-term contracts be determined under the percentage of completion method for federal income tax purposes. IRC Section 460(a).

[113] FASB ASC 740–10–25–25.

[114] FASB ASC 740–10–25–31.

[115] *Id.*

[116] *Id.*

[117] IRC Section 453(a). Under the tax laws, recapture income under section 1245 (or 1250) must be recognized in the year of disposition. IRC Section 453(i).

[118] FASB ASC 606–10–05–3; FASB ASC 606–10–05–4; FASB ASC 606–10–25–23.

arises because the book basis of the equipment exceeds its tax basis. The amount of the taxable temporary difference is $10,000, the excess of the book basis of the equipment over the tax basis of the equipment.

ILLUSTRATION 2-12: An entity receives an advance payment of $40,000 from a customer on July 1, 2022, for services required to be performed in the future. Under the tax laws, the entity is required to include the advance payment in taxable income upon receipt in 2022.[119] Under GAAP, the entity sets up a liability reflecting its obligation to provide services to the customer in the future.[120] The entity will include the advance receipt in financial income as it performs the services for the customer (decreasing its liability) in the future. A deductible temporary difference arises because the book basis of the liability exceeds its tax basis. The amount of the deductible temporary difference is $40,000, the excess of the book basis of the liability ($40,000) over its tax basis (zero).

ILLUSTRATION 2-13: An entity sets up a reserve for bad debts in the amount of $25,000 in 2022. Under the tax laws, the entity is not permitted a bad debt deduction until a debt becomes partially or completely worthless.[121] Under GAAP, the entity has a $25,000 expense in 2022 when it sets up the reserve account. A deductible temporary difference arises because the book basis of the reserve liability exceeds its tax basis. The amount of the deductible temporary difference is $25,000, the excess of the book basis of the reserve liability ($25,000) over its tax basis (zero).

§ 2.08 Deferred Tax Liabilities and Deferred Tax Assets

[1] In General

An entity must recognize a deferred tax liability or deferred tax asset for all temporary differences and net operating loss and tax credit carryforwards.[122] A deferred tax liability is the deferred tax consequences attributable to *taxable* temporary differences.[123] It is recognized when an asset has a higher book basis than tax basis or if a liability has a lower book basis than tax basis. It is measured using the applicable enacted tax rate and provisions of the enacted tax law.[124] For example, assume an entity has a taxable temporary difference of $100,000 and the applicable enacted tax rate is 21 percent (which is the current U.S. federal statutory tax rate for corporations). The entity

---

[119] *See, e.g.*, IRC Section 451(c); *Automobile Club of Michigan v. Commissioner*, 353 U.S. 180 (1957); *American Automobile Association v. United States*, 367 U.S. 687 (1961); *Schlude v. Commissioner*, 372 U.S. 128 (1963). *But see, e.g.*, IRC Section 455 and IRC Section 456; *Artnell v. Commissioner*, 400 F.2d 981 (1968); *Tampa Bay Devil Rays, Ltd. v. Commissioner*, 84 T.C.M. 394 (2002).

[120] FASB ASC 606–10–25–8; FASB ASC 740-10-25-20(c).

[121] IRC Section 166(a). Prior to enactment of the Tax Reform Act of 1986, a taxpayer was permitted under the tax laws to establish a reserve for bad debts. Old IRC Section 166(c).

[122] FASB ASC 740–10–25–29. As a general rule, separate deferred tax computations are made for each state and local tax jurisdiction in which deferred tax liabilities or assets are significant. If, however, there are no significant differences between the tax laws of the particular state and local tax jurisdictions, then an aggregate computation of deferred tax assets and liabilities is acceptable. *See* FASB Special Report, *A Guide to Implementation of Statement 109 on Accounting for Income Taxes: Questions and Answers*, Q & A 3 (1992).

[123] FASB ASC 740–10–20, *Glossary*.

[124] *Id.*

will set up a deferred tax liability of $21,000 with a $21,000 increase to deferred tax expense.

A deferred tax asset is the deferred tax consequences attributable to *deductible* temporary differences and net operating loss and tax credit carryforwards.[125] It is recognized if an asset has a lower book basis than tax basis or if a liability has a higher book basis than tax basis. Like a deferred tax liability, a deferred tax asset is measured using the applicable enacted tax rate and provisions of the enacted tax law.[126] For example, assume an entity has a deductible temporary difference of $80,000 and the applicable enacted tax rate is 21 percent. The entity will set up a deferred tax asset of $16,800 with a $16,800 decrease to deferred tax expense (or alternatively, a $16,800 increase to deferred tax benefit). Unlike a deferred tax liability, however, a deferred tax asset is reduced by a valuation allowance if, based on the weight of evidence available, it is more likely than not that some or all of a deferred tax asset will not be realized.[127]

Deferred tax expense or benefit is the change during the year in an entity's deferred tax liabilities or deferred tax assets.[128] For deferred tax liabilities and assets acquired in a purchase business combination during the year, it is the change since the combination date.[129] *Total income tax expense or benefit for the year is the sum of: deferred tax expense or benefit plus income taxes currently payable or refundable.*[130] See Illustration 2-14 for an example of computing total income tax expense.

> **ILLUSTRATION 2-14:** An entity has a beginning of the year balance in deferred tax liability of $500,000 and an end of the year balance of $900,000. It also has pretax financial income of $6 million and income tax payable for the year of $2.4 million. The deferred tax expense for the year is $400,000 ($900,000 ending balance in deferred tax liability less $500,000 beginning balance in deferred tax liability). The total income tax expense for the year is: $400,000 of deferred tax expense plus $2.4 million of current tax expense (income tax payable) equaling $2.8 million.

[2] Applicable Tax Rate

In concept, a deferred tax liability or asset represents the increase or decrease in taxes payable or refundable in future years as a result of temporary differences and carryforwards at the end of the current year.[131] In other words, the concept is an incremental or marginal concept.[132] The incremental or marginal tax effect is equal to: (a) the amount of taxes payable or refundable in future years *inclusive* of reversing temporary differences and carryforwards minus (b) the amount of taxes payable or refundable in future years *exclusive* of reversing temporary differences and carryforwards.[133] More succinctly, the future income tax cash flows with and without

---

[125] *Id.*

[126] *Id.*

[127] *Id.*

[128] FASB ASC 740–10–30–4.

[129] *Id.*

[130] FASB ASC 740–10–30–3.

[131] FASB ASC 740–10–10–3.

[132] *Id.*

[133] *Id.*

reversing temporary differences and carryforwards would be the incremental or marginal tax effect.[134]

FASB concluded that, except in the simplest situations, an incremental approach would be impossible, as a practical matter, to implement.[135] As a result, FASB decided to utilize a tax rate convention, referred to as the applicable tax rate, in measuring deferred tax liabilities and assets.[136] FASB also decided to utilize a valuation allowance in measuring deferred tax assets.[137]

The applicable tax rate with respect to a deferred tax liability or deferred tax asset is the enacted tax rate expected to apply to taxable income in the periods in which the deferred tax liability or asset is expected to be settled or realized.[138] Deferred taxes are not discounted.[139] Measurements are based on elections (for example, an election for a loss or tax credit carryforward instead of a loss or tax credit carryback) that are expected to be made for tax purposes in future years.[140] If Congress enacts changes in the tax laws and tax rates that become effective at a future date, then an entity must consider those future tax laws and tax rates in determining the tax rate to apply to temporary differences reversing in a future year(s).[141]

ILLUSTRATION 2-15:[142]

An entity has $900 of deductible temporary differences at the end of year two (the current year), which are expected to result in tax deductions of approximately $450 for each of years three and four. The enacted tax rates are 30 percent for years one and two, and 40 percent for years three and thereafter. The entity will record a deferred tax asset for the $900 of deductible temporary differences. The tax rate is 40 percent if the entity expects to realize a tax benefit for the deductible temporary difference by offsetting taxable income earned in future years. Alternatively, the tax rate is 30 percent if the entity expects to realize a tax benefit for the deductible temporary differences by loss carryback. Assume that the entity records a $360 deferred tax asset ($900 at 40 percent) to be realized by offsetting taxable income in future years, and taxable income and taxes payable in each of years one and two were $450 and $135, respectively. Realization of a tax benefit of at least $270 ($900 at 30 percent) is assured because carryback refunds totaling $270 may be realized even if no taxable income is earned in future years. Recognition of a valuation allowance for the other $90 ($360 minus $270) of the deferred tax asset depends on management's assessment of whether, based on the weight of available evidence, part or all of the tax benefit of the $900 of deductible temporary differences will not be realized at 40 percent tax rates in future years. Alternatively, if enacted tax rates are 40 percent for years one and two and 30

---

[134] *Id.*

[135] SFAS No. 109, paragraph 88.

[136] *Id.*

[137] *Id. See* Section 2.09 for discussion of the valuation allowance.

[138] FASB ASC 740–10–30–8 and FASB ASC 740–10–55–23.

[139] *Id.*

[140] FASB ASC 740–10–55–23.

[141] *Id.*

[142] FASB ASC 740–10–55–131 to FASB ASC 740–10–55–135. The Tax Cuts and Jobs Act (TCJA) repealed the two-year carryback period for net operating losses. IRC section 172.

percent for year three and thereafter, measurement of the deferred tax asset at a 40 percent tax rate could only occur if tax losses are expected in future years three and four.

If Congress enacts a phased-in change in tax rates, then an entity must determine when the deferred tax liabilities and assets will be settled and realized to calculate the applicable tax rate.[143] This is one of the few times in FASB ASC 740 when an entity must schedule when its temporary differences will reverse (i.e., when the deferred tax assets and liabilities will be settled).[144] If Congress has not enacted changes in the tax laws and tax rates that become effective in future years, then the tax laws and rates for the current year are used.[145] Illustration 2-16 provides an example of determining the applicable tax rate when Congress enacts a phased-in change in tax rates.

ILLUSTRATION 2-16:[146]

An entity has $2,400 of taxable temporary differences at the end of year two (the current year), which are expected to result in taxable amounts of approximately $1,200 per year for each of years three and four. The enacted tax rates are 35 percent for years one and two, 40 percent for years three and four, and 45 percent for years five and thereafter. The entity will record a deferred tax liability for the $2,400 of taxable temporary differences. The tax rate that is used to measure the deferred tax liability will differ depending on whether the tax effect of future reversals of the taxable temporary differences is in taxes payable for years one and two, years three and four, or years five and thereafter. The tax rate for measurement of the deferred tax liability is 40 percent whenever taxable income is expected in years three and four. If tax losses are expected in years three and four, however, the tax rate is (a) 35 percent if realization of a tax benefit for those tax losses will be by loss carryback to years one and two or (b) 45 percent if realization of a tax benefit for those tax losses in years three and four will be by loss carryforward to years five and thereafter.

A deferred tax asset for deductible temporary differences may be expected to be realized in future years through a carryback of a future net operating loss to the current or a prior year. Alternatively, a deferred tax liability for taxable temporary differences may be expected to reduce the refund claimed for a carryback of a future net operating loss to the current or a prior year. In either case, the deferred tax asset or deferred tax liability is measured using tax laws and rates for the current or prior year (i.e., the year for which a refund is expected to be realized based on loss carryback provisions of the tax law).[147]

Under U.S. tax law prior to 2018, if corporate taxable income exceeded a specified amount ($18,333,333), all taxable income was taxed, in substance, at a single flat tax rate of 35 percent.[148] FASB determined that deferred tax liabilities and assets should be

---

[143] FASB ASC 740–10–30–9.

[144] FASB 740–10–55–15. Reversing patterns of temporary differences may need to be scheduled in the following situations: (1) expected future taxable income eliminating the need for a valuation allowance; and (2) phased-in change on tax rates.

[145] FASB ASC 740–10–55–23.

[146] FASB ASC 740–10–55–129 and FASB ASC 740–10–55–130.

[147] FASB ASC 740–10–55–23.

[148] Old IRC Section 11.

measured using the enacted tax rate expected to apply to the *last* dollars of taxable income in the periods in which the deferred tax liability or asset was expected to be settled or realized.[149] As a result, the 35 percent rate was used for measuring a deferred tax liability or asset for entities in which graduated tax rates were not a significant factor.[150]

If graduated tax rates are a significant factor for an entity, then the entity must measure a deferred tax liability or asset using the average graduated tax rate applicable to the amount of estimated annual taxable income in the periods in which the deferred tax liability or asset is expected to be settled or realized.[151] FASB adopted the average graduated tax rate approach if graduated rates are a significant factor to prevent overstating deferred tax liabilities and assets.[152]

ILLUSTRATION 2-17:[153]

An entity has $1,500 of taxable temporary differences and $900 of deductible temporary differences at the end of year three (the current year), which are expected to result in net taxable amounts of approximately $200 for each of years four, five, and six. Enacted tax rates are 15 percent for the first $500 of taxable income, 25 percent for the next $500, and 40 percent for taxable income over $1,000. The deferred tax liability and asset for those reversing taxable and deductible temporary differences in years four, five, and six are measured using the average graduated tax rate for the estimated amount of annual taxable income in future years. Therefore, the average graduated tax rate will differ depending on the expected level of annual taxable income (including reversing temporary differences) in years four, five, and six. The average tax rate will be: (a) 15 percent if the estimated annual level of taxable income in years four, five, and six is $500 or less, (b) 20 percent if the estimated annual level of taxable income in years four, five, and six is $1,000 (15 percent for $500 and 25 percent for $500 averaging to 20 percent), or (c) 30 percent if the estimated annual level of taxable income in years four, five, and six is $2,000 (15 percent for $500, 25 percent for $500 and 40 percent for $1,000 averaging 30 percent).

As part of the Tax Cuts and Jobs Act (TCJA), Congress consolidated the graduated corporate tax rates into a single tax rate of 21 percent effective beginning in 2018. Other provisions of enacted tax laws must be considered in determining the tax rate to apply to certain types of temporary differences and carryforwards.[154] If the tax law provides for different tax rates to apply to ordinary income and capital gains, the difference in rates needs to be considered in determining the applicable tax rate.[155] For example,

---

149 SFAS No. 109, paragraph 89.

150 FASB ASC 740–10–30–9.

151 *Id.*

152 SFAS No. 109, paragraph 89.

153 FASB ASC 740–10–55–136 to FASB ASC 740–10–55–138.

154 FASB ASC 740–10–30–9.

155 FASB ASC 740–10–30–9 and FASB ASC 740–10–55–24. *See* FASB ASC 740–10–25–39 and FASB ASC 740–10–25–40 (a foreign jurisdiction taxes corporate income at a higher rate for undistributed income than distributed income but provides a tax credit for the excess when the previously taxed income is distributed in a later year; in the separate financial statements of the foreign entity, a deferred tax asset is not recognized for the future tax credits when the previously taxed income is distributed; rather, the tax credits reduce income tax expense when the credits are included in the foreign entity's tax return).

evidence based on all the facts and circumstances would determine whether an investor's deferred tax liability for the tax consequences related to the earnings of an investee should be measured using the tax rates for capital gains or the tax rates for dividends.[156] If the computation of a deferred tax liability for undistributed earnings is based on the tax rates for dividends, then the computation should also reflect any related dividends-received deductions, foreign tax credits, or taxes that would be withheld from the dividend.[157]

Entities must use regular tax rates in determining the amount of deferred taxes even if the entity is currently an alternative minimum tax (AMT) taxpayer and expects to always be an AMT taxpayer.[158] However, a deferred tax asset is recognized for AMT credit carryforwards.[159] The TCJA repealed the corporate alternative minimum tax effective beginning in 2018.[160] Similar principles apply in determining the applicable tax rate in jurisdictions other than the U.S. federal jurisdiction, such as foreign, state and local jurisdictions. In other words, the regular tax rate of the foreign, state or local jurisdiction must be used but consideration must be given to any interaction between that jurisdiction's regular tax system and any alternative tax system that it may have.[161]

Temporary differences usually do not reverse in equal annual amounts (as in Illustration 2-15, Illustration 2-16, and Illustration 2-17).[162] Therefore, a different average graduated tax rate might apply to reversals in different future years.[163] However, a detailed analysis to determine the net reversals of temporary differences in each future year usually is not needed because taxable income or losses (exclusive of reversing temporary differences in each of those future years) in each future year is simply an estimate.[164] As a result, an aggregate calculation is made using a single estimated average graduated tax rate based on estimated average annual taxable income in future years.[165] An entity must exercise its best judgment in dealing with unusual situations, such as an abnormally large temporary difference that will reverse in a single future year, or an abnormal level of taxable income that is expected for a single future year.[166] An entity should use the lowest graduated tax rate whenever the estimated average graduated tax rate would otherwise be zero.[167]

---

[156] FASB ASC 740–10–55–24.

[157] *Id.*

[158] FASB ASC 740–10–30–10; FASB ASC 740–10–30–11.

[159] FASB ASC 740–10–30–10.

[160] *But see* Section 2.22 for a discussion of the corporate AMT enacted as part of the Inflation Reduction Act of 2022 and scheduled to be effective beginning in 2023.

[161] FASB ASC 740–10–30–12. *See* FASB ASC 740–10–25–41 (a foreign jurisdiction taxes corporate income at a higher rate for undistributed income than distributed income but provides a tax credit for the excess when the previously taxed income is distributed in a later year; in the consolidated financial statements of a parent that includes a foreign subsidiary, if the parent is not utilizing FASB ASC 740–30–25–17 with respect to the unremitted earnings of the foreign subsidiary, it should recognize the deferred tax effects based on the distributed tax rate in the foreign jurisdiction; if the parent is utilizing FASB ASC 740–30–25–17 for the unremitted earnings of the foreign subsidiary, then the undistributed rate should be used in the consolidated financial statements).

[162] FASB 740–10–55–136 to FASB 740–10–55–138.

[163] *Id.*

[164] *Id.*

[165] *Id.*

[166] *Id.*

[167] *Id.*

[3] Annual Computation of Deferred Tax Liabilities and Deferred Tax Assets

[a] Basic Principles

In making the annual computation of deferred tax liabilities and assets, a five-step process is generally utilized for each tax-paying component in each tax jurisdiction.[168] The five steps are as follows:

(1) identify the types and amounts of existing temporary differences and the nature and amount of each type of net operating loss and tax credit carryforward and the remaining length of the carryforward period;[169]

(2) measure the total deferred tax liability for taxable temporary differences using the applicable tax rate;[170]

(3) measure the total deferred tax asset for deductible temporary differences and net operating loss carryforwards using the applicable tax rate;[171]

(4) measure deferred tax assets for each type of tax credit carryforward;[172] and

(5) reduce deferred tax assets by a valuation allowance.[173] The valuation allowance should be an amount sufficient to reduce the deferred tax asset to the amount that is more likely than not to be realized.[174]

Deferred tax liabilities and assets are adjusted for the effect of a change in tax laws or rates.[175] The effect is included in income from continuing operations for the period that includes the enactment date of the tax laws or rates.[176] If, for example, an entity has a deferred tax liability of $35,000 ($100,000 taxable temporary difference times 35 percent applicable tax rate) and Congress decreases the top tax rate from 35 percent to 21 percent, then the entity must decrease its deferred tax liability to $21,000 and decrease its deferred tax expense by $14,000 for the period that includes the enactment date. The net effect is to decrease income tax expense by $14,000, thereby increasing income from continuing operations by a corresponding amount. As a result, when Congress decreases the top U.S. federal tax rate, entities will have a one-time increase in earnings if they have net deferred tax liabilities (deferred tax liabilities in excess of deferred tax assets), while entities in a net deferred tax asset position (deferred tax assets in excess of deferred tax liabilities) will have a one-time decrease to earnings. In contrast, if Congress increases the top U.S. federal tax rate, entities that are in a net deferred tax liability position will have a one-time "hit" or charge to earnings as a result of the rate change while entities in a net deferred tax asset position will have a one-time increase in earnings.

---

[168] FASB ASC 740–10–30–5.

[169] FASB ASC 740–10–30–5(a).

[170] FASB ASC 740–10–30–5(b).

[171] FASB ASC 740–10–30–5(c).

[172] FASB ASC 740–10–30–5(d).

[173] FASB ASC 740–10–30–5(e).

[174] *Id.*

[175] FASB ASC 740–10–35–4.

[176] FASB ASC 740–10–45–15; FASB ASC 740–10–25–47.

When Congress increased the top corporate rate (from 34 percent to 35 percent) as part of the Omnibus Budget Reconciliation Act of 1993, it did so retroactively to January 1, 1993. An issue arose as to whether the tax effect of a retroactive change in tax rates should be measured utilizing temporary differences on the enactment date of August 10, 1993, or on the effective date of January 1, 1993, of the tax rate change. A FASB Task Force concluded that the tax effect of a retroactive change in tax rates should be measured using temporary differences and currently taxable income on the enactment date of August 10, 1993, with the cumulative tax effect included in income from continuing operations.[177] As a result, the tax effect of a retroactive change in tax rates is determined at the date of enactment using temporary differences and currently taxable income existing on the date of enactment.[178]

The TCJA decreased the top corporate tax rate from 35 percent to 21 percent. The date of enactment was December 22, 2017, and as a result deferred tax assets and liabilities had to be remeasured using a 21 percent corporate tax rate in the period including the enactment date. The effect is included in income from continuing operations.

An entity's tax status may change from nontaxable to taxable or from taxable to nontaxable.[179] For example, a partnership (nontaxable tax status) may convert to a corporation (taxable tax status) and vice versa.[180] If a nontaxable entity becomes a taxable entity then a deferred tax liability or asset must be recognized for temporary differences on the date that the nontaxable entity becomes a taxable entity.[181] If a taxable entity becomes a nontaxable entity, then a deferred tax liability or asset is eliminated on the date that the taxable entity becomes a nontaxable entity.[182] The effect of recognizing or eliminating a deferred tax liability or asset is included in income from continuing operations.[183] If an entity makes an election for a voluntary change in tax status, the change in status is recognized on the approval date (or on the filing date if approval is not necessary).[184] If an entity's tax status changes as a result of a change in tax law, then the change in status is recognized on the enactment date.[185]

---

[177] FASB Task Force, EITF Issue No. 93–13, *Effect of a Retroactive Change in Enacted Tax Rates that is Included in Income from Continuing Operations* (Sept. 23, 1993). The Task Force also concluded that the tax effect of items not included in income from continuing operations (e.g., discontinued operations, extraordinary items) that arose from the beginning of the current fiscal year and prior to the enactment date should be measured utilizing the enacted tax rate at the time the transaction was recognized for financial reporting purposes. The tax effect related to these items should also be included in income from continuing operations in the period of enactment.

[178] FASB ASC 740–10–25–48.

[179] FASB ASC 740–10–25–32.

[180] *Id.*

[181] *Id.*

[182] *Id. See* FASB Special Report, *A Guide to Implementation of Statement 109 on Accounting for Income Taxes: Questions and Answers*, Q & A 12 (1992) (change from taxable C corporation to non-taxable S corporation; the enterprise should continue to recognize a deferred tax liability for unrecognized net built-in gains, which is subject to tax under IRC Section 1374).

[183] FASB ASC 740–10–45–19.

[184] FASB ASC 740–10–25–33. If an entity makes an election to change its tax status early in year two (i.e., filed or approved, if approval is needed, early in year two) and prior to issuing financial statements for year one, the effect of the change in tax status is not recognized on the year one financial statements. FASB ASC 740–10–25–34.

[185] FASB ASC 740–10–25–33.

The future reversals of temporary differences may result in taxable and deductible amounts that offset each other.[186] The tax law determines whether such offset occurs.[187] The tax law also determines whether deductible temporary differences and loss carryforwards will offset taxable income that is expected to be earned in future years.[188] For example, under the U.S. tax laws, a corporation may deduct capital losses only to the extent of capital gains.[189] Any excess may be carried back three years and carried forward up to five years.[190] As a result, a tax benefit (i.e., deferred tax asset) is not recognized for deductible temporary differences that will result in future capital losses unless those capital losses will offset: (a) capital gains that are expected in future years, (b) other existing taxable temporary differences that will result in capital gains in future years, or (c) capital gains of the current year or prior years if within the carryback period (if carryback is expected).[191]

As a general rule, the particular year(s) in which a temporary difference results in a taxable or deductible amount is determined by the timing of the recovery of the asset or settlement of the liability to which the taxable difference relates.[192] For example, a taxable temporary difference arises when an entity makes an installment sale, reporting the gain for tax purposes under the installment method but recognizing the gain immediately for financial reporting purposes. The taxable temporary difference is related to the receivable generated by the installment sale. When the receivable is recovered (i.e., the receivable is collected), the taxable temporary difference results in a taxable amount. There are, however, exceptions to the general rule.[193] For example, a temporary difference between the tax basis and book basis of inventory for which cost is determined on a LIFO basis does not reverse when present inventory is sold in future years if it is replaced by purchases or production of inventory in those same future years.[194] As a result, a LIFO inventory temporary difference becomes taxable or deductible in the future year that inventory is liquidated and not replaced.[195]

For some assets or liabilities, such as depreciable assets, temporary differences may accumulate over multiple years and then reverse over multiple years.[196] For example, in the early years of a depreciable asset, taxable temporary differences may arise and accumulate if the entity utilizes accelerated depreciation for tax purposes and straight-line depreciation for financial reporting purposes. In the later years of the depreciable asset, as straight-line depreciation becomes more than accelerated depreciation, the taxable temporary differences will reverse. Future originating taxable temporary differences for existing depreciable assets (accelerated depreciation for tax purposes greater than straight-line depreciation for book purposes) and their subsequent reversals (the later years when straight-line depreciation becomes greater than

---

186 FASB ASC 740–10–55–12.

187 *Id.*

188 *Id.*

189 IRC Section 1211(a).

190 IRC Section 1212(a) (capital loss carryback permitted to three preceding taxable years and carried forward to the five succeeding taxable years).

191 FASB ASC 740–10–55–12.

192 FASB ASC 740–10–55–13.

193 *Id.*

194 *Id.*

195 *Id.*

196 FASB ASC 740–10–55–14.

accelerated depreciation) must be considered when assessing the likelihood of future taxable income for realization of a tax benefit (i.e., deferred tax asset) for existing deductible temporary differences, net operating losses and tax credit carryforwards.[197]

[b] Examples of Deferred Tax Assets and Deferred Tax Liabilities

ILLUSTRATION 2-18: An entity sold equipment with a book basis and tax basis of $20,000 on July 1, 2020, for $50,000, realizing a gain of $30,000. The equipment had $10,000 of recapture income under IRC Section 1245. The purchaser paid the entire purchase price in two years on July 1, 2022. Under the tax laws, the entity reported $10,000 of gain at the time of sale and reports the remaining $20,000 of gain for 2022 when the purchase price was received from the purchaser.[198]

Under GAAP, at the time of sale, the entity reported the entire gain of $30,000 in financial income. A taxable temporary difference arose in 2020 because the book basis of the receivable exceeds the tax basis of the receivable. The amount of the taxable temporary difference was $20,000 based on the excess of the book basis of the receivable ($50,000) over its tax basis ($30,000). Using an applicable tax rate of 21 percent, the entity had a deferred tax liability of $4,200 ($20,000 taxable temporary difference multiplied by 21 percent).

ILLUSTRATION 2-19: An entity purchased (and placed in service) equipment for $100,000 on January 1, 2017. The equipment had a five-year recovery period for tax purposes and financial accounting purposes. The amount of depreciation expense (straight-line method of depreciation) and depreciation deduction (200 percent declining balance method of depreciation with half-year convention) each year was as follows:

Year	Financial Accounting Depreciation	Tax Depreciation	Difference
2017	$20,000	$20,000	$ 0
2018	$20,000	$32,000	($12,000)
2019	$20,000	$19,200	$800
2020	$20,000	$11,520	$8,480
2021	$20,000	$11,520	$8,480
2022	$ 0	$5,760	($5,760)

In 2017, no temporary difference arose because the book basis of the depreciable asset ($80,000) was equal to its tax basis ($80,000). In 2018, a taxable temporary difference arose because the book basis for the depreciable equipment of $60,000 exceeded its tax basis of $48,000. The amount of the taxable temporary difference at the end of 2018 was $12,000. Using an

[197] *Id.*

[198] IRC Section 453(a) and (i).

applicable tax rate of 21 percent, the entity had a deferred tax liability of $2,520 ($12,000 taxable temporary difference multiplied by 21 percent).

ILLUSTRATION 2-20: An entity received an advance payment of $40,000 from a customer on December 31, 2020, for services required to be performed in the future. Under the tax laws, the entity included the advance payment in taxable income upon receipt in 2020. Under GAAP, the entity included none of the advance payment in income but rather set up a liability reflecting its obligation to provide services to the customer in the future. The entity will include the advance payment in financial income as it performs the services for the customer (decreasing its liability) in the future.

A deductible temporary difference arose in 2020 because the book basis of the liability exceeds its tax basis. The amount of the deductible temporary difference is the excess of the book basis of the liability ($40,000) over the tax basis for the liability ($0). Using an applicable tax rate of 21 percent, the entity has a deferred tax asset of $8,400 ($40,000 deductible temporary difference multiplied by 21 percent). If it is more likely than not that some or all of the deferred tax asset will not be realized, then the entity must reduce the deferred tax asset by a valuation allowance.

ILLUSTRATION 2-21: An entity had an operating loss of $100,000 for 2022. Under the current U.S. federal tax laws, the entity may not carry back the loss but may carry it forward for an unlimited number of years. Using an applicable tax rate of 21 percent, the entity has a deferred tax asset of $21,000. If it is more likely than not that some or all of the deferred tax asset will not be realized, then the entity must reduce the deferred tax asset by a valuation allowance.

ILLUSTRATION 2-22: An entity has a foreign tax credit of $50,000 for 2022. Under the tax laws, the entity may carry forward the foreign tax credit for up to ten years (assuming the foreign income taxes are not related to global intangible low-taxed income). The entity has a deferred tax asset of $50,000. If it is more likely than not that some or all of the deferred tax asset will not be realized, then the entity must reduce the deferred tax asset by a valuation allowance.

ILLUSTRATION 2-23: On December 1, 2022, a partnership made a check-the-box election to be taxed as a corporation effective January 1, 2023. Thus, the partnership made an election for a voluntary change in tax status. As a result, the change in status was recognized on the filing date because approval of the election is not necessary.

§ 2.09 Valuation Allowance

[1] In General

There are two main areas in accounting for income taxes (FASB ASC 740) in which an entity must make, at times, a difficult judgment call. The first involves the recognition of a deferred tax asset or deferred tax liability. An entity must recognize the financial statement effects of a tax position when it is more likely than not, based on the technical merits, that the position will be sustained upon examination.[199] The *more-likely-than-not* standard for recognition is discussed in detail in Chapter 3. The second judgment call an entity must make in accounting for income taxes (FASB ASC 740) involves recording of a valuation allowance with respect to a deferred tax asset. A valuation allowance is required for the portion of a deferred tax asset in which it is *more likely than not* that a tax benefit will not be realized.[200] The valuation allowance should be an amount sufficient to reduce the deferred tax asset to an amount that is more likely than not to be realized.[201] The valuation allowance is, in essence, a contra account. It operates in a similar manner as the Allowance for Doubtful Accounts, which is a contra account to an entity's Accounts Receivable.

FASB selected "more likely than not" rather than "probable" or some other standard in measuring a deferred tax asset because it believed that the criterion used in measuring a deferred tax asset should be one that produces accounting results that come closest to the expected outcome.[202] FASB intended "more likely than not" to mean a level of likelihood that is greater than 50 percent.[203]

FASB considered two approaches in measuring a deferred tax asset: an impairment approach and an affirmative judgment approach. An impairment approach to measuring a deferred tax asset would require recognition of a deferred tax asset unless the asset was impaired. An affirmative judgment approach would require recognition of a deferred tax asset based on a judgment that the asset will be realized. By selecting "more likely than not" as the criterion for measurement of a deferred tax asset, FASB intended to eliminate virtually any distinction between an impairment approach to measuring a deferred tax asset and an affirmative judgment approach to measuring a deferred tax asset.[204] As a result, in practice, there should be no substantive difference between the accounting results of either (a) the impairment approach (i.e., recognition of a deferred tax asset unless the likelihood of not realizing the future tax benefit is more than 50 percent) or (b) the affirmative judgment approach (i.e., recognition of a deferred tax asset if the likelihood of realizing the future tax benefit is more than 50 percent).[205] The approach adopted in SFAS No. 109 (FASB ASC 740), however, is generally referred to as an impairment approach.

It is possible that future realization of a tax benefit will be expected for a portion but not all of a deferred tax asset.[206] In this case, the entity needs to make a judgment to determine the portion of a deferred tax asset for which it is more likely than not that a tax benefit will not be realized.[207]

In determining whether a valuation allowance is needed, an entity must consider all available evidence—both positive and negative.[208] This would include, for example, information about an entity's current financial position as well information from its

---

[199] FASB ASC 740–10–25–5 and 6.

[200] FASB ASC 740–10–30–5.

[201] *Id.*

[202] SFAS No. 109, paragraph 96.

[203] SFAS No. 109, paragraph 97.

[204] SFAS No. 109, paragraphs 92 and 97.

[205] SFAS No. 109, paragraph 97.

[206] FASB ASC 740–10–30–24.

[207] *Id.*

[208] FASB ASC 740–10–30–17.

current year and previous years' operations.[209] In addition, whatever information is available regarding future years must also be considered.[210]

If an entity has cumulative losses in recent years, that is considered negative evidence and suggests the need for a valuation allowance with respect to its deferred tax asset. In fact, it may be difficult for the entity to conclude that a valuation allowance should not be recorded in the face of cumulative losses.[211] Some other examples of negative evidence include (but are not limited to) the following: (a) a history of net operating losses or tax credit carryforwards expiring unused;[212] (b) losses expected in the near future by a presently profitable entity;[213] (c) unresolved circumstances that, if unfavorably resolved, would adversely affect future operations and profit levels on a continuing basis in future years;[214] and (d) a short carryback or carryforward period so as to limit realization of the tax benefits of a significant deductible temporary difference that is expected to reverse in a single year or the entity operates in a traditionally cyclical business.[215] An entity's positive evidence suggests that a valuation allowance is not needed. Some examples of positive evidence that may overcome any negative evidence include the following: (a) existing contracts that will produce more than enough taxable income to realize the deferred tax asset based on existing sales prices and cost structures;[216] (b) appreciation in net assets (total values less total tax bases) in an amount sufficient to realize the deferred tax asset;[217] and (c) a strong earnings history exclusive of the loss that created the deferred tax asset (i.e., the net operating loss carryforward or deductible temporary difference) combined with evidence that the loss was an aberration.[218]

An entity must exercise its judgment in considering both negative and positive evidence.[219] The weight given to the various types of negative and positive evidence should be "commensurate with the extent to which it can be objectively verified."[220] The more negative evidence that exists creates a greater need for positive evidence and, in addition, makes it more difficult to support a determination that a valuation allowance is not needed for some or all of the deferred tax asset.[221] A cumulative loss in recent years is a significant piece of negative evidence and is difficult to overcome.[222]

The use of a valuation allowance permits an entity to manage its earnings from year to year.[223] The reason is that the more-likely-than-not standard is one of the most judgmental standards in accounting. For example, assume an entity has recorded a

---

[209] *Id.*

[210] *Id.*

[211] FASB ASC 740–10–30–21.

[212] FASB ASC 740–10–30–21(a).

[213] FASB ASC 740–10–30–21(b).

[214] FASB ASC 740–10–30–21(c).

[215] FASB ASC 740–10–30–21(d).

[216] FASB ASC 740–10–30–22(a).

[217] FASB ASC 740–10–30–22(b).

[218] FASB ASC 740–10–30–22(c).

[219] FASB ASC 740–10–30–23.

[220] *Id.*

[221] *Id.*

[222] *Id.*

[223] *See* Thomas Jaworski, *SEC Exams Reveal Flawed Valuation Allowance Processes*, 139 Tax Notes 127 (April 8, 2013).

deferred tax asset of $500,000. It is considering recording a $200,000 valuation allowance. If it does so, the net effect would be a (net) deferred tax asset of $300,000, which would reduce income tax expense for the year by $300,000, thereby increasing net income for the year by $300,000. If, however, the entity wishes to increase its net income for the year by $400,000 rather than $300,000, it merely needs to record a valuation allowance of only $100,000 rather than $200,000. This would decrease income tax expense by $400,000, thereby increasing net income for the year by $400,000. As a result, an entity may, by utilizing a valuation allowance, which is based on a very gray standard of more likely than not, adjust its net income upwards (reduce the valuation allowance) or downwards (increase the valuation allowance) from year to year.[224]

ILLUSTRATION 2-24:[225]

An entity has $900 of deductible temporary differences at the end of year three (the current year). The enacted tax rate is 40 percent for all years. A deferred tax asset is recognized at the end of year three in the amount of $360 ($900 times 40 percent). If the entity determines that it is more likely than not that $400 of the $900 of deductible temporary differences will not be realized, then a $160 valuation allowance ($400 times 40 percent) is recognized at the end of year three. The result is a *net* deferred tax asset of $200 ($360 deferred tax asset less $160 valuation allowance), which reduces income tax expense by $200. In year four, financial income and taxable income are as follows:

Financial loss	$ (50)
Reversing deductible temporary differences	(300)
Loss carryforward for tax purposes	$ (350)

The $50 financial loss in year four is additional negative evidence that must be weighed against available positive evidence to determine the amount of valuation allowance necessary at the end of year four. Deductible temporary differences and carryforwards at the end of year four are as follows:

Loss carryforward from year four	$ (350)
Unreversed deductible temporary differences	(600)
	$ (950)

[224] The literature is quite diverse as to whether entities utilize the valuation allowance to manage earnings. For articles suggesting little evidence of the use of valuation allowances for earnings management, *see, e.g.*, G. Visvanathan, *Deferred Tax Valuation Allowance and Earnings Management*, Journal of Financial Statement Analysis (1998); G.S. Miller & D.J. Skinner, *Determinants of the Valuation Allowance for Deferred Tax Assets under SFAS 109*, 73 The Accounting Review 213 (April 1998); C. Bauman, M. Bauman and R. Halsey, *Do Firms Use the Deferred Tax Asset Valuation Allowance to Manage Earnings?* 24 The Journal of the American Taxation Association No. 1 (Spring 2001); K. Kumar & G. Visvanathan, *The Information Context of the Deferred Tax Valuation Allowance*, 78 The Accounting Review No. 2 (April 2003). For articles suggesting evidence of the use of valuation allowances for earnings management, *see, e.g.*, C. Schrand & F. Wong, *Earnings Management Using the Valuation Allowance for Deferred Tax Assets Under SFAS No. 109*, Contemporary Accounting Research (2003); M. Frank & S. Rego, *Do Managers Use the Valuation Allowance Account to Manage Earnings Around Certain Earnings Targets?* The Journal of the American Taxation Association (Spring 2006); M. P. Bauman and C. R. Bowler, *FIN48 and Income Tax-Based Earnings Management: Evidence from the Deferred Tax Asset Valuation Allowance*, 25 Advances in Taxation 29 (2018).

[225] FASB ASC 740–10–55–124.

The $360 deferred tax asset recognized at the end of year three is increased to $380 at the end of year four ($950 times 40 percent). The entity determines that a $240 valuation allowance is necessary. Therefore, the $160 valuation allowance recognized at the end of year three is increased to $240 at the end of year four. The $60 net effect of those two adjustments (the $80 increase in the valuation allowance less the $20 increase in the deferred tax asset) results in $60 of income tax expense (i.e., deferred tax expense) that is recognized in year four, thereby lowering the entity's net income by $60.

If, however, the entity prefers to have its net income only lowered by $10 rather than $60 with respect to its deferred tax asset, it merely needs to record a valuation allowance of $190 (rather than $240) at the end of year four. This results in a net effect of only $10 (the $30 increase in the valuation allowance less the $20 increase in the deferred tax asset) rather than $60. As a result, net income is only lowered by $10 (rather than $60). The entity can partially control its net income for the year by adjusting its valuation allowance for its deferred tax asset.

As discussed, a valuation allowance affects both the balance sheet and the income statement. It is recorded on the balance sheet as a contra account to the entity's deferred tax asset(s). In addition, it impacts the income statement through income tax expense. An increase in the valuation allowance increases income tax expense for the year, and a decrease in the valuation allowance decreases income tax expense. A change in the valuation allowance also appears in the entity's effective tax rate reconciliation.

ILLUSTRATION 2-25: General Motors had the following tax rate reconciliation in its 2021 Annual Report (Note 17):

A reconciliation of the provision for income taxes compared with the amounts at the U.S. federal statutory rate was as follows:

	Years Ended December 31,		
	2021	2020	2019
Income tax expense at U.S. federal statutory income tax rate	$ 2,397	$ 1,558	$ 1,295
State and local tax expense	301	219	117
Non-U.S. income taxed at other than the U.S. federal statutory tax rate	36	(1)	166
U.S. tax impact on Non-U.S. income and activities	129	(160)	(197)
Change in valuation allowances	665	370	(233)
Change in tax laws	(93)	—	(122)
General business credits and manufacturing incentives	(492)	(366)	(420)
Settlements of prior year tax matters	11	(18)	—
Realization of basis differences in affiliates	(295)	(12)	—
Foreign currency remeasurement	28	(7)	74
Other adjustments	84	191	89
Total income tax expense	$ 2,771	$ 1,774	$ 769

As is evident from the tax rate reconciliation, General Motors reconciled using dollar amounts rather than percentages. General Motors increased its valuation allowances in 2020 and 2021 thereby increasing its income tax expense for such years.

[2] Sources of Income

In order to realize the tax benefit of a deductible temporary difference, net operating loss carryforward, or tax credit carryforward, an entity must have sufficient taxable income (of the appropriate character) within the carryforward (or carryback) period under the tax laws,[226] as shown in Illustration 2-26.

> **ILLUSTRATION 2-26:** An entity has a deductible temporary difference of $25,000, attributable to a reserve for bad debts established for financial accounting purposes. No reserve for bad debts is permitted under the tax laws, and therefore the entity employs the specific write-off method for bad debts. Using an applicable tax rate of 21 percent, the entity will record a deferred tax asset of $5,250. In order to realize the tax benefit of the deductible temporary difference of $25,000 (which created the deferred tax asset of $5,250), the entity needs taxable income in the future so that when it deducts its bad debts under the specific charge-off method, it has sufficient taxable income to utilize the deductions (and thereby reduce its income taxes for the future year).

FASB has identified four possible sources of taxable income that may be available under the tax laws to realize a tax benefit for deductible temporary differences, net operating losses and tax credit carryforwards.[227] The first source of taxable income is future reversals of existing taxable temporary differences.[228] More specifically, when the taxable temporary differences reverse in some future year(s), it will create taxable income equal to the amount of the reversal. For example, when an installment sale is made, a taxable temporary difference arises in the year of sale, which reverses when the entity later receives a payment from the purchaser of the property resulting in taxable gain in that later year. The taxable gain increases taxable income in the later year. Another common example of future reversals of existing taxable temporary differences involves an entity utilizing accelerated depreciation for tax purposes and straight-line depreciation for financial accounting purposes. In the early years of the depreciable asset, when the depreciation deduction for tax purposes is greater than the depreciation expense for financial accounting purposes, a taxable temporary difference arises. In the later years of the depreciable asset, when the taxable temporary difference reverses (i.e., depreciation expense each year is greater than the tax depreciation deduction), the lower depreciation deduction in a future year will result in greater taxable income in that future year.

A second source of taxable income to realize a tax benefit for deductible temporary differences and carryforwards is simply taxable income exclusive of reversing temporary differences and carryforwards.[229] The following illustration demonstrates the first and second sources of taxable income.

---

[226] FASB ASC 740–10–30–18.

[227] *Id.*

[228] FASB ASC 740–10–30–18(a).

[229] FASB ASC 740–10–30–18(b).

ILLUSTRATION 2-27:[230]

An entity has $2,400 of deductible temporary differences and $1,500 of taxable temporary differences at the end of year three (the current year). A deferred tax liability is recognized at the end of year three for the $1,500 of taxable temporary differences, and a deferred tax asset is recognized for the $2,400 of deductible temporary differences. All available evidence must be considered to determine if a valuation allowance is needed for some or all of the deferred tax asset. If evidence about one or more sources of taxable income is sufficient to support a determination that a valuation allowance is not needed, then other sources of taxable income do not need to be considered. For example, assume the entity earned $500 of taxable income in each of years one through three and there is no evidence to suggest it will not continue to earn that level of taxable income in future years. That level of future taxable income is more than sufficient to realize the tax benefit of $2,400 of tax deductions arising from reversing temporary differences (prior to 2018, over a period of at least 23 years—the year(s) of the deductions, two carryback years, and 20 carryforward years; beginning in 2018, net operating losses may not be carried back but may be carried forward indefinitely). Detailed forecasts, projections, or other types of analyses are unnecessary if expected future taxable income is more than sufficient to realize a tax benefit.

Alternatively, a valuation allowance is not needed if the weight of available evidence indicates that all $2,400 of tax deductions from future reversals of the deductible temporary differences will be realized by offsetting the $1,500 of taxable temporary differences and $900 of future taxable income exclusive of reversing temporary differences.

A third source of taxable income is taxable income in a prior carryback year(s) if a carryback for a net operating loss or tax credit is permitted under the tax laws.[231] For example, under the U.S. federal tax laws, net capital losses may be carried back three years by corporate taxpayers,[232] and certain foreign tax credits may be carried back one year.[233] Prior to 2018, net operating losses could be carried back two years. Beginning in 2018, however, net operating losses may no longer be carried back (but may be carried forward indefinitely). The following illustration demonstrates the third source of taxable income.

ILLUSTRATION 2-28:[234]

The situation is the same as in Illustration 2-27, except that if the deductible temporary differences will reverse within the next two years and taxable income in the current year exceeds $2,400, nothing needs to be known about future taxable income exclusive of reversing temporary differences because the deferred tax asset could be realized by carryback of a net operating loss to the current year. (Prior to 2018, net operating losses could be carried back two years. Beginning in 2018, however, net operating losses may no longer

[230] FASB ASC 740–10–55–120.

[231] FASB ASC 740–10–30–18(c).

[232] IRC Section 1212(a).

[233] IRC Section 904(c).

[234] FASB ASC 740–10–55–122.

be carried back, but may be carried forward indefinitely). More specifically, if there is zero or minimal taxable income in the next two years exclusive of reversing temporary differences, then the entity may carry back a net operating loss two years.[235] Other combinations of income may be available to eliminate any need for a valuation allowance. For example, a valuation allowance is not needed if the weight of available evidence indicates that all $2,400 of tax deductions from future reversals of the deductible temporary differences will be realized by offsetting (a) the $1,500 of taxable temporary differences and $900 of future taxable income exclusive of reversing temporary differences, (b) $2,400 of future taxable income exclusive of reversing temporary differences, (c) $2,400 of taxable income in the current or prior years by net operating loss carryback to those years, or (d) $2,400 of taxable income in one or more of the circumstances described above as a result of a tax-planning strategy.

A fourth source of taxable income is tax-planning strategies. For example, a strategy to accelerate taxable amounts to utilize an expiring net operating loss carryforward would be a classic example of a tax-planning strategy (prior to 2018, net operating losses could be carried forward for twenty years; beginning in 2018, net operating losses may be carried forward indefinitely).[236] Some other examples of tax-planning strategies would include (a) changing the character of taxable or deductible amounts from ordinary income or loss to capital gain or loss, and (b) switching from tax-exempt bonds to taxable bonds to generate taxable income.[237] Tax-planning strategies are discussed in detail below.

The evidence available about each of the four sources of taxable income may vary from year to year and will vary for different tax jurisdictions.[238] If evidence about one or more sources of taxable income is sufficient to support a conclusion that a valuation allowance is not necessary, then the other sources of taxable income may be disregarded.[239] An entity must consider each of the four sources of taxable income, however, to determine the amount of the valuation allowance that is recognized for deferred tax assets.[240]

SEC officials have stated that many times that they find boilerplate disclosures on valuation allowances in the management's discussion and analysis (MD&A) section of an entity's financial filing. Such boilerplate disclosures, which typically state that the entity considers the four sources of taxable income when determining the ability to realize deferred tax assets, do not provide sufficient information with respect to valuation allowances. The SEC staff may send a comment letter to the entity requesting greater disclosure of the sources of taxable income with respect to the deferred tax assets.[241] Some examples of SEC comments sent to entities include:

---

[235] IRC Section 172(b)(1)(A)(i).

[236] FASB ASC 740–10–30–18(d).

[237] *Id.*

[238] FASB ASC 740–10–30–18.

[239] *Id.*

[240] *Id.*

[241] *See* Thomas Jaworski, *SEC Concerned with Materiality of Corporate Tax Disclosures*, 141 Tax Notes 1168 (Dec. 16, 2013).

1. Tell us why you have a valuation allowance that covers most of your net deferred tax assets. In this regard, we note that you had positive income before taxes for each of the last three years. Tell us how you determined that these assets are not realizable under GAAP.

2. We note you have presented approximately $X in deferred tax assets at [date]. It also appears to us that you have not recorded a valuation allowance for such assets. Considering you have experienced losses for each quarter this fiscal year, please provide us with a detailed analysis of FASB ASC 740–10–30, including all the evidence you considered in determining that it was more likely than not you would be able to realize the benefits of substantially all of your deferred tax assets. In your response, please clarify for us how the forecasts used in your analysis at [date] compared to your actual results for the year to date.

[3] Tax-Planning Strategies

A tax-planning strategy is a possible source of taxable income that must be considered *only* in determining the amount of the valuation allowance required with respect to a deferred tax asset.[242] If the entity establishes the existence of a tax-planning strategy, then a valuation allowance may be not required for part or all of a deferred tax asset.[243] A tax-planning strategy is an action that an entity ordinarily would not take but would do so to realize a tax benefit for an expiring net operating loss or tax credit carryforward (prior to 2018, net operating losses could be carried forward for twenty years; beginning in 2018, net operating losses may be carried forward indefinitely).[244] For example, an entity may have a practice of deferring taxable income by structuring sales to qualify as installment sales for tax purposes.[245] This type of action is not a tax-planning strategy as the term is used in FASB ASC 740 because it is an action that is done in the normal course of business.[246] However, the entity's strategy to sell property at a gain and then lease it back for the sole purpose of generating taxable income in the year of sale so as to utilize an expiring net operating loss is a tax-planning strategy because it is not an action that the entity takes in the normal course of business.[247] A tax-planning strategy (which includes elections for tax purposes) must meet three general requirements to be treated as such under FASB ASC 740.[248] First, it must be prudent and feasible.[249] The question of whether or not a strategy is prudent goes to whether management would implement the strategy. If an action is not prudent, then management would probably not do it.[250] The question of whether or not a strategy is

242 FASB ASC 740–10–55–46.

243 *Id.*

244 *Id.*

245 FASB ASC 740–10–55–39.

246 *Id.*

247 *Id.*

248 FASB ASC 740–10–30–19; FASB ASC 740–10–55–39. Elections made for tax purposes that may be considered tax-planning strategies, assuming the requirements for tax-planning strategies are met, include the election of an affiliated group to file a consolidated tax return, the election to either deduct or credit foreign income taxes, and the election to forego carryback of a net operating loss. FASB ASC 740–10–55–40. As part of the Tax Cuts and Jobs Act, Congress repealed the two-year carryback period for net operating losses while allowing for an indefinite carryforward period.

249 FASB ASC 740–10–30–19; FASB ASC 740–10–55–39.

250 FASB ASC 740–10–55–39.

feasible goes to whether management has the ability to implement the strategy. If an action is not feasible, then management does not have the ability to do it.[251] Management must have the ability to implement the strategy and expect to do so unless the need is eliminated in future years.[252] For example, if income earned in a later year uses the entire amount of a net operating loss carryforward from the current year, then management would not have to apply the strategy.[253] Management must be in primary but not necessarily unilateral control in implementing the tax-planning strategy.[254]

The second requirement is that the action must be one that the entity ordinarily would not take but would do so to prevent a net operating loss or tax credit carryforward from expiring unused.[255] Management typically expects to employ a number of strategies for business or tax purposes. All of these expected strategies, except those that are expected to be employed for the utilization of carryforwards that would expire unused, are not tax-planning strategies as that term is used in FASB ASC 740.[256] However, those tax strategies expected to be employed to utilize a net operating loss or tax credit carryforward that would expire unused may be a tax-planning strategy.[257]

The third requirement is that the entity's action would result in realization of deferred tax assets.[258] The effect of tax-planning strategies must be recognized in the determination of the amount of a valuation allowance.[259] Tax-planning strategies do not have to be considered if positive evidence available from other sources is sufficient to support a conclusion that a valuation allowance is not necessary.[260] Tax-planning strategies can generally be categorized into one of two categories. The first category is tax-planning strategies to shift estimated future taxable income from one year to another year (i.e., a later year to an earlier year) so as to utilize an expiring net operating loss or tax credit carryforward.[261] For example, if an entity has a net operating loss that would otherwise expire unused at the end of next year, a tax-planning strategy to sell (i.e., factor) the entity installment sale receivables next year would accelerate the future reversal of taxable temporary differences for those gains on those installment sales.[262] The second category is tax-planning strategies that shift the timing of future reversals

[251] *Id.*

[252] FASB ASC 740–10–55–39.

[253] *Id.*

[254] FASB ASC 740–10–30–19.

[255] FASB ASC 740–10–30–19; FASB ASC 740–10–55–39.

[256] FASB ASC 740–10–55–39. A strategy to change from a taxable C corporation to a non-taxable S corporation is not a qualifying tax-planning strategy for an entity eligible to change but which has not done so. FASB ASC 740–10–55–48.

[257] FASB ASC 740–10–55–39. Management must make a reasonable effort to identify significant tax-planning strategies. If, however, there is sufficient evidence that taxable income from other sources is adequate to eliminate the need for a valuation allowance, then it is not necessary for management to search for tax-planning strategies. FASB ASC 740–10–55–41.

[258] FASB ASC 740–10–30–19; FASB ASC 740–10–55–39.

[259] FASB ASC 740–10–55–39. If, for example, an entity has two qualifying tax-planning strategies, it must recognize the effect of both tax-planning strategies and cannot recognize the effect of one tax-planning strategy in the current year and postpone recognition of the other tax-planning strategy to a later year. FASB Special Report, *A Guide to Implementation of Statement 109 on Accounting for Income Taxes: Questions and Answers*, Q & A 26 (1992).

[260] FASB ASC 740–10–55–39.

[261] FASB ASC 740–10–55–42.

[262] IRC Section 453B (disposition of an installment obligation triggers the gain inherent in the obligation).

of temporary differences.[263] For example, a deductible temporary difference may reverse many years in the future at a time when it is expected to provide no tax benefit. Therefore, a tax-planning strategy may be to accelerate the future reversal of a deductible temporary difference to offset taxable income in an early future year so as to realize a tax benefit for those deductible temporary differences.[264] Some specific examples of accelerating the future reversal of deductible temporary differences include (a) an entity making a larger than usual annual payment to reduce a long-term pension obligation, (b) an entity disposing of obsolete inventory to accelerate a tax deduction, and (c) an entity selling loans at their book bases (i.e., net of an allowance for bad debts) to accelerate a tax deduction for the allowance for bad debts.[265]

ILLUSTRATION 2-29:[266]

An entity has a $1,500 net operating loss that will expire at the end of next year. Its estimate of taxable income is approximately $1,000 per year for each of the next several years. The estimate of taxable income is based, in part, on the entity's present practice of making sales on the installment basis thereby resulting in temporary deferral of gains on installment sales under the tax laws. A tax-planning strategy to increase taxable income next year and realize the full tax benefit of the net operating loss carryforward might be to structure next year's sale in a manner that does not meet the tax rules to qualify as installment sales.[267] Another strategy might be to change next year's depreciation procedures for tax purposes (i.e., elect out of IRC Section 168(k) immediate expensing, use a slower depreciation method, a longer recovery period, not elect section 179 bonus depreciation) so as to create an additional amount of taxable income in the next year.

Tax-planning strategies might involve significant transaction costs.[268] For example, it is not unusual for transaction costs to run into the millions of dollars in planning and implementing a particular tax-planning strategy.[269] In addition, the entity might recognize a significant loss as a result of implementing a tax-planning strategy.[270] In both cases, the tax benefit recognized as a result of a tax-planning strategy should be net of any significant expenses and losses to implement the tax-planning strategy.[271] In addition, the expense or loss that reduces the amount of tax benefit should be net of any future tax benefit that would result from that expense or loss (i.e., deducting the expense or loss).[272]

---

[263] FASB ASC 740–10–55–43.

[264] *Id.*

[265] *Id.*

[266] FASB ASC 740–10–55–42.

[267] Alternatively, the entity could continue to make sales on the installment basis but simply elect out of the use of the installment method in reporting the gain. IRC Section 453(d) permits an election out of the installment method.

[268] FASB ASC 740–10–55–44.

[269] *See, e.g.*, Staff of the Joint Committee on Taxation, *Report of Investigation of Enron Corporation and Related Entities Regarding Federal Tax and Compensation Issues, and Policy Recommendations* (2003) (discussing 12 tax-motivated transactions planned and entered into by Enron with transaction costs as low as $100,000 (Project Valor) to as high as $16 million (Project Cochise)).

[270] FASB ASC 740–10–55–44.

[271] *Id.*

[272] *Id.*

ILLUSTRATION 2-30:[273]

An entity has a $900 net operating loss carryforward that will expire at the end of next year. The entity estimates that its taxable income next year will be $100. The entity has taxable temporary differences in the amount of $800, which would ordinarily result in taxable amounts of $400 in each of the next two years. The entity has a tax-planning strategy to accelerate the future reversal of all $800 of taxable temporary differences to next year. The estimated legal fees and other expenses to implement the tax-planning strategy are $150. The tax rate is 40 percent.

Without the tax-planning strategy, the entity would have $500 of taxable income next year ($100 of taxable income exclusive of reversing temporary differences plus $400 of reversing taxable temporary differences). As a result, only $500 of the net operating loss carryforward would be realized next year, and the remaining $400 of the net operating loss carryforward would expire unused. The entity would record a deferred tax asset of $360 ($900 net operating loss carryforward times 40 percent tax rate), which would be offset by a $160 valuation allowance ($400 unused net operating loss carryforward times 40 percent) resulting in a net deferred tax asset of $200.

With the tax-planning strategy, the entity would have $900 of taxable income next year ($100 of taxable income exclusive of reversing temporary differences plus $800 of reversing taxable temporary differences). The entire $900 net operating loss carryforward would then be utilized next year (beginning in 2018, a net operating loss may only offset 80 percent of taxable income). The $360 deferred tax asset would be offset by a valuation allowance of only $90, which is the amount of the expenses to implement the tax-planning strategy ($150) less the tax savings ($60) from deducting the implementation expenses ($150 times 40 percent).

A deferred tax liability is ordinarily recognized for all taxable temporary differences.[274] However, certain taxable temporary differences may or may not actually result in taxable amounts when those differences reverse in future years.[275] For example, the cash surrender value of life insurance over premiums paid may or may not result in taxable amounts in future years.[276] Also, the excess of book basis over tax basis of an investment in a domestic subsidiary may or may not result in taxable amounts in future years.[277] The determination of whether these differences are taxable temporary differences is not a tax-planning strategy as the term is used in FASB ASC 740.[278]

[4] Change in Valuation Allowance

A change in the beginning of the year balance of a valuation allowance that results from a change in judgment about the realizability of the related deferred tax asset is, as a general rule, included in income from continuing operations (and therefore included in

---

[273] FASB ASC 740–10–55–159 to FASB ASC 740–10–55–162.

[274] FASB ASC 740–10–55–46.

[275] *Id.*

[276] *Id. See* Section 2.07[2], Illustration 2–9.

[277] FASB ASC 740–10–55–46. *See* Section 2.16.

[278] *Id.*

the entity's effective tax rate reconciliation).[279] Exceptions to this general rule are provided with respect to a change in the valuation allowance of tax benefits in a business combination[280] and tax benefits that are allocated to the various components of shareholders' equity.[281]

FASB has addressed the issue of a change in valuation allowance due to transactions with or among the entity's shareholders.[282] The FASB concluded that a change in the valuation allowance regarding the realizability of the deferred tax asset caused by a transaction with or among shareholders is recognized in the income statement. For example, if a corporation with a net operating loss undergoes an ownership change, then the corporation's utilization of the net operating loss is limited under the tax laws.[283] If the corporation records a valuation allowance as a result of the ownership change, the tax effect is reflected on the income statement. However, if the transaction with or among shareholders changes the tax bases of the assets and liabilities of the entity, then a deferred tax asset or liability will be recorded and possibly a valuation allowance. The tax effects of recording a deferred tax asset or liability and a valuation allowance is reflected in shareholders' equity and not on the income statement. Any subsequent change in the valuation allowance is reflected on the income statement.

§ 2.10 Special Deductions

In certain cases, the tax laws may provide a deduction for entities engaged in a particular type of activity or industry. These special deductions are not matched by any expense of the entity so that the special deduction is, in essence, a permanent difference. For example, as part of the American Jobs Creation Act of 2004, Congress enacted a new deduction for entities engaged in manufacturing.[284] This deduction, referred to as the qualified production activities deduction, was generally equal to a maximum of nine percent of the entity's taxable income for the year. It was simply a benefit provided by Congress to entities engaged in manufacturing activity. The benefit (i.e., a deduction) lowered taxable income but had no impact on pretax financial income. Congress repealed the qualified production activities deduction as part of the Tax Cuts and Jobs Act (TCJA).

Also, as part of TCJA, Congress enacted a new special deduction—a tax deduction for foreign-derived intangible income (FDII).[285] The deduction, which is a permanent difference, is equal to 37.5 percent (21.875 percent for taxable years after 2025) of a domestic corporation's foreign-derived intangible income for the taxable year.

To calculate the amount of the deduction, a domestic corporation first computes its deduction-eligible income, which is generally its gross income less deductions, but excluding certain categories of gross income (and corresponding deductions) such as subpart F income and global intangible low-taxed income (GILTI). It then computes its foreign-derived deduction-eligible income, which is deduction-eligible income that is derived in connection with property sold for foreign use to a person who is not a US person, or services provided to any person, or with respect to property, not located within

---

279 FASB ASC 740–10–45–20 and FASB ASC 740–20–45–4.

280 *Id.*

281 *Id.*

282 FASB ASC 740–20–45–11.

283 IRC Section 382.

284 IRC Section 199.

285 IRC Section 250.

the United States. A domestic corporation must then compute its deemed intangible income. This is the excess of its deduction-eligible income over the deemed tangible income return, which is equal to 10 percent of the corporation's qualified business asset investment (QBAI). QBAI is the corporation's tangible depreciable property used in a trade or business.

The foreign-derived intangible income, for which the 37.5 percent deduction is applicable, is the amount that bears the same ratio to the deemed intangible income as the foreign-derived deduction-eligible income bears to the deduction-eligible income. Expressed as a formula, foreign-derived intangible income is:

$$\text{deemed intangible income} \times \frac{\text{foreign-derived deduction eligible income}}{\text{deduction eligible income}}$$

FASB provides that the tax benefit of a special deduction is recognized no earlier than when it is recognized on the tax return (as a deductible item).[286] As a result, the tax benefit of a special deduction is not anticipated for purposes of offsetting a deferred tax liability recognized for taxable temporary differences.[287] However, the tax benefit of a special deduction is recognized in determining the average graduated tax rate in measuring deferred tax assets or liabilities if graduated tax rates are a significant factor.[288] It is also recognized in determining the need for a valuation allowance for deferred tax assets.[289]

A special deduction can be contrasted to a tax rate reduction. For example, if Congress enacts a deduction for all manufacturing entities equal to nine percent of a manufacturer's taxable income, then assuming a tax rate of 35 percent, this could be viewed as essentially a tax rate reduction of 3.15 percent (35 percent times nine percent). Therefore, manufacturing entities could be viewed as being taxed at only 31.85 percent (35 percent less 3.15 percent) rather than 35 percent. If the manufacturing deduction is treated as a tax rate reduction for financial reporting purposes, then an entity with a net deferred tax liability would receive a one-time benefit by reducing its deferred tax liability with a corresponding decrease to deferred tax expense. This would lower income tax expense and decrease an entity's effective tax rate for the year.[290]

If the manufacturing deduction is treated as a special deduction for financial reporting purposes, then an entity's deferred tax liability is not reduced. If, however, part or all of the taxable temporary difference giving rise to the deferred tax liability reverses the next year, it will lower deferred tax expense the next year at the statutory tax rate of 35 percent. As a result, a special deduction (as opposed to a tax rate reduction) may lower deferred tax expense in a future year(s) and thereby decrease an entity's effective tax rate in a future year(s).

ILLUSTRATION 2-31: A manufacturing entity has a deferred tax liability of \$35,000 based on a taxable temporary difference of \$100,000 from year one. Congress enacts a deduction for manufacturing entities equal to nine percent

---

286 FASB ASC 740–10–25–37 and FASB ASC 740–10–30–13.

287 FASB ASC 740–10–25–37.

288 FASB ASC 740–10–25–37 and FASB ASC 740–10–30–13.

289 *Id.*

290 See Christopher H. Hanna, *Corporate Tax Reform: Listening to Corporate America*, 35 J. Corp. Law 283 (Jan. 2010).

of the entity's taxable income for year two to be effective beginning in year two. The statutory income tax rate is 35 percent.

If the manufacturing deduction is treated as a tax rate reduction of 3.15 percent, then the manufacturing entity will reduce its deferred tax liability at the end of year two from $35,000 to $31,850. The decrease of $3,150 is matched by a decrease to deferred tax expense of $3,150. As a result, income tax expense for year two is reduced by $3,150, thereby increasing net income for year two by $3,150. Assume the $100,000 taxable temporary difference reverses in its entirety in year three so that the manufacturing entity has $500,000 of taxable income in year three ($400,000 of taxable income arising during the year plus $100,000 of taxable income from the taxable temporary difference reversing). The entity is entitled to a $45,000 manufacturing deduction ($500,000 taxable income times nine percent). The entity will owe taxes of $159,250 ($455,000 taxable income times 35 percent). The entity will also have an offset to deferred tax expense of $31,850 so that its total income tax expense is $127,400. The entity's pretax financial income is $400,000. Its effective tax rate is 31.85 percent.

If, however, the manufacturing deduction is treated as a special deduction, no adjustment is made to the entity's deferred tax liability of $35,000 as a result of the enactment of the legislation. In year three, the entity will still owe taxes of $159,250 ($455,000 taxable income times 35 percent). However, the entity will also have an offset to deferred tax expense of $35,000 so that its total income tax expense is only $124,250. The $35,000 offset to deferred tax expense arises from the fact that the taxable temporary difference has reversed in its entirety in year three, thereby eliminating the need for any deferred tax liability at the end of year three. The entity's pretax financial income is $400,000. Its effective tax rate is only 31.0625 percent. Treating the manufacturing deduction as a special deduction (as opposed to a tax rate reduction) reduced the entity's effective tax rate in year three (when the taxable temporary difference reversed).

§ 2.11 Alternative Minimum Tax

An entity measures its deferred tax liability and asset for temporary differences and carryforwards using the regular tax rates.[291] If an entity has AMT credit carryforwards, it must record a deferred tax asset for the AMT credit carryforwards.[292] The entity must also reduce its deferred tax asset for AMT credit carryforwards by a valuation allowance if it is more likely than not that some or all of that deferred tax asset will not be realized.[293] As part of TCJA, Congress repealed the corporate alternative minimum tax but retained the individual alternative minimum tax. However, as part of the Inflation Reduction Act of 2022, Congress reintroduced a corporate alternative minimum tax with a 15 percent tax rate imposed on adjusted financial statement income.[294]

An entity must use regular tax rates in determining the amount of its deferred taxes even if the entity is currently an AMT (alternative minimum tax) taxpayer and expects

[291] FASB ASC 740–10–55–32.

[292] *Id.*

[293] *Id.*

[294] *See* Section 2.22[1] for discussion of the new corporate alternative minimum tax.

to always be an AMT taxpayer.[295] In order to understand FASB's reasoning in always requiring the use of regular tax rates, it is helpful to understand how the AMT operates. Generally, taxable income for regular tax purposes will differ from taxable income for AMT purposes because of either temporary items or preference items. Temporary items, such as depreciation differences, may cause the tentative minimum tax under the AMT to exceed the regular tax.[296] Temporary items, however, ultimately reverse over time. Therefore, if there is not a large amount of preference items, the total taxes paid over the life of the entity will be based on the regular tax system.[297]

An entity's preference items may also cause an entity's tentative minimum tax under the AMT to exceed its regular tax.[298] If the preference items are large enough, it may cause the entity to be subject, over its life, to the AMT system.[299] As a result, the AMT credit carryforwards would expire unused.[300] FASB believed, however, that it is not possible to predict whether an entity will always be an AMT taxpayer.[301] FASB also believed that it would be counterintuitive if the AMT provisions had the effect of reducing an entity's income tax expense for financial reporting when the provisions of the AMT are never beneficial to an entity.[302] Finally, FASB believed it would be counterintuitive to assume that an entity would permit its AMT credit carryforward to expire unused, which would occur if the entity was always an AMT taxpayer.[303]

§ 2.12 Tax Credits

Tax credits can be placed into one of two categories: nonrefundable credits and refundable credits. A nonrefundable credit reduces a taxpayer's tax liability dollar for dollar but can only reduce tax liability to zero. In contrast, a refundable credit, which also reduces tax liability dollar for dollar, creates a tax refund if the amount of the credit exceeds the taxpayer's tax liability. General business credits and foreign tax credits are nonrefundable credits. The employee retention tax credit is a refundable credit (with respect to payroll taxes).

A nonrefundable credit that is not transferable falls within FASB ASC 740. It reduces an entity's income tax expense and its effective tax rate. A nonrefundable credit may be transferable, meaning that it can reduce an entity's income tax liability or be transferred to a third party. The financial accounting treatment of such credits is not clear. One source indicates that the treatment should turn on the intent of the entity that generated the credit.[304] If the entity intends to use the credit, it should account for the credit under FASB ASC 740 (reduces the entity's income tax expense and its effective tax rate). If it intends to transfer the credit to a third party, it should account for the credit similar to a government grant.

---

[295] FASB ASC 740–10–30–10; FASB ASC 740–10–30–11.

[296] FASB ASC 740–10–55–31.

[297] *Id.*

[298] *Id.*

[299] *Id.*

[300] *Id.*

[301] FASB ASC 740–10–30–11.

[302] *Id.*

[303] *Id.*

[304] *See* Katie Morgan, Ken Kazmierski, Jenna Summer and Ashby Corum, *Accounting for Tax Credits* (KPMG—What's News in Tax) (Sept. 14, 2022).

The financial accounting treatment of a refundable credit is also not clear. It may fall outside of FASB ASC 740 and be treated as a government grant, even if the entity expects to apply it against its income tax liability.[305] An entity's accounting for government grants is usually analogized to IAS 20, Accounting for Government Grants and Disclosure of Government Assistance under the International Financial Reporting Standards (IFRS); FASB ASC 958-605, Not-For-Profit Entities—Revenue Recognition; or FASB ASC 450–30, Gain Contingencies.

An investment tax credit is a nonrefundable tax credit for the acquisition of an asset. An entity may use the "deferral method" or "flow-through method" in accounting for the investment tax credit with the deferral method being FASB's preferred approach.[306] Under the deferral method, the benefit of the investment tax credit is presented either as a reduction of the book basis of the property or as deferred income.[307] If the deferred benefit of an investment tax credit is presented as a reduction of the book basis of the property ("gross-up method"), it is subsequently recognized as a reduction to either depreciation expense or income tax expense. If, however, the deferred benefit of the investment tax credit is presented as deferred income ("income method"), it is amortized over the productive life of the property. FASB has indicated that the gross-up method may be preferable in many cases. Under the flow-through method, the credit is recognized as a reduction in income tax expense in the year it arises. A deferred tax asset is recognized for unused credits that are carried forward to future years. Any difference between the book basis and tax basis of the asset may result in a temporary difference for which a deferred tax asset or liability will need to be recognized.

§ 2.13 NOL and Tax Credit Carryforwards and Carrybacks

[1] Recognition of Tax Benefit for Carrybacks

Certain tax credits arising but not utilized in the current year may be carried back for a refund of taxes paid in prior years or carried forward to reduce taxes payable in future years.[308] Under current U.S. tax law, a net operating loss may not be carried back but may be carried forward indefinitely.[309] For corporations, net capital losses are carried back three years and carried forward five years.[310] Certain foreign tax credits are carried back one year (and carried forward ten years).[311] General business credits are carried back one year (and carried forward 20 years).[312] A receivable is recognized for the amount of taxes paid in prior years that are refundable by carryback of unused tax credits of the current year.[313]

---

[305] *Id.*

[306] FASB ASC 740–10–25–46.

[307] FASB ASC 740–10–45–27.

[308] FASB ASC 740–10–55–34.

[309] IRC Section 172.

[310] IRC Section 1212(a)(1).

[311] IRC Section 904(c).

[312] IRC Section 39.

[313] FASB ASC 740–10–55–34.

[2] Recognition of Tax Benefit for Carryforwards

A deferred tax asset is recognized for an operating loss carryforward or tax credit carryforward.[314] In addition, the entity must assess the need for a valuation allowance. Provisions in the tax laws that limit utilization of a net operating loss or tax credit carryforward are applied in determining whether it is more likely than not that some or all of the deferred tax asset will not be realized by reduction of taxes payable on taxable income during the carryforward period.[315]

The entity must forecast when the net operating loss or tax credit carryforward will be utilized and whether the carryforward might expire unused in determining the need for recording a valuation allowance. In 1997, Congress extended the carryforward period for net operating losses from 15 years to 20 years.[316] In 2004, Congress extended the carryforward period for excess foreign tax credits from five years to ten years.[317] The TCJA allows net operating losses to be carried forward indefinitely but limits their use to 80 percent of taxable income. As a result, it has become less likely for a net operating loss or excess foreign tax credit to expire unused. General business credits may be carried forward 20 years.

ILLUSTRATION 2-32:[318]

An entity has a net operating loss in year four of $8,800 (of which, $2,800 will be carried back to years two and three and $6,000 will be carried forward to future years; beginning in 2018, a net operating loss may no longer be carried back). The entity also has $3,800 of taxable temporary differences at the end of year four, and the enacted tax rate is 40 percent. At the end of year four, taxable income is not expected in years five and six and later years, and the entity concludes that a valuation allowance is necessary to the extent realization of the deferred tax asset for the net operating loss carryforward depends on taxable income (exclusive of reversing temporary differences) in future years.

In year four, $2,800 of the net operating loss is carried back to reduce taxable income in years two and three, and the taxes paid in those years are refunded. In addition, a $1,520 deferred tax liability is recognized for the $3,800 of taxable temporary differences ($3,800 times 40 percent), and a $2,400 deferred tax asset is recognized for the $6,000 net operating loss carryforward ($6,000 times 40 percent). However, because of the conclusion, at the end of year four, that taxable income is not expected in years five, six and later years, a valuation allowance is recognized for the amount by which the deferred tax asset exceeds the deferred tax liability. Therefore, the entity must recognize a valuation allowance of $880 ($2,400 deferred tax asset less $1,520 deferred tax liability) at the end of year four.

A net operating loss carryforward or tax credit carryforward from a prior year (for which the deferred tax asset was offset by a valuation allowance) may reduce taxable income that is attributable to certain revenues or gains that must be included in taxable

---

314 FASB ASC 740–10–55–35.

315 FASB ASC 740–10–55–36.

316 IRC Section 172(b)(1)(A).

317 IRC Section 904(c).

318 FASB ASC 740–10–55–149.

income for the year that the cash is received.[319] For financial reporting, however, there may have been no revenue or gain and a liability is recognized for the cash received.[320] As a result, a deductible temporary difference has arisen because the book basis of the liability (cash received) exceeds its tax basis (zero). Under these circumstances, in effect, the net operating loss or tax credit carryforward has simply been replaced by a deductible temporary difference, which will result in deductible amounts in future years.[321] The requirements for recognition of a tax benefit for deductible temporary differences and for net operating loss carryforwards are the same. Therefore, the manner of reporting the eventual tax benefit recognized is not affected by the intervening transaction reported for tax purposes.[322] Illustration 2-33 demonstrates this principle.

ILLUSTRATION 2-33:[323]

In its first year of operations, an entity has a financial and tax loss of $4,000. Assume the tax rate is 40 percent. At the end of year one, the entity records a deferred tax asset of $1,600 and also records a valuation allowance of $1,600.

In year two, the entity receives $2,500 as an advance payment for services to be rendered in future years. The entity includes $2,500 in taxable income but sets up a liability for $2,500 for financial reporting purposes. This is the only difference between financial income and taxable income. The $4,000 net operating loss carryforward from the end of year one is reduced to $1,500 at the end of year two because $2,500 of it is used to reduce taxable income (beginning in 2018, a net operating loss may only offset 80 percent of taxable income). The $2,500 reduction in the net operating loss carryforward becomes $2,500 of deductible temporary differences that will reverse and result in lower taxable income (relative to financial income) in the future when the services are performed.

The entity has no deferred tax liability to be offset when the deductible temporary differences reverse, the tax benefit when the deductible temporary differences reverse cannot be realized by a net operating loss carryback because no taxes have been paid, and the entity has had pretax losses for financial reporting since inception. Unless positive evidence exists that is sufficient to overcome the negative evidence associated with those losses, a valuation allowance of $1,600 continues to be recognized at the end of year two for the full amount of the deferred tax asset related to the $2,500 of deductible temporary differences and the remaining $1,500 of net operating loss carryforward.

Foreign tax credit carryforwards are generally treated the same as other tax credit carryforwards and are not limited to the amount of deferred tax liabilities recognized for undistributed foreign earnings. However, foreign tax credits generally are limited to the U.S. tax that would have been paid on the foreign source income,[324] and as a result, a

[319] FASB ASC 740–10–55–37.

[320] *Id.*

[321] *Id.*

[322] *Id.*

[323] FASB ASC 740–10–55–156.

[324] IRC Sections 901 through 904.

valuation allowance may be needed if utilization of the foreign tax credit is questionable. For example, assume an entity is earning foreign source income each year (through its foreign branch). If the entity is paying taxes on the foreign source income of 25 percent, it will generate a foreign tax credit carryforward of 4 percent (foreign tax rate of 25 percent less the U.S. corporate tax rate of 21 percent). As long as the entity pays a foreign tax at a rate higher than the U.S. tax rate and low-tax foreign source income is not available, then utilization of the foreign tax credit is questionable and a valuation allowance may be required.

§ 2.14 Regulated Enterprises

Regulated entities are not exempt from the requirement of accounting for income taxes.[325] The intricacies of the regulated rate process, in particularly with respect to taxes, is beyond the scope of this book—the interaction between tax law, tax accounting, and regulatory economic principles collide to create an extremely complex set of rules. This section provides a high-level overview with some simplified explanations and definitions.[326]

Income tax expense is usually treated no differently than any other operating expense to determine what a regulated company is allowed to earn. An important concept in income tax expense, in particular the negotiation between the company and the public utility commission along with any intervenors, is the normalization rule. The normalization rule is meant to ensure that tax incentives, such as tax credits and accelerated depreciation, do not flow immediately to lower operating expenses but are spread over a specified number of years. If not corrected, the penalty for a violation of the normalization rule is loss of the tax incentive.

There is a current component and a noncurrent component of income tax expense. The current component is the cash tax payments for the year, and the noncurrent component is referred to as the temporary difference or deferred taxes. As a result, a regulated entity must record a deferred tax asset or liability for its temporary differences. Deferred taxes have several roles in regulated companies.

The first consideration of deferred taxes is how it impacts a regulated company's earnings. To understand this process, assume the company took 100 percent expensing on a $100 capital expenditure and the tax rate is 35 percent. But for regulatory purposes, the $100 capital investment was capitalized and depreciated under the straight-line method over 10 years resulting in $10 of regulatory depreciation expense each year. There is a $90 temporary difference at the end of year one (book basis of $90 and tax basis of zero) resulting in a deferred tax liability of $31.50. As a regulated business, assume the company can earn eight percent on its "rate base," which is the company's investment in the business minus regulatory depreciation minus deferred tax liability (or increased by deferred tax assets). If the asset was placed in service on January 1 of Year 1, the company will earn $8. At the beginning of Year 2, the company's rate base is reduced to $58.50 ($100 capital investment minus $10 regulatory depreciation, minus $31.50 deferred tax liability). The company earns $4.68 in Year 2 ($58.50 rate base times eight percent). Rate base is reduced by deferred tax liabilities since the company recovered part of its investment from the U.S. government through an additional $31.50

---

[325] FASB ASC 980–740–25–1.

[326] For a plain-English write-up, *see* "Treatment of Income Taxes In Utility Ratemaking," a White Paper Prepared for The Oregon Legislative Assembly By Public Utility Commission of Oregon Staff, February 2005.

tax savings. To be consistent and avoid a potential violation of the normalization rule, a deferred tax asset should increase the rate base to the extent the deferred tax asset was attributable to a tax incentive subject to normalization.

Second, deferred taxes are subject to a three-step determination when a change in the underlying tax law gave rise to the deferred taxes, such as the reduction in the U.S. corporate tax rate from 35 percent to 21 percent under the TCJA. The three-step determination is as follows:

(1) Were the deferred taxes covered by the normalization rule?

(2) If the deferred taxes were not covered by the normalization rule, did the rate reduction benefit go to ratepayers or shareholders?

(3) If item 2 applies, was the change in deferred taxes offset by an equal entry to a regulatory asset/liability account? Different state public utilities commissions may have different approaches on how to return regulatory assets/liabilities to ratepayers.

For a company that is not regulated, any tax benefit or tax detriment due to a change in tax law flows directly to that company. For a regulated company, some of the tax incentives or detriments are essentially clawed back and go to the company's customers while other tax incentives flow directly to the company. The reduction in the U.S. corporate tax rate will flow entirely to customers but over many years. Another impact of the TCJA is that interest expense "properly allocable" to regulated utilities are not subject to the interest expense limitation.[327] However, regulated utilities are not allowed 100 percent expensing of depreciable tangible personal property.[328]

§ 2.15 Asset Purchases

[1] Business Combinations

One entity may acquire another entity in either a taxable business combination or a non-taxable business combination. If the acquisition is a taxable business combination, then the purchase price is allocated to the assets and liabilities of the acquired entity for both financial reporting and tax purposes. If the acquisition is a non-taxable business combination (such as an "A" reorganization), then the purchase price is allocated to the acquired entity's assets and liabilities for financial reporting purposes. For tax purposes, however, the tax bases of the assets and liabilities carry over to the acquiring entity.[329]

In June 2001, FASB issued SFAS No. 141, *Business Combinations* and SFAS No. 142, *Goodwill and Other Intangible Assets* (later FASB ASC 350). These two statements changed the accounting treatment for business combinations, goodwill and intangible assets. SFAS No. 141 eliminated pooling of interests accounting for business combinations effective for business combinations taking place after June 30, 2001. As a result, business combinations had to be accounted for under the purchase method of accounting. FASB ASC 350 does not allow goodwill to be amortizable for financial accounting purposes. Rather, goodwill is subject to periodic impairment testing and, to

[327] IRC Section 163(j).

[328] IRC Section 168(k).

[329] IRC Section 362(b).

the extent it is impaired, it must be written down or written off.[330] SFAS No. 141 and SFAS No. 142 (FASB ASC 350) did not, however, change the requirements in SFAS No. 109 (FASB ASC 740) for recognition of deferred taxes in a business combination.

In December 2007, FASB issued a revised version of SFAS No. 141, *Business Combinations.* SFAS No. 141(R) (FASB ASC 805) is effective for business combinations in which the acquisition date is on or after the beginning of the first annual reporting period beginning on or after December 15, 2008.[331] SFAS No. 141(R) (FASB ASC 805) made a number of changes to SFAS No. 141.[332] The purchase method of accounting was replaced by the acquisition method of accounting, which applies to all business combinations and requires an acquirer be identified for each business combination.[333] The acquirer is defined as "the entity that obtains control of one or more businesses in the business combination." The acquisition date is defined as the date that the acquirer achieves control.[334]

FASB ASC 805 requires that the assets acquired, liabilities assumed, and any noncontrolling interest in the acquiree be measured at the fair value on the acquisition date.[335] As a result, acquisition-related costs are recognized separately from the acquisition and are generally expensed.[336] The expensing of acquisition-related costs (with the exception of debt and equity issuance costs) provided for in FASB ASC 805 is a significant change from SFAS No. 141, which required capitalization of such costs. In addition, restructuring costs the acquirer expects to incur are also recognized separately from the acquisition.

An acquirer must recognize identifiable assets acquired and liabilities assumed as of the acquisition date (measured at their acquisition date fair values) only if it is more likely than not that the identifiable assets and liabilities meet the definition of an asset or liability under CON 6.[337] If the more likely than not standard is not met with respect to an identifiable asset or liability, then the costs are not part of applying the acquisition method. The acquirer accounts for the costs in its post-combination financial statements, in accordance with other GAAP principles (particularly FASB ASC 450). [338]

When one entity acquires another entity in a business combination, whether taxable or non-taxable, a deferred tax liability or asset is recognized for an acquired entity's taxable or deductible temporary differences (i.e., differences between the recognized values (i.e., book bases) and the tax bases of the acquired entity's assets and liabilities).[339] As a general rule, the differences between book bases and tax bases will be

---

[330] FASB ASC 350–20–35–7 (Deferred taxes are included in the carrying amount (i.e., book basis) of a reporting unit for purposes of determining whether goodwill impairment exists (i.e., comparing the fair value of a reporting unit with its carrying amount (i.e., book basis)).

[331] FASB ASC 805–10–65–1.

[332] FASB also issued a staff position that amended and clarified certain application issues with respect to SFAS No. 141(R) (FASB ASC 805). FSP No. FAS 141(R)–1 (April 1, 2009) (FASB ASC 805–20).

[333] FASB ASC 805–10–25–4.

[334] FASB ASC 805–10–25–6.

[335] FASB ASC 805–20–30–1.

[336] FASB ASC 805–10–25–23. Acquisition-related costs, generally referred to as transaction costs, include finder's fees; advisory, legal, accounting, valuation and other professional fees; general administrative costs; and the costs of registering and issuing debt and equity securities. *Id.*

[337] FASB ASC 805–20–25–2 and FASB ASC 805–20–25–19.

[338] FASB ASC 805–20–25–2.

[339] FASB ASC 805–740–25–3 and FASB ASC 805–740–05–1.

much more prevalent in a non-taxable business combination. A deferred tax liability is not recognized, however, for a difference between the book basis and the tax basis of goodwill if the goodwill is not amortizable for tax purposes, for leveraged leases, and for acquired temporary differences relating to the excess of the book basis over the tax basis of an investment in a foreign subsidiary or a foreign corporate joint venture that is essentially permanent in duration.[340]

FASB ASC 805 requires the acquirer to recognize goodwill as of the acquisition date.[341] Goodwill is measured as a residual, meaning that it is the excess of: the sum of the consideration transferred plus the fair value of any noncontrolling interest over the fair values of the identifiable net assets acquired.[342] FASB ASC 805 requires the acquirer to recognize contingent consideration at the acquisition date (measured at its fair value on that date).[343]

If a taxable business combination creates tax-amortizable goodwill, then a deferred tax liability is recognized over time as goodwill is amortized on the tax return over 15 years but not amortized for financial reporting (i.e., the tax basis of the goodwill will become less than the book basis of the goodwill as the tax basis is amortized for tax purposes). A similar situation arises with respect to indefinite lived intangible assets that are amortized for tax purposes but not for financial reporting purposes (i.e., the tax basis will become less than the book basis as tax amortization begins).

Purchased goodwill is deductible for tax purposes over a 15-year period.[344] The book basis and the tax basis of goodwill are each separated into two components as of the business acquisition date for purposes of the deferred tax calculations.[345] The first component of each is equal to the lesser of: goodwill for financial reporting or tax-deductible goodwill.[346] The second component of each is equal to the remainder (or excess) of each, i.e., the remainder, if any, of goodwill for financial reporting, or the remainder, if any, of tax-deductible goodwill.[347] Any future difference that arises between the book basis and tax basis of the first component of goodwill is a temporary difference that will give rise to a deferred tax liability or asset.[348]

If the second component of goodwill is an excess of tax-deductible goodwill over the book basis of goodwill, then the tax benefit for the excess is a temporary difference for

---

340 *Id.*

341 FASB ASC 805–30–30–1.

342 *Id.*

343 FASB ASC 805–30–25–5.

344 IRC Section 197. In enacting IRC Section 197 as part of the Omnibus Budget Reconciliation Act of 1993 (enactment date of August 10, 1993), Congress permitted companies the option of electing to retroactively apply it to business combinations occurring after July 25, 1991. A FASB Task Force concluded that the tax benefit related to tax-deductible goodwill in excess of the book basis of goodwill is included in income from continuing operations at the enactment date if the enterprise expects to retroactively apply IRC Section 197. FASB Task Force, EITF Issue No. 93–12, *Recognition and Movement of the Tax Benefit of Excess Tax-Deductible Goodwill Resulting from a Retroactive Change in Tax Law* (Sept. 23, 1993). A current tax benefit is reported for the retroactive amortization of goodwill (from the combination date to the enactment date). A deferred tax benefit is reported for the excess of tax-deductible goodwill (less the retroactive amortization) over the book basis of the goodwill.

345 FASB ASC 805–740–25–8.

346 *Id.*

347 *Id.*

348 *Id.*

which a deferred tax asset is recognized.[349] If the second component of goodwill is an excess of the book basis of goodwill over the tax-deductible goodwill, then no deferred taxes are recognized (either at the acquisition date or in future years).[350]

ILLUSTRATION 2-34:[351]

At the acquisition date, the reported amount (i.e., book basis) of goodwill is $600 (before adjustment for the tax benefit of goodwill) and the tax basis of goodwill is $900. For tax purposes, the amortization of goodwill will result in tax deductions of $60 in each of years one through fifteen. These deductions result in a tax benefit in years one through fifteen. For financial reporting, goodwill has not been impaired. The tax rate is 40 percent each year. At the acquisition date, the book basis of goodwill has to be adjusted for the tax benefit associated with goodwill. The computation is as follows ("simultaneous equations method"):

(Tax Rate ÷ (1 – Tax Rate) × Preliminary Temporary Difference = Deferred Tax Asset

Using the numbers in the example, the formula is: (40% ÷ (1 – 40%) × $300 = $200

Therefore, the book basis of goodwill is reduced to $400 at the acquisition date with a $200 deferred tax asset.

The goodwill is separated into two components, as follows:

	Book Basis	Tax Basis
First component (lesser of goodwill for financial reporting or tax-deductible goodwill)	$400	$400
Second component (remainder)	$ 0	$500
Total goodwill	$400	$900

One of the more significant changes made in accounting for business combinations is with respect to a bargain purchase.[352] A bargain purchase occurs in a business combination when, on the acquisition date, the total fair value of the identifiable net assets acquired exceeds the sum of the fair value of the consideration transferred plus any noncontrolling interest in the acquiree.[353] The bargain purchase element is recognized by the acquirer as gain and therefore included in earnings.[354] Previously, FASB treated the bargain purchase element as negative goodwill and allocated it as a pro rata reduction of the amounts otherwise assigned to the acquired assets.

In a business combination, the acquiring entity may recognize a valuation allowance with respect to a deferred tax asset recorded for the deductible temporary differences

---

349 *Id.*

350 *Id.*

351 FASB ASC 805–740–55–9.

352 FASB ASC 805–30–25.

353 FASB ASC 805–30–25–2.

354 *Id.*

attributable to the acquired entity's assets and liabilities, net operating loss carryforwards, or tax credit carryforwards on the acquisition date. Any decrease or elimination of the valuation allowance after the acquisition date and within the measurement period that results from new information about facts and circumstances that existed at the acquisition date is first used to reduce to zero the book basis of any goodwill created in the acquisition. Any additional decrease in the valuation allowance is treated as a bargain purchase.[355] Any change in the valuation allowance for an acquired entity's deferred tax asset that does not occur in the measurement period (and is not based on new information about facts and circumstances existing at the acquisition date) is reported as a reduction or increase to income tax expense (or as an adjustment to contributed capital).[356]

[2] Non-Business Combinations

FASB has provided little guidance on accounting for acquisitions of individual assets that are not business combinations in which the tax basis of an individual asset differs from its book basis.[357] FASB concluded that the tax effect of asset acquisitions that are not business combinations in which the tax basis differs from the book basis (i.e., purchase price) should not result in immediate income statement recognition.[358] Rather, if a deferred tax asset is created because the tax basis of an individual asset is greater than its book basis, then a corresponding decrease is made to the book basis of the asset.[359] If the book basis of the individual asset is reduced to zero, then any excess downward adjustment to the book basis is recorded as a deferred credit.[360] If a deferred tax liability is created because the book basis of the individual asset is greater than the tax basis, then a corresponding increase is made to the book basis of the asset.[361] In making the adjustment to the book basis of an individual asset, the deferred tax asset or liability must be grossed up ("simultaneous equations method").[362]

ILLUSTRATION 2-35:[363]

An entity pays $1 million for the stock of a corporation in a tax-free acquisition. The acquired corporation's sole asset is an FCC license with a tax basis of zero. The acquisition is an asset purchase that is not a business combination. The tax rate is 35 percent.

Because the book basis of $1 million in the FCC license exceeds the tax basis of zero, normally a deferred tax liability would be recognized equal to $350,000 ($1 million excess of book basis over tax basis times 35 percent). But no immediate income statement recognition is permitted; rather the deferred tax liability is applied to increase the book basis of the FCC license. Doing so will increase the amount of the deferred tax liability because the excess of book basis over tax basis will be increased. As a result, the deferred tax liability

---

[355] FASB ASC 805–740–45–2.

[356] *Id.*

[357] FASB ASC 740-10-25-49.

[358] FASB ASC 740–10–25–51.

[359] FASB ASC 740–10–55–171.

[360] FASB ASC 740–10–55–171 and FASB ASC 740–10–55–183.

[361] FASB ASC 740–10–55–177.

[362] FASB ASC 740–10–25–51.

[363] *Id.*

must be grossed-up to $538,462 ($350,000 deferred tax liability divided by (one minus the tax rate of 35 percent)). The FCC license will be recorded with a book basis of $1,538,462 ($1 million purchase price plus $538,462 deferred tax liability).

ILLUSTRATION 2-36:[364]

An entity acquires equipment in a foreign jurisdiction paying $100. The laws of the foreign jurisdiction permit the entity a deduction in excess of the amount paid for the equipment as an inducement to purchase the equipment. As a result, the entity's tax basis in the equipment is automatically increased to $150. The tax rate is 35 percent.

Because the tax basis of $150 exceeds the book basis of $100, normally a deferred tax asset would be recognized equal to $17.5 ($50 excess of tax basis over book basis times 35 percent tax rate). But no immediate income statement recognition is permitted; rather the deferred tax asset is applied to reduce the book basis of the equipment. Doing so will increase the amount of the deferred tax asset because the excess of tax basis over book basis will be increased. As a result, the deferred tax asset must be grossed-up to $27 ($17.5 deferred tax asset divided by (one minus the tax rate of 35 percent)). The equipment will be recorded with a book basis of $73 ($100 purchase price less $27 deferred tax asset).

In Illustration 2-36, the book basis of the equipment was reduced to $73. If the book basis is reduced to zero (as a result of grossing up the deferred tax asset), then a deferred credit is recorded that is equal to the excess of the deferred tax asset over the amount paid for the asset. The deferred credit is not a temporary difference and is amortized to income tax expense in proportion to the realization of the tax benefits that created the deferred credit.[365]

ILLUSTRATION 2-37:[366]

Same facts as Illustration 2-36 except that the entity acquires the equipment in a foreign jurisdiction paying only $50 (with a tax basis of $200). The tax rate is 35 percent.

Because the tax basis of $200 exceeds the book basis of $50, normally a deferred tax asset would be recognized equal to $52.5 ($150 excess of tax basis over book basis times 35 percent tax rate). But no immediate income statement recognition is permitted; rather the deferred tax asset is applied to reduce the book basis of the equipment. As a result, the deferred tax asset must be grossed-up to $81 ($52.5 deferred tax asset divided by (one minus the tax rate of 35 percent)). However, this would reduce the book basis of the equipment to ($31). The book basis cannot be less than zero so the equipment will have a book basis of zero. The tax basis of $200 exceeds the book basis of zero by $200 so that a deferred tax asset of $70 ($200 times 35 percent) will be recorded. The excess of the deferred tax asset of $70 over the purchase price of $50 is recorded as a deferred credit. This deferred credit of $20 is amortized into income tax

[364] FASB ASC 740–10–55–171.

[365] FASB ASC 740–10–25–51.

[366] FASB ASC 740–10–55–183.

expense in proportion to the realization of the tax benefits of the deferred tax asset.

§ 2.16 Investment in Corporations and Flow-Through Entities

When a parent entity includes the undistributed earnings of a subsidiary in its pretax financial income under either the consolidation method or the equity method, a temporary difference results.[367] In addition, it is presumed that all undistributed earnings of a subsidiary will be transferred to the parent entity.[368] The presumption may be overcome and therefore the parent entity should not accrue income taxes "if sufficient evidence shows that the subsidiary has invested or will invest the undistributed earnings indefinitely or that the earnings will be remitted in a tax-free liquidation."[369] However, a deferred tax liability is recognized for the excess of book basis over tax basis of an investment in a *domestic* subsidiary unless the tax law provides a means by which the investment can be recovered tax free.[370]

Probably the most common exception that will also have the most significant positive earnings impact is the exception for recognition of deferred taxes for undistributed earnings of a foreign subsidiary (or foreign corporate joint venture), which may require extensive tax planning.[371] A deferred tax liability is not recognized for the excess of book basis over tax basis of an investment in a foreign subsidiary (or foreign corporate joint venture) if there is sufficient evidence that the foreign subsidiary has invested or will invest the undistributed earnings indefinitely (i.e., the investment is essentially permanent in duration).[372] The remainder of this section will cover the recording of deferred taxes for different types of investees and the corresponding exceptions.

Deferred Taxes on Outside Basis Difference[373]

These rules can have materially different results based on whether they relate to domestic subsidiaries, foreign subsidiaries, or joint ventures. We provide below an expanded explanation of the pertinent provisions.

A company will record a deferred tax liability or deferred tax asset in the book-tax outside basis difference of its investment in a business entity (determined on a jurisdictional basis). The applicable tax accounting rule depends on two factors:

1. Whether the business entity is domestic or foreign in relation to the immediate parent entity.

---

367 FASB ASC 740.

368 FASB ASC 740.

369 FASB ASC 740–30–25–17.

370 FASB ASC 740–30–25–3, FASB ASC 740–30–25–5, FASB ASC 740–30–25–7 and FASB ASC 740–30–25–8. A deferred tax asset is also recognized for the excess of tax basis over book basis of an investment in a subsidiary or corporate joint venture that is essentially permanent in duration only if it is apparent that the temporary difference will reverse in the foreseeable future. FASB ASC 740–30–25–9. FASB has determined that the tax benefit for the excess of tax basis over book basis of an investment in a subsidiary that will be displayed as a discontinued operation is recognized when it is apparent that the temporary difference will reverse in the foreseeable future. FASB ASC 740–30–25–10.

371 FASB ASC 740–10–25–3. *See* FASB ASC 323–10–20 for a definition of *corporate joint venture*.

372 FASB ASC 740–10–25–3; FASB ASC 740–10–25–18.

373 FASB ASC 830-740-25-6 ("Differences between the tax basis and the financial reporting basis of an investment in a foreign subsidiary are referred to as outside basis differences.").

2. Whether the business entity is a subsidiary, corporate joint venture, 50 percent-or-less-owned investee, less than 20 percent-owned investee, or flow-through business.

Before discussing the rules, a few key terms need to be defined:

- Foreign versus domestic: The determination of whether an entity is foreign or domestic is made at each level in the corporate structure.[374] A common mistake is to classify any company incorporated in the United States as domestic while any company incorporated outside of the United States as foreign. First, it is not the country of incorporation that determines a company's status, but the country of tax domicile. Second, a company is domestic if it has the same tax domicile as its immediate parent company. **Example:** Example: Assume tax residency determines tax domicile in Country X and Country Y. A corporation (Parent) has its tax residency and therefore tax domicile in Country X. Its wholly-owned subsidiary (Sub) has its tax residency and therefore tax domicile in Country Y. Sub is considered a foreign subsidiary for purposes of applying the recognition provisions in FASB ASC 740–30. However, if Parent and Sub have their tax residencies and therefore tax domiciles in Country X, then Sub is considered a domestic subsidiary for purposes of applying the recognition provisions in FASB ASC 740–30. To the extent there is a tax treaty between two countries, the tax residency clause determines the tax domicile of the company.
- Subsidiary: A business entity that is consolidated for financial GAAP reporting. **Example:** Company is the controlling shareholder in Newco. Newco has two classes of common stock—Class A and Class B. The Class A has three votes per share while the Class B has only one vote per share. There are 100 outstanding shares of each class. Company owns 70 shares of the Class A stock which represents 52.5 percent of the voting power. Company's control is sufficient to consolidate Newco into the Company's GAAP financials.
- Corporate joint venture: A 50 percent-or-less-owned investee that no single investor controls, but the company is able to prevent the reversal of its outside book-tax basis difference. **Example:** Company and an unrelated party are each 50 percent shareholders in Newco. Newco's by-laws require a two-thirds vote on major corporate decisions including the declaration of dividends. Neither Company nor the other shareholder controls Newco. Since Company does not have voting control of Newco, Newco would not be a subsidiary of Company. However, the Company's 50 percent interest is enough to prevent Newco from declaring any dividends or taking any corporate action that would reverse the outside book-tax basis difference. Company would report its 50 percent ownership in Newco as a corporate joint venture.
- 50 percent-or-less-owned investee: A business entity that is typically at least 20 percent owned that is not a corporate joint venture and is reported

[374] Note that an exception to recording a deferred tax liability may apply if the lower-tier entity is domestic and more than 50 percent owned. *See* FASB ASC 740–30–25–7.

under the equity method of accounting under GAAP. **Example:** Company is a minority shareholder in Newco, owning 30 percent of Newco's common stock. The other 70 percent of Newco is owned by the majority shareholder. Newco's by-laws require a two-thirds vote on major corporate decisions including the declaration of dividends. Company clearly does not control Newco so Newco cannot be a subsidiary of Company. Company's ownership is insufficient to block the payment of dividends or major corporate decisions, so Newco cannot be a corporate joint venture. Company would report its investment in Newco under the equity method.

- Less than 20 percent-owned investee: A business entity where ownership is less than 20 percent and is not a corporate joint venture. **Example:** Company owns 10 percent of the stock in Newco. Newco stock is widely held. Newco's by-laws require a two-thirds vote on major corporate decisions including the declaration of dividends. The Company clearly does not control Newco so it cannot be a subsidiary of the Company. The Company's ownership is insufficient to block the payment of dividends or major corporate decisions so Newco cannot be a corporate joint venture. The Company does not own the requisite 20 percent for equity method treatment. The Company will report its 10 percent investment in Newco at cost or fair value.
- Flow-through entity: Any business entity in which the income is taxed at the investor level. **Example:** tax partnerships, U.S. limited liability companies, and S corporations would be reported as a flow-through investment.

There is no symmetry in the rules between recording a deferred tax liability and a deferred tax asset. Generally, a deferred tax liability must be recorded unless an exception is met, whereas a deferred tax asset cannot be recorded unless an exception is met.

Domestic Subsidiaries

General rule for deferred tax liabilities: Must be recorded.[375]

Exception: A deferred tax liability is not recorded if the investment can be recovered tax-free without significant cost and the entity expects ultimately to use that means of recovery.[376] In considering whether an investment can be recovered tax-free without significant cost, the inside tax basis of the subsidiary's assets must be compared to the outside tax basis of the investment to quantify the excess outside tax basis that would be lost if the company engaged in a tax-free recovery transaction (i.e., an asset sale). However, an asset sale that results in the loss of outside basis, which has value, cannot be considered a viable tax-free recovery of the basis difference since the loss of the outside basis is a significant cost. A potential planning idea is to interpose a foreign entity between two domestic entities to take advantage of the indefinite reinvestment doctrine. (The indefinite reinvestment doctrine is discussed in Section 4.04[2][c].)

General rule for deferred tax assets: Not recorded.

---

[375] FASB ASC 740–30–25–5.

[376] FASB ASC 740–30–25–7.

Exception: A deferred tax asset should be recorded if it is apparent that the temporary difference will reverse in the foreseeable future.[377] Although GAAP does not define *foreseeable future*, the major accounting firms believe it should be no more than twelve months.

Foreign Subsidiaries

General rule for deferred tax liabilities: Must be recorded.[378]

Exception: A deferred tax liability does not need to be recorded provided the indefinite reinvestment doctrine is met. (The indefinite reinvestment doctrine is discussed in Section 4.04[2][c].)[379]

General rule for deferred tax assets: Same as domestic subsidiary.

Exception: Same as domestic subsidiary.

Domestic Corporate Joint Venture

General rule for deferred tax liabilities: Same as domestic subsidiary.

Exception: None. A potential planning idea is to interpose a foreign entity between a domestic entity and a domestic corporate joint venture to take advantage of the indefinite reinvestment doctrine. (The indefinite reinvestment doctrine is discussed in Section 4.04[2][c].)

General rule for deferred tax assets: Same as domestic subsidiary.

Exception: Same as domestic subsidiary.

Foreign Corporate Joint Venture

General rule for deferred tax liabilities: Same as foreign subsidiary.[380]

Exception: A deferred tax liability is not recorded if the joint venture is permanent in duration and the indefinite reinvestment doctrine is met.[381] (The indefinite reinvestment doctrine is discussed in Section 4.04[2][c].)

General Rule for deferred tax assets: Same as foreign subsidiary.

Exception: Same as foreign subsidiary.

---

[377] FASB ASC 740–30–25–9.

[378] FASB ASC 740–30–25–5. In May 2019, the FASB issued Proposed ASU No. 2019–700, *Income Taxes (Topic 740): Simplifying the Accounting for Income Taxes*, which removes certain exceptions and simplifies other tax accounting rules. Historically, when a foreign subsidiary changes its classification to an equity method investment, no deferred tax liability will be recorded on the outside book-tax basis difference in the equity method investment. Similarly, when an equity method investment, which has a deferred tax liability from an outside basis difference, changes its classification to a foreign subsidiary, the company cannot reverse the deferred tax liability by asserting the indefinite reinvestment doctrine. These deferred tax positions are considered "frozen." Under Proposed ASU No. 2019–700, a deferred tax liability would be recorded on the outside basis difference when a foreign subsidiary changed its classification to an equity method investment. Similarly, the deferred tax liability on an equity method investment would be eliminated, in whole or in part, when it changed its classification to a foreign subsidiary and the company asserted the indefinite reinvestment doctrine.

[379] FASB ASC 740–30–25–17.

[380] As further support for not recording a deferred tax liability when the investment is permanent in duration, FASB ASC 740–10–25–30 provides an example in which the basis difference created by the excess of cash surrender value of life insurance over premiums paid is not recognized if the asset is expected to be recovered without tax consequence upon the death of the insured.

[381] FASB ASC 740–30–25–18.

50 Percent-or-Less-Owned Investee

General rule: Record both a deferred tax liability and deferred tax asset for foreign and domestic investees.[382]

Exception: No exceptions.

Less Than 20 Percent-Owned Investee

General rule: Record both deferred a tax liability and deferred tax asset for foreign and domestic investees.

Exception: No exceptions.

If a deferred tax liability or deferred tax asset is recorded, it must be computed for each jurisdiction that will impose income tax on that outside basis difference, while considering any tax credits or exemptions that will be available. However, there are also special rules that apply to the computation of the outside basis in arriving at the deferred tax liability and deferred tax asset. The special rules are due to currency adjustments and other adjustments, such as inflation indexation.

An outside basis difference is most frequently caused by earnings that have not been repatriated. A company's book basis in a subsidiary is increased by the subsidiary's earnings that have not been repatriated. Most countries do not allow an increase in the corresponding outside tax basis of the subsidiary. In such situations, the outside basis difference will reverse through dividends from the subsidiary, the sale of the subsidiary, the liquidation of the subsidiary, or a merger of the subsidiary into a related company.[383]

However, when a subsidiary's functional currency for U.S. GAAP is not the currency used to compute local income taxes, the carrying amounts of nonmonetary assets (e.g., fixed assets, common stock) are based on functional currency based on the historical exchange rates. The tax basis of an asset, in the functional currency, is typically determined when the asset is acquired using the spot exchange rate at the time of the transaction date. For example, assume a U.S. dollar functional currency company acquired an asset for $100 when the peso-to-USD exchange rate was 10 to 1. The local country tax basis is 1,000 pesos and the functional currency tax basis is $100. Assume the asset did not change in value and is worth $100 next year when the peso-to-USD exchange rate is 15 to 1. The sale of the asset for $100 would result in no U.S. GAAP gain. Since the asset is now worth 1,500 pesos, there is a 500-peso gain. Absent an exception, deferred taxes would need to be recorded on the 500 book-tax basis difference.

---

382 FASB ASC 740–30–25–5(b) and FASB ASC 740–30–25–9. In May 2019, the FASB issued Proposed ASU No. 2019–700, *Income Taxes (Topic 740): Simplifying the Accounting for Income Taxes*, which removes certain exceptions and simplifies other tax accounting rules. Historically, when a foreign subsidiary changes its classification to an equity method investment, no deferred tax liability will be recorded on the outside book-tax basis difference in the equity method investment. Similarly, when an equity method investment, which has a deferred tax liability from an outside basis difference, changes its classification to a foreign subsidiary, the company cannot reverse the deferred tax liability by asserting the indefinite reinvestment doctrine. These deferred tax positions are considered "frozen." Under Proposed ASU No. 2019–700, a deferred tax liability would be recorded on the outside basis difference when a foreign subsidiary changed its classification to an equity method investment. Similarly, the deferred tax liability on an equity method investment would be eliminated, in whole or in part, when it changed its classification to a foreign subsidiary and the company asserted the indefinite reinvestment doctrine.

383 According to ASC 740–30–25–19, "if circumstances change and it becomes apparent that some or all of the undistributed earnings of a subsidiary will be remitted in the foreseeable future but income taxes have not been recognized by the parent entity, it shall accrue as an expense of the current period income taxes attributable to that remittance."

In some cases, especially in hyperinflationary countries and countries that provide preferential tax treatment for capital gains, the local tax basis is subject to indexation for inflation. In such cases, the temporary difference for local tax purposes would include such adjustments to reflect the amount of local country tax upon the disposition of the shares in the investment. Such an adjustment would create a book-tax basis difference that might require deferred taxes.

There is an exception to booking these adjustments that provides there will be no "recognition of a deferred tax liability or asset for differences related to assets and liabilities that . . . are remeasured from the local currency into the functional currency using historical exchange rates and that result from changes in exchange rates or indexing for tax purposes."[384] Deferred taxes that have not been recorded will need to be recorded when there is a change in business circumstances. The held-for-sale guidance evaluates six criteria,[385] including (a) the company commits to market and sell the investment or asset under an approved plan, (b) the sale of the asset is probable within one year of the disposal decision, and (c) it is unlikely that the disposal plan will be withdrawn.

§ 2.17 Intraperiod Tax Allocation

An entity's income tax expense (or benefit) for the year must be allocated among the entity's continuing operations, discontinued operations, other comprehensive income, and items charged or credited to shareholders' equity.[386] This allocation is referred to as intraperiod tax allocation. The amount of income tax expense attributable to continuing operations is based on the pretax income (or loss) from continuing operations.[387] This amount of income tax expense (attributable to continuing operations) is then adjusted for the tax effects of a change in the beginning of the year balance of a valuation allowance due to a change in judgment as to the realizability of the related deferred tax asset, changes in tax laws or tax rates, changes in an entity's tax status, and tax-deductible dividends.[388]

Certain items are charged or credited directly to other comprehensive income or to components of shareholders' equity. The tax effects of these items are also charged or credited to other comprehensive income or to related components of shareholders' equity.[389] For example, certain changes in accounting principle or corrections of an error are adjustments to the beginning balance of retained earnings. As a result, the tax effects

---

[384] FASB ASC 740–10–25–3(f).

[385] FASB ASC 360–10–45.

[386] FASB ASC 740–20–45–2. The allocation of income tax expense between income from continuing operations and other items must include deferred taxes. As a result, both current tax expense and deferred tax expense must be allocated between income from continuing operations and other items. FASB ASC 740–20–45–1.

FASB has addressed the issue of the integrated tax system in France. FASB ASC 740–10–55–72 to FASB ASC 740–10–55–74. The French system integrates the shareholder and corporate level taxes by providing a shareholder a tax credit on dividends received. The tax credit is based on the taxes paid by the corporation when it pays the dividends. The FASB Task Force concluded that the taxes paid by the corporation when it pays the dividends is, in effect, a withholding tax for the benefit of the shareholders and should be recorded as part of shareholders' equity and not as an increase to income tax expense.

[387] FASB ASC 740–20–45–7.

[388] FASB ASC 740–20–45–8. *See* FASB ASC 830–740–25–2 (deferred taxes from temporary differences arising from a change in functional currency when an economy is no longer highly inflationary is recognized in other comprehensive income).

[389] FASB ASC 740–20–45–11.

of these items are also charged or credited to components of shareholders' equity (i.e., retained earnings). Tax effects charged to other comprehensive income or components of shareholders' equity include tax effects attributable to (a) adjustments in the opening balance of retained earnings due to a change in accounting principles or correction of an error, (b) gains and losses included in comprehensive income but not net income, such as the tax effects of unrealized gains and losses on available-for-sale securities, (c) an increase or decrease in contributed capital, (d) deductible temporary differences and carryforwards on the date that a corporation undergoes a quasi-reorganization, and (e) changes in the tax bases of assets and liabilities due to transactions among or with shareholders (which are included in shareholders' equity).[390]

In allocating income tax expense for the year, if there is one item other than continuing operations, then the portion of income tax expense remaining after allocation to continuing operations is allocated to that other item.[391]

ILLUSTRATION 2-38:[392]

An entity's pretax financial income and taxable income are the same. It has an ordinary loss from continuing operations of $500. It also has a capital gain from discontinued operations for the year of $900. The tax rate on ordinary income is 40 percent and the capital gains tax rate is 30 percent. Income taxes currently payable are $120 ($400 taxable income times 30 percent).

The tax effect of the $500 loss from continuing operations is a tax benefit of $200 ($500 loss multiplied by the 40 percent tax rate) because the entity does not consider the tax effects of items that are not included in continuing operations. Therefore, $200 of tax benefit is allocated to continuing operations. The difference between the $120 of income tax expense and the $200 tax benefit allocated to continuing operations is a $320 tax expense that is allocated to the discontinued operations.

If there are two or more items other than continuing operations, then the income tax expense is allocated first to continuing operations and the remainder is allocated to the other items proportionately to their effects on income tax expense for the year.[393] At times, the total of the individual effects of items other than continuing operations may not equal the remainder of the income tax expense after allocation to continuing operations. If this occurs, then the net loss items need to be separated from the net gain items.[394] The tax effect of the total of the net loss items is determined and ratably allocated to each of the net loss items.[395] The remaining amount (after allocation to continuing operations and net loss items) is allocated ratably to each net gain item.[396]

§ 2.18 Quasi-Reorganizations

If a corporation has a continuous run of losses each year, it may have a deficit balance in retained earnings. In some states, the deficit balance in retained earnings

---

390 *Id.*

391 FASB ASC 740–20–45–12.

392 FASB ASC 740–20–55–10.

393 FASB ASC 740–20–45–14.

394 *Id.*

395 *Id.*

396 *Id.*

may prevent the corporation from paying a dividend to its shareholders. To alleviate this hardship, a corporation may be permitted to undergo a quasi-reorganization in which the corporation's assets are revalued to current fair market value (i.e., a write-down of assets) and the deficit balance in retained earnings is eliminated (by reducing the balance in contributed capital).[397]

After a quasi-reorganization, an entity's accounting should be similar to that of a new entity.[398] A new entity would not have tax benefits attributable to net operating losses or tax credits that arose prior to the beginning of the new entity. If a corporation has deductible temporary differences and carryforwards on the date it undergoes a quasi-reorganization, the tax benefits attributable to such temporary differences and carryforwards are added to contributed capital when the tax benefits are recognized in later years.[399] If subsequent to a quasi-reorganization, a corporation determines that due to a change in circumstance a valuation allowance should be recognized (or increased) to offset a deferred tax asset recognized at the time of the quasi-reorganization, then a charge to income is appropriate.[400]

§ 2.19 Separate Financial Statements of a Subsidiary

An affiliated group of corporations may elect to file a consolidated tax return.[401] If an affiliated group elects to do so, it is referred to as a consolidated group and is generally treated as one taxpayer for purposes of the tax laws (i.e., all of the income and deductions of the group are pooled together in determining a single taxable income figure). If the members of the consolidated group issue separate financial statements, then the consolidated group must allocate its consolidated amount of current and deferred tax expense among its members.[402] FASB did not provide any particular allocation method but stated, in broad terms, that any method adopted "shall be systematic, rational, and consistent" with the principles in FASB ASC 740.[403] Treating each member of the group as if that member were a separate taxpayer.[404] FASB noted that several methods are expressly not permissible.[405] For example, a method that allocates only current taxes payable to a member of the consolidated group that has taxable temporary differences is not permissible.[406] The reason, of course, is that taxable temporary differences result in a recording of a deferred tax liability and therefore deferred tax expense.

Another impermissible method would be to allocate deferred taxes to a member of the group using a method other than the asset and liability method utilized in FASB ASC 740.[407] A final impermissible method would be to allocate no income tax expense

[397] FASB ASC 852–20.

[398] FASB ASC 852–740–55–4.

[399] FASB ASC 852–740–45–2.

[400] FASB ASC 852–740–55–5.

[401] IRC Section 1502.

[402] FASB ASC 740–10–30–27.

[403] *Id.*

[404] *Id.*

[405] *Id.*

[406] *Id.*

[407] *Id.*

(current or deferred) to a member of the consolidated group if the member has taxable income even if the consolidated group has no income tax expense for the year.[408]

An entity is not required to allocate consolidated tax expense to legal entities that are not subject to tax.[409] However, an entity may elect to allocate consolidated tax expense to legal entities that are not subject to tax and are disregarded (i.e., single member limited liability companies).[410] The election is not available for legal entities that are partnerships or other pass-through entities that are not wholly-owned.[411]

§ 2.20 Financial Statement Presentation

On its balance sheet, an entity reports deferred tax assets and deferred tax liabilities as assets and liabilities, respectively. An entity must classify deferred tax assets and liabilities as noncurrent amounts.[412] A particular tax-paying component of an entity within a particular tax jurisdiction, presents its deferred tax assets (and any valuation allowance) and deferred tax liabilities as a single noncurrent amount.[413] Offsetting or netting deferred tax assets and deferred tax liabilities is not permitted if attributable to different tax-paying components or different tax jurisdictions.

§ 2.21 Financial Statement Disclosure

An entity will disclose its net deferred tax liability or asset on its statement of financial position. However, the entity must also disclose the make-up of its net deferred tax liability or asset. This means that the entity must disclose the total of all deferred tax liabilities, the total of all deferred tax assets, and the total valuation allowance for its deferred tax assets.[414] The entity must also disclose the net change during the year in its total valuation allowance.[415]

An entity must also disclose the different types of its significant temporary differences and carryforwards.[416] If the entity is a public entity, it must also disclose the tax effects of its significant temporary differences and carryforwards.[417] If a public entity is not subject to income taxes because it is a pass-through entity, such as certain publicly traded partnerships, then the entity must disclose that its income is taxed directly to its owners and must also disclose the net difference between the tax bases and book bases of its assets and liabilities.[418] An entity must disclose in its financial statements the amount of income tax expense attributable to continuing operations and income tax expense attributable to other items, such as discontinued operations, other comprehensive income and retained earnings.[419] An entity must further disclose the significant components of its income tax expense attributable to continuing

---

408 *Id.*

409 FASB ASC 740–10–30–27A.

410 *Id.*

411 *Id.*

412 FASB ASC 740–10–45–4.

413 FASB ASC 740–10–45–6.

414 FASB ASC 740–10–50–2.

415 *Id.*

416 FASB ASC 740–10–50–5; FASB ASC 740–10–50–8.

417 FASB ASC 740–10–50–6.

418 FASB ASC 740–10–50–7; FASB ASC 740–10–50–16.

419 FASB ASC 740–10–50–10.

operations.[420] For example, two of the major components of income tax expense needed to be disclosed would be current tax expense (or benefit) and deferred tax expense (or benefit).[421] Other components of income tax expense attributable to continuing operations that would need to be disclosed include (a) investment tax credits, (b) government grants (if treated as a reduction of income tax expense), (c) the tax benefits of net operating loss carryforwards, (d) tax expense from allocating certain tax benefits to contributed capital, (e) adjustments to deferred tax asset or liability because of a change in tax laws or tax rates or a change in tax status, and (f) adjustment to the beginning balance of a valuation allowance because of a change in judgment as to the realizability of the related deferred tax asset.[422]

A public entity must reconcile, using either percentages or dollar amounts, income tax expense attributable to continuing operations with the amount of income tax expense that results from applying the U.S. federal statutory rates to pretax financial income from continuing operations.[423] This is generally referred to as the effective tax rate reconciliation. The entity must also disclose the nature and amount of each significant reconciling item.[424] If the entity is not a public entity, it may simply disclose the nature of each significant reconciling item and dispense with the numerical reconciliation.[425] Any other significant matter not otherwise evident from the disclosures must also be disclosed.[426] See Illustration 2-39 and Illustration 2-40 for examples of an effective tax rate reconciliation.

ILLUSTRATION 2-39: PepsiCo Inc. had the following effective tax rate reconciliation in its 2021 Annual Report (note 5):

	2021	2020	2019
U.S. Federal statutory tax rate	21.0 %	21.0 %	21.0 %
State income tax, net of U.S. Federal tax benefit	1.0	1.2	1.6
Lower taxes on foreign results	(1.6)	(0.8)	(0.9)
One-time mandatory transition tax - TCJ Act	1.9	—	(0.1)
Other, net	(0.5)	(0.5)	(0.6)
Annual tax rate	21.8 %	20.9 %	21.0 %

As is evident from the effective tax rate reconciliation, PepsiCo reconciled using tax percentages, beginning with the U.S. Federal statutory tax rate of 21

420 FASB ASC 740–10–50–9. The sum of the amounts disclosed as the components of income tax expense should equal the total income tax expense for continuing operations as reported in the statement of earnings for continuing operations. Insignificant components are aggregated and disclosed as a single amount (and then added to the significant components). FASB Special Report, *A Guide to Implementation of Statement 109 on Accounting for Income Taxes: Questions and Answers*, Q & A 18 (1992). Separate disclosure is required for the tax benefit of net operating loss carryforwards and tax credits and tax credit carryforwards that reduce current income tax expense or deferred income tax expense. *Id.*

421 FASB ASC 740–10–50–9.

422 *Id.*

423 FASB ASC 740–10–50–12.

424 *Id.* Rule 4–08(h) of SEC Regulation S-X requires disclosure of reconciling items that are five percent (or more) of the amount computed by multiplying pretax income by the statutory tax rate; i.e., any item that increases or decreases the tax rate by 1.05 percent or more. 17 CFR § 210.4–08—General notes to financial statements.

425 FASB ASC 740–10–50–13.

426 FASB ASC 740–10–50–14.

percent. PepsiCo's effective tax rate has remained fairly steady each year staying at about the U.S. Federal statutory rate.

ILLUSTRATION 2-40: Berkshire Hathaway, Inc. had the following effective tax rate reconciliation in its 2021 Annual Report (note 19):

	2021	2020	2019
Earnings before income taxes	$ 111,686	$ 55,693	$ 102,696
Hypothetical income tax expense computed at the U.S. federal statutory rate	$ 23,454	$ 11,696	$ 21,566
Dividends received deduction and tax-exempt interest	(457)	(448)	(433)
State income taxes, less U.S. federal income tax benefit	(417)	858	494
U.S. income tax credits	(1,860)	(1,519)	(942)
Goodwill impairments	—	1,977	20
Other differences, net	159	(124)	199
	$ 20,879	$ 12,440	$ 20,904
Effective income tax rate	18.7%	22.3%	20.4%

As is evident from the effective tax rate reconciliation, Berkshire Hathaway reconciled using dollar amounts rather than percentages but also provided the effective tax rate percentage each year.

If an entity has a net operating loss or tax credit carryforwards, it must disclose the amount and expiration dates of the loss or carryforwards.[427] It must also disclose any portion of a valuation allowance for which subsequent tax benefits will be credited directly to contributed capital.[428]

An entity that is a member of a consolidated group must disclose in its separately issued financial statements the total amount of current and deferred tax expense.[429] It must also disclose the amount of any tax-related balances due to or from another member of the consolidated group.[430] In addition, the entity must disclose the method by which the current and deferred tax expense is allocated among the members of the consolidated group and the nature and effect of any changes in the method.[431]

§ 2.22 Developments in Accounting for Income Taxes

[1] Corporate Alternative Minimum Tax

The TCJA repealed the corporate alternative minimum tax (AMT) effective for taxable years beginning after 2017. However, as part of the Inflation Reduction Act of 2022, which President Biden signed into law on August 16, 2022, Congress enacted a new corporate AMT, which was completely different than the version repealed five years earlier.[432] The new corporate AMT applies to an applicable corporation. An applicable corporation includes a U.S. corporation with average annual adjusted financial

---

[427] FASB ASC 740–10–50–3.

[428] *Id.*

[429] FASB ASC 740–10–50–17.

[430] *Id.*

[431] *Id.*

[432] *See* Christopher H. Hanna, Michelle Hanlon, Norman Richter and Michael Schler, *The Rise of the Minimum Tax*, 100 Taxes 55 (March 2022).

statement income of greater than $1 billion over a three taxable year period.[433] An applicable corporation also includes a foreign-parented corporation, if, in addition to meeting the $1 billion net income threshold, the U.S. average annual adjusted financial statement income exceeds $100 million over a three taxable year period. S corporations, REITs and RICs are not applicable corporations and therefore not subject to the new corporate AMT.

The tax base for the new corporate AMT is adjusted financial statement income, which is the net income or loss of the taxpayer set forth on the taxpayer's applicable financial statement for such taxable year, with certain adjustments.[434] An applicable corporation includes in its adjusted financial statement income its distributive share of partnership income, its proportionate share of income and losses of all of its CFCs, dividends and other income received from a foreign corporation that is not a CFC, all items of income from a foreign branch or disregarded entity, disregard any Federal income taxes as well as foreign income taxes, and make an adjustment for covered defined benefit plans and for depreciation expense.

Two separate rules apply to foreign tax credits under the corporate AMT. Foreign tax credits arising from foreign income taxes paid by CFCs (i.e., indirect FTCs) are limited to 15 percent of the U.S. shareholder's pro rata share of the CFC's net income. Direct foreign tax credits (foreign income taxes paid by the U.S. corporation or its disregarded entity) are not subject to the 15 percent limitation.

General business credits are limited to 75 percent of the net income tax as exceeds $25,000.

An applicable corporation is liable for the corporate AMT to the extent that its "tentative minimum tax" (15 percent of the adjusted financial statement income for the taxable year over the corporate AMT foreign tax credit for the taxable year) exceeds its regular Federal income tax liability plus its liability for the base erosion anti-abuse tax (BEAT). Any corporate AMT paid is carried forward and utilized as a credit to the extent the taxpayer's regular Federal income tax liability plus BEAT liability exceeds the tentative minimum tax.

An applicable corporation will record a deferred tax asset for the corporate AMT credit carryforward with a corresponding reduction in (deferred) tax expense. As a result, any corporate AMT paid will not impact the corporation's effective tax rate unless it records a valuation allowance against the deferred tax asset.

[2] Excise Tax on Stock Buybacks

As part of the Inflation Reduction Act of 2022, Congress enacted a one percent excise tax on a publicly traded U.S. corporation ("covered corporation") for the value of any of its stock that is repurchased by the corporation during the taxable year.[435] The term "repurchase" means a redemption of stock with regard to such corporation and any other economically similar transaction as determined by the Secretary of Treasury. The amount of repurchases subject to the tax is reduced by the value of any new stock issuance to the public and stock issued or provided to the employees of the corporation

[433] IRC section 55.

[434] IRC section 56A.

[435] IRC section 4501.

(or a specified affiliate of such corporation), including stock issued or provided pursuant to the exercise of stock options.

The acquisition of stock of a covered corporation by a specified affiliate of such covered corporation (from a person who is not the covered corporation or a specified affiliate of such covered corporation) is treated as a repurchase of the stock of the covered corporation by such covered corporation. A "specified affiliate" means, with respect to any corporation, any corporation more than 50 percent of the stock of which is owned (by vote or by value), directly or indirectly, by such corporation, and any partnership more than 50 percent of the capital interests or profits interests of which is held, directly or indirectly, by such corporation. A domestic or foreign subsidiary of a publicly traded U.S. corporation that performs the buyback for its U.S. parent triggers the one percent excise tax to the U.S. parent.

In the case of an acquisition of stock of a foreign publicly traded corporation ("applicable foreign corporation") by a specified affiliate of such corporation (other than a foreign corporation or a foreign partnership (unless such partnership has a domestic entity as a direct or indirect partner)) from a person who is not the applicable foreign corporation or a specified affiliate of such applicable foreign corporation, the specified affiliate is treated as a covered corporation with respect to such acquisition. The acquisition is treated as a repurchase of stock of a covered corporation by such covered corporation, and the adjustment to the amount of repurchases is determined only with respect to stock issued or provided by such specified affiliate to employees of the specified affiliate. A U.S. subsidiary of a foreign publicly traded corporation that buys back its foreign parent's stock is subject to the one percent excise tax. A foreign subsidiary that buys back its foreign publicly traded parent's stock is not subject to the one percent excise tax. A foreign publicly traded corporation that buys back its own stock is not subject to the one percent excise tax.

The provision excludes certain repurchases from the excise tax to the extent:

- the repurchase is part of a tax-free reorganization under section 368(a) and no gain or loss is recognized on such repurchase by the shareholder by reason of such reorganization;
- the repurchased stock or its value is contributed to an employer-sponsored retirement plan, employee stock ownership plan (ESOP), or similar plan;
- the total amount of stock repurchases within the year is less than $1 million;
- under prescribed regulations, the repurchase is by a dealer in securities in the ordinary course of business;
- the repurchase is by a regulated investment company (RIC) or real estate investment trust (REIT);
- the repurchase is treated as a dividend.

The excise tax is not deductible.

For financial accounting purposes, it appears that the excise tax is not treated as an expense of the corporation but rather bundled into the stock buyback. As a result, it impacts shareholders' equity and although it has no effect on the income statement line items (i.e., it is not an expense), it may impact earnings per share.

[3] Deemed Repatriation Tax

As part of the TCJA, Congress enacted a deemed repatriation tax as a transition to a new territorial international tax regime.[436] The transition tax is imposed on a corporation's accumulated post-1986 deferred foreign income as of November 2, 2017, or December 31, 2017, whichever is greater. The tax rate is eight percent, but a 15.5 percent rate is imposed on cash or cash equivalents. The tax may be paid in eight annual installments of eight percent for the first five years, 15 percent in year six, 20 percent in year seven and 25 percent in year eight.

The FASB staff determined that the deemed repatriation tax liability should not be discounted to present value.[437] The FASB staff, citing FASB ASC 740–10–30–8, noted the prohibition on the discounting of deferred taxes. The FASB staff believed that Subtopic 835–30, which addressed the imputation of interest, did not apply.

The transition tax on post-1986 foreign earnings can be satisfied by using net operating losses (NOLs), which are deferred tax assets. They will have to be remeasured to reflect the lowering of the corporate tax rate from 35 percent to 21 percent. Using NOLs to pay the transition tax will result in a different earnings impact when compared with a cash payment of the transition tax. This simple example illustrates the earnings difference between the two approaches.

> **ILLUSTRATION 2-41:** The Company has $1 million of post-1986 foreign earnings, for which it paid no foreign taxes. The Company has $1 million in an offshore bank account. The Company also has $1 million of NOLs composed entirely of U.S. source losses. Since the Company has a bank account with cash of $1 million, the transition tax rate is 15.5 percent for a total transition tax of $155,000.
>
> Situation 1: The Company decides to pay the transition tax in annual installments over eight years. There are no foreign tax credits so there is no proportionate gross-up; therefore, the taxable amount is $1 million. The Company will remeasure the $350,000 deferred tax asset on the $1 million NOL to $210,000, resulting in an earnings loss of $140,000. The Company's total earnings loss is $295,000 composed of the $155,000 transition tax and the $140,000 remeasurement of the deferred tax asset.
>
> Situation 2: The taxable amount is $1 million but the Company decides to use its NOLs to reduce it to zero. As a result, the company uses all its NOLs so that the $350,000 deferred tax asset is zero. The earnings impact is $350,000.

The difference between Situation 1 and Situation 2 is that in the latter, the Company had an incremental earnings costs of $55,000 (Situation 1 total tax expense of $295,000 and Situation 2 tax expense of $350,000). This is exactly the difference between the remeasured deferred asset of $210,000 for the NOL carryover and the $155,000 transition tax. Basically, the company utilized a $210,000 tax asset to pay for a $155,000 tax liability.

Companies should evaluate the earnings impact of using NOLs versus cash to pay the transition tax. A company should also evaluate the time value of money when using

---

[436] IRC section 965.

[437] FASB Staff Q & A, Topic 740, No. 2, Whether to Discount the Tax Liability on the Deemed Repatriation (Jan. 2018).

the cash option as well as other non-tax factors. Some companies will use NOLs despite the negative earnings impact. A capital intensive company may not be able fully to utilize its NOLs for many years and this is further exacerbated by 100 percent expensing under IRC Section 168(k) and the 80 percent of taxable income limitation on utilizing NOLs under IRC Section 172.

On August 9, 2018, Treasury published proposed regulations on the transition tax imposed on post-1986 foreign earnings under IRC Section 965 (with final regulations published on February 5, 2019). The transition tax is eight percent but it is 15.5 percent on a company's "cash position." As noted in the proposed regulations:

> The cash position of any specified foreign corporation is the sum of—(i) cash held by such foreign corporation, (ii) the net accounts receivable of such foreign corporation, and (iii) the fair market value of the following assets held by such corporation [each asset, a "cash equivalent asset"]: (I) Personal property which is of a type that is actively traded and for which there is an established financial market ["actively traded property"]. (II) Commercial paper, certificates of deposit, the securities of the Federal government and of any State or foreign government; (III) any foreign currency; (IV) Any obligation with a term of less than one year ["short-term obligation"]; and (V) Any asset which the Secretary identifies as being economically equivalent to any asset described in this paragraph [i.e., IRC Section 965(c)(3)(B)].

A company's cash position would include its investment in a consolidated foreign affiliate should the foreign affiliate be listed on a stock exchange. For example, a U.S. multinational owned more than 90 percent of a subsidiary and the multinational was listed on a local stock exchange. The multinational's investment in the foreign subsidiary was illiquid and not the equivalent of cash because it would take a long time to liquidate the investment without substantially lowering the foreign affiliate's stock price if a large number of shares hit the market causing an oversupply. Treasury considered and dismissed the stock's illiquid nature; the proposed regulation states the following:

> However, the Treasury Department and the IRS have determined that it would not be administrable to create individual regulatory exceptions to the statute in the absence of a statutory standard for liquidity because it would likely require introducing a facts-and-circumstances test that analyzes the liquidity of every asset, which would be difficult to administer. Furthermore, while some assets that would otherwise be treated as cash-equivalent assets could be excluded from a specified foreign corporation's cash position for being insufficiently liquid, other assets that are not treated as cash-equivalent assets but are liquid would need to be included in a specified foreign corporation's cash position. Accordingly, the proposed regulations do not introduce new regulatory exceptions to the definition of cash position. Proposed Regulation 1.965, page 102, Background.

It is indeed counterintuitive that an investment in a consolidated affiliate could be the equivalent of cash. In lieu of paying the additional 7.5 percent higher transition tax, a company could have acquired the minority shares and delisted the foreign subsidiary. This is unfortunate because the local listing is typically for bona fide business and portfolio risk management reasons. A local public listing allows the company to raise cost-effective capital. Local ownership can also mitigate political risks and it also allows a company to attract and retain local talent by issuing them stock compensation in the local affiliate.

[4] Corporate Alternative Minimum Tax Credits

The TCJA repealed the corporate alternative minimum tax (AMT) effective for taxable years beginning after 2017. Many corporations may have AMT credit carryforwards that arose when a corporation's AMT liability exceeded its regular tax liability. This excess generated an AMT credit carryforward with no expiration date.

Any AMT credit carryforward can be used to reduce the regular tax liability from 2018 through 2020. Any AMT credit carryforward that does not reduce regular income tax liability is eligible to be refunded: a 50 percent refund from 2018 through 2020 and a 100 percent refund in 2021.

The FASB staff determined that AMT credit carryforwards should not be discounted to present value.[438] The non-discounting applies whether the AMT credit carryforward is presented as a deferred tax asset or as a receivable. The FASB staff believed that FASB ASC 835–30, which addresses the imputation of interest, does not apply.

[5] Base Erosion and Anti-Abuse Tax (BEAT)

As part of the TCJA, Congress enacted a new taxing regime, the base erosion and anti-abuse tax (BEAT). The BEAT is a 10 percent (12.5 percent after 2025) minimum tax imposed on a U.S. corporation with average annual gross receipts of at least $500 million and base erosion payments equal to or exceeding three percent of its deductible payments.[439] A U.S. corporation computes its BEAT liability by increasing its taxable income by base erosion payments (generally, outbound deductible payments to a foreign related person) resulting in modified taxable income. This modified taxable income is multiplied by the 10 percent BEAT rate. If the BEAT liability is greater than the regular income tax liability, the U.S. corporation must pay the greater amount.

The FASB staff determined that an entity's deferred tax assets and liabilities should be measured using the statutory rate (21 percent) of the regular income tax system and not the lower BEAT rate (10 percent).[440] The FASB staff analogized the BEAT to the corporate AMT, which was repealed by the TCJA. When the corporate AMT was in effect, an entity measured its deferred tax assets and liabilities using the statutory rate (then 35 percent) under the regular income tax system and not the lower AMT rate: likewise with the BEAT and the current statutory rate.

The FASB staff noted that the increment effect of BEAT is recognized in the year the BEAT is incurred—as a negative permanent difference. In addition, the staff believed that an entity did not need to evaluate the potential impact of BEAT on the realization of deferred tax assets recognized under the regular income tax system. Realizations of the deferred tax assets under the regular income tax system would occur even if an incremental BEAT liability was owed for the same period.

FASB ASC 740 applies only to income taxes. Only an income tax is shown in the financial statements income tax expense line. Only an income tax goes into the

---

[438] FASB Staff Q & A, Topic 740, No. 3, Whether to Discount Alternative Minimum Tax Credits that Become Refundable (Jan. 2018).

[439] IRC Section 59A.

[440] FASB Staff Q & A, Topic 740, No. 4, Accounting for the Base Erosion Anti-Abuse Tax (Jan. 2018).

numerator in calculating the company's effective tax rate. Only an income tax is in the company's effective tax rate reconciliation table. Only an income tax is analyzed in the tax footnotes. The question is whether BEAT is an income tax as defined under FASB ASC 740. BEAT is a 10 percent tax on "modified taxable income," which comprises certain related-party payments to a foreign recipient that are deductible by the payor. The FASB has not issued a final decision on the proper classification of BEAT.

The FASB staff in their guidance notes that the BEAT is sufficiently similar to the alternative minimum tax, which the FASB previously concluded was an income tax. Unlike the minimum tax, a company does not receive a tax credit for the incremental BEAT that exceeds the regular tax. As a result, although the minimum tax does not increase the effective tax rate, the BEAT will. Despite this key difference, the FASB staff noted that the BEAT, like the minimum tax, was an incremental tax, so a company would not pay less than the statutory tax rate. Although the FASB guidance did not directly address the issue of whether BEAT was an income tax, due to the analogy between BEAT and the minimum tax, the prevailing view is that BEAT should be classified as an income tax.

Another BEAT issue is the impact of BEAT on minimum credit carryovers and NOLs carryovers. In the FASB guidance (FASB Staff Q&A, Topic 740, No. 4), it notes that "the staff also believes that an entity would not need to evaluate the effect of potentially paying the BEAT in future years on the realization of deferred tax assets recognized under the regular tax system because the realization of the deferred tax asset (for example, a tax credit) would reduce its regular tax liability, even when an incremental BEAT liability would be owed in that period." Although the FASB guidance does not require a company to consider the interaction of BEAT with the company's deferred tax assets, at least one major accounting firm believes the FASB guidance does not prohibit a company from considering the interaction. Should a company decide to include this interaction, the company may have to record a valuation allowance on deferred taxes recorded on minimum tax carryover and NOL carryover.[441]

[6] Global Intangible Low-Taxed Income (GILTI)

As part of the Tax Cuts and Jobs Act, Congress enacted a new regime for taxing the income of a controlled foreign corporation.[442] Generally, a U.S. shareholder of a controlled foreign corporation must include its share of the global intangible low-taxed income (GILTI). GILTI is the excess of a U.S. shareholder's total net foreign income over a deemed return of 10 percent on the foreign corporation's tangible depreciable assets less certain interest expense. The U.S. shareholder, if a domestic corporation, is permitted a 50 percent deduction of its GILTI, but the deduction is limited to the domestic corporation's taxable income.[443]

A domestic corporation is allowed a foreign tax credit of 80 percent of the foreign income taxes paid on GILTI. Unused foreign tax credits associated with GILTI cannot be carried back or forward (or used against other foreign-source income). A U.S. shareholder increases its tax basis in the stock of the foreign corporation for the GILTI inclusion.

---

[441] *See* "In depth: A look at current financial reporting issues: Frequently asked questions: accounting considerations of US Tax Reform," Q&A 4.2, PwC (Jan. 24, 2018).

[442] IRC section 951A.

[443] IRC section 250.

The FASB staff believed there were two different interpretations of FASB ASC 740 as it relates to GILTI, and that an entity could apply either interpretation.[444] An entity can recognize deferred taxes for temporary basis differences that are expected to reverse in future years as GILTI. This interpretation is consistent with the treatment of subpart F income under FASB ASC 740. Alternatively, an entity can account for taxes on GILTI as period costs. An entity must disclose its accounting policy related to GILTI inclusions in accordance with FASB ASC 235–10–50–1 through 50–3.

[7] Business Interest Expense Limitation

The TCJA limited the deduction of business interest expense. IRC Section 163(j) generally imposes a limit on the deductibility in any taxable year of "business interest" to 30 percent of "adjusted taxable income," as defined. There are exceptions for business interest "properly allocable," as defined, to regulated utilities, real estate, and farming. The amount of business interest that exceeds the 30 percent threshold will carry over and be recorded as a deferred tax asset. Although there is an indefinite carryover for the excess business interest, a full or partial valuation allowance may be required on the deferred tax asset absent positive evidence that the company will have sufficient adjusted taxable income in subsequent tax years. Section 2.09 covers valuation allowance in detail. An unfavorable factor is the definition of *adjusted taxable income*, which will change for tax years beginning on or after January 1, 2022. Between the effective date of TCJA and tax years beginning before January 1, 2022, *adjusted taxable income* is defined roughly as the equivalent of EBITDA (earnings before interest, taxes, depreciation, and amortization). For tax years on or after January 1, 2022, *adjusted taxable income* is defined as roughly the equivalent of EBIT (earnings before interest and taxes). Since companies have higher EBITDA than EBIT, the 30 percent threshold will be lower after the transition year, which could result in the suspension of additional business interest. The limitation will impact capital-intensive companies the most. A finding from a survey by Fitch Ratings yielded the following results:

> [The survey] found that 37 percent of issuers would lose part of their interest deduction under the EBITDA definition of income used for the first four years, while one in 10 would be unable to deduct at least half of their interest. Under the more restricted EBIT definition of taxable income, leaving out depreciation and amortization deductions, 64 percent said they would lose part of their interest deduction, and four in 10 said they'd lose half.[445]

Some publicly held companies have stated in SEC filings that they do not expect to realize benefits from disallowed interest deductions that may be carried forward indefinitely and as a result have recorded valuation allowances.[446] Companies could avoid or delay recording a valuation allowance as they evaluate planning ideas, such as shifting debt to foreign operations and using leasing arrangements, such as sale-and-leaseback for existing assets. The 100 percent deduction on foreign-source dividends allowed under IRC Section 245A may increase the likelihood that U.S. companies will

---

[444] FASB Staff Q&A, Topic 740, No. 5, Accounting for Global Intangible Low-Taxed Income (Jan. 2018).

[445] *See* Lydia O'Neal, *Highly Leveraged Firms Face Headwinds from GOP Tax Bill*, Daily Tax Report, Bloomberg Tax (Dec. 26, 2017).

[446] *See* Emily L. Foster, *Financials Reveal Hazards of Interest Deduction Limitation Rules*, 166 Tax Notes Fed. 1799 (March 16, 2020).

increase foreign debt to fund dividend payments and use the proceeds to reduce U.S. debt.

[8] Tax Cuts and Jobs Act of 2017 Disclosure—Examples

The Tax Cuts and Jobs Act, which was enacted on December 22, 2017, had significant accounting and disclosure consequences for reporting entities. On the same day the TCJA was enacted, the SEC staff issued Staff Accounting Bulletin No. 118 (SAB No. 118) to provide financial statement disclosure guidance for reporting periods that included December 22, 2017, and clarify reporting uncertainty resulting from the TCJA. FASB ASC 740–10–10–1 addresses the recognition of taxes payable (or refundable) for the current year and the recognition of deferred tax liabilities and deferred tax assets for the future tax consequences of events that have been recognized in an entity's financial statements or tax returns. The SEC staff noted that FASB ASC 740–10–25–47 addresses the accounting for income taxes upon a change in tax laws or tax rates. The SEC staff noted further that, pursuant to FASB ASC 740–10–35–4, the income tax accounting effect of a change in tax laws or tax rates includes, for example, adjusting (or re-measuring) deferred tax liabilities and deferred tax assets, as well as evaluating whether a valuation allowance is needed for deferred tax assets.

FASB ASC 740–10 does not, however, address certain situations in which the reporting entity does not have the necessary information available, prepared, or analyzed in reasonable detail for the reporting period in which the TCJA was enacted. In such a situation, SAB No. 118 generally permits the SEC registrant to recognize provisional amounts (or possibly reporting no amounts) reflecting the differences in the amount of tax the entity might owe until the SEC registrant has obtained, prepared, and analyzed the information necessary to report the results of the TCJA properly, provided this occurs by December 22, 2018 (the first anniversary of the enactment of the TCJA). Thus, throughout 2018 public companies continued to update their 2018 earnings based on the TCJA relating to balance sheet tax items through December 22, 2018 (such as remeasurement of deferred taxes due to corporate tax rates decreasing from 35 percent to 21 percent, the one-time IRC Section 965 international transition tax, adjustments to IRC Section 162(m) deferred taxes, etc.).

On February 14, 2018, the FASB issued a ASU No. 2018–02, which addresses certain "stranded" income tax effects in accumulated other comprehensive income resulting from the TCJA, as well as repatriation and alternative minimum tax credits, among other issues. During March 2018, FASB issued ASU No. 2018–05 to amend SEC paragraphs in FASB ASC 740, Income Taxes, to reflect SAB No. 118.

Below are five examples of portions of Form 10-Q tax disclosure reported by public companies in July 2018 relating to the TCJA, which are available at https://www.sec.gov/edgar/searchedgar/companysearch.html.

Kimberly Clark Corp., Form 10-Q, released July 24, 2018, for period ending June 30, 2018

On December 22, 2017, the U.S. government enacted comprehensive tax legislation commonly referred to as the Tax Cuts and Jobs Act (the "Tax Act"). The Tax Act made changes to the U.S. tax code, which included (1) reduced U.S. corporate tax rate from 35 percent to 21 percent, (2) implemented a base erosion and anti-abuse tax, (3) generally eliminated U.S. federal income taxes on dividends from foreign subsidiaries, (4) a new provision designed to tax global intangible low-taxed income ("GILTI") of foreign subsidiaries which allows for the possibility of utilizing foreign tax credits to offset the tax liability (subject to some limitations), (5) a lower effective U.S. tax rate on certain revenues from sources outside the U.S., and (6) a one-time transition tax on certain undistributed earnings of foreign subsidiaries.

In the period ended December 31, 2017, we recorded a provisional discrete net tax benefit associated with the Tax Act and related matters. In the first quarter of 2018, we recorded discrete net tax expense of $82 primarily related to new guidance issued affecting tax benefits we recorded in fourth quarter 2017 for certain tax planning actions taken in anticipation of the Tax Act.

As of June 30, 2018, the amounts recorded for the Tax Act remain provisional for the transition tax, the remeasurement of deferred taxes, and our reassessment of permanently reinvested earnings, uncertain tax positions and valuation allowances. These estimates may be impacted by further analysis and future clarification and guidance regarding available tax accounting methods and elections, earnings and profits computations, state tax conformity to federal tax changes and the impact of the GILTI provisions. At June 30, 2018, we were not able to reasonably estimate, and therefore have not recorded, deferred taxes for the GILTI provisions. We have not yet determined our policy election with respect to whether to record deferred taxes for basis differences expected to reverse as a result of the GILTI provisions in future periods or use the period cost method. We have, however, included an estimate of the current GILTI impact in our tax provision for 2018.

Visteon Corp., Form 10-Q, released July 26, 2018, for period ending June 30, 2018

Due to the timing of the Act and the substantial changes it brings, the SEC issued Staff Accounting Bulletin No. 118 ("SAB 118"), which provides registrants a measurement period to report the impact of the new U.S. tax law. During the measurement period, provisional amounts for the effects of the law are recorded to the extent a reasonable estimate can be made. To the extent that all information necessary is not available, prepared or analyzed, companies may recognize provisional estimated amounts for a period of up to one year following enactment of the Act.

For year-end 2017, the Company recorded provisional amounts for impacts of the Act in accordance with the guidance as of the date of the year-end filing, including the one-time transition tax on the mandatory deemed repatriation of foreign earnings, gross foreign tax credit carryforwards, the remeasurement of deferred taxes, and related valuation allowances. The Company will continue to refine provisional amounts surrounding the remeasurement of deferred taxes and information related to unremitted earnings from foreign affiliates to more precisely analyze and compute the remeasurement of deferred taxes and the impact of the transition tax under the Act, as well as other provisions of the Act, such as the global minimum income tax and base erosion tax provisions related to offshore activities and affiliated party payments, as more information and further guidance become available.

Allegion plc, Form 10-Q, released July 26, 2018, for period ending June 30, 2018

In March 2018, the FASB issued ASU 2018–05, "Income Taxes (Topic 740): Amendments to SEC Paragraphs Pursuant to SEC Staff Accounting Bulletin No. 118". The overarching purpose of ASU 2018–05 is to codify the guidance issued by the SEC related to income tax accounting implications due to the comprehensive U.S. tax legislation commonly referred to as the Tax Cuts and Jobs Act enacted on December 22,

2017 (the "Tax Reform Act"), as originally discussed within Staff Accounting Bulletin No. 118, Income Tax Accounting Implications of the Tax Cuts and Jobs Act (SAB 118) within ASC 740, Income Taxes. SAB 118, and now ASC 740 provide a measurement period, which in no case should extend beyond one year from the Tax Reform Act enactment date, during which a company acting in good faith may complete the accounting for the impacts of the Tax Reform Act. To the extent that a company's accounting for certain income tax effects of the Tax Reform Act is incomplete, the company can determine a reasonable estimate for those effects and record a provisional estimate in the financial statements in the first reporting period in which a reasonable estimate can be determined. If a company cannot determine a provisional estimate to be included in the financial statements, the company should continue to apply ASC 740 based on the provisions of the tax laws that were in effect immediately prior to the Tax Reform Act being enacted. At December 31, 2017, the Company recorded a provisional valuation allowance related to interest limitation carryforwards and other adjustments to the net deferred tax assets, with a corresponding discrete net tax charge of $22.8 million. On April 2, 2018, IRS Notice 2018–28 was issued to provide guidance to assist taxpayers in complying with providing transition guidance related to interest limitation carryforwards recorded at the enactment date. Management is in process of evaluating IRS Notice 2018–28 and assessing its impact on the provisional valuation allowance recorded at December 31, 2017. The Company will continue to analyze the effects of the Tax Reform Act on its Condensed and Consolidated Financial Statements. Additional impacts from the enactment of the Tax Reform Act will be recorded as they are identified during the measurement period as provided for in SAB 118, which extends up to one year from the enactment date. No adjustments were made to the provisional amounts previously recognized during the three or six months ended June 30, 2018.

Owens Corning, Form 10-Q, released July 25, 2018, for period ending June 30, 2018

The U.S. government enacted tax legislation commonly known as the U.S. Tax Cuts and Jobs Act of 2017 on December 22, 2017 (the "Tax Act"). The Tax Act made broad and complex changes to the U.S. tax code, including but not limited to, a reduction to the U.S. federal corporate income tax rate from 35 percent to 21 percent; a one-time transition tax on certain unrepatriated earnings of foreign subsidiaries (the "Transition Tax"); eliminating the corporate alternative minimum tax (AMT) and changing realization of AMT credits; changing rules related to uses and limitations of net operating loss (NOL) carryforwards created in tax years after December 31, 2017; changes to the limitations on available interest expense deductions; and changes to other existing deductions and business-related exclusions.

The SEC issued Staff Accounting Bulletin No. 118, "Income Tax Accounting Implications of the Tax Cuts and Jobs Act" ("SAB 118"), which provides guidance on the accounting for the tax effects of the Tax Act. SAB 118 provides a measurement period that should not extend beyond one year from the Tax Act enactment date to complete the accounting under ASC 740, "Income Taxes." The Company's accounting for the income tax effects of the Tax Act is incomplete. In accordance with SAB 118, we were able to make reasonable estimates on certain effects of the Tax Act resulting in a total provisional charge to the financial statements as of December 31, 2017. There have been no material changes to the provisional charges as disclosed in our 2017 Form 10-K. The Company was not yet able to make a reasonable estimate of the U.S. state tax effects of the Tax Act. Therefore, no provisional adjustment was recorded with respect to this item.

We are continuing to evaluate the estimates used to record and disclose the effects of the Tax Act.

Diamond Offshore Drilling, Inc., Form 10-Q, released July 30, 2018, for period ending June 30, 2018

In response to our interpretation of the Tax Reform Act, which was signed into law in late December 2017, we recorded a provisional net tax expense of $1.1 million during the fourth quarter of 2017, which included a charge relating to the one-time mandatory repatriation of previously deferred earnings of certain non-US subsidiaries that are owned either wholly or partially by our U.S. subsidiaries, inclusive of the utilization of certain tax attributes offset by a provisional liability for uncertain tax positions related to such attributes. Due to the timing of the enactment of the Tax Reform Act, there has been and continues to be a significant amount of uncertainty as to the appropriate application of a number of the underlying provisions, pending further guidance and clarification from the relevant authorities. In 2018, the U.S. Department of the Treasury and Internal Revenue Service issued additional guidance which we believe clarified certain of our tax positions taken in 2017 and, consequently, we reversed a $43.3 million liability for an uncertain tax position related to the toll charge in accordance with the Securities and Exchange Commission's Staff Accounting Bulletin No. 118, or SAB 118. SAB 118 allowed companies to report the income tax effects of the Tax Reform Act as a provisional amount based on a reasonable estimate, subject to adjustment during a reasonable measurement period, not to exceed twelve months, until the accounting and analysis under Topic 740 is complete.

We are still in the process of evaluating our estimate as it relates to the tax effect of (i) the mandatory, deemed repatriation aspect of the Tax Reform Act, (ii) the amount of deferred tax assets and liabilities subject to the income tax rate change from 35 percent to 21 percent and (iii) the ability to more likely than not realize the benefit of deferred tax assets, including net operating losses and foreign tax credits. We will continue to monitor developments in these areas and adjust our estimates throughout 2018, as and if necessary, as additional guidance and clarification becomes available.

§ 2.23 Planning in Accounting for Income Taxes

As a general rule, entities prefer recording deferred tax liabilities rather than deferred tax assets on the financial statements. The reason, of course, is that a deferred tax liability is recorded when tax deferral is taking place. For example, a deferred tax liability is recorded for an entity using accelerated depreciation for tax purposes and straight-line depreciation for financial reporting purposes. An entity also records a deferred tax liability when it uses the installment method for reporting the gain from the sale of property for tax purposes and immediate recognition of gain for financial reporting purposes. In both cases, the entity is deferring the paying of its taxes to the government, thereby taking advantage of the time value of money. Famed investor Warren Buffet, who is the chairman of Berkshire Hathaway, Inc., has noted the time value of money benefits for deferred tax liabilities and has written:

> Besides, Berkshire has access to two low-cost, non-perilous sources of leverage that allow us to safely own far more assets than our equity capital alone would permit: deferred taxes and "float," the funds of others that our insurance business holds because it receives premiums before needing to pay out losses.

> Both of these funding sources have grown rapidly and now total about $69 billion.
>
> Better yet, this funding to date has often been cost-free. Deferred tax liabilities bear no interest. And as long as we can break even in our insurance underwriting the cost of the float developed from that operation is zero. Neither item, of course, is equity; these are real liabilities. But they are liabilities without covenants or due dates attached to them. In effect, they give us the benefit of debt—an ability to have more assets working for us—but saddle us with none of its draw-backs.[447]

When an entity records a deferred tax asset, it is losing out on the time value of money. For example, if an entity receives an advance payment for services to be performed in the future, it must include the payment in income upon receipt for tax purposes and immediately pay taxes on that income. For financial reporting purposes, however, the entity sets up a liability reflecting the advance payment, and includes the payment in revenue over time as the services are rendered. In other words, taxes are being paid before the revenue is reflected on the financial statements. The entity is losing out on the time value of money because, when viewed from a financial reporting standpoint, the entity has prepaid its taxes, thus giving rise to the deferred tax asset.

Some entities, most notably Enron Corporation, utilized the recording of deferred tax assets to increase their net income each year.[448] Enron, which at one time was the seventh largest U.S. corporation according to Fortune magazine, planned a number of tax-motivated transactions from 1995 to 2001. Two of Enron's tax-motivated transactions can be characterized as "REMIC Carryover Basis Transactions."[449] Three of its tax-motivated transactions can be characterized as "Tax-Basis Step-Up Transactions."[450]

The REMIC Carryover Basis Transactions involved Enron acquiring REMIC residual interests. These interests would generate a substantial amount of tax losses in future years. Enron's tax basis in the REMIC residual interests greatly exceeded its book basis in the interests, thereby permitting Enron to record a deferred tax asset for the difference. Enron also recorded a balancing deferred credit equal to the amount of the deferred tax asset.[451] As a general rule, a deferred credit is taken into income (generally as an offset to income tax expense) over time "using a rational and systematic basis." However, Enron acquired other assets (such as corporate bonds) along with the REMIC residual interests. By doing so, it amortized the deferred credit into income over the life of the bonds. Enron reported the amortization of the deferred credit as "Other Revenue" on its financial statements.

---

[447] Berkshire Hathaway, Inc. 2006 Annual Report, pages 75–76.

[448] *See, e.g.*, Staff of the Joint Committee on Taxation, *Report of Investigation of Enron Corporation and Related Entities Regarding Federal Tax and Compensation Issues, and Policy Recommendations* (2003); N. Batson, Second Interim Report of Neal Batson, Court Appointed Examiner, In re Enron Corp. S.D.N.Y. (Bkr.) Case No. 01-16034 (AG) Jan. 21, 2003.

[449] N. Batson, Second Interim Report of Neal Batson, Court Appointed Examiner, In re Enron Corp S.D.N.Y. (Bkr.) Case No. 01–16034 (AG) Jan. 21, 2003, at 2–4 and 25–44.

[450] *Id.* at 5–6 and 45–68.

[451] Because Enron's book basis in the deferred credit exceeded its tax basis (zero), Enron also grossed-up its deferred credit.

The Enron bankruptcy examiner questioned Enron's financial accounting treatment of the acquisition of the REMIC residual interests.[452] More specifically, the bankruptcy examiner determined that the following was not in accordance with GAAP: (1) the recording of a deferred tax asset with respect to the acquisition of the REMIC residual interests; (2) the lack of recording of a valuation allowance with respect to the deferred tax asset; (3) the short amortization time frame for the deferred credit; and (4) the reporting of the amortization of the deferred credit as "Other Revenue."

The Tax-Basis Step-Up Transactions involved Enron acquiring depreciable assets in some future year. Enron's tax bases in the depreciable assets when it eventually acquired them would be substantially greater than its book bases in the assets. Enron recorded a deferred tax asset for the expected excess of the tax bases over the book bases in the depreciable assets with a corresponding decrease to deferred tax expense.

The Enron bankruptcy examiner also questioned Enron's financial accounting treatment of the expected acquisition of the depreciable assets.[453] The bankruptcy examiner determined that the following was not in accordance with GAAP: (1) the recording of a deferred tax asset when Enron did not yet own the depreciable assets but merely owned investments in various partnerships that owned the depreciable assets; and (2) the lack of recording of a valuation allowance with respect to the deferred tax asset.

Enron attempted to exploit the two judgment decisions that had to be made under SFAS No. 109 (a predecessor to FASB ASC 740). First, Enron recorded a deferred tax asset concluding that it was probable that the tax treatment on which the deferred tax item depended would be sustained in the event of an audit. Enron knew that the probable standard for recording a deferred tax asset (prior to the issuance of FIN 48 (FASB ASC 740–10)) was a gray area and a judgment call. In support of its treatment of recording a deferred tax asset for REMIC Carryover Basis Transactions and Tax-Basis Step-Up Transactions, Enron, as a general rule, obtained "should" opinion letters from various law firms in support of its tax treatment of the transactions. Second, Enron did not record a valuation allowance when it recorded its deferred tax assets for the REMIC Carryover Basis Transactions and Tax-Basis Step-Up Transactions. Recording of a valuation allowance would have defeated the purpose of recording the deferred tax asset, which was to increase net income each year. Enron knew that the measurement of a deferred tax asset (and valuation allowance) based on a more-likely-than-not standard was a gray area and a judgment call.

---

[452] N. Batson, Second Interim Report of Neal Batson, Court Appointed Examiner, In re Enron Corp S.D.N.Y. (Bkr.) Case No. 01–16034 (AG) Jan. 21, 2003, at 37–44.

[453] *Id.* at 63–68.

Chapter 3

UNCERTAIN TAX POSITIONS

Table of Sections

§ 3.01 Overview of FASB ASC 740–10

Guidance from the Financial Accounting Standards Board (FASB) concerning accounting for uncertainty in income taxes was issued on July 30, 2006, as FASB Interpretation No. 48 (FIN 48). This continued the seemingly unending flow of efforts by various governmental agencies to address the consequences to investors of business transactions of the past decade, including Sarbanes-Oxley (SOX), Public Company Accounting Oversight Board (PCAOB) pronouncements, revision of Circular 230 and so on. Like these other pronouncements, FIN 48 (later codified in FASB ASC 740–10) has had significant impact in the world of overlap between financial accounting and taxation.

In general, a company reflects the benefit of a tax position in its financial statements when a sufficient degree of confidence exists that the tax position will be sustained upon examination by the relevant taxing authority. Because of the extraordinary complexity and uncertainty inherent in the tax laws, however, some tax positions are naturally subject to legitimately varied interpretation, leading to uncertainty as to whether the tax position will ultimately be sustained. Prior to the issuance of FIN 48 (later codified in FASB ASC 740–10), some companies reported aggressive positions on their tax returns that arguably were supportable under the tax law but not realistically expected to be sustained. Many of these companies were also aggressive on audit risks, namely, the government is highly unlikely to identify the issue on audit. And, even if the issue was identified, the company would litigate the matter to the highest court and expect to prevail.

As discussed in Chapter 2, FASB ASC 740 presents standards of financial accounting and reporting for the effects of income taxes resulting from a company's activities and addresses many issues concerning accounting for income taxes. At one time, FASB guidance did not address the accounting for uncertainty in income taxes.

Prior to FIN 48, entities applied different interpretations to reflect uncertain tax positions in their financial statements, resulting in potential inconsistent calculations of the corresponding financial statement benefit.[1] This diversity in practice,[2] in turn, caused a lack of comparability in the financial reporting of income tax assets and liabilities by different companies.

FASB ASC 740–10 takes a two-step approach (consisting first of a minimum recognition threshold, and second, measurement) to account for uncertain income positions. This both increases the relevance and comparability of financial reporting of uncertain income taxes, and provides more financial information concerning those taxes.

FASB ASC 740–10 prescribes the requirements that a company must satisfy before recognizing the benefit of a tax position in its financial statements. It also provides guidance on the measurement of a recognized tax position benefit, derecognition of a tax position that has previously been recognized, classification of an uncertain tax position, accounting treatment of interest and penalties relating to uncertain tax positions, and financial disclosure of uncertain tax positions and the related accounting disclosure for interim periods.

When an uncertain tax position reduces the amount of income taxes otherwise owed, the company realizes an immediate economic benefit. Considerable time may elapse, however, before the tax position is accepted (implicitly or explicitly) by the taxing authority. FASB ASC 740–10 mandates that an entity (and, indirectly, its outside auditors who audit the entity's financial statements) undertake an affirmative evaluation of the technical merits of each tax position to determine if the position is "more likely than not" to be sustained. If a tax position does not meet the more-likely-than-not recognition threshold, FASB ASC 740–10 precludes the entity from recognizing any benefit of that position in its financial statements.

FASB ASC 740–10 imposes a two-step process in the evaluation of a tax position:

a. Recognition: The entity determines whether it is "more likely than not"[3] that a tax position will be sustained upon examination, including resolution of any related appeals or litigation processes, based on the technical merits of the position.

b. Measurement: If a tax position meets the "more-likely-than-not" recognition threshold, the entity measures[4] the amount of benefit to recognize in the financial statements. The tax position is measured at the largest amount of estimated benefit that has a greater than 50 percent likelihood of being realized upon settlement.

The objective of financial reporting is to provide information useful to investors, creditors, and other capital market participants in making well-informed financial decisions. In promulgating FIN 48, FASB noted that the benefits of financial statement

---

1 FIN 48, Appendix B, paragraph B2.

2 In developing the FASB ASC 740–10 recognition and measurement guidance, FASB considered the qualitative characteristics discussed in FASB Statement of Financial Accounting Concepts (CON) 2, *Qualitative Characteristics of Accounting Information*, which emphasizes that comparable information enables users to identify similarities in and differences between two sets of economic events. It was intended that FIN 48 establish a consistent threshold for recognizing current and deferred taxes.

3 *See* Section 3.04[2][a].

4 *See* Section 3.04[3].

information should justify the costs related to compiling and furnishing such information, which costs of course fall on the reporting company.[5] After discussions with regulators, preparers, and auditors of financial statements, FASB concluded that the increased cost of complying with the recognition and measurement rules would be outweighed by the expected benefit of improved and more comparable financial reporting resulting from a more consistent application of the FASB rules on accounting for income taxes to the recognition of tax benefits.[6]

Because FASB ASC 740–10 encompasses all uncertain income tax positions, a company's management and internal tax staff must seriously consider how and when they address the income tax consequences of their transactions. In particular, if the income tax consequences of a significant transaction are unclear, then prior to consummating a transaction, the company will not only continue to analyze the proper tax reporting (which process generally is not affected by FASB ASC 740–10), but also generally address the FASB ASC 740–10 impact of that income tax position. One consequence of the FASB rules on accounting for uncertain income tax positions is that certain proposed transactions that management historically might have decided to complete after accepting the corresponding tax risks now may not be consummated due to the adverse financial reporting disclosure imposed by FASB ASC 740–10.

An important and controversial provision of the FASB rules on accounting for uncertain income tax positions relates to financial statement disclosure. FASB ASC 740–10 provides for mandatory disclosure of the impact of those rules on a company's uncertain income tax positions. This includes for each annual period a tabular disclosure of the beginning and ending aggregate unrecognized income tax benefits resulting from FASB ASC 740–10, along with detailed information regarding any unrecognized tax benefit that is reasonably possible to significantly increase or decrease with the succeeding twelve-month period.[7]

As is readily apparent in this chapter, there are significant consequences to a company resulting from the imposition of the FASB rules on accounting for uncertain income tax positions. For example, each company must decide the manner in which the company's management exercises and documents its judgment on implementing various difficult, vague and uncertain tax and FASB ASC 740–10 standards. Further, it will be necessary for a company to determine how to successfully demonstrate to its external auditors that management's conclusions are reasonable and supportable, and that the provisions of FASB ASC 740–10 have been satisfied. In this context, the manner in which a company's outside auditor concludes that management's positions comply with FASB ASC 740–10, and how any disagreements are resolved, are at best unclear. In practice, this potential conflict between management and its outside auditors can be expected to result in some very interesting and potentially heated dialogue.

At a minimum, it appears prudent for management to establish internal written operating procedures relating to:

1. identification of those tax positions of the company which are uncertain under FASB ASC 740–10,

---

[5] FIN 48, Appendix B, paragraph B73.

[6] FIN 48, Appendix B, paragraph B74.

[7] *See* Section 3.08[1].

2. establishment of guidelines to determine the "unit of account" of its tax positions,[8]
3. documentation of management's analysis and conclusions regarding the recognized tax position,
4. implementation of procedures to measure the financial statement benefit of the recognized tax position, including how to determine and document the possible alternative outcomes of an uncertain tax position and assign probabilities and dollar amounts to those outcomes,
5. coordination of, and cooperation with, the company's outside auditors with respect to FASB ASC 740–10 tax positions and disclosure,
6. monitoring the outcome of a prior tax position (whether by settlement, expiration of statute of limitations, etc.) and establishing the manner in which the outcome affects financial reporting and disclosure, and
7. monitoring of new facts and information relating to a tax position that occurs subsequent to the date the company initially reports the position, and whether management's judgment and prior conclusions under FASB ASC 740–10 are altered based on those new facts. The extent to which documentation requirements and internal procedures are adopted by a company generally is based on management's judgment after considering all existing facts and circumstances.[9]

§ 3.02 Background and Rationale for FASB ASC 740–10

[1] FIN 48 Exposure Draft

Before the creation of the current FASB rules on accounting for uncertain income tax positions, diverse accounting practices had developed with respect to (i) the minimum confidence level required to recognize a financial statement benefit from a tax position, (ii) when a recognized tax benefit should be recorded for accounting purposes, and (iii) the amount of any valuation allowance. In practice, this lack of uniformity resulted in noncomparability of recorded tax assets and liabilities in financial statements of different companies.

For example, various companies had recognized uncertain but non-aggressive tax positions in their financial statements on a best estimate basis. Other companies (i) recognized a tax position if the position would be sustained on examination by the applicable taxing authority; and (ii) recorded an offsetting liability for a contingent loss either when the examination results became known or when it became probable that a payment would be made to the taxing authority.

Yet other companies recognized a financial statement benefit for tax positions to the extent and at the time they reported the tax positions on their tax returns. Under this approach, current or deferred tax assets and deferred tax liabilities were immediately recognized for financial accounting purposes when the related tax position was included on the tax return. Sometimes, a company's financial statements included a valuation allowance that correspondingly reduced any resulting deferred tax asset since the tax

[8] *See* Section 3.04[2][d].

[9] *See* Section 3.11.

benefit ultimately might not be fully realized. Other companies have identified various complex transactions and used gain contingency accounting to account for the tax benefits of those transactions. One of FASB's major objectives was to provide definitive guidance that was intended to reduce the diversity in practice and thus result in financial statements becoming more comparable. On July 14, 2005, FASB published a Proposed Interpretation, *Accounting for Uncertain Tax Positions—an interpretation of FASB Statement No. 109* ("FIN 48 Exposure Draft"),[10] that set forth proposed guidance for the recognition, derecognition, and measurement of tax positions, as well as certain disclosure requirements.

FASB received 118 comment letters on the FIN 48 Exposure Draft during the public comment period. Those comments were received from a broad spectrum of the business community, including preparers, financial institutions, each of the "Big 4" accounting firms, and various advocacy groups. After consideration of the issues and concerns raised by those public comments, participating in discussions with interested parties and much deliberation, FASB reconsidered and revised the FIN 48 Exposure Draft and, ultimately, issued the final version of FIN 48 in July 2006.

The staff of FASB prepared an outline of the comment letters titled "Uncertain Tax Position—Summary of Comment Letter Analysis", which was released by FASB during October 2005.[11] Among the provisions of the FIN 48 Exposure Draft that attracted the most public comment were: (i) the use of a dual threshold;[12] (ii) the use of "probable" as the recognition threshold;[13] (iii) nexus issues; (iv) the recognition concept of unit of account;[14] (v) the use of best estimate for measurement; and (vi) effective date issues.

[2] Original Rationale for FASB's UTP Rules

FASB summarized the issues that it deemed significant in formulating FIN 48 (later FASB ASC 740-10), and described its reasons for accepting or rejecting various conceptual approaches, in Appendix B "Background Information and Basis for Conclusions," which was attached to FIN 48.

Among the major substantive issues considered in promulgating final FIN 48 were:[15]

a. Whether the financial statement recognition of a tax position should presume that an individual tax position will be examined by a taxing authority.[16]

---

[10] Exposure Draft No. 1215-001.

[11] The FASB staff prepared the comment letter summary to facilitate an understanding of the issues raised by the public comments. That summary focused primarily on public comments received by FASB that related to each of the 11 issues identified in the "Notice for Recipients" section of the FIN 48 Exposure Draft. It should be noted, however, that the summary document was prepared and released for discussion purposes only, and was not intended to reflect the views of the FASB or its staff. Official positions of the FASB are determined only after extensive due process and deliberations.

[12] *See* Section 3.04[2][b].

[13] *Id.*

[14] *See* Section 3.04[2][d].

[15] FIN 48, Appendix B, paragraphs B7-B8.

[16] FIN 48, Appendix B, paragraph B18.

b. What effect does the nature of evidence supporting a tax position have on establishing recognition and measurement guidance.[17]

c. Whether a single methodology should be applied that combines recognition and measurement,[18] rather than treating recognition and measurement separately.[19]

§ 3.03 Application of FASB ASC 740–10

[1] Entities and Tax Positions Subject to FASB ASC 740–10

[a] Tax Position

FASB ASC 740–10 applies to all of an entity's income[20] tax positions[21] that are subject to the FASB rules on accounting for income taxes (FASB ASC 740).[22] For this purpose, the term "tax position" means a position taken in a previously filed tax return or expected to be taken in a tax return that is reflected in measuring current or deferred income tax assets and liabilities for interim or annual periods of the entity.[23] FASB ASC 740–10 specifically does not apply to taxes that are not primarily calculated on income, such as sales and value added taxes.[24] A tax position also includes, but is not limited to:

1. a decision not to file a tax return;
2. an allocation or a shift of income between jurisdictions;
3. the characterization of income or a decision to exclude reporting taxable income in a tax return; and
4. a decision to classify a transaction, entity, or other position in a tax return as tax exempt.[25]

---

[17] FIN 48, Appendix B, paragraph B27 (FASB ASC 740–10–05–6). FASB concluded that an evaluation of tax positions against a consistent benchmark is more operational than the other approaches it considered.

[18] For example, measuring tax assets and liabilities at fair value or using fair-value-type measurement techniques would combine recognition and measurement.

[19] FASB analyzed three alternative recognition methods that could be applied separately from the measurement threshold: (i) recognition when a tax position has met a minimum statutory threshold and additional amounts are not anticipated to be paid to settle underpayment controversies; (ii) recognition and derecognition based on a single threshold; and (iii) recognition when a tax position has met a specified confidence level and derecognition when the position falls below a specified confidence level. FIN 48, Appendix B, paragraph B8.

[20] FASB ASC 740–10 applies to all US federal income taxes, and foreign, state, and local (including franchise) taxes based on income. *See* FASB ASC 740–10–15–3 and FASB ASC 740–10–20.

[21] FASB specifically rejected limiting its rules on accounting for uncertain income tax positions only to tax positions that (a) are substantially uncertain (such as tax shelters, tax motivated positions, and listed transactions within the meaning of IRC Section 6706A(c)) or (b) involve nontaxable or nondeductible differences between financial statements and tax returns (sometimes referred to as permanent differences). FIN 48, Appendix B, paragraph B11.

[22] FIN 48, paragraph 3. FIN 48 (later codified in FASB ASC 740–10) took effect for fiscal years beginning after December 15, 2006.

[23] FASB ASC 740–10–20.

[24] In finalizing FIN 48, FASB considered and rejected broadly applying FIN 48 to all taxes, including non-income taxes. FIN 48, Appendix B, paragraph B10. FASB also concluded that restricting the FIN 48 rules only to uncertain tax positions, or tax positions with specified attributes, would create a rules-based standard that would both result in inconsistent application and add unnecessary complexity. FIN 48, Appendix B, paragraph B12.

[25] *See* FASB ASC 740–10–20.

FASB ASC 740–10 applies to all income tax positions of an "entity" that reports its financial results consistent with US generally accepted accounting principles (GAAP). An entity is broadly construed for this purpose to include not only business entities, but also not-for-profit organizations, pass-through entities, and entities whose tax liability is subject to 100 percent credit for dividends paid (for example, real estate investment trusts and registered investment companies) that are potentially subject to income taxes.[26] In this regard, FASB specifically rejected providing different recognition, measurement, disclosure, or transition standards for nonpublic entities and public entities.[27] ASU 2009–06 modified FASB ASC 740 by providing guidance for pass-through entities and tax-exempt organizations in the following three areas (i) definition of a tax position, (ii) attribution of income taxes to the entity or its owners, and (iii) financial statements of a group of related entities.

[b] Pass-Through and Tax-Exempt Entities

In Accounting Standards Update (ASU) 2009–06, on September 2, 2009, FASB issued guidance on the application of FIN 48 (FASB ASC 740–10) to pass-through entities (such as S corporations and partnerships) and tax-exempt non-profit entities, including eliminating the application of certain disclosure requirements.[28]

Subsequent to the adoption of FIN 48 (later FASB ASC 740–10), a number of questions arose regarding its application to pass-through entities and tax-exempt entities, which often are not subject to income tax in a particular jurisdiction. For example, a pass-through entity's disclosure obligations were unclear when a taxing jurisdiction required a pass-through entity to withhold taxes of its owners. ASU 2009–06 states that if, based on a taxing jurisdiction's laws and regulations income taxes paid by the entity are attributable to the entity, the amounts due to or from the taxing jurisdiction should be classified as an income tax and accounted for under FASB ASC 740.

Specifically, ASU 2009–06 added the following to the definition of a tax position: "An entity's status, including its status as a pass-through entity or a tax-exempt not-for-profit entity." ASU No. 2009–06 clarified that an entity's tax status as a pass-through or tax-exempt not-for-profit entity is a tax position subject to the recognition requirements

---

[26] FASB ASC 740–10–20. SFAS No. 109, paragraphs 186–189 pertained to private versus small public enterprises. FASB Staff Position (FSP) No. FIN 48–2 noted that although FIN 48 applies to (i) not-for-profit organizations, (ii) entities whose tax liability is subject to 100 percent credit for dividends paid (for example, real estate investment trusts and registered investment companies), and (iii) pass-through entities, such as partnerships and S corporations, many of those entities had not paid income taxes and had not applied the provisions of FAS 109, thus resulting in apparent confusion about whether and how FIN 48 applied to those companies.

[27] *See* FIN 48, Appendix B, paragraphs B68–B69. One FASB member questioned whether the same FIN 48 (FASB ASC 740–10) accounting guidance as is applicable to public companies should apply to nonpublic enterprises, considering the presumable low tax audit rate and potentially substantial FIN 48 (FASB ASC 740–10) compliance cost for small private companies. A FASB staff member explained, however, that smaller companies generally have fewer and less complex tax positions to evaluate, which should substantially reduce their FIN 48 (FASB ASC 740–10) compliance efforts. Another FASB member also asserted that FIN 48 (FASB ASC 740–10) generally should provide valuable information to financial statements users concerning the liquidity of nonpublic companies. *See* May 16, 2006 FASB Minutes. Based on public input, FASB initially determined that nonpublic enterprises do not need additional time beyond that provided to public enterprises to adopt the provisions of FIN 48 (FASB ASC 740–10). FASB reconsidered this position in FASB Staff Position (FSP) No. FIN 48–2 (Feb. 1, 2008) and extended the FIN 48 (FASB ASC 740–10) effective date for certain nonpublic enterprises until fiscal years beginning after December 15, 2007. In FSP No. FIN 48–3 (Dec. 30, 2008) (FASB ASC 740–10–65–1), FASB delayed the effective date to December 15, 2008. *See* Section 3.03[3].

[28] *See* FASB ASC 740–10–50–15 for the disclosure requirements that apply to these entities.

of FASB ASC 740–10–25–6. Thus, a pass-through or tax-exempt not-for-profit entity is required to use the recognition and measurement guidance in FASB ASC 740 when assessing those tax positions. In addition, ASU 2009–06 emphasizes that a pass-through or tax-exempt not-for-profit entity may have other tax positions that have to be assessed under FASB ASC 740, such as (i) whether an S corporation is subject to income taxes for built-in gains, (ii) whether an entity that has elected S corporation status continues to meet the requirements of a subchapter S corporation, (iii) whether all income qualifies for exemption from income tax under the jurisdiction's rules, and (iv) whether the entity has filed income tax returns in all of the appropriate jurisdictions where it has nexus that subjects it to state income tax.[29]

If a jurisdiction's laws and regulations attribute the income tax to the entity's owners, then amounts due to or from the taxing jurisdiction should be treated as a transaction with owners. ASU 2009–06 clarifies that attribution is not based on agreements between the entity and its owners or on who pays the income taxes.[30]

ILLUSTRATION 3-1:[31]

Partnership A, a state law partnership with partner 1 and partner 2 as its two partners, has nexus in State J. State J assesses an income tax on Partnership A and allows the partners to file a tax return and use their pro rata share of Partnership A's income tax payment as a payment against the tax liability of partner 1 and partner 2. Because the owners may file a tax return and utilize Partnership A's payment as a payment against their personal income tax, the income tax is attributed to the partners whether or not the partners file an income tax return. Because the income tax has been attributed to the owners of Partnership A, payments to State J for income taxes should be treated as a transaction with the owners.

An agreement between Partnership A and its two partners whereby Partnership A is obligated to reimburse partners 1 and 2 for taxes they owe to State J does not change the conclusion in Illustration 3-1 since the attribution of income taxes is based on State J's tax laws and regulations, rather than on agreements between Partnership A and its owners. If, however, the tax rules of State J indicated that partners 1 and 2 were not required to file income tax returns in State J and the tax payments made by Partnership A made on behalf of partners 1 and 2, then the State J income taxes are attributed to Partnership A.[32]

ILLUSTRATION 3-2:[33]

Corporation S, a corporation that has elected to be taxed as an S corporation, files an income tax return in State M. The State M tax laws and regulations provide that tax payments made by Corporation S are made on behalf of the shareholders of Corporation S, although State M can hold Corporation S and its owners jointly and severally liable for the non-payment

[29] *See* e.g., Example 32 (FASB ASC 740–10–55–223), Example 33 (FASB ASC 740–10–55–224), and Example 34 (FASB ASC 740–10–55–225).

[30] The determination of attribution should be made for each taxing jurisdiction where the entity is subject to income taxes.

[31] This illustration is based on FASB ASC 740–10–55–226, Example 35.

[32] FASB ASC 740–10–55–227, Example 36.

[33] This illustration is based on FASB ASC 740–10–55–228, Example 37.

of income taxes. Because the State M income taxes are attributed to the owners of Corporation S, the payment of the State M income taxes should be treated by Corporation S as a transaction with its owners.

The enactment of Section 1101 of the Bipartisan Budget Act of 2015[34] (the 2015 Act) on November 2, 2015, completely overhauled the rules relating to the imposition and collection of income tax assessments of partnerships (including limited liability companies taxed as partnerships). These rules generally were effective for tax years beginning in 2018, although a partnership could elect to apply the new provisions prior to 2018.[35] Subject to various exceptions and elections, the Internal Revenue Code for the first time imposed (and allowed the IRS to assess and collect) income tax relating to partnership assessments at the partnership (rather than the partner) level. Pursuant to an exception, a partnership with no more than 100 partners (none of whom are trusts or taxed as partnerships) could elect out of these audit rules on a year-by-year basis,[36] thus shifting the resolution and collection of the partnership tax adjustments to its partners. Further, the rules permitted those partnerships that either do not (or are not eligible to) elect out of these new provisions to shift some or all of the partnership tax payment responsibility to one or more of its partners either (i) by issuing special Schedule K-1 to its partners reflecting the partnership tax adjustments, or (ii) by causing one or more of its partners to file amended partners returns reflecting the partner's share of the assessment.[37] Significantly, for a partnership that does not elect out of these provisions and otherwise does not shift the obligation to pay partnership tax assessments to its partners, application of FASB ASC 740–10 to such partnership is unclear and potentially subjects the partnership to record audited financial statement tax reserves and disclosures for uncertain federal income tax positions. Thus, these partnership audit rules may cause some partnerships and limited liability companies, which previously never had a federal income tax liability, to become subject to the FASB ASC 740–10 reporting obligations.

[c] Consolidated Entities

ASU 2009–06 states when preparing financial statements of a related group of entities, the reporting group must consider the tax position of all entities within the group, regardless of whether the group consists of both taxable and nontaxable entities. Thus, the consolidated or combined financial statements of a related group of taxable and nontaxable entities must include all tax positions for each entity that is subject to income taxes or has income assigned to it from a pass-through entity. ASU 2009–06 clarifies that regardless of the tax status of the reporting entity, its financial statements should include all tax positions for each entity in the consolidated group.

ILLUSTRATION 3-3:[38]

Partnership X, a state law partnership with two partners, owns all of the stock of Corporation Y, a taxable corporation with unrecognized tax positions

[34] H.R. 1314, 114th Cong. (P.L. 114–74 2015). Section 1101 of the 2015 Act amends IRC Section 6221 through IRC Section 6223; IRC Section 6225 through IRC Section 6227; IRC Section 6231 through IRC Section 6235; and IRC Section 6241.

[35] Partnerships generally may elect to apply the new rules to partnership tax years that begin between the November 2015 enactment date of the rules and the 2018 effective date.

[36] *See* amended IRC Section 6223(b).

[37] *See* amended IRC Section 6226 and IRC Section 6225(c).

[38] This illustration is based on FASB ASC 740–10–55–229, Example 38.

and a related liability for unrecognized tax benefits. Partnership X and Corporation Y are required to issue consolidated financial statements. Partnership X should include in its financial statements the assets, liabilities, income and expenses of both Partnership X and Corporation Y, including those relating to the implementation of FASB ASC 740–10 to Corporation Y, even though Partnership X is a pass-through entity.

[d] Implementation Guidance on Certain Nonpublic Entities

In order to develop the guidance in ASU 2009–06, FASB issued FSP FIN 48–3 (FASB Staff Position No. FIN 48–3, "Effective Date of FASB Interpretation No. 48 for Certain Nonpublic Enterprises") and deferred the guidance in FASB ASC 740–10 on uncertainty in income taxes for certain nonpublic enterprises until the first annual financial statements for fiscal years beginning after December 15, 2008.

[2] Exclusion for Highly Certain or Immaterial Tax Positions

Because of the difficulty of defining an uncertain tax position, the rules on accounting for uncertain income tax positions apply to all income tax positions, regardless of how likely it is that the position will be supported by the tax law.[39] Although its application is broad, in practice FASB ASC 740–10 should not present implementation or interpretative difficulties to many everyday tax positions (e.g., a deduction for normal expenses such as payroll, utilities, etc.) since those positions typically are not controversial. Moreover, the effect of the rules on accounting for uncertain income tax positions often will be minimal on tax positions relating to significant but routine business transactions that clearly have a high level of certainty of being sustained.

ILLUSTRATION 3-4:[40]

USCo is a U.S.-based public corporation that intends to deduct on its tax return the payment of salaries to its employees. The salaries in question are not subject to any limitations on deductibility and none of the expenditures are required to be capitalized. USCo determines, based on a clear and unambiguous interpretation of the tax law, that the salaries are fully deductible.

The salary is clearly deductible based on applicable tax law and, accordingly, the tax position meets the recognition criterion. Management is very confident that the full amount of the deduction will be allowed. Accordingly, USCo would recognize the full amount of the tax position in the financial statements.

FASB ASC 740–10 states that it applies broadly to all[41] income tax positions that are accounted for under the FASB rules on accounting for income taxes. Although the rules on accounting for uncertain income tax positions do not specifically exempt tax positions that are de minimis, FIN 48 (FASB ASC 740–10) includes a qualifier at the end of its text stating "[t]he provisions of this Interpretation need not be applied to

---

39 *See* FIN 48, Appendix B, paragraph B12; FASB ASC 740–10–55–101.

40 This illustration is based on FASB ASC 740–10–55–100 and FASB ASC 740–10–55–101.

41 *See* FIN 48, Appendix B, paragraph B12.

immaterial items."[42] FASB does not provide guidance concerning what tax positions may be "immaterial" and thus exempt from FASB ASC 740–10. For example, it is unclear (i) if the determination of whether a position is immaterial is based solely on the dollar amount of the transaction, (ii) what the tax position in question is compared with to determine materiality, and (iii) whether similar or repetitive transactions must be aggregated. Questions naturally will arise when management attempts to identify and evaluate which tax positions are immaterial.

§ 3.04 Definitional Interpretations of FASB ASC 740–10—Recognition and Measurement of Tax Benefits

[1] In General

The literal language of FASB ASC 740–10 is interesting, but unenlightening in many respects, and raises a number of difficult interpretive issues. As discussed below, applying the standards of FASB ASC 740–10 to some fairly common transactions of a company involves the exercise of business judgment not only by a company's management (and, possibly, the company's outside tax advisor) but also by the company's independent auditors. To put these FASB rules in perspective, it is first appropriate to review the definitions provided by FASB relating to the recognition and measurement of the benefit of a tax position, followed by a consideration of some of the illustrations set forth in FASB ASC 740–10.

FASB ASC 740–10 prescribes rules for the financial statement recognition and measurement of uncertain tax positions in a tax return, along with guidance on:

1. reversing the prior recognition of a tax benefit based on new facts, referred to as "derecognition,"
2. classification of the benefit of those positions,
3. financial reporting of interest and penalties with respect to uncertain tax positions,
4. interim period accounting rules relating to tax positions, and
5. the manner in which uncertain tax positions are disclosed in financial statements.

[2] Recognition of Tax Benefits

[a] More-Likely-than-Not (MLTN) Standard

Under FASB ASC 740–10, an entity recognizes a benefit of a tax position in its financial statements, provided that it is more likely than not that the position will be sustained upon examination[43] based on the technical merits. For this purpose, the term "more likely than not" means a likelihood of more than 50 percent.

Satisfaction of the more-likely-than-not recognition threshold is dependent on the entity's belief that "it is entitled to the economic benefits associated with a tax

[42] Language following paragraph 24 of FIN 48.

[43] FASB ASC 740–10–25–6 defines "examined" and "upon examination" to include resolution of any related appeals or litigation.

position."[44] Although management is not required to obtain a tax opinion or even seek tax advice from its tax advisor to support its determination that a position meets the more-likely-than-not standard, FASB concluded that a legal tax opinion might serve as external evidence supporting management's judgment.[45] Management is permitted, however, to rely on other evidence, either in addition to or instead of a tax opinion, to support its conclusion that the recognition threshold is met. The level of relevant evidence that is necessary and appropriate to make this determination is a matter of management's judgment that depends on all available information.[46]

The more-likely-than-not standard raises a number of critical issues for management such as:

(1) how to determine that a substantive tax position will more-likely-than-not be sustained on examination;

(2) how to document management's judgment and conclusions with respect to a particular tax position;

(3) how to coordinate the application of the FASB rules on accounting for uncertain income tax positions with the entity's outside auditors, including resolving disputes when the auditors do not agree with management's conclusion that a tax position meets the more-likely-than-not threshold or the measurement amount of that position; and

(4) when will it be beneficial (even though not required) for management to seek a tax opinion from a qualified independent tax advisor that the more-likely-than-not threshold is satisfied?

It should be noted that obtaining a tax opinion from an independent tax advisor that concludes that it is more likely than not that an uncertain tax position will be sustained based on applicable tax law merely supports, but does not ensure, management's conclusion. FASB ASC 740–10 does not contain specific guidelines concerning what standards an opinion must adhere to and, under certain circumstances, management might be prohibited from relying on a tax opinion.[47] For example, an opinion might not be reliable for FASB ASC 740–10 purposes if it does not consider all material facts applicable to the transaction or the relevant tax authorities. Further, the entity's external auditor will likely request to review and retain a copy of any such tax opinion or tax advice to substantiate the auditor's FASB ASC 740–10 due diligence audit requirements. Furnishing a tax opinion prepared by the entity's external legal counsel to the entity's independent auditors, however, may waive the attorney-client privilege and possibly any work product doctrine privilege applicable to the opinion and thus permit the tax authority to obtain the opinion during an audit of the company.[48]

---

[44] *See* FASB ASC 740–10–25–6.

[45] *See* FIN 48, Appendix B, paragraph B34 (FASB ASC 740–10–25–6). FASB recommends that management should decide whether to obtain a tax opinion after evaluating the weight of all available evidence and the uncertainties of the applicability of the relevant statutory or case law.

[46] *See* FASB ASC 740–10–25–6.

[47] Section 9 of Exposure Draft No. 1215–001 listed an unqualified tax opinion based on objectively verifiable conditions as acceptable substantiation of management's conclusion concerning recognition. Final FIN 48 did not contain that provision.

[48] *See generally* Chapter 8 regarding attorney-client and related privileges. FASB ASC 740–10 raises critical issues regarding whether legal tax advice (including written tax opinions) obtained by a company to support its FASB ASC 740–10 conclusions will be protected by the attorney-client or work product privilege.

The assessment of whether a tax position meets the more-likely-than-not recognition threshold is a facts and circumstances determination based on management's judgment. FASB ASC 740–10 requires that the more-likely-than-not standard assume that the tax position in question will be examined by the applicable taxing authority with full knowledge of all relevant facts and information.[49] Further, the technical merits of a tax position must be based on consideration of relevant authorities in the tax law (e.g., legislation and statutes, legislative intent, regulations, rulings, and case law) and their applicability to the facts and circumstances of the tax position.[50]

Other tax disciplines apply a "more-likely-than-not" standard in various circumstances. For example, under Reg. § 1.6662–4(g)(4), a substantial understatement penalty will not be imposed on certain underreported federal tax items if the taxpayer reasonably believes that the tax treatment of the item is more likely than not the proper tax treatment. This standard is met if (i) the taxpayer analyzes the pertinent facts and authorities in the manner described in the tax regulations, and in reliance upon that analysis, reasonably concludes in good faith that there is a greater than 50 percent likelihood that the tax treatment of the item will be upheld if challenged by the Service; or (ii) the taxpayer reasonably relies in good faith on the opinion of a professional tax advisor, provided the opinion is based on the tax advisor's analysis of the pertinent facts and authorities as prescribed by the regulations and unambiguously states that the tax advisor concludes that there is a greater than 50 percent likelihood that the tax treatment of the item will be upheld if challenged by the Service. For this purpose, Reg. § 1.6662–2(g)(4) requires that the more likely than not standard be applied by ignoring the possibility that (i) a tax return will not be audited, (ii) the issue will not be raised on audit, or (iii) the issue will be settled.[51]

[b] Rejection of "Probable" Standard in the FIN 48 Exposure Draft

Under the FIN 48 Exposure Draft, the financial statement benefit of a tax position could not be recognized unless it was "probable"[52] that the tax position would be sustained based on existing tax law. FASB believed that the confidence level indicated by the "probable" standard was commonly understood by financial statement preparers, auditors, and regulators. Public comments and public roundtable discussions strongly criticized the "probable" threshold. Among the concerns identified with a "probable" recognition threshold included: (i) a systematic overstatement of tax liabilities because that threshold would not reflect anticipated cash flows; (ii) the lack of clear understanding and inconsistent application of the probable standard by companies; and (iii) minor changes in a company's confidence about a tax position could have a disproportionate financial statement effect under the standard.[53]

If the written tax advice is provided to the company's auditors as part of the tax accrual workpapers, the privilege might be lost.

[49] *See* FASB ASC 740–10–25–7.

[50] *See* FASB ASC 740–10–25–7.

[51] *See also* Reg. § 10.35(b)(4)(i) of Circular 230 which imposes various ethical standards on tax advisors who render written tax advice concerning a plan or arrangement with a significant purpose of tax avoidance or evasion, provided that the tax advice has a confidence level of more likely than not (greater than 50 percent) that a significant federal tax issue will be resolved in favor of the taxpayer.

[52] For this purpose, the definition of "probable" set forth in SFAS No. 5, paragraph 3.a (later FASB ASC 450–20–20) applied to the FIN 48 Exposure Draft. *See* FIN 48, Appendix B, paragraph B30.

[53] *See* FIN 48, Appendix B, paragraphs B31–B32.

In response to those concerns, the Board initially selected a dual-recognition threshold approach for recognition and derecognition purposes in which a tax position would be (i) recognized when it met the probable recognition threshold, and (ii) derecognized when it was more likely than not that the tax position would not be sustained.[54]

Public comments expressed the additional concern that a dual-recognition threshold would result in noncomparability when similar (or the same) tax positions that had been previously recognized no longer meet the probable recognition threshold but remain more likely than not.[55] Public comments also stated that a dual-recognition threshold would cause inconsistency between periods and a lack of comparability across enterprises.[56]

FASB also considered an approach that would require financial statement recognition when: (i) a tax position meets the minimum statutory threshold to avoid the payment of penalties, and (ii) it is not probable that an additional amount would be paid to the taxing authority to settle any underpayment controversies. The Board rejected that threshold on the basis that if fair value is disregarded as the measurement attribute for assets and liabilities, uncertainty should be reflected in a recognition standard that has a sufficiently high threshold to indicate that the enterprise is entitled to the economic benefits of a tax position.[57]

Based on the foregoing and to provide greater comparability and operationality, FASB adopted a single-threshold approach, with more likely than not as the recognition and derecognition criterion. FASB believed the "more likely than not" recognition threshold adequately addressed concerns about the overstatement of income tax expense and results in recognizing income tax benefits that better represent the amounts that will be ultimately realized.[58]

[c] Widely Understood Administrative Tax Practices and Precedents

Interestingly, FASB ASC 740–10 permits an entity to consider administrative practices and precedents of the relevant taxing authority, either with the entity or similar enterprises, to the extent that those practices and precedents are "widely understood."[59] Thus, to the extent that an administrative practice and precedent is broadly understood by preparers, tax practitioners, and auditors, a company is permitted to apply FASB ASC 740–10 by considering that administrative practice or precedent.

This rule was implemented after FASB became aware of certain administrative practices and precedents of taxing authorities which accept a limited number of tax

---

[54] *See* FIN 48, Appendix B, paragraph B31. FASB believed that this dual approach would be easier to apply, thus resulting in greater consistency in application, than a single "probable" threshold for both recognition and derecognition.

[55] *See* FIN 48, Appendix B, paragraph B32.

[56] *Id.*

[57] *See* FIN 48, Appendix B, paragraph B29.

[58] *See* FIN 48, Appendix B, paragraph B33.

[59] *See* FASB ASC 740–10–25–7. However, each tax position must be evaluated without consideration of the possibility of offset or aggregation with other positions. *See* FASB ASC 740–10–25–7. Thus, in evaluating the recognition of one tax position, management is not permitted to consider the possibility of negotiating and possibly conceding or settling a second more favorable position to obtain a favorable result with the first position, or to anticipate aggregating both positions in a unified resolution of its issues.

positions that may technically violate the tax law.[60] FASB concluded that permitting the consideration of administrative practices and precedents not only achieves greater consistency and comparability of financial statements but also consistently applies the financial reporting rules for uncertain tax positions resulting from those limited circumstances in which taxing authorities permit what might be deemed technical violations of the tax law.[61]

In determining whether a particular administrative practice or precedent might be applied by the taxing authority, however, an entity must presume that (i) the tax position will be examined and (ii) the taxing authority has the same information pertaining to the tax position that is available to the company.[62]

ILLUSTRATION 3-5:[63]

USCo adopts an internal policy whereby all depreciable property acquired for less than $2,000 is currently deducted in the year of purchase. The applicable tax rules require that the cost of property must be capitalized and does not permit immaterial purchases to be currently expensed. Based on USCo's audit experience and that of similar companies, along with discussions with its external tax advisors, USCo concludes that the taxing authority would not disallow USCo's deduction.

Although USCo's capitalization policy might be deemed a technical violation of the tax law, USCo determines that its capitalization policy is consistent with the administrative practices and precedents of the taxing authority and the practices of other companies that are regularly examined by the taxing authority. Further, based on its previous experience with other companies and consultation with its external tax advisors, USCo concludes that this administrative practice is widely understood. Accordingly, the more-likely-than-not recognition threshold has been met.

ILLUSTRATION 3-6:[64]

USCo is incorporated in state A and has filed returns in state A for the last 50 years. USCo has also conducted business in state B for the prior 20 years, but has never filed a state B tax return. In performing its due diligence, USCo reviews all of its open tax years in all possible jurisdictions in which it may have conducted business. Because no return was filed in state B, the statute of limitations for state B tax never commenced. Based on its understanding of the administrative practices and precedents of state B, USCo believes that state B will only review the last six years to determine if a state

---

[60] *See* FIN 48, Appendix B, paragraph B35. As set forth in the May 16, 2006 FASB Minutes, the FASB staff's research, including discussions with representatives of a taxing authority, indicated that taxing authorities have a particular administrative practice that is typically widely understood by taxpayers, tax practitioners and the taxing authority. These minutes indicate that this administrative practices and precedents concept is intended to deal with a limited number of tax positions that are technical violations of the tax law for which it is broadly understood that the taxing authorities, with access to all relevant facts, would not object. *See* May 16, 2006 FASB Minutes.

[61] FIN 48, Appendix B, paragraph B37.

[62] FIN 48, Appendix B, paragraph B36.

[63] This illustration is based on FASB ASC 740-10-55-91 and FASB ASC 740-10-55-92.

[64] This illustration is based on FASB ASC 740-10-55-94 and FASB ASC 740-10-55-95.

B return is due and a deficiency owed. Based on the foregoing, a liability for possible state B tax assessments is required only for the prior six-year period.

In Illustration 3-5, management of USCo formed its conclusion based on previous experience of a similar enterprise and current discussions with its external tax advisors, and in Illustration 3-6, it was assumed that management was familiar with the administrative practices and precedents of state B and it understood that state B would look back only six years in determining if a tax deficiency was due. These two examples, which are based on examples provided by FASB, appear to illustrate FASB's intent that consideration of widely understood practices or precedents of an applicable taxing authority is to be construed narrowly and generally applied only in limited circumstances.

There are many critical questions concerning what represents authoritative information to establish that a specific "practice or precedent" can be relied upon by an entity, and when that practice or precedent is "widely understood." Among the questions raised is whether oral confirmation by a representative of a taxing authority of an unofficial position of the taxing authority is dependable proof that the practice is widely understood. Does it matter whether the taxing authority representative is a senior or junior official, or that the entity has no specific knowledge that the taxing authority has applied this practice or precedent to other taxpayers? Likewise, how similar must the entity's facts be to other comparable taxpayers who have successfully applied the practice or precedent in question?

Presumably, an entity must continuously monitor the taxing authority's continued adherence to that policy and precedent.[65]

In that event, would it matter that the company was not aware of the change of policy? This situation is considered in Illustration 3-7.

ILLUSTRATION 3-7: Assume the same facts in Illustration 3-5, except that five years after USCo established its capitalization threshold of $2,000, based on its discussions with its external tax advisors at the time the company implemented the threshold, the taxing authority changes its auditing policy to permit the current deduction of otherwise capital expenditures, provided that the expenditure does not exceed $1,000. Both USCo and its new external tax advisors are unaware of this auditing policy change until a number of years thereafter. Since the company failed to reanalyze its initial capitalization policy concerning currently deducting the full amount of capital expenditures that do not exceed $2,000, has the company violated FASB ASC 740–10 when the taxing authority changed its internal procedure? It would appear the answer is yes, since USCo has an affirmative FASB ASC 740–10 duty to continually monitor new developments (including changes in law) that occur after it recognizes a financial benefit of a tax position.

[65] The May 16, 2006 FASB Minutes reflect discussions by the FASB staff that a change in administrative practices and precedents (for example, when a new commissioner is appointed) would be considered a change in estimate, not an error.

[d] Unit of Account

To calculate the financial benefit of an individual tax position, an entity must first determine the appropriate "unit of account" relating to that tax position.[66] After the proper unit of account is established, the entity then assesses whether the more-likely-than-not recognition threshold is met for the tax position for each unit of account. Identification of the appropriate unit of account is a factual determination based on management's judgment, considering the entity's individual facts and circumstances surrounding the tax position.[67] Although public comments to the FIN 48 Exposure Draft requested additional guidance concerning the unit of account concept, FASB concluded it is neither beneficial nor possible to define a unit of account for every circumstance.[68]

Because the recognition standard is imposed at the unit of account level, the determination of a unit of account for a particular tax position could have significant consequences. For example, if an entity characterizes a number of transactions as a single unit of account and determines that the overall income tax position of the combined unit of account fails the more-likely-than-not recognition standard, none of the benefit of the tax position will be recorded on the financial statements. Conversely, it may be possible that if the entity adopts a different unit of account method with respect to those transactions (e.g., resulting in multiple units of account), one or more units of account might individually satisfy the recognition standard.

Significantly, in selecting the appropriate unit of account, FASB specifically directs management to evaluate the manner in which the entity (i) prepares and supports its income tax return, and (ii) intends to address the tax position with taxing authorities during an examination.[69] The determination of a unit of account is another example of the type of potentially difficult issues on which management must exercise its judgment based on facts that may or may not occur in the future. Also, it should be noted that if two different entities with the same surrounding facts are presented with the same transaction, they each could properly decide upon a different unit of account. This might occur, for example, because one entity has an internal policy to avoid or minimize tax controversies and litigation, to the extent possible, while the other entity typically litigates its tax controversy rather than settling. Consider Illustrations 3-8 and 3-9.

ILLUSTRATION 3-8:[70]

During the year, USCo, a U.S.-based public corporation, incurred an equal amount of expenditures on four separate research projects. USCo intends to claim a $1 million research and experimentation (R&D) credit on its tax return made up of $250,000 of tax credits per project to reduce its current year tax liability. After review of each of the projects and the supporting documentation, USCo management determines that it is more likely than not that USCo will

---

66 *See* FASB ASC 740–10–25–13.

67 *Id.*

68 *See* FASB ASC 740–10–25–13.

69 *See* FASB ASC 740–10–25–13; FIN 48, Appendix A, paragraph A9. FASB expects the determination of how a company prepares its return positions and negotiates with tax authorities will vary with the facts and circumstances of a tax position and of a specific taxpayer. *See* FIN 48, Appendix B, paragraph B14. Further, the determination of the unit of account presumes that taxing authorities will evaluate the position and have full knowledge of all relevant information.

70 This illustration is based on FASB ASC 740–10–55–83 and FASB ASC 740–10–55–85.

sustain a total benefit of $650,000 for all four projects, consisting of $200,000 for each of the first three projects and $50,000 for the fourth project.

To measure the amount of FASB ASC 740–10 financial benefit to recognize from the R&D credit, management must first determine the appropriate unit of account. Due to the size of the expenditures for each project, the level both at which USCo obtains information to support its return and where it expects to address the issue with tax authorities, management decides to use each individual research project as the unit of account.

ILLUSTRATION 3-9:[71]

Assume the same facts as in Illustration 3-8, except that USCo management determines that it is more likely than not that the tax credits of only three projects will be sustained if challenged. The recognition threshold thus is met for the tax credits of those three projects. Due to the activities of the fourth project, the more-likely-than-not recognition threshold is not met and none of the tax credit benefits for the fourth project are recognized in USCo's financial statements, even though the tax positions associated with that project will be included in USCo's tax return. USCo recognizes a $600,000 financial statement benefit related to the first three projects but would not recognize a financial statement benefit related to the fourth project.

Generally, the unit of account selected by management should be consistently applied to similar positions of the company from period to period. However, if a change in facts and circumstances subsequently occurs that might change the proper unit of account, then management must evaluate those facts and circumstances. If new facts support a conclusion that a different unit of account is more appropriate, the entity must determine the recognition and measurement of the benefit of the tax position based on the new unit of account.[72]

ILLUSTRATION 3-10:[73]

Assume the same facts as in Illustration 3-8, except that in Year 2, USCo increases its spending on R&D projects and claims significantly larger research credits on its Year 2 tax return. Management concludes that the project level is no longer the appropriate unit of account for the research credits due to the significant increase in expenditures, advice of USCo's external tax advisors, and management's prior experience. Also, management anticipates that any audit conducted by the taxing authority for Year 2 will focus on functional expenditures.

Accordingly, USCo should reevaluate the unit of account for the tax credits for its Year 2 financial statements at a more detailed level than the individual project based on the new facts and circumstances.

---

[71] This illustration is based on FASB ASC 740–10–55–86.

[72] FASB ASC 740–10–55–89.

[73] This illustration is based on FASB ASC 740–10–55–88 and FASB ASC 740–10–55–89.

[3] Measurement of Tax Benefits

[a] Tax Position Fails to Satisfy MLTN Standard

If management initially determines that a tax position does not satisfy the more-likely-than-not recognition standard, then unless a subsequent recognition occurs,[74] the entity is not allowed to record any financial statement benefit attributable to the tax position reported in its return and interest expense and possibly penalties must be recorded. In that event, the measurement provisions of FASB ASC 740–10 do not apply. If, however, new facts and information arise concerning the tax position, then management must reevaluate its initial determination that the tax position did not meet the more-likely-than-not threshold. If a subsequent recognition of the tax position occurs, management then must apply the FASB ASC 740–10 measurement criteria at that time.

[b] Tax Position Satisfies MLTN Standard

A tax position that initially satisfies the more-likely-than-not recognition threshold will initially and subsequently be measured as the largest amount of tax benefit that is greater than a 50 percent likelihood of being realized upon settlement with a taxing authority, assuming the taxing authority has full knowledge of all relevant information.[75]

Significantly, management's calculation of the largest tax benefit that exceeds the 50 percent threshold is based on cumulatively aggregating each separately assigned probability (expressed as a percentage) for each possible outcome of the tax position as estimated by management.

More specifically, with respect to each recognized tax position, management must determine the amounts and probabilities of the possible outcomes that could result upon settlement of the tax position based on the facts, circumstances, and information available at the reporting date.[76] The total of the probabilities of the possible outcome must equal 100 percent. These possible outcomes along with their related probabilities are arranged from the highest dollar amount to the lowest dollar amount. The possible amount of benefits will range from zero to the total benefit based on the amount reported in the tax return.[77] The amount of the recognized tax benefit recorded in the financial statements equals the largest dollar amount outcome that cumulatively exceeds 50 percent. The measurement process is indicated in Illustration 3-11:

---

[74] *See* Section 3.05.

[75] *See* FASB ASC 740–10–30–7. On May 2, 2007, FASB issued FSP No. FIN 48–1, *Definition of "Settlement" in FASB Interpretation No. 48* (later FASB ASC 740–10–25–9), to provide guidance on how an enterprise should determine whether a tax position is effectively (rather than ultimately, as previously required) settled for the purpose of recognizing previously unrecognized tax benefits. *See* Section 3.05[1]. The FSP made conforming changes to FIN 48: the term "ultimately settled" (when used to describe recognition) was replaced with "effectively settled" and the terms "ultimate settlement" or "ultimately settled" (when used to describe measurement) were replaced with "settlement" or "settled."

[76] *Id.* The term "reporting date" refers to the date of the enterprise's most recent statement of financial position. See FASB ASC 740–10–30–7.

[77] *See* FIN 48, Appendix B, paragraph B43. FASB believed that the measurement required by FIN 48 would result in consistent and comparable measurement of tax positions and in more representative reporting than a best-estimate measurement. *See* FIN 48, Appendix B, paragraph B44.

ILLUSTRATION 3-11:[78]

USCo determines that a tax position resulting in a benefit of $100 qualifies for recognition and should be measured. USCo has considered the amounts and probabilities of the possible estimated outcomes as follows:

Possible Estimated Outcome	Individual Probability of Occurring (%)	Cumulative Probability of Occurring (%)
$100	5%	5%
80	25%	30%
60	25%	55%
50	20%	75%
40	10%	85%
20	10%	95%
0	5%	100%

Because $60 is the largest amount of benefit that is greater than 50 percent likely of being realized upon settlement, USCo recognizes a tax benefit of $60 in its financial statements.

Since taxpayers often settle a tax controversy to avoid the costs and hazards of litigation, FASB ASC 740–10 requires that the measurement of financial benefit be based on management's best judgment of the amount for which the entity would settle the tax position with the taxing authority.[79] It is not entirely clear how management properly exercises its judgment to predict how a taxing authority might settle a tax position, or if the taxing authority would entertain a settlement with respect to a particular tax position. For example, assume during a reporting period an entity's tax position is audited by a tax authority, which asserts penalties and interest on a proposed tax assessment. Assume that a taxing authority representative indicates that it will not settle the controversy. Presumably, management is permitted to consider the possibility that the taxing authority might settle the matter, and that the government representative is merely "playing hardball" as part of a litigation strategy.

ILLUSTRATION 3-12:[80]

USCo has determined that a tax position resulting in a benefit of $100 qualifies for the more-likely-than-not recognition standard and should be measured. Limited guidance exists about how a taxing authority will view the tax position. After considering all relevant information and the technical merits of the tax position, however, management believes it is likely it would settle for less than the full amount of the entire position when examined. Management has considered the amounts and the probabilities of the possible estimated outcomes:

---

[78] This illustration is based on FASB ASC 740–10–55–103 and FASB ASC 740–10–55–104.

[79] *See* FASB ASC 740–10–55–4.

[80] This illustration is based on FASB ASC 740–10–55–106 and FASB ASC 740–10–55–107.

Possible Estimated Outcome	Individual Probability of Occurring (%)	Probability of Occurring (%)
$100	25	25
75	50	75
50	25	100

Because $75 is the largest amount of benefit that is greater than 50 percent likely of being realized upon settlement, USCo recognizes a tax benefit of $75 in the financial statements.

Certain tax issues are typically viewed as "all or nothing" issues in that they do not easily lend themselves under substantive tax law to a settlement between the taxpayer and the taxing authority other than zero percent or 100 percent. For example, in a corporate transaction that is intended to be a tax-free reorganization described in IRC Section 368(a) or a tax-free spin-off transaction described in IRC Section 355, if one of the requirements of IRC Section 368(a) or IRC Section 355 is not satisfied, then the entire transaction might be taxable to the corporate shareholders.[81] If the transaction is challenged, the taxing authority often asserts (and may not settle on any basis other than) that the transaction is fully taxable.[82]

ILLUSTRATION 3-13: USCo is a U.S. public corporation that wholly owns an operating U.S. corporate subsidiary ("USSub"). USCo and an unrelated U.S. corporation ("PCo") negotiate the acquisition of USSub by PCo, whereby USSub would merge into PCo, with PCo surviving. In the merger, USCo, as the shareholder of USSub, would receive solely stock of PCo (constituting 15 percent of PCo's outstanding shares) in exchange for its USSub stock. It is intended that the merger be a reorganization transaction described in IRC Section 368(a)(1) and that neither USCo nor USSub recognize gain or loss as a result of the merger. During the negotiations of the merger, management of PCo expresses various alternative business plans for USSub, including the desire to sell a substantial portion of the USCo assets, along with various divisions of PCo, to a previously identified, unrelated buyer for cash. At the time of the merger, PCo had no written agreement in place to sell the USCo assets.

At the closing of the merger, USCo's outside tax advisor renders its tax opinion that it is more likely than not that the merger is described in IRC Section 368(a)(1) and that neither USCo nor USSub would recognize gain or loss from the merger. In the tax opinion, the tax advisor addressed the question whether the merger satisfied the continuity of business enterprise requirement set forth in Reg. § 1.368–1(d) in light of the possibility that PCo might sell

[81] Another example of possible "all or nothing" transactions is the characterization of an instrument as debt or equity for tax purposes. *But see* IRC section 385(a). Further, the Service sometimes officially states its litigation policy on specified tax issues, and on occasion has adopted a uniform position that it will not settle certain issues or will only settle at a specified settlement percentage (which may be less than the 50 percent recognition threshold).

[82] As discussed at Section 3.04[2][c], a company is not permitted to consider offsets or negotiations of other issues with the taxing authority when evaluating a tax position.

USCo assets after the merger. If the merger did not satisfy that requirement, then the transaction would be fully taxable to USCo and its shareholders.

A few months after the merger, USCo's management performs a recognition and measurement analysis. At that time, USCo's management learns that PCo is about to sell a substantial portion of the USSub assets for cash to the previously identified buyer. After considering all relevant information, management's confidence in the technical merits of the tax position is at the 51 percent likelihood of success level and thus exceeds the more-likely-than-not recognition threshold. But management believes it is likely that the Service would not settle on any basis except that the transaction does not constitute a Section 368(a) reorganization and is fully taxable.

The question to be addressed is whether management may calculate the probabilities of the possible estimated outcomes of the tax position based solely on two outcomes: (i) a zero percent probability of success with a $0 benefit outcome; and a 100 percent probability of success with a full tax benefit, thus permitting USCo to recognize the entire tax benefit from the merger in its financial statements.

FASB considered the procedures applicable to resolving disputes with taxing authorities and concluded that because many tax positions are settled based on qualitative evidence, the measurement criteria should rely on management's experience in similar matters with the relevant taxing authority.[83] In Illustration 3-13, in order to sustain the recognition of the tax position, USCo may be required to demonstrate that it would litigate the issue if challenged.

ILLUSTRATION 3-14:[84]

USCo determines that a tax position resulting in a benefit of $100 meets the more-likely-than-not recognition standard and should be measured. Recently, USCo settled the same position with the applicable taxing authority for future years. The facts surrounding the current tax position is substantially the same as the tax position that was settled with the taxing authority and the relevant tax rules have not changed since the settlement. Based on the settlement, USCo has a very high confidence level regarding the amount that will be realized and, thus, it is not necessary for management to evaluate other possible outcomes to measure the FASB ASC 740–10 amount of the position.

This illustration assumes that the facts surrounding the current tax position are consistent with the recently settled previous position. It is unclear when a change of facts will preclude the company from measuring the benefit of the tax position in question based on the prior settlement, but presumably that determination is left to the discretion of management.

---

[83] *See* FIN 48, Appendix B, paragraph B41. The Board initially selected best estimate, as the term is used in CON 7, *Using Cash Flow Information and Present Value in Accounting Measurements*, to measure tax benefits that were within the scope of FIN 48. The best estimate represents the single most likely amount in a range of possible estimated amounts. Some public responses to the FIN 48 Exposure Draft stated that a best-estimate measurement might yield counterintuitive results, especially if there was a wide dispersion of possible estimated outcomes, each with a low probability of being ultimately realized. FASB agreed with those comments, and decided to modify the approach. *See* FIN 48, Appendix B, paragraph B42.

[84] This illustration is based on FASB ASC 740–10–55–109.

As in other provisions of FASB ASC 740–10, FASB did not provide much direction concerning management's exercise of judgment to:

(i) reasonably predict how an uncertain tax position will be resolved with a taxing authority in the future, and

(ii) establish the amounts and probabilities of the possible outcomes that could be realized upon a resolution.

Needless to say, the limited guidelines contained in FASB ASC 740–10 to assist management in applying the measurement requirements are vague, consequently resulting in potential disagreements between an entity and its external auditors.

[4] Valuation Allowance and Tax-Planning Strategies

When a tax-planning strategy is contemplated as a source of future taxable income to support the realization of a deferred tax asset under FASB ASC 740–10–30–18,[85] the recognition and measurement rules applicable to uncertain tax benefits (discussed above) must be applied in determining the amount of available future taxable income,[86] as indicated in Illustration 3-15.

ILLUSTRATION 3-15:[87]

> USCo has a wholly owned subsidiary with certain deferred tax assets as a result of several years of losses from operations. Management of USCo has determined that it is more likely than not that the subsidiary will not generate sufficient taxable income to realize those deferred tax assets. Thus, USCo must recognize a full valuation allowance for those deferred tax assets. Management identifies tax-planning strategies that might enable the realization of those deferred tax assets. Although management believes that USCo will not be subject to penalties if the tax strategies are challenged, management concludes that it is not more likely than not that the strategies would be sustained upon examination based on the technical merits. Those tax strategies may not be used to reduce the valuation allowance for the deferred tax assets.[88]

In the context of transfer pricing matters,[89] some multinationals have sought, and will seek advance pricing agreements to address the need for certainty for FASB ASC 740–10 (FIN 48) purposes.[90] The Service's website outlines efforts to address the

---

[85] *See* Section 2.09[3].

[86] *See* FASB ASC 740–10–30–20.

[87] This illustration is based on FASB ASC 740–10–55–97, FASB ASC 740–10–55–98 and FASB ASC 740–10–55–98.

[88] Only a tax-planning strategy that meets the more-likely-than-not recognition threshold would be considered in evaluating the sufficiency of future taxable income for realization of deferred tax assets. *See* FASB ASC 740–10–55–98.

[89] *See* Chapter 9.

[90] *See generally IRS Official Says FIN 48 May Lead to Future Participation in APA Program*, BNA Daily Tax Report, at G-4 (Oct. 23, 2007). *See generally* Cym Lowell & Mark Thomas, *U.S. International Transfer Pricing*, Chapter 12 (Thomson Reuters) [*U.S. International Transfer Pricing*]. An additional aspect of transfer pricing and uncertain tax positions relates to transfer pricing adjustments made as a result of IRS examination or other procedures. *See U.S. International Transfer Pricing* ¶ 3.09[3]. *See also* Corum, Summer, and LeBlanc, *It Ain't Over Till It's Over, Part IV: Financial Accounting Implications of a Sustained Federal Transfer Pricing Adjustment*, Tax Management Transfer Pricing Report (May 14, 2015, Vol. 24, No. 01).

increasingly complex international tax issues involved in globalization and the efforts of multinationals (MNEs) to minimize their global effective tax rate costs.[91]

§ 3.05 Subsequent Recognition, Derecognition, and Measurement

[1] Subsequent Recognition, Derecognition, or Remeasurement of the Benefit of a Prior Tax Position

Under FASB ASC 740–10, an entity is required to continually monitor the uncertain tax positions reflected on prior year returns and reassess, and possibly adjust the corresponding book benefit, as new developments occur with respect to the prior tax positions. This requirement should be contemporaneously documented pursuant to the company's controls under Sarbanes Oxley as discussed in Chapter 6.

An entity is permitted to recognize the benefit of a tax position that previously failed to meet the more-likely-than-not recognition threshold in the first interim period that the position meets one of the following conditions:[92]

1. The more-likely-than-not recognition threshold is met by the reporting date.
2. The tax position is "effectively settled" through examination, negotiation or litigation.
3. The statute of limitations for the relevant taxing authority to examine and challenge the tax position has expired.

On May 2, 2007, FASB issued FSP No. FIN 48–1, *Definition of "Settlement" in FASB Interpretation No. 48* (later FASB ASC 740–10), to provide guidance on how an entity should determine whether a tax position is effectively (rather than ultimately, as previously required) settled for the purpose of recognizing previously unrecognized tax benefits. A tax position is considered to be effectively settled through examination if:

(a) the taxing authority has completed all of its required or expected examination procedures,[93]

(b) the entity does not intend to appeal or litigate any aspect of the tax position, and

(c) it is considered remote that the taxing authority would reexamine the tax position.[94]

In the event that an entity becomes aware that the taxing authority may examine or reexamine a tax position that was effectively settled, the entity is required to (a) consider the tax position no longer effectively settled and (b) reevaluate the tax position in

[91] *See* Bennett, *IRS Outlines Its Strategy to Administer, Enforce Complex International Tax Issues, BNA Daily Tax Report & Taxcore* (Oct. 25, 2007, No. 206, page I-1).

[92] *See* FASB ASC 740–10–25–8.

[93] Almost all major companies also wait for the Joint Committee on Taxation refund approval for any matters exceeding the $5 million threshold for C corporations. IRC Section 6405.

[94] FASB ASC 740–10–25–10; FASB ASC 740–10–25–11. As amended, the standard does not require a tax position to be specifically examined by the taxing authority to be considered effectively settled, although effective settlement of a position subject to an examination does not result in effective settlement of similar or identical tax positions in periods that have not been examined. *Id.*

accordance with FASB ASC 740–10.[95] Although an entity may obtain information during the examination process that enables it to change its assessment of the technical merits of a tax position or similar tax positions taken in other periods, the effectively settled conditions enumerated in FASB ASC 740–10–25–10 do not provide any basis for the entity to change its assessment of the technical merits of any tax position in other periods.[96]

Likewise, an entity must derecognize a previously recognized tax position in the first accounting period in which it is no longer more likely than not that the tax position would be sustained upon examination.[97] FASB ASC 740–10 specifically provides that use of a valuation allowance as defined in FASB ASC 740 cannot be used as a substitute for derecognizing the benefit of a tax position when the more-likely-than-not recognition threshold is no longer met.[98] If management becomes aware of new facts or information relating to a prior tax position, management must also reassess a possible change in measurement of the tax position.

One area of frequent adjustment involves transfer pricing issue resolution in periods subsequent to recording the tax position.[99] The net results of both the recording and resolution can be critical elements of the effective tax rate planning strategy of a multinational entity.

[2] Recognition, Derecognition, and Measurement Standards Applicable to Subsequent Change in Facts of Prior Tax Position

With respect to tax positions reported in an entity's tax return in a prior period, management must exercise its best judgment given the facts and information available at the subsequent reporting dates to determine if the tax benefit of a prior tax position should be:

1. Recognized because the tax position now satisfies the more-likely-than-not standard, but previously did not meet that standard;
2. Derecognized because the position no longer meets the more-likely-than-not threshold; or
3. Remeasured based on management's assessment of the new facts and information and application of the FASB ASC 740–10 measurement provisions.[100]

---

[95] FASB ASC 740–10–40–3.

[96] FASB ASC 740–10–25–12.

[97] *See* FASB ASC 740–10–40–2.

[98] *Id.* Further, the requirement to assess the need for a valuation allowance for deferred tax assets based on the sufficiency of future taxable income was unchanged by FIN 48. *See* Summary to FIN 48.

[99] *See* Chapter 9. *See also* Parker, *In April 14 Companies Report Changes to Reserves from Transfer Pricing Cases,* 23 BNA Transfer Pricing Rep. 94 (May 15, 2014); Parker, *February Search for Transfer Pricing Issues in SEC Filings Reveals 60 Companies, 12 APAs,* 22 BNA Transfer Pricing Rep. 1318 (Mar. 6, 2014).

[100] *See* FASB ASC 740–10–25–14. In its deliberations, FASB did consider adopting the rule that once the recognition threshold is met, there should be no subsequent recognition, derecognition, or remeasurement of the recognized tax benefit until the tax position is resolved, but rejected that view as inconsistent with the existing guidance for loss contingencies and FASB ASC 740. FIN 48, Appendix B, paragraph B45. FIN 48 clarified that a tax position need not be legally extinguished and its resolution need not be certain to subsequently recognize, derecognize or recalculate the benefit of the position. FIN 48, paragraph 12 (FASB ASC 740–10–25–14).

In considering the subsequent recognition and measurement of prior unrecognized tax positions, FASB initially considered and ultimately rejected whether specific external events should be required before a change in judgment occurs concerning the recognition of a tax position or the measurement of a recognized tax position.[101] During its deliberations, FASB also considered whether a subsequent change in recognition or measurement should be reported only when a tax position is resolved with certainty.[102] A final resolution of an entity's tax position is not required to subsequently recognize or measure tax positions and thus the recognition and measurement of a tax position at a reporting date should be based on management's best judgment given the facts and circumstances known at the reporting date.[103]

In this regard, FASB provides that information received subsequent to the reporting date should not be used to evaluate a tax position at the reporting date.[104]

Any subsequent change in judgment that causes a revision to recognition, derecognition, and measurement of the benefit of a tax position should result from management's evaluation of new information, rather than from a new evaluation or new interpretation by management of information that was available in a previous financial reporting period.[105] The scope of this standard is unclear. For example, if management was not aware of available information when it made its initial determination regarding realization and measurement of a tax position, is management permitted to subsequently consider the information on the basis that the information is new to management? What if management would have initially become aware of the information had it exercised reasonable due diligence, or alternatively, what if management initially ignored the information? It appears that the FASB rules preclude management from considering the information retroactively since the information was readily available.

> **ILLUSTRATION 3-16:** USCo is a U.S.-based public corporation that negotiates cross-border financing from an unrelated lender, which is a tax resident of a foreign country ("FCountry") that has in place a tax treaty with the U.S. The financing is nominally designated as preferred shares issued from USCo to the lender, but has many terms that are typically found in instruments that are properly characterized as debt for U.S. federal income tax purposes. The parties intend that the financing constitutes (i) debt for U.S. tax and treaty purposes, resulting in the "dividends" payable on the financing deducted by USCo as interest for tax purposes and subject to favorable U.S. withholding tax under the treaty (as compared to payments characterized as dividends), and (ii) equity for FCountry purposes, resulting in favorable benefits to the lender in FCountry. If the "dividend" payments were properly treated as dividends under the treaty, USCo would be required to withhold U.S. tax on those payments under the treaty.

---

[101] Some public comments to the FIN 48 Exposure Draft expressed the view that any information or evidence supporting a change in judgment should be objectively verifiable and that a triggering event would normally be required to subsequently recognize a tax benefit. FASB concluded in the FIN 48 Exposure Draft, however, that a change in estimate is a judgment that requires evaluation of all available facts and circumstances, even in the absence of a specific triggering event. *See* FIN 48, Appendix B, paragraph B46.

[102] *See* FIN 48, Appendix B, paragraph B47.

[103] *See* FIN 48, Appendix B, paragraph B47.

[104] *See* FIN 48, Appendix B, paragraph B47.

[105] *See* FASB ASC 740–10–25–14.

The internal tax director of USCo, who was involved in the negotiations of the terms of the financing and reviewed the draft documents, determined that based on his understanding of the terms of the financing, USCo has "substantial authority" pursuant to IRC Section 6662(d)(2)(B)(i) (but it is not more likely than not) to characterize the "dividend" payments as interest for U.S. tax and treaty purposes and as dividends for FCountry purposes. Based on the tax director's analysis, USCo deducts the "dividend" payments as interest, but records no financial accounting benefit for the tax position. Two years after consummating the financing, the tax director learns that the parties renegotiated various significant terms of the financing that were incorporated into the final financing documents. USCo's finance department did not realize that these revised terms potentially strengthened USCo's tax position and, thus did not provide the tax director with the final documents.

It is not clear under the FASB rules whether this company is permitted to re-analyze the characterization of the financing based on the final terms of the documents under these facts, especially since the company failed to provide its tax director with final documents.

If an entity initially relied on an external tax advisor to conclude that the benefit of a tax position cannot be recognized, but in a later reporting period the entity engages the same (or another) advisor who determines that the tax position can be recognized, does the subsequent advice constitute new information?[106]

ILLUSTRATION 3-17: Assume the same facts as in Illustration 3-16, except that the tax director (who is aware of the final terms of the financing when the financing is funded) engages an outside tax advisor ("Tax Advisor A") to provide its opinion concerning the U.S. tax treatment of the payments under the instrument denominated as "dividends." Tax Advisor A, who was not a sophisticated tax practitioner and who was not familiar with analyzing similar financing, concluded with little analysis that the financing more likely than not was equity for U.S. tax purposes and thus USCo was not entitled to any interest deduction.

USCo decided to deduct the "dividend" payments on the financing as interest on its return, but relied on the advice of Tax Advisor A to conclude that this tax position did not satisfy the recognition threshold because Tax Advisor A concluded that it was not more likely than not that the deduction of the "dividends" as interest would be sustained. Two years later, USCo hires a new tax advisor ("Tax Advisor B"), who is familiar with the analysis and arguments (favorable and unfavorable) relating to the U.S. tax treatment of these types of financing transactions. Tax Advisor B, who determines that the applicable tax law did not change since the financing was funded, furnishes USCo with tax advice concluding that based on the financing terms it is more likely than not that USCo is entitled to treat the "dividends" as deductible interest for U.S. tax purposes. After reviewing Tax Advisor B's detailed and well-reasoned tax

[106] Alternatively, if management initially concludes without the advice of an outside advisor that a position cannot be recognized, but in a subsequent period engages a tax advisor who concludes that the tax position satisfies the more-likely-than-not standard, is management permitted to treat the advisor's advice as new information in connection with the tax position?

advice, management believes that it is more likely than not that its interest deduction reported on its tax return would be sustained.

Under FASB ASC 740–10, it is not clear if USCo is permitted to reevaluate its position, even though a new outside tax advisor, rather than management, is reevaluating the prior tax position, especially since no facts or law have changed and both the relevant facts and legal authorities were readily available to management when the financing was consummated and the first financial statement was prepared.

Based on its deliberations concerning changes in management's judgment, FASB concluded that recognition and measurement of a tax benefit should be based on all information available at the reporting date, and that a subsequent change in facts and circumstances should be recognized in the period in which the change occurs.[107] Accordingly, a change in facts subsequent to the reporting date but prior to the issuance of the financial statements should be recognized in the period in which the change in facts occurs.[108]

FASB ASC 740–10 requires management of an entity to evaluate uncertainty and changes in uncertainty to determine if the entity is entitled to the benefits of a particular tax position. Thus, management is required to monitor changes in facts that occur subsequent to a reporting date and determine if the new facts alter management's judgment that the entity should continue to recognize the economic benefits of a tax position.[109]

ILLUSTRATION 3-18:[110]

USCo evaluated a tax position at its most recent reporting date, by considering all relevant tax authorities' sources of tax law, including a pending court case in which the taxing authority has fully disallowed a similar tax position with Company B, which is unrelated to USCo. Although USCo was aware of the pending litigation as of USCo's recent reporting date, USCo's management determined that the more-likely-than-not recognition threshold had been met. Subsequent to the reporting date, but prior to the issuance of the financial statements, the taxing authority prevailed in its litigation with Company B, and USCo concludes that it is no longer more likely than not that it will sustain the position.

FASB provides that "an entity shall derecognize a previously recognized tax position in the first period in which it is no longer more likely than not that the tax position would be sustained upon examination,"[111] and also indicates that "subsequent recognition, derecognition, and measurement shall be based on management's best judgment given the facts, circumstances, and

---

[107] The Big 4 accounting firms are clear that if the facts and law exist on the reporting date, and the entity did not take all the facts and law into account, this is an error. The correction, if large enough, would require a correction of the prior period financial statement, i.e., a restatement. If it is not large, the correction is recorded in the financial period the error was discovered.

[108] *See* FASB ASC 740–10–25–8. Although AS 2801 (AU Section 560)), *Subsequent Events,* defines two different types of events subsequent to a reporting date, it does not consider the perspective of a change in facts and resolution of uncertainty. Rather, AS 2801 evaluates whether information confirms the existence of a condition at a previous reporting date.

[109] *See* FIN 48, Appendix B, paragraph B40.

[110] *See* FIN 48, Appendix A, paragraphs A31–A32.

[111] FASB ASC 740–10–40–2.

information available at the reporting date."[112] Because the resolution of Company B's litigation with the taxing authority is the information that caused management of USCo to change its judgment about the sustainability of the position and that information was not available at the reporting date, the change in judgment would be recognized in the first quarter of the current fiscal year.

ILLUSTRATION 3-19: SoftCo is a U.S.-based technology company with global operations. The non-U.S. business is managed by a wholly-owned subsidiary, HoldCo, based in a country with a low tax rate which allows royalties, interest, and related expenses to be deducted in determining income subject to the low rate. Assume that HoldCo owns its own intangibles. All foreign subsidiaries of Holdco have agreements with HoldCo which determine the income of the subsidiaries via traditional one-sided transfer pricing methodologies (cost plus or TNMM)[113] with the residual income earned by HoldCo. SoftCo has studied the BEPS materials, which make it likely that the one-sided methodologies of HoldCo will need to be tested with a profit-split method (two-sided testing of combined income).[114]

In such a situation, the evaluation could have an impact on the recognition and measurement elements of FASB ASC 740–10.

[3] Financial Disclosure of Recognition, Derecognition, and Remeasurement of Prior Tax Position

FASB ASC 740–10 requires that the (i) subsequent recognition of a previously unrecognized tax position, (ii) derecognition of a prior recognized tax position, or (iii) remeasurement of a tax position that was recognized in a prior period all be accounted for as a discrete item in the period in which the change occurs.[115] A subsequent derecognition of a prior year tax position occurs in the first interim period in which the tax position no longer satisfies the recognition standard.[116] Likewise, the recognition of a previously unrecognized tax position occurs in the first financial reporting period in which that more-likely-than-not threshold is met.[117]

Application of FASB ASC 740–10 to a position taken in a prior interim period and, within the same fiscal year, adoption of a different FASB ASC 740–10 recognition, derecognition, or remeasurement analysis of that position, constitutes an integral part of the annual period which must comply with the provisions of FASB ASC 740–270–30–8, and FASB ASC 740–270.[118]

---

[112] FASB ASC 740–10–25–14.

[113] *See* Cym Lowell, Mark Thomas & Mark Levey, *International Transfer Pricing OECD Guidelines* Chapter 4 (Thomson Reuters) [*OECD Transfer Pricing*].

[114] *See OECD Transfer Pricing* Section 4.08.

[115] *See* FASB ASC 740–10–25–15. FASB decided that changes in judgments about the recognition, derecognition, and measurement of income tax positions covered by FIN 48 should be made consistent with APB 28 (FASB ASC 270–10) and FIN 18 (FASB ASC 740–270). FIN 48, Appendix B, paragraph B49. Further, during its initial deliberations of FIN 48, FASB concluded that the guidance in paragraph 194 of SFAS No. 109 should also apply to changes in judgment concerning the realization of tax benefits governed by FIN 48. FIN 48, Appendix B, paragraph B48.

[116] *See* FASB ASC 740–10–40–2.

[117] *See* FASB ASC 740–10–25–8.

[118] *See* FASB ASC 740–270–35–6. *See* Section 2.05.

§ 3.06 Interest and Penalties

[1] Recognition and Derecognition of Interest and Penalties

If a company is required to pay interest on an underpayment of income taxes, it must recognize the corresponding interest expense during the first accounting period in which the interest begins to accrue under the applicable tax law.[119] The recognized interest expense equals the applicable statutory rate of interest multiplied by the difference between the FASB ASC 740–10 recognized tax position and the tax position taken (or to be taken) in the company's tax return.[120] Significantly, FASB ASC 740–10 requires interest expense to be recognized for book purposes on the amount of a recognized tax position that is measured at less than 100 percent, even if the uncertain tax position meets the more-likely-than-not recognition standard.[121] Interest will continue to accrue for each reporting period until the tax position is resolved under FASB ASC 740–10.

If a tax position does not meet the minimum statutory threshold[122] to avoid payment of penalties, the company must recognize an expense for the amount of the statutory penalty in the period in which the entity claims or expects to claim the position in its tax return.[123] For this purpose, a company determines if the minimum statutory standard is met by:

1. Assuming the tax position will be examined by the relevant taxing authority having full knowledge of all relevant information;
2. Considering the technical merits of the tax position based on relevant tax authorities and their applicability to the particular facts and circumstances of the tax position, including widely known administrative practices and precedents of the relevant taxing authority in its dealings with similar enterprises with respect to that tax position; and
3. Evaluating each tax position without consideration of the possibility of offset or aggregation with other positions.[124]

If penalties were not recognized when the position was initially taken, the expense must be recognized beginning in the period in which the entity first determines that the minimum statutory threshold is not met.[125] Likewise, previously recognized interest and

---

[119] *See* FASB ASC 740–10–25–56.

[120] *Id.* See FIN 48, Appendix B, paragraph B53.

[121] In its deliberations, FASB considered whether the accrual of interest should be on (i) the amount of payment anticipated by the company to settle an underpayment controversy; or (ii) the difference between the tax benefit of the return tax position and the amount recognized in the financial statements. *See* FIN 48, Appendix B, paragraph B52. Because tax law determines the amount payable, the FIN 48 Exposure Draft indicated that interest should be accrued by applying the applicable statutory interest rate to the difference between the recognized tax position benefit and the return amount. Final FIN 48 (later FASB ASC 740–10) affirmed the approach set forth in the FIN 48 Exposure Draft.

[122] Some taxing authorities impose penalties only if the tax position meets certain requirements. For example, IRC Section 6662(d)(2)(B) provides that the substantial understatement penalty does not apply to an understatement of income tax if substantial tax authority exists supporting the tax position or the tax position is adequately disclosed in the company's tax return.

[123] *See* FASB ASC 740–10–25–57.

[124] *Id.* This criteria is also applied to assess whether a tax position meets the recognition more-likely-than-not threshold. *See* Section 3.04[2]; FASB ASC 740–10–25–7.

[125] *See* FASB ASC 740–10–25–57.

penalties associated with tax positions that initially did not meet the more-likely-than-not standard must be derecognized in the period that the standard is met. The determination of whether derecognition of previously recognized penalties and interest is appropriate is based on whether management believes that one of the following requirements is met by the current reporting date: (i) the more-likely-than-not recognition threshold is satisfied, (ii) the tax position is resolved through examination, negotiation or litigation, or (iii) the statute of limitations for the relevant taxing authority to examine and challenge the tax position has expired.[126]

[2] Classification and Disclosure of Interest and Penalties

FASB ASC 740 does not provide guidance on the classification of interest and penalties.[127] FASB decided that the classification of interest and penalties should be treated as an accounting policy election. To assist users of financial statements in understanding the accounting for income taxes, the policy election and the amount of interest and penalties recognized in the financial statements should be disclosed in the notes to the financial statements.[128]

Based on the company's accounting policy election and the application of FASB ASC 740–10: (a) recognized interest may be classified in the financial statements as either income taxes or interest expense; and (b) recognized penalties may be classified in the financial statements as either income taxes or another expense classification.[129]

FASB considered whether a provision for the anticipated payment of interest or penalties (or both) should be recognized in the financial statements. FASB noted that the tax law of many jurisdictions requires the payment of:

(i) penalties when a specified confidence level for a substantive tax position does not exist; and

(ii) interest when there has been an underpayment of income taxes.[130]

To ensure completeness of the financial statements, FASB concluded that a liability should be recognized when it is deemed incurred under the relevant tax law.[131] Accordingly, consistent with accrual accounting, the financial statements:[132]

(i) should reflect interest beginning in the period that it would begin accruing according to the relevant tax law; and

---

[126] *See* FASB ASC 740–10–25–57. These requirements are the same as those applied to determine if a tax position should be recognized in a period subsequent to the period in which management initially determined that the position did not meet the more-likely-than-not threshold. *See* Section 3.05[1]; FASB ASC 740–10–25–8.

[127] *See* FIN 48, Appendix B, paragraph B50. Public comments to the FIN 48 Exposure Draft requested that FASB provide guidance on classification. In initial deliberations of FIN 48, FASB considered whether to provide guidance on classification and concluded that the guidance should be more properly considered in its short-term convergence project on accounting for income taxes, if at all.

[128] *See* FASB ASC 740–10–50–19 and FIN 48 Appendix B, paragraph B50.

[129] *See* FASB ASC 740–10–45–25. Those elections are required to be consistently applied by the company.

[130] *See* FIN 48, Appendix B, paragraph B51.

[131] *Id.*

[132] *Id.*

(ii) should reflect penalties in the first period the tax position was taken in a tax return that would give rise to the penalty, based on the provisions of the relevant tax law.[133]

§ 3.07 Classification

As a result of applying the principles of FASB ASC 740–10, the amount of benefit recognized and measured in the statement of financial position may differ from the amount taken (or expected to be taken) in a tax return for the current year, generally resulting in one of the following:

1. An increase in a liability for income taxes payable or a reduction of an income tax refund receivable,
2. A reduction in a deferred tax asset or an increase in a deferred tax liability,
3. Both (1) and (2).

A liability is created (or the amount of a net operating loss carryforward or amount refundable is reduced) for an unrecognized tax benefit because it represents an entity's potential future obligation to the taxing authority for a tax position that was not recognized pursuant to FASB ASC 740–10.[134] An entity that presents a classified statement of financial position must classify a liability associated with an unrecognized tax benefit as a current liability (or reduce the amount of a net operating loss carryforward or tax refundable) to the extent the entity anticipates payment (or receipt) of cash within one year or the operating cycle, if longer.[135] FASB ASC 740–10 precludes the combination of the liability for unrecognized tax benefits (or reduction in amounts refundable) with deferred tax liabilities or assets.[136]

A tax position recognized pursuant to FASB ASC 740–10 in the financial statements may also affect the tax bases of assets or liabilities, thus changing or creating temporary differences.[137] For this purpose, a taxable and deductible temporary difference is a difference between the amount of an item reported in the financial statements and the tax basis of an item as determined by applying the recognition and measurement provisions of FASB ASC 740–10.[138] A liability recognized pursuant to FASB ASC 740–10 is not classified as a deferred tax liability unless it arises from a taxable temporary difference (for example, a difference between the tax basis of an asset or a liability calculated by applying FASB ASC 740–10 and its reported amount in the statement of financial position).[139]

[133] Public comments to the FIN 48 Exposure Draft expressed concern that the requirements for recognition of interest and penalties would lead to systematic overstatement of liabilities followed by subsequent reversals into income. During deliberations, FASB considered whether recognition of interest should be based on management's best estimate of the amount that would ultimately be paid to the tax authority upon settlement. However, because the recognition threshold was reduced from probable in the FIN 48 Exposure Draft to more likely than not in final FIN 48, FASB concluded there would not be an overstatement of liabilities. FIN 48, Appendix B, paragraph B53.

[134] *See* FASB ASC 740–10–25–16.

[135] *See* FASB ASC 740–10–45–11; FIN 48, Summary to FIN 48.

[136] *See* FASB ASC 740–10–45–11.

[137] *See* FASB ASC 740–10–25–17. *See also* Section 2.02[2], regarding temporary differences.

[138] *See* FASB ASC 740–10–25–17.

[139] *See* FASB ASC 740–10–45–12; FIN 48, Summary to FIN 48.

FASB considered whether the difference between the as-filed tax position and the FASB ASC 740–10 recognized amounts should be classified as a deferred tax liability or as a current or noncurrent liability.[140] Since the liability associated with that difference results from the reduction of an income tax paid or currently payable, FASB reasoned that the amount should not be classified as a deferred tax liability unless the liability arises from a taxable temporary difference.[141]

Public comments to the FIN 48 Exposure Draft argued that because the timing of payments of an uncertain tax position is not clear, the liability should be classified as a current liability.[142] FASB considered those comments but also acknowledged that long delays are possible or likely between filing a tax return and a settlement of the tax positions on that return. In fact, FASB noted that several years[143] may elapse between filing a tax return and settlement with taxing authorities. Based on the foregoing, FASB concluded that the proper classification of uncertain tax positions should be based on management's assessment of the timing of the ultimate payment to taxing authorities.[144] The portion of the liability that is expected to be paid in the next year (or operating cycle, if longer) should be thus classified as a current liability.[145]

These issues are addressed in Illustration 3-20:

ILLUSTRATION 3-20:[146]

In year 1, USCo acquired an intangible asset for $15 million that has an indefinite life for financial statement purposes and is, therefore, not subject to amortization. Under the tax rules, USCo is certain that the full amount of the intangible is ultimately deductible, but it is uncertain as to the timing of the deduction. USCo decides to deduct the entire cost of the asset in year 1 on its tax return. USCo has determined that this tax position qualifies for the more likely than not recognition standard. USCo determines further that it is 25 percent likely it would realize an immediate deduction upon settlement with the taxing authorities, and it is certain it could sustain a 15-year amortization for tax purposes. Based on these facts, the largest benefit in year 1 that is greater than 50 percent likely of being realized upon settlement is the tax effect

---

[140] *See* FIN 48, Appendix B, paragraph B54. FASB initially concluded that the liability created from applying FIN 48 should be classified as a current liability under the guidance in ARB 43, Chapter 3A (later FASB ASC 210–10–45), since the liability is similar to a due-on-demand note. Because taxing authorities could issue an assessment and a demand for payment, FASB reasoned that the liability is appropriately classified as due on demand. However, some members of FASB indicated that this reasoning, and therefore the guidance in ARB 43, Chapter 3A (later FASB ASC 210–10–45), might apply only to the as-filed tax liability. *See* FIN 48, Appendix B, paragraph B57.

[141] *See* FIN 48, Appendix B, paragraph B54. In determining the appropriate classification of that difference, FASB considered the potential timing of any settlement with the taxing authority, the characteristics of the liability, and the guidance in ARB 43, Chapter 3A, "Working Capital Current Assets and Current Liabilities," (later FASB ASC 210–10) on the classification of tax liabilities. *See* FIN 48, Appendix B, paragraph B55.

[142] *See* FIN 48, Appendix B, paragraph B59.

[143] For example, months or years may elapse before a return might be selected for examination and it might be many more months or years before the company appeals and litigates the assessments proposed by the audit. FIN 48, Appendix B, paragraph B56.

[144] *See* FIN 48, Appendix B, paragraph B59.

[145] *Id.* FIN 48 (FASB ASC 740–10) did not change the classification requirements for deferred taxes. See Summary to FIN 48.

[146] This illustration is based on FASB ASC 740–10–55–111 and FASB ASC 740–10–55–112.

of $1 million (the year 1 deduction from straight-line amortization of the asset over 15 years).

USCo should reflect a year 1 deferred tax liability for the tax effect of the temporary difference created by the difference between the financial statement basis of the asset of $15 million and the tax basis of the asset computed in accordance with FIN 48 ($14 million, i.e., the $15 million cost of the asset reduced by $1 million of amortization). USCo will also reflect a tax liability for the tax imposed on the difference between the as-filed tax position ($15 million deduction) and the amount of the deduction that is considered more likely than not of being sustained ($1 million). Further, USCo must determine if it should accrue for statutory penalties as well as interest expense on the difference between the amounts reported in the financial statements and the tax position taken in its tax return.

It is interesting that in the above illustration, which is set forth in Appendix A to FIN 48, USCo's treatment of the full $15 million cost as currently deductible does not meet the more-likely-than-not recognition threshold, yet the example applies the measurement criteria based on a possible settlement of the issue using a 15-year amortization for tax purposes. It appears that this application of FASB ASC 740–10 may be limited to those tax positions that involve a temporary difference between tax and book.

§ 3.08 Disclosures

[1] Tabular Reconciliation Required

One controversial aspect of FASB ASC 740–10 is the requirement that a company disclose the following items at the end of each annual reporting period:[147]

1. A tabular reconciliation of the total amounts of unrecognized tax benefits at the beginning and end of the period, which will include at a minimum:
   - (a) The gross amounts of the increases and decreases in unrecognized tax benefits as a result of tax positions taken during a prior period.
   - (b) The gross amounts of increases and decreases in unrecognized tax benefits as a result of tax positions taken during the current period.
   - (c) The amounts of decreases in the unrecognized tax benefits relating to settlements with taxing authorities.

[147] *See* FASB ASC 740–10–50–15 and FASB ASC 740–10–50–15A. Note that pursuant to ASU 2009–06, the following requirements do not apply to nonpublic entities: first, a tabular reconciliation of the total amounts of unrecognized tax benefits at the beginning and end of the period (which will include at a minimum: (a) the gross amounts of the increases and decreases in unrecognized tax benefits as a result of tax positions taken during a prior period, (b) the gross amounts of increases and decreases in unrecognized tax benefits as a result of tax positions taken during the current period, (c) the amounts of decreases in the unrecognized tax benefits relating to settlements with taxing authorities, and (d) reductions to unrecognized tax benefits as a result of a lapse of the applicable statute of limitations), and, second, the total amount of unrecognized tax benefits that, if recognized, would affect the effective tax rate. After consulting with FASB's Private Company Financial Reporting Committee (PCFRC) and other constituents, FASB concluded that these disclosure requirements were unduly burdensome for private entities and were not useful to users of private entities' financial statements.

   (d) Reductions to unrecognized tax benefits as a result of a lapse of the applicable statute of limitations.

2. The total amount of unrecognized tax benefits that, if recognized, would affect the effective tax rate.
3. The total amounts of interest and penalties recognized in the statement of operations and the total amounts of interest and penalties recognized in the statement of financial position.
4. For positions for which it is reasonably possible that the total amounts of unrecognized tax benefits will significantly increase or decrease within 12 months of the reporting date:
   (a) The nature of the uncertainty;
   (b) The nature of the event that could occur in the next 12 months that would cause the change; and
   (c) An estimate of the range of the reasonably possible change or a statement that an estimate of the range cannot be made.
5. A description of tax years that remain subject to examination by major tax jurisdictions.

FASB decided that a tabular reconciliation of the amounts of unrecognized tax benefits at the beginning and end of the period provides financial statement users with valuable information about a significant and sensitive estimate (and any change in the measurement of that estimate) based on the company's judgment.[148]

Some individual members of FASB who favored the tabular reconciliation believed that certain required minimum line items were necessary to (i) explain the change in the beginning and ending balances of unrecognized tax benefits and (ii) avoid meaningless boilerplate disclosures.[149] Other individual FASB members disagreed with this approach and either preferred to provide financial statement preparers flexibility to describe the changes in the beginning and ending balances[150] or favored allowing preparers to provide the beginning and ending balance of the unrecognized tax benefits and a qualitative description of the reason(s) for the change in the balance.[151]

In an attempt to simplify income tax disclosures, FASB considered the disclosure requirements in SFAS No. 5 (later FASB ASC 450) and AICPA Statement of Position 94–6, *Disclosure of Certain Significant Risks and Uncertainties* (later FASB ASC 275-10), but decided that codifying and enumerating required disclosures in its rules on

---

[148] *See* FIN 48, Appendix B, paragraph B63. At the May 16, 2006 FASB meeting, FASB approved (by a vote of four to two) the requirement of a tabular reconciliation, including certain required line items in the reconciliation relating to the changes in the balance of the unrecognized tax benefits. *See* May 16, 2006 FASB Minutes.

[149] *See* May 16, 2006 FASB Minutes.

[150] This minority view also desired internal consistency within SFAS No. 109, which does not require extensive disclosures for valuation allowances relating to deferred tax assets. *See* May 16, 2006 FASB Minutes.

[151] This individual FASB member also expressed concern that the disclosure requirements prior to implementing FIN 48 would be very time consuming and complex for companies and this FIN 48 reconciliation would add to that burden and complexity without providing significant incremental information compared to a qualitative description of the reason(s) for the change in the balance of unrecognized tax benefits. *See* May 16, 2006 FASB Minutes.

accounting for uncertain income tax positions would increase comparability of financial statements of companies and reduce complexity.[152]

In considering whether its rules on accounting for uncertain income tax positions should require additional disclosures, FASB considered the information that financial statement users find useful. Public comments from financial statement users requested a wide array of disclosures. In connection with finalizing its rules on accounting for uncertain income tax positions, FASB considered those requests. Some FASB members concluded that additional disclosures were not necessary because a more-likely-than-not recognition threshold was sufficiently high to address the uncertainty of tax positions. Other members believed the more-likely-than-not recognition threshold was not sufficiently high to capture the effects of uncertainty and that a tabular reconciliation of the beginning and ending balances of the liability for unrecognized tax benefits would be appropriate.[153]

As noted above,[154] there can be material financial accounting elements relating to government assistance provided by domestic or foreign governmental units. This has been highlighted by the European Union investigations relating to so-called state aid.[155] As the potential significance of these matters has evolved, the FASB in late 2015 issued Proposed ASU No. 2015–340, *Government Assistance (Topic 832): Disclosures by Business Entities about Government Assistance*. It would require a business entity to disclose in its financial statements information that would allow investors/analysts to assess the effect of government assistance. This would include disclosure of the nature and significant terms and conditions of the assistance, including a general description of the categories of assistance, such as grants, tax incentives, and so on. The disclosure should also include the form in which the assistance was received (e.g., cash), disclose whether the assistance has been recognized in the financial statements including the accounting policies replied upon for the recognition, and identify by line item the benefit of the assistance on the balance sheet and income statement. Finally, if practical, the amount of assistance received that has not been recognized in the financial statements.

At a meeting in June 2016, the FASB voted to reverse the proposed decision to include in the proposed government assistance disclosure requirements assistance falling under FASB ASC 740. Companies had expressed concern that such inclusion would impose significant cost burdens. Accordingly, the Board concluded that such matters would be better addressed under the ongoing FASB ASC 740 disclosure project. FASB also affirmed that the rules would apply only to legally enforceable agreements and not to general tax provisions any company can claim (whatever this may be defined to mean).

Subsequent period disclosure issues are discussed below, at Section 3.10.

[2] Road Map for Tax Authority

Public comments to the FIN 48 Exposure Draft expressed concern that the requirement of a tabular reconciliation is inappropriate because it provides a "roadmap" for taxing authorities, and asserted that the relationship between a taxpayer and a

---

[152] *See* FIN 48, Appendix B, paragraph B61.

[153] *See* FIN 48, Appendix B, paragraph B62. Application of the disclosure provisions is discussed in Section 3.11.

[154] *See* Section 3.05[2].

[155] *Id.*

taxing authority should be viewed analogous to parties in a lawsuit. FASB dismissed those arguments for several reasons.[156]

First, FASB rejected the analogy of a taxing authority with a counterparty in a lawsuit since a counterparty acts in its own particular interest, while a taxing authority is acting in the broader public interest in regulating compliance with self-reporting income tax laws. Second, FASB expressed the view that requiring disclosures at the aggregate level does not reveal information about individual tax positions but instead provides information that is useful to users of financial statements. Third, FASB acknowledged that the Service has instituted[157] a detailed reconciliation requirement that provides information regarding differences between amounts reported in a company's income tax return and in its financial statements.[158]

The May 16, 2006 FASB Minutes set forth various related observations from individual FASB members and the FASB staff related to the FIN 48 disclosure requirements. For example, the FIN 48 disclosure recommended by the FASB staff was intended to provide relevant information to financial statement users that they do not presently have access to, but not information that is so detailed that it furnishes taxing authorities or competitors with an advantage or "roadmap." The staff thus attempted to balance the competing objectives of users of financial statements and preparers in recommending financial disclosure generally based on aggregate rather than individual amounts. Further, the FASB staff concluded that the information needed to comply with FIN 48 disclosures would be available without any significant incremental costs to the company.[159]

Some members of FASB and its staff also concluded that most public and large non-public companies already provided the Service a more detailed and effective "roadmap" in its Schedule M-3 than would be provided by the FIN 48 disclosures requirement.

---

[156] *See* FIN 48, Appendix B, paragraph B64. Based on the May 16, 2006 FASB Minutes, the FASB staff stated that public comments also raised the concern that the FIN 48 disclosure would provide too much information to a company's competitors.

[157] IRS Form 1120, US Corporate Income Tax Return, contains Schedule M-1 on which the taxpayer reconciles taxable net income with the increase or decrease in surplus for the taxable year. Effective for tax years ending on or after December 31, 2004, the Service replaced Schedule M-1 with Schedule M-3 for corporations with assets of $10 million or more. Schedule M-3 provides a complete reconciliation from financial accounting net income to taxable income in a standardized and detailed format. Rev. Proc. 2004–45, 2004–31 IRB 140, permits a taxpayer with significant book-tax difference transactions to report the transaction on Schedule M-3, rather than on IRS Form 8886, "Reportable Transaction Disclosure Statement." Treasury regulations issued August 1, 2007 (TD 9350) eliminated as a category of reportable transactions under Treas. Reg. § 1.6011–4 transactions with a significant book-tax difference. *See also* Rev. Proc. 2004–45, sections 4.02 and 4.03, which provide an alternative disclosure procedure for corporations with total assets of less than $10 million, partnerships, and S corporations. That disclosure procedure allows entities to file an incomplete Schedule M-3 to satisfy their IRC Section 6011 disclosure obligations.

[158] In FASB's view, this reconciliation requirement and those similar to it are the sources of information that taxing authorities use to focus their examination. FIN 48, Appendix B, paragraph B64.

[159] *See* May 16, 2006 FASB Minutes. The FASB staff also noted that currently the Service is empowered to seek the total amount of a company's liability for unrecognized tax benefits. Furthermore, the FASB staff stated that based on informal discussions with financial statement preparers, tax practitioners, and the Service, it appears that a company's liability for unrecognized tax benefits may be meaningless for companies with permanent establishment or nexus in a variety of jurisdictions since a taxing authority might not know if the liability relates to taxes attributable to its jurisdiction or another jurisdiction. *See* May 16, 2006 FASB Minutes.

Additionally, the FASB staff stated that it appeared that several states were exploring enhanced disclosures like the Schedule M-3.[160]

Despite the views expressed by FASB in 2006 that FIN 48 disclosure should not cause information about a company's individual uncertain tax positions to be publicly divulged, many companies were concerned that uncertain tax position disclosure may provide IRS and possibly other tax authorities with a roadmap to discover possible uncertain tax issues, resulting in return examination.

In particular, some companies fear that the requirements of paragraph 21(d) of FIN 48 (now FASB ASC 740–10–50–15) may provide the taxing authority with too much tax-sensitive information. Under the UTP rules, when it is "reasonably possible" that the total amount of unrecognized tax benefits of tax positions will "significantly" change within 12 months of the financial reporting date, the company must disclose the "nature of the uncertainty" and the "nature of the event" that would cause the change.[161] Further, the UTP rules require the company to (i) estimate the range of the reasonably possible change to the company's unrecognized tax benefits, or (ii) provide a statement that an estimate of the range cannot be made.[162] The FASB rules on reporting uncertain income tax positions do not provide specific guidance as to when the total tax benefits are "reasonably possible" to "significantly" change. Further, no standards are provided as to how specific the UTP disclosure needs to be regarding either the "nature of the uncertainty" or the "nature of the event" that results from a possible change in a company's unrecognized tax benefits. With respect to estimating the reasonably possible range of significant change to unrecognized tax benefits, it is possible that many companies will conclude that an estimate cannot be made.

The Service likewise believes that UTP disclosures may provide it with details about tax reserves that may reveal vulnerable income tax positions. The Service issued a field examiners' guide on FIN 48 (later FASB ASC 740–10)[163] addressing whether UTP disclosures are a roadmap for the Service:

> Question #1: Are FIN 48 Disclosures a Roadmap for the IRS?
>
> Answer #1:
>
> The disclosures required under FIN 48 should give the Service a somewhat better view of a taxpayer's uncertain tax positions; however, the disclosures still do not have the specificity that would allow a perfect view of the issues and amounts at risk. For example, there may be a contingent tax liability listed in the tax footnotes of a large multi-national taxpayer with a description called

---

[160] Another FASB member acknowledged that although the disclosed information may not provide any incremental information to the Service, such disclosure might provide incremental information to other taxing authorities, for example, other foreign countries, thus possibly increasing the company's taxes. *See* May 16, 2006 FASB Minutes.

[161] Some examples of events that might cause a significant change in the succeeding 12-month period to a company's unrecognized tax benefits are expiration of the statute of limitations for an uncertain income tax position within the ensuing 12 months, or issuance of an adverse tax decision with respect to a tax position taken by a company on its prior year return.

[162] Paragraph 21(e) of FIN 48 (later FASB ASC 740–10–50–15) also requires companies to disclose a description of the tax years that remain subject to examination by major tax jurisdictions. For multinational companies and/or those that are subject to tax in numerous states, this disclosure may be challenging.

[163] Service Large and Mid-size Business Division (LMSB) Memorandum (LMSB–04–0507–045) on FIN 48 Implications—Field Examiners' Guide (May 2007). For discussion of the Service's "policy of restraint" in regard to tax accrual workpapers (TAW), *see* Chapter 8.

"tax credits;" however, tax credits could be US, foreign, or state tax credits. So the "tax credits" in this example may or may not in this case have a US tax impact.

Even with the lack of specificity, tax footnotes included in financial statements, including FIN 48 disclosures, should be carefully reviewed and analyzed as part of the audit planning process. For example, if a taxpayer reflecting a contingent tax liability in the year under audit for Subpart F income does not reflect Subpart F in the tax return, questions could develop about why Subpart F income does not appear in the tax return, but is mentioned in the tax footnotes as creating a contingent tax liability.

Revenue Agents should not be reluctant to pursue matters mentioned in FIN 48 disclosures, but should be mindful of our policy of restraint on Tax Accrual Workpapers (TAW) and not cross over the boundaries contained there. If for example, there is discussion in the tax footnotes about a contingent tax liability being reversed because the statute of limitations related to the transfer of an intangible asset has expired, even though the statute may have run on that particular issue, this provides insight into how the taxpayer may be treating other intangible assets in other years where the statute of limitations is still open. In this example, this is public information that can be used without violating the TAW's policy.

Significantly, in early 2010, the IRS announced that it was proposing to require that certain taxpayers disclose their uncertain federal income tax positions on their tax return. In September, 2010, IRS issued the final version of Schedule UTP, to accompany the 2010 tax returns of certain large corporations. For further discussion of Schedule UTP, see Section 3.11.

[3] Convergence of Financial Accounting, Financial Reporting, and Tax

There is a consistent trend in financial accounting, financial reporting, and taxation to require transparency with respect to material items. Disclosure requirements from the FASB are noted above, as are the evolving tax reporting requirements under the country-by-country regime finalized in late 2015,[164] with effective dates in 2016. The focus of these changes is in different directions. Financial accounting and reporting rules are intended to provide information to investors and other interested parties about the financial health of a company (including focus on foreign earnings of U.S.-based companies).[165] Tax disclosures, on the other hand, are typically designed to provide tax authorities with appropriate data to determine whether a company has complied with its tax obligations.

It has been suggested that the financial disclosure evolutions have been fueled by public angst about the tax reporting habits of multinational companies (MNEs).[166] In the continuing stream of public criticism of the tax planning processes of MNEs, the bedrock

---

[164] *See* Section 9.10[2].

[165] *See* Section 4.04[2][c].

[166] *See* Parker, *Financial Reporting in the BEPS Era: Are FASB and the SEC the New Watchdogs?* Tax Management Transfer Pricing Report (Apr. 30, 2015, Vol. 23, No. 25); Parker, *SEC: New Country-by-Country Reporting Rule for Oil and Gas Industry Postponed to 2016*, Tax Management Transfer Pricing Report (Apr. 16, 2015, Vol. 23, No. 24).

reality of international tax planning is seldom recognized. Countries enact tax laws and procedures to develop their own tax base (at the expense of other countries). Like water going downhill, MNE planning strategies then utilize the most efficient path (i) to take advantage of new opportunities created by the new regimes; and (ii) to minimize transfer pricing exposures, imposition of exit, or other taxes on the movement of intangibles or other assets, and so on.

As with many financial accounting or tax policy changes, initial fears of the potential draconian consequences of disclosure, both for tax and financial accounting purposes, have largely proven to be less severe than initially contemplated. These processes have become routine on all sides, with reporting companies providing a far greater range of information than was the case prior to FASB ASC 740–10 with the IRS having access to the UTP information.

Perhaps the clearest impact of the disclosure requirements is on the nature of the relationship between reporting companies and their independent auditors, which must ascertain whether the respective standards have been satisfied to allow reporting of certain tax benefits.

§ 3.09 Request by Service for UTP Workpapers

A controversial issue that arises regarding financial statement reporting of uncertain tax positions is whether the Service is permitted to, and will, request the uncertain-tax-position workpapers during an audit of a company or otherwise. This raises various issues relating to attorney-client privilege, work product doctrine, and IRC Section 7525 (tax accountant privilege).[167] As stated above, the FASB rules on accounting for uncertain income tax positions contains detailed and specific rules that require the disclosure of unrecognized tax benefits relating to uncertain income tax positions, which information is presented in financial statements.[168] Although that disclosure is on an aggregate basis,[169] rather than on an issue-by-issue basis, UTP workpapers typically will include a separate analysis of each uncertain income tax position of the company.[170]

The Service currently exercises a "policy of restraint" whereby it only requests a taxpayer's tax accrual workpapers in limited and unusual circumstances and for listed transactions.[171] Significantly, the Service has issued a chief counsel memorandum[172]

---

167 *See* Chapter 8.

168 Companies should take great care with respect to the UTP documents that are provided to its outside auditors since such information might not be protected by the work product doctrine. To preserve the attorney-client privilege with respect to legal advice rendered in connection with a specified uncertain tax position which it is anticipated may be litigated, a company should avoid providing those documents to the FASB ASC 740–10 auditors (or other third parties).

169 *See* Section 3.08. As an exception to aggregate disclosure, the effect of FASB ASC 740–10 on a company's uncertain income tax position must be separately stated if it is reasonably possible that the total amounts of unrecognized tax benefits will significantly increase or decrease within the ensuing twelve-month period, in which event FASB ASC 740–10 requires disclosure of the nature of the uncertainty, the nature of the event that could occur within twelve months to cause a change, and an estimate of the range of change or a statement that an estimate cannot be made.

170 As discussed in Section 3.05, a company is also required to monitor subsequent changes to its income tax positions, which could result in financial statement disclosure of revisions to a company's uncertain tax positions, including the disclosure of a position that previously was not required to be disclosed.

171 *See* Section 8.05[3].

172 Chief Counsel Memorandum, AM 2007–0012 (Mar. 22, 2007), which was released June 8, 2007. Compare reported statements of Jeff Bosch of the Service's Large and Mid-Size Business Division, 2007 FRW

that expresses the view that workpapers that are prepared to support a company's compliance with the FASB rules on accounting for uncertain income tax positions are tax accrual workpapers that are subject to the Service's policy of restraint as outlined in Internal Revenue Manual Section 4.10.20.2(2).[173]

Likewise, after initially determining that its policy of restraint does not apply to effective tax rate reconciliation workpapers,[174] the IRS has reconsidered and concluded (without public explanation or analysis) that its restraint policy does apply to rate reconciliation workpapers.[175] Further, any financial statement disclosure of a company's uncertain income tax positions as required by FASB ASC 740–10 and filed with the SEC is publicly available to the Service and not covered by the Service's restraint policy.

In September 2010, IRS issued the Schedule UTP, which requires tax reporting of information about uncertain tax positions.[176]

§ 3.10 Subsequent Disclosure Issues

[1] Overview

As discussed above,[177] FASB ASC 740–10 requires each public entity to disclose in its financial statements, at the end of each annual reporting period, a reconciliation of the total beginning and ending unrecognized tax benefits for the period (including (i) the aggregate increases and decreases resulting from tax positions arising both in a prior and the current period, and (ii) decreases from settlements and from termination of statute of limitations).[178]

ILLUSTRATION 3-21:[179]

USCo, a calendar year taxpayer, files a U.S. federal income tax return. The statute of limitations has expired on all USCo's tax periods ending before 2001. Assume that in the first quarter of 2007 the Service commences an exam of USCo's U.S. income tax returns for 2002 through 2004, which should be completed by the end of 2008. As of December 31, 2007, the Service has proposed certain significant adjustments to USCo's transfer pricing and research credits tax positions. Although it is unclear if the company will challenge the proposed adjustments, these adjustments would not result in a

---

112–9, *IRS Considering Changing Policy on FIN 48 Workpapers* (Tax Analysts, June 11, 2007) (acknowledging that Chief Counsel of Service has advised that FIN 48 workpapers are considered tax accrual workpapers that are subject to Service policy of restraint, but noting that his agency will reevaluate and possibly consider changing that policy in the near future with respect to requests for tax accrual tax workpapers covered by FIN 48).

173 *See* Section 8.05[6].

174 IRS Chief Counsel Notice (CC–2007–015) (June 20, 2007).

175 IRS Chief Counsel Notice (CC–2008–008) (Dec 31, 2007). *See* Section 8.05[6].

176 *See* Section 3.11.

177 *See* Section 3.08[2].

178 FASB ASC 740–10 also requires disclosure of (i) the total unrecognized tax benefits that if recognized would affect the effective tax rate (FASB ASC 740–10–50–15A); (ii) the total amounts of interest and penalties recognized in the statement of operations and the statement of financial position (FASB ASC 740–10–50–15); and (iii) a description of tax years that remain subject to examination by major tax jurisdictions (FASB ASC 740–10–50–15). Further, FASB ASC 740–10–50–19 requires a company to disclose its policy on interest and penalty classification in footnotes to the financial statements. As discussed below, FASB ASC 740–10–50–15 requires various disclosure of UTP liability relating to the succeeding 12-month period.

179 This illustration is based on FIN 48, Appendix A, paragraph A33 (later FASB ASC 740–10–55–217).

material change to its financial position. It is reasonably possible that an additional payment in the range of $80 to $100 million will be made by the end of 2008.

Upon implementing FIN 48 as of January 1, 2007, USCo increased its liability for unrecognized tax benefits by approximately $200 million, which was accounted for as a reduction to its January 1, 2007 balance of retained earnings. Included in the balance at December 31, 2007 was $60 million of tax positions the deductibility of which is highly certain but the timing of the deductibility is uncertain. Because of the impact of deferred tax accounting, other than interest and penalties, the disallowance of the shorter deductibility period would not affect the annual effective tax rate but would accelerate the payment of cash to the taxing authority to an earlier period.

USCo recognizes accrued interest and penalties related to its unrecognized tax benefits as interest expense and penalties in operating expenses. During the years ended December 31, 2007, 2006, and 2005, USCo recognized approximately $10 million, $11 million, and $12 million in interest and penalties. USCo had approximately $60 and $50 million for the payment of interest and penalties accrued at December 31, 2007, and 2006, respectively.

A reconciliation of the beginning and ending amount of unrecognized tax benefits is as follows:

	(in thousands)
Balance at January 1, 2007	$ 370,000
Additions based on tax positions related to current year	10,000
Additions for tax positions of prior years	30,000
Reductions for tax positions of prior years	(60,000)
Settlements	(40,000)
Balance at December 31, 2007	$ 310,000

[2] Disclosure of Possible Recognition of Unrecognized Tax Benefits Within Succeeding 12-Month Period.

If a significant increase or decrease in total unrecognized tax benefits within the subsequent 12-month period is "reasonably possible," FASB ASC 740–10–50–15 requires disclosure of (a) the nature of the uncertainty, (b) the event causing the adjustment, and (c) either an estimated range of the amount of the possible tax position adjustment (or a statement that an estimate cannot be make).

Much debate and speculation has occurred as to whether these financial disclosure requirements provide the Service with a "roadmap" to a company's uncertain tax positions.[180] The SEC also monitors compliance by public companies with the FASB disclosure rules in their Form 10-K and 10-Q filings.[181] The disclosures included in SEC filings by public companies, including the 12-month disclosure under FASB ASC 740–

[180] *See* Section 3.08[2] and Section 3.09. UTP disclosures can also be expected to be reviewed by state and local taxing authorities, along with relevant foreign taxing jurisdictions.

[181] *See* Section 3.10[5].

10–50–15, have thus far been rather general, with generic depictions of the reporting company's aggregate unrecognized tax benefits.[182]

Even though public disclosure under the financial accounting rules for disclosure of uncertain tax positions may not provide a tax authority with a detailed roadmap of a company's questionable tax positions, such information does furnish the tax authority with a clear view of the "tip" of the potential uncertain tax position iceberg.[183] It can be expected that the IRS will concentrate on a company's UTP disclosure to determine what possible issues to review upon audit and what documents to request from, and questions to pose to, the taxpayer in the Information Document Requests (IDRs) that IRS makes during its audits.

The FASB ASC 740–10 requirement that a company provide financial statement disclosure relating to decreases in unrecognized tax benefits resulting from settlements with the taxing authority raises interesting issues. FASB ASC 740–10–25–8 states that a company is permitted to recognize the book benefit of any unrecognized tax position when that position is "effectively settled." FASB ASC 740–10–25–9[184] addresses when completion of a tax audit constitutes effective settlement of a tax position thus permitting the company to recognize the tax position benefit based on the completed audit.

Effective settlement occurs upon termination of an audit provided: (i) the tax authority has fully completed its exam, including any appeals and administrative reviews, (ii) the company does not intend to appeal or litigate the tax position, and (ii) subsequent examination or reexamination of the tax position is "remote." Significantly, the "remote" standard set forth in clause (iii) is applied by evaluating the tax authority's policy on reopening closed examinations.[185] If should be noted that if an exam occurs for the given tax year, a tax position need not be specifically reviewed by the tax authority to satisfy the "effectively settled" standard and, thus, upon completion of an audit that satisfies the above criteria, all uncertain tax positions generally are effectively settled based on the terms of the audit.[186]

---

[182] For example, one reporting company disclosed under FIN 48 that it is "difficult to project how unrecognized tax benefits will change over the next 12 months but is reasonably possible that they should change significantly." Another public company's FIN 48 disclosure stated that as of January 1, 2007, its liabilities for unrecognized tax benefits was approximately $945 million, and assuming that an IRS audit [relating to transfer pricing] is satisfactorily completed and assuming application of the proposed transfer pricing adjustments related to the company's transfer pricing tax positions to subsequent periods, the company believes it is reasonably possible that liabilities for unrecognized tax benefits may decrease by $350 million to $600 million within the next 12 months. Another illustrative FIN 48 disclosure set forth in a public filing with the SEC stated that it is "reasonably possible that [Company's] existing liabilities for uncertain tax benefits may increase or decrease within the next twelve months primarily due to the progression of audits in process or the expiration of statutes of limitation. [The Company] cannot reasonably estimate a range of potential changes in such benefits due to the unresolved nature of the various audits."

[183] Through mandatory training, the Service has instructed its auditors how to analyze FASB ASC 740–10 financial disclosures. *See* IRS LMSB Memorandum (LMSB 04–0507–044) *Updating Tax Accrual Workpaper Policy Following FIN 48* (May 10, 2007), reprinted in BNA Daily Tax Rep. at G-7 Jun. 27, 2007) (implementation of 6-hour mandatory CPE program providing guidance to Service auditors on how to use FIN 48 information and disclosure to conduct risk assessments). See also reported comments of Robert Adams, senior adviser to commissioner of the Service Large and Midsize Business Division, reported in 2007 Financial Reporting Watch 134–11 (Jul. 12, 2007) (through training, agents will use UTP disclosures as an audit tool).

[184] *See* Section 3.05[1].

[185] For purposes of this evaluation, the company must presume that the taxing authority is fully aware of all applicable information relating to the uncertain tax position.

[186] Effective settlement of a tax position for a specific tax period does not occur unless an audit is performed and completed for that tax period, even if similar or identical tax positions exist in other tax periods

[a] Reopening of Completed Tax Audit

A critical issue in recording an unrecognized tax benefit upon conclusion of an audit is whether it is remote that the tax authority will reopen the completed audit. Section 4.01(1) of Rev. Proc. 2005–32[187] provides that an agreed case is closed after examination when the Service furnishes the taxpayer with written notification of either the adjustments to the taxpayer's tax liability or acceptance of the taxpayer's tax return without change.[188] An examination involving an unagreed income issue is not closed until the period for filing a petition with the United States Tax Court has expired, as specified in the statutory notice of deficiency or notice of determination issued to the taxpayer.

Pursuant to the Internal Revenue Manual,[189] the Service's administrative practice generally has been not to reopen an audit to make an adjustment except for (i) fraud, malfeasance, collusion, concealment or misrepresentation of a material fact; (ii) a substantial error in the closed audit based on an established Service position; or (iii) circumstances indicating failure to reopen would be a serious administrative omission.[190] A serious administrative omission includes a limited examination involving a potentially abusive tax issue that was not reviewed, such as a reportable transaction within the meaning of Treas. Reg. § 1.6011–4(b).[191]

Although the Service has stated that it has no plans to modify its policy against reopening examinations absent exceptional circumstances, Service officials acknowledged that the additional disclosure of uncertain tax positions might result in more reopenings of completed audits.[192]

ILLUSTRATION 3-22:[193]

USCo, a public reporting corporation, does not report $75 million of dividend income on its 2007 U.S. federal income tax return based on uncertainty in the tax law. USCo's management has determined that this tax

---

that have been examined and closed. Also, it appears that uncertain tax positions relating to carryforward tax attributes in a specified carryover period, such as the use of a net operating loss carryover in a year subsequent to the year of the loss, are not effectively settled except to the extent that the specified carryover period (rather than the tax period during which the loss or other tax attribute arose) is subject to a closed audit.

[187] 2005–32 IRB 1206.

[188] A refund matter that is subject to review by the Joint Committee on Taxation under IRC Section 6405 is not closed until Joint Committee review and follow-up are complete. Further, a tax exam that is resolved with a closing agreement under IRC Section 7121 is not closed until the closing agreement is signed by an appropriate Service official. Rev. Proc. 2005–32.

[189] IRM Section 1.2.1.4.1, P–4–3 (Dec. 21, 1984).

[190] *See generally* IRC Section 7605(b) (only one audit of taxpayer generally permitted each taxable year unless the Service, after investigation, notifies the taxpayer in writing that an additional inspection is necessary). *See also* Rev. Proc. 2005–32, 2005–32 IRB 1206 (procedures for reopening examinations under IRC Section 7605(b), including when proceeding is deemed closed after IRS examination).

[191] Section 5.01(3) of Rev. Proc. 2005–32. Guidance regarding when an uncertain tax position is effectively settled for FIN 48 purposes offers the taxpayer an incentive to timely complete an audit in order to book the unrecognized tax benefits of the tax positions for the year of the audit. In addition, a taxpayer may accelerate the recognition of tax benefits for book purposes through other administrative procedures of the Service, including (i) industry issue resolution, (ii) pre-filing agreements (PFAs), (iii) advance pricing agreements (APAs), (iv) the fast track appeals program, and (v) the accelerated issue resolution.

[192] IRS LMSB Memorandum (LMSB–04–0507–045) on *FIN 48 Implications—LMSB Field Examiners' Guide Q & A 9*, reprinted in Daily Tax Rep. at G-7 (Jun. 27, 2007).

[193] This illustration is based on an example set forth in IRS LMSB Memorandum (LMSB–04–0507–045) on *FIN 48 Implications—LMSB Field Examiners' Guide*, reprinted in Daily Tax Rep. at G-7 (Jun. 27, 2007).

position satisfies the more likely than not recognition standard. USCo properly books 60 percent of the tax benefit on its financial statement, and creates a reserve for the unrecognized tax benefit relating to this position. During 2009, the Service audits USCo's 2007 tax return, but does not propose an adjustment for the dividend issue and closes the case. Upon completion of the audit, management concludes that it is remote that the Service would reopen the examination of the issue based on the Service's policy, and that the dividend income position is effectively settled. USCo thus reverses the contingent tax liability and records the unrecognized tax benefit for the position.

After the audit, if the dividend position is effectively settled within the meaning of FASB ASC 740–10–25–9, USCo will recognize in its financial statements the previously unrecognized tax benefit attributable to the dividend income. Assume that the Service completely overlooked the dividend issue during its audit and that the examiner, as part of her routine post-audit procedures, reviews USCo's financial statement disclosure relating to reductions in USCo's unrecognized tax benefits resulting from settlements and disclosure of reasonably possible recognition of unrecognized tax benefits in the succeeding 12-month period. Query if the examiner notices that USCo discloses a significant reduction in its unrecognized tax positions whether the Service will be inclined to reopen the audit to determine if there has been a serious administrative omission under IRM Section 1.2.1.4.1, P–4–3.

[b] Termination of Statute of Limitations Period

An issue similar to effective settlements with the Service of completed audits arises when the statute of limitations relating to a significant uncertain tax position is scheduled to expire within the next 12 months. As noted above, FASB ASC 740–10–50–15 requires a company to disclose the total amount of unrecognized tax benefits that, on a reasonably possible basis, will decrease within 12 month of the company's financial statement reporting date. The company must report of (i) the nature of the applicable uncertainty and event, and (ii) an estimate of the benefit reduction (or a statement that an estimate cannot be made).

ILLUSTRATION 3-23: The facts are the same as in Illustration 3-22, except that the Service does not audit USCo. Within 12 months of expiration of the applicable limitations period for 2007 (the tax year in which the dividend occurred), USCo discloses in its financial statements that it is reasonably possible that the full amount of liability for the unrecognized tax benefit relating to the dividend income issue will be eliminated due to the termination of the statute of limitations. Service Examination reviews the public disclosure and commences an audit of USCo for 2007 and prepares IDRs relating to the disclosure.

Illustration 3-23 highlights various interesting tax issues that might arise in connection with financial statement disclosure of tax positions. For example, USCo may determine that it is strategically advantageous not to extend the statute of limitations if requested by the Service.[194] Query how specific USCo's disclosure must be (i.e., how

[194] Audit Technique Guidelines, published in IRS LMSB Memorandum (LMSB–04–0507–045) on *FIN 48 Implications—LMSB Field Examiners' Guide*, reprinted in Daily Tax Rep. at G-7 (Jun. 27, 2007), alert Service auditors that taxpayers may desire to tightly control the statute of limitations during an audit, especially if the taxpayer has a motivation to release the contingent tax liabilities into earnings for financial accounting purposes.

general can the disclosure of the uncertainty relating to the dividend income be under FASB ASC 740–10).

[3] Disclosures Revealed in Public Filings

[a] General

Uncertain tax position disclosures have been very general in nature, and many disclosures of specific issues have discussed either existing audits (which the applicable tax authority is obviously already aware of) or broadly described issues (such as transfer pricing positions without mention of the specific issue or foreign jurisdiction involved).[195] Based on a limited review of SEC annual reports for public companies for the year ending December 31, 2011, the disclosures of uncertain tax positions under the FASB's UTP rules continue to involve a substantial amount of uncertain tax benefits.[196] It does not appear that the disclosures to date have provided the taxing authorities with a clear roadmap of a company's uncertain tax positions.[197]

[b] Retained Earnings Adjustment at Adoption

The cumulative effect of initially adopting the FASB rules on accounting for uncertain income tax positions had to be separately reflected in the beginning retained earnings balance (or other appropriate components of equity or net assets in the statement of financial position).[198] The cumulative adjustment equaled the difference between the net assets and liabilities recognized in the previous statement of financial position and the recognized net assets and liabilities resulting from adoption of FASB's UTP rules.[199] Accordingly, a company whose liability for unrecognized income tax benefits increased as a result of adopting the FASB rules on accounting for uncertain

---

[195] *See generally*, Wright, *10–Q FIN 48 Disclosures Show Firms Uncertain About How Transfer Pricing Positions Will Be Viewed,* 16 Transfer Pricing Report 123 (Tax Mgt. Jun. 27, 2007) (reviewing the first quarter 2007 SEC filings made by 30 large multinational companies between April 1, 2007 and May 11, 2007 which made transfer pricing disclosures and setting forth in annotated form the transfer pricing disclosures for those companies). *See generally The Seigel Tax Reserve Report 2008 Full Year Update* (based on analysis of 2008 SEC annual reports of 790 public companies having annual revenue of at least $2 billion, concluded that only 67 percent satisfactorily complied with the minimum disclosure requirements, with the greatest noncompliance consisting of failure to disclose the total amount of interest and penalties expensed, closely followed by inadequate disclosure of the "12-month look forward" requirement of paragraph 21(d) of FIN 48 (FASB ASC 740–10–50–15)).

[196] *See* Wright, *Ford Motor Co. Lists $1.8 Billion In Unrecognized Tax Benefits for 2011,* Daily Tax Rep., at I-1 (Apr. 11, 2012) (noting that Ford Motor Co. reported $1.8 billion in unrecognized tax benefits for the year ending Dec. 31, 2011, an increase of $700 million from the prior year, and disclosed several transfer pricing disputes in unnamed jurisdictions from 1994; and selected other filing companies likewise disclosed unrecognized tax benefits based on a variety of tax issues ranging from transfer pricing matters and the expiration of statutes of limitations to research and development tax credits).

[197] Interestingly, it has been suggested that FASB ASC 740–1 (FIN 48) insurance might be an effective tool for companies to mitigate the UTP risk and insure against the tax, interest, and penalties in the event an insured tax position is successfully challenged by a taxing authority. *See* Tax Executives Institute, *FIN 48: Insurance for When the IRS Doesn't Recognize What You Did* (Aug. 31, 2009).

[198] *See* FIN 48, paragraph 23. For the year in which FIN 48 was adopted, this cumulative effect had to be disclosed in the statement of financial position as of the FIN 48 adoption date. *See* FIN 48, paragraph 24. With respect to companies applying purchase accounting, however, the cumulative effect of adopting FIN 48 had to be recorded as an adjustment to goodwill. *See* FIN 48, paragraph 23. Another 2007 study, Zion and Varshney, *Peeking Behind the Tax Curtain* (Credit Suisse) (May 18, 2007) reviewed 361 S&P 500 companies and found that 62 of the companies each disclosed in excess of $500 million of unrecognized tax benefits (36 of those companies reported over $1 billion of unrecognized tax benefits). This report studied the correlation between each company's unrecognized tax benefits to the company's market capitalization.

[199] *See* FIN 48, paragraph 23.

income tax positions in essence obtained a one-time "free pass" since the corresponding book adjustment was to reduce retained earnings, rather than reduce the company's profit (or increase the company's loss) on its profit and loss (P&L) statement.[200]

> **ILLUSTRATION 3-24:** USCo deducted an amount on its 2005 U.S. federal income tax return that results in a tax benefit of $10 million. USCo applied pre-FIN 48 accounting rules to create a tax reserve of $6 million on its financial statements and reflected a book benefit of $4 million for that tax position. USCo determined that this tax position did not satisfy the more-likely-than-not recognition standard and, therefore, USCo was not entitled to recognize any of the tax benefit relating to that deduction when FIN 48 (FASB ASC 740–10) became effective. Upon adopting FIN 48 (FASB ASC 740–10), USCo had to increase its liability for unrecognized tax positions, and correspondingly reduced the beginning balance of its retained earnings by the unrecognized tax benefit of $4 million. This decrease in the beginning balance of retained earnings (along with the other cumulative increases and decreases to retained earnings resulting from implementing FIN 48 (FASB ASC 740–10)) was not reflected in USCo's book income or loss.

The cumulative adjustment to retained earnings, which only applies with respect to adoption, raised the potential of "smoothing out" a company's earnings by (i) over-accruing the FIN 48 (FASB ASC 740–10) liability upon implementing FIN 48 (FASB ASC 740–10), and (ii) releasing the excess FIN 48 (FASB ASC 740–10) liability in subsequent periods to increase book income and improve financial earnings. Of course, financial statement disclosure of a significant decrease to a company's beginning retained earnings upon adoption might have alerted the Service to the possibility of pre-2007 tax positions that did not meet the more likely than not standard and thus might have drawn unwanted attention to those return filing positions.

This situation could likewise have arisen for those companies that adopted aggressive tax positions prior to FIN 48 but established small tax reserves on their financial statements. Conversely, a company that recorded a significant reduction to its retained earnings balance pursuant to FIN 48 (FASB ASC 740–10) might simply be the result of the application of the provisions of ambiguous tax law to complex business transactions. FIN 48 (FASB ASC 740–10) provided those companies with a potential "free pass" by increasing the company's tax reserve without a corresponding book expense recorded on its income statement (i.e., the corresponding entry is a reduction to beginning retained earnings) upon adoption. On the other hand, those companies that were conservative in reporting their pre-FIN 48 (FASB ASC 740–10) transactions and other activities for both tax and accounting typically would have had a relatively small adjustment to their liability for uncertain tax positions when FIN 48 (FASB ASC 740–10) became effective.

[c] Quarterly SEC Disclosure—Interim Reporting Clarified

Although FASB ASC 740–10–50–15 mandates financial statement disclosure at the end of each annual reporting period, public companies are required to disclose events

---

[200] Of course, those companies that increased retained earnings when FIN 48 became effective (because they reduced their initial FIN 48 liabilities), and later are required to adjust their historic uncertain tax positions by increasing their FIN 48 (FASB ASC 740–10) liability, will be disadvantaged by increasing their book income.

that have occurred since the previous year end that have a material impact on the company under applicable SEC reporting rules. Upon adoption of a new accounting pronouncement during an interim reporting period, the SEC staff has generally required, pursuant to Rule 10–01(a)(5) of Regulation S–X, that all disclosures required by the new accounting pronouncement (i) be provided in the interim Form 10-Q period financial statements, and (ii) continue to be provided in each subsequent interim period until annual financial statements are filed on Form 10.

[d] Annual Disclosure—Examples

As noted above,[201] the FASB rules on accounting for uncertain income tax positions require a company to annually disclose in its financial statements, among other items, a reconciliation of the total beginning and ending unrecognized tax benefits for the period, including the aggregate increases and decreases to tax positions from both the current and prior years, and decreases from tax settlements and lapses of tax statute of limitations.

Below are four representative FIN 48 disclosures made by public companies in their annual Form 10-K or other filings with the SEC, which are available at https://www.sec.gov/edgar/searchedgar/companysearch.html.

> Twitter, Inc., Form 10-K, filed February 16, 2022, for period ending December 31, 2021
>
> At December 31, 2021, the Company had $2.39 billion of U.S. federal, $1.36 billion of U.S. state, $151.5 million of Ireland, and $55.6 million of Brazil net operating losses. The federal and state net operating losses will begin to expire in 2034 and 2024, respectively, if not utilized. The Ireland and Brazil net operating losses have no expiration date. The Company also has $494.8 million and $349.4 million of U.S. federal and state research credit carryforwards, respectively. The U.S. federal credit carryforward will begin to expire in 2027, if not utilized. The majority of state research tax credits have no expiration date. A small portion of state research tax credits will begin to expire in 2030, if not utilized. Additionally, the Company has California Enterprise Zone Credit carryforwards of $16.4 million which will begin to expire in 2023, if not utilized. Utilization of the U.S. net operating loss and credit carryforwards may be subject to an annual limitation due to the ownership change limitations provided by the Internal Revenue Code of 1986, as amended (the Code), and similar state provisions. Utilization of the foreign net operating losses may be subject to limitation based on the nature of income earned. Any annual limitation may result in the expiration of net operating losses and credits before utilization.
>
> As of December 31, 2021, the Company had $401.4 million of unrecognized tax benefits, of which $309.5 million could result in a reduction of the Company's effective tax rate, if recognized. The remainder of the unrecognized tax benefits would not affect the effective tax rate due to the full valuation allowance recorded for California and Massachusetts deferred tax assets.

[201] *See* Section 3.08[1].

A reconciliation of the beginning and ending amount of unrecognized tax benefit is as follows (in thousands):

	Year Ended December 31,		
	2021	2020	2019
Gross unrecognized tax benefits at the beginning of the year	$ 354,598	$ 419,858	$ 332,314
Increases related to prior year tax positions	3,365	5,943	54,743
Decreases related to prior year tax positions	(5,296)	(99,540)	(2,537)
Increases related to current year tax positions	50,468	28,337	35,338
Statute of limitations expirations	(1,770)	—	—
Gross unrecognized tax benefits at the end of the year	$ 401,365	$ 354,598	$ 419,858

Total unrecognized tax benefits are recorded on the Company's consolidated balance sheets as follows (in thousands):

	December 31,	
	2021	2020
Total unrecognized tax benefits balance	$ 401,365	$ 354,598
Amounts netted against related deferred tax assets	(369,312)	(331,339)
Unrecognized tax benefits recorded on consolidated balance sheets	$ 32,053	$ 23,259

The Company recognizes interest and/or penalties related to income tax matters as a component of income tax expense. During the years ended December 31, 2021, 2020, and 2019, the Company recognized immaterial amounts of interest and penalties in income tax expense. As of December 31, 2021and 2020, the Company had $7.6 million and $7.2 million of interest and penalties included in uncertain tax positions, respectively.

The Company is subject to taxation in the United States and various foreign jurisdictions. Earnings from non-U.S. activities are subject to local country income tax. The material jurisdictions where the Company is subject to potential examination by tax authorities include the United States, California and Ireland. The Company believes that it has reserved adequate amounts for these jurisdictions. The Company's 2007 to 2020 tax attributes remain subject to potential examination by the United States and California, and its 2017 to 2020 tax years remain subject to potential examination in Ireland. The Company remains subject to potential examination in various other jurisdictions that are not expected to result in material tax adjustments. The Company does not believe that its unrecognized tax benefits will materially change within the next 12 months.

La-Z-Boy Inc., Form 10-K, filed June 21, 2022, for period ending April 30, 2022

As of April 30, 2022, we had a gross unrecognized tax benefit of $1.0 million related to uncertain tax positions in various jurisdictions. A reconciliation of the beginning and ending balance of these unrecognized tax benefits is as follows:

(Amounts in thousands)	Fiscal Year Ended (53 weeks) 4/30/2022	(52 weeks) 4/24/2021	(52 weeks) 4/25/2020
Balance at the beginning of the period	$ 1,069	$ 1,030	$ 1,069
Additions:			
Positions taken during the current year	121	176	174
Positions taken during the prior year	10	35	106
Reductions:			
Positions taken during the prior year	(23)	(19)	—
Decreases related to settlements with taxing authorities	—	—	(211)
Reductions resulting from the lapse of the statute of limitations	(140)	(153)	(108)
Balance at the end of the period	$ 1,037	$ 1,069	$ 1,030

We recognize interest and penalties associated with uncertain tax positions in income tax expense. We had approximately $0.4 million accrued for interest and penalties as of April 30, 2022 and April 24, 2021.

If recognized, $0.9 million of the total $1.0 million of unrecognized tax benefits would decrease our effective tax rate. We do not expect that the net liability for uncertain income tax positions will significantly change within the next 12 months. The remaining balance will be settled or released as tax audits are effectively settled, statutes of limitation expire, or other new information becomes available.

Our U.S. federal income tax returns for fiscal years 2019 and subsequent are still subject to audit. In addition, we conduct business in various states. The major states in which we conduct business are subject to audit for fiscal years 2018 and subsequent. Our foreign operations are subject to audit for fiscal years 2012 and subsequent.

Cash paid for taxes (net of refunds received) during the fiscal years ended April 30, 2022, April 24, 2021, and April 25, 2020, was $38.6 million, $40.5 million, and $24.7 million, respectively.

Tessco Technologies, Inc., Form 10-K, filed May 26, 2022, for period ending March 27, 2022

As of March 27, 2022 and March 28, 2021, the Company had no unrecognized tax benefits.

The Company's accounting policy with respect to interest and penalties related to tax uncertainties is to classify these amounts as part of the provision for income taxes. The total amount of interest and penalties related to tax uncertainties recognized in the Consolidated Statements of Income (Loss) was $0 for fiscal years 2022, 2021 and 2020. The cumulative amount included in the Consolidated Balance Sheets as of March 27, 2022 and March 28, 2021 was $0.

Apple, Inc., Form 10-K, filed October 29, 2021, for period ending September 25, 2021

Uncertain Tax Positions

As of September 25, 2021, the total amount of gross unrecognized tax benefits was $15.5 billion, of which $6.6 billion, if recognized, would impact the Company's effective tax rate. As of September 26, 2020, the total amount of gross unrecognized tax benefits was $16.5 billion, of which $8.8 billion, if recognized, would have impacted the Company's effective tax rate.

The aggregate change in the balance of gross unrecognized tax benefits, which excludes interest and penalties, for 2021, 2020 and 2019, is as follows (in millions):

	2021	2020	2019
Beginning balances	$ 16,475	$ 15,619	$ 9,694
Increases related to tax positions taken during a prior year	816	454	5,845
Decreases related to tax positions taken during a prior year	(1,402)	(791)	(686)
Increases related to tax positions taken during the current year	1,607	1,347	1,697
Decreases related to settlements with taxing authorities	(1,838)	(85)	(852)
Decreases related to expiration of the statute of limitations	(181)	(69)	(79)
Ending balances	$ 15,477	$ 16,475	$ 15,619

The Company is subject to taxation and files income tax returns in the U.S. federal jurisdiction and many state and foreign jurisdictions. Tax years after 2015 for the U.S. federal jurisdiction, and after 2014 in certain major foreign jurisdictions, remain subject to examination. Although the timing of resolution and/or closure of examinations is not certain, the Company believes it is reasonably possible that its gross unrecognized tax benefits could decrease in the next 12 months by as much as $1.2 billion.

[4] SEC Monitoring of UTP Disclosures

A public company's disclosure under the FASB rules on accounting for uncertain income tax positions is reviewed not only by the company's independent auditors as part of their financial audit, but also by the SEC when the company submits its Form 10-K and 10-Qs. The staff of the SEC reviews a reporting company's annual and quarterly SEC filings and monitors the company's compliance with the disclosure rules. Set forth are typical illustrations (annotated) of comments made by the SEC staff relating to FIN 48 (later FASB ASC 740–10) disclosure based on the company's preliminary filing, and the reporting company's response, which are available at www.sec.gov/edgar.

Sample Company 1

SEC Comment.

Based on the information in note ___, we calculate your domestic federal effective tax rate for the U.S. in 2015 to be ___ %. Please explain to us the reasons why the domestic federal effective tax rate was so much higher than your statutory rate.

Company Response.

The Company respectfully advises that the Staff appears to have calculated the ___ % domestic federal effective tax rate based on the Company's 2015 federal current and deferred taxes of $ ___ billion and U.S. pre-tax income of $ ___ billion disclosed in Note of the Company's Form 10-K. Included in the Company's 2015 federal current income tax expense are the effects of unrecognized tax benefits related to licensing arrangements between wholly-owned entities measured under the criteria of ASC 740–10–25–16 as further discussed in response to questions below, which increased the effective tax rate in 2015. In addition, the effective tax rate in 2015 was further increased by the impact of taxes on non-deductible share-based compensation which have the effect of increasing the domestic federal effective tax rate.

SEC Comment.

We note from your remarks in an earnings call dated ___, 2016, that you anticipate your full year GAAP tax rates to be ________ % on a percentage basis and that you expect your tax rate will decline further over time and resemble those for your global peers over the next several years. Please tell us the reasons for your expectation of a decreasing effective tax rate from ___ % in 2015 to ___ % on a percent-age basis.

Company Response.

The Company respectfully advises the Staff that, as discussed in the Company's earnings call dated ________, 2016, the Company anticipates that its GAAP effective tax rate will decrease from ___ % in 2015 to a lower effective tax rate in 2016. This expectation is primarily due to a forecasted increase in the proportion of consolidated pre-tax income being earned in jurisdictions with tax rates lower than the United States. Additionally, the Company noted the following trend in the MD&A; section of its Form 10-Q filing for the first quarter of 2016: Our effective tax rate in the first quarter of 2016 decreased compared to the same period in 2015, primarily due to an increase in pre-tax income in jurisdictions with tax rates lower than the United States.

The Company intends to indefinitely reinvest a majority of its 2016 foreign earnings pursuant to ASC 740–10–25–3(a)(1) such that the Company expects that it will not accrue the incremental U.S. tax in 2016 on those earnings, reducing the effective tax rate accordingly. In 2015, the Company was unable to indefinitely reinvest in these countries as the countries were in a cumulative deficit position. The Company further advises the Staff that as discussed in response to the question below, the Company will make the disclosures required by ASC 740–30–50–2 related to undistributed earnings of subsidiaries in future filings to the extent the disclosure is applicable.

SEC Comment.

We note that your domestic income before provision for income taxes decreased from $ _____ billion in 2014 to $ _____ billion in 2015. Conversely, we note that your foreign income before provision for income taxes increased from a loss of $ _____ million in 2014 to income of $ _____ billion in 2015. Please tell us what caused this shift. In addition, identify for us the jurisdictions in which you generate significant pre-tax income and the related amounts that comprise the $ ___ billion of foreign pre-tax income in 2015. Please also clarify the jurisdictions that comprise the $ ___ million foreign pre-tax loss in 2014. Last, tell us how this shift affected your consolidated effective tax rate, and describe and quantify for us any reasons that offset the effects of this shift in 2015.

Company Response.

The Company respectfully advises the Staff that the shift in domestic income before provision for income taxes from 2014 to 2015 was related to certain transactions between wholly-owned entities that occurred in 2014 but that did not recur in 2015. The shift in pretax income related to the Company's foreign subsidiaries provided a benefit to its consolidated effective tax rate since this pre-tax income was earned in jurisdictions with tax rates lower than rates in the United States. The effect of the shift in pretax income related to the Company's foreign subsidiaries was, however, offset by the effects of unrecognized tax benefits related to the licensing arrangements between wholly-owned entities pursuant to ASC 740–10–25–16. This unrecognized tax benefit comprised the majority of the increase to the current year tax positions disclosed in the roll-forward of gross unrecognized tax benefits noted in Note ___, Income Taxes, on the Company's Form 10K and as further discussed in response to the question, below.

The Company further advises the Staff that its significant jurisdictions are the US and ______. The substantial majority of the $ _____ billion of foreign pre-tax income in 2015 and $ _____ million of foreign pre-tax loss in 2014 were from the foreign jurisdiction of ______.

SEC Comment.

We note your gross unrecognized tax benefits increased from $ _____ billion at December 31, 2014, to $ _____ billion at December 31, 2015. Please explain to us where this increase is presented in your reconciliation of the U.S. federal statutory income tax rate to your effective tax rate.

Company Response.

The Company respectfully advises the Staff that pursuant to ASC 740–10–25–6, the increase in its gross unrecognized tax benefits is related to a number of uncertain tax positions, not all of which impact the Company's effective tax rate. To the extent that there is an impact to the effective tax rate, the change in the unrecognized tax benefit is allocated to the respective line items in the effective tax rate reconciliation as required by Regulation § 210.4–08(h)(2) (e.g., unrecognized tax benefits related to U.S. federal tax credits from research and development are netted against the "Research tax credits" line item and unrecognized tax benefits related to certain transactions between wholly-owned entities affecting non-U.S. operations are netted against the "Effects of non-U.S. operations" line item).

SEC Comment.

Please provide the disclosures required by ASC 740–30–50–2 related to undistributed earnings of subsidiaries and corporate joint ventures, or tell us why they are not required.

Company Response.

The Company respectfully advises the Staff that ASC 740–30–50–2 requires the disclosure of information related to deferred tax liabilities not recognized for taxable temporary differences because of the exceptions to the comprehensive recognition of deferred tax liabilities. The disclosures required by ASC 740–30–50–2 were not required because the Company did not have any material jurisdictions in cumulative surplus positions where deferred tax liabilities had not been recorded. Furthermore, the only instance where the Company has not recognized a deferred tax liability relates to subsidiaries that were in cumulative deficits as of December 31, 2015 and accordingly no deferred tax liabilities would be required. The cumulative deficits were related to the entities that are attributable to the foreign jurisdiction of ___. All of the Company's other entities have provided residual deferred taxes as disclosed in Note ________________________. Income Taxes, of the Company's Form 10-K. The Company respectfully advises the Staff that as discussed in response to question 1, above, the Company will make the disclosures required by ASC 740–30–50–2 related to undistributed earnings of subsidiaries in future filings to the extent they become applicable.

Sample Company 2

SEC Comment.

In connection with the recognition of the loss related to the settlement of the ________ Proceeding, we note that you recognized a tax benefit of $ _____ billion net of a $ _____ billion uncertain tax position due to the uncertainty related to the deductibility of the final settlement payment. Disclosure in your Form 10-K for the fiscal year ended December 31, 2013 states that a deferred tax benefit of $ _____ million was recognized as you concluded that it is more likely than not that ___ % of the $_million loss recognized in _____ will be deductible for U.S. tax purposes. Please tell us why an uncertain tax position for the deferred tax benefit recognized was not deemed necessary as of December 31, 2015, but was deemed necessary as of March 31, 2014. Refer to FASB ASC 740–10–30.

Company Response.

The Company evaluated the tax treatment of future payments attributable to the _____ Proceeding under the more-likely-than-not standard of FASB ASC 740–10–25–5 for the fiscal year ended December 31, 2013. Applying that standard, the Company determined that ___ % of any future payment related to the ______________ Proceeding would be deductible up to an estimated threshold and that___% would not be deductible. The contingent loss recorded at December 31, 2013_, was below the amount the Company determined is deductible under the more-likely-than-not standard of FASB ASC 740–10–25–5; and therefore, there was no uncertain tax position related to the amount recorded at December 31, 2013. The additional contingent loss recorded for the quarter ended March 31, 2014, was in excess of the amount the Company determined is deductible under the more-likely-than-not standard of FASB ASC 740–10–25–5. Accordingly, with respect to such excess amount, the Company recognized an uncertain tax position because it is expected that there will be a difference between the amount claimed on a tax return and the amount recorded as a tax benefit for financial statement purposes.

Sample Company 3

SEC Comment.

Reference is made to the disclosures regarding Notices of Proposed Adjustment from the IRS for the ___ and ___ calendar years relating to transfer pricing with your foreign subsidiaries. Please explain to us how you consider and historically considered transfer pricing when evaluating tax contingencies and the required tax contingency disclosures. In doing so, please tell us when you received the Notices of Proposed Adjustment, the approximate time you learned of the IRS position on your transfer pricing, why your tax contingencies at December 31, 2009, December 31, 2010, and March 31, 2011 are significantly less than the approximate $ ___ billion potential federal income tax expense impact disclosed and how you have satisfied the disclosure requirements of ASC 740–10–50–15d.

<u>Company Response</u>.

As part of our quarterly close process, Tax and Accounting team members review and evaluate our existing and new uncertain tax positions, including those related to transfer pricing. They consider all relevant facts and circumstances including communications from tax authorities, statutes of limitations, relevant court cases, existing legislation and other information. In addition, for purposes of meeting the disclosure requirements of ASC 740–10–50–15d, they evaluate whether it is reasonably possible that the total amount of income tax contingencies will significantly increase or decrease within twelve months of the relevant reporting date.

Since the 20 ___ establishment of our European headquarters, we have consistently disclosed that transfer pricing is a significant component of our tax contingencies. In our 20 10-K, we disclosed that we transferred assets from the U.S. to other countries with the establishment of our European headquarters, which may result in transfer pricing exposure. Specifically, . . ., we transferred certain of our operating assets in 2006 and 2010 from the U.S. to international locations. These transfers resulted in taxable income and exposure to additional taxable income assertions by taxing jurisdictions. Additionally, in each 10-K from 20 ___ to 20 ___, we consistently disclosed that transfer pricing is a primary component of our tax contingencies.

The IRS audited our transfer pricing relating to our___ and federal tax returns through an examination which principally took place between _____ and ___. On __________, we received a Notice of Proposed Adjustment ("+") from the IRS that proposed an adjustment to a portion of our transfer pricing. The NOPA was not material and represented approximately ___% of the $ _____ billion in potential federal tax expense contingencies that we subsequently disclosed. On __________, we received a draft valuation report from consultants hired by the IRS, which included a valuation of assets transferred as part of the establishment of our European headquarters, and the IRS asked us to comment on the report. Representatives from the Company, the IRS, and the consultant met several times between __________ and __________ to discuss, among other things, this report. On __________, we received the final valuation report from the consultant, which revised and modified the __________ draft but retained the same valuation. On __________, we received a second NOPA which relied on the consultants' final January report and which, together with the first NOPA, resulted in our disclosure of the approximate $ _____ billion potential federal income tax expense impact. This second NOPA was our first official notification from the IRS regarding its preliminary position on the potential incremental transfer pricing impact. Even NOPAs, however, are proposed adjustments that are preliminary in nature and subject to negotiation and change until the IRS examination team issues the Revenue Agent's Report at the conclusion of the audit.

Based on our interpretation of the relevant regulations and case law, including a recently-issued, taxpayer-favorable tax court decision that provides further support to our analysis, we disagree with the two transfer pricing NOPAs. Accordingly, we intend to vigorously contest these two NOPAs, and to pursue all available administrative and, if necessary, judicial remedies. However, because of the amounts involved in the second NOPA, we disclosed in our First Quarter 20 10-Q that these NOPAs proposed an increase to our U.S. taxable income, which would result in additional federal tax expense over a seven-year period beginning in 20___totaling approximately $ _____ billion, subject to interest.

Our reserves for income tax contingencies at __________ of $_____ million, at __________ of $_____ million, and at __________ of $_____million, represent management's best judgment given the facts, circumstances, and information available at the time. We consider many factors when evaluating and estimating our tax positions and tax benefits, which may require periodic adjustments and which may not accurately forecast actual outcomes. We believe that our existing reserves for income tax contingencies, which include amounts related to transfer pricing, among other tax contingencies, but are less than the amounts proposed by the IRS in these two transfer pricing NOPAs, represent adjustments that are more than 50% likely of being realized.

<u>Sample Company 4</u>

<u>SEC Comment</u>.

The revised disclosure included in your response to our comment addresses the nature of the events that could occur in the next 12 months, but it does not appear to address the requirement of ASC 740–10–50–15(d)(1) for disclosure of the nature of the uncertain tax position. Please revise your disclosure in future filings. Also refer to ASC 740–10–55–217.

<u>Company Response</u>.

We acknowledge the Staff's comment and we will provide these additional disclosures in future filings beginning with our Form 10-Q for the quarter ended June 30, 2016. Using the disclosure in our Form 10-Q for the quarter ended March 31, 2016 as an example, the following is an illustration of future proposed disclosures (proposed new disclosures shown in underlined and bolded text), updated from our previous response:

The Company is currently under examination by the Internal Revenue Service for the 20_ through 20_ tax years and [state] Tax Board for the 20_ and 20_ tax years. At this time, the Company is not able to estimate the potential impact that the examination may have on income tax expense. If the examinations are resolved unfavorably, there is a possibility it may have a material negative impact on the Company's results of operations. At March 31, 2016 and December 31, 2015, the Company's gross unrecognized tax benefits was $ _____ million and $ _____ million, respectively. If recognized, $ _____ million of these unrecognized tax benefits (net of federal benefit) at March 31, 2016 would be recorded as a reduction of future income tax provision. These unrecognized tax benefits relate primarily to unresolved matters with taxing authorities regarding the Company's transfer pricing positions and tax positions based on the Company's interpretation of certain U.S. trial and appellate court decisions, which remain subject to appeal and therefore could be overturned in future periods. The Company's existing tax positions will continue to generate an increase in unrecognized tax benefits in subsequent periods. Management believes events that could occur in the next 12 months and cause a material change in unrecognized tax benefits include, but are not limited to, the completion of examinations by the U.S. or foreign taxing authorities and the expiration of statute of limitations on the Company's tax returns. Although the completion, settlement and closure of any audits is uncertain, it is reasonably possible that the total amount of unrecognized tax benefits will materially increase within the next 12 months. However, given the number of years remaining that are subject to examination, the range of the reasonably possible change cannot be estimated reliably.

<u>Sample Company 5</u>

<u>SEC Comment</u>.

You indicate that tax contingencies and other tax liabilities increased due to transfer pricing developments in certain foreign tax jurisdictions. Explain the nature and effect of these transfer pricing developments. In addition, tell us what consideration was given to enhancing your disclosure to indicate the possible impact on your effective tax rate if certain tax jurisdictions are taxed at a higher rate as a result of these developments. Further, consider disclosing the amount of foreign income before taxes for each tax jurisdiction that has a lower tax rate than your statutory tax rate.

<u>Company Response</u>.

The increase in our tax contingencies balance in the third quarter of fiscal year___primarily relates to accruals for transfer pricing developments in connection with a tax audit in the foreign jurisdiction of _____. These developments primarily relate to our acquisition of __________ and subsequent integration into ________. As the potential related tax liability is creditable in the US, for which we recorded an increase in other long-term assets, these developments do not have a material impact on our effective tax rate and therefore we determined that the developments did not warrant further disclosure. The foreign jurisdictions that have a material impact on our effective tax rate are ________________, _____, and ___. We disclose these in our MD&A and our tax footnote. In addition, we quantify and disclose the collective impact of these jurisdictions on our effective tax rate in our effective tax rate reconciliation in our income tax footnote annually in our Form 10-K. We considered disclosing income before income taxes by country but believe our disclosures convey the material drivers of our effective tax rate and are consistent with the current rules and regulations. If the distribution of our income materially changes, we will modify our tax disclosures in future filings.

<u>SEC Comment</u>.

You disclose that the ________ acquisition was structured in a manner that enabled you to utilize a substantial portion of the cash, cash equivalents, short-term investments and long-term investments held by certain of your foreign subsidiaries in a tax efficient manner. Please explain to us the ways in which the structure of the acquisition was tax efficient.

Company Response.

The Company advises the Staff that in preparation for the closing of the________acquisition, the Company arranged to jointly fund and acquire______'s U.S. operations (including ________ Corporation which is the U.S. parent entity) with one of the Company's non U.S. affiliates and, through post transaction closing integration steps, caused the Company's non U.S. affiliate to acquire the key non U.S. affiliates of________ while __________ (the U.S. parent of the Company) acquired and retained the U.S. affiliates and the remaining non U.S. affiliates of ________. Given the substantial value of ______'s key foreign entities relative to ______'s overall value, a significant portion of the Company's offshore cash, cash equivalents, short-term investments and long-term investments were used in the public ________ transaction and in turn funded the acquisition of ________'s key foreign affiliates. The utilization of the Company's non-U.S. cash in the acquisition in the foregoing manner was more tax efficient than had the Company's offshore earnings been repatriated to the U.S.

SEC Comment.

We note from your tax rate reconciliation that the impact of your foreign income taxed at lower than the federal rate was a benefit of $ _____ billion in 2016 which was more than your computed expected income tax provision of $ _____ million. Please tell us the amount and nature of each significant reconciling item included in the benefit and briefly describe the factual circumstances of your tax holiday, the per share effects of the tax holiday, and the date upon which the special tax status terminates. Revise future filings to include all of the disclosures required by ASC 740–10–50–12 and SAB Topic 11C.

Company Response.

The Company advises the Staff that the Company's foreign jurisdiction of_____ manufacturing operations are currently subject to numerous tax holidays granted to the Company based on its investment in property, plant and equipment in the foreign jurisdiction of___. The Company's tax holiday periods in the foreign jurisdiction of ______ expire at various times in the future, however, the Company actively seeks to obtain new tax holidays. The Company does not expect the future expiration of any of its tax holiday periods in the foreign jurisdiction of_____ to have a material impact on its effective tax rate. In fiscal 2016, the aggregate dollar benefits derived from these tax holidays was approximately $ ___________ million and increased the Company's basic net income per common share by $ _____. The remaining material components of foreign income taxed at a rate lower than the U.S. are earnings accrued in the foreign jurisdiction of_____ at a _____ % statutory tax rate and earnings accrued by ________'s offshore technology company which is resident in the foreign jurisdiction of ___________ at a 0% statutory tax rate. At their statutory rates, the income accrued in these jurisdictions provides a rate benefit compared to the U.S. of $ _____ billion. These two jurisdictions plus the tax holiday in the foreign jurisdiction of ___ make up ___ % of the total $

___________ billion benefit of foreign income taxes at a lower rate than the federal rate.

SEC Comment.

In future filings, revise the Provision of Income Taxes section of Management's Discussion and Analysis to include a more robust discussion of these foreign income related tax benefits, including the likely impact on your future results and the periods over which you expect they will have the impact. Refer to Item 303(a)(3) of Regulation S-K.

Company Response.

In response to the Staff's comment, in future filings, the Company will revise the language that was used in "Income Taxes" in the Company's Annual Report on Form 10-K for the year end March 31, 2016 to read as follows:

The foreign tax rate differential benefit primarily relates to the Company's operations in the foreign jurisdiction of _____, the foreign jurisdiction of ________ and the foreign jurisdiction of ______. The Company's manufacturing operations the foreign jurisdiction of are currently subject to numerous tax holidays granted to the Company based on its investment in property, plant and equipment in the foreign jurisdiction of _____. The Company's tax holiday periods in the foreign jurisdiction of ________ expire at various times in the future, however, the Company actively seeks to obtain new tax holidays. The Company does not expect the future expiration of any of its tax holiday periods in the foreign jurisdiction of ________ to have a material impact on its effective tax rate. The aggregate dollar benefits derived from these tax holidays approximated $ __________________________ million, $ ________ million and $ ___ million in fiscal 2016, 2015 and 2014, respectively. The geographic dispersion of earnings and losses contributes to the period-to-period changes in the Company's effective tax rates. Approximately ___ % of the Company's current year earnings from continuing operations before income taxes was generated in the U.S. at a combined federal and state effective tax rate that is higher than the Company's overall effective tax rate. The Company is also subject to taxation in many other jurisdictions where it has operations. The effective tax rates that the Company pays in these jurisdictions vary widely, but they are generally lower than the Company's combined U.S. federal and state effective tax rate. The Company's domestic statutory tax rates for fiscal years 2016 and 2015 were approximately ___ %. The Company's non-U.S. blended statutory tax rates for fiscal years 2016 and 2015 were much lower than this. The difference in rates applicable in foreign jurisdictions results from a number of factors, including lower statutory rates, historical loss carry-forwards, financing arrangements and other factors. The Company's effective tax rate has been, and will continue to be impacted by the geographical dispersion of the Company's earnings and losses. To the extent that domestic earnings increase while the foreign earnings remain flat or decrease, or increase at a lower rate, the Company's effective tax rate will increase.

Public companies must disclose the results in their public financial reports filed with the SEC. Tax publications publish these results, which are doubtlessly reviewed by

IRS examination teams together with the uncertain tax position data.[202] When important events occur in the international or transfer pricing worlds, each company must reassess its posture and disclosures.[203]

§ 3.11 Tax Return Disclosure of Uncertain Tax Positions

In 2010, the Service took a giant step with respect to the ongoing issues relating to transparency between financial accounting and tax treatment of uncertain tax positions. Specifically, the IRS Commissioner announced that business taxpayers would have to complete a newly-created schedule on their tax returns identifying their uncertain tax positions and the amount that would be at issue if the item were completely disallowed (the FIN 48 Return Schedule Initiative).[204] At the time of this announcement it certainly seemed to meet the definition of a tax bombshell.

[1] Background

Since the adoption of FIN 48 (later codified in FASB ASC 740–10) in 2006,[205] there has been a rather amazing evolution in the relationship between competing forces in the tax arena:

1. IRS need to defend the U.S. tax base against under-reporting;
2. Government studies indicating a huge tax gap due to tax planning;
3. Corporate imperative to reduce costs in a competitive global marketplace;
4. Financial Accounting Standards Board determination to preclude abuses of the ambiguity between financial accounting and tax treatment of uncertainty in tax positions, perceived as the means by which Enron, WorldCom, and other financial frauds were perpetrated on the public;
5. Federal government need for revenue due to heavy spending; and
6. Auditor responsibility to become the enforcer of the FASB guidance contained in FASB ASC 740–10. For all companies issuing financial statements based on U.S. GAAP standards, the first round of confrontation relating to the defense of uncertain tax positions has been with the company's own financial auditor. Examination by the IRS or

[202] *See*, for example, *Securities and Exchange Commission Financial Statements Filed During February 2016, Detailing Transfer Pricing Issues*, Tax Management Transfer Pricing Report (Mar. 17, 2016, Vol. 24) (listing the transfer pricing disclosures of forty-plus companies).

[203] For example, there was a vital Tax Court opinion in a transfer pricing case in late 2015, *Altera Corp. v. Commissioner,* 145 TC 91 (2015), relating to the treatment of certain stock-based compensation costs in the context of so-called cost-sharing agreements; see *U.S. International Transfer Pricing* ¶ 2.03[14]. The *Altera* case has required each MNE with material transfer pricing issues to reassess their effective tax rate disclosures. *See* Parker, *Twenty-Seven Companies Cite Altera in SEC Filings*, Tax Management Transfer Pricing Report (Dec. 10, 2015, Vol. 24, No. 15). Of course, MNEs must remain ever vigilant: The Court of Appeals for the Ninth Circuit reversed the Tax Court's judgment in June 2019. *See Altera Corp. v. Commissioner,* 926 F.3d 1061 (9th Cir. 2019). *See also* Andrew Velarde, *Tech Giants Give First Glimpse of Altera's Financial Impact*, 95 Tax Notes Int'l 550 (Aug. 5, 2019).

[204] *See* Announcement 2010–9, 2010–7 IRB 408. *See generally* Moses, *Practitioners React to IRS Disclosure Proposal, Discuss How Privilege Applies to Benchmarking Studies,* 18 BNA Transfer Pricing Rep. 1083 (Feb. 25, 2010). Proposed regulations promulgated in 2011 declared authority for the UTP Schedule. The operative provision of the regulations simply declares the authority to require the UTP Schedule, which does not seem to involve a serious issue in any event. *See IRS proposes rules allowing service to require uncertain tax position disclosure,* 172 Daily Tax Rep., at G-3 (Sept. 8, 2010).

[205] *See* Section 3.02.

other tax authorities would occur at a later point in time. The current reality of dealing with auditors on these issues is a process that has evolved to be similar in nature to tax authority examinations, which reflects the nature of the duties of the auditor in today's world. This evolution has also raised the level of diligence required by Board Audit Committees to make sure that the disclosure and audit process is conducted in a manner consistent with the policies of the Board of Directors.

As these evolutions have occurred, the IRS has stated that it is training its Examination Teams to adapt to the heightened disclosures under FASB ASC 740–10 to streamline the audit process. At the same time, corporate taxpayers expressed concern about the extent to which the disclosures under the FASB rules for accounting for uncertain income tax positions would provide a "roadmap" for IRS examinations although this concern has shown, over the last 15 years, to be unfounded. There has also been anxiety in the taxpayer community over the extent of privilege or work product protection for the financial accounting uncertain-tax-position workpapers, an issue that has been with us for some time.

One other consequence of this evolution has been the growth in the Service's alternative dispute resolution programs.[206] For companies that have used such programs to address their uncertain tax positions, the imposition of the FASB rules on uncertain tax positions has been a non-event.

[2] Announcement 2010–9

It was into this evolving process that the IRS Commissioner in January 2010 introduced the "FIN 48 Return Schedule Initiative." The new schedule promised by the Commissioner was to be required to be included with returns filed after the schedule was released.

Specifically, the Service announced that it was considering changes to reporting requirements regarding certain large business taxpayers' uncertain tax positions in order to improve tax compliance and administration. The new schedule was to require disclosure of positions with a concise description their magnitude, but not the taxpayer's risk assessment or tax reserve amounts. While the Service has the authority to compel such disclosure under Supreme Court precedent, it has had a "policy of restraint" which it declared will continue.[207]

[3] Schedule UTP

Schedule UTP and the accompanying Instructions require[208] that, beginning with the 2010 tax year, certain public or privately held corporations with both uncertain tax positions and assets equal to or exceeding $100 million must file Schedule UTP for their 2010 (and following) tax years if they, or a related party, issued audited financial statements. The dollar threshold is currently $10 million, see below. These types of corporations are the ones affected:

- Corporations required to file Form 1120;

---

[206] *See* Chapter 9.

[207] *See* Section 8.05[3].

[208] Announcement 2010–75, 2010–41 IRB 428.

- Insurance companies required to file Form 1120-L; and
- Foreign corporations required to file Form 1120-F.

Schedule UTP need not have been filed for short tax years ending in 2010. Also, tax positions taken in years before 2010 need not be reported in a later year even if a reserve is recorded in audited financial statements issued in 2010 or later.

Worldwide assets are used to determine whether a corporation that files a Form 1120-F (including a protective return) must file Schedule UTP.

A corporation's assets equal or exceed $10 million for this purpose if the amount reported on any of the following is at least $10 million:

- Page 1, Item D of Form 1120, or
- the higher of the beginning or end of year total assets amounts reported on Schedule L of Form 1120-L, or Form 1120-PC, or
- the higher of the beginning or end of year total worldwide assets reported on Form 1040-F, Schedule L, Line 17 (if Schedule were prepared on a worldwide basis).

The total asset threshold was $100 million in 2010 and 2011, reduced to $50 million starting with 2012 tax years and to $10 million for 2014 and later tax years.[209]

[a] Key Elements of Schedule UTP

In the Schedule and accompanying Instructions, IRS made a number of clarifications and added some new guidance. IRS clarified, for example, that temporary differences must be reported on Schedule UTP.[210] Additional guidance follows.

[i] Audited Financial Statement

An audited financial statement is one on which an independent auditor expresses an opinion. Compiled or reviewed financial statements are excluded from the definition of "audited financial statement."[211]

[ii] Required Information

For each reported tax position on Schedule UTP, the corporation must report the primary sections and subsections of the Internal Revenue Code associated with it; identify whether the reported tax position is a temporary or permanent difference or both; provide the employer identification number of any pass-through entity involved; indicate whether it is a major tax position; and rank the tax position by size.

On October 11, 2022, the IRS released a new draft Schedule UTP for the 2022 tax year requiring five additional items to be reported for each tax position: if disclosing a tax position contrary to a rule otherwise reportable on Form 8275, identify the rule; if disclosing a tax position contrary to a regulation otherwise reportable on Form 8275-R, identify the regulation; identify the location of the tax position by form or schedule and by line number and give the incremental amount included on the line related to the tax position taken.

---

[209] *Id.*

[210] *Id.*

[211] *Id.*

[iii] Concise Description

The corporation must provide a concise description of the tax position, including a description of the relevant facts affecting the tax treatment of the position and information that reasonably can be expected to apprise IRS of the identity of the tax position, its amount, unit of account, and the nature of the controversy. This is based upon and similar to the information required to be reported on Form 8275. A corporation should not include an assessment of the hazards of a tax position or an analysis of the support for or against the tax position.[212]

For tax positions which would otherwise be reported on Forms 8275, Disclosure Statement, or 8275-R, Regulation Disclosure Statement, the concise description of UTPs in Schedule UTP, Part III, should include the information required under those forms.

If the corporation is disclosing a position contrary to a rule (such as a code provision or IRS revenue ruling) reportable on Form 8275, it must identify the rule by name. For tax positions reportable on Form 8275-R, the corporation must enter the full citation for each regulation for which it has taken a contrary position. The citation should specify the section number, including all designations of smaller units (lettered or numbered subsections, paragraphs, subparagraphs, and clauses) to which the contrary position relates. For example, a corporation should enter "1.482–7(d)(1)(iii)" instead of "482 regs" or "1.482–7."

On October 11, 2022, the IRS released a new draft Schedule UTP for the 2022 tax year providing additional guidance on adequate disclosure for the concise description. A "description of the relevant facts affecting the tax treatment of the position" should include all information pertaining to the nature, amount, or timing of the tax position uncertainty. An example is a corporation claiming a current year tax deduction for the cost of fixing the roof of a building. The description should indicate why it was determined that the work was performed to keep the asset in normal operating condition and why the costs do not improve or extend the useful life of the asset. The "identity of the tax position" should provide information that further defines the primary IRC section(s), rule, or regulation section listed in the Schedule UTP. Examples include identification of a 15-year depreciable life assigned to land improvement assets under section 168 or indicating that a request has been filed in accordance with Rev. Rul. 90-38 to change from an erroneous method of accounting for advanced payments. "The nature of the controversy or potential controversy" can include a description of the legal issues presented by the facts. It should identify the specific entity, country, or transaction to which the tax position relates; the character of income; the type of expense; the relationship of the tax position to other assets or activities; and whether the uncertainty relates to computational issues, substantiation issues, sampling methodologies, or legal interpretation.

[iv] Ranking

If a corporation does have to file Schedule UTP, then it must rank all reported tax positions on that Schedule. The ranking is to be based on the size of the U.S. federal income tax reserve that is recorded for the position taken in the return. For this purpose, the reserve includes interest and penalties. Furthermore, "tax positions" does include transfer pricing and other valuation positions.

---

[212] *Id.*

Also, the corporation has to designate those tax positions for which the reserve exceeds 10 percent of the aggregate amount of the reserves for all of the tax positions reported on the schedule.

However, no size need be determined for the following tax positions: tax positions for which no reserve was created based on an expectation to litigate. These positions can be assigned any ranking by the corporation.

Ranking is intended to allow IRS to more accurately evaluate the materiality of the issues reported on the schedule, and to impose less burden on corporations, than the previously-proposed "maximum tax adjustment" reporting requirement.

This method relies on the reserve computations that corporations already must perform for audited financial statement purposes, and, unlike the "maximum tax adjustment" proposal, does not require disclosure of the actual amounts of the tax reserves.[213]

[v] Penalties

The instructions do not provide specific instructions regarding penalties. However, IRS's Announcement 2010–75 did say that complete and accurate disclosure of a tax position on the appropriate year's Schedule UTP is to be treated as if the corporation filed a Form 8275 or Form 8275-R regarding the tax position. A separate Form 8275 or Form 8275-R need not be filed to avoid certain accuracy-related penalties with respect to that tax position. In the case of a transaction that is not a reportable transaction, IRS said, it will treat a complete and accurate disclosure of a tax position on Schedule UTP as satisfying the disclosure requirements of Code Sec. 6662(i).[214]

[vi] Record a Reserve

Schedule UTP seeks the reporting of tax positions consistent with the reserve decisions made by the corporation for audited financial statement purposes.

IRS requires reporting of tax positions taken in a return for which reserves were created under applicable financial accounting standards or for which no reserve was created because of an expectation to litigate. A tax position is reported on Schedule UTP once (1) a reserve for a tax position is recorded, and (2) a tax position is taken on a return regardless of the order in which those two events occur.

A corporation may rely on the reserve decisions it made for financial statement purposes to complete Schedule UTP; that is, the corporation is not expected to reassess at the time the schedule is completed those reserve decisions previously made for financial statement purposes.[215]

[vii] Related Party

Corporations report their own tax positions on Schedule UTP and do not report the tax positions of a related party.

For corporations included in multiple audited financial statements, the recording of a reserve in any audited financial statement in which the corporation is included triggers

---

[213] *Id.*

[214] *Id.*

[215] *Id.*

reporting of the tax position if the tax position is taken on a return filed by the reporting corporation.[216]

[viii] Reserve Not Recorded Based on Administrative Practice

IRS eliminated its proposed requirement to report tax positions for which no reserve was created due to a widely-understood administrative practice. However, IRS said it will continue to explore ways to assess the impact of these tax positions on overall tax compliance.[217]

[ix] Reserve Not Recorded Based on Expectation to Litigate

Corporations are not required to report tax positions that are either:

- immaterial under applicable financial accounting standards, or
- sufficiently certain so that no reserve is required under those standards.

Thus, a tax position that a corporation would litigate, if challenged, but that is clear and unambiguous, or is immaterial, does not have to be reported on Schedule UTP.[218]

[x] Tax Position Taken in a Tax Return

Schedule UTP requires the reporting of U.S. federal income tax positions but not foreign or state tax positions. However, a corporation must report a United States federal income tax position taken in a return that arises out of uncertainty with regard to a foreign tax position (e.g., foreign tax credits) if a reserve for United States federal income tax was recorded to reflect that uncertainty.[219]

[xi] Unit of Account

IRS emphasized that the unit of account should be applied consistently with the guidance in FASB ASC 740–10.[220]

ILLUSTRATION 3-25:[221]

Corporation A and Corporation B each have two individual research projects and each anticipates claiming research and development credit arising out of their projects. Corporation A chooses each individual research credit as the unit of account for GAAP financial reporting purposes, since the corporation accumulates information for the tax return at the project level and expects IRS to address the issues during an examination of each project separately. Corporation B determines that the appropriate unit of account for GAAP financial reporting purposes is the functional expenditures, based on the amount of its expenditures, the anticipated credits to be claimed, its previous experience, and the advice of its tax advisors. Based on the unit of account used for financial reporting purposes, Corporation A must use each project as the

[216] *Id.*

[217] *Id.*

[218] *Id.*

[219] *Id.* An example of the UTP Schedule with respect to transfer pricing positions is set out at Cym Lowell & Mark Martin, *U.S. International Taxation: Practice and Procedure* ¶ 14.07[12][f] (Thomson Reuters) [*U.S. International Taxation: Practice and Procedure*]. Preparing for an IRS examination of the UTP schedule is discussed at ¶ 14.07[12][g].

[220] Announcement 2010–75, 2010–41 IRB.

[221] Instructions to Schedule UTP (Dec. 2019), Example 6.

unit of account for Schedule UTP reporting purposes, and Corporation B must use functional expenditures as its unit of account for Schedule UTP reporting, regarding the research and development credit.

A corporation that uses its entire tax year as a unit of account under IFRS or another method of accounting may not do so for Schedule UTP reporting, but must identify a unit of account based on FASB ASC 740–10 principles or by using any other level of detail that is consistently applied if that identification is reasonably expected to apprise IRS of the identity and nature of the issue underlying a tax position taken in the tax return.[222]

[xii] Information Sharing

IRS will generally not provide Schedule UTP information to foreign governments except where there is a reciprocal arrangement with the foreign government regarding uncertain-tax-position information.[223] (For example, the foreign government might be collecting similar information for its own tax administration purposes, and agree to make the information available to IRS in a similar manner.) Even where reciprocity does exist, IRS will weigh other factors, including the relevance of the information to the foreign government. In many cases the information would be irrelevant. In practice, the IRS often issues IDRs related to Schedule UTP to increase understanding of the underlying factual and legal issues, even though it does not request the underlying workpapers in normal examinations not involving tax shelters.

[4] Future Examinations Involving Schedule UTP

It can reasonably be anticipated that Schedule UTP will be an important element in future examinations.

There is an inevitable tension within the Service and between an Examination Team and the taxpayer concerning Schedule UTP and its underlying workpapers. The Service has continued to indicate that it will adhere to its "policy of restraint."[224] In practice, the IRS often issues IDRs related to Schedule UTP to increase understanding of the underlying factual and legal issues, even though it does not request the underlying workpapers in normal examinations not involving tax shelters.

[5] Relationship of Schedule UTP to Financial Accounting Disclosure Decision-Making

As the Schedule UTP is used in preparing pertinent U.S. corporate income tax returns, an inevitable issue will be the relationship between the FASB ASC 740–10 analysis and the Schedule UTP for tax return purposes. The essential question will be the extent to which the Schedule UTP reporting will be consistent with the FASB ASC 740–10 disclosure that was made for financial statement purposes.

There are a variety of issues that will occur as this process evolves for each entity, including at least the following:

---

222 Announcement 2010–75, 2010–41 IRB.

223 *See U.S. International Taxation: Practice and Procedure* ¶ 9.03.

224 *See* Section 8.05[3].

[a] Difference in Analysis Between Financial Accounting and Schedule UTP

While the FASB ASC 740–10 analysis is undertaken for financial accounting purposes and Schedule UTP compliance is undertaken for tax purposes, the underlying purposes of the two analyses are the same. FASB ASC 740–10 is required for tax provision purposes. The IRS has obviously been frustrated with the lack of transparency in financial statement disclosures as well as the assertion of attorney-client privilege or work product protections relating to workpapers and other underlying analyses.

The ultimate purpose of the Schedule UTP is to obtain such transparency, at least for purposes of IRS Examination Team issue identification.

[b] Extent of Symmetry

Once the FASB ASC 740–10 process is complete for financial accounting purposes, the next step for an entity's tax department will be to prepare the Schedule UTP for the tax return. The tax return will of course be filed at a later point in time than the issuance of the audited financial statement.

In the case of transfer pricing matters, the process is somewhat different, though the ultimate analysis seems to be essentially the same as for other tax positions.

[c] Internal Documentation

A logical approach to preparing internal documentation for the Schedule UTP would be to begin with the FASB ASC 740–10 workpapers. Each tax position or unit of account could be evaluated in terms of whether a different definition should be used for the Schedule UTP.

[6] Comments About the Schedule UTP Initiative

The Schedule UTP initiative continues the revolution that has occurred in transparency concerning tax positions. The process began in the late 1980s in the United States, in the transfer pricing context. The state of play at that point was that taxpayers would take whatever position they thought appropriate on specific issues, await IRS examination, and then address any issue that was discovered. This was like the process of growing mushrooms, which grow the best in the dark with manure as fertilizer. In other words, a common strategy was to maintain tax positions in as much secrecy as possible unless or until the Service discovered an issue (the Mushroom Period).

In 1988, the Service complained in the famous "White Paper" that the process of discovering transfer pricing issues was unduly difficult, and the taxpayer had an overwhelming advantage.[225] As a result, Congress enacted the transfer pricing penalties in 1990 which required that taxpayers prepare contemporaneous documentation of their transfer pricing policies.[226] When IRS Examination Teams commence audits, this documentation is typically the second IDR that is served on the taxpayer (the first is for listed transactions). This effectively ended the Mushroom Period, at least for transfer pricing matters, and ushered in a world of at least partial transparency. It was "partial"

---

[225] *See U.S. International Transfer Pricing* ¶ 2.02[11][b].

[226] *Id. at* ¶ 10.04.

in the sense that taxpayers were only required to identify how they determined the pricing results reflected in their income tax returns.

Following the corporate financial scandals of the late 1990s, Congress enacted Sarbanes-Oxley in 2002,[227] which required the maintenance of controls with business entities. The control process became something that was addressed by financial auditors, and began changing the nature of the relationship between taxpayers and their auditors.

From a taxation transparency standpoint, the promulgation of the FASB rules on accounting for uncertain tax positions in 2006 took the transparency process a giant step forward, requiring a process for quantifying the potential loss of tax benefits from uncertain tax positions.[228] As noted above, this has resulted in real time evaluation of tax positions between taxpayers and auditors. The IRS began training examiners in how to evaluate and use the information disclosed in financial statements, as it respected its traditional "policy of restraint" concerning request for tax accrual (or uncertain tax position) workpapers.

It is apparent that the Service was not satisfied with the amount of information that was provided via the uncertain-tax-position disclosures. Examination Teams have been required to request details from taxpayers being examined, which, not unexpectedly, can be cumbersome, contentious process.

The Schedule UTP initiative seemed to be a game changer when it was initially proposed, drawing fire from the taxpayer community. Despite the initial concern over Schedule UTP, experience has shown that it is perhaps more effective at causing taxpayers to self-police the aggressiveness of their tax positions than it is at identifying issues of the IRS to examine.

Commentators have observed that the UTP filings seem to reveal few actual disclosures,[229] as IRS officials note that the UTP schedules reveal little that is useful for purposes of oversight of transfer pricing (one of the objects of the process) or for other oversight purposes.[230] In short, there is a rather general feeling that the UTP process has not only had little impact on taxpayer behavior, but has generally been a waste of time on all sides.[231] Whether the Service will revamp the process to obtain what it believes to be useful information remains to be seen. On October 11, 2022, the IRS issued

---

[227] *See* Chapter 6.

[228] *See* Chapter 3.

[229] *See* J. Richard Harvey, *Schedule UTP—Why So Few Disclosures?* 139 Tax Notes 69 (April 1, 2013). Interestingly, a March 23, 2018 report from the Treasury Inspector General for Tax Administration entitled, *The Uncertain Tax Position Statement Does Not Contain Sufficient Information to Be Useful in Compliance Efforts* (Reference No. 2018–30–023) maintains that Schedule UTP lacks the information needed for the IRS to use it as originally intended (i.e., to target noncompliance efficiently). The report finds that Schedule UTP provides little more than a confirmation that certain issues existed. The report concludes that without expanding the details reported on Schedule UTP—such as requiring more detailed descriptions of the reported tax position or dollar amounts of disclosed positions—the goals in implementing Schedule UTP will not be realized and recommends either modifying Schedule UTP to include more details or eliminating the requirement to file Schedule UTP.

[230] *See Schedule UTP Filings Reveal Little of Use About Section 482 Issues, Maruca Says,* 21 BNA Transfer Pricing Rep. 1027 (Feb. 21, 2013).

[231] *See Practitioners Question UTP Filings' Influence on Taxpayer Behavior,* Daily Tax Rep., at G-10 (May 12, 2014).

a new draft UTP schedule for 2022 requesting additional information that "will improve the form's usefulness."[232]

[a] Issues for the Tax Department

While the consequences of the Schedule UTP initiative continue to unfold, tax departments continue to face the following issues.

Refinement of "Unit of Account" Determinations. These define the position for which measurement will need to be made. For example, in the transfer pricing context is there one unit of account on a global basis or multiple units?

Expectation of More Focused Examinations. The IRS continues to face significant examination resource limitations. As a consequence, tax departments should expect fewer, but more focused, examinations. Further, following the increase in uncertain tax positions brought about by tax reform, Schedule UTP may play a revitalized role in the identification of problems.

More Scrutiny from Audit Committees. Our experience is that Audit Committees have become increasingly zealous in evaluating the FASB ASC 740–10 process. Given the increase in uncertain tax positions, it can be anticipated that the level of scrutiny will increase to assure that the process of complying with the UTP rules under FASB ASC 740–10, negotiating with the financial auditor, and complying with the tax return disclosure schedule, subject to penalties, is: (i) consistent; and (ii) unlikely to result in earnings discontinuities in the event the financial disclosure process claims a greater level of benefit from critical tax positions than survives IRS examination.

Increased Willingness to Consider ADR Programs. As the price of uncertainly seems to continually escalate, both with auditors and the Service, tax departments may have increasingly open minds about using the Service's advance determination programs to get issues "off the table."[233]

Ongoing Concerns about "Policy of Restraint." Service officials continue to indicate that the "policy of restraint" with respect to exercise of its ability to request production of tax accrual or related workpapers, will remain intact with respect to the UTP Schedule as well as for FASB ASC 740–10.[234] On the other hand, the essence of the Schedule UTP initiative seems plainly to be an effort to short circuit the entire process, as noted above.[235]

Foreign Tax Examinations. It can also be anticipated that foreign tax authorities will request information from the UTP Schedule, or underlying FASB ASC 740–10, with respect to issues being examined in such countries, especially with transfer pricing matters.

[b] Developing Issues

The UTP process is an American evolution reflecting the perceived need for greater disclosure concerning potential liabilities for uncertain tax positions. As noted, U.S.

---

[232] IRS Statement about Uncertain Tax Positions (UTP) Reporting (Oct. 11, 2022, updated Oct. 19, 2022).

[233] *See* Chapter 9.

[234] *See* Section 8.05[3].

[235] *See* Bertoldo, *IRS Chief Counsel Wilkins Downplays the Gutting of the Policy of Restraint,* Daily Tax Rep., at J-1 (Apr. 13, 2010).

public companies must disclose the results in their public financial reports filed with the SEC. Tax publications publish these results, which are doubtless reviewed by IRS examination teams together with the uncertain tax position data. When important events occur in the international or transfer pricing worlds, each company must continually reassess its posture and disclosures.[236] This will certainly be the case with the issues arising from the 2017 U.S. Tax Act,[237] as well as the ongoing focus on tax-base protection globally (BEPS 2.0).[238]

---

[236] For example, there has been vital litigation in this area (*Altera Corp. v. Commissioner,* 145 TC 91 (2015), rev'd, 926 F.3d 1061 (9th Cir. 2019)), relating to the treatment of certain stock compensation costs in the context of so-called cost-sharing agreements, that has required each MNE with material transfer pricing issues to reassess their effective tax rate disclosures. *See U.S. International Transfer Pricing* ¶ 2.03[14], Chapter 13A; *also see* Parker, *Twenty-Seven Companies Cite Altera in SEC Filings,* 24 Tax Mgt Transfer Pricing Rep. (Dec. 10, 2015).

[237] *See* Section 1.03[1].

[238] *See* Section 1.03[2].

Appendix 3.1

FASB ASC 740–10 CHECKLIST

1. Identify material income tax positions of the company that are uncertain under FASB ASC 740–10.
2. Establish guidelines to determine the "unit of account" of the company's income tax positions.
3. Document management's analysis and conclusions regarding the recognition of uncertain tax positions.
4. Implement procedures to measure the financial statement benefit of the recognized tax position, including how to determine and document the possible alternative outcomes of an uncertain tax position and assign probabilities and dollar amounts to those outcomes.
5. Calculate the FASB ASC 740–10 interest and, if applicable, penalty amounts applicable to the company's unrecognized income tax positions.
6. Coordinate the company's outside auditors with respect to FASB ASC 740–10 tax positions and disclosure thereof.
7. Monitor the outcome of prior tax positions (whether by settlement, expiration of statute of limitations, etc.) and establish the manner in which those outcomes affect financial reporting and disclosure.
8. Monitor new facts and information relating to a tax position that occur subsequent to the company's reporting date, and whether management's judgment and prior conclusions under FASB ASC 740–10 are altered based on those new facts.

Chapter 4

PERMANENT VERSUS TEMPORARY DIFFERENCES

Table of Sections

§ 4.01 Introduction

From a tax law standpoint, tax deferral is viewed as a significant benefit for a corporation. Even if tax rates remain constant over time, there is a time value of money benefit to defer paying taxes. From an accounting standpoint, however, tax deferral is viewed, on many occasions, as a minor benefit. Exclusions (and deductions that are equivalent to exclusions, such as the deduction for foreign-derived intangible income) are seen as a much greater benefit to Fortune 500 companies and other publicly held corporations (referred to in this chapter as "Corporate America"),[1] which highly covets such items, that it refers to as permanent differences. Permanent differences may increase a corporation's net income and therefore its earnings per share (EPS) while also reducing a corporation's effective tax rate. In contrast, tax deferral items, referred to as temporary differences for financial accounting purposes, do not immediately increase a corporation's net income or its EPS, and also do not reduce a corporation's effective tax rate. The primary benefit of temporary differences, which may not be applicable in all cases, is to temporarily increase a corporation's cash flow, which while certainly not unimportant, is not seen as significant a benefit to corporate management as increasing the corporation's net income or EPS or decreasing its effective tax rate.

§ 4.02 Background on Financial Income

[1] General Principles

A public corporation is required to compute its income for financial accounting purposes each year in accordance with generally accepted accounting principles (GAAP). The resulting income figure is generally referred to as pretax financial income or pretax book income (PTBI).[2] The corporation will also compute its income tax expense for the year, which is subtracted from pretax financial income, resulting in the corporation's net income. In addition, a corporation's income is generally subject to taxation by federal,

---

1 For purposes of this chapter, the term "Corporate America" will refer to public corporations that are required to file financial statements with the SEC.

2 "Pretax financial income" is sometimes referred to as pretax book income (PTBI), income before taxes (or earnings before taxes), income for financial reporting purposes or income for book purposes. *See* Donald E. Kieso, et al., *Intermediate Accounting* 1054 (16th ed. 2016).

most state and several local taxing authorities. As a result, a corporation must also compute its income for tax purposes in accordance with the applicable tax statutes and regulations of these various jurisdictions. The resulting income figure is referred to as taxable income.[3] In almost all cases, a corporation's taxable income will differ from its pretax financial income. In fact, the determinations of taxable income for these various jurisdictions almost always differ from each other and also from pretax financial income. These differences primarily reflect the different objectives behind the various taxing authorities and the accounting rules.[4]

The tax rules are designed to provide equitable and efficient determination of tax liability and subsequent collection of revenue and also to provide incentives for corporations and individuals to engage in a particular activity based upon the priorities and revenue needs of the various taxing authorities.[5] The financial accounting rules are designed to paint a picture of the corporation's operations that is consistent in its measurement on both an annual basis and across entities such that creditors, shareholders, management and any other properly interested persons can evaluate the absolute and relative performance of the corporation. The Financial Accounting Standards Board (FASB) has written:

> The objective of general purpose financial reporting is to provide financial information about the reporting entity that is useful to present and potential investors, lenders, and other creditors in making decisions in their capacity as capital providers. . . Those decisions involve buying, selling, or holding equity and debt instruments and providing or settling loans and other forms of credit.[6]

While the rules for determining pretax financial income are fairly rigorous and based upon underlying economic assumptions and principles, the various taxing authorities have promulgated laws and regulations that do not necessarily follow rules grounded on the economic theories of financial reporting but rather may be based on political, social, or economic objectives. In addition, the difference between a corporation's taxable income and its pretax financial income may be due to tax planning strategies engaged in by the corporation, resulting in lower taxable income relative to pretax financial income.[7]

The differences between taxable income and pretax financial income give rise to tax differences. Some of these differences are permanent differences and others are temporary differences (sometimes referred to as timing differences). Permanent differences are (i) items that enter into pretax financial income but *never* into taxable income, or (ii) items that enter into taxable income but *never* into pretax financial

---

3 IRC Sections 11 and 63(a).

4 *See Thor Power Tool Co. v. Commissioner*, 439 U.S. 522 (1979) ("The primary goal of financial accounting is to provide useful information to management, shareholders, creditors and others properly interested; the major responsibility of the accountant is to protect these parties from being misled. The primary goal of the income tax system, in contrast, is the equitable collection of revenue; the major responsibility of the Internal Revenue Service is to protect the public fisc.").

5 *See, e.g.*, Michelle Hanlon, *What Can We Infer about a Firm's Taxable Income from Its Financial Statements?* 56 Nat'l Tax J. 831, 833 (2003); Myron S. Scholes, et al., *Taxes and Business Strategy: A Planning Approach* Appendix 2.2 (3rd ed. 2004); *Gil B. Manzon, Jr. & George A. Plesko, The Relation Between Financial and Tax Reporting Measures of Income*, 55 Tax L. Rev. 175, 180 (2002).

6 *See* FASB, Statement of Financial Accounting Concepts No. 8 (CON 8), Conceptual Framework for Financial Reporting, Chapter 1, "The Objective of General Purpose Financial Reporting" (Sept. 2010; amended Dec. 2021).

7 *See* Hanlon, supra note 5, at 833.

income. Temporary differences are generally (i) items that enter into pretax financial income earlier than when the item enters into taxable income, or (ii) items that enter into taxable income earlier than when the item enters into pretax financial income.[8]

[2] The Focus of Corporate Management

Before discussing permanent differences and temporary differences in detail, it may be helpful to summarize the financial indicators that are critical to corporate management. The following is an excerpt from a Microsoft press release for its earnings for the quarter ended March 31, 2022:

> REDMOND, Wash.—April 26, 2022—Microsoft Corp. today announced the following results for the quarter ended March 31, 2022, as compared to the corresponding period of last fiscal year:
>
> - Revenue was $49.4 billion and increased 18%
> - Operating income was $20.4 billion and increased 19%
> - Net income was $16.7 billion and increased 8% GAAP (up 13% non-GAAP)
> - Diluted earnings per share was $2.22 and increased 9% GAAP (up 14% non-GAAP)[9]

As a general proposition, which is supported by the Microsoft press release, corporate management (and the business community) is extremely focused on the income statement, often called the statement of income or statement of earnings. In business parlance, it is usually referred to as the P & L statement (i.e., profit and loss statement). The income statement is the "report that measures the success of a corporation's operations for a given period of time."[10] In looking at the income statement, several key items stand out. First, revenue and income are viewed as the primary indicator of the performance of corporate management.[11] Revenues increased 18 percent from the corresponding quarter a year earlier, indicating a growing business. Microsoft's net income for the second quarter was $16.7 billion, an eight percent increase from the same quarter a year earlier. Its operating income was $20.4 billion, a 19 percent increase from the quarter a year earlier. In many cases, the board of directors of a public corporation will focus on the income of the corporation in evaluating the performance of corporate management. Investors and analysts will also look at a company's income in evaluating the company's performance.[12]

---

[8] *See* Section 2.07.

[9] *See* https://www.microsoft.com/en-us/investor/earnings/fy-2022-q3/press-release-webcast.

[10] Kieso, supra note 2, at 154.

[11] *Id.* at 155 ("So far, our discussion has highlighted the importance of information in the income statement for investment and credit decisions, including the evaluation of the company and its managers."); id. at 167 ("A company customarily sums up the results of its operations in one important figure: net income."); Joanne M. Flood, *Wiley GAAP 2021: Interpretation and Application of Generally Accepted Accounting Principles* 52 (2021) ("In financial reporting, performance is primarily measured by net income and its components, which are provided in the income statement.").

[12] A subset of pretax financial income is operating income, sometimes referred to as income from continuing operations. Operating income differs from pretax financial income in that the latter figure includes several additional items, such as discontinued operations and extraordinary items. *See* Kieso, supra note 2, at 162–167. Another item on the income statement that is critical is revenues. Corporate management will, in almost all cases, focus on increasing revenues from period to period.

Corporate management desires a sufficient amount of income each quarter to try to meet or exceed the expectations of Wall Street so that the market price of the stock will increase.[13] One effect of an increasing stock price is to increase the value, if any, of management's stock options.[14] Generally, corporations prefer, if possible, to show steady growth each period in income rather than wild swings in income from period to period.[15] Attempting to smooth out a corporation's income from period to period is referred to as "earnings management."[16]

While corporate management focuses on income, the financial world generally focuses intently on a corporation's (diluted) EPS. More specifically, EPS is considered to be the most significant business indicator in the financial world.[17] In the press release, Microsoft reported that its diluted EPS was $2.22 cents per share, an increase of nine percent from the quarter a year earlier. A corporation's basic EPS is equal to its income available to common shareholders (i.e., income from continuing operations (operating income) or net income less dividends on preferred stock) divided by the weighted average number of common shares of its stock outstanding.[18] Its diluted EPS is computed as if all convertible securities (outstanding convertible preferred shares, convertible debentures, stock options, and warrants) were exercised.[19] Because EPS is calculated using the corporation's net income (and operating income), both EPS and net income are directly related (i.e., a higher net income will lead to a higher EPS). A corporation must disclose its EPS on the face of its income statement.[20]

A public corporation must also disclose its effective tax rate reconciliation in the footnotes to its financial statements filed as part of the Form 10-K.[21] This disclosure is

---

[13] Under the Securities and Exchange Act of 1934, public companies, usually referred to as reporting companies, must file a quarterly report on Form 10-Q for each of the first three quarters of the company's fiscal year. The Form 10-Q will contain the company's financial statement showing the company's financial results for the quarter. Securities and Exchange Act of 1934, Rule 13a–13. A public company must also file an annual report on Form 10-K. The Form 10-K will contain complete audited financial statements. Securities and Exchange Act of 1934, Rule 13a–1. Most reporting companies do not file a Form 10-Q for their last fiscal quarter but include the last fiscal quarter's financial results in the Form 10-K.

[14] *See* Kieso, supra note 2, at 155–156.

[15] *See, e.g.*, Staff of the Joint Committee on Taxation, *Present Law and Background Relating to Corporate Tax Reform: Issues of Conforming Book and Tax Income and Capital Cost Recovery*, JCX–16–06, at 17–18 (2006) [*JCT Book-Tax Report*].

[16] *See, e.g.*, Kieso, supra note 2, at 155 (earnings management is "often defined as the planned timing of revenues, expenses, gains and losses to smooth out bumps in earnings"). *See also* Section 1.05.

[17] *See, e.g.*, Kieso, supra note 2, at 167 ("However, the financial world has widely accepted an even more distilled and compact figure [than net income] as the most significant business indicator—earnings per share (EPS)."); Flood, supra note 11, at 124 ("Earnings per share (EPS) is an indicator widely used by investors to gauge the profitability of a corporation.").

[18] FASB ASC 260–10–45–10 (basic earnings per share). A corporation computes its basic EPS using both net income and operating income resulting in two EPS figures. FASB ASC 260–10–45–11.

[19] FASB ASC 260–10–45–16 (diluted earnings per share).

[20] FASB ASC 260–10–45–2 (entities with only common stock outstanding must present basic EPS for net income and income from continuing operations on the face of the income statement; all other entities must present both basic EPS and diluted EPS for net income and income from continuing operations on the face of the income statement with equal prominence).

[21] FASB ASC 740–10–50–12. FASB requires that a public entity disclose a reconciliation of "(a) the reported amount of income tax expense attributable to continuing operations for the year to (b) the amount of income tax expense that would result from applying domestic federal statutory tax rates to pretax income from continuing operations." *Id.* In computing and disclosing this reconciliation, a public entity may use actual dollar amounts or percentages. *Id.* A public entity will also disclose its estimated effective tax rate as part of the Form 10-Q, which is filed quarterly with the SEC. FASB ASC 740–270–30. The estimated amount and nature of each significant reconciling item should be disclosed. Rule 4–08(h) of SEC Regulation S-X requires disclosure of reconciling items that are five percent (or more) of the amount computed by multiplying pretax

referred to as the "tax footnote." Generally, a public corporation desires that its effective tax rate be comparable to or lower than the industry average. More specifically, a corporation wants a lower effective tax rate than its main competitors.[22] The effective tax rate is computed by dividing the corporation's income tax expense attributable to operating income by its operating income (sometimes referred to as "income from continuing operations").[23] The income tax expense includes current tax expense and deferred tax expense.[24] The deferred tax expense is computed based on a corporation's tax deferral items (i.e., its temporary differences). Because the tax effects of the deferral items are included in deferred tax expense and therefore income tax expense, a corporation's effective tax rate is not impacted (i.e., reduced) by tax deferral items.

§ 4.03 Exemptions and Permanent Differences

[1] General Principles

In the Internal Revenue Code, Congress provides a number of exclusion provisions.[25] These are provisions in which the item of income or gain is not taxed under the federal income tax laws. Some common examples of exclusion items include interest on state and local bonds;[26] proceeds of life insurance;[27] gifts, bequests, devises and inheritances;[28] certain gains on the sale of a principal residence;[29] physical personal injury damages;[30] and various employee benefits.[31] In each case, Congress has some policy reason as to why the item in question is not taxed. The policy reason is usually of a social, economic or political nature. For example, in 1913, Congress enacted the exemption for interest income on state and local bonds based on the idea that taxing such income "would impose an unconstitutional burden on the borrowing power of state and local governments."[32] Congress has retained the exclusion as a revenue sharing

---

income by the statutory tax rate; i.e., any item that increases or decreases the tax rate by 1.05 percent or more. 17 CFR § 210.4–08—General notes to financial statements.

[22] *See, e.g.*, Roger D. Wheeler, et al., *Session 7: Opportunities and Obstacles in Designing a U.S. Business Tax System for 2010 and Beyond*, 86 Taxes 115, 120 (2008) (Statement of Roger D. Wheeler: "I used to be a corporate tax executive, and, you know, statutory rates, we had them, but I never focused on statutory rates very much. It was always the effective rates. That is sort of how you earned your stripes, you focused on that, you tried to do better than somebody else and getting your effective rate lower."); *Martin D. Sullivan, Reported Corporate Effective Tax Rates Down Since Late 1990s*, 118 Tax Notes 882 (2008) ("Effective corporate tax rates, as reported to shareholders and to the Securities and Exchange Commission, play a critical role in a corporation's bottom line. The profit numbers universally cited in the financial press are after-tax figures, so corporate tax managers can contribute significantly to a corporation's reported profits by managing the effective tax rate.").

[23] FASB ASC 740–10–50–12. Operating income is a subset of pretax financial income.

[24] FASB ASC 740–10–30–3 ("Total income tax expense or benefit for the year is the sum of deferred tax expense or benefit and income taxes currently payable or refundable"); FASB ASC 740–10–50–9 (two significant components of income tax expense attributable to continuing operations for the year are current tax expense (or benefit) and deferred tax expense (or benefit)).

[25] *See* Internal Revenue Code, part III (Sections 101–140) (listing a number of items specifically excluded from gross income).

[26] IRC Section 103(a).

[27] IRC Section 101(a).

[28] IRC Section 102(a).

[29] IRC Section 121.

[30] IRC Section 104(a)(2).

[31] IRC Sections 105, 106, 119, 127, 129 and 132.

[32] *See* Boris I. Bittker & Lawrence Lokken, *Federal Taxation of Income, Estates and Gifts* ¶ 15.1.1 (3rd ed., 1999).

arrangement with the state and local governments.[33] Allowing the exclusion permits the state and local governments to borrow at lower interest rates than taxable bonds of similar quality.

When an item of income or gain is excluded from a corporation's gross income (and therefore taxable income) it leads to a difference between the corporation's taxable income and its pretax financial income. More specifically, that item of income or gain, while excluded from taxable income, is included in pretax financial income. As a result, pretax financial income is greater than taxable income by the excluded amount. For financial accounting purposes, the excluded amount is referred to as a permanent difference.

Permanent differences are items that (i) enter into pretax financial income but never into taxable income; or (ii) enter into taxable income but *never* into pretax financial income. As a result, these items create a difference between pretax financial income and taxable income that will not reverse over time, i.e., they are permanent differences. FASB has not defined permanent differences; however, in defining temporary differences, FASB has written:

> Some events do not have tax consequences. Certain revenues are exempt from taxation and certain expenses are not deductible. In the United States, for example, interest earned on certain municipal obligations is not taxable and fines are not deductible.[34]

FASB appears to be describing permanent differences as events that do not have tax consequences, with the two broad categories being revenues exempt from taxation and expenses that are not deductible. Permanent differences arise primarily because of a variety of tax provisions enacted by Congress to achieve certain purposes, such as political, social and economic objectives.[35] As noted by FASB, these tax provisions generally include exclusions of certain revenues from taxable income and limiting (or disallowing) certain expenses as a deduction in computing taxable income.

> **ILLUSTRATION 4-1:** A corporation owns state and local bonds. It receives $50,000 of interest on the bonds in Year 1. Under the tax code, interest on state and local bonds is excluded from gross income and therefore never enters into the computation of taxable income.[36] However, such interest enters into the computation of pretax financial income. As a result, a difference of $50,000 is created in Year 1 between taxable income and pretax financial income. This difference is permanent—it will not reverse over time. This is an example of a permanent difference that is favorable to the corporation.

> **ILLUSTRATION 4-2:** A public corporation pays its chief executive officer a salary of $1.4 million in Year 1. The salary payment of $1.4 million is an

---

[33] *Id.*

[34] FASB ASC 740–10–10–1. FASB utilized the term "permanent difference" by writing "nontaxable or nondeductible differences between financial statements and tax returns (sometimes referred to as permanent differences)." Accounting for Uncertainty in Income Taxes, FIN 48, paragraph B11. The Accounting Principles Board, which was the predecessor to FASB, had defined a permanent difference as "[d]ifferences between taxable income and pretax accounting income arising from transactions that, under applicable tax laws and regulations, will not be offset by corresponding differences or 'turn around' in other periods." Accounting for Income Taxes, APB Opinion No. 11, paragraph 13.f.

[35] *See* Kieso, supra note 2, at 1066.

[36] IRC Section 103(a).

expense on the corporation's income statement; however, for tax purposes the corporation may only deduct $1 million as a result of the limitation for certain excessive employee remuneration under IRC Section 162(m).[37] The $400,000 difference between the $1.4 million expense on the income statement and the $1 million deduction on the tax return is a permanent difference, which enters into the computation of pretax financial income but never into taxable income. This is an example of a permanent difference that is unfavorable to the corporation.

Some other common examples of items of permanent difference that enter into the computation of pretax financial income but not taxable income include: expenses incurred in generating tax-exempt income,[38] the 50 percent limitation on deduction of meals,[39] fines and penalties resulting from a violation of law,[40] proceeds from life insurance carried by the entity on key employees,[41] and premiums paid for life insurance carried by the entity on its key employees.[42] Some permanent differences enter into the computation of taxable income but not pretax financial income. One common example of a permanent difference that enters into the computation of taxable income but not pretax financial income is percentage depletion of natural resources in excess of their cost.[43] Another example is the dividends-received deduction for corporate recipients of dividends, as indicated in Illustration 4-3:[44]

ILLUSTRATION 4-3: A corporation owns two percent of the stock of XYZ Corporation. During the year, the corporation receives $10,000 of dividends from XYZ Corporation. The corporation includes the $10,000 of dividends in its pretax financial income and its taxable income. For tax purposes, the corporation is entitled to a 50 percent dividends-received deduction in computing its taxable income.[45] In computing its pretax financial income, however, the corporation simply includes the entire amount of the dividend resulting in a permanent difference of $5,000 between taxable income and pretax financial income (equal to the amount of the dividends-received deduction).

Permanent differences can be interpreted in one of two ways.[46] The broad interpretation of permanent differences includes any item that creates a difference between pretax financial income and taxable income that is not temporary. A narrower interpretation of the term permanent difference includes only items that create a difference between pretax financial income and taxable income that are not temporary but that also appear in the effective tax rate reconciliation in the financial statements (i.e., the tax footnote). For

---

[37] IRC Section 162(m).

[38] IRC Section 265.

[39] IRC Section 274(n).

[40] IRC Section 162(f).

[41] IRC Section 101(a)(1).

[42] IRC Section 264(a)(1).

[43] IRC Section 613.

[44] IRC Sections 243–246A.

[45] IRC Section 243.

[46] *See* Lillian F. Mills & George A. Plesko, *Bridging the Reporting Gap: A Proposal for More Informative Reconciling of Book and Tax Income*, 56 Nat'l Tax J. 865, 873 fn. 9 (2003).

example, prior to 2017, the expensing of nonqualified stock options could create an item that would be treated as a permanent difference under a broad interpretation of the term (i.e., a book-tax difference that is not temporary) but would not be treated as a permanent difference item under the narrower interpretation (i.e., it does not appear in the effective tax rate reconciliation).[47]

Public companies that must report certain financial statements with the SEC must file Form 10-K pursuant to the Securities Exchange Act of 1934.[48] In the notes to the financial statements, the company discloses its effective tax rate.[49] The effective tax rate shows either the percentage or dollar amount of taxes paid based on financial income.[50] Permanent differences may affect a company's effective tax rate and therefore its earnings per share. For example, assume a company receives an amount that it includes in revenues in computing its pretax financial income but not in gross income in computing its taxable income. The item may have the effect of reducing the company's effective tax rate and increasing its earnings per share. In contrast, if a company pays an amount that is not deductible for tax purposes but is an expense for purposes of computing pretax financial income (such as a fine), the company's effective tax rate will increase as a result of the expense and its earnings per share will be reduced.

ILLUSTRATION 4-4: A corporation has pretax financial income of $200,000 for 2021 and 2022. In 2021, it pays a non-deductible fine of $10,000, and in 2022 it receives $20,000 of tax-exempt interest that it includes in revenue but not gross income.

	2021	2022
Pretax financial income	$ 200,000	$ 200,000
Permanent differences:		
Non-taxable revenue	$ 0	$ 20,000
Non-deductible expense	$ 10,000	$ 0
Taxable income	$ 210,000	$ 180,000
Statutory tax rate	21%	21%
Total tax expense	$ 44,100	$ 37,800
Effective tax rate	22.05%	18.9%

---

47 In March 2016, FASB issued Accounting Standards Update (ASU) No. 2016–09, Compensation-Stock Compensation: Improvements to Employee Share-Based Payment Accounting, which affirmed its decision to require entities to recognize all excess tax benefits and all tax deficiencies as income tax expense or benefit in the income statement. The Board also affirmed its decision to remove the requirement to delay recognition of an excess tax benefit until the tax benefit is realized.

48 *See* Securities Exchange Act of 1934, Section 13(a).

49 FASB ASC 740–10–50–12. The reconciliation may be accomplished utilizing percentages or dollar amounts. The estimated amount and nature of each significant reconciling item should be disclosed. Rule 4–08(h) of SEC Regulation S-X requires disclosure of reconciling items that are 5 percent (or more) of the amount computed by multiplying pretax income by the statutory tax rate; i.e., any item that increases or decreases the tax rate by 1.05 percent or more. 17 CFR § 210.4–08—General notes to financial statements.

50 *Id.* Some companies show both percentages and dollar amount in computing their effective tax rate.

The permanent differences impact the effective tax rate. The $10,000 non-deductible fine in 2021 increased taxable income (relative to pretax financial income) thereby increasing current tax expense and therefore total income tax expense. Increasing the total income tax expense raised the effective tax rate to 22.05 percent, which is higher than the statutory tax rate of 21 percent in 2021. The $20,000 non-taxed revenue decreased taxable income (relative to pretax financial income) thereby decreasing current tax expense and therefore total income tax expense. Decreasing the total income tax expense lowered the effective tax rate to 18.9 percent, which is lower than the statutory tax rate of 21 percent in 2022.[51]

ILLUSTRATION 4-5: Berkshire Hathaway, Inc. had the following tax rate reconciliation in its 2021 Annual Report (note 19):

Income tax expense is reconciled to hypothetical amounts computed at the U.S. federal statutory rate for each of the three years ending December 31, 2021 in the table below (in millions).

	2021	2020	2019
Earnings before income taxes	$ 111,686	$ 55,693	$ 102,696
Hypothetical income tax expense computed at the U.S. federal statutory rate	$ 23,454	$ 11,696	$ 21,566
Dividends received deduction and tax-exempt interest	(457)	(448)	(433)
State income taxes, less U.S. federal income tax benefit	(417)	858	494
U.S. income tax credits	(1,860)	(1,519)	(942)
Goodwill impairments	—	1,977	20
Other differences, net	159	(124)	199
	$ 20,879	$ 12,440	$ 20,904
Effective income tax rate	18.7%	22.3%	20.4%

Berkshire Hathaway's dividends-received deduction (and tax-exempt interest) reduced its effective tax rate in years 2019, 2020 and 2021.

[2] Examples of Permanent Differences

[a] Deduction for Foreign-Derived Intangible Income

As part of the Tax Cuts and Jobs Act, Congress enacted a tax deduction for foreign-derived intangible income.[52] The deduction is equal to 37.5 percent (21.875 percent for taxable years after 2025) of a domestic corporation's foreign-derived intangible income for the taxable year.[53] The deduction is limited by the domestic corporation's taxable income for the year.[54]

In computing the amount of the deduction, a domestic corporation first computes its deduction-eligible income, which is generally its gross income less deductions but

[51] For purposes of this Illustration, operating income is assumed to equal pretax financial income. This is an important assumption because the effective tax rate is determined based on the corporation's operating income and not its pretax financial income. As a result, some permanent differences may not impact the corporation's effective tax rate if the permanent difference merely affects pretax financial income and not operating income. *See* supra note 12 for a discussion of the difference between operating income and pretax financial income.

[52] IRC Section 250.

[53] IRC Section 250(a)(1).

[54] IRC Section250(a)(2).

excluding certain categories of gross income (and corresponding deductions) such as subpart F income and global intangible low-taxed income (GILTI).[55] It then computes its foreign-derived deduction-eligible income, which is its deduction-eligible income derived in connection with property sold for foreign use to a person who is not a United States person or services provided to any person, or with respect to any property, not located within the United States.[56] A domestic corporation must then compute its deemed intangible income, which is the excess of its deduction-eligible income over the deemed tangible income return of the corporation.[57] The deemed tangible income return is equal to 10 percent of the corporation's qualified business asset investment (QBAI).[58] QBAI is the corporation's tangible depreciable property used in a trade or business.

The foreign-derived intangible income, for which the 37.5 percent deduction is applicable, is the amount that bears the same ratio to the deemed intangible income as the foreign-derived deduction eligible income bears to the deduction eligible income.[59] Expressed as a formula, foreign-derived intangible income is:

$$\text{deemed intangible income} \times \frac{\text{foreign-derived deduction eligible income}}{\text{deduction eligible income}}$$

ILLUSTRATION 4-6: A domestic corporation has deduction-eligible income of $100 million. It has foreign-derived deduction eligible income of $40 million. The domestic corporation has tangible depreciable property with a basis of $90 million. Its deemed intangible income is $91 million ($100 million of deduction-eligible income less $9 million deemed tangible income return). Its foreign-derived intangible income is $36.4 million ($91 million times 40 percent), which qualifies for a 37.5 percent deduction. The deduction of $13.65 million is a permanent difference for the domestic corporation.

ILLUSTRATION 4-7: The Boeing Company had the following tax rate reconciliation in its 2018 Annual Report (note 6):

The following is a reconciliation of the U.S. federal statutory rate to our effective income tax rates:

	Years ended December 31,		
	2018	**2017**	**2016**
U.S. federal statutory tax	**21.0%**	35.0%	35.0%
Foreign derived intangible income	**(4.7)**	—	—
Federal audit settlements	**(3.6)**	—	—
Research and development credits	**(1.8)**	(1.6)	(5.0)
Excess tax benefits	**(1.6)**	(2.1)	(1.8)
Other provision adjustments	**1.3**	(0.2)	(0.3)
Impact of Tax Cuts and Jobs Act	**(1.0)**	(12.6)	—

55 IRC Section 250(b)(3).

56 IRC Section 250(b)(4).

57 IRC Section 250(b)(2).

58 IRC Section 250(b)(2)(B).

59 IRC Section 250(b)(1).

Tax on non-US activities	**0.3**	(0.9)	(0.5)
Tax basis adjustment			(7.6)
U.S. manufacturing activity tax benefit		(1.3)	(3.7)
Effective income tax rate	**9.9%**	16.3%	13.0%

Boeing's deduction for its foreign-derived intangible income (FDII) reduced its effective tax rate by 4.7 percentage points in 2018 (the first year the FDII deduction was available).

[b] Research Credit

In 1981, Congress enacted a research credit because it believed that "a substantial tax credit for incremental research and experimental expenditures [would] overcome the resistance of many businesses to the significant cost of staffing, supplies and certain computer charges which must be incurred in initialing or expanding research programs."[60] Until 2015, Congress never made the credit a permanent part of the tax laws but rather renewed the credit almost continuously since 1981. As part of the Protecting Americans from Tax Hikes (PATH) Act of 2015, Congress permanently extended the research credit.[61]

The amount of the research credit is equal to 20 percent of the excess of the qualified research expenses for the taxable year over the base amount.[62] "Qualified research" is defined as research with respect to which the expenditures may be treated as specified research and experimental expenditures under section 174, which is undertaken for the purpose of discovering information which is technological in nature, and the application of which is intended to be useful in the development of a new or improved business component of the taxpayer, and substantially all of the activities of which constitutes elements of a process of experimentation for a particular purpose (i.e., a new or improved function, performance, or reliability or quality).[63] Qualified research expenses is the sum of in-house research expense and contract research expenses.[64] The base amount is the greater of: the fixed base percentage times the average annual gross receipts for the preceding four taxable years or 50 percent of the qualified research expenses for the year.[65] As a result, the maximum credit is ten percent of qualified research expenses (20 percent of the excess of qualified research expenses over 50 percent thereof).[66] A taxpayer may elect the alternative simplified credit in which case the credit is equal to 14 percent of the qualified research expenses for the taxable year that exceeds 50 percent of the average qualified research expenses for the three previous years.[67]

ILLUSTRATION 4-8: Texas Instruments had the following tax rate reconciliation in its 2018 Annual Report (note 5).

---

60 H.R. Rep. No. 201, 97th Cong., 1st Sess. 111 (1981).

61 P.L. No. 114–113 (Dec. 18, 2015).

62 IRC Section 41(a)(1).

63 IRC Sections 41(d)(1) and (d)(3).

64 IRC Sections 41(d)(1), (d)(2) and (d)(3).

65 IRC Section 41(c).

66 *See* Bittker & Lokken, supra note 32, at ¶ 27.4.2.

67 IRC Section 41(c)(4).

Principal reconciling items from the U.S. statutory income tax rate to the effective tax rate (provision for income taxes as a percentage of income before income taxes) are as follows:

	For years ended December 31,		
	2018	**2017**	**2016**
U.S. statutory income tax rate	21.0%	35.0%	35.0%
U.S. tax benefit for foreign derived intangible income	(5.3)	—	—
U.S. Tax Act transitional non-cash expense	4.2	—	—
U.S. Tax Act enactment-date effects and measurement period adjustments	(0.7)	12.7	
U.S. tax on global intangible low-taxed income	0.4	—	—
U.S. tax benefit for manufacturing	—	(1.6)	(1.5)
U.S. excess tax benefit for stock compensation	(2.0)	(4.1)	(3.0)
U.S. R & D tax credit	(1.3)	(1.1)	(1.2)
U.S. non-deductible expenses	0.2	0.2	0.3
Non-U.S. effective tax rates	0.1	(2.5)	(3.7)
Impact of changes to uncertain tax positions—	0.7	0.6	
Other	(0.1)	0.1	0.6
Effective tax rate	16.5%	39.4%	27.1%

As seen in Texas Instruments' effective tax rate reconciliation, the deduction for foreign-derived intangible income (FDII) and the R&D tax credit are permanent differences. In 2018, they reduced Texas Instruments' effective tax rate by 5.3 percentage points and 1.3 percentage points, respectively.

§ 4.04 Tax Deferral and Temporary Differences

[1] General Principles

Probably the most common view of tax deferral among tax academics and practitioners is the interest-free loan analogy, which equates tax deferral to an interest-free loan from the government to the taxpayer.[68] The U.S. government has certainly viewed tax deferral in this manner. For example, in November 1984, the Treasury Department released its report, titled *Tax Reform for Fairness, Simplicity, and Economic Growth.* This report is commonly referred to as *Treasury I.* In *Treasury I*, the Treasury Department described tax deferral as the "Federal Government effectively provid[ing] to the taxpayer an interest-free loan equal to the deferred tax liability. The value of tax deferral is greater, the longer the deferral and the higher the taxpayer's marginal tax

[68] Some other views of tax deferral include the percentage exclusion view and the yield exemption view. For purposes of this discussion, it is not relevant what view of tax deferral is utilized. For a discussion of the various views of tax deferral, *see, e.g.*, Stanley S. Surrey, *Pathways to Tax Reform* 120–125 (1973); Michael J. Graetz & Anne L. Alstott, *Federal Income Taxation: Principles and Policies* 297–303 (9th ed., 2022); Christopher H. Hanna, *Comparative Income Tax Deferral: The United States and Japan* 13–28 (2000).

rate."[69] The Treasury then provided the following chart showing the effective tax rate per dollar of income deferred by a taxpayer in the 50 percent marginal tax bracket.[70]

	Deferral Period (in years)					
Interest rate	1 year	3 years	5 years	10 years	20 years	30 years
4 percent	48.1	44.4	41.1	33.8	22.8	15.4
6 percent	47.2	41.0	47.4	27.9	15.6	8.7
8 percent	46.3	39.7	34.0	23.2	10.7	5.0
10 percent	45.4	37.6	31.0	19.3	7.4	2.9
12 percent	44.6	35.6	28.4	16.1	5.2	1.7

As the chart demonstrates, at a six percent interest rate, a ten-year deferral period effectively reduces a 50 percent marginal tax rate to only 27.9 percent.[71] If the interest rate is 12 percent and the deferral period is 30 years, then a 50 percent marginal tax rate is effectively reduced to 1.7 percent, almost equivalent to complete exclusion.

In the Internal Revenue Code, Congress has provided a number of tax deferral provisions. Generally, a deferral provision falls into one of two categories: (1) an item of income or gain that is not currently taxed but rather is taxed in a later year, or (2) a deduction or loss that is accelerated from a future year to the current year.[72] In both cases, a tax savings is achieved for the current year with an offsetting increase in taxes in a later year. However, even with constant tax rates, the taxpayer is benefiting from the deferral through the time value of money. In other words, the taxpayer can take the immediate tax savings in the current year and invest it so that when the offsetting increase in taxes takes place in a later year, the taxpayer will pay the increased taxes and still have some amount of the invested taxes left over. Some common examples of deferral provisions in the tax laws include accelerated depreciation,[73] section 179 expensing,[74] the installment method for reporting gain from an installment sale[75] unrealized appreciation in property,[76] and expensing of tangible depreciable property with a recovery period of twenty years or less.[77]

When an item of income or gain is deferred from a corporation's gross income (and therefore taxable income) it may lead to a current difference between the corporation's taxable income and its pretax financial income. More specifically, that item of income or

---

[69] *See* United States Department of the Treasury, *Tax Reform for Fairness, Simplicity and Economic Growth* (*Treasury I*) (Nov. 1984) at 126.

[70] *See id.* at 127.

[71] The formula for computing the effective tax rate in the table provided by the Treasury Department is:

$T/(1 + i)^n$ where:

T = tax rate

i = interest rate

n = years in the deferral period.

[72] *See, e.g.*, Hanna, supra note 68, at 1.

[73] IRC Section 168.

[74] IRC Section 179.

[75] IRC Section 453.

[76] IRC Section 1001.

[77] IRC Section 168(k).

gain, while deferred from taxable income, may be currently included in pretax financial income. As a result, pretax financial income is greater than taxable income by the deferred amount. In a later year, however, when the deferred amount is included in gross income (and therefore taxable income), taxable income will be greater than pretax financial income by the deferred amount. As a result, the deferred amount creates a temporary difference between taxable income and pretax financial income, which reverses in a later year when the deferred amount is included in taxable income. For financial accounting purposes, the deferred amount is referred to as a temporary difference, many times referred to by practitioners as a timing difference.[78]

The Financial Accounting Standards Board (FASB) has defined a temporary difference as occurring when the tax basis of an asset or liability differs from its financial reporting basis (i.e., book basis).[79] For example, assume a corporation purchases equipment for $100,000 and immediately places it in service. In the first year, assume the corporation's depreciation deduction for tax purposes is $20,000 but its depreciation expense for financial accounting purposes is only $15,000.[80] As a result, the tax basis of the equipment is $80,000 ($100,000 less $20,000 of tax depreciation) at the end of year one and its book basis is $85,000 ($100,000 less $15,000 of book depreciation). Because the tax basis differs from the book basis, a temporary difference of $5,000 has arisen. This temporary difference of $5,000 will eventually reverse out and be eliminated as the equipment becomes fully depreciated, at which time its tax basis and book basis will both be zero.

[2] Examples of Tax Deferral Provisions and Temporary Differences

The Internal Revenue Code contains a number of tax deferral provisions, which are, in almost all cases, temporary differences under the financial accounting rules. Three common tax deferral provisions will be discussed: (1) installment sales of property, (2) accelerated depreciation for equipment, and (3) foreign source income of foreign subsidiaries of U.S. parent corporations.

[a] Installment Sales of Property

Under the Code, a taxpayer that makes an installment sale of property at a gain may recognize the gain in gross income under the installment method.[81] An installment

---

[78] In 1967, the Accounting Principles Board issued Opinion No. 11, entitled Accounting for Income Taxes. In the opinion, the APB defined a timing difference as "[d]ifferences between the periods in which transactions affect taxable income and the periods in which they enter into the determination of pretax accounting income. Timing differences originate in one period and reverse or 'turn around' in one or more subsequent periods." Accounting for Income Taxes, APB Opinion No. 11, paragraph 13.e. Although APB 11 was superseded by SFAS No. 109 and FASB ASC 740, some practitioners still use the term "timing difference" in describing a "temporary difference."

[79] FASB ASC 740–10–20. If a corporation's tax basis in an asset is greater than its book basis in the asset, a *deductible* temporary difference is created resulting in a deferred tax asset. If a corporation's tax basis in an asset is less than its book basis in the asset, a *taxable* temporary difference is created resulting in a deferred tax liability. *Id.*

[80] The difference between the amount of the depreciation deduction and the depreciation expense may be due to the use of an accelerated method of depreciation for tax purposes and the straight-line method of depreciation for financial accounting purposes, the use of a longer recovery period for financial accounting purposes than for tax purposes, or a different placed in service date for financial accounting purposes than for tax purposes.

[81] IRC Section 453(a). In fact, the installment method is mandatory unless the taxpayer elects for it not to apply. IRC Section 453(d).

sale arises when property is sold at a gain and at least one payment is to be received by the seller after the close of the year in which the sale occurred.[82] Congress enacted the installment sale rules in 1926, when arguably tax deferral and time value of money were not widely recognized issues.[83] In more recent times, tax law academics have written about and discussed the tax deferral benefits of the installment sale rules.[84] One commonly accepted view is that the tax that is being deferred can be analogized to an interest-free loan from the government.[85] For example, assume a corporation makes an installment sale of property with a basis of $200,000 and a sales price of $1 million. The buyer will pay $500,000 down and an additional $500,000 (with interest) in one year. The corporation recognizes a gain of $400,000 in year one and an additional $400,000 of gain in year two.[86] Assuming a 21 percent corporate tax rate, the corporation pays $84,000 ($400,000 gain times 21 percent) of taxes in year one and an additional $84,000 of taxes in year two. The corporation has deferred paying taxes of $84,000 for one year. This deferral can be viewed as the government loaning the corporation $84,000 for one year with no interest due.[87]

For financial accounting purposes, the corporation's pretax financial income remains unchanged as a result of the corporation's use of the installment method for tax purposes. Under the financial accounting rules, a corporation is generally not permitted to use the installment method in computing its pretax financial income.[88] It must report the entire amount of gain at the time of sale. Therefore, in the above example, the corporation will report the entire $800,000 of gain in revenue in year one (i.e., the year of sale) regardless of whether the corporation uses the installment method for tax purposes.

In measuring net income, income tax expense is an item that is aggregated with other expenses, then subtracted from total revenues, in arriving at net income. Because the corporation only pays taxes in year one on $400,000 of gain, it appears that the income tax expense for year one will only reflect $84,000 of taxes ($400,000 of gain times

---

[82] IRC Section 453(b)(1).

[83] Revenue Act of 1926, Pub. L. No. 20, section 212(d). The Supreme Court has written that the purpose for the enactment of the installment sale method was "to relieve taxpayers who adopted it from having to pay an income tax in the year of sale based on the full amount of anticipated profits when in fact they had received in cash only a small portion of the sales price. Another reason was the difficult and time-consuming effort of appraising the uncertain market value of installment obligations." *Commissioner v. South Texas Lumber Co.*, 333 U.S. 496, 503 (1948).

[84] *See, e.g.*, Martin D. Ginsburg, *Teaching Tax Law After Tax Reform*, 65 Wash. L. Rev. 595, 617 (1990); Daniel I. Halperin, *The Time Value of Money—1984*, 23 Tax Notes 751 (1984); Christopher H. Hanna, *The Virtual Reality of Eliminating Tax Deferral*, 12 Amer. J. Tax Pol'y 449 (1995); Lee A. Sheppard, *Ginsburg Discusses Taxing the Privilege of Tax Deferral in Installment Sales*, 27 Tax Notes 457 (1985).

[85] In 1987, Congress enacted IRC Section 453A imposing an interest charge on the tax being deferred under the installment method, in a sense, recognizing that the seller of the property is, in essence, receiving an interest-free loan from the government. Pub. L. No. 100–203, 101 Stat. 1330–382 (1987). The interest charge only applies, however, on installment obligations arising from the sale of property, if the total amount of installment obligations that arose during the year and were outstanding at the end of the year exceeded $5 million. IRC Section 453A. *See* Christopher H. Hanna & Samuel Olchyk, *Interest Under Section 453A(c): Is It or Isn't It?* 56 Tax Notes 1345 (1992).

[86] In computing the amount of gain recognized each year, the corporation must compute the selling price, total contract price, gross profit and gross profit ratio from the installment sale. Treas. Reg. § 15a.453–1(b)(2).

[87] *See Treasury I*, supra note 69, at 129 ("Charging interest on the amount of the deferred tax liability for taxpayers electing the installment method would make the tax law neutral as to the financing of property sales and would end use of installment sales as a vehicle for tax deferral.").

[88] *See* FASB ASC 606–10–05–3; FASB ASC 606-10-05-4; FASB ASC 606-10-25-8.

21 percent tax rate). However, the $400,000 of gain that will be recognized for tax purposes in year two is a temporary difference. As a result, the corporation will in year one record a deferred tax liability of $84,000 ($400,000 temporary difference times 21 percent tax rate), reflecting the fact that it will pay the $84,000 of taxes in year two. In recording the deferred tax liability of $84,000, the corporation will also, in year one, show deferred tax expense of $84,000, which when added to the current tax expense of $84,000 in year one equals the income tax expense for year one of $168,000. Consequently, the deferral of $84,000 of taxes from year one to year two does not increase net income for the corporation in year one.[89] The corporation will report net income of $632,000 in year one ($800,000 gain less $168,000 of income tax expense) even if the gain is recognized in gross income for tax purposes over two years through use of the installment method. In other words, for financial accounting purposes, it is as if the entire gain were taxed in year one.

	Income Statement (Installment Method Used for Tax Purposes)	Income Statement (Installment Method Not Used for Tax Purposes)
Revenues:		
Gain	$800,000	$800,000
Current Tax Expense	$84,000	$168,000
Deferred Tax Expense	$84,000	$0
Net Income	$632,000	$632,000

As previously stated, corporate management is focused on net income, earnings per share, and effective tax rate. The corporation's use of the installment method for tax purposes did not affect its net income for the year of sale of the property, which remained unchanged at $632,000 whether or not the installment method was used for tax purposes. The corporation's EPS is computed based on its net income for the year, and consequently, the corporation's use of the installment method has no effect on its EPS for the year of sale of the property. If, for example, the corporation had 100,000 shares of stock outstanding, its EPS would be $6.32 ($632,000 net income divided by 100,000 shares) whether or not the installment method was used for tax purposes. As a result, the key business indicator in the financial world is unaffected by a temporary difference (i.e., use of the installment method for tax purposes).[90]

Corporate management is also very interested in the corporation's effective tax rate. In computing the effective tax rate, the corporation's income tax expense is divided by its operating income. In the above example, operating income is assumed to equal net income before income tax expense or more simply pretax financial income. Therefore, operating income is equal to $800,000 ($632,000 net income plus income tax expense of $168,000). The effective tax rate is equal to $168,000 (income tax expense) divided by $800,000 (operating income) or 21 percent. The 21 percent effective tax rate, which the

[89] FASB considered the issue of discounting deferred taxes to present value but determined not to do so. SFAS No. 109, paragraph 5.b; FASB ASC 740-10-30-8. Discounting is discussed in detail at Section 4.05[3].

[90] Temporary differences may impact a corporation's earnings per share in future years. *See* Section 4.05[2].

corporation will disclose in a footnote to its financial statements filed with the Form 10-K, is unchanged whether or not the installment method was used for tax purposes. In other words, temporary differences do not affect a corporation's effective tax rate. The reason is that temporary differences create deferred taxes that are included in income tax expense along with current tax expense.

[b] Accelerated Depreciation for Equipment

Under the Code, a corporation may depreciate tangible personal property under an accelerated method of depreciation.[91] The general rule for the depreciation method is the 200 percent declining balance method of depreciation, sometimes referred to as double declining balance method of depreciation.[92] If a corporation elects, it may use the 150 percent declining balance method of depreciation or the straight-line method of depreciation.[93] For financial accounting purposes, a corporation will depreciate an asset over its useful life.[94] If the number of years specified for tax purposes for depreciation deductions for an asset does not fall within a reasonable range of the asset's useful life, then the depreciation deductions for tax purposes may not be used as depreciation expenses for financial reporting purposes.[95] Although accelerated methods of depreciation (such as the double declining balance) are acceptable methods for financial reporting purposes,[96] many corporations use the straight-line method of depreciation for two reasons: (1) it results in a greater amount of pretax financial income (at least in the early years of the depreciable asset) as opposed to an accelerated depreciation method, and (2) it is simple to use.

Similar to a corporation's use of the installment method, a corporation's use of accelerated depreciation merely creates a temporary difference between pretax financial income and taxable income. For example, assume a corporation purchases equipment for $1 million (and places it in service) on January 1, 2017. It uses accelerated depreciation for tax purposes (200 percent declining balance with the half-year convention) and straight-line depreciation for financial accounting purposes, in both cases, over a five-year recovery period/useful life. The following table shows the depreciation expense, depreciation deduction, book basis of the equipment and tax basis of the equipment each year.

---

[91] IRC Section 168.

[92] IRC Section 168(b)(1).

[93] IRC Sections 168(b)(2)(C) and 168(b)(3)(D).

[94] FASB ASC 360–10–35–3.

[95] FASB ASC 360–10–35–9.

[96] FASB ASC 360–10–35–7.

Year	(a) Depreciation Expense (Accounting)	(b) Depreciation Deduction (Tax)	(c) Difference ((a) – (b))	(d) Book Basis	(e) Tax Basis	(f) Difference ((d) – (e))
2017	$200,000	$200,000	0	$800,000	$800,000	0
2018	$200,000	$320,000	($120,000)	$600,000	$480,000	$120,000
2019	$200,000	$192,000	$8,000	$400,000	$288,000	$112,000
2020	$200,000	$115,200	$84,800	$200,000	$172,800	$27,200
2021	$200,000	$115,200	$84,800	0	$57,600	($57,600)
2022	0	$57,600	($57,600)	0	0	0

In 2017, the tax and book depreciation are the same. But in 2018, the corporation has $120,000 *more* of tax depreciation deduction than book depreciation expense with respect to the equipment. The tax basis of the equipment is $120,000 lower than the book basis of the equipment creating a temporary difference of $120,000. As a result, in 2018, the corporation will record a deferred tax liability of $25,200 ($120,000 times 21 percent) with a corresponding increase to deferred tax expense of $25,200.

Assume that, in 2018, the corporation has revenues of $20 million and its only expenses were depreciation and income taxes. The following table shows the corporation's income statement for 2018 if it uses accelerated depreciation for tax purposes or straight-line depreciation for tax purposes:

	Income Statement (Accelerated Depreciation Used for Tax Purposes)	Income Statement (Straight-Line Depreciation Used for Tax Purposes)
Revenues:	$20,000,000	$20,000,000
Expenses:		
Depreciation Expense	$ 200,000	$ 200,000
Operating Income	$19,800,000	$19,800,000
Current Tax Expense	$ 4,132,800	$ 4,158,000
Deferred Tax Expense	$ 25,200	$ 0
Net Income	$15,642,000	$15,642,000

The corporation's net income will be the same whether it uses accelerated depreciation or straight-line depreciation for tax purposes. The reason is that the tax benefit from the excess of accelerated depreciation over straight-line depreciation is recorded for financial accounting purposes as a deferred tax liability of $25,200 with a corresponding increase to deferred tax expense. As a result, the corporation's net income remains at $15,642,000 for 2018. The corporation's EPS will also be the same whether it uses accelerated depreciation or straight-line depreciation for tax purposes.

In addition, the corporation's effective tax rate is also unaffected by use of accelerated depreciation for tax purposes. In the above example, operating income (and pretax financial income) is $19.8 million. The effective tax rate is $4.158 million (income tax expense) divided by $19.8 million (operating income) or 21 percent. The effective tax rate is 21 percent whether or not the corporation uses an accelerated depreciation method for tax purposes. As a result, accelerated depreciation does not increase a corporation's net income or its EPS, and does not lower a corporation's effective tax rate.

[c] Foreign Source Income of a Foreign Subsidiary of a U.S. Corporation

Under the financial accounting rules, if a corporation owns 20 percent or more of the voting stock of another corporation (whether domestic or foreign) but not more than 50 percent, then the investor corporation is presumed, in the absence of predominant evidence to the contrary, as having "significant influence" over the investee corporation.[97] The investor corporation will account for its investment in the investee corporation under the equity method of accounting, which treats the income of the investee corporation as flowing through to the investor corporation.[98] Deferred taxes are not recorded on the investor corporation's equity investment in the investee corporation. If the investor corporation owns more than 50 percent of the outstanding stock of the investee corporation, then the investor corporation is referred to as the parent corporation and the investee corporation is referred to as the subsidiary corporation.[99] The parent corporation will include in its consolidated financial statement its share of the income of the subsidiary and the subsidiary's assets and liabilities.[100]

In computing the U.S. parent's book basis in its foreign subsidiary stock, the book income of the foreign subsidiary flows through to the U.S. parent.[101] As a result, for financial accounting purposes, the U.S. parent will increase its basis in the stock of the foreign subsidiary.[102] For tax purposes, prior to 2018, however, none, or only a portion of, the income of the foreign subsidiary would flow through to the U.S. parent. As a result, the U.S. parent's book basis in its foreign subsidiary will generally be greater than its tax basis. Under the financial accounting rules, the excess of book basis over tax basis in an asset is a temporary difference leading to the recording of a deferred tax

---

[97] FASB ASC 323–10–15–8. An investment of less than 20 percent of the voting stock of another corporation leads to a presumption that the investor corporation does not have significant influence over the investee corporation unless such influence can be demonstrated.

[98] FASB ASC 323–10–35–4.

[99] *See* FASB ASC 810–10–15–8. For tax purposes, only if the investor corporation owns 80 percent or more of the investee corporation, is the investor corporation referred to as the parent corporation and the investee corporation as the subsidiary corporation. *See, e.g.*, IRC Sections 332, 337, and 1504.

[100] FASB ASC 810.

[101] FASB ASC 810 (consolidation). Under the equity method, the income will flow through the foreign corporation to its U.S. shareholder. FASB ASC 323–10–35–4. In essence, the income of the foreign corporation is aggregated with the income of its U.S. shareholder. If the U.S. shareholder and foreign corporation file consolidated financial statements, the income of the foreign subsidiary is aggregated with the income of its U.S. parent. Both the equity method and consolidation, in essence, aggregate the income of the foreign corporation with its U.S. shareholder. As a result, the equity method is sometimes referred to as "one line consolidation." *See* Joanne M. Flood, *Wiley GAAP: Financial Statement Disclosure Manual* ch. 19 (2021).

[102] FASB ASC 810 (consolidation). FASB ASC 323–10–35–4 ("An investor adjusts the carrying amount of an investment for its share of the earnings or losses of the investee subsequent to the date of investment.").

liability with a corresponding increase to deferred tax expense.[103] The difference in the outside basis of the foreign subsidiary must be temporary before a deferred tax liability applies. For instance, where there is no foreign capital gains tax and no U.S. tax on the sale of a foreign subsidiary, and it is management's intent to sell the foreign subsidiary to recover its investment, the outside book and tax basis difference will not give rise to a deferred tax liability.

This determination must be done on a jurisdictional basis, so each jurisdiction that has the right to impose income tax on an outside basis difference, as such difference reverses, must be evaluated and recorded. The outside basis difference is generally due to undistributed earnings. This concept is based on the presumption that all undistributed earnings of a subsidiary will be ultimately transferred to the parent company. The tax impact of this hypothetical distribution may be based on the assumption that the unremitted earnings are distributed in the current period and that the parent company receives the benefit of all viable tax planning alternatives and available tax credits and deductions. The income tax expense of the parent should include taxes that would be withheld if the undistributed earnings had been remitted as dividends.[104]

However, if the book basis is lower than the tax basis, a deferred tax asset is not recorded. FASB ASC 740–30 provides that a deferred tax asset will only be recorded when an investment in the foreign subsidiary is essentially permanent in nature and the temporary difference will reverse in the foreseeable future.[105] Although a deferred tax asset and prepaid tax share similar economic attributes, they are different from a GAAP perspective. The distinction between a prepaid tax and a deferred tax asset is that, in the case of a prepaid tax, the tax rate has been fixed at the time of the transaction. As a result, the prepaid tax is not adjusted for fluctuations in tax rates and currency exchange rates. A deferred tax asset, however, is subject to periodic adjustments due to any fluctuation in tax rates and currency exchange rates.[106]

Under the financial accounting rules, FASB has provided an exception to the recording of a deferred tax liability with respect to the excess of book basis over tax basis in the stock of a foreign subsidiary if there is a showing of sufficient evidence that the foreign subsidiary has invested or will invest its undistributed earnings indefinitely (i.e., the investment is essentially permanent in duration).[107] This exception to the recording

---

[103] FASB ASC 740–30–25–5; FASB ASC 740–30–25–7; and FASB ASC 740–10–20 (book basis over tax basis in an asset is a taxable temporary difference).

[104] FASB ASC 740–30–25–3; FASB ASC 740–30–25–6.

[105] The GAAP literature does not define "foreseeable future," but the major accounting firms believe it should be within twelve months, although there have been situations where companies recorded the deferred asset without recognition actually occurring for several years.

[106] FASB ASC 740–10–35–4; FASB ASC 740–10–45–15.

[107] FASB ASC 740–30–25–18; FASB ASC 740–30–25–17 ("The presumption that all undistributed earnings will be transferred to the parent entity may be overcome, and no income taxes shall be accrued by the parent entity, if sufficient evidence shows that the subsidiary has invested or will invest the undistributed earnings indefinitely or that the earnings will be remitted in a tax-free liquidation."). The indefinite reinvestment doctrine may also apply to earnings from foreign corporate joint ventures. A corporate joint venture is an entity owned and operated by a small group as a separate and specific business or project for the mutual benefit of the members of the group. Typically, the entity is formed in order to share risks and rewards in developing a new market, product or technology, or to combine complementary technological knowledge, or to pool resources in developing production or other facilities. *See* FASB ASC 323–10–20 Glossary.

of a deferred tax liability is referred to as the APB 23 provision, named after Opinion No. 23 issued by the Accounting Principles Board in 1972.[108]

When the Accounting Principles Board enacted APB 23 (later FASB ASC 740–30) in April 1972, several members of the Board dissented to the omission of a requirement providing for deferred income taxes.[109] The dissenting members believed that the earnings of the foreign subsidiary were being accounted for under the accrual method while the related income taxes were being accounted for under the cash method.[110] They viewed this as completely contrary to the concept of deferred tax accounting for other businesses.[111] In addition, the dissenting members believed that the accounting distinction for over 50 percent investors (no deferred income taxes) and 50 percent or less investors (accounting for deferred income taxes) was completely artificial.[112]

FASB revisited APB 23 with the enactment of FAS 109 in 1992. FASB changed many parts of APB 23, but retained an exception for the recognition of a deferred tax liability with respect to a more than 50 percent investment in a foreign corporation (i.e., a foreign subsidiary as defined for financial accounting purposes).[113]

Since the exception only applies to a *foreign* subsidiary, that classification must be determined. Whether a subsidiary is domestic or foreign is made with respect to the immediate shareholder of the subsidiary. Thus, application of the doctrine to the unrepatriated earnings of a Country X subsidiary (FCo) is not permitted if it is held by a Country X corporation. However, if FCo is owned by a Country Y corporation, the doctrine may be applied to avoid the establishment of a deferred tax liability with respect to U.S. withholding tax on repatriation of the earnings to a Country Y parent. The indefinite reinvestment doctrine is not applicable to subsidiaries of the holding company when both the holding company and the subsidiary are tax domiciled in the same country.

Although the GAAP literature does not define when a company and its subsidiary are domestic or foreign, it is commonly understood that tax residency is determined by each jurisdiction's tax law. Unlike the U.S., a company's tax residency may be a country other than the country of incorporation. Since this determination is made for each parent company and subsidiary, local law is applied to determine whether an entity is a tax resident in that country. If an entity that is disregarded for U.S. tax purposes is, nevertheless, a tax resident under local law, it would render that entity a subsidiary in that country for FASB ASC 740–30. In addition to evaluating each company and its subsidiaries, the determination is made for each taxing jurisdiction. The temporary difference in the outside basis of a foreign subsidiary is based on the local tax basis of that subsidiary and the parent company's tax basis as determined under the tax law of the country in which the parent company is tax resident. The parent company could be subject to local country tax and home country tax should it sell its subsidiary. Finally,

---

108 FASB ASC 740–30.

109 APB Opinion No. 23, APB 23 Dissent (1972).

110 *Id.*

111 *Id.*

112 *Id.*

113 FASB ASC 740–30–25–18. FASB stated in SFAS No. 109, paragraph 169, that it had retained an exception for the recognition of a deferred tax liability with respect to a more than 50 percent investment in a foreign corporation "because of (a) the complexity in measuring the deferred tax liability for foreign undistributed earnings, (b) the need to compromise and (c) the omission of discounting."

there are foreign currency considerations because the outside tax basis is generally denominated in the local country's currency which could be different than the GAAP reporting currency.

> **ILLUSTRATION 4-9:** USCo is incorporated in the United States. FCo is a wholly-owned subsidiary that is incorporated in Country F. There is a tax treaty between the United States and Country F. A company is tax resident in Country F if its mind and management is in Country F. Since the board of directors of FCo resides in the United States, Country F determined that FCo is tax resident in the United States. Under U.S. tax law, tax residency is determined by place of incorporation. FCo would be tax resident in Country F under U.S. tax law. The tax treaty provides that when a company has dual tax residency, the law of Country F takes precedence. As a result, FCo is tax resident in the United States. USCo and FCo are both domestic companies under GAAP. USCo cannot assert the indefinite reinvestment doctrine and must record deferred taxes on the basis difference in FCo.

FASB ASC 740–30–25–17 and FASB ASC 740–30–25–19 set forth the criteria to meet the indefinite reinvestment doctrine. FASB ASC 740–30 requires sufficient evidence that the subsidiary has invested or will invest the undistributed earnings indefinitely. The parent company should have evidence of specific plans for reinvestment of the earnings which demonstrate that the remittance of the earnings will be postponed indefinitely. FASB ASC 740–30 looks to the past experience of the company as well as plans for future operations, remittances, and investments. In order to substantiate a position that undistributed earnings will not be remitted, it may be necessary to examine the projected working capital needs of the parent corporation, debt maturities of the parent corporation, and expected sources of income to service parent debt and to fund dividends and other anticipated domestic needs of the parent.

FASB ASC 740–30–05–4 sets forth the following non-exclusive list of factors that would be considered by the parent and subsidiary in determining whether undistributed earnings will be permanently reinvested:

a. financial requirements of the parent company;

b. financial requirements of the subsidiary;

c. operational and fiscal objectives of the parent company, both long-term and short-term;

d. remittance restrictions imposed by governments;

e. remittance restrictions imposed by lease or financing agreements of the subsidiary;

f. tax consequences of the remittance.

FASB ASC 740–30–05–5 concludes with the statement that "[h]owever, the parent company may control the events that create the tax consequences," which implies the electivity of the exception.

If circumstances change and it becomes apparent that part or all of the undistributed earnings of the foreign subsidiary will be remitted in the foreseeable future, then the parent entity must accrue for the current period, income tax expense attributable to the remittance.[114]

The indefinite reinvestment doctrine can be applied on an entity-by-entity, year-by-year, or quarter-by-quarter basis. Further, it appears that the doctrine can be applied to a specific amount of earnings of a specific foreign subsidiary.[115] Due to this high level of flexibility and electivity, companies' decisions to assert and change their assertion on the indefinite reinvestment doctrine have been subject to heightened scrutiny by the Securities and Exchange Commission, as discussed later in this section. In 2015, HP Inc. earned $4.7 billion before taxes and booked a tax liability of $178 million for a 3.8 percent effective tax rate. As explained in the following illustration, the indefinite reinvestment doctrine was the major factor behind the extremely low effective tax rate. As discussed later in this section, the Tax Cuts and Jobs Act renders it unnecessary for a U.S. multinational company to assert the indefinite reinvestment doctrine to achieve a low effective rate.

ILLUSTRATION 4-10: The rate reconciliation table that appears in the financial statements of HP Inc. (note 6) for fiscal year ending October 31, 2015, illustrates the impact of the indefinite reinvestment doctrine on the effective tax rate of a company. In 2015, the effective tax rate of HP Inc. was reduced by 16.2 percentage points as a result of utilizing the doctrine. In 2014 and 2013, the effective tax rates were reduced by an equally impressive 12.9 percentage points and 24.5 percentage points, respectively.

"The differences between the U.S. federal statutory income tax rate and HP's effective tax rate were as follows:

	For the fiscal years ended October 31		
	2015	**2014**	**2013**
U.S. federal statutory income tax rate	35.0%	35.0%	35.0%
State income taxes, net of federal tax benefit	(4.6)%	0.4%	0.1%
Lower rates in other jurisdictions, net	(16.2)%	(12.9)%	(24.5)%
Valuation allowances	(23.4)%	1.7%	3.8%
Uncertain tax positions	10.1%	(2.3)%	4.1%
Other, net	(2.9)%	1.6%	3.0%
	3.8%	23.5%	21.5%

"The jurisdictions with favorable tax rates that have the most significant effective tax rate impact in the periods presented include Puerto Rico, Singapore, China, Malaysia, Ireland and Netherlands. To the extent that HP plans to reinvest earnings of these jurisdictions indefinitely outside the United States, U.S. taxes have not been provided on those indefinitely reinvested earnings."

In 2015, the 16.2 percentage point reduction in the effective tax rate increased HP's earnings by $760 million. In 2013 and 2014, HP's earnings were increased by,

[114] FASB ASC 740-30-25-19.

[115] *See* Section 1.05.

respectively, $1.6 billion and $840 million as a result of the indefinite reinvestment doctrine.

A major strategic business shift is another catalyst to no longer assert the indefinite reinvestment doctrine. In 2015, General Electric announced its intention to sell its massive GE Capital division and use $50 billion of the proceeds to fund a share repurchase. General Electric will accrue $12 billion in taxes to repatriate the sale proceeds. This followed an announcement by eBay in early 2014 that it would accrue $3 billion in taxes to repatriate $9 billion. The $6 billion of after-tax cash would provide eBay with financial flexibility to capitalize on opportunities which the company believed are increasingly in the U.S. Once a company gets to a critical size, it is very difficult, if not impossible, to reinvest foreign earnings in projects that generate an acceptable financial return. A company that is willing to distort its portfolio so it is overly weighted in foreign investments simply exacerbates its capital inflexibility problem.

The SEC has increased its scrutiny of U.S. multinational enterprises by asking them to substantiate claims of indefinite reinvestment pursuant to FASB ASC 740–30–25–17 (formerly APB 23).[116] The increased scrutiny appears to be due to the significant amounts of offshore cash held by U.S. multinationals. Some examples of SEC comments issued to U.S. multinational enterprises with respect to undistributed earnings of foreign subsidiaries include:

1. We also note your disclosures on page X that you are not able to reasonably estimate the amount of undistributed foreign earnings that are considered to be reinvested indefinitely outside the United States. Please clarify for us why you cannot make an estimate of this amount. As applicable, please revise your MD&A [management discussion and analysis] liquidity section to discuss how your indefinite reinvestment in foreign operations may affect your liquidity.

2. We note your disclosure that you have not provided for U.S. federal and state income and foreign withholding taxes on your non-U.S. continuing operations subsidiaries undistributed earnings. Please explain to us how your accounting complies with paragraph 740–30–25–3 of the FASB Accounting Standards Codification. In this regard, to the extent that you believe you qualify for the exception outlined in paragraph 740–30–25–17 of the FASB Accounting Standards Codification, please explain to us your basis for this conclusion in light of your disclosure in the preceding paragraph that in part because of your ability to repatriate earnings, you believe it is more likely than not that sufficient taxable income will be generated to realize the net deferred tax assets.

A few years prior, in a set of "form" comment letters in the spring of 2011, the SEC requested a number of companies to (1) disclose and quantify the top two countries that impacted their worldwide tax rates, and (2) disclose in the Management Discussion and Analysis (MD&A) section the amount of U.S. tax the company would pay to repatriate foreign earnings. The SEC wants the company to disclose that certain cash is "not available" for U.S. operations unless the company incurs U.S. and other taxes.

---

[116] *See* Amanda Athanasiou, *SEC Scrutinizing Claims of Indefinite Reinvestment Overseas*, 74 Tax Notes Int'l 919 (June 9, 2014).

The industries with a large amount of earnings that asserted the indefinite reinvestment doctrine are the pharmaceutical and high-tech electronic sectors. The offshore cash presented a dilemma, in particular for such companies. Because the earnings are mostly from low-tax and no-tax countries, the cash is trapped offshore and the only long-term way to get that money back into the U.S. was to pay U.S. tax.[117]

The Tax Cuts and Jobs Act reduced the value of the indefinite reinvestment doctrine as a result of the enactment of the global intangible low-taxed income (GILTI) regime, which taxes most of the income of a foreign subsidiary on an annual basis to its U.S. shareholder. However, there continues to be value in making the APB 23 assertion when foreign earnings are subject to additional taxes, such as a dividend withholding tax or U.S. state and local taxes upon repatriation. Some companies have decided to no longer assert the indefinite reinvestment doctrine for earnings subject to the transition tax, thereby accruing the other non-U.S. federal income taxes. By accruing all these taxes, these companies could repatriate such earnings in the future without incurring the earnings impact of the tax. If the indefinite reinvestment doctrine is not asserted on previously taxed income, any foreign-currency-exchange impact and change-in-law impact will need to be recorded each reporting period.

ILLUSTRATION 4-11: Texas Instruments had the following tax rate reconciliation in its 2018 Annual Report (note 5).

Principal reconciling items from the U.S. statutory income tax rate to the effective tax rate (provision for income taxes as a percentage of income before income taxes) are as follows:

	For years ended December 31,		
	2018	**2017**	**2016**
U.S. statutory income tax rate	21.0%	35.0%	35.0%
U.S. tax benefit for foreign derived intangible income	(5.3)	—	—
U.S. Tax Act transitional non-cash expense	4.2	—	—
U.S. Tax Act enactment-date effects and measurement period adjustments	(0.7)	12.7	
U.S. tax on global intangible low-taxed income	0.4	—	—
U.S. tax benefit for manufacturing	—	(1.6)	(1.5)
U.S. excess tax benefit for stock compensation	(2.0)	(4.1)	(3.0)
U.S. R & D tax credit	(1.3)	(1.1)	(1.2)
U.S. non-deductible expenses	0.2	0.2	0.3
Non-U.S. effective tax rates	0.1	(2.5)	(3.7)
Impact of changes to uncertain tax positions—	0.7	0.6	
Other	(0.1)	0.1	0.6

[117] The cash is not really trapped offshore but directly or indirectly finds its way back to the U.S. For instance, many companies' foreign subsidiaries use the cash to purchase U.S. government bonds or U.S. corporate bonds.

Effective tax rate	16.5%	39.4%	27.1%

Texas Instruments asserted the indefinite reinvestment doctrine for 2017 and 2016 reducing their effective tax rate by 2.5 percentage points and 3.7 percentage points, respectively. For 2018, Texas Instruments continued to assert the indefinite reinvestment doctrine but only for its non-cash operating assets. As to cash being held by its foreign subsidiaries, Texas Instruments wrote: "However, withholding taxes in certain non-U.S. jurisdictions will be incurred upon repatriation of available cash to the United States. A provision has been made for deferred taxes on these undistributed earnings to the extent that dividend payments from these subsidiaries are expected to result in a withholding tax liability." This increased Texas Instruments' effective tax rate by 0.1 percentage point for 2018.

In some cases, certain U.S. companies may find it beneficial to treat the earnings as not permanently reinvested, making appropriate demonstration that reinvestment opportunities are in the United States. Accordingly, it would record the deferred tax liability. It may make this determination even though it has uses for the earnings in foreign locations.

Why would companies take this approach (i.e., not make the APB 23 assertion)? There could be a variety of reasons. For example, the company may have taken aggressive transfer pricing or other planning approaches and prefers not to address treatment of the planning approaches under FASB ASC 740–10,[118] the U.S. uncertain tax position disclosure for tax purposes,[119] or similar considerations in its home countries. In view of the potential issues, benefits as well as difficulties, noted above with respect to the indefinite reinvestment doctrine, it has continued to be a subject of controversy.[120]

As a practical matter, the decision whether to remit earnings of a foreign subsidiary in today's global economy is highly dependent upon the tax consequences of repatriation. The tax consequences of remitting earnings of a foreign subsidiary may be neutral in the event of income entitled to the 245A 100 percent dividends-received deduction enacted under the TCJA or the U.S. tax on income subject to the subpart F regime is fully offset by foreign tax credits.

Prior to the TCJA, the impact of the U.S. tax regime, exacerbated to some extent by the favorable accounting treatment of FASB ASC 740–30 may have distorted economic decision-making. For example, assume a company wanted to construct a new factory at a cost of approximately $100 million, and the company had adequate funds for the project in undistributed low-taxed earnings of its foreign subsidiary. Assume further that based on normal non-tax considerations (such as proximity to market, customs duties, availability of raw materials and adequate labor force, and availability of utilities and

---

118 *See* Section 9.03.

119 *See* Chapter 3. *See also Cook Lightly Grilled*, The Economist, May 25, 2013, at 65; Foroohar, *The Coming Corporate Crackdown*, Time, June 3, 2013, at 20; Hook & Yadron, *Apple CEO, Lawmakers Square Off Over Taxes*, Wall Street Journal, May 22, 2013, at 1; Puzzanghera, *Apple's Tax Shelters Faulted; It Avoids Paying Billions on Overseas Income Through a Web of Subsidiaries, a Senate Panel Finds*, Los Angeles Times, May 21, 2013; *In Face of Criticism, Apple CEO Says Company Has Paid All Taxes*, BNA Daily Tax Rep., May 22, 2013, at GG-1; *Senators: Apple Shifted Billions Offshore Using "Weaknesses" in Tax Law*, BNA Daily Tax Rep., May 5, 2013, at G-5.

120 *See* Parker, *Financial Reporting in the BEPS Era: Are FASB and the SEC the New Watchdogs?* 23 BNA Transfer Pricing Rep. 1603 (Apr. 30, 2015).

other infrastructure issues), the company was indifferent as to whether to locate the new factory in the United States or in a specific foreign location.

Utilizing undistributed earnings of a foreign subsidiary that have not been subject to local tax (possibly because the local jurisdiction imposes no tax, or provides pro-growth incentives, such as highly accelerated tax depreciation, or pursuant to a tax holiday) to construct the factory in the United States (whether or not such funds are obtained by the U.S. parent company via loan or by repatriation, or the foreign subsidiary constructs and owns the U.S. factory) would incur a U.S. tax liability of $35 million (utilizing the 35 percent U.S. corporate tax rate in effect prior to enactment of TCJA). As a result, the company would be required to repatriate sufficient funds from its foreign subsidiary to have $100 million after taxes to construct the factory in the United States. A 35 percent U.S. corporate tax on $154 million repatriated earnings would be approximately $54 million dollars, leaving the company with $100 million after taxes to construct the factory. Due to the constructive dividend rule of IRC Section 956, the outcome was similar where the foreign subsidiary constructs and owns the U.S. factory, the difference being the company would repatriate $54 million to pay the U.S. tax. Therefore, the total cost to the company of the new factory in the United States was, in essence, $154 million.

In contrast, construction of the factory in a non-U.S. location would permit use of the foreign subsidiary's accumulated earnings without incurring additional U.S. tax and would achieve the $100 million cost objective. This effect, which was clearly a disincentive to invest in the United States, has been referred to as the "lock-out effect" or the "negative investment credit." Congress, realizing the adverse impact on the U.S. economy of such practices (such as loss of jobs), enacted IRC Section 245A as part of the TCJA that provides a 100 dividends-received deduction for certain repatriated earnings of a foreign subsidiary beginning on January 1, 2018, and prior to that, Congress enacted IRC Section 965 as part of the American Jobs Creation Act of 2004 ("AJCA"), allowing a one-time repatriation of earnings at an effective tax cost of 5.25 percent. Although the lock-out effect was certainly real to a U.S. multinational company, whether the lock-out effect had a negative, neutral, or even positive impact on the U.S. economy is beyond the scope of this treatise.[121]

The impact of a change in circumstances that affects the indefinite reinvestment doctrine is reflected in income tax expense for the period in which the change of circumstances occurs.[122] A change in the domestic cash needs of a company may require the planned repatriation of earnings of a foreign subsidiary that is subject to significant dividend withholding taxes, which were subject to the indefinite reinvestment doctrine in prior periods. Under these circumstances, the income tax expense associated with the repatriation of the earnings from prior periods will increase current period tax expense even though the pre-tax earnings for the current period remain unaffected. Consequently, the change in circumstances results in an increase in the company's effective tax rate.

In the past, many companies have accumulated undistributed earnings of foreign subsidiaries operating in developing countries under a tax holiday or generated revenues

[121] *See* Marples and Gravelle, *Tax Cuts on Repatriation Earnings as Economic Stimulus: An Economic Analysis*, Congressional Research Service (May 27, 2011); Marr and Highsmith, *Tax Holiday for Overseas Corporate Profits Would Increase Deficits, Fail to Boost the Economy, and Ultimately Shift More Investment and Jobs Overseas*, published by Center on Budget and Policy Priorities (June 23, 2011).

[122] FASB ASC 740–30–25–19.

in tax havens. Many of these companies increased their after-tax earnings per share by applying the indefinite reinvestment doctrine. In some situations, the governments of the host countries (e.g., the Philippines) became unstable, causing many companies to forgo the tax and financial accounting benefits of permanent reinvestment in order to insure the safety of their liquid assets. Repatriation of these earnings, particularly from first-tier foreign subsidiaries, resulted in a one-time increase to the company's effective tax rate and a decrease in reported earnings per share.

In contrast, there may be circumstances in which a company wishes to apply the indefinite reinvestment doctrine to earnings accumulated in previous accounting periods. For example, a company initially intending to repatriate the foreign tax earnings of its foreign subsidiary may instead decide to significantly increase the manufacturing facility in the foreign country. Use of the earnings to finance such expansion would be considered a change in circumstances, which would invoke the indefinite reinvestment doctrine. Consequently, the deferred tax liability previously established with respect to such earnings would be eliminated, resulting in a decrease of tax expense for the current period.[123]

The industries with a large amount of earnings that asserted the indefinite reinvestment doctrine were the pharmaceutical and high-tech electronic sectors. The offshore cash presented a dilemma, in particular for such companies. Because the earnings are mostly from low-tax and no-tax countries, the cash is trapped offshore and the only long-term way to get that money back into the U.S. is to pay U.S. tax.[124] If a company's weighted average cost of capital is 10 percent, money sitting offshore earning an ultra-low interest rate will hit break-even at four years. In other words, if investors expect a company to earn 10 percent after-tax on assets, paying a combined U.S. tax of 40 percent is economically similar to holding the cash offshore for four years generating practically no earnings.

ILLUSTRATION 4-12: Company A and Company B are U.S. companies that are identical. They each own a foreign subsidiary with $1 million of earnings that have not been subject to any foreign tax. They each have $650,000 of debt at a 10 percent interest rate. Company A decides to repatriate the $1 million while Company B decides to assert the indefinite reinvestment doctrine. Company A pays down debt with the after-tax repatriated foreign earnings. Company B earns no interest income on the foreign cash. Company A and Company B made no additional investments in the next five years. Assume the U.S. federal income tax rate is 35 percent and that the impact of state and local taxes is ignored for purposes of this example.

	Company A	Company B
Foreign Cash After Repatriation	0	$1,000,000
U.S. Cash After Debt Repayment	350,000	0
Tax Expense on Repatriation	(350,000)	0
U.S. Debt	0	(650,000)
5 Years of Interest Income on Foreign Cash	0	0

123 *Id.*

124 The cash is not really trapped offshore but directly or indirectly finds its way back to the U.S. For instance, many companies' foreign subsidiaries purchase U.S. government bonds or U.S. corporate bonds.

5 Years of Interest Expense on Debt	0	(325,000)
Tax Shield on Interest Expense Deduction	0	113,750
Net Cash	0	138,750

Clearly, Company B is better off by the amount of $138,750 by not repatriating the foreign earnings. However, if in the next year, Company B needs to repatriate the $1 million to fund U.S. business needs, Company B will incur the $350,000 U.S. tax expense and would be $211,250 worse off. That is what happened with General Electric and eBay. The TCJA put many companies into this economic scenario. Assume the TCJA was enacted the next year and Company B's $1 million of foreign cash was subject to a 15.5 percent transition tax of $155,000. Instead of being $138,750 better off, Company B is now $16,250 worse off than Company A.

Since investors and analysts increasingly judge a company by its quarterly results, five years is an eternity in the investment world and not many companies are willing to do something, even if it is something beneficial to the company, to miss earnings forecasts. As discussed, eBay announced during its first quarter 2014 earnings release that it will no longer assert the indefinite reinvestment doctrine on $9 billion of foreign earnings, and it recorded a $3 billion tax expense. "We are an acquisitive company and we need to ensure we have the resources available to capitalize on targets that become available," said Bob Swan, eBay's chief financial officer. As the prospect of another one-time repatriation holiday and comprehensive international tax reform diminished, more companies began to change their positions on the indefinite reinvestment doctrine. Of course, the TCJA changed that landscape and, in hindsight, some companies would have been better off holding their earnings offshore and asserting the indefinite reinvestment doctrine. For instance, assuming all of eBay's $9 billion of earnings were in cash or cash equivalents, the transition tax under the TCJA would have been $1.3 billion versus the $3 billion pre-TCJA. What this does not consider is the time value of the $6 billion after-tax cash eBay received in 2014 versus waiting until 2018 to receive $7.7 billion.

The indefinite reinvestment doctrine may be asserted on "previously taxed earnings." However, most companies do not make such an assertion since a deferred tax liability has already been accrued for the federal income tax. But without the assertion the company must accrue other taxes, such as local country dividend withholding tax and U.S. state and local taxes. The transition tax enacted under TCJA dramatically increased the amount of previously taxed earnings.[125] If the indefinite reinvestment doctrine is not asserted on previously taxed earnings, any foreign currency exchange impact will be recorded as a cumulative translation adjustment and allocated to other comprehensive income.[126] Furthermore, if the indefinite reinvestment doctrine is not asserted on previously taxed earnings, the impact of any change in law, such as a change in the local country dividend withholding tax rate, must be recorded each reporting period.

In addition to foreign subsidiaries, the indefinite reinvestment doctrine may also apply to earnings from foreign corporate joint ventures. A corporate joint venture is an entity owned and operated by a small group as a separate and specific business or project for the mutual benefit of the members of the group typically to share risks and rewards

---

[125] IRC Section 965.

[126] FASB ASC 830-740–45-2; FAS 52, paragraph 24.

in developing a new market, product or technology, or to combine complementary technological knowledge, or to pool resources in developing production or other facilities.[127] Each member of the joint venture has the ability to participate, directly or indirectly, in the overall management of the joint venture and owns an interest other than as a passive investor. Since the indefinite reinvestment doctrine does not apply to domestic corporate joint ventures, some companies insert a foreign subsidiary between the parent company and the corporate joint venture.[128] The benefit is mitigating, if not outright eliminating, earning fluctuations due to deferred taxes that are recorded each reporting period. Such non-business planning can be avoided if U.S. GAAP conformed to IFRS by extending the doctrine to domestic corporate joint ventures.

§ 4.05 Reflections on Permanent and Temporary Differences

[1] General Principles

Corporate America highly covets permanent differences. Permanent differences may increase a corporation's net income, increase a corporation's EPS, and may decrease a corporation's effective tax rate. In contrast, temporary differences do not increase a corporation's net income, do not increase a corporation's EPS, and do not lower a corporation's effective tax rate. As a result, Corporate America does not covet temporary differences nearly as much as it covets permanent differences.

[2] Advantages of Temporary Differences

While Corporate America prizes permanent differences much more than temporary differences, that does not mean that temporary differences are irrelevant. A temporary difference may increase a company's cash flow.[129] The statement that "Happiness is a positive cash flow" is certainly true.[130] For small and new companies, cash flow is considered to be the single most important element for survival.[131] For publicly traded companies, corporate management focuses on the income statement while also controlling the company's cash flow. Investors also focus on the income statement but may look at a company's cash flow in assessing the company's liquidity, financial flexibility and overall performance.[132]

An increase in cash flow may help a company in many different ways. Famed investor Warren Buffet, who is the chairman of Berkshire Hathaway, Inc., has noted the time value of money benefits for temporary differences (which create deferred tax liabilities) and has written:

---

[127] FASB ASC 323-10-20 Glossary. *See also* Section 2.16.

[128] FASB 740-30-25-5.

[129] In 1970, the SEC required that companies registered with the SEC include a funds flow statement, which is the predecessor to the cash flow statement, in their annual SEC filings. *See* Lanny G. Chasteen, et al., *Intermediate Accounting* 1063 (2d ed. 1987).

[130] *See* Kieso, supra note 2, at 221.

[131] *Id.*

[132] *Id.* at 191. Some analysts look at deferred taxes and try to determine when they could turnaround to evaluate a company's future operating cash flow, which impacts dividend payout and funding growth without issuing more shares that generally are dilutive to earnings. In other words, temporary differences can drive performance metrics that impact share value and earnings. Depending on assumptions used, if a fully taxable company was able to defer taxes, the value of that deferral approaches the tax rate. A company that earns 79 cents per share in earnings will, theoretically, be able to increase future earnings by almost 21 cents. If this was played out forever that means a company's future earnings will be one dollar a share without any change in the business's profitability.

> Besides, Berkshire has access to two low-cost, non-perilous sources of leverage that allow us to safely own far more assets than our equity capital alone would permit: deferred taxes and "float," the funds of others that our insurance business holds because it receives premiums before needing to pay out losses. Both of these funding sources have grown rapidly and now total about $69 billion.
>
> Better yet, this funding to date has often been cost-free. Deferred tax liabilities bear no interest. And as long as we can break even in our insurance underwriting the cost of the float developed from that operation is zero. Neither item, of course, is equity; these are real liabilities. But they are liabilities without covenants or due dates attached to them. In effect, they give us the benefit of debt—an ability to have more assets working for us—but saddle us with none of its drawbacks.[133]

Another way that increasing cash flow can help is by paying down debt. A reduction in debt has several advantages. Many companies believe that "removing debt enhances the quality of the balance sheet" and thereby permits credit to be obtained more readily at a lower cost.[134] In addition, loan covenants typically limit the amount of debt a company may have.[135] Deferred tax liabilities are not typically treated as debt for this purpose thereby giving, as Buffet notes, some of the advantages of debt without the drawbacks. Finally, a reduction in debt decreases the "debt to total assets ratio." The ratio is calculated as total debt (both current and long-term liabilities) divided by total assets.[136] The higher a corporation's debt to total assets ratio is, the greater the risk that the corporation may be unable to meet its obligations as they mature.[137]

A reduction in interest expense also has several advantages. First, it increases net income for the year, which, in itself, is a valuable benefit for the company. Moreover, it is an above the income tax expense line on the income statement meaning that it increases pretax financial income for the year, which is an even greater benefit for a company than simply increasing net income.[138] Second, a reduction in interest expense also increases the "times interest earned ratio." This ratio is determined by dividing the sum of pretax financial income and interest expense by interest expense.[139] The higher a corporation's times interest earned ratio is, the greater the probability that the corporation can meet its interest payments as they come due.[140] The times interest earned ratio is an important ratio to long-term creditors and stockholders in determining the long-run solvency of the corporation.[141]

> **ILLUSTRATION 4-13:** In its 2005 Annual Report, Best Buy reported total liabilities of $5.845 billion, total assets of $10.294 billion, interest expense of

[133] Berkshire Hathaway, Inc. 2006 Annual Report at 75–76, berkshirehathaway.com/2006ar/2006ar.pdf.

[134] *See* Kieso, supra note 2, at 740.

[135] *Id.*

[136] *Id.* at 742.

[137] *Id.* at 743.

[138] The reduction in interest expense should increase pretax financial income by a greater amount than the increase in net income because of the dilution by income tax expense. For illustration, using a 21 percent tax rate, a reduction in interest expense of $100 will increase pretax financial income by $100 but will only increase net income by $79.

[139] *See* Kieso, supra note 2, at 743.

[140] *Id.*

[141] *Id.*

$44 million, income tax expense of $509 million, and net income of $984 million.[142] Best Buy's debt-to-asset ratio is $5.845 billion divided by $10.294 billion equaling 56.8 percent. This is considered a relatively high debt to asset ratio.[143] Best Buy's times interest earned ratio is $1.537 billion ($984 million of net income plus $44 million of interest expense plus $509 million of income tax expense) divided by $44 million equaling 35 times. Best Buy's interest coverage of 35 times indicates that it can easily meet its interest payments when they come due.[144]

Rather than paying down debt, a company may use an increase in cash in its business operations to increase its pretax financial income (and therefore net income) in future years.[145] Increasing its pretax financial income will also increase the company's EPS. As a result, temporary differences may not have an immediate impact on net income or EPS but may have a future impact by paying down debt or increasing income from business or investment operations.[146]

Because of the importance of the income statement to corporate management, if a permanent difference and a temporary difference both create an equal net present value of future cash flows, corporate management will favor the permanent difference over the temporary difference because of its positive impact on net income, EPS, and effective tax rate.[147] In fact, corporate management may even sacrifice net present value of future cash flows in exchange for a net income and EPS benefit.

[3] Why Temporary Differences Are Unimportant to Corporate America

If there are advantages to temporary differences, why are some companies so focused on permanent differences and almost indifferent to temporary differences?[148] There may be several reasons for this. First, as demonstrated, temporary differences do not provide an immediate impact on the income statement. In other words, they do not increase net income for the period in which the temporary difference arises and therefore do not immediately increase EPS. They also do not have an immediate impact on the company's effective tax rate. Rather, a temporary difference creates a deferred tax

---

[142] Best Buy 2005 Annual Report at https://s2.q4cdn.com/785564492/files/doc_financials/2005/BestBuyAR05.pdf.

[143] *See* Donald E. Kieso, et al., *Intermediate Accounting*, 12th ed. (2007) at 696.

[144] *Id.*

[145] Generally, a company will utilize an increase in cash in its business operations if it can earn at least the weighted average cost of capital.

[146] The cash flow and balance sheet benefits of temporary differences may be valuable to a corporation that is the target of a takeover or a corporation that is putting itself up for sale.

[147] *Cf. JCT Book-Tax Report*, supra note 15, at 20–33 (noting how the investment tax credit, in contrast to expensing or accelerated depreciation, lowers a corporation's effective tax rate but then focuses on net present value of cash flows in determining what is desirable to taxpayers).

[148] Some items that lead to differences between pretax financial income and taxable income are, in a sense, permanent differences but are treated as temporary differences under the financial accounting rules. For illustration, assume a corporation acquires a depreciable asset with a book basis of zero and a tax basis of $100,000. The corporation will depreciate the asset upon acquisition. For financial accounting purposes, the corporation will have no depreciation expense because its initial book basis is zero. For tax purposes, however, the corporation will, over the asset's applicable recovery period, have $100,000 of depreciation deductions. As a result, taxable income over the asset's applicable recovery period will be $100,000 less than its financial income over the same time period. This difference is permanent—it will not reverse over time. *See, e.g.*, Second Interim Report of Neal Batson, Court Appointed Examiner, Appendix J, In re Enron Corp., No. 01–16034 (AJG) Bankr. (S.D.N.Y. Jan. 21, 2003).

liability on the company's balance sheet. This means that the company is deferring the payment of some taxes; however, the taxes that are deferred are treated as deferred tax expense for the year that the temporary difference arises. As a result, the income statement reflects in full the taxes that will be paid in the future. In other words, the company takes a current charge to earnings for the deferred taxes even though the taxes may not be paid for many years.[149]

A company is not permitted to discount deferred taxes even if the timing of paying the deferred taxes is known with some or even exact precision.[150] For example, assume a company makes an installment sale of property in 2018 in which the gain is $1 million and the sales price will be paid in its entirety in 2021. Using a 21 percent corporate tax rate, the company will record a deferred tax liability of $210,000 and a deferred tax expense of $210,000 in 2018. The company is not permitted to discount the $210,000 deferred tax liability (and deferred tax expense) to its present value. If discounting of the deferred tax liability and corresponding deferred tax expense were permitted, then the deferral of the $210,000 of tax would provide an immediate benefit on the income statement equal to the excess of $210,000 over the present value of $210,000 (discounted three years).

The APB, which was the predecessor to FASB, addressed the issue of discounting deferred taxes.[151] The APB wrote that it was "giving attention" to the issue of whether certain long-term deferred taxes should be discounted as recommended in an Accounting Research Study.[152] The APB concluded that "[p]ending further consideration of this subject and the broader aspects of discounting as it is related to financial accounting in general" deferred taxes should not be accounted for on a discounted basis.[153] If deferred taxes were discounted, then it would provide an immediate benefit on the income statement. But, because discounting is prohibited, temporary differences provide no immediate income statement benefit.[154]

Because deferred taxes are not discounted, coupled with the possibility that corporate management is focused on the current period rather than looking ahead to future periods, temporary differences may simply just not be that important. Temporary differences may provide an immediate impact on the cash flow statement, but this is

---

[149] It is not uncommon for a chief financial officer to ask the tax advisor, "Has the item in question already hit the income statement?" What this generally means is whether the corporation has fully accounted for the deferred tax consequences of the item. If so, then no current or future income statement benefit will result from the item (except for an increase in cash flow that may lead to a future income statement benefit).

[150] FASB ASC 740–10–30–8.

[151] APB Opinion No. 10, Tax Allocation Accounts—Discounting (1966).

[152] *Id. See also* Accounting Research Study No. 9, Interperiod Allocation of Corporate Income Taxes.

[153] APB Opinion No. 10, Tax Allocation Accounts—Discounting (1966).

[154] In some cases, deferred taxes may, in essence, be discounted. If the base amount, for which deferred taxes are calculated, is a discounted amount, then the deferred taxes are also, in a sense, discounted. *See* APB Opinion No. 10, Tax Allocation Accounts—Discounting (1966) ("Messrs. Davidson and Weston do not agree with the conclusion of the Board that further use of the discounting (or present value) technique in measuring the current cost of deferred income taxes is not acceptable, pending further consideration of this subject by the Board. They point out that Accounting Research Study No. 9 concluded that this method is required whenever the interest factor is significant. They recognize that the Board is attempting to prevent the development of an alternative practice until it has had an opportunity to consider the subject matter thoroughly and form an opinion thereon. On the other hand, the Board has required use of the discounting technique in measuring the present value of obligations due in the future in (a) the capitalization of leases (Opinion No. 5—paragraph 15) and (b) the accrual of pension costs (Opinion No. 8—paragraphs 23 and 42). They find it difficult to reconcile these inconsistent positions of the Board on similar questions of measurement.").

generally considered to be of lesser importance to corporate management and investors than the income statement unless the company is in a cash flow crisis.

A second reason why companies may not prize temporary differences is that the deferral period relating to the temporary difference may be quite short. In other words, not all temporary differences are created equal. Some temporary differences may not reverse for many years, thereby creating a much larger benefit to the company than a temporary difference that reverses, for example, in one or two years.

In some cases, however, temporary differences that reverse in a relatively short time period may actually create a deferral period of an indefinite nature. For example, if a company purchases equipment in which it utilizes accelerated depreciation for tax purposes and straight-line depreciation for financial accounting purposes, it will recognize a deferred tax liability in depreciating the equipment. The amount of the deferred tax liability will start to decrease as the financial accounting depreciation begins to exceed the tax depreciation for the year, which may occur in just a few years. If, however, the company continues to purchase equipment, a new deferred tax liability will be created with the respect to the new equipment that can be viewed as, in essence, replacing the old deferred tax liability. When viewed in the aggregate, the total deferred tax liability may not change very much from year to year. As a result, the company is achieving an indefinite deferral of taxes.[155]

Another reason a number of companies may not value temporary differences is that many companies have paid zero corporate income taxes to the U.S. government despite showing net income on the income statement and a positive effective tax rate in the tax footnote to the financial statements. Apparently, this was prevalent in the late 1990s and early 2000s.[156] It may also be prevalent in 2020.[157] If a company is paying no federal income taxes to the U.S. government, then temporary differences are of little to no benefit; however, permanent differences can still be of significant benefit. To illustrate, assume a corporation has net income of $500 million and has no tax liability to the U.S. government. In addition, the corporation has $10 million of permanent differences increasing the corporation's net income to $510 million. The permanent differences will increase the corporation's EPS. They may also lower the corporation's effective tax rate. As a result, the permanent differences are still beneficial to the corporation even though

[155] FASB recognized the indefinite deferral aspect of deferred tax liabilities with respect to items such as depreciation on equipment in SFAS No. 109, paragraphs 203–205. In deciding what approach to adopt with respect to deferred taxes FASB considered what is known as the "partial recognition of deferred taxes." Under this approach, a deferred tax liability is not recognized if the cumulative amount of temporary differences for a particular recurring item, such as depreciation, does not reverse in future years because new originating differences offset reversing differences. In SFAS No. 109, paragraphs 203–205 FASB rejected such an approach noting that "the deferred tax consequences of a depreciation difference for a particular depreciable asset ordinarily will result in a sacrifice [reverse resulting in taxes owed] in future years."

[156] *See, e.g.*, United States General Accounting Office, *Tax Administration: Comparison of the Reported Tax Liabilities of Foreign- and U.S.-Controlled Corporations, 1996–2000* (Feb. 2004) (from 1996 to 2000, a large percentage of U.S. controlled corporations with either assets of at least $250 million or gross receipts of at least $50 million had no tax liability; the percentages with no tax liability were 32.7 percent in 1996, 35.5 percent in 1997, 37.8 percent in 1998, 40.9 percent in 1999, and 45.3 percent in 2000); Robert S. McIntyre & T.D. Coo Nguyen, *Corporate Income Taxes in the Bush Years* (Sept. 2004) (82 of the 275 largest U.S. corporations paid no income taxes in at least one year from 2001 to 2003); United States General Accounting Office, *Tax Administration: Comparison of the Reported Tax Liabilities of Foreign-and U.S.-Controlled Corporations, 1998–2005* (July 2008).

[157] *See, e.g.*, Matthew Gardner and Steve Wamhoff, *55 Corporations Paid $0 in Federal Taxes on 2020 Profits, Institute on Taxation and Economic Policy* (April 2021) at https://itep.sfo2.digitaloceanspaces.com/040221-55-Profitable-Corporations-Zero-Corporate-Taxes.pdf.

it has no U.S. tax liability for the year. In contrast, temporary differences would be of no benefit to the corporation because it is not paying any taxes to the U.S. government so no taxes are being saved in the current year as a result of the deferral.[158]

It is important to distinguish a company's taxes paid to the U.S. government from its effective tax rate. For example, Enron Corporation paid no federal income taxes in the years 1996 to 1999, yet reported in those years, effective tax rates of 31.7 percent, (598.3) percent, 20.0 percent and 9.2 percent, respectively, in its financial statements.[159] In addition, Enron reported consolidated net income of $584 million, $105 million, $703 million and $893 million, respectively, in its financial statements for the years 1996 through 1999.[160] So even though Enron reported significant amounts of net income for the period 1996 through 1999, and reported positive effective tax rates in three out of four years from 1996 through 1999, it paid no federal income taxes during that period.[161]

A number of reasons may exist to explain why a corporation may show net income and a positive effective tax rate in its financial statements yet pay no taxes to the U.S. government. It may, for example, have a net operating loss that it is carrying forward eliminating its U.S. tax liability.[162] In Enron's case, it had a large net operating loss that it was carrying forward each year, eliminating its tax liability each year.[163] A net operating loss does not reduce net income and it does not appear in the effective tax reconciliation.[164] As a result, a corporation may continue to show net income and a positive effective tax rate while having its entire taxable income offset by a net operating loss carryforward.

In addition, a corporation may show net income for financial accounting purposes and no taxable income through the use of tax-motivated transactions, which may employ permanent differences, temporary differences or a combination of the two.[165] These tax-

---

[158] The temporary differences may create, increase or preserve a net operating loss of the corporation that can be carried forward indefinitely. IRC Section 172. Increasing a net operating loss carryforward is generally considered to be a minor benefit to a corporation.

[159] *See* Enron Annual Report 1999 at picker.uchicago.edu/Enron/EnronAnnualReport1999.pdf (Enron's net income and effective tax rates for 1997, 1998 and 1999) [*Enron Annual Report 1999*]; Enron Annual Report 1998 at picker.uchicago.edu/Enron/EnronAnnualReport1998.pdf (Enron's net income and effective tax rates for 1996, 1997 and 1998) [*Enron Annual Report 1998*]; Staff of the Joint Committee on Taxation, *Report of Investigation of Enron Corporation and Related Entities Regarding Federal Tax and Compensation Issues, and Policy Recommendations*, JCS–3–03, vol. I at 5 (2001) (Enron's federal tax liability from its federal income tax returns) [*JCT Enron Report*].

[160] *See* Enron Annual Report 1999 at 41; Enron Annual Report 1998 at 45; JCT Enron Report at 7.

[161] Enron utilized temporary differences that were, in essence, permanent differences in a number of (now) well-publicized transactions. In 1996 to 1999, Enron had no need for temporary differences because it was not paying any taxes to the U.S. government. Enron could, however, utilize permanent differences to increase its net income, increase its EPS, and lower its effective tax rate. *See* Section 2.23.

[162] A corporation may also have a large amount of excess tax credits that it is carrying forward reducing its tax liability to the U.S. government in future years.

[163] *See* Enron Annual Report 1999 at 51; Enron Annual Report 1998 at 55; JCT Enron Report at 5–6.

[164] A corporation with a net operating loss carryforward creates a deferred tax asset on the corporation's balance sheet. (FASB ASC 740–10–25–29; FASB ASC 740–10–30–5). The deferred tax asset may be subject to a valuation allowance. (FASB ASC 740–10–30–5 and FASB ASC 740–10–30–17; FASB ASC 740–10–30–18; FASB ASC 740–10–30–19; FASB ASC 740–10–30–20; FASB ASC 740–10–30–21; FASB ASC 740–10–30–22; FASB ASC 740–10–30–23). If a corporation records a valuation allowance with respect to its net operating loss carryforward, then that means that the corporation has determined that it may not utilize a portion of its carryforward due to a lack of taxable income in the future. The valuation allowance would affect the corporation's effective tax rate.

[165] Much has been written on the disparity between book income (i.e., net income for financial accounting purposes) and taxable income. *See, e.g.*, Hanlon, supra note 5; Manzon & Plesko, supra note 5; Written Testimony of Commissioner of Internal Revenue Mark Everson before Senate Committee on Finance on

motivated transactions, sometimes referred to as corporate tax shelters,[166] seemed to have reached their zenith in the late 1990s and early 2000s, about the same time as reports showing many corporations paying no taxes to the U.S. government.[167]

Finally, some corporations' tax departments may best be described as "compliance shops." In such corporations, corporate management may not place much emphasis on tax planning, and, as a result, may not place much value, if any, on the benefits of temporary differences.[168] This may be particularly true with regard to corporations that have large net operating loss carryforwards or a significant amount of excess tax credits.

Compliance Concerns Relative to Large and Mid-Size Businesses, IR–2006–94, June 13, 2006; Michelle Hanlon, et al., *Evidence for the Possible Information Loss of Conforming Book Income and Taxable Income*, 48 J. Law & Econ. 407 (2005); Mihir Desai, *The Divergence Between Book and Tax Income*, in James Poterba (ed.), Tax Policy and the Economy 17 (2003); George Plesko and Lillian Mills, *Bridging the Reporting Gap: A Proposal for More Informative Reconciling of Book and Tax Income*, MIT Working Paper 4289–03 (2003); Alison Bennett, *2004 Figures Show Big Discrepancy Between Book, Tax Profits Among Firms*, BNA Daily Tax Report G-8 (Nov. 28, 2006) (In 2004, publicly-traded companies reported $554 billion in book income and only $394 billion in taxable income; companies may have reduced their taxable income by about $35 billion through "potentially abusive transactions").

[166] For a discussion of corporate tax shelters, *see, e.g.*, United States Department of the Treasury, *The Problem of Corporate Tax Shelters: Discussion, Analysis, and Legislative Proposals* (July 1999); Staff of the Joint Committee on Taxation, *Study of Present Law Penalty and Interest Provisions as Required by Section 3801 of the Internal Revenue Service Restructuring and Reform Act of 1998 (Including Provisions Relating to Corporate Tax Shelters)*, JCS–3–99 (July 1999); *Symposium: Business Purpose, Economic Substance, and Corporate Tax Shelters*, 54 SMU L. Rev. 3 (2001); *Symposium on Corporate Tax Shelters, Part I*, 55 Tax L. Rev. No. 2 (2002); *Symposium on Corporate Tax Shelters, Part II*, 55 Tax L. Rev. No. 3 (2002).

[167] Treasury had promulgated regulations in which significant book-tax differences were required to be disclosed in certain cases. Treas. Reg. § 1.6011–4(b)(6) (now removed) (significant book-tax difference is a transaction in which the amount for tax purposes of any item of income, gain, expense or loss differs by more than $10 million on a gross basis from the amount of the item for book purposes; the disclosure requirement applies to reporting companies under the Securities Exchange Act of 1934 and business entities that have $250 million or more in gross assets for book purposes). In Notice 2006–6, 2006–1 C.B. 385, the Internal Revenue Service eliminated the category of transactions with a significant book-tax difference from the categories of reportable transactions. In 2004, Treasury and the Internal Revenue Service released Schedule M-3, Net Income (Loss) Reconciliation For Corporations With Total Assets of $10 Million or More. In general, for taxable years ending on or after December 31, 2004, any corporation (or U.S. consolidated tax group) required to file a U.S. Corporation Income Tax Return, that reports total assets at the end of the corporation's (or U.S. consolidated tax group's) taxable year that equal or exceed $10 million on Schedule L, Form 1120 is required to complete and file Schedule M-3. Rev. Proc. 2004–45, 2004–2 C.B. 140.

[168] One reason why a corporation's tax department may simply be acting as a "compliance shop" is the shortage of available tax professionals to meet the growing demands on a corporation's tax department. *See* Jay J. Levine, *Resource Challenges for Tax Departments Could Become Opportunities*, BNA Daily Tax Report, J-1 (Aug. 24, 2006) (not enough tax professionals to meet the growing demands on a corporation's tax department; FAS 109 and information technology were the two most important areas of "core competency").

Chapter 5

SARBANES-OXLEY—AUDITOR INDEPENDENCE: IMPACT ON TAX SERVICES

Table of Sections

§ 5.01 Introduction and Background

As a result of the corporate finance and accounting scandals in the United States in 2001 and 2002, Congress enacted the Sarbanes-Oxley Act of 2002 (SOX) to prescribe a broad range of limitations on the services that auditors of public companies[1] may provide while maintaining their requisite independence for purposes of issuing audit opinions concerning such companies.[2] A violation of these rules could require a company to change auditors or obtain a re-audit of its financial statements.[3] Moreover, an accounting firm violating these rules could be subject to discipline by the Public Company Accounting Oversight Board (PCAOB).[4] While these limitations have had a noticeable impact on the provision of tax advice by audit firms, concerns still remain that the investments that accounting firms have made in providing non-audit services can become a distraction to

[1] Although SOX applies to "issuers," we use the more general term "public companies" (including references to a company or companies) in this chapter for ease of reading. "Issuers" are defined to include all types of registrants that file disclosure documents with the Securities and Exchange Commission, including U.S. public companies and non-U.S. companies that have securities listed on a U.S. exchange or traded in Nasdaq (e.g., ADR programs). *See* Securities Exchange Act of 1934 (Exchange Act) § 10A(f).

[2] *See generally* Bostelman, et al., *Enactment of Broad Accounting, Corporate Governance Reform Act Brings New Prohibitions, Requirements for Executives and Auditors,* 34 BNA Sec. Reg. & Law Rep. 1281 (Aug. 5, 2002); Goodman, *The Taxpayer's and Tax Advisor's Guide to Sarbanes-Oxley,* Tax Analysts Doc No 2003–17937 (Aug. 4, 2003); *ANALYSIS: Accounting Reform Act Affects Corporate Tax Departments—Sarbanes-Oxley Accounting Reform Act Affects Corporate Tax Departments,* 160 Daily Tax Rep., at J-1; Moses, *New Law Will Force Taxpayers to Reconsider Using Same Firm for Audits, Transfer Pricing,* 11 Tax Mgmt. Transfer Pricing Rep. 319 (Aug. 7, 2002).

[3] 17 CFR § 240.10A–2 provides that "[i]t shall be unlawful for an auditor not to be independent * * *."

[4] PCAOB Release No. 2005–014 (July 26, 2005).

the firms' audit practices, jeopardizing their independence for purposes of issuing audit opinions.[5]

Title II of SOX, addressing "auditor independence," added new subsections to Section 10A of the Securities Exchange Act of 1934 (Exchange Act § 10A). Specifically, SOX Section 201 added subsection (g) to Exchange Act § 10A, which specifies a number of non-audit services that an audit firm may not provide to an audit client. Section 201 also added subsection (h), which provides that non-audit services that are not prohibited under SOX and Securities and Exchange Commission's (SEC's) rules must be pre-approved by the company's board audit committee. SOX also added a number of other provisions directed at auditor independence, although we have focused on the provisions related to tax services.[6]

Two decades later, it appears the same concerns have gotten more severe.[7]

§ 5.02 Scope of Services Provided by Auditors

SOX Section 201 added Exchange Act § 10A(g), which provides that it shall be "unlawful" for a registered public accounting firm that performs an audit of a company's financial statements (and any person associated with such a firm) to provide to that company, contemporaneously with the audit, any non-audit services, including the nine categories of prohibited services. However, SOX also added Exchange Act § 10A(h), which provides that the provision of any non-audit service, including tax services, that is not described as a prohibited service, can be provided by the auditor without impairing the auditor's independence "only if" the service has been pre-approved by the company's board audit committee. Thus, other than the list of nine prohibited services set forth in Exchange Act § 10A(g), an auditor can provide non-audit services to an audit client, provided the company obtains approval from its board audit committee for such services. The nine categories of prohibited non-audit services set forth in Exchange Act § 10A(g) are as follows:

- Bookkeeping or other services related to the accounting records or financial statements of the audit client;
- Financial information systems design and implementation;
- Appraisal or valuation services, fairness opinions, or contribution-in-kind reports;
- Actuarial services;
- Internal audit outsourcing services;
- Management functions or human resources;

---

5 *See* Thomas Jaworski, *Non-Audit Services Could Distract Accounting Firms, PCAOB Fears*, Tax Analysts Doc 2014–28596 (Dec. 4, 2014); Thomas Jaworski, *Year in Review: Non-Audit Tax Work Reemerges as a Possible Independence Risk*, 146 Tax Notes 34 (Jan. 5, 2015); Thomas Jaworski, *SEC Enforcement Focusing on Non-Audit Services, Accounting Fraud*, Tax Analysts Doc 2015–4381 (Feb. 24, 2015).

6 For example, SOX Sections 203, 204 and 206 address (i) mandatory rotation of audit partners, (ii) matters that must be reported to the audit committee, and (iii) audit firm conflict of interest issues, respectively. For an expanded discussion of these areas, *see* Final Rule: Strengthening the Commission's Requirements Regarding Auditor Independence, SEC Release No. 33–8183.

7 *SEC Questions Auditor Independence as Firm's Advisory Work Booms*, Daily Tax Report (Bloomberg), (Nov. 3, 2021).

- Broker or dealer, investment adviser, or investment banking services;
- Legal services and expert services unrelated to the audit; and
- Any other service that the PCAOB determines, by regulation, is impermissible.

These rules do not limit the scope of non-audit services provided by an accounting firm to a non-audit client.

The principles of independence underlying the foregoing rules are predicated on three guiding principles which, if violated, would impair the auditor's independence: (1) an auditor cannot function in the role of management, (2) an auditor cannot audit his or her own work, and (3) an auditor cannot serve in an advocacy role for his or her client.[8]

In the following sections we examine the pertinent provisions of the foregoing rules as applied to tax services.

§ 5.03 Appraisal and Valuation Services

SOX amended Exchange Act § 10A to include subparagraph (g)(3), which provides that an accounting firm (and any person associated with that firm) cannot provide "appraisal or valuation services, fairness opinions, or contribution-in-kind reports" for an audit client of the firm. The Securities and Exchange Commission's (SEC) rules elaborate on the prohibition, providing that an accountant is not "independent" if it provides:

> Any appraisal service, valuation service, or any service involving a fairness opinion or contribution-in-kind report for an audit client, unless it is reasonable to conclude that the results of these services will not be subject to audit procedures during an audit of the audit client's financial statements.[9]

Of course, even if it is reasonable to conclude that the results of appraisal or valuation services will not be subject to audit procedures during an audit of the audit client's financial statements, any such service would need to be approved by the company's audit committee, as provided in Exchange Act § 10A(h).

The SEC has defined valuation and appraisal services as follows:

> Appraisal and valuation services include any process of valuing assets, both tangible and intangible, or liabilities. They include valuing, among other things, in-process research and development, financial instruments, assets and liabilities acquired in a merger, and real estate.[10]

In addition, the SEC has explained its interpretation of Exchange Act § 10A(g)(3) as follows:

> We continue to believe that providing these services to audit clients raises several independence concerns. When it is time to audit the financial statements, it is likely that the accountant would review his or her own work, including key assumptions or variables that underlie an entry in the financial statements. Also, if the appraisal methodology involves a projection of future

---

[8] *See* SEC Release No. 33–8183, § II.B.

[9] 17 CFR § 210.2–01(c)(4)(iii).

[10] *See* SEC Release No. 33–8183, § II.B.3.

> results of operations and cash flows, some believe that the accountant that prepares the projection may be unable to evaluate skeptically and without bias the accuracy of that valuation or appraisal. Accordingly, the rules we are adopting prohibit the accountant from providing any appraisal service, valuation service or any service involving a fairness opinion or contribution-in-kind report for an audit client, unless it is reasonable to conclude that the results of these services will not be subject to audit procedures during an audit of the audit client's financial statements.
>
> Our rules do not prohibit an accounting firm from providing such services for non-financial reporting (e.g., transfer pricing studies, cost segregation studies, and other tax-only valuations) purposes. Also, the rule does not prohibit an accounting firm from utilizing its own valuation specialist to review the work performed by the audit client itself or an independent, third-party specialist employed by the audit client, provided the audit client or the client's specialist (and not the specialist used by the accounting firm) provides the technical expertise that the client uses in determining the required amounts recorded in the client financial statements. In those instances, the accountant will not be auditing his or her own work because a third party or the audit client is the source of the financial information subject to the audit. Additionally, the quality of the audit may be improved where specialists are utilized in such situations.[11]

An interesting element of the SEC's interpretation of Exchange Act § 10A(g)(3) is that the prohibition of providing appraisal and valuation services does not extend to "services for non-financial reporting (e.g., transfer pricing studies, cost segregation studies, and other tax-only valuations) purposes."[12] Thus, the SEC's interpretation indicates that "tax-only" appraisal and valuation services are permissible, with the apparent rationale being that such services do not impact financial reporting. As evident throughout this text, this apparent assumption that tax-only services do not impact financial reporting would be an erroneous assumption in many instances. For example, transfer pricing matters, especially pricing involving intangible property, often generate significant tax uncertainly that may require analysis by the audit firm. For example, the IRS has touted its "successful" settlement in the U.S. Tax Court transfer pricing case of *GlaxoSmithKline Holdings (Americas) Inc. v. Commissioner*, which the IRS characterized as the "largest tax dispute in the history of the Internal Revenue Service."[13] According to the IRS, the taxpayer was to pay the Internal Revenue Service approximately $3.4 billion in tax.[14]

In light of the potential exposure of transfer pricing and other tax matters, it appears that the upper bookend of the SEC's rule is that tax-only appraisal and valuation services, including transfer pricing and other tax-only valuation services, are permissible "unless it is reasonable to conclude that the results of these services will * * * be subject to audit procedures during an audit of the audit client's financial statements."[15] A more reasonable and consistent application of the SEC's rule is to

---

[11] *Id.*

[12] *Id.*

[13] *See* IR 2006–142 (Sept. 11, 2006).

[14] *Id.*

[15] 17 CFR § 210.2–01(c)(4)(iii).

prohibit such services. One has to stretch to reconcile the prohibition against "legal services and expert services unrelated to the audit" with the permissible expert valuation tax services that are related to the audit. Ted Baker Plc, a U.K. fashion brand, replaced KPMG as its auditor and announced it overvalued its inventory by as much as £25 million.[16] Two years earlier, KPMG was fined £2.1 million by the U.K. Financial Reporting Council when KPMG admitted to conflict of interest when KPMG was an expert witness for the company in a court proceeding.

Consider an example where Global Audit & Co. provided transfer pricing studies supporting the principal tax planning strategies underlying a restructuring. As a result of the restructuring, the operating margins of its client, USCo and its foreign affiliates went from 14 percent and 30 percent to 11 percent and 5 percent, respectively, with the bulk of the post-restructuring profit being shifted to another subsidiary, Int'lCo, which was organized in a low tax jurisdiction. There will likely be transfer pricing exposure in the countries in which the foreign affiliates conduct business, which could lead to examination issues in the U.S., as well as potential correlative adjustments once such cases are resolved. These uncertain tax positions will need to be addressed for FASB ASC 740–10 purposes.[17] Thus, if Global Audit & Co. provided audit services to USCo, Global Audit & Co. will need to review and evaluate the FASB ASC 740–10 analysis of the restructuring. In such circumstances, subparagraph (g)(3) of Exchange Act § 10A should preclude Global Audit & Co. from preparing transfer pricing studies supporting the principal tax planning strategies underlying the restructuring, as it is reasonable to conclude that such services will be subject to audit procedures during an audit of USCo's financial statements.[18]

Although tax appraisal and valuation services clearly introduce independence issues, both the client and the audit firm have interpreted the SEC interpretation of Exchange Act 10A(g)(3) as blessing transfer pricing studies, cost segregation studies, and other tax-only valuations. When audit clients use a third-party firm to perform such services, the audit firm usually makes it very clear that to audit the studies and valuation properly, the audit firm must perform a nearly complete study and valuation for validation. Audit firms will typically not audit the tax studies under normal audit standards and the common reason for expanding the scope of the audit outside such standards is that the audit firm possesses tax expertise. That internal expertise demands a heightened level of scrutiny, often-times requiring a tax study and valuation to be completely and independently done by the audit firm to validate the third party's work. And this is just the tip of the iceberg. If the audit firm's tax study and valuation do not match up exactly with the third-party study, the client may need to accrue a higher reserve for the additional tax liability or may not recognize the benefit at all where the more-likely-than-not standard of FASB ASC 740–10–25 is not met. There are numerous situations in which the study and valuation meet the more-likely-than-not standard required to recognize a tax benefit under FASB ASC 740–10–25 in the opinion of the client or third-party firm, but not in the opinion of the audit firm. The more-likely-than-not standard is commonly quantified as being more than 50 percent and it is not unusual for the audit firm's own study and valuation to get very close to, but not over, the 50 percent threshold. That hairline difference would prevent the client from

[16] *See* Michael Kapoor, *KPMG Resigns as Ted Baker Auditor After Accounting Errors*, Bloomberg Law News (June 1, 2020).

[17] *See* Chapter 3, which addresses uncertain tax positions.

[18] *See* SEC Release No. 33–8183 § II.B.3.

recognizing any tax benefit associated with the study and valuation. Certain studies are very costly, such as complex transfer-pricing matters, which means the company will not only be paying twice for this costly study-once to the third-party firm and once again to the audit firm-but also greatly increases the chance that it will not be able to accrue the tax benefits due to minor differences between the two studies. Audit clients often capitulate and seek audit committee approval for the audit firm to perform such studies and valuations with full recognition of the independence dilemma.

The 2009 case involving Caterpillar, Inc.[19] (the "Caterpillar case") vividly demonstrates the concerns noted. The Caterpillar case involves a suit brought by a one-time global tax strategy manager of Caterpillar (the "plaintiff"). The plaintiff asserted that he was demoted because he complained that an offshore holding company structure implemented by Caterpillar violated U.S. tax law.

The essence of the plaintiff's apparent concern regarding the holding company structure was that the structure lacked economic substance. Apparently, the plaintiff had expressed concern to his superiors about the so-called "Swiss Tax Structure," asserting it was a scheme to improperly avoid over $2 billion in U.S. income tax.[20] According to the plaintiff, PricewaterhouseCoopers, LLP ("PwC") was the "primary architect of the Swiss Tax Structure."[21] This is particularly interesting in the context of SOX because at the time at issue PwC was Caterpillar's public auditor.[22] Thus, the issues described above were actually present in the Caterpillar case, where PwC allegedly devised a tax structure that saved material U.S. taxes and then was responsible for auditing its own work. PwC was both auditor and tax adviser for Caterpillar and maintains that the firm's concurrent delivery of tax and audit services complied with both the letter and spirit of all applicable regulations.[23] Nonetheless, U.S. regulators and the European Union continue to express concern about the role that auditors play in their clients' tax planning.[24]

§ 5.04 Legal Services

SOX amended Exchange Act § 10A to include subparagraph (g)(8), which provides that a public accounting firm (and any person associated with that firm) cannot provide "legal services" for an audit client of the firm. The SEC rules elaborate on the prohibition, providing that an accountant is not "independent" if it provides:

> any service to an audit client that, under circumstances in which the service is provided, could be provided only by someone licensed, admitted, or otherwise qualified to practice law in the jurisdiction in which the service is provided.[25]

---

[19] *Schlicksup v. Caterpillar, Inc. et al.*, Docket No. 1:09-cv-01208 (C.D. Ill. June 12, 2009).

[20] *See* Order dated May 24, 2011 and filed in *Schlicksup v. Caterpillar, Inc. et al*, Docket No. 1:09-cv-01208 (C.D. Ill. June 12, 2009).

[21] *Id.*

[22] *Id.*

[23] *See* Thomas Jaworski, *Year in Review: Non-Audit Tax Work Reemerges as a Possible Independence Risk*, 146 Tax Notes 34 (Jan. 5, 2015).

[24] *See* Section 5.05.

[25] 17 CFR § 210.2–01(c)(4)(ix). *See* SEC Office of the Chief Accountant, *Application of the Commission's Rules on Auditor Independence, Frequently Asked Questions, Prohibited Non-Audit Services*, Q1 (2001), where the SEC noted that the standard includes all legal services and does not apply only to appearance in court or solely to litigators.

In explaining this rule, the SEC has noted that a lawyer's core professional obligation is to zealously advance its clients' interests within the bounds of the law.[26] The SEC further noted its position that "an individual cannot be both a zealous legal advocate for management or the client company, and maintain the objectivity and impartiality that are necessary for an audit."[27]

In promulgating these rules, the SEC recognized that the rule may prevent auditors from providing tax services in jurisdictions where a license to practice law is required to provide such services. However, the SEC noted that, in such situations, it would "consider whether the provision of the service would be prohibited in the United States as well as in the foreign jurisdiction," and it encouraged accounting firms and foreign regulators to consult with the staff to address these issues.[28]

The SEC has recognized that advocacy associated with litigating tax matters would impair the objectivity and impartiality of an auditor, noting that "accountants would impair their independence by representing an audit client before a tax court, district court, or federal court of claims."[29] While the SEC has implied that assistance with tax audits and appeals would be permissible non-audit tax services,[30] it has also made clear that a fundamental principle underlying the auditor independence rules is that an auditor cannot serve in an advocacy role for his or her client.[31] An auditor should not provide representation of an audit client in tax controversy matters, as such services involve advocacy of the client's position which is antithetical to the independence required to perform the audit function.

ILLUSTRATION 5-1: A U.S. company (USCo) owns a 25 percent interest in a real estate investment partnership (Partnership). The remaining 75 percent interest in the Partnership is owned by Partners 2, 3 and 4 in equal portions (i.e., 25 percent each). The Partnership owns a 10-acre parcel of raw land (Blackacre) in an area that is undergoing substantial real estate development. USCo and another partner (Partner 2) in the Partnership believe that the Partnership should sell Blackacre and re-invest the proceeds in another parcel of raw land that is currently available (Whiteacre). USCo and Partner 2 note that the gain arising from the sale of Blackacre can be deferred under IRC Section 1031 provided the proceeds arising from the sale of the Land are invested in the purchase of Whiteacre. Partners 3 and 4 do not want the Partnership to sell Blackacre.

To accommodate the desires of USCo and Partner 2, the Partnership divides Blackacre into four equal 2.5 acre portions and distributes a portion to USCo and Partner 2, respectively, and retains the remaining five acres. USCo then sells its 2.5-acre portion of Blackacre and directs the sales proceeds to be delivered to a qualified intermediary. Through the qualified intermediary, USCo purchases a portion of Whiteacre. On its Year 1 tax return, USCo takes

---

[26] *See* SEC Release No. 33–8183, § II.B.9.

[27] *Id.*

[28] *Id.*

[29] *Id.*

[30] *Id.*, § II.H.

[31] *Id.*, § II.B.

the position that the gain arising from its sale of Blackacre is deferred under IRC Section 1031.

Subsequently, in connection with examining USCo's Year 1 tax return, the IRS issues information document requests (IDRs) regarding the gain realized on USCo's sale of Blackacre. In connection with issuing these IDRs, the examining agent informally tells USCo's tax director that the IRS has concern about whether IRC Section 1031 applies to defer the gain realized on USCo's sale of Blackacre. Specifically, the examining agent notes that USCo may not have held Blackacre for productive use in a trade or business or for investment,[32] as it acquired the 2.5-acre interest in Blackacre with the immediate intention of selling it and using the proceeds to purchase an interest in Whiteacre.

Global Audit & Co. is USCo's auditor. Global Audit & Co. was familiar with USCo's sale of the 2.5-acre interest in Blackacre and its subsequent purchase of an interest in Whiteacre. In addition, an individual in Global Audit & Co.'s national office in Washington, D.C. is a well-known expert in IRC Section 1031. For these reasons, the tax director of USCo was considering engaging Global Audit & Co. to assist USCo in responding to the IDRs and dealing with the IRS regarding the tax consequences associated with the sale of the 2.5-acre interest in Blackacre.

The SOX Section 201 issue presented by Illustration 5-1 is whether Global Audit & Co. can represent USCo before the IRS regarding the tax consequences associated with the sale of the 2.5-acre interest in Blackacre. If this non-audit service is allowable, the tax director will then need to obtain the approval of USCo's audit committee before Global Audit & Co. can provide such service, as provided in Exchange Act § 10A(h).

In the controversy context, the process of advocating the taxpayer's position begins during the examination stage of the case and continues until the case is resolved.[33] In Illustration 5-1, Global Audit & Co. would begin to shape its position that the gain arising from the sale of Blackacre should be deferred under IRC Section 1031 in connection with preparing written responses to the IDRs. Of course, Global Audit & Co. would provide all non-privileged information requested but, most importantly, it would highlight facts that would be favorable to USCo's position. In addition, it would begin to develop the arguments defending the return position taken by USCo. Eventually, Global Audit & Co. would affirmatively make arguments and alternative arguments in support of USCo's position. In sum, Global Audit & Co. would use all factual and legal arguments available to vigorously defend the tax return position taken by USCo.

Under these circumstances, there is no question that, if Global Audit & Co. was properly handling the matter with the IRS, it would not be objective and impartial in its dealings with the IRS. Instead, Global Audit & Co. would be zealously advocating for USCo. Thus, Global Audit & Co. should not provide representation before the IRS regarding the tax consequences associated with the sale of the 2.5-acre interest in

---

[32] *See* IRC Section 1031(a)(1).

[33] *See* Michael Saltzman and Leslie Book, *IRS Practice and Procedure* ¶ 8.11 (Thomson Reuters) [*IRS Practice and Procedure*].

Blackacre, as such services involve advocacy of USCo's tax return position which is antithetical to the independence required to perform the audit function.[34]

An audit firm does not have to be physically present at the proceedings to be an advocate. During proceedings, the audit firm can continue to provide advocacy support to the client and its counsel. Once the client has expended time and resources with the audit firm, it is unlikely the client will want to replicate this costly effort in the proceedings. The expansion of audit firms into many services, mostly through acquisitions of consulting firms and technology firms, will increase the potential for greater client advocacy by audit firms across a growing and broad spectrum.

There are a variety of practical issues posed by the "legal services" rules. The practice of law certainly goes beyond litigation. In fact, only a very small percentage of lawyers are litigators, with many providing legal advice.

Accounting firms, particularly in the firms' national practice group, are staffed with lawyers who gained their experience in many of the country's top law firms. These lawyers are doing the same type of work at the accounting firms that they were doing at the law firms. If they were practicing law at the law firm, they are continuing to do so at the accounting firms. If you cut off the letterhead in memoranda prepared by law firms and accounting firms, are they not indistinguishable? Such memoranda are drafted predominantly by the accounting firms' lawyers, not their accountants. Take a look at the footnotes in the memoranda prepared by accounting firms and you will find that they almost always follow the lawyer's bible for citations-the Bluebook. Accounting firms are also increasing its hire of government and in-house counsel.[35] The former author of this chapter was a law firm partner and is currently an accounting firm partner; the current author of this chapter was an accounting firm partner and is now an in-house legal counsel for a public company. Both authors are lawyers, not accountants, and are not performing services other than practicing law, whether employed by an accounting firm or a law firm. Although the distinction between how a lawyer practices in a law firm as opposed to how a lawyer practices in an accounting firm may seem questionable as a practical matter, it is not questionable for SOX purposes. It is certainly questionable that the distinction is vital from an attorney-client privilege standpoint.[36] Indeed, when lawyers move from law firm to accounting firm, it is common practice for continuing clients to take steps to maintain privilege.[37]

In late summer 2017, a major global accounting firm announced the launch of its law firm, which would be located in the U.S. even though the firm would not practice law in the U.S.[38] The firm would only provide foreign legal consulting for U.S.-based companies that are not audit clients. In 2019, an alliance was formed by the law firm Epstein Becker Green and Big 4 accounting firm, Deloitte.[39] Under the alliance, Deloitte Legal will offer employment law and workforce management services to clients. In

---

34 *See* SEC Release No. 33–8183, § II.B.

35 *See* Yvonne Juris, *EY Hires Former Microsoft Tax Atty with Treasury Experience*, Law360 (Oct. 11, 2019).

36 *See* Section 8.01[3][b].

37 *See* Section 8.01[3].

38 *See* Peter Burkholder, *Law Firm, Regulators Keep Eye on Big Four Move to Legal Services, Bloomberg* BNA (Oct. 17, 2017). *Also see* Jason Tashea, *Sleeping Giant: Should BigLaw firms worry about increasing competition from the Big Four accounting firms?* ABA Journal (Sept. 2018).

39 *See* Sam Skolnik, *Epstein Becker Green, Deloitte Form New 'Strategic Alliance*, Bloomberg Law (May 7, 2019).

countries where accounting firms may offer legal services, Epstein Becker Green will refer their clients to Deloitte. In return, Deloitte will refer their U.S. clients to Epstein Becker Green as a preferred provider since accounting firms cannot practice law in the U.S.

Some states may open the floodgates to accounting firms' offering legal services. To make legal services more affordable to the poor and middle class, several Western states are considering relaxing their bar ethics rules by allowing ownership of law firms by nonlawyers. Law firms will find it difficult to counter such a proposal with a monopolistic position provided the states ensure there is a level playing field. The field may be level, but it's a battle between David and Goliath because "the Big Four's war chests are exponentially larger than those of even the country's richest law firms, and their tech capabilities are often greater."[40]

The Big 4 Accounting firms continue to expand into legal services traditionally handled by law firms where they cannot practice law. In a brand survey, the Big 4 dominate in providing alternative legal services with the Big 4 in the top 5 spots.[41] The Big 4 have ambitious plans to grow their legal services business.[42] The Big 4 have a huge technology advantage over law firms. Some predict that within a decade large law firms[43]and large alternative legal services providers will be indistinguishable.[44] This path could be preferable and more lucrative for the Big 4 than to lobby states to allow them to own law firms, which is likely to be accompanied by some stiff terms.[45] This migration to a comprehensive professional services model is driven by market demand, and the PCAOB is well aware of the expansion of accounting firms into legal services. [46] Law firms are understandably concerned about this and increasingly view accounting firms as competitors (as well as strategic partners in servicing client needs) as a growing number of lawyers join accounting firms. The authors have seen firsthand that a significant percentage of the graduates from the masters in tax law program are hired by accounting firms. Each of the Big 4 accounting firms employs around 2,000 lawyers worldwide. Accounting giant Ernst & Young is awaiting ratification from its partners to split the audit business from the non-audit tax and consulting business.[47] Once the split is completed, the consulting business can expand into additional legal services.[48]

---

[40] *See* Sam Skolnik and Amanda Iacone, *Big Four May Gain Legal Market Foothold With State Rule Change*, Bloomberg Tax (April 11, 2019).

[41] *See Acritas Global Alternative Legal Brand Index 2019. See also* Michele Gorman, *EY Law Leads Big 4 Among Global Alternative Legal Brands*, Law360 (Oct. 9, 2019).

[42] *See* Sam Skolnik, *EY Aims To Double Legal Services Revenue Over Next 12 Months*, Daily Tax Report (Aug. 5, 2020).

[43] *See, e.g.*, Sam Skolnik, *Deloitte Takes Aim at U.S. Legal Services Market with Tech Unit*, Bloomberg Law (July 13, 2020); Sam Skolnik, *Deloitte Buys Tech Driven Law Firm, Doubles U.K. Legal Line-Up*, Bloomberg Tax (Nov. 3, 2020); Sam Skolnik, *Deloitte Augments Legal Business Services with New Contracts Team*, Bloomberg Law (Aug. 30, 2021); Michael Kapoor, *Big Four Invests Billions in Tech, Reshaping Their Identifies*, Bloomberg Law (Jan. 2, 2020).

[44] *See* Sam Skolnik, *Big Law, Big Four Best Off When They Cooperate, Panelists Say*, Bloomberg Law (Feb. 4, 2020).

[45] *See* Sam Skolnik, *Deloitte Not Ready to Practice Law in the U.S., Tax Unit Chief Says*, Bloomberg Law (Aug. 16, 2021).

[46] *See* Michael Kapoor, *EY to Double Size of U.K. Consulting Arm to 10,000 People*, Bloomberg Law (April 5, 2022).

[47] *See* Jean Eaglesham, *EY Leaders Green Light Split Plan*, Wall St. J. (Sept. 8, 2022).

[48] *See* Joe Patrice, *The Big 4 Are Coming, But Maybe Not For The Law Firms . . . Yet*, Above the Law (Sept. 27, 2022).

While many law firms continue to ignore the threat from the Big 4, some law firms are leveling the playing field by expanding into non-legal consulting services which provides clients a greater menu of integrated professional services.[49] They are simply following the Big 4's path to success. One major accounting firm's U.S. Chair has openly stated that "a multidisciplinary firm, from our perspective, is the best way to deliver audit quality."[50] The rationale for a multidisciplinary firm harks back to the pre-SOX era: "PwC auditors rely on the expertise of their tax accounting colleagues, for example, to help verify tax expenses and liabilities and how the benefits of the 2017 tax law should be reported on their clients' financial statements. And cybersecurity professionals lend advice to the auditors on controls needed to secure financial records."[51] Similar to the pre-SOX era, tax and consulting services are propelling the growth of the major accounting firms. The largest global law firms are dwarfed by the Big 4.

§ 5.05 Tax Services

[1] SEC Guidance

SOX amended Exchange Act § 10A to include subparagraph (h), which provides that a public accounting firm may engage in any non-audit service, "including any tax services," that is not a prohibited service for an audit client, but only if the activity is approved in advance by the audit committee of the company. As such, Congress intended that auditors may provide tax services to their audit clients.

Consistent with Congressional intent, the SEC has explained that "accountants may continue to provide tax services such as tax compliance, tax planning, and tax advice to audit clients, subject to the normal audit committee preapproval requirements * * *."[52] However, the SEC has cautioned that "merely labeling a service as a 'tax service' will not necessarily eliminate its potential to impair [auditor] independence."[53] Thus, prior to approving any tax work by its auditor, the audit committee of the company must ascertain whether such services could impair the independence of the accountant. In this regard, the SEC has noted, for example, that accountants would "impair their independence by representing an audit client before a tax court, district court, or federal court of claims."[54] Also, the SEC has cautioned that "audit committees also should scrutinize carefully the retention of an accountant in a transaction initially recommended by the accountant, the sole business purpose of which may be tax avoidance and the tax treatment of which may be not supported in the Internal Revenue Code and related regulations."[55] Another area of concern for the SEC involves "scope creep," where work that was originally acceptable can evolve into a prohibited activity as time passes.[56]

---

[49] *See, e.g.*, Sam Skolnik, *Global Law Leaders Said to Ignore Big Four Threat*, Bloomberg Law (April 6, 2021); Aebra Coe, *BigLaw to Big Four: Anything You Can Do, We Can Do Better*, Law360 (Aug. 27, 2020).

[50] *See* Amanda Iacone, *PwC's U.S. Chair Defends Audit, Consulting Mix*, Bloomberg Tax (March 6, 2019).

[51] *Id.*

[52] *See* SEC Release No. 33–8183, § II.B.11.

[53] *Id.*

[54] *Id.*

[55] *Id.*

[56] *See* Thomas Jaworski, *Non-Audit Tax Work Reemerges as a Possible Independence Risk*, 146 Tax Notes 34 (Jan. 5, 2015).

Other than situations involving tax litigation and solely tax-oriented transactions recommended by the auditor, the SEC has provided very little guidance regarding how an audit committee should evaluate whether proposed tax services by the auditor could impair the auditor's independence. In connection with its discussion of the disclosure of fees paid to the auditor in annual periodic reports, the SEC has implied that tax compliance, tax planning, and tax advice would be permissible tax services.[57] Moreover, it implied that assistance with tax audits and appeals, tax advice related to mergers and acquisitions, employee benefit plans and requests for rulings or technical advice from taxing authorities would be permissible tax services.[58]

However, the lack of direct guidance in this area will require audit committees to analyze proposed tax services using the following three principles underlying the auditor independence rules: (1) an auditor cannot function in the role of management, (2) an auditor cannot audit his or her own work, and (3) an auditor cannot serve in an advocacy role for his or her client.[59]

In this light, it appears that tax compliance is the only truly safe tax service that an auditor can provide to an audit client, as tax planning, advice and controversy services could violate one or more of the three principles underlying the auditor independence rules. Tax compliance is highly susceptible of scope creep since the auditor is now in a better position to identify and propose aggressive interpretations of the tax law, propose tax planning idea to reduce taxes for subsequent tax years, and suggests ways to mitigate exposure on uncertain tax positions. Tax planning and advice may violate the principle that an auditor cannot audit its own work. As evident throughout this text, a company's tax positions may have an impact on financial reporting and, in some instances, the impact can be very substantial.[60]

Moreover, although the SEC has specifically indicated that tax litigation services would impair the independence of an auditor, it appears that any tax controversy service could violate the fundamental principle that an auditor cannot serve in an advocacy role for his or her client. As stated above, in the tax controversy context, the process of advocating the taxpayer's position begins during the examination stage of the case and continues until the case is resolved.[61] Thus, it appears an auditor should not provide representation of an audit client in tax controversy matters, as such services involve advocacy of the client's position which is antithetical to the independence required to perform the audit function.[62] In some situations, advocacy can begin as early as tax compliance. It is not uncommon when deciding what tax position to take on the return, the auditor could discuss the merits of various reporting positions, such as impact on cash taxes, earnings, penalties and interest, and likelihood of detection on audit.

Another interesting issue is whether an auditor can represent its audit client in obtaining tax authority agreement on a tax position. For example, can an auditor assist an audit client in obtaining a private letter ruling, a pre-filing agreement, an advance pricing agreement or competent authority agreement? These situations may involve

---

[57] Id, § II.H.

[58] *Id.*

[59] Id, § II.B.

[60] *See GlaxoSmithKline Holdings (Americas) Inc. v. Commissioner*, IR 2006-142 (Sept. 11, 2006), discussed at Section 5.03.

[61] *See IRS Practice and Procedure* ¶ 8.11.

[62] *See* SEC Release No. 33–8183, § II.B.11.

material tax issues the resolution of which could impact the financial reporting of the company, suggesting that the auditor would be auditing its own work. On the other hand, if tax authority agreement is obtained, there will be no ambiguity regarding the tax position at issue. A conflict arises when the auditor insists there is an ambiguity and suggests the ambiguity be eliminated by obtaining tax authority agreement; and then, because the audit firm has the necessary expertise, the audit firm performs the services necessary to secure a favorable agreement from the tax authority. Nonetheless, there appear to be three areas of difficulty in connection with having an auditor represent an audit client in a private letter ruling, pre-filing agreement, advance pricing agreement, competent authority agreement or similar tax authority agreement. The first would be how to handle the financial statement implications of the matter under review by the tax authority prior to the time an agreement is reached with the tax authority. Particularly in the advance pricing agreement and competent authority context, this period of time could include several financial statement cycles. The second issue would be how to handle the financial statement implications of the matter if tax authority agreement cannot be achieved, and the company must take a filing position without tax authority approval. The final concern with having the auditor handle a private letter ruling, pre-filing agreement, advance pricing agreement, competent authority or similar matter with a tax authority is the fact that such proceedings involve advocating the position of an audit client, which is inconsistent with one of the three fundamental principles underlying the auditor independence rules.[63]

[2] PCAOB Guidance

Although the PCAOB has promulgated specific rules regarding auditor independence in the context of tax services (discussed immediately below), the PCAOB continues to review independence problems that can arise from a firm's performance of non-audit tax advisory services, and it will issue a referral to the SEC if a firm's practices raise concerns.[64] The PCAOB continues to monitor concerns expressed by investors about auditors' performance of tax services that may put the firm in a position to audit its own work or perform as an advocate for the client.[65] The PCAOB's strategic plan for 2017 to 2021 provides that the PCAOB will "monitor audit practice for emerging threats to independence and develop appropriate responses, with a view to the PCAOB reporting on the evolution and structure of audit and non-audit services, including tax consulting services, offered by accounting firms and possible implications of their multi-disciplinary business model to independence, audit quality, and investor protection."[66] The PCAOB 2018–2022 Strategic Plan introduces several new values and core strategies. The Strategic Plan focuses on four primary strategic priorities:

- **Effective Oversight.** We will drive continuous improvement in the quality of audit services and more clearly communicate our assessment of the quality we observe.

---

[63] *See* SEC Release No. 33–8183, § II.B.

[64] *See* Thomas Jaworski, *Non-Audit Services Could Distract Accounting Firms, PCAOB Fears*, Tax Analysts Doc 2014–28596 (Dec. 4, 2014).

[65] *See* Thomas Jaworski, *Year in Review: Non-Audit Tax Work Reemerges as a Possible Independence Risk*, 146 Tax Notes 34 (Jan. 5, 2015).

[66] *Public Company Accounting Oversight Board Strategic Plan: Improving the Quality of the Audit for the Protection and Benefit of Investors 2017—2021* (Nov. 20, 2017).

- **Innovation.** We will be more innovative in our oversight activities—particularly with respect to our approach to inspections and standard setting—and at the same time prepare for significant market-driven changes in the audit profession.
- **Improved Engagement.** We will engage more often and more directly with a broader array of investors, as well as with audit committees, preparers, and our other stakeholders to promote robust and timely dialogue regarding the quality of audit services.
- **Process and Culture Optimization.** We will optimize our operations and enhance the culture of our organization.

Most stakeholders should benefit from improved guidance and oversight by the PCAOB of non-audit services that impair an auditor's independence.

[a] Confidential and Aggressive Tax Position Transactions

Under PCAOB Rule 3522,[67] an audit firm is not independent of its audit client if the firm, or any affiliate of the firm, during the audit and professional engagement period, provides any non-audit service to the audit client related to marketing, planning, or opining in favor of the tax treatment of a "confidential" or "aggressive tax position" transaction.[68]

[i] Confidential Transactions

Under PCAOB Rule 3501(c)(i)(1), the term "confidential transaction" means a transaction that is offered to a taxpayer under "conditions of confidentiality" and for which the taxpayer has paid an advisor a fee.

It is important to note that the auditor's independence may be impaired even if the conditions of confidentiality are imposed by tax advisors who are not employed by or affiliated with the audit firm.[69] In such circumstances, the firm, or any affiliate of the firm, cannot provide any non-audit service to the audit client related to marketing, planning, or opining in favor of the confidential transaction.[70] In order to determine whether a transaction has been offered to a taxpayer under conditions of confidentiality, the audit firm may rely on a representation from its audit client, provided the firm does not know, or have reason to know, that such representation is incorrect or incomplete.[71]

Under PCAOB Rule 3501(c)(i)(2), a transaction is considered to be offered to a taxpayer under "conditions of confidentiality" if the advisor who is paid the fee places a limitation on disclosure by the taxpayer of the tax treatment or tax structure of the transaction and the limitation on disclosure protects the confidentiality of the strategy.[72]

---

[67] On July 26, 2005, the PCAOB adopted certain ethics and independence rules addressing tax services, contingent fees, and certain related general ethics and independence standards. PCAOB Release No. 2005–014. PCAOB Staff Questions and Answers regarding the Ethics and Independence Rules were issued by the PCAOB on April 3, 2007.

[68] PCAOB Rule 3522. *See* PCAOB Release No. 2005–014, § II.B.3. The PCAOB will not apply Rule 3522 to tax services that a registered public accounting firm completed no later than June 18, 2006. PCAOB Release No. 2005–020.

[69] *See* PCAOB Staff Questions and Answers at Q1 and A1 (April 3, 2007).

[70] *See* PCAOB Rule 3522(a).

[71] *See* PCAOB Staff Questions and Answers at Q2 and A2 (April 3, 2007).

[72] *See* PCAOB Release No. 2005–014, § II.B.3.b.

For this purpose, the rule provides that a transaction is treated as confidential even if the conditions of confidentiality are not legally binding on the taxpayer. However, the rule also provides that a claim that a transaction is proprietary or exclusive is not treated as a limitation on disclosure if the advisor confirms to the taxpayer that there is no limitation on disclosure of the tax treatment or tax structure of the transaction.[73]

> **ILLUSTRATION 5-2:** A U.S. company (USCo) is contemplating the sale of a wholly-owned subsidiary (Subsidiary). The value of the Subsidiary is approximately $100x, and USCo has a tax basis in its shares of the Subsidiary's stock of $10x. Global Audit & Co. is USCo's auditor. Global Audit & Co. is aware of USCo's intention to sell the Subsidiary and approaches USCo with a plan that, after a series of transactions, would increase USCo's tax basis in the Subsidiary to $100x. Moreover, this plan (Plan) would not impose any additional economic cost to USCo, other than professional and other related fees incurred to implement the Plan. Global Audit & Co. generally advises USCo of the technique that could be used to increase USCo's tax basis in the Subsidiary to $100x but advises USCo that the full details of the Plan cannot be revealed unless USCo signs a "license agreement" (License Agreement). Under the terms of the License Agreement, USCo can disclose the Plan to anyone, but each disclosure will require USCo to pay a license fee to Global Audit & Co. in the amount of $1 million. The License Agreement makes clear that the license fee is due upon any disclosure to a person other than an employee of USCo, including a disclosure to the law firm that provides most of USCo's outside legal advice.

The issue in Illustration 5-2 is whether the License Agreement imposes a limitation on USCo's disclosure of the tax treatment or tax structure of the transaction and whether such limitation protects the confidentiality of the strategy.[74] Although the License Agreement technically does not limit USCo's disclosure of the Plan, the fact that USCo is required to pay a $1 million fee upon any such disclosure serves as an actual impediment to USCo's disclosure of the Plan, even to its external legal advisors. Moreover, this actual limitation on the disclosure of the Plan is clearly intended to protect the confidentiality of the strategy. As such, it appears that the Plan is being offered to USCo under "conditions of confidentiality."[75]

As noted earlier, the expansion of accounting firms into many services, mostly through acquisitions of consulting firms and technology firms, increasingly enables accounting firms to sidestep this restriction by cloaking certain proprietary transactions with impenetrable technology. Going back to Illustration 5-2, let's say the tax basis was increased from $10x to $100x through a series of complex derivative contracts that were executed through accommodating offshore banks. The complex derivatives being used and the offshore banking system are confidential and were devised by the accounting firm's quantitative engineers, very much like the mathematicians at the hedge funds who wrote sophisticated algorithms to execute the over-the-counter trades, which generated the tax basis bump. Although the PCAOB is aware of the independence risks posed by accounting firms' multi-disciplinary business model, regulators should not underestimate accounting firms' technological prowess and capability to work around

---

[73] PCAOB Rule 3501(c)(i)(2). *See* PCAOB Release No. 2005–014, § II.B.3.b.

[74] *Id.*

[75] *Id.*

restrictions. Major global accounting firms have massive resources and employ thousands of attorneys (see Section 5.04).

[ii] Aggressive Tax Position Transactions

Under PCAOB Rule 3522(b),[76] an audit firm is not independent if the firm, or an affiliate of the firm, provides an audit client any service related to marketing, planning, or opining in favor of the tax treatment of a transaction that satisfies the following three criteria:

- the transaction was initially recommended, directly or indirectly, by the audit firm;
- a significant purpose of the transaction is tax avoidance; and
- the proposed tax treatment of the transaction is not at least more likely than not to be allowed under applicable tax laws.

The second prong of the test set forth in PCAOB Rule 3522(b) uses the phrase "significant purpose of which is tax avoidance," and the PCAOB has defined the term "tax avoidance" to include acceleration of deductions into earlier taxable years and deferral of income to later taxable years. Moreover, the PCAOB recognized that this standard set a low threshold and specifically noted that it did not use a term that might seem to establish a higher threshold, such as requiring an evaluation of whether the "sole purpose" of a transaction is tax avoidance.[77]

The third prong of the test set forth in PCAOB Rule 3522(b) uses the term "more likely than not to be allowable under applicable tax laws." The PCAOB has noted that to satisfy this standard the audit firm must establish, based on an analysis of the pertinent facts and authorities, that there is a greater than 50-percent likelihood that the tax treatment of the transaction would, if challenged, be upheld.[78] Moreover, the PCAOB noted that, to satisfy this test, an auditor's analysis must be objectively reasonable and well-founded at the time the analysis is conducted.[79]

There is an inherent conflict when a firm marketing a transaction is also opining on whether the transaction meets the greater-than-50-percent-likelihood criterion. There is certainly no widget manufacturer with a marketing campaign proclaiming that the widget is unlikely to perform as advertised. Self-policing one's product and services is bad policy. At a minimum, an unrelated firm, preferably a reputable law firm that is authorized to practice law in the jurisdiction, should provide the opinion on whether the transaction satisfies the greater-than-50-percent-likelihood requirement. Without such safeguards, it quickly becomes a race to the bottom as increasingly aggressive transaction seek to barely clear the 50 percent threshold.

PCAOB Rule 3522(b) confirms that any transaction characterized as a "listed transaction" within the meaning of Treas. Reg. § 1.6011.1–4(b)(2) would render the audit firm to not be independent.[80] However, if the IRS designates a transaction as a listed transaction subsequent to the time the audit firm marketed, planned, or opined in favor

---

[76] *See* PCAOB Release No. 2005–014, § II.B.3.a.

[77] *Id.*

[78] *Id.*

[79] *Id.*

[80] *Id.*

of the tax treatment of the transaction, the audit firm does not automatically lose its independence.[81] Instead, the determination regarding the firm's independence will be made based on all the facts and circumstances available at the time it marketed, planned, or opined in favor of the tax treatment of the transaction.[82] This analysis would include whether the tax treatment of the transaction was, at the relevant time, at least more likely than not allowable under pertinent tax laws. Nonetheless, even if the audit firm was independent at the time the tax transaction was executed, the listing of the transaction could still impair the firm's independence, where (for example) the firm and the client become mutually interested in defending the tax treatment of the transaction.[83] The listed transaction barrier isn't much of a barrier because many aggressive transactions are "off-the-shelf," so they can be implemented very quickly. Prior to the requirement that taxpayers must self-report uncertain tax positions on their tax returns, it could take years before the IRS audits the aggressive transaction.[84]

[b] Tax Services for Persons in Financial Reporting Oversight Roles

PCAOB Rule 3523[85] generally provides that an audit firm is not independent if the firm provides any tax service to a person in a financial reporting oversight role[86] at the audit client, or an immediate family member of such person, during the audit and professional engagement period. These rules are designed to address certain concerns related to auditor independence when auditors sell personal tax services to individuals who play a direct role in preparing the financial statements of the audit client.[87]

These rules prohibit tax services during the "audit and professional engagement period." This phrase includes two distinct periods of time: (i) the audit period, which is the period covered by any financial statements being audited or reviewed; and (ii) the professional engagement period, which is the period beginning at the earlier of the time the firm signs the engagement letter or begins its work. Thus, under Rule 3523, a firm is not independent of the audit client if the firm, or an affiliate of the firm, provided tax services to a person covered by Rule 3523 during the audit period but before the professional engagement period.[88] As such, the rule effectively prevents a firm from accepting a new audit client when the firm, or an affiliate of the firm, provided tax

---

[81] *See* PCAOB Staff Questions and Answers at Q4 and A4 (April 3, 2007).

[82] *Id.*

[83] *Id.*

[84] The compliance requirement is known as the "Schedule UTP, Uncertain Tax Position Statement." The final Schedule UTP was issued on September 24, 2010. *See* Section 3.11.

[85] On July 26, 2005, the PCAOB adopted certain ethics and independence rules addressing tax services, contingent fees, and certain related general ethics and independence standards. PCAOB Release No. 2005–014. PCAOB Staff Questions and Answers regarding the Ethics and Independence Rules were issued by the PCAOB on April 3, 2007. On July 24, 2007, the PCAOB proposed an amendment to Rule 3523 and adjusted the implementation schedule. PCAOB Release No. 2007–008. On April 22, 2008, the PCAOB adopted the amendment to Rule 3523. PCAOB Release No. 2008–002.

[86] The term "financial reporting oversight role" means a role in which a person is in a position to or does exercise influence over the contents of the financial statements or anyone who prepares them, such as when the person is a member of the board of directors or similar management or governing body; chief executive officer; president; chief financial officer; chief operating officer; general counsel; chief accounting officer; controller; director of internal audit; director of financial reporting; treasurer; or any equivalent position. PCAOB Rule 3501(f)(i).

[87] *See* PCAOB Release No. 2005–014, § I.

[88] The PCAOB announced that it will not apply Rule 3523 to tax services provided on or before April 30, 2008, when those services were provided during the audit period and were completed before the professional engagement period began. *See* PCAOB Release No. 2007–008, § V.

services to such a person during the period covered by any financial statements to be audited or reviewed.[89] On April 22, 2008, the PCAOB amended Rule 3523 so that it would not prohibit tax services that precede the beginning of the professional engagement period.[90] The SEC approved the PCAOB's amendment.[91]

Accounting firms continue to test the boundaries of the type of professional services they can legally provide to audit clients and their employees. One of the major accounting firms held a webcast and podcast for their clients in October 2018 entitled "How can financial wellness pay off for you and your people?" Here is an excerpt from the invitation:

> Employee financial stress can be a major distraction for your employees, but it can also strain your company through high turnover and loss of productivity.
>
> In fact, 83 percent of HR professionals say financial stress in employees negatively impacted work performance.
>
> With your bottom line being so closely linked to your workers' finances, having a comprehensive financial wellness plan can help boost your employees' bottom line and, ultimately, yours. Join the upcoming Ernst & Young LLP Personal Finance webcast as we feature a live panel discussing:
>
> - Why financial wellness benefits are now equally important as traditional employee benefits
> - Key elements of a financial wellness program
> - How financial wellness can aid in recruitment and retention efforts
> - Examples from peer HR professionals about why they chose to offer financial wellness to their workforce and the impact it has made

One of the four panelists was the accounting firm's "Employee Financial Services Leader." It is difficult to imagine financial planning that does not include tax services, which audit firms are prohibited from offering to employees of their audit clients that are involved in financial reporting. The big accounting firms appear to be comfortable following the letter of the independence rules as opposed to the spirit of the rules. Lax enforcement of the independence rules together with the lack of rules that are concise and clear will continue to erode auditor independence.

Similar to the era before SOX in 2002, after a series of recent company failures the question of the lines of demarcation for auditor independence are coming up again. Tax and consulting services are propelling the growth of the major accounting firms.

The major accounting firms clearly have ambitious expansion in mind. If the SEC and PCAOB do not ensure auditor independence, the damage to today's economy will dwarf what happened in the pre-SOX era.

Due to the expansion of accounting firms into many services, the PCAOB should expand the prohibited services beyond tax services. Similar to Merrill Lynch, UBS, and Fidelity, accounting firms provide personal financial services that include (1) investment

---

[89] *See* PCAOB Release No. 2007–008, § II.

[90] PCAOB Release No. 2008–003.

[91] SEC Release No. 34–58415.

planning, (2) philanthropy, (3) insurance and risk management, (4) family offices, and (5) estate, trust, and gift planning and compliance.[92]

[3] European Commission Guidance

In June of 2014, the European Commission ("the EU") finalized stricter requirements that will preclude audit firms from providing any prohibited non-audit tax services, which include preparing tax forms, calculating payroll taxes, and providing support during examinations by tax authorities. The requirements took effect in 2016, but EU member states have the option to allow the statutory auditors to provide tax and valuation services when the services are immaterial to or have no direct effect on the audited financial statements.[93] The EU requirements provide some carve-outs from the prohibited non-audit tax services, but commentators have indicated that it may be relatively difficult to meet the underlying conditions of those exceptions.[94] Moreover, commentators have noted that, in many cases, effective in 2016, public companies domiciled in the EU that are subject to these requirements must select a tax service provider that is not their normal auditor.[95]

§ 5.06 Audit Committee Approval of Non-Audit Services

SOX amended Exchange Act § 10A to include subparagraph (h), which provides that an accounting firm may engage in any non-audit service for an audit client, but only if the activity is not a prohibited activity and such activity is approved in advance by the audit committee of the company. SOX Section 202 amends Exchange Act § 10A to add subparagraph (i), which provides that the audit committee of a public company must pre-approve all audit and non-audit services provided by the auditor to the public company. The SEC rules elaborate on the audit committee approval requirement, providing that non-audit services may be (1) approved in advance by the audit committee; or (2) pre-approved pursuant to policies and procedures established by the audit committee.[96] In addition, the SEC rules allow the audit committee to approve certain non-audit services that were inadvertently not approved by the audit committee in advance of the performance of such services.[97]

[1] Pre-Approval of Non-Audit Services

The SEC rules sanction two methods the audit committee can use to approve non-audit services. Under the first method, the audit committee may approve non-audit services prior to the time that the audit firm is engaged by the company to perform those services.[98] Under the second method, the engagement may be commenced pursuant to pre-approval policies and procedures established by the audit committee of the company, provided (1) the policies and procedures are detailed as to the particular service, (2) the audit committee is informed of each service, and (3) such policies and procedures do not

---

92 For example, *see* PwC, Personal financial services, at https://www.pwc.com/us/en/industries/private-company-services/personal-financial-services.html.

93 *See* Thomas Jaworski, *Year in Review: Non-Audit Tax Work Reemerges as a Possible Independence Risk*, 146 Tax Notes 34 (Jan. 5, 2015).

94 *See* Thomas Jaworski, *EU Ban on Non-Audit Tax Services Might Alarm U.S. Multinationals*, Tax Analysts Doc 2014–20179 (Aug. 29, 2014).

95 *Id.*

96 17 CFR § 210.2–01(c)(7)(i)(A) and (B).

97 17 CFR § 210.2–01(c)(7)(i)(C).

98 17 CFR § 210.2–01(c)(7)(i)(A).

include delegation of the audit committee's responsibilities under the Exchange Act to management.[99] With regard to the third element of these pre-approval rules, the PCAOB has noted that:

> the inquiry the auditor should engage in when proposing to provide tax services to an audit client is whether, in the particular case, the company has the capacity to make its own decisions regarding the proposed tax matter, such that the auditor would not be in the position of performing management functions or making management decisions for the company.[100]

The SEC has provided an example of one method of pre-approval of non-audit services, where one or more members of the audit committee who are independent board directors pre-approve non-audit services and report such decisions to the full audit committee at each of its scheduled meetings.[101] Another important element of audit committee pre-approval is that the audit committee's policies for the pre-approval of non-audit services by the auditor must be disclosed by the company in its periodic annual reports.[102]

Under PCAOB Rule 3524,[103] the PCAOB has established guidelines for seeking audit committee pre-approval to perform for an audit client any permissible tax service. In seeking such approval, the rule provides that the audit firm must describe, in writing, to the audit committee of the company:

(1) the scope of the service, the fee structure for the engagement, and any side letter or other amendment to the engagement letter, or any other agreement (whether oral, written, or otherwise) between the firm and the audit client, relating to the service; and

(2) any compensation arrangement or other agreement, such as a referral agreement, a referral fee or fee-sharing arrangement, between the registered public accounting firm (or an affiliate of the firm) and any person (other than the audit client) with respect to the promoting, marketing, or recommending of a transaction covered by the service.[104]

In addition, PCAOB Rule 3524 provides that the audit firm must discuss with the audit committee of the company the potential effects of the services on the independence of the firm.[105] Moreover, the audit firm must document the substance of its discussion with the audit committee of the company.[106]

---

[99] 17 CFR § 210.2–01(c)(7)(i)(B).

[100] PCAOB Release No. 2005–014, § II.C.

[101] *See* SEC Release No. 33–8183, § II.D.

[102] *Id.*

[103] On July 26, 2005, the PCAOB adopted certain ethics and independence rules addressing tax services, contingent fees, and certain related general ethics and independence standards. PCAOB Release No. 2005–014. With respect to tax services provided to audit clients whose audit committees pre-approve tax services pursuant to policies and procedures, PCAOB Rule 3524 does not apply to any of these tax services that were begun by April 20, 2007. PCAOB Release No. 2006–001. Regarding tax services pre-approved on an engagement-by-engagement basis, PCAOB Rule 3524 does not apply to any tax service pre-approved on an engagement-by-engagement basis before June 18, 2006. PCAOB Release No. 2005–020; PCAOB Release No. 2006–001.

[104] PCAOB Rule 3524(a).

[105] PCAOB Rule 3524(b).

[106] PCAOB Rule 3524(c).

In promulgating the foregoing rules regarding audit committee approval, the PCAOB noted that the timing and method by which auditors describe for, and discuss with, audit committees proposed tax services will necessarily vary depending on different audit committees' procedures.[107] For example, the PCAOB noted that, for companies whose audit committees meet annually to consider proposed non-audit services, it would be appropriate for auditors to provide the disclosures and conduct the discussions required by PCAOB Rule 3524 at that annual meeting.[108] Moreover, the PCAOB noted that, if the audit committee has policies in place that delegate authority to pre-approve non-audit services to one committee member and require reporting of any services approved by such delegate at the next scheduled audit committee meeting, it would be appropriate for auditors to provide the member holding the delegated authority a description of the service that complies with PCAOB Rule 3524. However, the PCAOB also noted that, in such circumstances, the auditor should ultimately discuss the service with the full audit committee.[109]

PCAOB Rule 3525 implements the pre-approval requirement by directing auditors to take certain steps as part of seeking audit committee pre-approval of internal control-related non-audit services.[110] The steps are meant to make sure that audit committee members have relevant information so they can make informed decisions on how the performance of internal control-related services may affect independence.[111] PCAOB Rule 3525 requires a registered public accounting firm that seeks pre-approval of a client's audit committee to perform otherwise permissible internal control-related non-audit services to:

- Describe, in writing, to the audit committee the scope of the proposed service;
- Discuss with the audit committee the potential effects of the proposed service on the firm's independence; and
- Document the substance of the firm's discussion with the audit committee.

[2] Inadvertent Error Exception to Approval of Non-Audit Services

The SEC rules also allow the audit committee to approve non-audit services provided by the auditor and not initially recognized as non-audit services. To qualify for this exception to the general requirement of pre-approval, the rules provide that the following conditions must be satisfied:

(1) The aggregate amount of all such services provided constitutes no more than five percent of the total amount of revenues paid by the audit client to its accountant during the fiscal year in which the services are provided;

[107] PCAOB Release No. 2005–014, § II.C.

[108] *Id.*

[109] *Id.*

[110] PCAOB Release No. 2007–005. The SEC approved Rule 3525 on July 25, 2007. *See* SEC Press Release 2007–144. PCAOB Rule 3525 is effective and required for integrated audits conducted for fiscal years ending on or after Nov. 15, 2007. However, earlier adoption was permitted.

[111] PCAOB Release No. 2007–005, § 3.

(2) Such services were not recognized by the company at the time of the engagement to be non-audit services; and

(3) Such services are promptly brought to the attention of the audit committee of the company and approved prior to the completion of the audit by the audit committee or by one or more members of the audit committee who are members of the board of directors to whom authority to grant such approvals has been delegated by the audit committee.[112]

Because of the condition that the services were not recognized as non-audit services prior to the commencement of the engagement, this exception is limited to situations where the company inadvertently failed to identify such services as non-audit services and have them approved by the audit committee.

§ 5.07 Contingent Fees

Under PCAOB Rule 3521,[113] an audit firm is not independent of its audit client if the firm, or any affiliate of the firm, during the audit and professional engagement period, provides any service or product to the audit client for a contingent fee or a commission, or receives from the audit client, directly or indirectly, a contingent fee or commission. For this purpose, the term "contingent fee" means any fee established for the sale of a product or the performance of any service pursuant to an arrangement in which no fee will be charged unless a specified finding or result is attained, or in which the amount of the fee is otherwise dependent upon the finding or result of such product or service.[114] However, a fee is not a "contingent fee" if the amount is fixed by courts or other public authorities and not dependent on a finding or result.[115] Also, a "value-added" fee is not considered a contingent fee, although the SEC and the PCAOB have indicated that they will closely monitor the use of value-added fees to determine whether a fee labeled a "value added" fee is in fact a contingent fee.[116]

§ 5.08 Disclosure of Audit and Non-Audit Fees and Non-Audit Service Policies

To allow investors to evaluate the independence of a company's auditor, the SEC has mandated disclosure of fees paid to the auditor and policies in place to permit approval of non-audit services provided by the auditor.[117] Specifically, the SEC rules provide that the company must disclose in its annual periodic reports, under the caption

---

[112] 17 CFR § 210.2–01(c)(7)(i)(C).

[113] On July 26, 2005, the PCAOB adopted certain ethics and independence rules addressing tax services, contingent fees, and certain related general ethics and independence standards. PCAOB Release No. 2005–014. The PCAOB did not apply Rule 3521 to contingent fee arrangements that were paid in their entirety, converted to fixed fee arrangements, or otherwise unwound before June 18, 2006. PCAOB Release No. 2005–020.

[114] PCAOB Rule 3501(c)(ii). *See* PCAOB Release No. 2005–014, § II.B.2.

[115] *Id.*

[116] *Id.*

[117] In addition, PCAOB independence standards require the auditor to provide certain information to the audit committee about independence that could assist the audit committee in fulfilling its oversight of the audit firm. On April 22, 2008, the PCAOB adopted proposed Ethics and Independence Rule 3526, *Communication with Audit Committees Concerning Independence*, which requires the auditor, before accepting an initial engagement with the company and annually thereafter, to describe in writing to the company's audit committee all relationships between that firm or any of its affiliates and the company or persons in a financial reporting role at the company that could reasonably be thought to affect the accounting firm's independence. PCAOB Release No. 2008–003. The SEC approved Rule 3526 on August 22, 2008. SEC Release No. 34–58415.

Audit Fees, the aggregate fees billed for each of the last two fiscal years for professional services rendered by the auditor in connection with, or reasonably related to, the performance of the audit of the company's financial statements.[118]

In addition to disclosing fees paid to the auditor for audit services, the company must disclose in its annual periodic reports, under the caption Tax Fees, the aggregate fees billed in each of the last two fiscal years for professional services rendered by the auditor for tax compliance, tax advice, and tax planning; moreover, the disclosure must include a description of the nature of the services comprising the fees disclosed under the Tax Fee category.[119] The SEC has recognized that certain tax services may be properly attributable to the audit function and, therefore, has stated that an appropriate allocation of those fees may be included in the audit fee category.[120]

The company must also disclose in its annual periodic reports, under the caption All Other Fees, the aggregate fees billed in each of the last two fiscal years for products and services provided by the auditor, other than Audit and Tax Fees; such disclosure must also describe the nature of the services comprising the fees disclosed under the All Other Fees category.[121]

In addition to disclosing fees paid to the audit firm, the company must also disclose any policies it has in place regarding pre-approval of non-audit services by the audit firm.[122] The SEC has indicated that these disclosures should provide a clear, concise and understandable description of these policies and procedures.[123] Alternatively, the SEC has indicated that companies could include a copy of those policies and procedures with the information delivered to investors and filed with the SEC.[124]

Moreover, if the audit committee approves any fees paid to the auditor that were not pre-approved but were approved pursuant to the inadvertent error exception described in Section 5.06[2], the percentage of such fees to the total fees paid to the auditor must be disclosed.[125] Additionally, the company must disclose the specific processes in place that monitor activities where the inadvertent error exception is utilized.[126]

§ 5.09 Impact of Auditor Independence Rules

In the following sections we examine the impact of the auditor independence rules on the various parties who have an interest in the manner in which tax advice is obtained and implemented by companies.

---

[118] 17 CFR § 240.14a–101 Schedule 14A, Item 9(e). Under another category, Audit-Related Fees, the company must disclose the aggregate fees billed in each of the last two fiscal years for assurance and related services by the auditor that are reasonably related to the performance of the audit or review of the company's financial statements and are not reported under Audit Fees. 17 CFR § 240.14a–101 Schedule 14A, Item 9(e).

[119] *Id.*

[120] *See* SEC Release No. 33–8183, § II.H.

[121] 17 CFR § 240.14a–101 Schedule 14A, Item 9(e).

[122] *Id.*

[123] *See* SEC Release No. 33–8183, § II.H.

[124] *Id.*

[125] 17 CFR § 240.14a–101 Schedule 14A, Item 9(e).

[126] *See* SEC Release No. 33–8183, § II.H.

[1] Impact on Companies

From the standpoint of companies, it seems likely that outside tax advice will increasingly (maybe generally) be sought from advisors other than the auditor, since non-audit tax services would require, at the very least, audit committee advance approval. As discussed more fully in Section 5.05, it appears that tax compliance could be the only truly safe tax service that an auditor can provide to an audit client, as tax planning, advice and controversy services could violate one or more of the three principles underlying the auditor independence rules. Moreover, as also discussed in Section 5.05, it appears that any tax controversy service could violate the fundamental principle that an auditor cannot serve in an advocacy role for his or her client. In addition, as noted in Section 5.05, there appear to be serious concerns in connection with having an auditor represent an audit client in a private letter ruling, pre-filing agreement, advance pricing agreement, competent authority agreement or similar tax authority agreement matter.

If it becomes common to seek such advice from advisors other than a company's auditor, there will certainly be a change in the dynamics of tax planning and tax advice. The audit of the company's tax provision is inevitably a potentially contentious matter, with clear concerns and objectives on both sides. There have been anecdotal reports of situations in which an auditor has tactfully threatened adverse consequences if tax services potentially pertaining to provision determination are not performed by the auditor. Companies must also weigh the higher audit costs as well as the risks of an adverse outcome when the auditor does not perform the tax services subject to a tax-provision determination. Such obvious conflicts of interest could be curtailed by imposing restrictions on auditors from providing tax advice to their audit clients. But as noted, there continues to be pressure to use audit firms, and the audit firms have also found ways around certain restrictions.

Nevertheless, it seems likely that companies will seek material tax planning services from non-auditor advisors. This would appear to be beneficial to companies in any event. The overall interest of the company is to find an appropriate means of reducing its effective tax rate. This, in turn, means strategies must be developed that will succeed and not be subject to years of contest in the United States and one or more other countries or be subject to a penalty that would ultimately increase the effective tax rate or reduce pre-tax earnings. In the case of advice provided by the auditor itself, it has often seemed, in pre-SOX periods, that there was scant independent scrutiny of the advice from the standpoint of provision analysis. It often appeared that the audit function accepted planning work done by its own colleagues in the tax area without scrutiny or review, regardless of how aggressive the advice may have been. On the other hand, it has also often seemed that any advice rendered by an advisor other than the auditing firm's colleagues was subjected to the most searching of scrutiny to make appropriate provision determinations. Thus, the auditor's review of tax work provided by other professionals should allow the company to accurately evaluate its tax positions.

With the increasing spread of penalty and examination regimes in international taxation in many countries, as well as the heightened scrutiny of common strategies for reducing effective tax rates, it seems apparent that the interests of the company are best protected by assuring that aggressive tax strategies are evaluated carefully, without the potentially conflicting interest of an auditor's auditing function examining the tax planning work of its colleagues.

It also seems inevitable that a corporate tax department benefits from evaluating both its auditor[127] and other advisors in the process of determining who can provide the expertise that is needed for a specific project. In short, it appears that SOX will have a salutary effect from the overall standpoint of companies, certainly from the perspective of the audit committee.

[2] Impact on Auditors

From the standpoint of audit firms, it seems likely that the auditing function will be better executed if material tax advice is provided by other advisors. In this way, the auditor can conduct its own examination of the advice for provision or other purposes without being limited by considerations of collegiality. The net result is likely to be a more carefully screened process.

It may also be that the level of services and fees earned by the auditor need not necessarily diminish, even from the client in question. To the extent that material tax planning benefits are accrued in the financial results for the period in question, analysis of such planning for tax provision purposes will obviously need to be undertaken. It may be that the level of tax work from such analysis will partly compensate for the "loss" of the tax planning work to other advisors and, most importantly, allow audit firms to perform more tax planning work for non-audit companies.

> **Illustration 5-3:** Four accounting firms execute a tax planning idea for their respective audit client, each earning $100 in tax services revenues. Alternative, they are prohibited from providing such tax planning services to their audit clients. Each accounting firm now implements the tax planning idea for a non-audit client. Again, they each earn $100 for providing tax services but to a non-audit client. In addition, each firm will now thoroughly audit the tax planning idea implemented by its audit client. The firm charges $40 for the audit. Each firm has increased revenues from $100 to $140!

Of course, this is an over-simplification since in reality, one firm would strive to implement the tax planning for the three non-audit clients and its audit client, earning $400 in revenues. At the very least, the provision determination process is likely to evolve in the era of separation of audit from planning activities.

It also seems apparent that the inevitable reluctance of audit committees to allow the auditor to perform non-audit tax services, as well as the fuzzy boundary line of prohibited tax, valuation and legal services, requires auditing firms to hone their skills in competing for work with other non-audit advisors of companies for which they do not serve as auditors. At the very least, this makes the process of selecting such advisors likely to be based on the advisor's expertise and not on the audit firm's real or implied threat of higher audit costs due to heightened audit standards and full or partial loss of the tax provision benefit.

[3] Impact on Non-Audit Advisors

In the case of other advisors, limitations on a company from using its own auditor for significant tax planning work can provide greater opportunities to submit proposals for projects and be included in "beauty-contest" lineups for new projects. In many

[127] A statement of the benefits of using the auditor for tax services is set out in *AICPA Official Cites Benefits of Continuing to Use External Auditors for Tax Services,* Daily Tax Rep., at G-7, June 3, 2005.

companies, the auditor has often had an understandable edge in obtaining tax planning assignments, since it has such a significant on-site presence and knowledge of the company. The opening of such work to a broader range of potential advisors can plainly be beneficial to those other advisors that have expertise to offer with respect to the project in question. In fact, tax executives at many companies concur that the accounting firms are splitting a bigger pie as evidenced by the growing audit fees and global revenues, much of this explosive revenue growth coming in the post-SOX era. Deloitte's revenues, for example, grew over 80 percent in the ten-year span of 2006 to 2016, from $20 billion to $36.8 billion. KPMG revenues grew from $22.7 billion in 2011 to $32.1 billion in 2021, which is almost 50 percent over a 10-year period.

[4] Impact on Investing Public

Needless to say, the intended beneficiaries of SOX are investors who, hopefully, are less likely to be defrauded by the types of conflict-of-interest-laden professional services that are reported to have been at the heart of so many business scandals. In the context of taxation, several of these celebrated collapses involved U.S.-based companies conducting extensive tax haven activities, or formerly U.S.-based companies that have expatriated to foreign tax haven locations. While SOX does not preclude such activities from recurring in the future to other companies, it certainly erects significant safeguards to increase the likelihood that the auditor will carefully scrutinize all material transactions without the baggage of the obvious conflicts of interest. These safeguards would be more effective if the accounting industry was not dominated by four major accounting firms. In many respects, they are indistinguishable in terms of tax expertise and the planning transactions they market. Any one of the firms is unlikely to render an unfavorable audit opinion on a transaction that the firm itself is performing for other companies. Although the Big 4 dominance will continue to grow, greater independence could be achieved by requiring opinions on tax transactions to be issued by an independent and reputable law firm.

§ 5.10 Relationship to Global Tax Evolutions

As noted at Section 1.03, there are a wide range of global tax evolutions occurring at a rapid pace. The SOX issues discussed in this chapter will inevitably recur for multinational groups as they adapt their tax-rate strategies to these realities. The critical issues will concern the extent to which independence considerations impact auditor involvement. In a world in which country-by-country reporting data will expose the group to potentially searching tax examinations throughout its global operations, which anyhow may become public in due course, the independence and objectivity of the auditor is likely to be an important element of comfort to the Board, investors, senior management, and other constituents. There are certainly countervailing considerations. The auditor may have unique insight to the group. On the other hand, in the event of material challenge from tax authorities, confidentiality of the underlying planning may be important (see Section 8.01, attorney client privilege in international planning contexts and Section 8.02, application to tax accrual work papers). In addition, such issues may receive further guidance from the PCAOB as it implements its strategic plan. The International Ethics Standards Board of Accountants ("IESBA"), the global organization that sets ethical standards for professional accountants, proposed prohibiting most consulting work for audit clients. IESBA's code of conduct is followed by 120 countries. The proposal was in response to a growing need to reinforce auditor independence. Tax advisory and tax planning services would be allowed provided they are supported by tax authority, or established practice that have not been challenged by tax authorities, or have a legal basis are likely to prevail. In the United Kingdom, lawmakers are seeking a separation of the Big 4's consulting an audit businesses.[128] The U.K.'s Financial Reporting Council has asked the Big 4 to operationally separate the audit business by June 2024.[129] Some firms are not waiting for regulators to clamp down and taking the initiative to separate their consulting business.[130] EY shocked the accounting and consulting world when its executives approved a plan to split the audit business from its non-audit business.[131] The split must be ratified by EY's 13,000 worldwide partners. The split should increase the independence of the audit. Unless the split proves favorable, the other major accounting firms will not follow EY's lead so massive independence concerns will remain.

---

[128] *See* Martin Croucher, *Big Four Increase Market Share Despite Increased Scrutiny*, Law360 (Oct. 28, 2019).

[129] *See* Aoife White and Hugo Miller, *Big Four Face Big Split as Watchdog Sets Separation Deadline*, Bloomberg Law (July 6, 2020).

[130] *See* Amanda Iacone, *PwC Splits Tax Practice Between Audit, Advisory in Restructuring*, Bloomberg Tax (June 15, 2021). *See also* Mark Maurer and Jean Eaglesham, *Accounting Firm EY Considers Split of Audit, Advisory Businesses*, Wall St. J. (May 26, 2022) (appeared in Wall St. J. print edition on May 27, 2022 as "Accounting Giant EY Weighs Global Split").

[131] *See* Jean Eaglesham, *EY Leaders Green Light Split Plan*, Wall St. J. (Sept. 8, 2022).

Appendix 5.1

AUDIT COMMITTEE PRE-APPROVAL POLICY

XYZ, Inc. Audit Committee

Policies and Procedures Concerning Pre-Approval of Non-Audit Services

January ___, 20__

The following are the policies and procedures concerning the pre-approval by the Audit Committee of the Board of Directors (the "Audit Committee") of XYZ, Inc. (the "Company") of the Company's independent auditors to perform non-audit services for the Company.

The Audit Committee must pre-approve all permitted non-audit services (including the fees and terms thereof) to be performed for the Company by the Company's independent auditors that are not prohibited by law.

1. Prohibited Services

The Audit Committee may not approve the performance of the following services for the Company by the Company's independent auditor, and the Company's independent auditors shall not perform any of the following non-audit services for the Company:

- Bookkeeping or other services related to the accounting records or financial statements of the Company;
- Financial information systems design and implementation;
- Appraisal or valuation services, fairness opinions, or contribution-in-kind reports;
- Actuarial services;
- Internal audit outsourcing services;
- Management functions or human resources;
- Broker or dealer, investment adviser, or investment banking services;
- Legal services and expert services unrelated to the audit; and
- Any other service that the PCAOB determines, by regulation, is impermissible.

2. Guiding Principles

Moreover, even if the proposed non-audit service is not one of the foregoing prohibited services, the Audit Committee shall consider whether such service would impair the independence of the audit firm. In this regard, the Audit Committee should be mindful of the following principles, as the violation of any one of these principles would impair the independence of the audit firm:

- The auditor cannot function in the role of management;

- The auditor cannot audit its own work; and
- The auditor cannot serve in an advocacy role for the Company.

3. ***Engagement Arrangements***

All engagement arrangements for non-audit services shall be in writing, and the terms of such engagement shall be in accordance with applicable SEC and PCAOB rules and regulations. The audit firm shall not require the Company to enter into any arrangement containing conditions of confidentiality. In addition, the Company shall not hire the audit firm to provide non-audit services related to any transaction or arrangement that would be characterized as an aggressive tax position under pertinent rules and regulations. Also, the Company shall not hire the audit firm to perform any non-audit services on a contingent fee or contingent commission basis.

4. ***Designated Member Pre-Approval Process***

The Audit Committee shall annually appoint one of its members, who is an independent member of the Board of Directors of the Company (the "Member"), to grant pre-approval of non-audit services provided by the independent auditor.

a. ***Covered Services***

Prior to approving any non-audit service by the audit firm, the Member shall determine the scope of the proposed non-audit service, the fee structure for the engagement, and any other agreement (whether oral, written, or otherwise) between the Company and the audit firm, relating to the proposed service. The Member shall determine compliance with the engagement arrangement principles outlined in *Paragraph 3.* (above).

The Member shall only pre-approve non-audit services that are not "prohibited services," as described in *Paragraph 1.* (above), and the Member shall consider the "guiding principles" outlined in *Paragraph 2.* (above) in determining whether to approve the non-audit services in question. The Member may ask the audit firm to provide a written statement explaining why the proposed non-audit services are not prohibited services and do not otherwise impair the independence of the auditor.

b. ***Ratification of Pre-Approved Services***

The Member shall report all non-audit services provided by the Company's audit firm and approved pursuant to the procedure outlined in this *Paragraph 4.* to the Audit Committee at the next regularly scheduled meeting of the Audit Committee, and such services must be ratified and approved by a majority of the members of the Audit Committee.

Chapter 6

MANAGEMENT ASSESSMENT AND AUDITOR ATTESTATION OF INTERNAL CONTROLS

Table of Sections

§ 6.01 Background

Section 404(a) of the Sarbanes-Oxley Act of 2002[1] (SOX) directed the Securities Exchange Commission (SEC) to prescribe rules that require each annual report that a company[2] files pursuant to Section 13(a) or 15(d) of the Securities Exchange Act of 1934 (Exchange Act) to contain an internal control report: (1) stating management's responsibility for establishing and maintaining an adequate internal control structure and procedures for financial reporting; and (2) containing an assessment, as of the end of the company's most recent fiscal year, of the effectiveness of the company's internal control structure and procedures for financial reporting.

Under SOX Section 404(b), auditors must attest to, and report on, management's annual report of its assessment of the company's internal control structure and procedures for financial reporting.[3] SOX Section 404(b) further provides that this attestation must be made in accordance with standards adopted by the Public Company Accounting Oversight Board (PCAOB).[4]

This chapter provides an overview of internal controls, management's obligation to establish and maintain an adequate internal control structure and procedures for financial reporting, and management's obligation to annually assess and report on such internal control structure and procedures. It also touches on the auditor's attestation of internal control over financial reporting. This chapter begins by laying out the general rules and procedures for internal controls, followed by the application of these rules and procedures to the company's tax department and, in particular, the calculation of the tax provision. It will be assumed for purposes of this chapter that accounting for the tax provision is the responsibility of the tax department or the tax department has material involvement in the preparation of the tax provision.

---

1 15 U.S.C. § 7262.

2 Although SOX applies to "issuers," we use the more general terms company or companies in this chapter for ease of reading. "Issuers" are defined to include all types of registrants that file disclosure documents with the SEC, including U.S. public companies and non-U.S. companies that have securities listed on a U.S. exchange or traded in Nasdaq (e.g., ADR programs). *See* Exchange Act § 10A(f).

3 15 U.S.C. § 7262.

4 *Id.*

§ 6.02 Internal Controls

Under SOX Section 404(a), management has an obligation to establish and maintain an adequate internal control structure and procedures for financial reporting. Internal controls have been used by companies to improve profitability and to assist management in achieving its goals. Thus, internal controls serve many purposes, including promoting efficiency, reducing risk, quality controls, forecasting and planning, and ensuring the reliability of financial statements and compliance with laws and regulations.[5]

The *Internal Control—Integrated Framework* created by the Committee of Sponsoring Organizations of the Treadway Commission (COSO) is a widely recognized and utilized framework for internal controls.[6] The COSO framework establishes a common definition of internal control to serve the needs of companies, independent public accountants, legislators, and regulatory agencies, and to provide a broad framework of criteria against which companies could evaluate and improve their control systems.

The COSO framework divides internal control into three broad objectives:[7]

- Effectiveness and efficiency of operations;
- Reliability of financial, nonfinancial, and internal reporting;[8] and
- Compliance with applicable laws and regulations.

The first category addresses a company's business objectives, including performance and profitability goals and safeguarding of resources. The second category relates to the preparation of reliable financial statements. The third category deals with complying with those laws and regulations to which the company is subject. It is important to note that SOX Section 404(a) and related SEC rules and guidance relate only to the second objective of the COSO framework, i.e., reliability of financial reporting.[9] Although SOX was primarily directed at public financial reporting, compliance with laws that would impact a company's financial results is also an objective (see SEC Release No. 33–83238).

Under the COSO framework, internal control is a process, implemented by a corporation's board of directors, management, and other personnel, designed to provide reasonable assurance that:

---

[5] Title I of Pub. L. 95–213 (1977).

[6] *See* COSO, *Internal Control—Integrated Framework* (2013). COSO is sponsored by five major professional associations in the United States: the American Accounting Association, the American Institute of Certified Public Accountants, Financial Executives International, The Institute of Internal Auditors, and the Institute of Management Accountants. Information on COSO can be obtained at www.coso.org.

[7] The 2013 COSO Internal Control—Integrated Framework maintains the same three objectives the 1992 version had. For an in-depth discussion of COSO's 2013 Internal Control Framework, *see* Avellant, *Practical Guide to Internal Control,* Chapter B1 (Thomson Reuters), available on Checkpoint, http:// checkpoint.riag.com. In August 2017, COSO released its latest guidance, *Enterprise Risk Management: Integrating with Strategy and Performance*, which addresses the emerging risks that a company's board and management should focus on—while emphasizing the importance of the company's culture and information technology—and seeks to assist boards on meeting oversight responsibility.

[8] The 2013 COSO Internal Control—Integrated Framework expanded the reporting objective to include nonfinancial and internal reporting objectives.

[9] SEC Release No. 33–8762, § I, note 15 (Dec. 13, 2006).

- They understand the extent to which the company's operational objectives are being achieved;
- They understand the extent to which the company's reporting objectives (financial, nonfinancial and internal) are being achieved; and
- Applicable laws and regulations are being complied with.[10]

The effectiveness of internal control is the state or condition of this process at one or more points in time.

The process of internal control consists of five interrelated components under the COSO framework—control environment; risk assessment; control activities; information and communication; and monitoring. Each of these components is described more fully below:[11]

- Control Environment. The control environment component is considered the foundation of all other components of internal control. The control environment sets the tone of a corporation. Factors entering into and making up the control environment include the integrity, ethical values and competence of the corporation's people; management's philosophy and operating style; the way management assigns authority and responsibility, and organizes and develops its people; and the involvement and direction provided by the board of directors and the audit committee.[12]
- Risk Assessment. Every corporation faces a range of risks from internal and external sources. These risks must be continually assessed, even as economic, industry, regulatory and operating conditions continue to change. Risk assessment involves establishing consistent, linked objectives; identifying, analyzing, and evaluating risks to achieving those objectives; and forming a basis for determining how the risks should be managed. Mechanisms are needed to identify and deal with the special risks associated with change.[13]
- Control Activities. Control activities are the policies and procedures that address the risks identified in risk assessment and help ensure management directives are carried out. Control activities are "internal controls" in the most widely recognized sense of the term. These activities occur throughout the corporation, at all levels and in all functions. Types of control activities include authorizations, verifications, reviews, approvals, information system controls, physical controls, and segregation of duties.[14]
- Information and Communication. The information and communication component relates to the identification, capture, and communication of financial, operating, or other information to those who need it in a form

---

[10] COSO, *Internal Control—Integrated Framework* (2013), Chapter 1.

[11] The 2013 COSO Internal Control—Integrated Framework maintains the five integrated components of internal control.

[12] *Id.* at Chapter 2.

[13] *Id.* at Chapter 3.

[14] *Id.* at Chapter 4.

and timeframe that allows such people to carry out their responsibilities. The communication component also relates to internal controls; the communication must indicate that control responsibilities must be taken seriously, and it must provide a means to convey information to appropriate personnel.[15]

- Monitoring. Monitoring refers to the process of assessing the quality and effectiveness of internal controls over time. This is accomplished on an ongoing basis through management and supervisory activities. It is also accomplished through periodic, separate evaluations. The scope and frequency of separate evaluations will depend on an assessment of risks and the effectiveness of ongoing monitoring procedures. An element of monitoring includes reporting internal control deficiencies to appropriate personnel.[16]

Under the COSO framework, there is a direct relationship between the three categories of objectives, which are what a corporation strives to achieve, and the five components, which represent what the corporation needs to achieve in order to reach the objectives.[17] This 3-objectives-by-5-components matrix is applied to the corporation as a whole, to each distinct operating unit, and to each functional activity, forming a three-dimensional analysis. This three-dimensional analysis and standard of effectiveness constitute the COSO framework for internal control.[18]

§ 6.03 Management Assessment and Reporting of Internal Controls

SOX Section 404(a) directed the SEC to prescribe rules that require each annual report that a company files pursuant to Section 13(a) or 15(d) of the Exchange Act to contain an internal control report: (1) stating management's responsibility for establishing and maintaining an adequate internal control structure and procedures for financial reporting; and (2) containing an assessment, as of the end of the company's most recent fiscal year, of the effectiveness of the company's internal control structure and procedures for financial reporting.[19]

[1] Framework for Evaluating Internal Control

Although the SEC did not adopt the COSO Framework as the standard for an internal control evaluation framework, it did state that the "COSO Framework satisfies our criteria and may be used as an evaluation framework for purposes of management's annual internal control evaluation and disclosure requirements."[20] In rejecting a specific framework that management must use to evaluate internal controls over financial

---

15 *Id.*

16 *Id.* In January 2009, COSO issued "Guidance on Monitoring Internal Control Systems," which is designed to assist organizations of any size or structure in developing efficient means to monitor the continued operating effectiveness of internal control related to financial reporting, operational, and compliance control objectives.

17 17 CFR § 240.13a–15(f).

18 COSO, *Internal Control—Integrated Framework* (2013) Chapter 1.

19 *See* 17 CFR § 240.13a–15(f).

20 *Id.* On May 14, 2013, COSO updated its framework. The updated framework permanently replaced the 1992 edition as of December 15, 2014.

reporting, the SEC expressed its belief that the methods of conducting assessments of internal control over financial reporting will, and should, vary from company to company.[21] The SEC also believed that it was impractical to prescribe a single methodology that meets the needs of every company.[22]

The SEC issued guidance on May 16, 2005, emphasizing that management, not the auditor, is responsible for determining the appropriate nature and form of internal controls for the company as well as their evaluation methods and procedures.[23] In addition, the SEC noted that "[r]egistered public accounting firms should recognize that there is a zone of reasonable conduct by companies that should be recognized as acceptable in the implementation of Section 404."[24]

The SEC indicated that "a one-size fits all, bottom-up, check-the-box approach that treats all controls equally is less likely to improve internal controls and financial reporting than reasoned, good faith exercise of professional judgment focused on reasonable, as opposed to absolute, assurance."[25]

Companies and auditors needed to focus on the central purpose of the SOX internal control requirement, which was the preparation of reliable financial statements that are materially accurate. As such, the SEC emphasized that the internal control review process should focus on identifying material weaknesses that have, as indicated by their very definition, more than a remote likelihood of leading to a material misstatement in the financial statements.[26] The SEC stated that "[t]he desired approach should devote resources to the areas of greatest risk and avoid giving all significant accounts and related controls equal attention without regard to risk."[27]

Absent clear and detailed guidance, many companies spent tremendous internal and external resources in identifying, creating, and documenting processes and controls that were task-centric. The ineffectiveness of the SOX implementation is evidenced by the number of material tax deficiencies that were reported by companies several years after the SOX control rules were issued and implemented.[28]

Management is not permitted to conclude that the company's internal control is effective if there are one or more material weaknesses in the company's internal control. For this purpose, a material weakness is defined as "a deficiency, or combination of deficiencies, in internal control over financial reporting such that there is a reasonable possibility that a material misstatement of the registrant's annual or interim financial statements will not be prevented or detected on a timely basis."[29]

---

[21] *Id.*

[22] *See* SEC Release No. 34–54122 (July 11, 2006).

[23] Commission Statement on Implementation of Internal Control Reporting Requirements, Press Release No. 2005–74 (May 16, 2005).

[24] *Id.*

[25] *Id.*

[26] Staff Statement on Management's Report on Internal Control over Financial Reporting (May 16, 2006) available at http://www.sec.gov/info/accountants/stafficreporting.htm#9.

[27] *Id.*

[28] *See* Lynford E. Graham and Jean C. Bedard, *Deficiencies in Tax-Related Internal Controls Detected Under Sarbanes-Oxley Section 404*, American Accounting Association Annual Meeting-Tax Concurrent Sessions (Aug. 5, 2011).

[29] 17 CFR § 240.12b–2; Rule 1–02(a)(4) of Regulation S-X [17 CFR § 210.1–02(a)(4)]; *see also* SEC Release No. 34–55928.

A company's principal executive officer and principal financial officer must certify that they have disclosed "significant deficiencies" in the design or operation of internal control over financial reporting that are reasonably likely to adversely affect the company's ability to record, process, summarize and report financial information, to the external auditor and the company's audit committee, with the intended result that these parties can more effectively carry out their respective responsibilities with regard to the company's financial reporting. A significant deficiency is defined as follows:

> A deficiency, or a combination of deficiencies, in internal control over financial reporting that is less severe than a material weakness, yet important enough to merit attention by those responsible for oversight of the registrant's financial reporting.[30]

Unlike the definition of material weakness, the definition of a significant deficiency does not include a likelihood component (that is, reasonable possibility that an error would not have been detected or prevented in a timely manner). This reflects the SEC's belief that the focus of the term "significant deficiency" should be on the communications required to take place among management, the audit committee, and the independent auditor.[31]

Management should evaluate the design of its internal controls to determine whether they adequately address the risk that a material misstatement in the financial statements would not be prevented or detected in a timely manner.[32] Thus, it is management's responsibility to determine the areas that pose a risk of a material misstatement and evaluate whether extant controls are adequate to address that risk. The purpose of this principle is to promote efficiency by allowing management to focus on those controls that are needed to adequately address appropriate areas of risk.

It is management's responsibility to determine the appropriate evidence necessary for the evaluation. This allows management to focus resources on high-risk areas.

Management can decide the range of controls to use, including policies, procedures, and activities designed to address financial reporting risks. There are a wide range of controls and they may be automated or manual, including reconciliations, variance analyses, segregation of duties, review and approval authorizations, safeguarding and accountability of assets, error or fraud detection and prevention, or disclosure.[33] Controls may also be preventive, detective or a combination of both.

If management determines that its controls are not adequately designed to address financial reporting risks, a deficiency exists that must be evaluated to determine whether it is a material weakness.

§ 6.04 Auditor Attestation of Internal Controls

Under SOX Section 404(b), auditors must attest to, and report on, management's annual report of its assessment of the company's internal control structure and procedures for financial reporting.[34] The SEC's rules implementing this requirement

---

[30] 17 CFR § 240.12b–2; Rule 1–02(a)(4) of Regulation S-X [17 CFR § 210.1–02(a)(4)].

[31] *See* SEC Release No. 34–56203.

[32] *Id.*

[33] SEC Release No. 34–55929, § II.A.1.b, note 27.

[34] 15 U.S.C. § 7262. When enacted, the SOX Section 404(b) requirement of an independent audit of internal control over financial reporting applied to all issuers. However, under its administrative authority,

provide that management's annual report on internal control over financial reporting must include:

> the registered public accounting firm's attestation report on the registrant's internal control over financial reporting in the registrant's annual report containing the disclosure required by this Item.[35]

The SEC approved PCAOB Auditing Standard No. 5 on July 25, 2007.[36] Auditing Standard No. 5 (AS 2201) was designed to achieve four objectives:

1. *Focus the Internal Control Audit on the Most Important Matters.*
2. *Eliminate Procedures that Are Unnecessary to Achieve the Intended Benefits.*
3. *Make the Audit Clearly Scalable to Fit the Size and the Complexity of Any Company.*
4. *Simplify the Text of the Standard.*

To express an opinion on the company's internal control over financial reporting, the auditor must plan and perform the audit to obtain reasonable assurance about whether a "material weakness" exists as of the date specified in management's assessment.[37]

The auditor must review the control environment of the company, including the following elements:

- Whether management's philosophy and operating style promote effective internal control over financial reporting;
- Whether sound integrity and ethical values, particularly of top management, are developed and understood; and

---

the SEC deferred the applicability of this requirement to non-accelerated filers. In 2010, the Dodd-Frank Wall Street Reform and Consumer Protection Act (Sec. 989G, Pub. L. No. 111–203) amended SOX Section 404 by adding SOX Section 404(c), which permanently exempts non-accelerated filers from the Section 404(b) requirement. The exemption applies to an issuer that is neither a large accelerated filer nor an accelerated filer, as those terms are defined in Rule 12b–2 of the Exchange Act. In general, an accelerated filer is an issuer with market capitalization of at least $75,000,000. Further, pursuant to the Dodd-Frank Act (Sec. 989G(b), Pub. L. No. 111–203), the SEC is charged with looking for ways to provide relief from the burden of complying with SOX Section 404(b) to issuers with market capitalization of between $75 and $225 million. In addition to dealing with compliance burdens of existing issuers, the SEC is also to consider whether lessening the SOX Section 404(b) burden will encourage companies to list on U.S. exchanges for their initial public offerings. Under another provision of the Dodd-Frank Act (Sec. 989I, Pub. L. No. 111–203), the Comptroller General is charged with carrying out a study on the impact of the amendments made to SOX Section 404(b). In 2012, the Jumpstart Our Business Startups Act (JOBS Act) (Pub. L. No. 112–106, § 103) amended Section 404(b) to exempt emerging growth companies from the requirement of an independent audit of internal control over financial reporting. An emerging growth company is an issuer that had total annual gross revenues of less than $1 billion (indexed for inflation) during its most recently completed fiscal year. The emerging growth company definition applies only to companies that initially issue common equity securities to the public after December 8, 2011. An entity remains an emerging growth company until (1) the last day of its fiscal year during which it had total annual gross revenues of $1,000,000,000 (indexed for inflation) or more (2) the last day of the fiscal year following the fifth anniversary of the date of its first sale of registered common equity securities, (3) the date on which it has, during the previous 3-year period, issued more than $1,000,000,000 in non-convertible debt, or (4) the date on which it meets the definition of a "large accelerated filer." Section 2(a) of the Securities Act (15 U.S.C. § 77b(a)), and Section 3(a) of the Exchange Act (15 U.S.C. § 78c).

[35] 17 CFR § 229.308(b).

[36] SEC Release No. 34–56152.

[37] PCAOB News Release, May 24, 2007.

- Whether the Board or audit committee understands and exercises oversight responsibility over financial reporting and internal control.[38]

The severity of a deficiency in internal control over financial reporting does not depend on whether a misstatement actually has occurred but rather on whether there is a reasonable possibility that the company's controls will fail to prevent or detect a misstatement.[39]

If there are deficiencies that, individually or in combination, result in one or more material weaknesses, the auditor must express an adverse opinion on the company's internal control over financial reporting.[40]

The PCAOB has expressed concern about whether auditors are conducting a sufficient evaluation of internal controls related to tax structuring activities, particularly when the audit firm has been involved in the planning of such activities.[41]

§ 6.05 Internal Control for Financial Reporting of Tax Matters

Under SOX, management must (i) establish and maintain adequate internal control procedures for financial reporting; and (ii) assess the effectiveness of these procedures at the end of the company's most recent fiscal year. The corporate tax function plays an important role in the proper preparation of the financial statement tax accounts in accordance with GAAP and, therefore, must be part of establishment, maintenance, and evaluation of a company's internal control over financial reporting. This section addresses these matters.

[1] Establishing Tax Department Controls

Under SOX Section 404(a), management has an obligation to establish and maintain adequate internal control procedures for financial reporting. Prior to SOX, companies used internal controls to improve accuracy of financial reporting, calculation of return on investments, and to identify potential tax planning opportunities. However, SOX elevated the importance of this topic with more specific guidance and reporting requirements, making it appropriate to review internal controls generally and, in the context of this publication, tax department controls specifically.

The SEC rules require internal controls to provide reasonable assurance regarding the reliability of financial reporting and preparation of financial statements in accordance with GAAP and, more specifically, require policies and procedures to (1) maintain records reflecting transactions; (2) ensure recording of transactions to permit preparation of GAAP financial statements, and proper authorization of transactions by management and directors; and (3) prevent or detect theft or on other unauthorized disposition of assets.[42] In this context, the tax department financial statement control objectives would be to assure proper preparation of the financial statement tax accounts in accordance with GAAP and to prevent theft of assets.

---

38 PCAOB AS 2201, ¶ 24.

39 PCAOB Audit Standard No. 5 (AS 2201) Checklist.

40 PCAOB Audit Standard No. 5 (AS 2201) Checklist.

41 *See* Thomas Jaworski, *Year in Review: Non-Audit Tax Work Reemerges as a Possible Independence Risk*, 146 Tax Notes 34 (Jan. 5, 2015). An auditor's independence when providing tax services to its clients is covered in Section 5.05.

42 17 CFR § 240.13a–15(f).

[2] Controls over Preparation of Financial Statement Tax Accounts and Disclosures—Overview

Both the Interpretive Guidance and AS 2201 require an initial identification of material financial statement amounts or disclosures and an evaluation of whether a misstatement of these amounts or disclosures could result in a material misstatement to the financial statements.[43] Applying this top-down approach[44] to the tax elements of the financial statements, the critical areas to initially examine include (i) the provision for income taxes in the income statement; (ii) the balance sheet statement of deferred tax assets and liabilities; and (iii) disclosures in the tax footnote, including disclosures related to uncertain tax positions (the "tax financial statement elements"). The financial statement should obviously be subject to appropriate internal control procedures. Specifically, these procedures should extend to underlying account balances, transactions or other supporting information that have a meaningful bearing on the tax financial statement elements, including the activities required to initiate, authorize, process, and record such matters (the "underlying activities").[45]

After risks associated with the underlying account balances and activities have been identified, controls should be designed and implemented to address these risks. The types of control activities that should be considered include authorizations, verifications, reviews, approvals, information system controls, automation controls, physical controls, and segregation of duties.[46]

Once controls have been designed and implemented, these controls must be monitored and evaluated.

[a] Controls over Specific Situations

In preparing the financial statement,[47] the tax department must ensure that it is prepared in accordance with GAAP.[48] The internal controls should extend to the underlying activities associated with the financial statement impacted by tax. Controls should be developed for all such underlying activities. Set forth below are control activities for several key tax GAAP items that companies should consider adopting:

a. Book-Tax Differences: Accounts are analyzed to determine the proper income tax treatment. If the income tax treatment is different from the book treatment, there is a book tax difference. As discussed in Chapter 4, this difference can be temporary or permanent. A temporary difference is timing based, such as depreciation, while a permanent difference is not timing based, such as investment tax credits. At least annually, material accounts, and accounts with significant year-over-year variance should be examined to confirm that (1) the type of revenues or expenses booked to the account has not changed, and (2) the income tax laws have not

---

[43] *Id.*

[44] *Id.*

[45] *See* SEC Release No. 34–55929, § II; AS 2201, ¶ 34.

[46] COSO, *Internal Control—Integrated Framework* (2013), Chapter 7.

[47] As noted in Section 2.21, the tax financial statement elements include: (i) the provision for income taxes in the income statement, including the statement of current and deferred income tax expense; (ii) the balance sheet statement of deferred income assets (liabilities); and (iii) the disclosures in the tax footnote, including disclosures related to uncertain tax positions.

[48] 17 CFR § 240.13a–15(f).

changed. All new accounts should be analyzed for book-tax differences. As a check that book-tax differences are correct, another team could identify all changes in facts and all changes in law followed by a determination of all the tax accounts that could be impacted.

A situation with a higher likelihood of error is where no deferred taxes have been recorded because when the account was first analyzed, it was determined there was no difference between the income tax treatment and the book treatment. For example, interest expense incurred during construction of an asset must be allocated to that asset. Similar to the direct construction costs, the allocated interest expense is capitalized for both income tax and for GAAP. As a simplification, let us presume that book depreciation and tax depreciation are the same. The capitalized interest expense will not have a book-tax difference. However, let us say the company determines on audit that the asset qualifies for accelerated depreciation or expensing. The company's depreciation deduction for income tax will be higher than the book depreciation, giving rise to a book-tax difference. The company, unfortunately, did not make a similar tax accounting change to reflect that income tax on the capitalized interest expense is similarly accelerated based on the same appreciation methodology applied to the direct construction costs. There continues to be no book-tax difference on the capitalized interest expense. If this error is not caught prior to the expiration of the statute of limitation, the company will write-off the missing tax payable. Had the error been identified prior to the expiration of the statute, the company would file an amended return to correct the mistake and also record a tax refund (which is a tax payable) and a deferred tax liability. Once the company is barred from securing tax refund, the only entry on its financial statement is the deferred tax liability. What would have been a temporary book-tax difference, which has no earnings impact, has transformed into a permanent tax liability, which has a negative earnings impact. One control is an annual review of all tax research memoranda that address the tax treatment of assets and liabilities that are still on the balance sheet.

b. Deferred Taxes on Legal Entity Outside Basis Differences: Section 2.16 discusses the need for deferred tax liabilities for an investment in a foreign subsidiary or foreign corporate joint venture. Also covered in Chapter 2 is the need for deferred taxes for an investment in domestic entities. At least annually and whenever a transaction is contemplated or completed, the outside book-tax basis difference should be evaluated for deferred taxes. Unless an exception applies, deferred tax liabilities or deferred tax assets must be recorded.

c. Adjustment to Tax Provision Based on Filed Return: Differences between the tax provision and the tax return for each account should be recorded. If the difference is timing based, such as whether an expenditure should be capitalized or currently deducted, this is a balance sheet only entry and has no earnings impact. However, if this change results in the underpayment of estimated taxes, the underpayment interest expense or overpayment interest refund would be recorded to earnings. If the difference is permanent, such as the amount of investment tax credits, this will impact earnings including any interest expense or interest refund. There should be clear internal guidelines on when these adjustments should be recorded. For instance, amounts below a certain dollar threshold are not recorded until the tax return is filed, while amounts above the threshold are recorded once the amount has been determined.

d. Adjustment to Tax Accounts Based on Settled Audit Issues: The adjustment may be initiated by the company or by the government auditor. Once the matter is settled or effectively settled, the company will record the difference between the amount reflected in the tax return, the settled amount, any interest or penalties, and the company's reserves for tax, interests, and penalties. Any settled issue that gives rise to a corollary adjustment in any open tax years must also be recorded to those open years. For instance, the government denies a current deduction for an expenditure but allows it to be capitalized and depreciated over five years; the company would record a deferred tax asset for those years. The company should clear all relevant tax accounts for each year prior to the expiration of the statute of limitations. Any tax accounts not cleared prior to the expiration of the statute of limitations must be cleared through earnings. Using the same example, the government denies a current deduction for an expenditure but allows it to be capitalized and depreciated over five years. If the company fails to take the depreciation deduction in any of the subsequent years and the statute of limitations has expired for those years, the deferred tax asset that was recorded must be written off to earnings. There should be procedures in place, such as a comprehensive checklist, to ensure the company does not finalize the audit and allow the statute of limitations to expire prior to clearing all relevant tax accounts for that year. In a cross-border transaction, to the extent an agreed-upon audit adjustment in one jurisdiction gives rise to a corollary adjustment in the other jurisdiction, the company should consider a protective filing in the second jurisdiction—or if there is a tax treaty between the two jurisdictions, a competent authority filing—to protect the corollary adjustment from being statute barred.

e. Deferred Tax Assets and Valuation Allowance: Section 2.09 discusses the requirement to record a valuation allowance against a deferred tax asset, such as a carryover of a net operating tax loss or tax credit. Tax departments will sometimes not record a deferred tax asset because they do not believe the company will benefit from the tax loss or the tax credit. Although the earnings impact of not recording a deferred tax asset is similar to recording a deferred tax asset with an offsetting valuation allowance, the former approach skips an important control. Without a complete inventory of deferred tax assets, the evaluation of the valuation allowance each reporting period will be incomplete. Not only could this lead to an accounting error, but it could also result in missed opportunities to monetize the deferred tax asset. Equally important, it may give rise to a reporting error in the company's financial statement since valuation allowances should be disclosed in the Management Discussion and Analysis section of the company's financial filings with the SEC.

f. Nonroutine Transactions: A company such as a retailer could open hundreds of new stores and they are typically so similar that there are very few, if any, unique income tax, indirect tax, and tax accounting issues. For transactions that are not routine, the company should prepare a comprehensive memorandum that analyzes the GAAP treatment, income taxes, indirect taxes, tax compliance, tax accounting, and tax reserves for both income tax and indirect taxes. The advantage of a single comprehensive memorandum versus separate memoranda prepared by each tax functional group is that it forces everyone to work off a common set of facts and presumptions. The memorandum should be reviewed at least annually but preferably each reporting period for changes in fact or law. A common nonroutine transaction is a business combination, and due to the highly complex income tax and tax accounting rules, extra care should be taken. Section 7.04 discusses the tax accounting for business combinations. As noted in Section 7.04, the SEC has not objected to a company's limiting the scope of its internal control to exclude recent business combinations. From a practical perspective, while the acquirer has access to a seller's data room that houses thousands and even millions of documents, it is nearly impossible for the acquirer to apply its controls to many years of financial records.

g. Tax Rate Reconciliation: A rate reconciliation between the statutory tax rate and the effective tax rate is required in the Management Discussion and Analysis section of the company's financial filings with the SEC. The reconciliation is a check to ensure permanent differences have been identified and recorded. But this presumes the permanent differences that were recorded are accurate. A company can only get this assurance by implementing the controls discussed above. Furthermore, it is best practice to incorporate tax rate reconciliations along with other reconciliations in tax analyses for tax planning, mergers and acquisitions, and tax controversies. This mitigates, if not eliminates, computational errors that are recorded in the company's financial statements.

h. Tax Balance Sheet "Walk": The best analogy for this is balancing a checkbook. Using the ending balance on December 31 of the prior year and the ending of the current reporting period, the company should "walk" from the prior balance to the current balance. The change in the balance can be attributable to several things, such as change in deferred taxes, utilization of carryforward net operating tax losses, and so forth. Depending on the complexity of the company, there can be mini-walks, such as the change in deferred taxes for each major subsidiary.

i. Cross-Border Matters: Additional control issues may also arise in connection with international business.

j. Critical Process User Manuals: The combination of lean staffing, high turnover, and increased complexity presents another risk—that of not having the necessary key personnel available to complete critical tasks required to compute the tax provision. One approach to this problem is to prepare step-by-step user manuals for the critical tasks. This user manual should be reviewed and tested. When key personnel are unavailable, the user manual provides a level of assurance that the tax provision can be and was correctly prepared. It may take someone longer to complete the tasks, but it provides higher assurance it was done correctly and the reviewer can use the manual to examine the work done.

k. Running Parallel: When there is a change in the method that a tax task is performed, to check the new method, the tax department can perform one, and preferably, both control tests. Before using the new method for the current accounting period, use the new method to perform the task and compare it against results for prior accounting periods. Once the tax department decides to use the new method for the current accounting period, it performs the task using both the new method and the old method. This is commonly known as "running parallel."

A company could have a unique situation that would require it to design comprehensive controls in specialized areas of tax accounting. Designing effective controls require a team approach where the team must possess deep expertise in both the technical subject but also the detailed processes in computing and recording the tax entry. The Tax Cuts and Jobs Act 2017 (TCJA) is such a unique situation. Since tax systems were not designed to compute many of the new laws, companies used a combination of internally prepared spreadsheets or professional services firms' spreadsheets. A couple of the suggestions noted above were used to test and verify the results, namely, rate reconciliation and balance sheet walk.

Below are several uncommon or nonintuitive issues triggered by the TCJA that could be on a company's control list to ensure proper GAAP tax accounting:

- U.S. Deferred Taxes: Fully schedule out the turn-around of U.S. temporary differences because only temporary differences that turn within the ten-year window are adjusted from the pre-TCJA 35 percent tax rate to the post-TCJA 21 percent tax rate.
- Non-U.S. Deferred Taxes: Companies that no longer assert indefinite reinvestment need to schedule the turn-around of non-U.S. temporary differences because only temporary differences that turn within the 10-year window may be repatriated and entitled to the 100 percent dividends-received deduction under IRC Section 245A.
- Global Intangible Low-Taxed Income (GILTI): Companies should not presume that having a foreign statutory tax rate and foreign effective tax rate higher than the GILTI rate will result in no GILTI tax. A company that is not in a U.S. cash paying position is not entitled to the IRC Section 250 deduction, which is economically equivalent to losing any tax operating losses or tax credits that could have reduced or eliminated the payment of federal cash taxes. Net operating tax losses and carryover tax credits are reflected on the financial balance sheet as deferred tax assets. The company may need to record a valuation allowance against deferred tax assets because GILTI prevents the company from recognizing the value of the deferred tax assets.
- Fines and Penalties: Payment to government agencies will only be deductible if the government agency files IRS Form 1098-F (required by

IRC Section 6050X), which states that the payment constitutes restitution or remediation of property to be compliant with the law that was violated. IRS Form 1098-F was not released in time for calendar year taxpayers filing their 2018 tax returns. Taxpayers will not be denied the deduction, however, but they must establish that the payment constitutes restitution or remediation to be compliant with the law that was violated. (IRC Section 162(f); also see Notice 2018–23).

- Executive Compensation: The IRC Section 162(m) limitation for executive compensation remains at $1 million but the TCJA eliminated certain exceptions that allow a deduction for compensation above the $1 million threshold. These changes to the deductibility of executive compensation will require a company to write off deferred tax assets. The TCJA did include a transition rule for executive compensation granted under a written binding contract (See Section 13601(e)(2) of TCJA). The transition rule introduced much uncertainty on the proper tax accounting for several situations. For instance, many companies' executive compensation plans allow their boards to exercise downward discretion on the amount ultimately paid to the executives. The downward discretion may not meet the binding contract requirement under the transition rule. In Notice 2018–68, the IRS strongly implied that negative discretion was not a binding written contract. This uncertainty may require the company to write off or record a valuation allowance on the underlying deferred tax asset. There is a real irony, perhaps unintended, in the binding contract requirement. Downward discretion provides the board with the right to reduce executive compensation should the company's performance fall short despite meeting all the prescribed performance metrics. It is impossible to identify every conceivable situation in designing an executive compensation plan. As a result, downward discretion allows the board to align executives' compensation with shareholders' return. A board exercises good corporate governance when it applies downward discretion. When executives receive compensation that is not aligned with shareholders' return, it typically signifies poor corporate governance. The grandfathered clause rewards companies with poor corporate governance while punishing companies with strong corporate governance. Although the underlying principle of IRC Section 162(m) may be solid—namely to not have taxpayers subsidize excessive executive compensation—a transition rule that continues to reward companies that pay excessive compensation while punishing companies that rein in excessive compensation with downward adjustment clauses is difficult to comprehend. The transition rule presents a huge gray area that will require a robust GAAP (FASB ASC 740–10) analysis.

- Employee Benefits: TCJA eliminated or reduced the tax deduction for many employee fringe benefits provided by companies. One such benefit defies common sense: the valuation of employer-provided parking. For example: A company leases two office buildings, one in the city and the other in a suburban commercial area. Both office buildings include parking stalls for the buildings' occupants. Next to the city office building is a private parking structure that charges a monthly rent of $250. As for the suburban commercial building, there is ample nearby non-metered street parking. It is completely reasonable that the value of the employer parking in the city office building should be $250, and the value of the employer provided parking in the suburban commercial building is de minimis. Treasury provided interim guidance in Notice 2018–99 which provides the taxpayer may use any reasonable method but then goes on to set forth a multi-step determination to arrive at the nondeductible parking expenses. This can result in a spartan subterranean parking garage's being valued similarly to premium office space. In Notice 2018–99, the IRS sets forth the computation methodology to arrive at the amount of nondeductible expense. It is a two-step determination. The first step is to factor in all costs (except depreciation) to compute the nondeductible expenses for the parking spots; taxpayers cannot use the market value of the parking spot. These costs include utilities costs, insurance, property taxes, repairs and maintenance, lease payment, security, and other labor costs. For example, a company leases a 20-story building with two stories of subterranean parking, a street-level retail floor, and the remaining 17 floors as high-quality office space. The company's annual lease payment is $200,000. The two floors of parking are allocated $20,000 of the lease payment. The fact that the office space, without the parking, would command $195,000 is irrelevant. And the fact that the company could lease those same parking spots for $5,000 is irrelevant. Although nearby companies could arrange to sublease each other's parking spots to circumvent this punitive outcome, it is not practical. The company's facilities personnel services the entire building and the company's security system is integrated for the entire building. The second step is to determine the number of parking spots reserved for employees versus the number of spots available to customers. The deduction denied is the product of these two amounts. In our example, if 80 percent of the parking spots are reserved for employees, the nondeductible expenses are $16,000 ($20,000 expenses allocated to the parking spaces times 80 percent employee reserved spots). Companies will need to determine whether to follow the Notice, in its entirety, partially, or not at all, and perform a GAAP (FASB ASC 740–10) analysis and measurement.

- Company Foundations: The excess executive compensation limit under IRC Section 162(m) also applies to tax-exempt organizations. A for-profit organization cannot deduct excess compensation while a tax-exempt organization is charged an excise tax. Many companies have charitable foundations, and it is not uncommon for company executives to also be officers of the foundation. The U.S. Treasury shocked the non-profit community when it issued Notice 2019–09. Since a foundation and a company can be related, Notice 2019–09 provides that to determine the foundation's excess compensation, the compensation of the company's executives' will be attributed to the foundation if the executives are also officers of the foundation. In addition to the company's losing the deduction, the foundation now pays an excise tax, which means the after-tax cost of the compensation is higher than the compensation. It defies logic that a dollar of deduction ends up costing a $1.21. Foundations have several options: (1) file the return and report no excise tax due, (2) do not file a return because there is no tax due, (3) file a return and pay the excise tax and later file a refund claim, or (4) file for an extension and hope the issue is resolved by the time the extension is due. In options (1), (2) and (4), there is a tax reserve issue. In option (3) the foundation already paid the tax, but it does have a tax reserve issue and will record a tax payable if the foundation meets the tax reserve more-likely-than-not threshold. Of course, the ultimate self-help is to not allow the company's executives to serve on the foundation. Although the company's executives will continue to make major decisions for the foundation, they will now need to do so through proxies that will serve on the foundation, which will add another layer of inefficiencies.

- State Conformity: States conform to the IRC in one of three ways: rolling conformity, fixed date conformity, or selective conformity. Rolling conformity states automatically adopt provisions of the IRC as enacted (i.e., on a continual basis). Fixed-date-conformity states follow the IRC as of a certain fixed date, and legislative action is typically required to update the state income tax laws to conform to the IRC as of a specific date. Finally, selective-conformity states adopt only certain IRC provisions, certain provisions as of a specific date, or make material changes to key IRC provisions. For instance, California is typically defined as a selective conformity state because it does not fully conform to the IRC, instead incorporating specific IRC sections. Generally, where California does conform to specific IRC sections, it conforms to the IRC as in effect at a certain date. As states conform to the TCJA, it will impact a company's state tax expense accrual and, furthermore, state deferred taxes may require remeasurement or valuation allowances. Since state tax expense is deductible for Federal income tax purposes, any change to state tax expense and state deferred taxes will also impact federal tax expense and federal deferred taxes.

- Base Erosion and Anti-abuse Tax: A company subject to the base erosion and anti-abuse tax (BEAT) must measure deferred taxes using the statutory tax rate, not the BEAT tax rate. To the extent BEAT increases a company's tax above the statutory rate, the excess will be recognized in the period incurred. [FASB Staff Q&A No. 4]

- Transition Tax on Foreign Earnings: Companies may decide to repatriate foreign earnings since they would no longer incur additional U.S. Federal taxes after the payment of the transition tax. The companies may even accrue any associated foreign dividend withholding tax and U.S. state taxes under SAB 118 and remove these tax expense from adjusted GAAP earnings. By recording the transition tax, local dividend tax, and U.S. state tax in the TCJA financial reporting period, it would result in higher future GAAP earnings when excess foreign cash is repatriated. A change in the currency exchange rate should not result in a remeasurement of the deferred tax liability accrued for the foreign dividend withholding tax even where the subsidiary's tax liability is based on a currency that is different from the GAAP functional currency of the subsidiary's parent company that is liable for the dividend withholding tax. For example, the functional currency of the parent company of a foreign subsidiary is the U.S. dollar (USD). The subsidiary has $100 of GAAP earnings. The foreign subsidiary pays taxes in pesos. On the measurement date, the exchange rate is 10 pesos to 1 USD. The local country dividend withholding tax rate is 20 percent. The dividend withholding tax on the distribution of $100 would be 200 pesos ($100 distribution times 10 pesos exchange rate times 20 percent withholding tax rate). The 200 pesos is converted to $20, which is the deferred tax liability recorded. At the end of the next quarter, the exchange rate is 12 pesos to one USD. The distribution of the $100 would give rise to a dividend withholding tax of 240 pesos ($100 distribution times 12 pesos times 20 percent withholding tax rate). The 240 pesos is converted to $20. Therefore, a change in the currency exchange rate does not change the deferred taxes for the dividend withholding tax.

- Dividends-Received Deduction: The TCJA reduced the dividends-received deduction under IRC Section 243. To the extent a company must record deferred taxes for dividends to be paid to eliminate the book-tax outside basis difference, the deferred taxes must be remeasured to reflect the change in the less generous dividends-received deduction. The dividends-received deduction pre-TCJA and post-TCJA are listed in this chart—

Ownership	Pre-TCJA	Post-TCJA
Less than 20%	70%	50%
20% to 80%	80%	65%
80% or more	100%	100%

This is not an exhaustive list and each company's unique tax profile could certainly give rise to other uncommon or nonintuitive TCJA-related tax issues that will have GAAP tax accounting impact. Many of the items listed are not unique to TCJA but equally applicable to any tax reform and change in tax law in general.

Tax department controls must be evaluated as part of the control environment at the company. As such, the philosophy, operating style, integrity, and ethical values of the tax department are important to the overall control environment of the company. In this regard, the tax department should consider implementing its own code of conduct or further adapting the company's code of conduct to specific tax department situations.

[3] Controls to Prevent Theft of Assets

Companies are required to have controls in place to prevent or detect theft or other unauthorized disposition of assets.[49] Moreover, AS 2201 requires the auditor to identify and review the controls that management has implemented to prevent or timely detect the unauthorized acquisition, use, or disposition of the company's assets that could result in a material misstatement of the financial statements.[50]

The company's overall payment, procurement, and authorization controls should address the risk of the unauthorized acquisition, use, or disposition of the company's assets. However, specific risks related to the tax department should also be considered and addressed as part of the company's overall control procedures or as part of the tax department's control procedures. For example, two risks that should be addressed are theft of tax refund checks and misappropriation of funds by virtue of creating a false tax authority payee. Strong controls at the company's treasury department will prevent these two primary risks. An indirect form of theft is under-reporting tax expense to increase performance-based bonuses. This is particularly problematic when subjectivity is involved, such as recording tax reserves and valuation allowances. There could be pressure outside of the tax department to take aggressive tax positions.

[4] General Tax Department Controls

As an element of an effective control environment, the tax department should periodically review its human, technology and other resources to determine whether such resources are adequate to perform the functions of the tax department.[51] Also, retention of key personnel should be considered, with the associated evaluation of compensation and benefit packages.[52] In addition, technology and information systems should be periodically reviewed and evaluated to ensure that back-up systems are adequate to address a failure of such systems that could significantly affect operations.[53] Moreover, the tax department should periodically review training programs for existing personnel, as well as training for new hires. This training should, obviously, include tax and accounting training, along with department's policies, procedures and culture. This became very difficult to accomplish during COVID and perhaps even post-COVID. During the spring of 2020, many tax professionals worked remotely and new employees were onboarded remotely. Even after the danger of COVID has passed, many employees will continue to work remotely for all or part of the time. It also challenged traditional thinking that certain tasks must be or are best performed in the office. It also challenged traditional thinking that employees that have been trained internally must or are best at performing certain tasks. Professional service firms were quick to latch onto this new paradigm and have created or expanded their outsourcing models to perform these remote tasks.

As an element of maintaining appropriate personnel and training such personnel, the tax department should also consider developing job descriptions for each position in the tax department. These descriptions should include the level of competence needed for each particular job, as well the appropriate level of knowledge and skill (competence)

---

[49] 17 CFR § 240.13a–15(f).

[50] *See* PCAOB AS 2201, ¶ 34.

[51] COSO, *Internal Control—Integrated Framework* (2013), Chapter 5.

[52] *Id.*

[53] *Id.*

necessary to fill such position.[54] Moreover, the roles and responsibilities of members of the department should be clearly defined.[55] In this regard, the tax department should consider developing an organizational chart that depicts the different functions handled by each person and the people to whom they report.

The foregoing general control and ethical matters, as well as controls over the financial statement impacted by tax, should be the subject of documentation, whether through policy manuals, codes of conduct or an overall document addressing of such matters.

---

54 *Id.*

55 *Id.*

Chapter 7

SPECIFIC SITUATIONS

Table of Sections

§ 7.01 In General

The financial accounting principles involving tax matters addressed in this text are often, perhaps even generally, stated in the dry, technical terms of professional jargon. The concepts come alive via illustrations, which we have sprinkled generously throughout the book. We have endeavored to utilize a full range of direct and indirect income tax subjects to illustrate application of the pertinent financial accounting concepts. Another means of facilitating application of the pertinent principles in practice is to focus on specific technical taxation issues, which is, frankly, the manner in which the process will actually be carried out.

Accordingly, the purpose of this Chapter 7 is to provide a catalogue of specific substantive tax matters that commonly arise followed by the financial accounting determinations. For each such issue, we will use an illustration, and set out the financial accounting issues that will need to be addressed, referencing the pertinent text discussion in this book. We will also note the pertinent technical tax issues to be addressed with respect to such situations.

The specific format for each special situation will generally be as follows:

General Principles

Illustration

Technical Tax Matters

Financial Accounting for Income Taxes (FASB ASC 740)

General Principles of Deferred Taxes

SOX

There may be variations in this format based on the nature of the matters pertinent to a specific situation. We will note the U.S. income tax matters, financial accounting for income tax matters, and SOX considerations that we find to be important in each situation.

As noted in Chapter 1, the essential purpose of this text is to address the elements that have made the intersection of the financial accounting and tax worlds so complex. As we have prepared this text, we have become duly impressed by the magnitude of the task facing finance, accounting and tax executives, consultants, analysts and commentators in trying to bring light to the complicated intersection caused by the related financial accounting, substantive tax and tax accounting rules that need to be digested and understood in specific situations while ensuring the process and procedures to accomplish this are SOX compliant.

This book is not intended to be a treatise solely on financial accounting or solely on corporate income taxation. Rather, it is focused on the intersection of those subjects. Accordingly, we have done our best to identify the issues that need to be addressed in this area of intersection and to offer our commentary on how such issues can be addressed in the idiosyncratic facts and circumstances of specific cases. Our hope is that this chapter will facilitate your navigation in the intersection, as we have tried to illuminate the process of applying all of the various principles and requirements in the context of specific tax issues or positions.

§ 7.02 Advance Payments for Services

General Principles

For financial accounting purposes, if an entity receives an advance payment for services[1] to be rendered in future years, the entity must set up a liability reflecting its obligation to provide services in the future.[2] Due to the offsetting liability, the advance payment is not included in the entity's revenue upon receipt. As the entity provides the services, it will include the advance payment into revenue. For tax purposes, as a general rule, the advance payment is included in gross income upon receipt.[3]

ILLUSTRATION 7-1: An entity receives an advance payment of $40,000 from a customer on July 1, 2022, for services required to be performed in the future. Under the tax laws, the entity, as a general rule, is required to include the advance payment in gross income upon receipt in 2022. Under GAAP, the

1 In the case of advance payments for goods, similar issues will need to be addressed.

2 FASB ASC 606–10–25–8; FASB ASC 740-10-25-20(c).

3 IRC Section 451(c).

entity sets up a liability reflecting its obligation to provide services to the customer in the future. The entity will include the advance receipt in revenue as it performs the services for the customer (decreasing its liability) in the future. A deductible temporary difference has arisen because the advance payment is included in taxable income before it is included in financial income. The amount of the deductible temporary difference is $40,000, the excess of the book value of the liability ($40,000) over its tax basis (zero).

Technical Tax Matters

As a general rule, an accrual method taxpayer that receives an advance payment for services must include the entire amount in gross income upon receipt.[4] There are a very limited number of situations in which an advance payment is included in gross income over time as the services are rendered rather than upon receipt. In the first situation, the taxpayer may elect to include a portion of the advance payment in gross income in the taxable year in which such payment is received, and include the remaining portion of such advance payment in gross income in the following year.[5]

In the second situation, an accrual method taxpayer may defer inclusion of an advance payment for services if "the extent and time of performance are so certain, and related items properly accounted for with such clarity, that a system of accounting involving deferral of prepaid income is found clearly to reflect income."[6] This exception is based on the Seventh Circuit's holding in *Artnell v. Commissioner*,[7] which involved the Chicago White Sox baseball team deferring from gross income advance payments received for baseball games to be played in the future.[8]

Financial Accounting for Income Taxes (FASB ASC 740) Recognition and Measurement of Deferred Taxes

In the context of Illustration 7-1, if the entity includes the advance payment in gross income upon receipt, its tax position should be certain and thus, as a general rule, no recognition issues should arise. If, however, the entity arranged the advance payments for a potentially non-business purpose (such as absorbing a soon to be expiring net operating loss), an uncertainty may relate as to whether the structure of the transaction would be recharacterized as a tax avoidance transaction.[9]

An uncertainty could also arise where, for example, the entity in Illustration 7-1 took the tax position that no part of the advance payment was currently taxable on the basis that the "extent and time of performance" of the services was certain, i.e., the *Artnell* exception. The normal range of recognition issues would need to be addressed with respect to such potential uncertainty.

The entity would need to determine whether its position to defer all of the advance payment meets the more-likely-than-not recognition threshold of FASB ASC 740–10–

---

4 IRC Section 451(c)(1)(A).

5 IRC Section 451(c)(1)(B).

6 *Artnell v. Commissioner*, 400 F.2d 981, 984 (7th Cir. 1968).

7 400 F.2d 981 (7th Cir. 1968).

8 The Tampa Bay Devil Rays, another professional baseball team, successfully invoked the *Artnell* exception to the general rule for advance payments for services. *Tampa Bay Devil Rays, Ltd. v. Commissioner*, 84 T.C. M. 394 (2002).

9 *See generally* Boris I. Bittker & James S. Eustice, *Federal Income Taxation of Corporations and Shareholders* ¶ 8.07[2][a] (7th ed., 2000) [*Federal Income Taxation of Corporations and Shareholders*].

25–5. If it does, then the entity must measure the allowable tax benefit for financial accounting purposes that may be recorded on the entity's financial statements (see Chapter 3). The taxpayer in Illustration 7-1 meets the more-likely-than-not recognition threshold, so the next step is to measure the amount of tax benefit to be recognized. The measurement probability table prepared by management is set out below (with the possible estimated outcomes based on the entity having varying amounts of income subject to a 21 percent corporate tax rate). The example assumes the 21 percent corporate tax rate applies to all years. The first outcome in the measurement probability table is an $8,400 tax benefit ($40,000 deduction for the advance payment times 21 percent corporate tax rate). The second outcome is the tax benefit will be denied in its entirety.

Possible Estimated Outcome	Individual Probability of Occurring (%)	Cumulative Probability of Occurring (%)
$8,400	85%	85%
0	15%	100%

Because the tax benefit from the entity's tax position that has a cumulative probability of occurring that is greater than 50 percent is $8,400, the entity would be able to recognize the full tax benefit and would not be required to recognize a liability for the after-tax interest on the underpayment of taxes and any potential penalties.

The entity receiving the advance payment in Illustration 7-1 is presumed to be the principal in the service agreement. On March 17, 2016, the FASB finalized amendments to the new revenue guidance in Accounting Standards Update (ASU) 2016–08, *Revenue from Contracts with Customers (Topic 606): Principal versus Agent Considerations (Reporting Revenue Gross versus Net)*, which provides that if the entity that receives the advance payment is an agent, the entity reports the advance payment on a net basis.[10] For instance, if the entity in Illustration 7-1 receives a 10 percent commission from the service provider, the entity would recognize $4,000 of revenue from the $40,000 advance payment. The classification between principal and agent is based on an evaluation of several "indicators," the most important being control of the good or service before it is transferred to the customer.

General Principles of Deferred Taxes

When an entity receives an advance payment for services, it will set up a liability reflecting its obligation to provide services to the customer in the future.[11] This results in a deductible temporary difference equal to the excess of the book basis of the liability over its tax basis. As a result, the entity will record a deferred tax asset equal to the applicable tax rate multiplied by the deductible temporary difference. The entity must reduce its deferred tax asset by a valuation allowance if it is more likely than not that some or all of that deferred tax asset will not be realized. As the services are performed, the entity will reduce the liability and include a corresponding amount in revenue.

If the entity defers inclusion in gross income of the advance payment for services, then its tax treatment is more closely aligned with its financial accounting treatment of

---

[10] FASB ASC 606–10–55–36 to 606–10–55–40.

[11] FASB ASC 606–10–25–8; FASB ASC 740-10-25-20(c).

the advance payment. For example, if the entity utilizes the *Artnell* exception, then its tax treatment may parallel the financial accounting treatment. As a result, a temporary difference should not arise and therefore no deferred tax asset (or deferred tax liability) should be recorded.

If the entity utilizes IRC Section 451(c)(1)(B)—enacted by the TCJA largely to codify Rev. Proc. 2004–34—to defer inclusion in gross income of part or all of the advance payment for services, then unless the entity is utilizing the same time frame of deferral for both tax purposes and financial accounting purposes, a temporary difference will arise. For example, if the entity receives an advance payment of $40,000 on July 1, 2022, with half of the services to be performed in 2023 and the remaining half of the services to be performed in 2024, then the entity will have a $40,000 liability (i.e., unearned revenue) in 2022 for tax and financial accounting. Since the entity elects deferral under IRC Section 451(c)(1)(B), it has no gross income in 2022, so no temporary difference has arisen in 2022. In 2023, the entity includes $20,000 in revenue for financial accounting purposes and all $40,000 in gross income for tax purposes. As a result, in 2023, a deductible temporary difference of $20,000 has arisen equal to the excess of the entity's book basis of $20,000 in its liability over its tax basis of zero. The entity will record a $4,200 deferred tax asset in 2023 equal to the applicable tax rate of 21 percent multiplied by the deductible temporary difference of $20,000. The entity must reduce its deferred tax asset by a valuation allowance, as discussed in Section 2.09, if it is more likely than not that some or all of that deferred tax asset will not be realized.

To the extent the tax method of accounting is different from the book method and the company wants its tax method to conform to the book method, the company will be required to file a notice of change in accounting method. Some changes of accounting method require the approval of the U.S. Secretary of the Treasury, while others are automatic provided the proper tax form (Form 3115) has been timely filed. Treasury has provided guidance that allows taxpayers to change their accounting method to be consistent with the GAAP revenue recognition accounting method.[12] Although there should be minimal direct impact on the tax provision and cash taxes, there could be an indirect earnings impact that would have a commensurate tax provision impact. For instance, where the company's bonus and other compensation plans are based on revenues, the new revenue recognition rules could impact the company's compensation costs. A change in compensation expense will impact the tax provision.

SOX

The SOX Section 404 considerations in the context of advance payments are to assure that the entity has sufficient controls in place so that appropriate procedures are created and followed to determine the proper tax and financial accounting treatment of the advance payments. A common control is to reconcile the tax accounts by analyzing each temporary difference and have support on when that difference will turn. Unless reconciliation is performed, the statute of limitations may preclude the taxpayer from amending the return to reflect a missed tax deduction or an erroneous income inclusion.

In the scenario above, assume the entity did not defer the advance payment and included $40,000 in gross income in 2022 and recorded a $8,400 deferred tax asset. The

[12] FASB ASC 606, Revenue from Contracts with Customers. Rev. Proc. 2018–49 modifies Rev. Proc. 2018–29 and Rev. Proc. 2018–31. The guidance is effective May 10, 2018, which is the date Rev. Proc. 2018–29 was issued.

entity's tax return preparer may not know services attributable to this advance payment will be performed in 2023 and 2024, so the tax return preparer could incorrectly pick up GAAP revenues of $20,000 in the 2023 tax return and another $20,000 in the 2024 tax return. The entity ends up reporting $80,000 of gross income on the $40,000 advance payment. The $8,400 deferred tax asset will never turn if the statute of limitations has expired on filing amended returns for 2023 and 2024 to correct the erroneous income inclusions. This would result in the $8,400 deferred tax asset being written off, which increases income tax expense in the year of the write-off.

The entity had only $40,000 of gross (and taxable) income and should have paid only $8,400 of taxes. But the entity actually reported $80,000 of taxable income and paid $16,800 of taxes. The entity paid $8,400 more in taxes than it was legally obligated to pay. By reconciling the tax accounts, the taxpayer would have found a "dangling" deferred tax asset of $8,400. Similar to balancing a checkbook, the taxpayer's "tax checkbook" would not balance and be off by $8,400. If the opportunity to correct this tax reporting error is no longer available, as the statute of limitations has expired to file amended returns for 2023 and 2024, the taxpayer will need to take a $8,400 earnings loss by writing off the $8,400 deferred tax asset.

The proper year to write off the deferred tax asset is the year the statute of limitations expired. For Illustration 7-1, the $8,400 of deferred tax asset would be split equally between 2023 and 2024 since $20,000 of the GAAP revenues was recognized in 2023 and another $20,000 was recognized in 2024. Each tax year had a $4,200 deferred tax asset. In addition to the tax return reporting error, if the company did not write off the deferred tax asset in the proper year, it would be a tax accounting control deficiency that could also trigger a restatement of the company's financial statements (as discussed in Chapter 6).

Corporate tax departments are, understandably, well aware of changes in tax law and have procedures in place to ensure proper compliance. However, changes in GAAP rules, particularly outside of the tax accounting area of FASB ASC 740, *Income Taxes,* are rarely known or tracked by tax departments. The revenue recognition standard (FASB ASC 606), initially introduced in 2014, may require a timely submission requesting an accounting method change. Failure to submit the change could leave the company with no choice other than to file its return using an improper method. Since the IRS may force the company to change to the proper method of accounting, the company now must evaluate its filing position under the recognition standard of FASB ASC 740–10 (see Chapter 3).

§ 7.03 Bad Debts

General Principles

For financial accounting purposes, an entity will record an Allowance for Doubtful Accounts (also known as "Allowance for Uncollectible Accounts" or "Reserve for Bad Debts"), which is generally an estimate of the receivables that will prove to become uncollectible.[13] For tax purposes, an entity must use the specific charge off method for bad debts and is not permitted a bad debt deduction based on estimates.[14]

13 FASB ASC 450.

14 IRC Section 166.

ILLUSTRATION 7-2: An entity has credit sales of $100,000 in Year 1. It estimates that approximately two percent (or $2,000) will be uncollectible. The entity records a $2,000 increase to its Allowance for Doubtful Accounts with a $2,000 bad debt expense. For tax purposes, the entity may take a bad debt deduction only with respect to debts that are partially or totally worthless during the year.

Technical Tax Matters

Since 1986, an entity is not permitted to use a reserve method in accounting for bad debts for tax purposes. An entity may only take a bad debt deduction when a debt is either partially or totally worthless.[15] In determining whether a debt is either partially or totally worthless, all pertinent evidence, including the value of the collateral securing the debt and the financial condition of the debtor must be considered.[16] A deduction is permitted if "the surrounding circumstances indicate that a debt is worthless and uncollectible and that legal action to enforce payment would in all probability not result in the satisfaction of execution on a judgment."[17] If a debt is partially worthless, then the amount that has become worthless is allowed as a deduction but only to the extent it is charged off during the year on the entity's accounting books.[18] As a result, in the case of partially worthless debts, there is a tax/book conformity rule: a tax deduction is permitted for a partially worthless debt as long as it has been written off on the taxpayer's accounting books.

At times, the government may acknowledge that a debt is partially or totally worthless but disagree as to what year the debt became worthless.[19] To alleviate some of the problems of an entity selecting the wrong year in deducting a bad debt, Congress has extended the statute of limitations for refund claims based on bad debts from the normal three years to seven years.[20]

Financial Accounting for Income Taxes (FASB ASC 740) Recognition and Measurement of Deferred Taxes

In the context of bad debts, the uncertain tax position revolves around the proper application of the law to the facts to determine whether and when a debt is partially or totally worthless. These issues can be difficult to resolve, and the resolution may be challenged by IRS examination teams. Therefore, the recognition and measurement analysis will need to consider the likelihood of success through the final determination process. The entity needs to determine whether its position to deduct a particular amount of bad debt expense for tax purposes meets the more likely than not recognition threshold of FASB ASC 740–10–25–5. If it does, then the entity must measure the allowable tax benefit for financial accounting purposes that may be recorded on the entity's financial statements.[21]

---

[15] *Id.*

[16] Treas. Reg. § 1.166–2.

[17] Treas. Reg. § 1.166–2(b).

[18] Treas. Reg. § 1.166–3.

[19] *See* Boris I. Bittker & Lawrence Lokken, *Federal Taxation of Income, Estates and Gifts* ¶ 33.3.1 (3rd ed., 1999) [*Federal Taxation of Income, Estates and Gifts*].

[20] IRC Section 6511(d)(1).

[21] FASB ASC 740–10–30–7.

SOX

The SOX Section 404 considerations in the context of bad debts are to assure that the entity has sufficient controls in place so that appropriate procedures are created and followed to determine the proper tax and financial accounting treatment of the partial or complete worthlessness issues. Similar to the controls for advanced payments for services, a reconciliation of the deferred tax account is necessary to ensure tax deductions for bad debts are reflected on tax returns or amended tax returns prior to the expiration of the statute of limitations. However, bad debts present control challenges that are absent in almost all other areas, particularly where the company has thousands and even millions of customer accounts. In many situations, the company must utilize a percentage or amount that is based on historical experience due to the sheer magnitude of the number of claims, and the constantly changing facts for each claim. Both the financial accounting work and the tax compliance work in this bad-debt arena is one of the most prone to error, and neither the businesses involved nor the government tax auditors have the resources to fully comply with the rules. Taxpayers should consider using statistical sampling to reduce the tax compliance burden, as well as reducing audit risk and the complexity of the FASB recognition threshold. This risk is further reduced by reaching advance agreement with the IRS audit team on such an approach.

§ 7.04 Business Combinations

General Principles

Business combinations, restructuring, divestures, joint venture and other major corporate transactions really picked up post-COVID, including supply chain challenges with emerging conflicts around the globe. There has also been an increase of activity by hedge funds, private equity firms and activist investors. Often, a critical element is whether the transaction will be taxable or tax-free. Another equally important consideration is the financial accounting consequences from the transaction. In today's sophisticated and complex business environment, the tax and accounting analyses of major transactions are not always free from doubt, leading to interesting reporting and compliance issues.

ILLUSTRATION 7-3: USCo, a U.S. publicly held corporation, wholly owns an operating U.S. corporate subsidiary (USSub). USCo and an unrelated U.S. corporation (PCo) negotiate the acquisition of USSub by PCo, whereby USSub will merge into PCo, with PCo surviving. In the merger, USCo, as the shareholder of USSub, will receive solely stock of PCo (constituting 15 percent of PCo's outstanding shares) in exchange for its USSub stock. It is intended that the merger be a tax-free "A" reorganization (described in IRC Section 368(a)(1)(A)) and that neither USCo nor USSub recognize gain or loss as a result of the merger. During the negotiations of the merger, management of PCo expresses various alternative business plans for USSub, including the desire to sell a substantial portion of the USSub assets, along with various divisions of PCo, to a previously identified buyer for cash. At the time of the merger, PCo had no written agreement in place to sell the USSub assets.

At the closing of the merger, USCo's outside tax advisor renders its tax opinion that it is more likely than not that the merger is a tax-free "A" reorganization and that neither USCo nor USSub will recognize gain or loss from the merger. In the tax opinion, the tax advisor addressed the question whether the merger satisfied the continuity of business enterprise (COBE) requirement (set forth in Treas. Reg. § 1.368–1(d)) in light of the possibility that PCo might sell a substantial portion of USSub assets after the merger. If the merger did not satisfy the COBE requirement, then the transaction would be fully taxable to USSub and USCo. A few months after the merger, PCo is about to sell a substantial portion of the USSub assets for cash to the previously identified buyer.

Technical Tax Matters

The tax-free acquisition of a target corporation is typically structured to satisfy one of the acquisitive reorganization transactions described in IRC Section 368(a). If the acquisition meets Section 368(a), then the target shareholders do not recognize gain or loss on the receipt of stock issued by the acquirer in the transaction and the tax basis of the target assets are not adjusted based on the purchase price.[22] Among the various forms of reorganizations are a simple merger of the target corporation into the acquirer corporation (or into a single member limited liability company of the acquirer) with the acquirer corporation surviving (an "A" reorganization).[23] Another form of acquisitive reorganization is a forward triangular merger whereby the target corporation merges into a wholly-owned corporate subsidiary of the acquirer corporation (a "Forward Triangular Merger").[24] An acquisition may also be structured tax-free where a wholly-owned corporate subsidiary of the acquirer corporation mergers into the target corporation (a "Reverse Triangular Merger").[25]

Each of these Section 368 reorganization transactions must comply with a different set of tax requirements to be tax-free, although in each type of transaction, the target shareholders receive stock of the acquirer and possibly other non-stock consideration. In each of these reorganization transactions, the target's historic business or historic assets must be continued to be used by the acquirer (the "continuity of business enterprise" requirement).[26] Further, in both the Forward Triangular Merger and the Reverse Triangular Merger, substantially all of the target's properties must either remain in the target (in the case of a Reverse Triangular Merger) or be acquired by the acquirer's subsidiary (in the case of a Forward Triangular Merger).[27]

In each of these reorganizations, the target shareholders receive acquirer corporation stock, and possibly other merger consideration, in exchange for their target stock. In an "A" reorganization and a Forward Triangular Merger, an example in the regulations concluded the transaction satisfied the continuity of interest requirement when forty percent of the merger consideration consisted of stock of the acquirer corporation.[28] In a Reverse Triangular Merger, the acquirer must acquire at least eighty

---

[22] IRC Section 354 (nonrecognition to target shareholders), IRC Section 361 (nonrecognition to target corporation), and IRC Section 362(b) (transferred basis in target assets to acquiring corporation).

[23] IRC Section 368(a)(1)(A). Treas. Reg. § 1.368–2(b)(1)(iii) Example 2 (merger of target corporation into a disregarded entity of acquiring corporation in exchange for stock of the acquiring corporation).

[24] IRC Section 368(a)(2)(D).

[25] IRC Section 368(a)(2)(E).

[26] Treas. Reg. § 1.368–1(d).

[27] *See generally* Rev. Proc. 77–37, 1977–2 C.B. 568 (paragraph 3.04 stating that for advance ruling purposes the "substantially all" test is satisfied by meeting the 90/70 test; 90 percent of the net assets and 70 percent of the gross assets).

[28] Treas. Reg. § 1.368–1(e)(2)(v), Example 1.

percent of the target stock solely in exchange for voting stock of the acquirer corporation.[29]

IRC Section 338 generally permits a unilateral election by a corporate acquirer of the stock of a target corporation to treat the stock acquisition as an asset acquisition for tax purposes.[30] In order to make the election, 80 percent of the shares of the target must be acquired by purchase from sellers unrelated to the acquirer within a 12-month period. The advantage of this election has been diminished, if not eliminated, by TCJA on the acquisition of a foreign target company. The foreign target's tax attributes, such as earnings and profits and foreign tax credits, disappear in a constructive asset acquisition. Since foreign source dividends will effectively not be subject to U.S. federal tax because of the 245A 100 percent dividends-received deduction, resetting tax attributes to zero provide minimal, if any, U.S. Federal income tax benefits. There may continue to be value for state tax planning, which will depend on the state taxation of foreign dividends. Otherwise, the Section 338 election generally has no consequences to the seller of the foreign subsidiary and results in a fair market value tax basis of all of the assets of the foreign subsidiary, including goodwill, to the corporate acquirer.[31] It should be noted that this "fresh start" tax basis is applicable only for purposes of determining the earnings and profits of the foreign subsidiary for U.S. tax purposes. Additional depreciation and amortization deductions resulting from the stepped-up basis will reduce the post-acquisition earnings and profits of the foreign subsidiary and will increase the foreign tax credits associated with dividend distributions. Low earnings and profits can be a detriment in a post-Section 245A world. Distributions in excess of earnings and profits will lower the U.S. parent company's U.S. tax basis in the foreign subsidiary, and if there is insufficient tax basis, it (the excess) will be treated as taxable capital gain.[32]

The Section 338 election eliminates all pre-acquisition earnings and profits of the foreign subsidiary and eliminates the foreign tax pool, which the acquirer could elect as tax credits, relating to the pre-acquisition period. The potential adverse consequences of elimination of the pre-acquisition tax pool should be weighed against the benefits of fresh start tax basis and amortizable goodwill. The Section 338 election has no impact for local law purposes and the tax bases of the assets remain at historic costs when calculating local income tax liability. Similarly, the Section 338 election has no direct impact on the determination of the book bases of the assets or the book basis of the shares of the acquired foreign subsidiary. However, the acquisition accounting principles along with the concepts of push down accounting and the goodwill methodology of FASB ASC 350 may produce results that are similar to a Section 338 election.

---

[29] IRC Section 368(a)(2)(E).

[30] *See generally Federal Income Taxation of Corporations and Shareholders* ¶ 10.42.

[31] In cases where the target subsidiary is a controlled foreign corporation (CFC), the buyer's Section 338 election could result in the taxation of subpart F income to the U.S. seller. Typically, a well-advised U.S. seller will be aware if such an election would produce adverse tax consequences and will prohibit the availability of such election in the contract of sale or reflect such adverse consequences in the pricing.

[32] IRC Section 301(c)(2), (3).

Financial Accounting for Income Taxes (FASB ASC 740) Recognition and Measurement of Deferred Taxes

In the context of Illustration 7-3, management of USCo must first determine if it is more likely than not that the merger will be a tax-free reorganization.[33] If the more-likely-than-not recognition threshold is met, then management must measure the benefit of the deferred gain considering possible settlement of the issue.[34] Assume that in Illustration 7-3, management considers all relevant information, and determines that the more-likely-than-not recognition threshold is met. Management believes it is likely that the IRS would not settle on any basis except that the transaction does not constitute a tax-free reorganization and is therefore a fully taxable transaction. USCo thus measures the benefit of the deferred gain resulting from the merger by identifying two outcomes and calculating the probabilities of the outcomes along with the tax benefit of the outcomes: (i) a zero percent probability of success with no tax benefit; and (ii) a 100 percent probability of success with the full tax benefit and thus recognize the entire tax benefit from the merger in its financial statements. Management determines that the full benefit should be recorded for financial statement purposes. Although it may not be uncommon to use a binary approach in a significant transaction, such as a major corporate merger with significant taxes, it is much less likely in lesser tax matters. It is suspect when a company that settled almost every dispute with the tax authorities would represent that it would litigate one or more lesser tax matters all the way to the highest court in the land.

A significant consideration in the business combination process may be the recognition and measurement analysis of the target corporation, including the measurement probability table and financial statement disclosure of pre-acquisition income tax positions of the target that are uncertain. Accordingly, it may be advisable for an acquiring company to seek a representation or warranty that the target company warrants the propriety of its recognition and measurement analysis. In addition to seeking a representation and warranty, the acquirer could include an indemnification clause that requires the seller to compensate the acquirer for any additional taxes, including interest and penalties, for pre-acquisition income tax positions. The acquirer should consider a holdback of the sale proceeds when collection of any indemnification will be difficult, if not impossible, such as with a publicly traded target corporation or if the seller is a holding company that can easily liquidate. These risk mitigation actions should facilitate the due diligence that should be performed by the acquirer.

When there is a payment by the seller to the acquirer pursuant to an indemnification clause that requires the seller to compensate the acquirer for additional taxes incurred, the payment reduces the acquirer's GAAP tax expense. For income tax, the payment is a purchase price adjustment; and for a taxable transaction, the payment will be reflected in the IRC Section 1060 computations. The indemnification clause typically covers tax underpayments as well as tax overpayments by the seller. In an overpayment situation, the acquirer makes a payment to the seller.

General Principles of Deferred Taxes

There is a fair amount of historical background on the applicable GAAP tax principles that should help readers understand the accounting for transactions that have

[33] FASB ASC 740–10–25–5 to FASB ASC 740–10–25–17.

[34] FASB ASC 740–10–30–7.

been completed years ago. This section also covers a fair amount of non-tax GAAP principles that apply to business combinations to help the reader gain an understanding of the significant interdependence with the tax GAAP principles. The GAAP rules have changed over the years and while the text will mention the "methods" used to account for business combinations during the different chronological periods, descriptions of these GAAP methods goes beyond this text. What the text does do is provide a comprehensive discussion on the GAAP and tax treatment of goodwill due to the significant attention it has garnered.

One entity may acquire another entity in either a taxable business combination or a non-taxable business combination (i.e., a tax-free reorganization).[35] If the acquisition is a taxable business combination, then the purchase price is allocated to the assets and liabilities of the acquired entity for both financial accounting and tax purposes. If the acquisition is a non-taxable business combination (such as an "A" reorganization), then the purchase price is allocated to the acquired entity's assets and liabilities for financial accounting purposes. For tax purposes, however, the tax bases of the assets and liabilities of the target corporation carry over to the acquiring entity.[36]

In June 2001, FASB issued SFAS No. 141, *Business Combinations* and also SFAS No. 142, *Goodwill and Other Intangible Assets* (FASB ASC 350). These two statements changed the accounting treatment for business combinations, goodwill and intangible assets. SFAS No. 141 eliminated pooling of interests accounting for business combinations effective for business combinations taking place after June 30, 2001. As a result, business combinations had to be accounted for under the purchase method of accounting. SFAS No. 142 (FASB ASC 350) no longer allowed goodwill to be amortizable for financial accounting purposes. Rather, goodwill was subject to periodic impairment testing and, to the extent it was impaired, it had to be written down or written off.[37] The rule did not, however, change the requirements in SFAS No. 109 (FASB ASC 740) for recognition of deferred taxes in a business combination.[38]

In December 2007, FASB issued a revised version of SFAS No. 141, *Business Combinations*.[39] The revised version made a number of changes to SFAS No. 141.[40] The purchase method of accounting was replaced by the acquisition method of accounting, which applied to all business combinations and required an acquirer be identified for each business combination.[41] Unlike SFAS No. 141, SFAS No. 141(R) (FASB ASC 805) provided a definition of the acquirer—defined as "the entity that obtains control of one or more businesses in the business combination." The acquisition date was defined as the date that the acquirer achieves control.[42] SFAS No. 141(R) was codified as part of FASB ASC 805.

---

[35] *See* Section 2.15[1].

[36] IRC Section 362(b).

[37] FASB ASC 350–20–35–7 (deferred taxes are included in the carrying amount (i.e., book basis) of a reporting unit for purposes of determining whether goodwill impairment exists (i.e., comparing the fair value of a reporting unit with its carrying amount (i.e., book basis)).

[38] SFAS No. 141, and SFAS No. 142 (FASB ASC 350).

[39] SFAS No. 141(R) (FASB ASC 805).

[40] FASB also issued a staff position that amended and clarified certain application issues with respect to SFAS No. 141(R) (FASB ASC 805). FSP No. 141(R)–1 (April 1, 2009) (FASB ASC 805–20).

[41] FASB ASC 805–10–25–4.

[42] FASB ASC 805–10–25–6.

FASB ASC 805 requires that the assets acquired, liabilities assumed, and any noncontrolling interest in the acquiree be measured at the fair value on the acquisition date.[43] As a result, acquisition-related costs are recognized separately from the acquisition and are generally expensed.[44] The expensing of acquisition related costs (with the exception of debt and equity issuance costs) in FASB ASC 805 is a significant change from SFAS No. 141, which required capitalization of such costs. In addition, post-acquisition restructuring costs the acquirer expects to incur are also recognized separately from the acquisition.

An acquirer must recognize identifiable assets acquired and liabilities assumed as of the acquisition date (measured at their acquisition date fair values) only if it is more likely than not that the identifiable assets and liabilities meet the definition of an asset or liability under CON 6.[45] If the more likely than not standard is not met with respect to an identifiable asset or liability, then the costs are not part of applying the acquisition method. The acquirer accounts for the costs in its post-combination financial statements, in accordance with other GAAP principles (particularly FASB ASC 450).[46]

When one entity acquires another entity in a business combination, whether taxable or non-taxable, a deferred tax liability or asset is recognized for an acquired entity's taxable or deductible temporary differences (i.e., differences between the recognized values (i.e., book bases) and the tax bases of the acquired entity's assets and liabilities).[47] A deferred tax liability is not recognized, however, for a difference between the book basis and the tax basis of (a) goodwill if the goodwill is not amortizable for tax purposes, (b) for leveraged leases, and (c) for acquired temporary differences relating to the excess of the book basis over the tax basis of an investment in a foreign subsidiary or a foreign corporate joint venture that is essentially permanent in duration.[48]

FASB ASC 805 requires the acquirer to recognize goodwill as of the acquisition date.[49] Goodwill is measured as a residual, by taking the consideration transferred by the buyer and adding it to the fair value of any noncontrolling interest and reducing that sum by the fair values of the identifiable net assets acquired.[50]

FASB ASC 805 also requires the acquirer to recognize contingent consideration at the acquisition date (measured at its fair value on that date).[51]

If a taxable business combination creates tax-amortizable goodwill, then a deferred tax liability is recognized on the acquisition date and it is reversed over time as goodwill is amortized on the tax return but not amortized for financial reporting (i.e., the tax basis of the goodwill will become less than the book basis of the goodwill as it is amortized for tax purposes). A similar situation arises with respect to indefinite lived intangible assets

---

[43] FASB ASC 805–20–30–1.

[44] FASB ASC 805–10–25–23. Acquisition-related costs, generally referred to as transaction costs, include finder's fees; advisory, legal, accounting, valuation and other professional fees; general administrative costs; and the costs of registering and issuing debt and equity securities. *Id.*

[45] FASB ASC 805–20–25–2 and FASB ASC 805–20–25–19.

[46] *Id.*

[47] FASB ASC 805–740–25–2.

[48] FASB ASC 805–740–25–3.

[49] FASB ASC 805–30–30–1.

[50] *Id.*

[51] FASB ASC 805–30–25–5.

that are amortized for tax purposes but not for financial reporting purposes (i.e., the tax basis will become less than the book basis as tax amortization begins).

Since 1993, purchased goodwill has been deductible for U.S. Federal income tax purposes over a 15-year period.[52] The book basis and the tax basis of goodwill are each separated into two components as of the acquisition date for purposes of the deferred tax calculations.[53] The first component of each is equal to the lesser of: goodwill for financial reporting or tax-deductible goodwill. The second component of each is equal to the remainder (or excess) of each, i.e., the remainder, if any, of goodwill for financial reporting, or the remainder, if any, of tax-deductible goodwill. Any future difference that arises between the book basis and tax basis of the first component of goodwill is a temporary difference that will give rise to a deferred tax liability or asset.

For the second component of goodwill, if tax-deductible goodwill is greater than the book basis of goodwill, then the tax benefit will be recognized for the deferred tax asset. However, if the book basis of goodwill is greater than the tax-deductible goodwill, then no deferred tax liability is recognized (either at the acquisition date or in future years).

One of the more significant changes made in accounting for business combinations is with respect to a bargain purchase.[54] A bargain purchase occurs in a business combination when, on the acquisition date, the total fair value of the identifiable net assets acquired exceeds the sum of the fair value of the consideration transferred plus any noncontrolling interest in the acquiree.[55] The amount of the bargain purchase is recognized by the acquirer as gain and therefore included in earnings.[56] Previously, FASB treated the amount of the bargain purchase as negative goodwill and allocated it as a pro rata reduction of the amounts otherwise assigned to the acquired assets (i.e., as a reduction of the book bases of the acquired assets).

In a business combination, the acquiring entity may recognize a valuation allowance with respect to a deferred tax asset recorded for the deductible temporary differences attributable to the (a) acquired entity's assets and liabilities, (b) net operating loss carryforwards, or (c) tax credit carryforwards on the acquisition date. Any decrease or elimination of the valuation allowance after the acquisition date and within the measurement period that results from new information about facts and circumstances that existed at the acquisition date will reduce any goodwill created in the acquisition.[57] The acquisition goodwill cannot be reduced below zero and any additional decrease in the valuation allowance is treated as a bargain purchase.[58] Any change in the valuation

---

52 IRC Section 197. In enacting IRC Section 197 as part of the Omnibus Budget Reconciliation Act of 1993 (enactment date of August 10, 1993), Congress permitted companies the option of electing to retroactively apply it to business combinations occurring after July 25, 1991. A FASB Task Force concluded that the tax benefit related to tax-deductible goodwill in excess of the book basis of goodwill is included in income from continuing operations at the enactment date if the enterprise expects to retroactively apply IRC Section 197. FASB Task Force, EITF Issue No. 93–12, *Recognition and Movement of the Tax Benefit of Excess Tax-Deductible Goodwill Resulting from a Retroactive Change in Tax Law* (Sept. 23, 1993). A current tax benefit is reported for the retroactive amortization of goodwill (from the combination date to the enactment date). A deferred tax benefit is reported for the excess of tax-deductible goodwill (less the retroactive amortization) over the book basis of the goodwill.

53 FASB ASC 805–740–25–8.

54 FASB ASC 805–30.

55 FASB ASC 805–30–25–2.

56 *Id.*

57 FASB ASC 805–740–45–2(a).

58 *Id.*

allowance for an acquired entity's deferred tax asset that does not occur in the measurement period, which is one year from the transaction date, and is not based on facts and circumstances existing at the acquisition date is reported as a reduction or increase to income tax expense (or as an adjustment to contributed capital).[59]

FASB issued an exposure draft on April 28, 2014 addressing "push-down" accounting when control of the target company is achieved in multiple steps.[60] The exposure draft gives the target company the option to apply push-down accounting in the reporting period that it is controlled by another company. To illustrate, a foreign company owns 30 percent in a U.S. company. The U.S. company files quarterly financial statements on a calendar year basis. The foreign company acquires another 60 percent in the U.S. company on October 15, 2017. The U.S. company has the option to apply push-down accounting in the third quarter of 2017. The Emerging Issues Tax Force reached a final consensus on Issue 12-F and it was ratified by FASB at their October 8, 2014 meeting and released in November 2014 as ASU 2014–17, *Business Combinations: Pushdown Accounting.*

Subsequent sale, in whole or in part, of a business acquired in a non-taxable transaction could present both income tax and financial reporting complexities, as illustrated in this next example.

ILLUSTRATION 7-4: USCo acquires 100 percent of Acquired, a publicly traded U.S. company, for $500. Acquired has operating assets with a tax basis of $40 and book basis of $100. USCo's combined federal and state statutory tax rate is 30 percent. The fair market value of the operating assets is $450. Unlike tax, there is no difference between the book outside basis and the book inside basis. The book and tax outside and inside bases of the acquired business are set forth in the two tables—

	Book	Tax	Deferred Tax
Outside Basis in Target	100		
Original assets			
FMV step up (book only step-up)	350		
Goodwill	50		
Total Purchase Price	500	500	–
Inside Basis of Target			
Original assets	100	40	18
FMV step up (book only step-up)	350	0	105
Goodwill	50	0	0
Total Purchase Price	500	40	123

[59] FASB ASC 805–740–45–2(b).

[60] FASB Proposed ASU, April 28, 2014, on EITF Issue No. 12-F, *Recognition of New Accounting Basis (Pushdown) in Certain Circumstances.*

As shown in the calculations, since there was $123 of deferred taxes on the balance sheet, there must be an offsetting $123 of asset. For simplicity, add $123 of intangible assets so USCo gets back to $500 on its balance sheet.

To illustrate a point, assume USCo sells the stock of Acquired on the same day for $500. As expected, there is no book and tax gain or loss. However, here is what happens if Acquired sells all its assets for $500—

	Book	**Tax**
Sales Price	500	500
Basis	623	40
Gain/(Loss)	(123)	460
Current Tax Benefit/(Expense)	0	(138) (460 x 30% Tax Rate)
Deferred Tax on Balance Sheet		123
Additional Tax Benefit/(Expense)	(15)	(15)
Net Earnings/(Loss)	(138)	

When Acquired sells all the assets for $500, there is a book loss of $138. It's not a coincidence that the book loss is exactly equal to current tax liability of $138.[61] To see why the book loss is appropriate, shift to the income tax side. The tax gain of $460 less the taxes of $138 results in tax earnings and profits of $322. This will increase Acquired's outside tax basis from $500 to $822. After the sale of Acquired's assets, there will be net proceeds of $362 ($500 sale price less $138 tax payment). When the net proceeds are distributed to USCo, the outside tax basis in Acquired is reduced by $362, so the outside basis goes from $822 to $460. The book basis is zero, so there is a book-tax outside basis difference of $460. When USCo sells the Acquired stock for zero consideration, USCo will have a $460 tax loss. Absent any restriction on the use of the tax loss, the tax will reduce USCo's tax liability by $138, which is a tax benefit. The $138 book loss on the sale of Acquired's assets matches the $138 book tax benefit on the sale of the Acquired stock. But USCo cannot recognize the $138 deferred tax asset from the outside book-tax basis difference in the Acquired stock unless the book-tax difference will reverse in the foreseeable future.[62] Basically, there is a so-called off-balance-sheet deferred tax asset of $138 that USCo cannot currently recognize.

The deferred taxes on the outside basis difference in Illustration 7-4 could not be recognized until that difference reverses in the foreseeable future, but there are situations where a deferred tax liability and sometimes a deferred tax asset must be recognized. Audit firms and companies have begun to focus on this area as transactions and planning structures and the rules for deferred taxes have become more complex. The rules are more fully explained in Section 2.16.

The objective of pushing down the acquisition method of accounting is to allocate the cost of the acquisition to all of the assets of the target subsidiary for financial

[61] The $138 book loss is the $123 of book loss on the sale and the additional $15 of tax expense incurred. The additional tax expense is due to the $138 of tax on the sale being higher than the $123 of deferred taxes.

[62] FASB ASC 740–30–25–9.

accounting purposes.[63] Like the Section 338 election discussed in the Tax Technical Matters section, push down accounting (sometimes referred to as "new basis accounting") does not affect either the local statutory books or the basis of the subsidiary's assets for local tax purposes. The purchase price to be allocated among the assets will include liabilities assumed in the acquisition, including liabilities of the target foreign subsidiary. The amount of the purchase price in excess of the fair market value of the tangible assets and the non-goodwill intangible assets of the target foreign subsidiary will be allocated to goodwill pursuant to the principles of FASB ASC 350 (for financial accounting purposes) and IRC Section 1060 (for tax purposes). Because the principles governing recognition of liabilities differ significantly for purposes of U.S. tax and financial accounting, the amount of the purchase price and, therefore, the amount allocated to goodwill and potentially other assets could differ significantly for U.S. tax and financial accounting purposes.[64]

FASB ASC 350 and FASB ASC 740 provide that deferred taxes will not be provided with respect to goodwill that is not deductible for tax purposes (either through amortization or direct write-off).[65] Amortization of tax-deductible goodwill to the extent of book goodwill will result in a temporary difference and the establishment of a deferred tax liability. The amount of any goodwill that exists for tax purposes in excess of book goodwill, when amortized and realized for tax purposes, is applied to first reduce book goodwill related to the acquisition and second to non-current intangible assets related to the acquisition. Only when such goodwill and non-current intangible assets have been reduced to zero will amortization of goodwill for tax purposes reduce income tax expense.

ILLUSTRATION 7-5: USCo purchases all of the shares of JCo, which is incorporated and exclusively doing business in Country J, for $100,000 from a resident of Country J. The tax rate in Country J is 45 percent. The fair market value of the tangible and non-goodwill intangible assets of JCo is $60,000, and the Country J tax basis of JCo's assets is $20,000. JCo's financial statements immediately prior to the acquisition reflect an unfunded pension liability of $10,000,[66] a reserve for cleanup of an abandoned manufacturing site of $15,000, and net deferred tax liabilities of $8,000.[67] Applying the principles of push

---

[63] SFAS No. 141, Business Combinations (June 2001).

[64] In cases where the cash purchase price exceeds the fair market value of tangible and non-goodwill intangible assets, any differences between liabilities considered for U.S. tax and financial accounting purposes will be reflected in goodwill. In cases where the cash price is less than the fair market value of the tangible and non-goodwill intangible assets (bargain purchase), the difference between tax and financial statement liabilities will be reflected in the basis of these assets. Generally, allocation to tangible assets and non-goodwill intangible assets is substantially identical for both book purposes and U.S. tax purposes, as both methodologies are based on the fair market value of the relevant assets. However, allocation of purchase price to inventory for book purposes is typically based on net replacement value of the inventory while allocation to inventory for tax purposes can be based on comparative sales value of the inventory (estimated value of the inventory at sales price reduced by estimated selling costs) as described in Rev. Proc. 77–12, 1977–1 CB 569. When inventory is handled differently for these purposes, the difference will be reflected in differing allocations to goodwill for book and U.S. tax purposes.

[65] FASB ASC 350–20–35–61; FASB ASC 805–740–25–3.

[66] Under the laws of Country J, the unfunded pension liability is deductible when accrued. Therefore, JCo will not establish a deferred tax asset with respect to this liability.

[67] The net deferred tax liabilities of $8,000 prior to the acquisition reflected on JCo's financial statements consist of a deferred tax asset of $6,750 with respect to the cleanup reserve, and deferred tax liabilities of $14,750 with respect to tax depreciation in excess of book depreciation in prior periods.

down accounting for financial accounting purposes, JCo will reflect a deferred tax liability of $18,000 and goodwill of $83,000 computed as follows:

Purchase price to be allocated:	
Cash purchase price	$100,000
Pension liability assumed	10,000
Cleanup reserve	15,000
Existing deferred tax liability (eliminated)	0
Deferred tax liability (45 percent Country J tax rate of excess of $60,000 over $20,000)	18,000
Total purchase price to be allocated	143,000
Less: Allocated to tangible and non-goodwill intangible assets	
(fair market value)	60,000
Allocated to goodwill (residual method)	83,000

Note that the existing deferred tax liability on the financial statements of JCo, prior to the acquisition, has been eliminated. Pursuant to FASB ASC 805–740–25–9 and FASB ASC 350, no deferred tax asset is established with respect to the local book and tax difference of goodwill. USCo's tax basis in its shares of JCo is $100,000; similarly, USCo's book basis in its shares of JCo is also $100,000. Since USCo purchased JCo for $100,000, USCo's book basis and tax basis (both U.S. tax basis and Country J tax basis) should be $100,000. Deferred taxes would not have to be provided, as required by ASC 740–30–25–9, since there is no outside book-tax basis difference.

ILLUSTRATION 7-6: Assume USCo makes an election under IRC Section 338 with respect to the acquisition of JCo. Pursuant to this election, the purchase price of JCo is allocated to the assets of JCo for purposes of determining earnings and profits of JCo in subsequent years. For this purpose, the purchase price of JCo is considered to be $100,000 as the liabilities for unfunded pensions and cleanup reserves are not considered for tax purposes because of the principles of IRC Section 404(a)(5) in the case of the unfunded pension liability and the failure to meet the "all events" test has not been satisfied in the case of the cleanup reserve. As a result, for purposes of determining earnings and profits, the U.S. tax basis of JCo's tangible assets and non-goodwill intangible assets is $60,000 and the tax basis in JCo's goodwill is $40,000.

Assume JCo's earnings in the first year subsequent to the acquisition are $30,000 prior to deductions for depreciation and amortization. Further assume that JCo's assets are depreciable over a five-year life under the straight-line method for purposes of U.S. GAAP financial statements, local tax and U.S. tax earnings and profits. Country J also reduced its tax rate from 45 percent to 35 percent. JCo will reduce the deferred tax liability established as a result of the excess of book basis over tax basis in JCo's assets by $4,000 to $14,000 (the remeasured deferred taxes is equal to $18,000 multiplied by (35 percent tax rate divided by 45 percent tax rate)). This adjustment to the deferred tax liability resulting from the rate change will decrease income tax expense for the current year even though creation of the deferred liability did not initially result in a charge to tax expense.[68] The results of the year for JCo, including deductions for depreciation and amortization, are as follows:

	GAAP	Local Tax	U.S. E&P
Income before depreciation and amortization	$30,000	$30,000	$30,000
Depreciation	(12,000)	(4,000)	(12,000)
Goodwill amortization	0	0	(2,667)
Pre-tax Income	18,000	26,000	15,333
Tax Expense			
Foreign Tax Benefit/(Expense)	(6,300)	(9,100)	(9,100)
Rate Change Benefit/(Expense)	4,000	0	0
Total Tax Benefit/(Expense)	(2,300)	(9,100)	(9,100)
Types of Earnings			
Book retained earnings	15,700		
Local statutory retained earnings		16,900	

Assume that JCo makes a distribution to USCo of an amount equal to or greater than its U.S. earnings and profits of $6,233 ($15,333 U.S. pre-tax income minus $9,100 foreign tax expense). JCo's income tax expense for GAAP purposes for the year will be $6,300 ($18,000 pre-tax GAAP income multiplied by 35 percent Country J tax rate). The actual tax paid to Country J will be $9,100 ($26,000 local pre-tax income multiplied by 35 percent Country J tax rate); the additional $2,800 will be charged against the deferred tax liability of $18,000 from push down accounting rather than income tax expense. The correct technical procedure to arrive at the amount charged to deferred tax liability is to multiply $8,000, which is the difference between GAAP and local pre-tax income, by the 35 percent Country J tax rate. The distribution will result in a taxable dividend to USCo of $6,233; however, USCo is entitled to a 100 percent dividends-received deduction under IRC Section 245A. Any distribution in excess of $6,233 will be treated as a non-taxable return of capital, and if there is insufficient tax basis, it will be treated as taxable capital gain.[69]

Finally, it is noteworthy that following a distribution of $6,233, USCo's book basis in the shares of JCo will exceed its U.S. tax basis by $9,467, which is simply the difference between book retained earnings of $15,700 and the U.S. earnings and profits of $6,233. Because JCo will have no earnings and profits remaining, any distributions from JCo to USCo will be treated as return of capital under U.S. tax principles (see IRC Section 301(c)(2)) and will not result

[68] The initial balance sheet following acquisition of JCo reflected an increase in goodwill as a result of the creation of the deferred tax liability.

[69] IRC Section 301(c)(2), (3).

in additional U.S. tax until the total return of capital distributions exceeds the original tax basis of $100,000. After all the capital has been distributed, any additional distributions will result in a taxable capital gain to USCo.[70] As it appears impossible for JCo to make such a distribution in the foreseeable future, other than through a taxable liquidation of all or some of its business, it is questionable whether a deferred tax liability should be established with respect to this book and tax outside basis difference if USCo did not assert the indefinite reinvestment doctrine. See Section 2.16 for a discussion on deferred taxes on book-tax outside basis difference. Since U.S. GAAP is rule-based (unlike IFRS that is principle-based), there is no exception to recording a deferred tax liability even on an unlikely, if not impossible, scenario.

SOX

The SOX Section 404 considerations in the context of business combinations are to assure that the entity has sufficient controls in place so that appropriate procedures are created and followed to determine the proper tax and financial accounting treatment of business combination transactions. In this regard, a critical issue will concern the data that is used to allocate the purchase price among the various categories of assets, which may be a critical element in the successful resolution of future tax disputes involving business combination transactions.

The deal structure with respect to the target's tax assets and liabilities may introduce tracking obligations. For instance, the consideration paid for the target could reflect the value of the target's tax attributes, such as tax credit carryforwards, or it may exclude the target's tax attributes. In the latter situation, there could be material post-acquisition adjustments, principally due to changes agreed with government tax auditors and expiration of the statute of limitations on tax years with material uncertain tax positions. To the extent that these tax liabilities are contractual obligations of the target's former shareholders pursuant to a tax indemnification clause, these adjustments are purchase price adjustments and would not be income tax expense to the target's former shareholders.

ILLUSTRATION 7-7: Same facts as Illustration 7-5, above, where USCo's wholly-owned U.S. corporate subsidiary (USSub) is acquired by another U.S. corporation (PCo) in exchange for stock of PCo. USSub had an uncertain tax position for U.S. Federal income tax for tax year 2020 but pursuant to FASB ASC 740–10 was able to recognize the entire $100 tax benefit. USCo and PCo agreed that any pre-acquisition tax liabilities or benefits will be settled in cash once these assets and liabilities are absolutely certain. After the acquisition, the uncertain tax position was raised by the IRS and the parties settled. In the settlement, USSub conceded $40 to the government. USCo remits $40 to PCo and treats the payment as a purchase price adjustment. Contrast this to what would have happened had the business combination not occurred. The $40 settlement payment to the IRS and the state, net of federal tax benefit for the state tax deduction, would be recorded as an income tax expense. In both cases, the settlement is shown on USCo's 2020 Federal consolidated tax return and state tax return. USCo's consolidated tax accounts would have a $40 payable due to the $40 income tax expense from the tax settlement with the IRS and

[70] IRC Section 301(c)(3).

the state; the payable will be eliminated when USCo remits a $40 payment to the IRS and the state. That would not be the case in the business combination because instead of an income tax expense, a $40 purchase price adjustment would have been recorded; USCo's tax accounts would not reconcile because without the income tax expense, no tax payable would be set up and without the tax payable, the tax payment to the IRS would not zero out. The controls need to take into account anomalies such as the one in this Illustration. This Illustration raises another commercial matter. The $40 purchase price adjustment paid by USCo to PCo would reduce the gain on the sale of USSub. If it turns out that the lower gain results in lower taxes to USCo, the $40 payment would actually cost USCo less than $40. Contrast that outcome to what would have happened had USCo not sold USSub: the $40 tax payment would have reduced earnings by the full $40. PCo's tax basis in USSub is unchanged since the $40 purchase price adjustment is offset by the $40 tax payment. Since the 30 percent tax rate used in the Illustration is a combined federal and state tax rate, the federal tax benefit of state taxes are blended into the 30 percent combined rate.

For complex or large business combinations, a "second chair" arrangement can help reduce tax risks. The second chair is a tax professional with significant experience in business combinations. The tax professional is independent of the team working on the business combinations. While it does increase costs, it is well worth having another pair of eyes that are sufficiently removed from the team to provide an unbiased assessment of the tax issues and risks.

One question that was posed to the SEC regarding business combinations was as follows: If a registrant consummates a material purchase business combination during its fiscal year, must the internal control over financial reporting of the acquired business be included in management's report on internal control over financial reporting for that fiscal year?[71] The SEC has stated that while it expects management's report on internal control over financial reporting to include controls at all consolidated entities, it acknowledges that it might not always be possible to conduct an assessment of an acquired business's internal control over financial reporting in the period between the consummation date and the date of management's assessment.[72] In these instances, the SEC does not object to management referring in the report to a discussion in the registrant's Form 10-K regarding the scope of the assessment and to the disclosure noting that management excluded the acquired business from management's report on internal control over financial reporting. If this reference is made, however, management must identify the acquired business excluded and indicate the significance of the acquired business to the registrant's consolidated financial statements. Notwithstanding management's exclusion of an acquired business's internal controls from its annual assessment, a registrant must disclose any material change to its internal control over financial reporting due to the acquisition. In addition, the period in which management may omit an assessment of an acquired business's internal control over financial reporting from its assessment of the registrant's internal control may not extend beyond

[71] Office of the Chief Accountant, *Division of Corporation Finance: Management's Report on Internal Control Over Financial Reporting and Disclosure in Exchange Act Periodic Reports—Frequently Asked Questions* (revised Sept. 24, 2007), Question 3.

[72] *Id.*

one year from the date of acquisition, nor may the assessment be omitted from more than one annual management report on internal control over financial reporting.[73]

The tax law and financial tax accounting on business combinations may be one of the most, if not the most, complex in the tax universe, and cross-border business combinations significantly elevate that complexity. The number of tax practitioners that have mastered this area are probably in the low single digits, as a percentage, of all practitioners in the mergers and acquisitions practice area. Comprehensive SOX controls can mitigate the risks associated with this complexity.

§ 7.05 Business Expenses

General Principles

Companies incur numerous operating costs in the conduct of their business that typically are currently deductible as ordinary and necessary business expenses.[74] Many exceptions exist, however, that limit or preclude the current deductibility of costs incurred by a company in its business. For example, a business cost may be (i) subject to the capitalization rules[75] and recovered through depreciation,[76] amortization,[77] or on disposition[78] or (ii) simply not deductible (such as a fine or excessive executive compensation).[79] Further, a purported ordinary and necessary business expense may be properly characterized as a non-deductible expenditure (such as a payment by a corporation to its sole shareholder that is designated as salary, but in substance constitutes a non-deductible dividend for tax purposes). Thus, even if a business expenditure is not required to be capitalized, the proper tax treatment of a business expenditure might not be clear, thus raising various issues regarding its proper characterization for tax purposes.

> **ILLUSTRATION 7-8:** OilCo is a U.S.-based multinational corporation that has many wholly-owned foreign corporate subsidiaries engaged in different segments of its global business. In foreign country X, the local OilCo subsidiary (XCo) has been engaged in seeking to increase its market share in the face of an extremely competitive environment. XCo has incurred significant operating losses in this process. The decision to compete in Country X was made by the OilCo Board of Directors as a strategic matter. An inter-company agreement, styled as an "Operating Agreement," exists between OilCo and XCo relating to the Country X business. One provision of the agreement is that OilCo will reimburse XCo for certain categories of expenses, denominated as "market development expenses." In 2022, OilCo funded XCo's market development expenses by making a payment to XCo in the amount of $25 million. OilCo deducts the entire $25 million expense on its 2022 Federal income tax return based on an opinion of legal counsel that concludes that it is more likely than

[73] *Id.*

[74] IRC Section 162(a).

[75] IRC Section 263 (relating to capitalization rules); 263A (uniform capitalization rules). Treas. Reg. § 1.446–1(a)(4)(ii) requires a taxpayer to properly classify expenditures made during the year between capital expenditures and deductible expenses.

[76] IRC Section 167.

[77] *See, e.g.*, IRC Section 195 (start-up expenditures); IRC Section 197 (intangible assets).

[78] IRC Section 1001(a).

[79] *See, e.g.*, IRC Section 162(f) (relating to non-deductibility of certain fines and penalties); IRC Section 162(m) (certain excessive employee remuneration).

not that the payment of the market development expense is deductible as an ordinary and necessary business expense. Management of OilCo has determined that the proper unit of account for uncertain income tax accounting purposes is OilCo's payment to XCo. The tax benefit of the $25 million deduction is $7.5 million (based on a 30 percent combined U.S. federal and state income tax rate).

Technical Tax Matters

A taxpayer may deduct "all the ordinary and necessary expenses paid or incurred during the taxable year in carrying on any trade or business."[80] With certain exceptions, these business expenses include salaries,[81] travel,[82] rent,[83] utilities, supplies, repairs, maintenance and insurance premiums.[84] Various requirements must be met before an expense may be deducted as a business expense, including that the expense be "ordinary and necessary" to the conduct of a business, and the deduction be permitted pursuant to the company's method of accounting (e.g., the economic performance rules must be met for accrual method taxpayers).[85] There are numerous exceptions to the current deduction of a business expenditure. For example, if the cost is incurred in connection with the purchase or construction of an asset, the company typically is required to capitalize the cost.[86] Further, some expenses are statutorily nondeductible, such as fines and penalties paid to a governmental agency in violation of a law,[87] and illegal bribes, kickbacks, or unlawful payments to a governmental official or employee.[88] Moreover, some expenses require compliance with special substantiation provisions to be deducted.[89]

Financial Accounting for Income Taxes (FASB ASC 740) Recognition and Measurement of Deferred Taxes

Using the facts in Illustration 7-8, assume that management of OilCo has determined that OilCo's deduction of the $25 million payment to XCo is uncertain under the tax law. Thus, OilCo management must determine the financial accounting consequences resulting from that uncertain tax position. The main recognition issues are (i) what is the proper unit of account with respect to OilCo's payment to XCo,[90] and (ii) is it more likely than not that OilCo is entitled to currently deduct the payment.[91] If the

---

80 IRC Section 162(a).

81 Under IRC Section 162(a)(1), an ordinary business deduction is permitted for a reasonable allowance for salaries or other compensation for personal services actually rendered.

82 IRC Section 162(a)(2) generally permits a company to deduct costs incurred by an employee for traveling away from home in connection with and directly related to the employer's business, including meals and lodging expenses to the extent they are not extravagant. *But see* IRC Section 274 (disallowance of entertainment expenses).

83 *See* IRC Section 162(a)(3).

84 Treas. Reg. Section 1.162–1(a).

85 IRC Section 461(h) (the all events test is not met any earlier than when economic performance occurs).

86 *See generally* IRC Section 263; 263A.

87 *See* IRC Section 162(f).

88 *See* IRC Section 162(c)(1). Other examples of business costs that are not deductible include IRC Section 162(m) (excessive executive compensation), IRC Section 280G (precluding a deduction for certain excess golden parachute compensation payments made in connection with a change of control of the employer), and IRC Section 162(k) (disallowing costs incurred to redeem a shareholder's stock).

89 *See* IRC Section 274(d).

90 FASB ASC 740–10–25–13.

91 FASB ASC 740–10–25–5 to FASB ASC 740–10–25–17.

more-likely-than-not recognition threshold is met, management of OilCo must then determine what is the measurement of the allowable tax benefit that may be recorded on OilCo's financial statements.[92]

Identification of the appropriate unit of account is determined by reference to the applicable facts and circumstances based on management's judgment. As stated in the Illustration above, management of OilCo has determined that the appropriate unit of account for the marketing development expense is the expense itself.

After the proper unit of account is established, the next step is to determine whether OilCo's tax position can be recognized, i.e., whether it is more likely than not that OilCo's tax position will be sustained upon examination by the taxing authority, including resolution of any related appeals or litigation, based on the technical merits of the position. There are a number of technical issues to analyze with respect to the tax position.[93] For instance, the following issues might need to be addressed: (i) is the payment a non-deductible contribution by OilCo to the capital of XCo, (ii) if the payment is not a non-deductible contribution, does the payment constitute an ordinary and necessary business expense of OilCo, (iii) if the payment is an ordinary and necessary business expense, have the economic performance rules been satisfied to permit a current deduction, (iv) does any other provision of the tax law require any portion of the payment to be capitalized by OilCo or otherwise limit a current deduction and (v) if the payment is deductible, is it foreign source expense or US source expense. Although the first and second issues could have an earnings impact, the latter two would not have an immediate earnings impact because there should only be a temporary timing difference. The last issue could also have a negative earnings impact depending on OilCo's foreign tax credit position.

Assume OilCo concludes that the more-likely-than-not recognition threshold is met with respect to the current deduction of the payment made by OilCo to XCo, based in part on tax counsel's opinion[94] that concludes that it is more likely than not that OilCo should be permitted to deduct the payment to XCo as an ordinary and necessary business expense.

If OilCo's tax position meets the more-likely-than-not recognition threshold,[95] then OilCo must measure the amount of the tax benefit to reflect in OilCo's financial statements with respect to the tax position. OilCo is permitted to record a benefit for the amount that has a cumulative probability of occurring that is greater than 50 percent.

Under Illustration 7-8 and disregarding the impact on OilCo's foreign tax credit position, the full benefit of OilCo's deduction is $7.5 million based on the entire tax

---

[92] FASB ASC 740–10–30–7.

[93] For tax purposes, it is possible that a taxing authority may disallow in part or whole the current deduction of the OilCo payment.

[94] Although FASB ASC 740–10–25 does not require OilCo to obtain an opinion to support its position that the Section 162 tax position satisfies the more-likely-than-not recognition threshold, it may be prudent for OilCo to consider obtaining an opinion to show its independent auditors that it exercised good faith in determining whether the tax position would be sustained. *See* Chapter 8 on the potential loss of attorney-client privilege when an opinion is shared with the independent auditors.

[95] If OilCo's uncertain tax position does not satisfy the more-likely-than-not recognition threshold, then OilCo is not entitled to recognize on its financial statements any tax benefit from the deduction of the XCo payment, and OilCo is required to make financial statement disclosures with respect to the applicable interest and penalty costs attributable to the tax deduction. *See* Chapter 3.

2025) of a domestic corporation's foreign-derived intangible income for the taxable year.[97]

In computing the amount of the deduction, a domestic corporation first computes its deduction-eligible income, which is generally its gross income less deductions but excluding certain categories of gross income (and corresponding deductions) such as subpart F income and global intangible low-taxed income.[98] It then computes its foreign-derived deduction eligible income, which is its deduction-eligible income that is derived in connection with property sold for foreign use to a person who is not a United States person or services provided to any person, or with respect to any property, not located within the United States.[99] A domestic corporation must then compute its deemed intangible income, which is the excess of its deduction-eligible income over the deemed tangible income return of the corporation.[100] The deemed tangible income return is equal to 10 percent of the corporation's qualified business asset investment, generally referred to as qualified business asset investment (QBAI).[101] QBAI is the corporation's tangible depreciable property used in a trade or business.[102]

The foreign-derived intangible income, for which the 37.5 percent deduction is applicable, is the amount which bears the same ratio to the deemed intangible income as the foreign-derived deduction eligible income bears to the deduction eligible income.[103] Expressed as a formula, foreign-derived intangible income is:

$$\text{deemed intangible income} \times \frac{\text{foreign-derived deduction eligible income}}{\text{deduction eligible income}}$$

Financial Accounting for Income Taxes (FASB ASC 740) Recognition and Measurement of Deferred Taxes

The deduction for foreign-derived intangible income is a special deduction.[104] It is a permanent difference impacting (decreasing) a corporation's effective tax rate.

General Principles of Deferred Taxes

FASB provides that the tax benefit of a special deduction is recognized no earlier than when it is recognized on the tax return (as a deductible item). As a result, the tax benefit of a special deduction is not anticipated for purposes of offsetting a deferred tax liability recognized for taxable temporary differences. However, the tax benefit of a special deduction is recognized in determining the average graduated tax rate in measuring deferred tax assets or liabilities if graduated tax rates are a significant factor. It is also recognized in determining the need for a valuation allowance for deferred tax assets.

---

[97] IRC Section 250(a)(1), (3).

[98] IRC Section 250(b)(3).

[99] IRC Section 250(b)(4).

[100] IRC Section 250(b)(2).

[101] IRC Section 250(b)(2)(B).

[102] IRC Section 951A(d).

[103] IRC Section 250(b)(1).

[104] FASB ASC 740–10–25–37. *See* Section 2.10.

SOX

The SOX Section 404 considerations in the context of FDII are the resources the company uses to compute the tax deduction for FDII, including an internal spreadsheet or software from one of the major accounting firms to calculate the quantitative amount of the deduction and the legal support for the method the company uses in computing the deduction. The company should evaluate its method each reporting period taking into consideration developments from the taxing authorities, along with views expressed by academia, peers, industry groups, and professional firms.

§ 7.07 Global Intangible Low-Taxed Income

General Principles

The United States has historically taxed U.S. corporations on all their income regardless of geographic origin—that is, on worldwide income. Under that framework, in the case of income earned by a foreign subsidiary, there would be no income recognition by its U.S. parent unless or until dividends were paid by the foreign subsidiary to the U.S. parent, subject to the application of certain regimes in the Code that accelerated the recognition of such income, such as subpart F.[105] As part of the Tax Cuts and Jobs Act, Congress substantially changed the taxation of income earned by a foreign subsidiary of a U.S. parent. Generally, beginning in 2018, a controlled foreign corporation's income can fall into one of three categories: (1) tested income/global intangible low-taxed income (GILTI), (2) subpart F income, and (3) residual income (net deemed tangible income return).

Technical Tax Matters

Generally, a U.S. shareholder of a controlled foreign corporation must include its share of the global intangible low-taxed income (GILTI).[106] GILTI is the excess of a U.S. shareholder's total net tested (foreign) income over a deemed return of 10 percent on the foreign corporation's tangible depreciable assets less certain interest expense.[107] The U.S. shareholder, if a domestic corporation, is permitted a 50 percent deduction of its GILTI, but the deduction (along with the FDII deduction) is limited to the domestic corporation's taxable income.[108]

A domestic corporation is allowed a foreign tax credit of 80 percent of the foreign income taxes paid on GILTI.[109] Unused foreign tax credits associated with GILTI cannot be carried back or forward (or used against other foreign source income).[110] A U.S. shareholder increases its tax basis in the stock of the foreign corporation for the GILTI inclusion.[111]

[105] *See generally* IRC Sections 951–965. There are also other such regimes in the Code, such as the passive foreign investment company (PFIC) rules. IRC Sections 1291–1298. The principles noted below for dealing with differences between financial and tax accounting will operate in a similar fashion in the case of these other regimes.

[106] IRC Section 951A(a).

[107] IRC Section 951A(b).

[108] IRC Section 250.

[109] IRC Section 960(d).

[110] IRC Section 904(c).

[111] IRC Section 951A(f); 961.

Financial Accounting for Income Taxes (FASB ASC 740) Recognition and Measurement of Deferred Taxes

An investor corporation owning at least 20 percent but no more than 50 percent of the voting stock of an investee corporation will generally report income of the investee corporation under the equity method for financial accounting purposes because the investor corporation is considered to have "significant influence."[112] If an investor corporation owns more than 50 percent of the voting power of the investee corporation, then the investor corporation is generally referred to as the parent and the investee corporation is the subsidiary.[113] The parent will report income of the subsidiary under the consolidation method for financial accounting purposes. Under either the equity method or the consolidation method, the investor corporation's book basis in the investee corporation will increase (or decrease) by the income (or loss) of the investee corporation. For tax purposes, the investor corporation's tax basis in the investee corporation will increase (or decrease) as a result of tested income (loss) and subpart F income. U.S. multinationals experienced a massive subpart F inclusion due to the transition to a hybrid territorial/worldwide regime enacted under the TCJA.[114]

General Principles of Deferred Taxes

The FASB staff believed there were two different interpretations of FASB ASC 740 as it related to GILTI, and that an entity might apply either interpretation.[115] An entity can recognize deferred taxes for temporary basis differences that are expected to reverse in future years as GILTI. This interpretation is consistent with the treatment of subpart F income under FASB ASC 740. Alternatively, an entity can account for taxes on GILTI as period costs. An entity must disclose in its financial statements its accounting policy related to GILTI inclusions.[116] To illustrate, The Proctor & Gamble Company included the following language in its Form 10-K filed on August 5, 2022: "We have elected to account for the tax effects of Global Intangible Low-Taxed Income (GILTI) as a current period expense when incurred." In contrast, Pfizer Inc. included the following language in its 2021 Form 10-K:

> The TCJA subjects a U.S. shareholder to current tax on global intangible low-taxed income earned by certain foreign subsidiaries. The FASB Staff Q&A, Topic 740, No. 5, Accounting for Global Intangible Low-Taxed Income, states that we are permitted to make an accounting policy election to either recognize deferred taxes for temporary basis differences expected to reverse as global intangible low-taxed income in future years or provide for the tax expense related to such income in the year the tax is incurred. We elected to recognize deferred taxes for temporary differences expected to reverse as global intangible low-taxed income in future years.

Unused foreign tax credits associated with GILTI cannot be carried back or forward and the proper corporate tax accounting is to write off any excess foreign tax credits. It is incorrect to record a deferred tax asset with a full valuation allowance for the GILTI excess foreign tax credits.

---

112 FASB ASC 323–10–15–8.

113 FASB ASC 810–10–15–8.

114 IRC Section 965.

115 FASB Staff Q & A, Topic 740, No. 5: Accounting for Global Intangible Low-Taxed Income (Jan. 2018).

116 FASB ASC 235–10–50–1 to 235–10–50–3.

The U.S. shareholder is permitted a 50 percent deduction of its GILTI, but the deduction (along with the FDII deduction) is limited to the domestic corporation's taxable income. This limitation is economically equivalent to eliminating the value of any tax loss or tax credit that reduces taxable income. Since net operating losses and tax credits are reflected on the financial balance sheet as deferred tax assets, the company may need to record a valuation allowance against such deferred tax assets. A company that decides to recognize deferred taxes for temporary basis differences that are expected to reverse in future years as GILTI (versus as a period cost), may need to record a valuation allowance against deferred tax assets arising from NOLs and tax credits due to the company's inability to avail itself of the IRC Section 250 deduction.

SOX

The SOX Section 404 considerations in the context of GILTI are avoiding the presumption that a foreign statutory tax rate or foreign effective tax rate higher than the GILTI rate should result in no GILTI tax. The company should evaluate the need for a valuation allowance or the reduction of a previously recorded valuation allowance for NOLs and tax credits due to the company's ability to avail itself of the IRC Section 250 deduction. Another control consideration is the use of an internal spreadsheet or a software from one of the major accounting firms to calculate the quantitative amount of the GILTI and the legal support for the method the company uses in computing it.

§ 7.08 Base Erosion and Anti-Abuse Tax (BEAT)

Technical Tax Matters

As part of the Tax Cuts and Jobs Act, Congress enacted a new taxing regime, the base erosion and anti-abuse tax (BEAT).[117] The BEAT is a 10 percent (12.5 percent after 2025) minimum tax imposed on a U.S. corporation with average annual gross receipts of at least $500 million and base erosion payments equal to or exceeding three percent of its deductible payments. A U.S. corporation computes its BEAT liability by increasing its taxable income by base erosion payments (generally, outbound deductible payments to a foreign related person) resulting in modified taxable income. Modified taxable income is multiplied by the 10 percent BEAT rate. If the BEAT liability is greater than the regular income tax liability, the U.S. corporation must pay the greater amount.

Financial Accounting for Income Taxes (FASB ASC 740) Recognition and Measurement of Deferred Taxes

The FASB staff determined that an entity's deferred tax assets and liabilities should be measured using the statutory tax rate (21 percent) of the regular income tax system and not the lower BEAT rate (10 percent).[118] The FASB staff analogized the BEAT to the corporate alternative minimum tax (AMT), which was repealed as part of the Tax Cuts and Jobs Act. When the corporate AMT was in effect (i.e., prior to 2018), an entity measured its deferred tax assets and liabilities using the statutory rate (then 35 percent) under the regular income tax system and not the lower corporate AMT rate. The same result occurs with the BEAT. Unlike the repealed corporate AMT, the BEAT is a permanent tax since there is no tax credit for BEAT paid, which means there is no temporary difference that will lead to the recording of deferred taxes.

---

[117] IRC Section 59A.

[118] FASB Staff Q & A, Topic 740, No. 4, Accounting for the Base Erosion Anti-Abuse Tax (Jan. 2018).

The FASB staff noted that the incremental effect of BEAT is recognized in the year the BEAT is incurred—as a negative permanent difference. In addition, the staff believed that an entity does not need to evaluate the potential impact of the BEAT on the realization of deferred tax assets recognized under the regular income tax system. Realizations of the deferred tax assets under the regular income tax system would occur even if an incremental BEAT liability is owed for the same period.

General Principles of Deferred Taxes

FASB ASC 740 applies only to income taxes. Only an income tax is shown in the financial statements' income tax expense line. Only an income tax goes into the numerator in calculating the company's effective tax rate. Only an income tax is in the company's effective tax rate reconciliation table. Only an income tax is analyzed in the tax footnotes. The issue is whether BEAT is an income tax as defined under FASB ASC 740. The BEAT is a 10 percent tax on "modified taxable income," which includes certain related-party payments to a foreign recipient that are deductible by the payor.

The FASB staff in their guidance notes that the BEAT is sufficiently similar to the repealed corporate AMT tax, which the FASB previously concluded was an income tax. Unlike the repealed corporate AMT, a company does not receive a tax credit for the incremental BEAT tax that exceeds the regular tax. As a result, although the repealed corporate AMT did not increase the effective tax rate, the BEAT will. Despite this key difference, the FASB staff notes that the BEAT, like the repealed corporate AMT, is an incremental tax, so a company will not pay less than the statutory tax rate. Although the FASB guidance did not directly address the issue as to whether the BEAT is an income tax, due to the analogy between BEAT and the repealed corporate AMT, the prevailing view is that BEAT should be classified as an income tax.

Another BEAT issue is the impact of the BEAT on AMT credit carryovers and NOL carryovers. The FASB has noted that its "staff also believes that an entity would not need to evaluate the effect of potentially paying the BEAT in future years on the realization of deferred tax assets recognized under the regular tax system because the realization of the deferred tax asset (for example, a tax credit) would reduce its regular tax liability, even when an incremental BEAT liability would be owed in that period."[119] Although the FASB guidance does not require a company to consider the interaction of BEAT with the company's deferred tax assets, at least one major accounting firm believes the FASB guidance does not prohibit a company from considering the interaction. Should a company decide to include this interaction, the company may have to record a valuation allowance on deferred taxes recorded on AMT carryover and NOL carryover.[120]

SOX

The SOX Section 404 considerations in the context of BEAT are careful considerations of the different corporate tax accounting positions that may be available. The company should evaluate its method each reporting period taking into consideration developments from the taxing authorities, along with views expressed by academia, peers, industry groups, and professional firms. Another SOX control issue is the use of

---

[119] *Id.*

[120] *See* "In depth: A look at current financial reporting issues: Frequently asked questions: accounting considerations of US Tax Reform," Q&A 4.2, PwC, January 24, 2018 (updated as of March 7, 2018).

an internal spreadsheet or software from one of the major accounting firms to calculate the BEAT.

§ 7.09 Depreciation—Real Property

General Principles

For financial accounting purposes, depreciable real property, such as a building, is generally depreciated using the straight-line method of depreciation over an estimated useful life ranging from 15 to 50 years.[121] For tax purposes, depreciable real property is also depreciated using the straight-line method but over a fixed time frame (27.5 years for residential rental property or 39 years for nonresidential real property).[122]

ILLUSTRATION 7-9: An entity purchases a building for $1 million (and places it in service) on January 1, Year 1. It uses straight-line depreciation for tax purposes and also uses straight-line depreciation for financial accounting purposes. For tax purposes, the entity depreciates the building using an applicable recovery period of 39 years. For financial accounting purposes, it uses a useful life of 45 years. The salvage value is $50,000, which is treated as zero for tax purposes. The following table shows the depreciation expense, depreciation deduction, book basis of the building and tax basis of the building each year.

Year	(a) Depreciation Expense (Accounting)	(b) Depreciation Deduction (Tax)	(c) Difference ((a) – (b))	(d) Book Basis	(e) Tax Basis	(f) Difference ((d) – (e))
Year 1	$21,111	$24,573	($3,462)	$978,889	$975,427	$3,462
Year 2– Year 39	$21,111	$25,641	($4,530) per year	$176,671 (end of Year 39)	$1,068 (end of Year 39)	$175,603 (end of Year 39)
Year 40	$21,111	$1,068	$20,043	$155,560	$0	$155,560
Year 41– Year 45	$21,111	$ 0	$21,111 per year	$50,000 (end of Year 45)	$0 (end of Year 45)	$50,000 (end of Year 45)

The entity's accounting depreciation expense is $21,111 per year computed as follows: $950,000 depreciation base ($1,000,000 original cost less $50,000 salvage value) divided by 45 years (useful life). The entity's tax depreciation deduction is $25,641 per year computed as follows: $1 million cost basis divided by 39 years (applicable recovery period). For the first year, however, the tax depreciation deduction is only $24,573 ($25,641 times 11.5/12 months) reflecting the mid-month convention.

---

121 FASB ASC 360–10–35–3.

122 IRC Section 168(c).

Technical Tax Matters

For tax purposes, a depreciation deduction is permitted for a reasonable allowance for the exhaustion, wear and tear (including a reasonable allowance for obsolescence) of investment property or trade or business property.[123] Since 1981, tangible depreciable property is depreciated under the accelerated cost recovery system (ACRS).[124] In determining the amount of depreciation deduction of an asset for a particular period, generally four items must be known: (1) the applicable depreciation method,[125] (2) the applicable recovery period,[126] (3) the applicable convention,[127] and (4) the tax basis of the asset. In the case of depreciable real property, an entity must use the straight-line method as its applicable depreciable method.[128] It must also use the mid-month convention, treating the depreciable real property as being placed in service on the mid-point of the month it is actually placed in service.[129] Finally, depreciable real property has an applicable recovery period of either 27.5 years (if it is residential rental property) or 39 years (if it is nonresidential real property).[130] There is also an alternative depreciation system (ADS); if this is elected or required to be used by the entity, then residential rental property has a recovery period of 30 years and nonresidential real property has a recovery period of 40 years.[131] The TCJA requires the taxpayer to use the alternative depreciation system if the taxpayer elects out of the business interest deduction limitation.[132]

Financial Accounting for Income Taxes (FASB ASC 740) Recognition and Measurement of Deferred Taxes

In Illustration 7-9, the tax position should be certain because the tax benefit of the depreciation deduction should be consistent with the depreciation deduction filed on the company's tax return. However, an issue may arise, for example, if the company took a tax position that arguably some component portion of the building is subject to depreciation deduction over a recovery period of less than 39 years (e.g., the company characterizes a structural component of the building as subject to a less than 39-year recovery period). Much of these disputes have been resolved by the tangible personal property regulations that were issued on September 13, 2013.[133] In that event, the typical recognition and measurement issues would need to be addressed with respect to that potentially uncertain tax position, including (i) what is the proper unit of account with respect to depreciation deduction, (ii) is it more likely than not that the structural component is properly depreciated over a recovery period of less than 39 years, and (iii) if the more-likely-than-not threshold is met, what is the measurement of the allowable tax benefit for financial accounting purposes that may be recorded on the company's financial statements. Another potential area for dispute is the placed-in-service date.

---

[123] IRC Section 167(a).

[124] IRC Section 168.

[125] IRC Section 168(b).

[126] IRC Section 168(c).

[127] IRC Section 168(d).

[128] IRC Section 168(b)(3).

[129] IRC Section 168(d)(2) and (d)(4)(B).

[130] IRC Section 168(c).

[131] IRC Section 168(g).

[132] IRC Sections 163(j)(7)(A)(ii) and 168(k)(9).

[133] Treas. Reg. Section 1.263(a)–1(f).

There is also a natural tension between book and tax on the placed-in-service date. A later placed-in-service date would delay the start of book depreciation which increases financial earnings. In contrast, an earlier placed-in-service date gives rise to higher tax depreciation deductions, which translates to lower cash taxes, in the year the asset is placed in service. This lower cash tax is only temporary because it is offset by higher cash taxes in the last year of the tax life of the asset.

General Principles of Deferred Taxes

For financial accounting purposes, long-lived assets (many times referred to as either "fixed assets" or "property, plant and equipment") are depreciated over time.[134] In determining the amount of depreciation expense of an asset for a particular period, generally three items must be known: (1) the depreciable base for the asset, (2) the asset's useful life, and (3) the method of cost apportionment for the asset. The depreciable base of an asset is equal to the original cost of the asset less its salvage value. The asset's useful life is an estimate based on physical factors (such as wear and tear) and economic factors (such as obsolescence). The method of cost apportionment may be a straight-line method, an accelerated method or units of production method.

In the case of depreciable real property (e.g., a building), the book depreciation expense may differ from the tax depreciation deduction each year for several reasons. First, the building's accounting useful life may differ from the building's applicable tax recovery period.[135] Second, salvage value is taken into account for financial accounting purposes but is treated as zero for tax purposes.[136] Finally, depreciation for financial accounting purposes begins when the building is placed in service; however, for tax purposes, the mid-month convention applies to treat the building as placed in service on the mid-point of the month it is actually placed in service.[137]

If the book basis of the building exceeds its tax basis, a taxable temporary difference is created.[138] As a result, the entity will record a deferred tax liability. If the book basis of the building is less than its tax basis, the entity will record a deferred tax asset for the deductible temporary difference.[139] The entity will also need to determine if a valuation allowance is needed on the deferred tax asset.[140]

Another financial accounting principle that could also give rise to permanent book-tax difference, such as a valuation allowance, for real property is the "allowance for funds used during construction" (AFUDC), which applies only to regulated entities (e.g., company that transmits electricity to retail and residential customers). AFUDC reflects the book earnings the company will receive from the capital invested in the project during construction. The result is book income with no book tax expense. AFUDC is not a taxable event so there is a permanent book-tax difference. AFUDC increases the book basis in the underlying asset. Once the property is placed in service, the additional book

---

[134] FASB ASC 360–10–35–1.

[135] FASB ASC 360-10-35-9 ("If the number of years specified by the Accelerated Cost Recovery System of the Internal Revenue Service (IRS) for recovery deductions for an asset does not fall within a reasonable range of the asset's useful life, the recovery deductions shall not be used as depreciation expense for financial reporting.").

[136] FASB ASC 360-10-35-4; IRC Section 168(b)(4).

[137] FASB ASC 360-10-35-4; IRC Section 168(d).

[138] *See* Section 2.07 and Section 2.08.

[139] *Id.*

[140] *See* Section 2.09.

depreciation from AFUDC is also a permanent book-tax difference. There are two permanent differences that exactly offset each other (book income from capital invested in the project during construction and additional book depreciation expense). The cumulative permanent book-tax differences sum to zero once the property is fully depreciated for book purposes.

Although the TCJA was effective January 1, 2018, for calendar-year companies, temporary book-tax differences that were generated for the nine days between December 22 (the TCJA's enactment date) and December 31, would be recorded at the lower 21 percent corporate tax rate.[141] For the vast majority of book-tax differences, the nine days would be de minimis. However, companies with a large variance between their forecasted book-tax differences and the actual book-tax differences would have a material remeasurement for those nine days.

For example, a company forecasted pension liability of $12 million in 2017 and assume, for simplicity, that the liability is uniform throughout the year. The recognition of pension book expense (and the corresponding liability) often occurs prior to the recognition of the related tax deduction, which generally occurs when the pension liability is funded with cash. The company recorded a deferred tax asset of $350,000 each month ($1 million monthly deductible temporary difference times 35 percent federal corporate tax rate) and expected to record $4.2 million of deferred tax asset in Year 1. In mid-February of 2018, the actuaries determined the forecasted pension liability for 2017 was actually twice as large as originally forecasted. In the absence of the TCJA, the company would have simply doubled the deferred tax asset to $8.4 million. However, since the additional $12 million in pension liability falls within the nine-day window (December 22 to 31, 2017), the deferred tax asset related to that increase is only $2.52 million ($12 million deductible temporary difference times 21 percent federal corporate tax rate). The company's total deferred tax asset in Year 1 for the pension liability should be $6.72 million ($4.2 million plus $2.52 million). Since many companies have financial accounting/tax systems based on the 35 percent tax rate, the GAAP income tax benefit generated by the system would be $8.4 million. The company would need a manual contra entry of $1.68 million to arrive at a net deferred tax asset of $6.72 million.

The dilemma is that most companies would need to perform this time-consuming analysis before they could conclude the amounts are immaterial and do not need to be recorded. However, once the amounts have been computed, it would be better simply to record the entries to create headroom should post-SEC filing errors be identified. The additional headroom may mitigate the need for a restatement of the financial statements. As rule of thumb, cumulative errors that exceed five percent of the reported earnings trigger a potential restatement of the financial statements. Continuing with the example above, assume the company has $100 million in earnings. The threshold for potential restatement is $5 million ($100 million reported earnings times five percent cumulative error rate). After filing the financial statements, the company identified $4 million of errors. If the company did not record the $1.68 million deferred tax adjustment, the cumulative error would be $5.68 million. This is above the five percent threshold of $5 million, which could lead to the company's restating its financial statements. Had the company recorded the $1.68 million deferred tax adjustment to correct the deferred taxes on the pension expense, the only errors were the $4 million of errors and this would be below the $5 million threshold. While an error could be below

[141] Securities and Exchange Commission, Staff Accounting Bulletin No. 118 (Dec. 22, 2017).

the threshold to restate the company's financial statements, it does not mean the error is not a deficiency in management's internal control, as discussed in Chapter 6.

SOX

The SOX Section 404 considerations in the context of real property are to assure that the entity has sufficient controls in place so that appropriate procedures are created and followed to determine the proper tax and financial accounting treatment of the expenditures. One common control is to reconcile the tax accounts. In addition to balancing the tax accounts, the company could analyze each temporary difference and assemble documentation showing when that difference will turn. Unless reconciliation is performed, the statute of limitations may preclude the taxpayer from amending the return to reflect a missed tax deduction. Generally, it is after the property is placed in service that such controls and procedures come into play, primarily due to subsequent repairs, improvements and spare parts for the property. Both the accounting rules and tax rules have de minimis rules that allow a current expense for de minimis capital expenditures. Since book depreciation is generally lower than tax depreciation for long-lived assets, the tax accounts should show deferred tax liabilities. There should be a procedure in place to identify deferred tax assets for further analysis. For instance, the analysis could identify an impairment charge, as discussed in Section 7.12, as the cause for the anomaly.

§ 7.10 Foreign Tax Credits

General Principles

The adoption of a hybrid territorial/worldwide tax system under TCJA has changed the importance of foreign tax credits and related planning structures. The availability of foreign tax credits for tax calculation and resultant financial accounting purposes can be a complex or simple matter, depending, as always, on the facts and circumstances at hand. In the financial accounting context, a common issue concerns carryforward of foreign tax credits and their treatment as deferred tax assets for financial accounting purposes.

> **ILLUSTRATION 7-10:** An entity has excess foreign tax credits of $50,000 for 2022 that it will carry forward to future years. Under the tax laws, the entity carries back any excess foreign tax credits one year and carries forward any excess foreign tax credits for up to ten years (the foreign income taxes are not attributable to global intangible low-tax income). The entity will have a deferred tax asset of $50,000. If it is more likely than not that some or all of the deferred tax asset will not be realized, then the entity must reduce the deferred tax asset by a valuation allowance. Assuming a valuation allowance is not required in this example, a deferred tax asset of $50,000 will be recognized.

Technical Tax Matters

The foreign tax credit provisions provide a means of allowing U.S. corporate taxpayers to avoid the incidence of double taxation of income earned from foreign sources where income taxes are paid to foreign governments. In essence, the pertinent provisions provide that a U.S. corporate taxpayer may credit against its U.S. tax liability income taxes (or taxes in lieu of income taxes) paid to foreign taxing authorities.[142] There are

---

[142] IRC Section 901.

limitations on the amount of foreign tax that may be credited.[143] Congress has segregated categories of income, general and passive, into "baskets" and applying the limitations to each such category to minimize the ability of taxpayers to credit foreign income taxes paid with respect to one type of income against other types of income. The TCJA added two baskets for global intangible low-taxed income (GILTI) and foreign branch income.[144] As a result, there are currently four categories or baskets of income for foreign tax credit purposes: (1) general category income, (2) passive category income, (3) foreign branch income, and (4) GILTI. Under current U.S. tax law, excess foreign tax credits are carried back one year and carried forward ten years.[145] However, foreign tax credits in the GILTI basket may not be carried back or forward and therefore are lost if not utilized in the current year.

An emerging area of contention is whether the foreign tax is an income tax since only income taxes are allowed as foreign tax credits.[146] Until the corporate tax rate was lowered to 21 percent under the TCJA, the widening gap between the U.S. statutory tax rate and a foreign country tax rate, foreign earnings that are repatriated or subject to subpart F do not bring with them sufficient foreign tax credits to offset the U.S. tax. To attract U.S. investments, foreign countries may disguise non-income levies, such as fees and royalties, as an income tax. Lowering the U.S. tax burden on earnings from investments in such a country increases that country's competitiveness. Treasury issued final regulations in December 2021 dramatically changing the requirements of whether a foreign income tax is creditable for U.S. tax purposes.[147] It should be noted that while there is commonality, whether a levy is an income tax for foreign tax credit purposes is independent of whether a levy is a "tax based on income" for ASC 740 purposes.[148]

Another emerging concern by the IRS is foreign business enterprises controlled by U.S. companies conceding disputed local country income taxes because the local income taxes will give rise to a foreign tax credit that lowers the U.S. companies' U.S. taxes. Companies are increasingly having to rely on tax opinions by local country tax controversy counsel to help document that the foreign tax redeterminations and related payments were not voluntary. In general, the IRS has become much more stringent with its documentation and substantiation requirements during examinations.

Financial Accounting for Income Taxes (FASB ASC 740) Recognition and Measurement of Deferred Taxes

In the context of foreign tax credit carryforwards, there do not appear to be recognition and measurement issues, unless there is an uncertain tax position that created the foreign tax liability. In such an event, a loss of the underlying tax issue could cause an increase in foreign tax liability with a corresponding increase in the foreign tax credit carryforward.[149]

---

143 IRC Section 904.

144 IRC Section 904(d).

145 IRC Section 904(c).

146 IRC Section 901 and Treas. Reg. § 1.901–2. A foreign tax credit is allowed for a foreign tax that is paid in lieu of an income tax. IRC Section 903.

147 T.D. 9959, IRB 2022–3 (Jan. 18, 2022).

148 FASB ASC 740–10–15.

149 A similar issue arises in the NOL carryforward context.

Because the U.S. tax laws provide only a one-year carryback of excess foreign tax credits, a portion of the foreign tax credits related to taxes paid in year one may become separated from the underlying foreign source income. Any foreign tax credits that cannot be utilized in the current year or the prior year may be carried forward to each of the ten subsequent years. U.S. tax law also allows taxpayers the option of taking credits for accrued foreign taxes for foreign-source income that is not allowed the 245A 100 percent dividends-received deduction; however, the accrued foreign taxes must be paid within two years.[150] Consequently, the distribution at the end of year one or at any other intervening year may create a need to establish a valuation allowance that would not have been necessary had the distribution been appropriately timed for tax purposes. In considering whether or not to establish such a valuation allowance, the company will take into consideration its foreign tax credit limitation resulting from other operations.[151] Local country tax planning could actually be detrimental. For instance, assume there is a $10 temporary difference due to a foreign subsidiary electing under local law to use accelerated tax depreciation and by doing so, the local taxes are accrued but are not paid within two years. Since foreign taxes were accrued but not paid within two years, there would be no accompanying foreign tax credits when there is an actual or constructive distribution of earnings to the U.S. parent. If the U.S. parent does not have excess foreign tax credits, it would pay U.S. cash taxes for the shortfall. It is not uncommon for complex multinational companies to have local standalone earnings and cash flow performance metrics that do not factor in the global consolidated impact of local decisions. In this example, a local country timing benefit may be a fraction of the permanent US tax expense.

The deferred tax liability based on the difference between the book and tax basis of the shares of foreign subsidiary includes the imposition of a local country's dividend withholding tax. Establishing a deferred tax liability based on future withholding taxes is grounded on the assumption that, absent the assertion of the indefinite reinvestment doctrine, all earnings will be repatriated to the ultimate parent and a withholding tax is a tax liability of the parent that the foreign subsidiary remits to the government on behalf of parent. Clearly there are methods and techniques for repatriating earnings that permanently avoid imposition of the withholding tax. For example, the U.S. parent could sell the shares of foreign subsidiary to an unrelated party. Although IRC Section 1248 would, at the time of sale, impose U.S. tax on the unremitted earnings of the foreign subsidiary that would not qualify for the 245A 100 percent dividends-received deduction on the foreign-source portion of the Section 1248 dividend, local country tax may not be imposed on the sale.[152] Further, depending on the tax status and nationality of the purchaser, the potential withholding tax may not be fully reflected in the sales price of the shares. Nonetheless, the deferred tax liability resulting from the potential withholding tax on repatriation of the foreign earnings will be reflected on the U.S.

[150] IRC Section 905(c).

[151] FASB ASC 740 specifically allows a deferred tax asset to be recognized relating to foreign tax credits provided the company's structure and other tax attributes indicate such credits can be utilized without the need for a valuation allowance. FASB ASC 740–10–30–5.

[152] Most countries impose a capital gains tax on the sale of shares but many will also provide an exemption for qualifying capital gains, such as the "participation exemption" provided by many European countries, or defer to the home country of the seller, provided the seller is resident in a country that has a tax treaty with FCo's country.

parent company's books and in the computation of the U.S. parent company's tax expense.[153]

In the event the shares of the of the foreign subsidiary are ultimately sold without imposition of a local withholding tax, the deferred tax liability would be eliminated by reduction of the tax expense in the year of sale. On the other hand, repatriation of the foreign earnings that defers, but does not permanently avoid, the imposition of local withholding tax through other techniques, such as IRC Section 956 investments in U.S. property, would not reduce or eliminate the deferred tax liability attributable to the potential dividend withholding tax. The TCJA provides that repatriations of earnings through transactions covered by IRC Section 956 (i.e., investments in U.S. property) would no longer result in the imposition of U.S. taxation at the time of such transactions.[154]

General Principles of Deferred Taxes

Foreign tax credit carryforwards are not limited to the amount of deferred tax liabilities recognized for undistributed foreign earnings. However, foreign tax credits generally are limited to the U.S. tax that would have been paid on the foreign source income, and as a result, a valuation allowance may be needed if the recoverability of the foreign tax credit is questionable. For example, in Illustration 7-10, the entity has a foreign tax credit carryforward of $50,000. As long as the entity pays more foreign taxes than U.S. taxes on the foreign pre-tax earnings and other low-tax foreign source income, then the recoverability of the excess foreign tax credit is questionable and a valuation allowance may be required. One should not assume that a simple comparison of a foreign country's statutory rate against the U.S. statutory rate determines whether there will be excess foreign tax credits or a shortfall of foreign tax credits. Similar to the U.S. tax system, a foreign country could offer many tax incentives. A country with a high statutory rate could have an effective tax rate below the U.S. statutory rate due to such incentives.

Certain foreign tax credits arising from but not utilized in the current year are carried back for a refund of taxes paid in a prior year or carried forward to reduce taxes payable in future years. The entity must forecast when a foreign tax credit carryforward will be utilized and whether the carryforward might expire unused in determining the need for recording a valuation allowance. There are both favorable and unfavorable factors that will increase or decrease the need for a valuation allowance. Under current U.S. tax law, certain excess foreign tax credits are carried back one year and carried forward ten years, and the number of baskets has been reduced from nine to four, so that it is less likely that credits will expire unused than in prior periods when the carryforward period was shorter (i.e., five years). The recent addition of the "global intangible low-taxed income" and foreign branch income baskets by the TCJA will operate to limit cross-crediting. The reduction in the U.S. Federal income tax rate from

---

[153] FASB ASC 740 provides that, in the case of domestic subsidiaries, a deferred tax liability is not required to be recognized in cases where the tax law provides a methodology for the company to recover the investment in the subsidiary tax-free and the company intends to utilize such method. FASB ASC 740–30–25–7. FASB notes that examples include tax-free liquidations of 80 percent or more owned subsidiaries (FASB ASC 740–30–25–7(a).) and also certain mergers (FASB ASC 740–30–25–7(b)). It must be noted that this treatment is limited to domestic subsidiaries and does not appear to be applicable to a company's intention to utilize a method to recover unremitted earnings of a foreign subsidiary without including local withholding tax.

[154] T.D. 9859, 84 Fed. Reg. 23716 (May 23, 2019).

35 percent to 21 percent may result in more foreign tax credits that cannot be utilized. A tax receivable is recognized for the amount of taxes paid in prior years that are refundable by carryback of unused (foreign) tax credits of the current year.[155]

An interesting issue arises when the taxpayer elects to deduct foreign taxes but with the intention to subsequently change that election and claim foreign tax credits prior to the expiration of the statute of limitations.[156] Taxpayers typically engage in this election switch to increase cashflow when foreign tax credits cannot be utilized to reduce current taxes, while a deduction will lower taxable income, which reduces cash taxes. The better view is that the taxpayer should account for the foreign tax credits in the current period, including recording any deferred tax asset and determine whether a valuation allowance is needed. As noted, the TCJA has generally diminished the value of planning ideas such as changing the election to deduct foreign taxes.

In situations where the 245A 100 percent dividends-received deduction is inapplicable, the company will only have foreign tax credits by electing to treat foreign taxes as a credit and not default to deducting foreign taxes. Not electing to treat foreign taxes as a credit could result in a worldwide effective tax rate in excess of the U.S. statutory rate. Though counter-intuitive, there are situations where the effective tax rate is actually higher when the company elects to credit foreign income taxes. This typically happens when the foreign tax credits cannot be utilized, thereby requiring a full or partial valuation allowance. Electing to treat foreign income taxes as a credit requires a Section 78 gross-up of the dividends, which increases the U.S. tax on the distribution of the foreign earnings. This is illustrated as follows:

ILLUSTRATION 7-11: USCo is a publicly traded multinational company incorporated in the United States. FCo is a wholly-owned subsidiary of USCo and is incorporated in Country F. FCo is subject to tax in Country F and no other country. The tax rate in Country F is 21 percent and Country F does not impose a withholding tax on dividends remitted to the United States. Assume the U.S. income tax rate is 21 percent, and the impact of state and local taxes is ignored for purposes of this example. During the taxable year, FCo has Country F taxable income of $100 and incurs a Country F tax liability of $21. FCo's pre-tax U.S. earnings and profits is also $100. USCo also has $100 of expenses allocated to foreign source income. FCo remits a $79 dividend to USCo. Assume the dividend is from foreign income earned on or after January 1, 2018, and is not eligible for the 245A 100 percent dividends-received deduction. USCo's U.S. tax on the $79 dividend is computed both with a foreign tax credit and a deduction to illustrate the effective tax rate difference between these two options.

	Credit	**Deduction**
Amount of distribution	$79	$79
U.S. earnings and profits of FCo ($100 minus $21 Country F taxes)	$79	$79

[155] FASB ASC 740–10–55–34.

[156] IRC Section 901. The taxpayer may change its election for a ten-year period regardless of whether the statute of limitations has expired. IRC Section 6511(d)(3)(A); Treas. Reg. § 301.6511(d)–3(a).

Deemed paid foreign tax credits (79/79 times $21)	$21	0
U.S. foreign source income to calculate foreign tax credit limitation		
FCo dividend ($79 plus $21 Section 78 gross up)	$100	n/a
Expenses allocated to foreign source income	($100)	n/a
Foreign source income	0	n/a
U.S. foreign tax credit limitation (21 percent times zero)	0	n/a
Foreign tax credit allowed (lower of $21 or $0)	0	n/a
Tentative U.S. tax (Credit = 21 percent times $100: Deduction = 21 percent times $79)	$21	$16.59
U.S. tax on FCo dividends	$21	$16.59
Effective tax rate on FCo's $100 of pre-tax earnings	42%	37.59%

The impact of the company's decision to treat foreign taxes as a credit or a deduction must be disclosed in the company's financial statements in the rate reconciliation table.[157] Other items also disclosed in the rate reconciliation table are permanent differences, various tax credits and the impact of foreign operations subject to taxation at rates either in excess of or less than the U.S. statutory tax rate.

SOX

The SOX Section 404 considerations in the context of foreign tax credits are to assure that the entity has sufficient controls in place so that all appropriate procedures are created and followed to determine the proper tax and financial accounting treatment of foreign tax credits. Responsibility for foreign tax credit matters is typically in the tax department of a corporation, so the appropriate control would be to ensure that the foreign credit limitation has been determined appropriately. In the case of foreign tax credit carryforwards, an appropriate task is to monitor the expiring carryforwards to assure that they do not expire unused. Finally, prior to the enactment of the TCJA, companies that have asserted the indefinite reinvestment doctrine are generally very lax in compiling and analyzing data to support the foreign earnings and profits pool, the foreign tax pool, and the allocation of U.S. tax deductions to foreign source income. The expansion of subpart F to include GILTI will require companies to have the tax documentation and data necessary to calculate the amount of deemed paid foreign taxes and the amount of foreign tax credits that may be utilized to support the foreign tax credit. Such support requires evidence of the underlying tax payments, such tax receipts or some other acceptable documentation. Wire transfers and cancelled checks typically are not sufficient. This may be difficult to assemble when many years have elapsed between the tax payments and the time when the tax credits are claimed on the returns

157 FASB ASC 740–10–50; 17 CFR § 210.4–08—General notes to financial statements.

and audited by the tax authorities. Companies should collect tax receipts and documentation on a contemporaneous basis.

§ 7.11 Intangibles and Goodwill

General Principles

The explosive growth of technology has resulted in intangible assets being a major asset class that includes goodwill. It is often straightforward to identify the cost, useful life, and other elements that are pertinent to the ability of the entity to amortize the cost of the intangible asset for tax and book purposes. In many situations, the entity may want to claim a rapid deduction for tax purposes and have the asset deemed to be non-amortizable for financial accounting purposes (so that its earnings are not reduced by the amortization of an asset that may actually have an indefinite useful life). However, the flip side is that the rapid introduction of new technologies means equally fast obsolescence of existing technologies that will trigger potentially large impairment charges against earnings.[158] For U.S. income tax purposes, purchased goodwill is amortizable over a 15-year period.[159] For financial accounting purposes, goodwill is not amortizable but is reduced if it is impaired.[160]

ILLUSTRATION 7-12:[161] At the acquisition date, the book basis and tax basis of goodwill are $600 and $900, respectively. For tax purposes, the amortization of goodwill will result in tax deductions of $60 in each of years one through fifteen. Those deductions result in a current tax benefit in years one through fifteen. For financial accounting purposes, goodwill has not been impaired and, as a result, the entity does not write down its goodwill.

Technical Tax Matters

The technical taxation principles relating to amortization of intangibles have evolved over the years.[162] The accelerated cost recovery system rules are available only for tangible property.[163] Under traditional depreciation principles, intangibles were eligible for depreciation over a useful life if this could be determined with reasonable accuracy, such as for patents and copyrights.[164] An intangible asset, the useful life of which was not limited, would not receive an allowance for depreciation.[165] Not surprisingly, taxpayers sought to develop strategies to depreciate or amortize assets that have many of the characteristics of goodwill but also a limited useful life that can be estimated with reasonable accuracy, even achieving success in some circumstances. In many business combinations, the acquiring corporation would allocate the purchase price to depreciable tangible assets and intangible assets other than goodwill (such as

---

[158] *See* Section 7.12 (Impairment).

[159] IRC Section 197.

[160] FASB ASC 350–20–35–1.

[161] FASB ASC 805–740–55–9.

[162] *See generally Federal Taxation of Income, Estates and Gifts* ¶ 23.4.1.

[163] *See* IRC Section 168(a).

[164] *See* Treas. Reg. § 1.167(a)–3(a).

[165] *Id.*

covenants not to compete).[166] These strategies occupied a significant amount of judicial and administrative attention.

Congress addressed these matters in 1993 with the enactment of IRC Section 197, which allows the cost of an "amortizable section 197 intangible" to be amortized ratably over 15 years, beginning with the month in which the intangible is acquired.[167] The term *amortizable section 197 intangible* includes goodwill, going concern value, covenants not to compete, customer lists, and most other intangibles held in connection with a trade or business or an investment activity.[168] In enacting IRC Section 197, Congress intended "to simplify the law regarding the amortization of intangibles" by allowing virtually all intangible property acquired by purchase to be depreciated over an amortization period (of 15 years), which is longer than the period previously used for many arguably depreciable assets (e.g., customer lists and deposit base) and clearly depreciable assets (e.g., covenants not to compete and patents).[169] IRC Section 197 eliminates the issues of whether an intangible's useful life can be estimated with reasonable accuracy and, if so, the length of that useful life.[170] Not surprisingly, there are many technical issues that have to be addressed under IRC Section 197 to determine whether amortization is appropriate.[171]

Financial Accounting for Income Taxes (FASB ASC 740) Recognition and Measurement of Deferred Taxes

One entity may acquire another entity in either a taxable business combination or a non-taxable business combination (i.e., a tax-free reorganization). If the acquisition is a taxable business combination, then the purchase price is allocated to the assets and liabilities of the acquired entity for both financial accounting and tax purposes. If the acquisition is a non-taxable business combination (such as an "A" reorganization), then the purchase price is allocated to the acquired entity's assets and liabilities for financial accounting purposes. For tax purposes, however, the tax bases of the assets and liabilities of the target corporation carry over to the acquiring entity.[172]

FASB ASC 805 requires that the assets acquired, liabilities assumed, and any noncontrolling interest in the acquiree be measured at the fair value on the acquisition date.[173] As a result, acquisition-related costs are recognized separately from the acquisition and are generally expensed.[174] The expensing of acquisition-related costs (with the exception of debt and equity issuance costs) provided for in FASB ASC 805 is a significant change from SFAS No. 141, which required capitalization of such costs. In

---

166 *Newark Morning Ledger Co. v. United States*, 507 U.S. 546, 550 (1993) (the Court allowed the purchaser of a newspaper to depreciate the portion of the purchase price allocable to "paid subscribers").

167 IRC Section 197(a), IRC Section 197(b). *See* Treas. Reg. § 1.197–2(f).

168 IRC Sections 197(c) and (d).

169 *See generally Federal Taxation of Income, Estates and Gifts* ¶ 23.4.1.

170 Amendments to the regulations, adopted in 2004, allow taxpayers to amortize many intangibles not covered by IRC Section 197 over 15 or 25 years. *See* Treas. Reg. § 1.167(a)–3(b)(1).

171 *See generally Federal Taxation of Income, Estates and Gifts* ¶ 23.4.1.

172 IRC Section 362(b).

173 FASB ASC 805–20–30–1.

174 FASB ASC 805–10–25–23. Acquisition-related costs, generally referred to as transaction costs, include finder's fees; advisory, legal, accounting, valuation and other professional fees; general administrative costs; and the costs of registering and issuing debt and equity securities. *Id.*

addition, restructuring costs the acquirer expects to incur are also recognized separately from the acquisition.

An acquirer must recognize identifiable assets acquired and liabilities assumed as of the acquisition date (measured at their acquisition date fair values) only if it is more likely than not that the identifiable assets and liabilities meet the definition of an asset or liability under CON 6.[175] If the more likely than not standard is not met with respect to an identifiable asset or liability, then the costs are not part of applying the acquisition method. The acquirer accounts for the costs in its post-combination financial statements, in accordance with other GAAP principles (particularly FASB ASC 450).[176]

When one entity acquires another entity in a business combination, whether taxable or non-taxable, a deferred tax liability or asset is recognized for an acquired entity's taxable or deductible temporary differences (i.e., differences between the recognized values (i.e., book bases) and the tax bases of the acquired entity's assets and liabilities).[177] A deferred tax liability is not recognized, however, for a difference between the book basis and the tax basis of goodwill if the goodwill is not amortizable for tax purposes, for leveraged leases, and for acquired temporary differences relating to the excess of the book basis over the tax basis of an investment in a foreign subsidiary or a foreign corporate joint venture that is essentially permanent in duration.[178]

FASB requires the acquirer to recognize goodwill as of the acquisition date.[179] Goodwill is measured as a residual, by taking the sum of the consideration transferred by the buyer and adding it to the fair value of any noncontrolling interest and reducing that sum by the fair values of the identifiable net assets acquired.[180] FASB also requires the acquirer to recognize contingent consideration at the acquisition date (measured at its fair value on that date).[181]

If a taxable business combination creates tax-amortizable goodwill, then a deferred tax liability is recognized on the acquisition date and it is reversed over time as goodwill is amortized on the tax return but not amortized for financial reporting (i.e., the tax basis of the goodwill will become less than the book basis of the goodwill as it is amortized for tax purposes). A similar situation arises with respect to indefinite lived intangible assets that are amortized for tax purposes but not for financial reporting purposes (i.e., the tax basis will become less than the book basis as tax amortization begins).

Since 1993, purchased goodwill is deductible for U.S. Federal income tax purposes over a 15-year period.[182] The book basis and the tax basis of goodwill are each separated

---

[175] FASB ASC 805–20–25–2 and FASB ASC 805–20–25–19.

[176] *Id.*

[177] FASB ASC 805–740–25–2.

[178] FASB ASC 805–740–25–3.

[179] FASB ASC 805–30–30–1.

[180] *Id.*

[181] FASB ASC 805–30–25–5.

[182] IRC Section 197. In enacting IRC Section 197 as part of the Omnibus Budget Reconciliation Act of 1993 (enactment date of August 10, 1993), Congress permitted companies the option of electing to retroactively apply it to business combinations occurring after July 25, 1991. A FASB Task Force concluded that the tax benefit related to tax-deductible goodwill in excess of the book basis of goodwill is included in income from continuing operations at the enactment date if the enterprise expects to retroactively apply IRC Section 197. FASB Task Force, EITF Issue No. 93–12, Recognition and Movement of the Tax Benefit of Excess Tax-Deductible Goodwill Resulting from a Retroactive Change in Tax Law (Sept. 23, 1993). A current tax benefit is reported for the retroactive amortization of goodwill (from the combination date to the enactment date). A

into two components as of the acquisition date for purposes of the deferred tax calculations.[183] The first component of each is equal to the lesser of: goodwill for financial reporting or tax-deductible goodwill. The second component of each is equal to the remainder (or excess) of each, i.e., the remainder, if any, of goodwill for financial reporting, or the remainder, if any, of tax-deductible goodwill. Any future difference that arises between the book basis and tax basis of the first component of goodwill is a temporary difference that will give rise to a deferred tax liability or asset.

For the second component of goodwill, if tax-deductible goodwill is greater than the book basis of goodwill, then the tax benefit is recognized as a deferred tax asset. However, if the book basis of goodwill is greater than the tax-deductible goodwill, then no deferred tax liabilities will be recognized (either at the acquisition date or in future years).

In Illustration 7-12, at the acquisition date, the book basis of goodwill is $600 (before adjustment for the tax benefit of goodwill) and the tax basis of goodwill is $900. For tax purposes, the amortization of goodwill will result in tax deductions of $60 in each of years one through fifteen. These deductions result in a tax benefit in years one through fifteen. For financial reporting, goodwill has not been impaired. The combined U.S. federal and state tax rate is 30 percent each year. At the acquisition date, the book basis of goodwill has to be adjusted for the tax benefit associated with goodwill. The computation is as follows ("simultaneous equations method"):[184]

> Tax Rate ÷ (1 – Tax Rate) × Preliminary Temporary Difference = Deferred Tax Asset
>
> Using the numbers in the example, the formula is: 30% ÷ (1 – 30%) × $300 = $129

Therefore, the book basis of goodwill is adjusted by the $129 of deferred tax asset so it is $471 at the acquisition date. As discussed above, the goodwill is separated into two components as follows:

	Book Basis	Tax Basis
First component (lesser of goodwill for financial reporting or tax-deductible goodwill)	$471	$471
Second component (remainder)	$0	$429
Total goodwill	$471	$900

One of the more significant changes made in accounting for business combinations is with respect to a bargain purchase.[185] A bargain purchase occurs in a business combination when, on the acquisition date, the total fair value of the identifiable net assets acquired exceeds the sum of the fair value of the consideration transferred plus any noncontrolling interest in the acquiree.[186] The bargain purchase element is

deferred tax benefit is reported for the excess of tax-deductible goodwill (less the retroactive amortization) over the book basis of the goodwill.

[183] FASB ASC 805–740–25–8; FASB ASC 805–740–25–9.

[184] FASB ASC 805–740–55–9.

[185] FASB ASC 805–30–25.

[186] FASB ASC 805–30–25–2.

recognized by the acquirer as gain and therefore included in earnings.[187] Previously, FASB treated the bargain purchase element as negative goodwill and allocated it as a pro rata reduction of the amounts otherwise assigned to the acquired assets (i.e., as a reduction of the book bases of the acquired assets).

In a business combination, the acquiring entity may recognize a valuation allowance with respect to a deferred tax asset recorded for the deductible temporary differences attributable to the acquired entity's assets and liabilities, net operating loss carryforwards, or tax credit carryforwards on the acquisition date. Any decrease or elimination of the valuation allowance after the acquisition date and within the measurement period that results from the company's discovering facts and circumstances that existed at the acquisition date will reduce any goodwill created in the acquisition. The acquisition goodwill cannot be reduced below zero and any additional decrease in the valuation allowance is treated as a bargain purchase.[188] Any change in the valuation allowance for an acquired entity's deferred tax asset outside of the measurement period (and is not based on facts and circumstances existing at the acquisition date) is reported as a reduction or increase to income tax expense (or as an adjustment to contributed capital). Due to the different earnings impact based on whether the adjustment is made within or without the measurement period, companies should carefully examine all potential material adjustments within the measurement period.

SOX

The SOX Section 404 considerations in the context of intangibles and goodwill are to assure that appropriate procedures are created and followed to determine the proper tax and financial accounting treatment of intangibles and in particular the more complex goodwill issues throughout the entity. When a business combination is pursued for business synergies, management may allocate the book goodwill to entities that will benefit from the combination. Book goodwill could also be allocated when a business is reorganized. This could present complexities in reconciling numerous tax accounts and eliminations. One approach is to compute the expected results by disregarding the management allocation and compare that against the cumulative balances in the accounts of the entities that were allocated the accounting goodwill. The allocation of book goodwill will also change the outside book basis of the impacted entities without changing the outside tax basis. This could create a deferred tax liability that must be recorded, and an offsetting deferred tax asset in a related entity that cannot be recorded. Section 2.16 discusses whether a deferred tax liability or deferred tax asset should be recorded on the outside book-tax basis difference of entities engaged in business combinations.

§ 7.12 Impairment

General Principles

As discussed in Section 7.11, goodwill is subject to periodic impairment testing. Impairment testing is also required under Topic 323, *Investments—Equity Method and Joint Ventures,* for joint ventures and investments that are accounted for under the

[187] *Id.*

[188] FASB ASC 805–740–45–2.

equity method. The company will take an immediate write-off against its earnings for the impairment charge.

> **ILLUSTRATION 7-13:** USCo owns Sub, which is a C corporation. Sub owns a U.S. factory that manufactures widgets. Due to foreign competition, the factory has incurred several years of book losses. USCo takes an impairment charge and writes its $1 million book investment in Sub down to zero.

Technical Tax Matters

A taxpayer that owns a security is permitted a loss deduction for the security if it becomes worthless during the year.[189] The taxpayer is treated as having sold the worthless security on the last day of the taxable year.[190] A security is defined as a share of stock in a corporation, a right to subscribe to a share of stock in a corporation, or an evidence of indebtedness, issued by a corporation or government, with interest coupons or in registered form.[191] If the taxpayer is a domestic corporation and the security is in an affiliated corporation, the taxpayer may be entitled to an ordinary loss deduction.[192] A taxpayer may also claim a loss deduction on abandonment or worthlessness of a partnership interest.[193]

Financial Accounting for Income Taxes (FASB ASC 740) Recognition and Measurement of Deferred Taxes

The accounting for impairment is complex and a fair amount of judgment is required, see FASB ASC 323, *Investments—Equity Method and Joint Ventures*. There is a certain level of commonality between the valuation allowance principle covered in Section 2.09, and the accounting for impairments. For instance, FASB ASC 323–10–35–31 provides that "[a] series of operating losses of an investee or other factors may indicate that a decrease in value of the investment has occurred which is other-than-temporary and which should be recognized even though the decrease in value is in excess of what would otherwise be recognized by application of the equity method." The difference between the impairment charge and any current tax deduction from a decline in the value of the business asset is a temporary difference resulting in deferred taxes. In Illustration 7-13, USCo would record a deferred tax asset of $210,000 (assuming a 21 percent tax rate) at the same time it recorded the $1 million impairment charge resulting in a net earnings loss of $790,000 provided the deferred tax asset does not require a valuation allowance.

There are scenarios where this temporary difference could become, in effect, a permanent difference due to a valuation allowance. When an asset is impaired without a corresponding current tax deduction, the temporary difference is recorded as a deferred tax asset. The negative earnings impact of the impairment has been mitigated by this tax benefit. The deferred tax asset is subject to a valuation allowance evaluation.

There are even scenarios where the company does not even get to the valuation allowance evaluation because the company cannot record the deferred tax asset. Assume

---

[189] IRC Section 165(g).

[190] IRC Section 165(g)(1).

[191] IRC Section 165(g)(2).

[192] IRC Section 165(g)(3).

[193] *See, e.g.*, IRC Section 165(a); Rev. Rul. 93–80, 1993–2 C.B. 239; *MCM Investment Management, LLC v. Commissioner*, T.C. Memo. 2019–158 (2019).

the impaired asset is an investment in a corporate entity. In Illustration 7-13, assume USCo owns only 30 percent of Sub. To recover this book-tax difference would require the sale of the 30 percent interest in Sub. FASB ASC 740–30–25–9 does not allow the accrual of deferred taxes where the deferred taxes will turn only on the sale of the asset and such sale is not contemplated by the company. As discussed in detail in Section 2.16, this rule applies to investments in subsidiaries and corporate joint ventures. The indefinite reinvestment doctrine can only be asserted for foreign subsidiaries and foreign corporate joint ventures. Whether the subsidiary or corporate joint venture is foreign will depend on their country of tax residency and the country of tax residency of their parent company. To be classified as foreign, the parent company must be tax resident in a country different that its subsidiary or its interests in the corporate joint venture.

Typically, an impairment charge indicates a declining business investment and, as expected, the company may not view such an investment as strategic any longer and may be more than willing to part with it. The company must be careful balancing its strategic position on the investment with the financial/tax accounting treatment. As noted, impairment results in a deferred tax asset. When an asset is impaired, the book basis is reduced so there would be lower book depreciation. The tax depreciation deduction is unchanged since the impairment is not a taxable event. If as a result of the impairment, there is a net deferred tax asset, the valuation allowance analysis will look at when that deferred tax asset flips to a deferred tax liability. This cross-over point is how long the company needs to hold the impaired investment to avoid taking a valuation allowance on the deferred tax asset. If the company's management does not intend to keep the investment until this cross-over point, this could result in a partial or full valuation allowance. The impairment rules look at whether the investment will be recovered dollar-for-dollar. If the company does not hold the investment but intends to sell it and the tax loss is a capital loss, which the company cannot utilize due to not having sufficient capital gains,[194] the company will need a valuation allowance on the deferred tax asset that represents the capital loss. However, if the company intends to hold the investment long enough that the deferred tax asset flips to a deferred tax liability, it can avoid recognizing a valuation allowance.

ILLUSTRATION 7-14: Similar to Illustration 7-13, USCo records a $1 million impairment charge on its investment in Sub. The impairment charge was on January 1 of Year 6. In Year 1, USCo contributed $3 million to Sub to fund Sub's acquisition of the U.S. factory for $3 million. Assume book depreciation is straight-line over 20 years resulting in annual book depreciation of $150,000 from Years 1 through 5, but dropping down to $83,333 thereafter due to the impairment. For simplicity, tax depreciation is also straight-line, but over 15 years so there is an annual tax depreciation of $200,000 (ignore half-year convention). The schedule of book-tax temporary differences for the U.S. factory is as follows:

[194] IRC Section 1211(a).

Year	Book Depreciation	Tax Depreciation	Difference	Deferred Tax Asset/(Deferred Tax Liability)
1	$150,000	$200,000	($50,000)	($10,500)
2	150,000	200,000	(50,000)	(21,000)
3	150,000	200,000	(50,000)	(31,500)
4	150,000	200,000	(50,000)	(42,000)
5	150,000	200,000	(50,000)	(52,500)
Impairment	1,000,000		1,000,000	157,500
6	83,333	200,000	(116,667)	133,000
7	83,333	200,000	(116,667)	108,500
8	83,333	200,000	(116,667)	84,000
9	83,333	200,000	(116,667)	59,500
10	83,333	200,000	(116,667)	35,000
11	83,333	200,000	(116,667)	10,500
12	83,333	200,000	(116,667)	(14,000)
13	83,333	200,000	(116,667)	(38,501)
14	83,333	200,000	(116,667)	(63,001)
15	83,333	200,000	(116,667)	(87,501)
16	83,333	0	83,333	(70,001)
17	83,333	0	83,333	(52,501)
18	83,333	0	83,333	(35,001)
19	83,333	0	83,333	(17,501)
20	83,333	0	83,333	0

Immediately after the impairment, the cumulative deferred tax asset is $157,500. It is not unusual for management simultaneously to announce the company has retained some New York investment banking firm to evaluate alternatives for the impaired investment. This could be strong evidence that the company intends to dispose of the company. The $157,500 of deferred tax asset could be subject to a full valuation allowance. At the time of the impairment, the book basis of the investment is $1,250,000 and the tax basis is $2 million. If the investment is sold for the impaired book value of $1,250,000 there is no book gain or loss but there is a $750,000 tax loss. If the tax loss is a capital loss and USCo does not have any capital gain, the $750,000 capital loss would not result in a $157,500 tax benefit ($750,000 loss times 21 percent tax rate). USCo would need a valuation allowance on the $157,500 deferred tax asset that represents the capital loss. However, if USCo intends to hold the investment until Year 12, which is another seven years after the impairment, the deferred tax asset will have flipped to a deferred tax liability of $14,000. A management assertion that it intends to hold the investment for another seven years could allow USCo to avoid recognizing the valuation allowance on the $157,500 of deferred tax asset.

SOX

A common misunderstanding is that not all impairment charges will be mitigated by a corresponding reduction in financial accounting tax expense. There could be no deferred tax asset and even if the company is allowed to record a deferred tax asset, it could be offset by a full or partial valuation allowance. In certain situations, the company could restructure its investments to allow it to record the deferred tax asset and to avoid a valuation allowance. For instance, in Illustration 7-14, converting Sub from a regarded entity to a disregarded entity could allow USCo to record a deferred tax asset that it otherwise could not have recorded.

§ 7.13 Joint Ventures

General Principles

International joint ventures have become familiar vehicles for the conduct of international business. Typically, such ventures, or joint operating arrangements, are conducted between unrelated parties for the purpose of exploiting specific business opportunities. There has been an increase in joint ventures between related parties primarily for two reasons. First, companies have accumulated large cash positions outside of the U.S. due to the indefinite reinvestment doctrine asserted by these companies and when such cash is trapped at the local country level, an equity investment with a sister subsidiary may be desirable. Even after the U.S. shifted to a hybrid territorial/worldwide tax regime by enacting TCJA, U.S. companies could continue to assert the indefinite reinvestment doctrine due to local country taxes and U.S. state taxes on repatriation. Second, a joint venture may be an effective vehicle to shift earnings to low tax countries. Many of the discrete issues discussed in this chapter can arise in joint venture contexts.

For example, there are a variety of financial accounting, valuation, and transfer pricing issues to be addressed in related party joint venture situations. Other than transfer pricing, many of these issues are present in joint ventures with third parties. For purposes of the illustration, we will use the following abbreviations for financial accounting (FA), international financial accounting rules (IFRS), tax (T) and transfer pricing (TP) with respect to joint ventures (JV) as illustrated in the following hypothetical transaction:

ILLUSTRATION 7-15: XCo and YCo are unrelated parties located in different countries. They contemplate establishing a JV to conduct a business in a third country. They ask their respective advisors "what are the transfer pricing related issues that we need to address as we negotiate our joint venture ("JV") agreement?" An advisor could respond using the following diagram and following outline of comments:

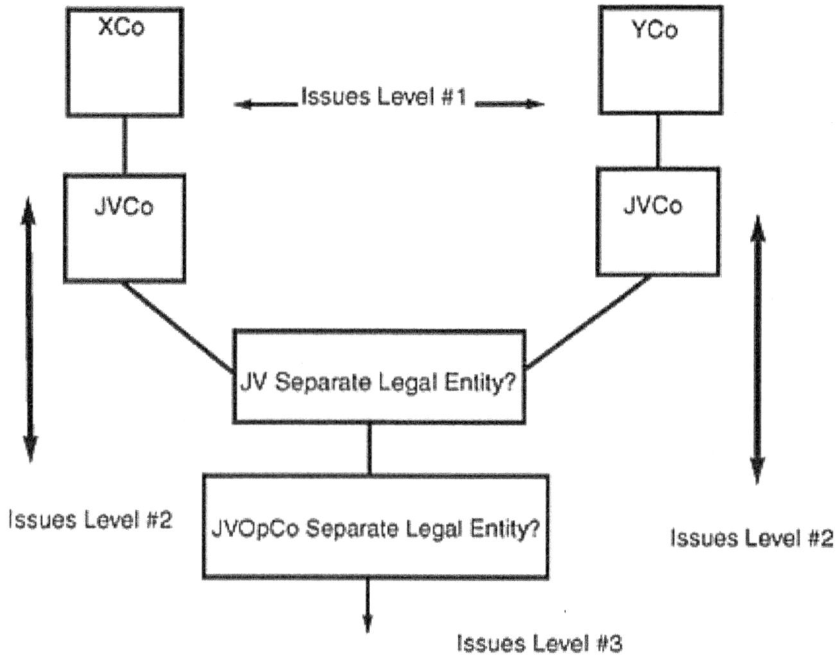

Issues Level #1: At the participant level for one or all parties (Participant Level)

At the participant level, relevant issues may include:

1. Valuation of tangible assets to be contributed or made available to the joint venture (such as land rights, used equipment, or buildings). There may also be need for an allocation of a purchase or transactional price between assets that are and are not subject to depreciation or amortization. [FA, IFRS, T]
2. Valuation of intangible assets (normally intellectual property, such as brand, patent, license, work force, know-how, or other potential items). This can also involve enterprise valuation where businesses or legal entities are to be transferred, or made available, to the joint venture. [FA, IFRS, T, TP]
3. Valuation of services to be provided to the joint venture. [FA, T, TP]
4. Evaluation of currency, capital, or guarantee matters. [FA, IFRS, T, TP]
5. Functional currency of the participant. [FA, IFRS, T]
6. Impact of valuations on licenses and other documentation that must be secured in the host country to operate the joint venture enterprise.
7. Identifying and reconciling local financial accounting standards and IFRS differences.

8. Coordination and advising of valuation and transfer pricing matters, including conducting transfer pricing studies for tax compliance or submission for advance pricing agreements.

Issues Level #2: At the JV or JVOpCo level (Venture Level)

The functional currency of the venture can be a major point when the parties are subject to different financial accounting standards (U.S. GAAP, IFRS, etc.). The denomination of revenues, expenses, and debt could have different financial earnings implications to the participants. Although a participant could execute derivative contracts and hedges to mitigate the currency impact, it is costly and could lead to a tax whipsaw situation where hedging gains are taxable while hedging losses are subject to a valuation allowance. The level of ownership and control is another key consideration since it could impact the financial reporting of the Venture's earnings (e.g., consolidated earnings, equity earnings) and the need to record deferred taxes on the outside book-tax basis difference in the investee, as discussed in Section 2.16.

The principal transfer pricing issue at the venture level will be whether the participants and joint venture are under "common" or "effective control" in the pertinent countries (as discussed with respect to Illustration 7-15). The country in which operations are conducted may be highly concerned as to whether the dealings between the venture and the participants or among the venture's group of controlled entities are arm's length in nature.

If there is any ground for concern about control, each of the matters noted at the Participants Level will have implications at the Venture Level, whether or not joint venture companies are formed.

Issues Level #3: At the project level (Local Country Level)

Again, each of the matters noted above will have implications at the Local Country Level. There may also be additional issues, including the following:

1. Licensing requirements.
2. Financial reporting standards, such as the functional currency of the joint venture entity.
3. Tax compliance matters, including local or regional taxation, and national taxation, including the functional currency used in determining taxable income.
4. Customs valuation.
5. International taxation matters—such as withholding obligations on some or all payments made to the participants or third parties; local taxable presence of the participants; presence of a "permanent establishment, treaty availability; or others, depending on the situation.
6. Transfer pricing documentation requirements.
7. Availability and desirability of an advance pricing agreement to minimize transfer pricing exposures and provide certainty.

8. Evaluation of "uncertain tax positions" where applicable, such as in U.S. GAAP situations, either at the Venture Level or Participants Level.
9. Local investment incentives that could be impacted by transfer pricing.

In short, there are a wide range of valuation, financial accounting, tax, and transfer pricing issues inherent in any international joint venture. Analysis of each of these issues, or others that may be appropriate in the context of specific situations, will ultimately lead to appropriate respective terms in establishing the joint venture.

SOX

There are both known and unknown differences between each participant's preferred tax reporting position on matters, in particular, the items listed above, both at the participant level and the joint venture level. Known differences should be resolved and the agreed position reflected in the joint venture agreement. The joint venture agreement should clearly set forth a procedure to resolve differences that may arise subsequent to the execution of the agreement. A common SOX failure is not having someone responsible for monitoring the tax and commercial terms in the joint venture agreement and providing timely notification as required by the agreement.

§ 7.14 Life Insurance

General Principles

Life insurance policies have grown in popularity and sophistication to serve a variety of business needs, ranging from funding deferred compensation plans to mitigating the economic impact from the unexpected death of key employees. When an entity purchases a whole life insurance policy on one of its corporate executives, then part of the premium payment it makes is an expense and part is a cash reserve, which is an asset on the statement of financial position.[195] For tax purposes, no portion of the premium is deductible.[196] Rather, the entire premium payment is capitalized as part of the entity's basis in the life insurance policy.

ILLUSTRATION 7-16: A corporation purchases a $1 million whole life insurance policy on one its corporate executives with the corporation the beneficiary on the policy. The corporation pays a premium of $10,000 per year. Part of the premium is for life insurance protection and part of the premium is for the cash reserve (i.e., cash surrender value). For financial accounting purposes, the corporation will expense the portion of the premium for life insurance protection of the corporate executive and will also set up an asset for the cash reserve portion of the premium. For tax purposes, however, no portion of the premium is deductible with the result that the entire premium payment is capitalized as part of the basis in the life insurance policy. Consequently, a

---

[195] FASB ASC 325–30. *See, e.g.*, FASB, Technical Bulletin No. 85–4, Accounting for Purchases of Life Insurance (Nov. 1985); FASB Task Force, EITF Issue No. 06–5, Accounting for Purchases of Life Insurance—Determining the Amount That Could Be Realized in Accordance with FASB Technical Bulletin No. 85–4 (June 15, 2006; Sept. 7, 2006).

[196] IRC Section 264(a)(1).

difference arises between the book basis and the tax basis of the life insurance policy.

Technical Tax Matters

A corporation may not deduct the premiums paid on a life insurance policy of one of its corporate executives if the corporation is the beneficiary under the policy.[197] However, if the executive dies and the corporation collects the face amount of the policy, the entire proceeds are excluded from the corporation's gross income.[198]

Financial Accounting for Income Taxes (FASB ASC 740) Recognition and Measurement of Deferred Taxes

In Illustration 7-16, the tax position should be certain and thus no recognition and measurement issues should arise.

General Principles of Deferred Taxes

If a corporation purchases a whole life insurance policy on one of its corporate executives with the corporation the beneficiary of the policy and the corporate executive later dies, then the corporation will receive the face amount of the policy and will record a gain for financial accounting purposes equal to the excess of the face amount of the policy over the cash surrender value. For tax purposes, however, the entire proceeds of the policy are excluded from gross income. In Illustration 7-16, if the corporate executive dies and the corporation receives $1 million when the cash surrender value is $300,000, the corporation will record a gain of $700,000 for financial accounting purposes. For tax purposes, however, the entire $1 million is excluded from gross income. As a result, the excess of the cash surrender value over the premiums paid becomes a permanent difference. This favorable permanent difference has led hedge funds to quietly offer products known as "insurance dedicated funds" that use a private placement insurance policy for hedge fund clients to invest in certain investments, such as the hedge fund, and allow profits to accumulate tax free until the client dies and the beneficiaries are paid out.[199]

If, however, the corporation intends to surrender the policy for its cash surrender value, any difference between the cash surrender value and its book basis is gain (or loss) for purposes of financial accounting and the corporation records a tax expense (or benefit) on the gain (or loss). In other words, unless the corporation asserts that it intends to hold the policy to term, the corporation must record tax expense on the book earnings. For tax purposes, the difference between the cash surrender value and the corporation's basis in the policy is gross income (or a deduction) to the corporation.[200] As a result, the excess of cash surrender value over the premiums paid becomes a temporary difference.[201]

---

[197] *Id.*

[198] IRC Section 101(a)(1).

[199] *See* Sonali Basak and Tom Metcalf, *Insurance Is the Hot New Way to Avoid Taxes*, Bloomberg (June 28, 2017).

[200] IRC Section 61(a). A corporation's basis in the life insurance policy is the aggregate of premiums paid. IRC Section 72(e)(5).

[201] FASB ASC 740–10–25–30.

SOX

A key SOX Section 404 control is that for each reporting period, the corporation should re-evaluate its assertion on whether it intends to hold the policy to term or whether it is likely the policy may be surrendered. Many of the considerations for this assertion are similar to the assertion on the indefinite reinvestment doctrine, such as the company's cash needs. A related consideration in making this assertion is the earnings volatility. To illustrate, the company has $1,000 of book gain from life insurance policies and the company's combined federal and state tax rate is 30 percent. If the company asserts that it will hold the policies to term, there is no tax expense so the company's earnings are increased by the entire $1,000. If the company does not assert it will hold the policies to term, the tax expense is $300 leaving earnings of $700. The assertion could magnify earnings shortfall during an economic down cycle because not only will operating profits suffer, but book losses on insurance policies will not be mitigated by tax benefits. Of course, the corporation could change its assertion and could surrender the policy for cash provided such a change is supportable (e.g., change in assertion made during an economic downturn). Similar to the indefinite reinvestment doctrine, when the assertion is changed, the company must record the deferred taxes that have not been recorded during the period it asserted it would hold the policies to term. To support management's assertion, comprehensive and contemporaneous documentation in support of the assertion must be prepared.

§ 7.15 Net Operating Losses

General Principles

Net operating losses ("NOLs") raise a multitude of interesting and challenging tax and financial accounting issues. There are a number of limitations on the use of NOLs. These include restrictions resulting from a change of control of the loss corporation and use of a corporation's NOLs under the separate return limitation year rules ("SRLY") after the loss corporation is acquired by a consolidated group. Another limitation is application of the so-called tax shelter reportable transaction rules of Treas. Reg. § 1.6011–4 for losses created in a potentially tax motivated manner. The TCJA further limits NOLs to 80 percent of taxable income and no longer allows carryback of NOLs, but does allow an indefinite carryforward.[202] Further, NOLs raise a host of financial accounting issues, including what financial earnings benefit a company is entitled to report with respect to its NOL.

ILLUSTRATION 7-17:[203]

USCo, a U.S. corporation, has a wholly-owned subsidiary (USSub) with certain deferred tax assets as a result of several years of losses from operations (i.e., net operating losses). The amount of the losses, which are not in dispute, consist of legitimate operating expenditures that are all currently deductible. Likewise, there is no uncertainty regarding the amount of USCo's gross income from which USCo's operational loss was offset.

Management of USCo has determined that it is more likely than not that the subsidiary will not generate sufficient taxable income to realize those deferred tax assets. Thus, USCo must recognize a full valuation allowance for

[202] IRC Section 172.

[203] FASB ASC 740–10–55–97; FASB ASC 740–10–55–98.

those deferred tax assets. Management however identifies tax-planning strategies that might enable the realization of those deferred tax assets. Although management believes that USCo will not be subject to penalties if the tax strategies are challenged by the taxing authority, management concludes that it is not more likely than not that the strategies would be sustained upon examination based on the technical tax merits. Those tax strategies may not be used to reduce the valuation allowance for the deferred tax assets.[204]

Technical Tax Matters

If, for a given taxable year, a corporation's deductions exceed its gross income, the corporation has an NOL equal to the excess.[205] Prior to the TCJA, a corporation's NOL was generally carried back as a deduction to the corporation's second taxable year preceding the year in which the loss was incurred, and then to the first preceding year.[206] To the extent any portion of the NOL remained, the NOL was permitted to be carried forward to each of the loss corporation's succeeding 20 years, until either fully offset by taxable income, or subject to a restriction under the tax laws.[207] Under the TCJA, however, NOLs arising in tax years beginning after December 31, 2017, are limited to 80 percent of taxable income. The new law also generally repeals the carryback provisions, and provides for the indefinite carryforward of NOLs arising in tax years ending after December 31, 2017, as opposed to the prior 20-year carryforward. Thus, corporations will be required to track two categories of NOLs.[208] A corporation's capital losses are only deductible against capital gains,[209] and can be carried back to the three taxable years preceding the loss year and forward to the five succeeding taxable years.[210]

Special limitations apply to a NOL carryover of a non-parent member of an affiliated group of corporations that files a U.S. consolidated federal income tax return if the loss was incurred while the loss corporation was not a member of the group, i.e., a separate return limitation year (SRLY) under Treas. Reg. § 1.1502–1(f). Very generally, such losses can only be used against the income of the loss members (and certain affiliates) unless the loss corporation experienced a change of control under IRC Section 382(g) in connection with joining the group.[211]

If an NOL arises from foreign operations, the NOL may be subject to special limitations. For example, if the NOL constitutes an overall foreign loss (OFL) (i.e., the loss generally consists of the excess of deductions allocated to foreign-source gross income over such foreign-source gross income), the loss corporation may be required to recognize taxable income with respect to that OFL under certain circumstances. A loss corporation is required to recapture its OFL by treating as United States source income

---

[204] Only a tax-planning strategy that meets the more-likely-than-not recognition threshold would be considered in evaluating the sufficiency of future taxable income for realization of deferred tax assets. *See* FASB ASC 740–10–55–98.

[205] IRC Section 172(c).

[206] *See* former IRC Section 172(b).

[207] *See, e.g.*, IRC Section 382.

[208] The Coronavirus Aid, Relief, and Economic Security (CARES) Act (Pub. L. No. 116–136, March 27, 2020) included a temporary change to the carryback of net operating losses. An NOL generated in tax years 2018, 2019 and 2020 could be carried back for up to five years.

[209] IRC Section 1211(a).

[210] IRC Section 1212(a)(1). A corporate capital loss carryback or carryover is treated as a short-term capital loss in the year to which it is carried and is available to offset corporate capital gains in that year.

[211] Treas. Reg. § 1.1502–21(g).

a portion of the taxpayer's foreign source taxable income.[212] Further, limits are placed on a so-called dual consolidated loss of a U.S. corporation. A dual consolidated loss generally means an NOL of a corporate member of a U.S. consolidated group that is subject to the income tax of another country "on a residence basis" or otherwise without regard to whether such income is from sources in or outside of such foreign country.[213] Subject to various exceptions, a dual consolidated loss generally cannot be used against the income of the other members of the loss corporation's consolidated group.

Another limitation applies with respect to a "loss transaction" which is defined as a transaction in which a taxpayer claims a loss under IRC Section 165 of at least (i) with respect to a corporation, $10 million in any single taxable year or $20 million in any combination of taxable years; or (ii) with respect to an individual, partnership which has one or more non-corporate partners, an S corporation, or a trust, $2 million in any single taxable year or $4 million in any combination of taxable years; and (iii) for individuals or trusts, $50,000 in any single taxable year if the loss arises with respect to a IRC Section 988 transaction (as defined in IRC Section 988(c)(1) relating to foreign currency transactions).[214] In determining if a transaction results in a taxpayer claiming a reportable transaction loss for multiple years, only losses claimed in the taxable year that the transaction is entered into and the five succeeding taxable years are aggregated.

Financial Accounting for Income Taxes (FASB ASC 740) Recognition and Measurement of Deferred Taxes

In Illustration 7-17, there is no uncertainty in USCo's tax position regarding its NOL, thus no issues arise with respect to its operating loss. However, USCo does not expect to generate sufficient taxable income in the future to utilize its NOL. To seek to resolve this issue, USCo contemplates implementing a tax-planning strategy to create taxable income to offset its NOL. USCo determines, however, that it is not more likely than not that such strategy will be sustained on the technical tax merits. In this situation, the recognition and measurement rules that are generally applicable to uncertain income tax benefits are also applied to determine the amount of available future taxable income (if any) for purposes of calculating the valuation allowance attributable to the deferred tax assets resulting from USCo's NOL under FASB ASC 740–10–30–18. Thus, USCo is not permitted to consider the proposed strategy to recognize future taxable income in reducing the valuation allowance for its deferred tax assets.[215]

The TCJA added a new category of income of controlled foreign corporations—global intangible low-taxed income (GILTI). U.S. corporate shareholders of CFCs are allowed a deduction under IRC Section 250 that reduces the effective tax rate to 10.5 percent for taxable years on or after 2018 and before 2025. However, the deduction is limited to the company's taxable income, which means the deduction is eliminated for a company with NOLs. Due to the loss of the GILTI deduction, a company with carryover NOLs will not realize the full value of the NOL. The following example illustrates the mechanics of the

---

[212] IRC Section 904(f) and Treas. Reg. § 1.904(f)–2(a).

[213] *See* IRC Section 1503(d) and Treas. Reg. § 1.1503–2(b)(1).

[214] Treas. Reg. § 1.6011–4.

[215] Only a tax-planning strategy that meets the more-likely-than-not recognition threshold would be considered in evaluating the sufficiency of future taxable income for realization of deferred tax assets. *See* FASB ASC 740–10–55–98.

GILTI calculation for a company with and without NOLs and assuming there are no foreign tax credits associated with the GILTI income.

	No NOLs	NOLs
US Gross Income		
Non-GILTI Income	0	0
GILTI Income	$100	$100
Total Before Deductions	100	100
US Deductions		
NOL Deduction	0	(100)
GILTI Deduction	(50)	0
Total Deductions	(50)	(100)
US Taxable Income	50	0
US Tax Rate	21%	21%
US Tax Payable	$10.5	$0

The $100 of NOL, using a 21 percent corporate income tax rate, is recorded as a $21 deferred tax asset. In the table, utilizing the $100 of NOLs was only better than the no NOL scenario by $10.50. The company may need to determine whether it should record a valuation allowance against the NOL deferred tax asset. According to one firm, FASB supports both views: (a) valuation allowance on the NOL, and (b) no valuation on the NOL.[216] This is a FASB accounting election and once the election is made, the company may only change to the other method if the other method is a preferred method.[217] At this time, the FASB has not indicated which method is the preferred method or whether there is even a preferred method.

General Principles of Deferred Taxes

Net operating loss carryforwards create deferred tax assets. A corporation will record a deferred tax asset equal to the amount of the NOL carryforward multiplied by the applicable tax rate. For example, if a corporation has an NOL carryforward of $1 million, using an applicable tax rate of 21 percent, the corporation will record a deferred tax asset of $210,000. The corporation must reduce its deferred tax asset by a valuation allowance if it is more likely than not that some or all of that deferred tax asset will not be realized. Because the NOL carryforward period is indefinite, a corporation may not record any valuation allowance or record only a small valuation allowance for its deferred tax asset. The benefit of a long or even indefinite carryforward period may be limited when a higher threshold must be satisfied to avoid recording a valuation allowance and that higher threshold is triggered where the corporation has sustained cumulative book losses in recent years.[218] Many corporations recorded valuation

---

[216] *Tax reform triggers need for new accounting policy—Assessing the impact of GILTI on realizability of NOLs*, In depth, PwC (Aug. 8, 2018).

[217] FASB ASC 250–10–45–2.

[218] FASB ASC 740–10–30–21.

allowances on NOLs generated during the "Great Recession" triggered by the 2007 financial crises.

In Illustration 7-17, USCo has determined that its tax planning strategies do not satisfy the more-likely-than-not recognition threshold. As a result, USCo's tax planning strategies may not be used to reduce the valuation allowance for its deferred tax assets. However, if the tax planning strategy could reduce the valuation allowance, the costs of implementing the strategy will be reflected in the valuation allowance reduction.

In the cross-border setting, the earnings impact of a valuation allowance on the foreign NOL could be offset, in full or in part, by the recognition of a loss upon disposition of the shares in the foreign subsidiary provided the company is allowed to record a deferred tax asset for the higher tax basis in the foreign subsidiary than its outside book basis. A deferred tax asset on the foreign subsidiary is allowed if it is apparent that the temporary difference will reverse in the foreseeable future.

Another tax accounting issue involving NOLs, as well as other deferred tax assets such as tax credit carryfowards, that typically catches tax professionals by surprise is "variable interest entities" (VIEs). The VIE area is highly complex with a fair amount of subjectivity and the discussion here is highly simplified to illustrate the tax accounting and SOX considerations. Basically, a VIE is an accounting fiction where a legal entity that is owned by an unrelated party is consolidated into the company's financial statements when certain conditions are met (see FASB ASC 810–10). A VIE is any entity in which the company has a controlling financial interest. There are a number of ways that control is satisfied, including an entity that is shielded by financial loss by the company.

> **ILLUSTRATION 7-18:** Sub is wholly owned by USCo. Sub owns a factory and has a contract with Company A to produce widgets exclusively for Company A. Company A must accept a minimum amount of widgets each year or pay a penalty. The price of the widget is direct costs and a "fee" for Sub's investment in the factory plus a profit that is adjusted to the Consumer Price Index. The contract term is 30 years and the factory's useful life under GAAP is 35 years. Sub has a put option to sell the factory to Company A at the end of the 30-year contract for $1,000. Company A has an option to buy the factory from Sub for $1,020. The agreement along with the two options has effectively ensured Sub's factory is highly unlikely to incur losses but neither will Sub have economic upside in the factory. As a result of the arrangement, Sub is a VIE which Company A must consolidate into its financials.
>
> Company A could encounter some surprising tax accounting results. For instance, assume Company A is profitable and has no losses and further assume the Sub forecasts NOLs in the first few years after the factory is placed in service (due to accelerated tax depreciation) but fully expects to utilize the NOLs. The USCo consolidated group has an abundance of NOLs that are subject to a full valuation allowance. While the USCo group may, collectively, have NOLs subject to a valuation allowance, Sub on a stand-alone basis would not have a valuation allowance on its separate company NOLs since the agreement with Company A practically assures Sub will be profitable over the useful life of the factory.

Query whether Company A should consolidate the valuation allowance for the Sub's stand-alone NOLs. Company A's tax expense and effective tax rate will be higher should Sub's valuation allowance be consolidated into Company A. Company A could argue that the valuation allowance should not be consolidated since (a) Sub, on a stand-alone basis, would not have a valuation allowance, or (b) if Company A actually owned Sub, Company A is profitable and would absorb Sub's NOLs so there would be no deferred tax asset to which a valuation allowance would apply. Both arguments are very rational, but, unfortunately, that is not the view embraced by the major accounting firms. The firms' view is that once a legal entity is a VIE, the company must consolidate the entire VIE. This view is interesting because the VIE is an accounting fiction (where a company is presumed to own the VIE), but unlike the tax law for substance-over-form matters, in this context the fiction is not fully played out. More importantly, the undisputed goal of financial accounting is to provide investors and other interested parties with a transparent view of the company. Imposing a nonexistent tax expense on a company is not reconcilable with good financial accounting and is another example of not seeing the forest through the trees.

SOX

The SOX Section 404 considerations in the context of net operating losses are to assure that the entity has sufficient controls in place so that appropriate procedures are created and followed to determine the proper tax and financial accounting treatment of net operating loss issues. Although the TCJA provides an indefinite carryforward of NOLs, many other taxing jurisdictions do not. Therefore, the expiration of NOL carryforwards and when tax planning must be implemented should be carefully monitored. An opportunity that sometimes eludes even the most sophisticated corporations is structuring dispositions and joint ventures to generate taxable income or capital gains to be absorbed by NOL carryforward and capital loss carryforward. The bias among tax professionals and management is to structure transactions to defer, not accelerate, taxes. Periodically communicating such tax attributes to various parties within the corporation, particularly large multinational conglomerates, will increase the likelihood that a pending transaction is not so far along that changing the deal structure will require conceding material terms to the other party. Too often, these types of macro tax issues are confined within the domain of the tax department.

§ 7.16 Permanent Establishment

General Principles

International tax planning arrangements often involve activities of one affiliate located in a country undertaking certain activities in a second country. The tax administration of the second country may view such activities to rise to the level of a taxable presence in its country. An assertion of tax deficiency in the second country raises a serious potential issue with respect to double taxation of the enterprise, in the absence of a treaty between the countries. In the treaty context, the taxable presence issue is referred to as a "permanent establishment" (PE). In the current world of international taxation, these PE issues have become endemic as local tax administrations seek to expand their domestic tax bases, or prevent their diminution via international tax planning.

ILLUSTRATION 7-19: USCo is a U.S.-based multi-national entity operating a worldwide manufacturing, distribution, and servicing business. USCo provides to customers (1) hardware; (2) software; and (3) installation services (which are provided with intangible property developed by USCo).

USCo invests heavily in research and development (technology intangibles), as well as in brand and image advertising (marketing intangibles). These intangibles contribute a significant part of USCo's profitability.

The goods and services are provided similarly in every commercially significant market of the world, with adaptations to the unique circumstances of specific markets. In the country of Domina, which has a ten percent tax rate, USCo has a wholly-owned Dominia subsidiary that operates a call center (DomCo). Dominia and the United States have a treaty based on the U.S. Model Tax Treaty. DomCo has received an economic incentive from national and local government units, as well as a preferential income tax regime. DomCo and USCo have entered a "Call Center Services Agreement," pursuant to which DomCo will provide call center services for USCo and its international affiliates. The transfer pricing methodology under the agreement is the cost-plus method with a mark-up of five percent.

The Call Center Services Agreement provides that USCo will provide to DomCo all intangible property relating to the conduct of the call center operations with respect to USCo products and procedures, as well as all customer referrals. In other words, DomCo will not be responsible for developing the DomCo protocols or seeking customers. Rather, its function is limited to operating the call center pursuant to the policies and procedures, and to the customers, provided by USCo.

USCo has considered whether DomCo's activities constitute a dependent agent PE of USCo in Dominia, such that an allocation of a portion of the profits or losses of USCo should be made for Dominia tax purposes. USCo has determined that DomCo is a not a dependent agent PE of USCo and therefore USCo does not have a PE in Dominia.

Technical Tax Matters

The concept of a PE is critical to the application of many important treaty provisions. For example, the existence of a PE in a contracting state is necessary for the taxation by that state of the business profits of a resident of the other state. When business is conducted in a treaty country through a PE, the state in which the PE is located may tax the enterprise on a net basis on the income that is attributable to the permanent establishment. The PE concept is relevant in determining which contracting state may tax certain gains or "other income."

The term PE is defined in Article 5 of the 2016 U.S. Model Treaty. A PE is a "fixed place of business through which the business of an enterprise is wholly or partly carried on."[219] Under this definition, the place of business must be "fixed" in the sense that a particular building or physical location is used by the enterprise for the conduct of its business. It must also be foreseeable that the enterprise's use of the building or other

[219] U.S. Model Tax Treaty, art. 5(1).

physical location will be more than temporary. To this general definition, the Model Treaty, like most U.S. treaties, adds a list of specific facilities that are presumptively treated as permanent establishments.[220] This list is illustrative and not exclusive.

A corporation looking to enter a foreign market frequently will conduct some aspect of its operations in that market through agents. For tax purposes, a question arises whether the activity or place of business of the agent may be attributed to the foreign principal, causing the principal to have a PE in the foreign country that would subject it to tax there. If the agent is a broker, general commission agent, or any other agent of an independent status, who is acting in the ordinary course of his or her business as an independent agent, then the activity of the agent will not result in the foreign principal having a PE.[221] There are three conditions that must be satisfied to rely on this provision: (1) the agent must be both legally and economically independent of the principal; (2) the agent must be acting in the ordinary course of its business in carrying out activities on behalf of the principal; and (3) the agent does not habitually exercise in the country an authority to conclude contracts that are binding on the principal.[222] The agent will cause the principal to have a PE if the type of contracts that the agent has authority to conclude relate to the essential business operations of the principal, rather than ancillary activities. The activities of the agent must also be of a type that if exercised through a fixed place of business by the principal would constitute a PE. Thus, if the agent's activities are limited to those activities of a preparatory or auxiliary character, as described in Article 5(4) of the Model Treaty, the agent cannot cause the principal to have a PE even if it has the authority to conclude contracts. If the local agent is not an independent agent, then the activities undertaken by the agent for the foreign principal will constitute a PE of the principal.[223]

The evolution of multinational business has placed increasing strain on traditional PE—taxable presence in a specific country—and transfer pricing concepts. Such evolution includes electronic commerce, global financial dealing, service-provider, complex strategic business alliances, and related arrangements. The U.S. Competent Authority has indicated that there are limitations on its ability to compromise on certain PE issues.

Financial Accounting for Income Taxes (FASB ASC 740) Recognition and Measurement of Deferred Taxes

PE issues in foreign countries pose interesting issues under the FASB rules on accounting for uncertain income tax positions, due to the aggressive nature of some tax authorities with respect to PE and PE allocation matters. Even though the U.S. company may feel its tax position is certain (i.e., no PE in the foreign country), the foreign taxing authority may assert a novel and/or radical PE theory.

After identifying the proper unit of account, the next step in the recognition and measurement process is that USCo must determine whether it is more likely than not that its tax position of no PE in Dominia will be sustained upon examination, including resolution of any related appeals or litigation processes, based on the technical merits of the position, assuming that the position will be examined by the appropriate taxing

[220] U.S. Model Tax treaty, art. 5(2).

[221] U.S. Model Tax Treaty, art. 5(6).

[222] U.S. Model Tax Treaty, art. 5(5).

[223] *Id.*

authority that has full knowledge of all relevant information. In Illustration 7-19, the pertinent tax authorities would be the United States (in the case of USCo) and the Dominia tax authority in the case of DomCo. Assume that USCo has determined that it is more likely than not that it does not have a PE in Dominia and therefore it owes no taxes to Dominia due to the presence of a treaty between the United States and Dominia.

The last step in the analytical process is measurement. Specifically, a tax position that meets the more-likely-than-not recognition threshold is measured to determine the amount of benefit to recognize in the financial statements. The tax position is measured as the amount of benefit that has a cumulative probability of occurring that is greater than 50 percent. In Illustration 7-19, because there is a tax treaty between the U.S. and Dominia, and the Dominia tax rate of 10 percent is less than the U.S. tax rate of 21 percent, in theory, there should be no possibility of double taxation. USCo would only need to evaluate its tax position for accrual of penalties and interest expense to Dominia. Although the foreign tax credit rules are beyond the scope of this section, there are several situations in which the taxes paid to Dominia would not offset the USCo's U.S. tax liability. First, for instance, it is possible that any taxes that USCo pays to Dominia may be treated as a voluntary tax unless it exhausts all effective and practical administrative remedies in Dominia.[224] If the tax to Dominia is determined to be a voluntary tax, then USCo may be denied a foreign tax credit for the Dominia taxes. Second, the inability to utilize the Dominia tax as a credit against USCo's tax liability could result in double taxation. For instance, USCo may not have sufficient foreign source income, which could be due to the allocation of tax deductions related to U.S. expenses or the additional Dominia tax is paid outside of the one-year carryback period for excess foreign tax credits. If double taxation does arise, USCo may need to prepare a measurement probability table.

SOX

The SOX Section 404 considerations in the context of PE matters are to assure that the entity, USCo in Illustration 7-19, has sufficient controls in place so that any PE issues are addressed and controlled from an exposure standpoint as early as possible, and that such internal controls are followed with respect to the increasingly arcane nature of PE assertions by tax authorities in many countries. Experienced international practitioners have learned, often the hard way, that what may appear "arcane" to U.S. tax professionals are quite intuitive to local tax practitioners. Retaining qualified local practitioners and gaining some basic understanding of local culture would attune the U.S. tax practitioner to potential PE assertions and perhaps allow for proactive planning to mitigate the risk. In fact, top-tier multinational companies often provide cultural training to project teams prior to the first meeting with local partners in joint ventures. Internal controls should include review of the contractual arrangements between USCo and DomCo and frequent monitoring by tax department personnel to ensure that the activities of DomCo and its employees are in accordance with the contractual arrangements. As a result of increased cooperation and sharing of information between countries, such as national security initiatives to combat terrorism, a country can easily ascertain how long employees have been in the country through airline flight logs and even the potential level of business conducted. The Organisation for Economic Co-Operation and Development in their Base Erosion and Profit Project requires country-by-country reporting and that will allow countries to get a deeper look into a company's

[224] *See, e.g.*, Treas. Reg. § 1.901–2(a)(2); Rev. Rul. 77–267, 1977–2 C.B. 243.

global operations. Thus, a country's taxing authorities could be armed with data that the tax department does not possess and which cannot be readily extracted from the company's systems.

§ 7.17 Research and Development/Experimental Expenditures

ILLUSTRATION 7-20: During the year, USCo, a U.S.-based public corporation, incurred an equal amount of expenditures on four separate research projects. USCo intends to claim a $1 million research and development credit on its tax return, made up of $250,000 of tax credits per project, to reduce its current year tax liability. After review of each of the projects and the supporting documentation, USCo management determines that it is more likely than not that the tax credits of only three projects will be sustained if challenged.

Technical Tax Matters

Prior to the TCJA, a taxpayer expensed its research or experimental expenditures paid or incurred in connection with the taxpayer's trade or business. The TCJA provided that specified research or experimental expenditures that are paid or incurred in tax years beginning after December 31, 2021, should be capitalized and amortized ratably over a five-year period, and if such expenditures are incurred outside of the U.S., the amortization period is increased to fifteen years.[225]

The amount of the research credit is equal to 20 percent of the excess of the qualified research expenses for the taxable year over the base amount.[226] "Qualified research" is defined as research with respect to which the expenditures may be treated as specified research or experimental expenditures under section 174, which is undertaken for the purpose of discovering information which is technological in nature, and the application of which is intended to be useful in the development of a new or improved business component of the taxpayer, and substantially all of the activities of which constitutes elements of a process of experimentation for a particular purpose (i.e., a new or improved function, performance, or reliability or quality).[227] Qualified research expenses is the sum of in-house research expense and contract research expenses.[228] The base amount is the greater of: the fixed base percentage times the average annual gross receipts for the preceding four taxable years or 50 percent of the qualified research expenses for the year.[229] As a result, the maximum credit is ten percent of qualified research expenses (20 percent of the excess of qualified research expenses over 50 percent thereof). A taxpayer may elect the alternative simplified credit in which case the credit is equal to 14 percent of the qualified research expenses for the taxable year that exceeds 50 percent of the average qualified research expenses for the three previous years.[230]

---

225 IRC Section 174(a).

226 IRC Section 41(a)(1).

227 IRC Sections 41(d)(1) and (d)(3).

228 IRC Sections 41(d)(1), (d)(2) and (d)(3).

229 IRC Section 41(c).

230 IRC Section 41(c)(4).

Financial Accounting for Income Taxes (FASB ASC 740) Recognition and Measurement of Deferred Taxes

Illustration 7-20 raises a number of recognition and measurement issues that management of USCo must address. First, USCo must determine the appropriate unit of account in order to measure the financial accounting benefit that it can recognize from the research credit. Identification of the appropriate unit of account is determined by reference to the applicable facts and circumstances based on management's judgment. Assume that management of USCo determines that (i) due to the size of the expenditures for each project, and (ii) the level both at which USCo obtains information to support its return, and where it expects to address the issue with tax authorities, each individual research project should be a separate unit of account.

After the proper unit of account is established, the next step in the process is to determine whether the benefit resulting from the research credit can be recognized for financial accounting purposes. For Illustration 7-20, this determination is dependent upon whether it is more likely than not that USCo's tax position regarding the research credit will be sustained upon examination by the taxing authority, including resolution of any related appeals or litigation, based on the technical merits of the return position. Management of USCo concludes that it is more likely than not that the research credit applicable to three of the projects will be sustained based on the technical merits. Accordingly, the tax credits of those three projects will be recognized since they meet the more-likely-than-not recognition threshold. Assume, however, due to the activities of the fourth project, management of USCo determines that the return position of the research credit for that project does not satisfy the more-likely-than-not recognition threshold and, thus, none of the tax benefits of the credit for that project are recognized in USCo's financial statements. Based on these facts and assumptions, USCo recognizes a financial statement benefit related to the three projects that satisfied the more-likely-than-not threshold and recognizes no financial statement benefit related to the fourth project.

The next step is to measure the amount of the tax benefit to recognize in USCo's financial statements with respect to the research credit claimed on USCo's return for the first three projects. USCo is permitted to record the benefit of the tax position that has a cumulative probability of occurring that is greater than 50 percent. Based on the measurement probability table prepared by management, USCo will be permitted a benefit on its financial statements with respect to the tax credit for the first three projects.

General Principles of Deferred Taxes

For financial accounting purposes, research and development costs are expensed as incurred.[231] As a result, if the costs are deducted for tax purposes and expensed for financial accounting purposes, no temporary difference arises. However, beginning in 2022, for tax purposes, specified research or experimental expenditures are capitalized and amortized ratably over a five-year period, and if such expenditures are incurred outside of the U.S., the amortization period is increased to fifteen years. As a result, a deductible temporary difference arises. The research and development credit is a permanent difference, lowering a corporation's effective tax rate.

---

[231] FASB ASC 730–10–25–1.

If the amount of the research and development credit for the taxable year exceeds the amount allowable as a deduction for such taxable year for qualified research expenses or basic research expenses, then the amount chargeable to capital account for the taxable year for such expenses is reduced by the amount of such excess.[232] The result is a lower deduction amount for qualified research expenses or basic research expenses. However, a corporation may make an election to reduce its research and development credit rather than reducing its deduction for qualified research expenses or basic research expenses.[233] If the election is made, the amount of the credit is equal to the excess of the amount of credit over the amount of the credit multiplied by the federal corporate tax rate of 21 percent. For example, if the corporation has a research credit for the year of $1 million, it may elect to reduce its credit to $790,000 rather than reducing the capitalized amount of qualified research expenses or basic research expenses.

SOX

The SOX Section 404 considerations in the context of the research deduction and credit is intended to assure that the entity has sufficient controls in place so that any qualifying activities have been identified and issues are addressed and controlled from an exposure standpoint. There are several common issues in the research credit area. The first is the diverse understanding, or misunderstanding, of what constitutes research, particularly by the non-tax community. An engineer, by training, solves many common technical challenges and typically does not consider her work to be "research." Not only does that make it challenging for the tax department to identify qualifying research, but also when the engineer is interviewed by the IRS agent, the engineer may agree with the agent that the activity is not research.

A second risk area is proving the employee was, indeed, contributing to a research project. This can be difficult if an employee's job title does not match the employee's actual role and responsibilities on the research project. This risk is more likely in companies with smaller or less frequent research activities, because when a research opportunity presents itself, the company will pull together a project team from throughout the organization. Companies typically do not change people's job title for short-term special assignments. For example, it will be tough to convince an IRS agent that an "Accounts Manager" was actually doing lab work. But due to the Accounts Manager's strong financial skills with spreadsheets, she designed a spreadsheet to analyze lab results.

A third area is tasks performed by third parties for the research project. To qualify for the research credit, the company must bear the risk of failure. It is not uncommon for the company's lawyer and procurement department personnel to insist on shifting this risk to the vendor. The vendor may agree to assume the risk, but the scope of the engagement is scaled back to reflect this shift in risk. However, the scope is subsequently increased through a series of change orders to the original contract. In a project that has a lot of unknowns, it is not uncommon for change orders to equal, if not exceed, the original contract price. On a macro basis, the risk is really borne by the company; however, the contract language betrays that reality and introduces unnecessary audit risk. Educating the company's contract lawyers and procurement department could help reduce the audit risk without compromising the company's legal rights.

---

232 IRC Section 280C(c)(1).

233 IRC Section 280C(c)(2).

§ 7.18 State Tax

General Principles

State income tax issues are playing an increasingly important role in a company's tax management function due to, among other factors, (i) the expansion of many companies' business to multiple state jurisdictions, and (ii) various states seeking to raise state revenues in times of budget deficits by revamping its tax rules and procedures and expanding its audit functions. A major uncertainty is whether states will conform or selectively conform to Federal tax laws and changes to such law. Coupled with these developments is the uncertainty surrounding state taxation of ecommerce through internet sales. In *South Dakota v. Wayfair, Inc.*,[234] the U.S. Supreme Court likely muddied things further and may accelerate Congressional action that has seen spurts of activity over the past decade. For ease of discussion, taxes imposed by counties, cities, and other local taxing jurisdictions are also encompassed in "state income tax."

Although each state has its own state tax statutes and regulations, in very general terms, for state tax purposes, a company's non-business income is often allocated to a particular jurisdiction (often the commercial domicile of the taxpayer), while its business income is apportioned among the various states in which the company does business. Many states require (and some permit) combined reporting of a taxpayer and its affiliates. Interestingly, many of these same issues exist with respect to a company's operations in foreign countries. For example, if a U.S. company is engaged in a trade or business in a foreign jurisdiction (or conducts its foreign operations through a permanent establishment in a country having a treaty with the U.S.), the analysis below is generally applicable to those situations as well.

Checklist of Potential Tax Issues or Positions

1. Has the company commenced operations in a new state during the year, and, if so, is the company subject to tax in that state?
2. Has the company reviewed all of the open tax years in jurisdictions in which the company may have conducted business? Has the company filed all applicable state income tax returns for prior years in states in which it has nexus and is subject to tax? If not, in what states should the company be filing?
3. Does the company pay royalties or management fees to an affiliated entity in a low-tax jurisdiction?
4. Is the company's sole contact with a particular low-tax state the ownership of an intangible for which it receives royalties from affiliates located in high-tax states?
5. Is the company's sole activity in the state internet sales?
6. If the company has not filed all state income tax returns where it arguably should be filing, what is the maximum possible assessment (tax, interest and penalties) arising therefrom?

[234] 138 S. Ct. 2080 (2018).

7. Does the applicable state taxing authority have an official or unofficial policy regarding how many years it imposes tax, penalties and interest on non-filing taxpayers?
8. Does the state jurisdiction have an amnesty program for taxpayers who voluntarily approach the state and agree to file prior year returns?
9. Do the states where the company currently files returns have an exchange of information program with other states?
10. In determining the scope of state taxation, is the state a separate return state, an economic nexus state, or some type of combined state?
11. Other than separate return states, most states use a multifactor formula to determine the amount of taxable income taxed by the state. Common factors are sales, property, and payroll. What is the state multifactor formula?

ILLUSTRATION 7-21:[235]

USCo is incorporated in state A and has filed returns in state A for the last 20 years. USCo has never filed a state tax return in state B, even though it has also conducted business in state B for the prior 20 years and would be subject to state B tax during that period. Because no return was filed in state B, the statute of limitations for state B income tax never commenced. Based on its understanding of the administrative practices and precedents of state B, USCo believes that state B will only review the last six years to determine if a state B return is due and a deficiency owed.

Technical Tax Matters

Each state has its own laws and regulations that tax both in-state companies and also out-of-state companies that conduct some level of activity in the state.[236] Generally, a state's right to impose (i) an income tax, (ii) a franchise tax (whether on income or capital),[237] or (iii) a gross receipts tax[238] is limited, for example, by the commerce clause and due process clauses of the Fourteenth Amendment to the U.S. Constitution. Further, Federal Public Law 86–272 enacted in 1959 generally restricts a state from taxing the net income of a company whose only activity with the state is the solicitation of orders for the sale of tangible personal property, provided that orders are accepted and the goods shipped from a location outside of the state.

Over the past ten years, there have been various efforts to enact legislation that will allow the states to collect sales and use tax directly from out-of-state business entities. A number of states and professional organizations have also been active in introducing

[235] *See* FASB ASC 740–10–55–94.

[236] Various states impose no state income tax on business activities.

[237] FASB ASC 740-10-15-4(a). If a franchise tax is partially based on income, then deferred tax assets and liabilities are recognized and accounted for under FASB ASC 740. FASB ASC 740–10–55–26; FASB ASC 740–10–55–139 to FASB ASC 740–10–55–144 (example 17 illustrating application of FASB ASC 740 to a franchise tax).

[238] Interestingly, in its deliberations, the FASB staff expressed the view that the Texas margin tax, which is imposed on Texas sourced adjusted gross revenues of certain entities, is based substantially on a measure of income and thus should be treated as an income tax for SFAS No. 109 (FASB ASC 740) accounting purposes. As a result, it appears that the Texas margin tax should be subject to FIN 48 (FASB ASC 740–10) as an income tax. *See* Minutes of FASB Meeting on Potential FSP: Texas Franchise Tax (Aug. 2, 2007).

legislation that would standardize payroll tax withholding obligations when employees travel to other states for business. Until *South Dakota v. Wayfair, Inc.*, the U.S. Supreme Court had confirmed the limitations on a state's right to tax, including the right to impose tax on out-of-state business entities. Then, in a remarkable turn of events, the Supreme Court invalidated the long-standing physical presence standard test it had previously upheld in *Quill Corp. v. North Dakota*.[239] Taxpayers can reasonably expect the states to be even more aggressive in asserting nexus in the wake of the *Wayfair* decision. Reporting positions will need to be appropriately reevaluated.

Financial Accounting for Income Taxes (FASB ASC 740) Recognition and Measurement of Deferred Taxes

In Illustration 7-21, USCo is subject to tax in state B but has not filed a state B income tax return. Although FASB ASC 740–10 mandates that USCo assume that state B will audit USCo and, based on the facts and circumstances, determine that USCo should have filed in prior years, FASB ASC 740–10 permits management of USCo to consider widely understood administrative practices of state B in assessing and reporting the uncertain tax position resulting from not filing in state B. A critical issue is whether USCo must disclose the tax exposure for all open years (i.e., all 20 years since the statute of limitations has not commenced in state B) or only for the last six years consistent with USCo's understanding that state B will only impose back taxes for the last six years. Although FASB ASC 740–10 does not provide detailed guidance as to when a tax authority's administrative practices and procedure is widely understood, it appears that USCo's determination for FASB ASC 740–10 purposes that it has only six years of tax, penalty and interest exposure is reasonable if this determination is based on the experience of (i) USCo as to how state B handles non-filers, (ii) other entities that have been assessed by state B for failing to file returns, and (iii) state B tax practitioners.

Since state taxes are deductible in arriving at Federal taxable income, separate tax accounts should be maintained for the Federal tax impact of the state tax deduction. This area can be particularly cumbersome depending on whether interest on tax overpayments and underpayments, as well as penalties on underpayments, are recorded as pre-tax financial income or as tax expense. The former is the preferred tax accounting approach and companies that are on the preferred approach cannot switch to any other approaches. It's also easier to do the tax accounting under the preferred method. Companies that treat interest and penalties as tax expense, the latter approach, should set up additional accounts to track the gross interest and penalties and the underlying Federal and state tax impact. For instance, interest payments but not necessarily penalties are deductible for Federal taxable income and state taxable income. The state tax deduction for interest expense would lower state taxes and that in turn will reduce the Federal deduction for state taxes. Reconciling these tax accounts when the tax, interest, and penalties are paid is equally complex. It appears most companies are using the preferred approach, thereby avoiding these complexities.

The turnaround of state book-tax differences should be forecasted and taken into account to determine state deferred taxes. State deferred taxes should be adjusted each reporting period due to changes in enacted state tax law, changes in the timing of the turnaround of book-tax differences, and changes in the multifactor formula when book-tax differences turn-around.

---

[239] 504 U.S. 298 (1992).

ILLUSTRATION 7-22: USCo owns two U.S. subsidiaries. ACo is incorporated in State A and only does business in State A. BCo is incorporated in State B and only does business in State B. State A is a separate return state so it only taxes ACo's profits from State A. State B is a combined state based on economic nexus. Under State B's economic nexus rule, ACo and BCo are combined. State B applies a multifactor formula in determining the amount of combined taxable income subject to State B tax. The multifactor formula is equally weighted between sales, property, and payroll. These are the sales, property, and payroll for ACo and BCo in Year 1:

	Sales	Property	Payroll	Total
ACo	$100,000	$75,000	$25,000	$200,000
BCo	$190,000	$95,000	$15,000	$300,000

In Year 1, ACo had $20,000 of taxable income and BCo had $60,000 of taxable income. State B combined taxable income is $80,000. Since BCo's sales, property, and payroll is 60 percent of the combined sales, property, and payroll, State B will tax $48,000, which is 60 percent of the combined group's taxable income of $80,000.

Due to higher state tax depreciation than book deprecation, at the end of Year 1, ACo had state book-tax differences of $45,000 and BCo had state book-tax differences of $35,000. State A's tax rate is 8 percent and State B's tax rate is 10 percent. State A deferred tax liability is $3,600 ($45,000 times 8 percent). State B deferred tax liability could be very complex. If the business mix does not change during the turnaround period of the State B deferred taxes, the calculation is quite simple. State B combined book-tax difference is $80,000, so State B deferred tax liability is $4,800 ($80,000 times 60 percent times 10 percent). However, USCo does expect faster growth in State A than State B, so the State B combined taxable income that is subject to State B tax will decline each year. For simplicity, State A and State B book-tax differences have the same turnarounds, and State B combined taxable income is positive during the turnaround period. The tax department converts these projections to a percentage of State B combined taxable income subject to State B tax:

	State B %	Turn-Around	Tax Rate	State B Deferred Taxes
Year 2	55%	$20,000	10%	$1,100
Year 3	50%	$20,000	10%	$1,000
Year 4	45%	$20,000	10%	$900
Year 5	40%	$20,000	10%	$800
				$3,800

If forecasted change in the cumulative sales, property, and payroll in State B is 60 percent of the forecasted change for both states combined, the State B deferred taxes would be $4,800.

Illustration 7-22 assumed positive taxable income in the turn-around period. Had there been State B combined net operating losses during the turnaround year, state deferred tax assets would be worth less due to State B's declining apportionment percentage as compared to the static scenario. State deferred taxes are often computed using the static approach and that can be problematic, particularly if a company has publicly announced growth plans, major divestments, workforce reduction, outsourcing, or other major business changes. Companies can expect heightened scrutiny of state deferred taxes as they become a more material component of the financial balance sheet. The reduction of the federal corporate tax rate from 35 percent to 21 percent and the switch to the hybrid territorial/worldwide tax regime should result in state taxes being a larger percentage of a company's total taxes.

In May 2019, the FASB issued Proposed ASU No. 2019–700, *Income Taxes (Topic 740): Simplifying the Accounting for Income Taxes*, which removes certain exceptions and simplifies other tax accounting rules. State franchise tax that is based on both income and non-income factors, such as capital or revenues, will be bifurcated with the amount based on income to be recorded according to FASB ASC 740 and the remainder, if any, as a non-income-based tax.[240]

SOX

The SOX Section 404 considerations in the context of state tax issues are to assure that the entity has sufficient controls in place so that appropriate procedures are created and followed to determine the proper tax and financial accounting treatment of state tax issues. In this regard, the company should scrutinize sales activities of the company, or its representatives, in states where it is believed not to have a taxable presence, nexus, to assure that sales personnel are not signing contracts or otherwise conducting business in such states. The company should also monitor the business travel of its employees to ensure it withholds and remits payroll taxes to the appropriate jurisdictions. Companies that are not currently using the preferred approach in accounting for interest and penalties should consider adopting it in order to simplify the accounting. Doing so will minimize the likelihood of a tax accounting error.

States that use an economic nexus standard in defining the combined group introduces another control challenge. The tax department should evaluate the company's dynamic business environment to determine when an affiliated company has gained nexus or lost nexus with the combined group. This exercise is particularly relevant when a company is restructuring its organization, buying businesses, divesting businesses, growing very quickly in a certain business segment, or altering its strategic course. These business events will also impact state deferred taxes as described in Illustration 7-22. The preference is for the tax department to have a seat at the table when these matters are being discussed versus being notified after decisions have been made.

---

[240] FASB ASC 740–10–15–4(a). If a franchise tax is partially based on income, then deferred tax assets and liabilities are recognized and accounted for under FASB ASC 740. FASB ASC 740–10–55–26; FASB ASC 740–10–55–139 to FASB ASC 740–10–55–144 (example 17 illustrating application of FASB ASC 740 to a franchise tax).

§ 7.19 Stock Options—Expensing

General Principles

One of the most visible and contentious issues in financial accounting in recent times has been the treatment of stock options. Financial accounting rules that took effect in 2006 require entities to expense stock options, reducing much of the prior attractiveness of issuing stock options (i.e., compensation with no expense).[241]

Pursuant to ASU No. 2016–09, all income tax expense will be recognized, which will match the deductions taken on a tax return and no tax benefits will be recorded to additional paid in capital (APIC). Furthermore, the requirement that the company must reduce income tax payable before it can recognize the income tax benefit has been removed. However, any tax benefits that have been suspended due to the deduction not reducing tax payable are all recorded to APIC. Although recognition of all tax expense in financial earnings will eliminate differences with the tax return, it introduces volatility to the effective tax rate, which means volatility to earnings. FASB ASC 718 provides that compensation expense be based on a forecasted value of the equity award.

To illustrate, assume a company issues a single stock option that is exercisable at $10 and is valued at $2 on the date of grant. The company's compensation expense is $2. Assume the share price is $25 when the option is later exercised. The company has a tax deduction for compensation expense of $15. Using a 25 percent combined federal and state tax rate, the deduction results in a tax benefit of $3.75. A $3.75 tax benefit associated with a $2 book compensation expense will distort the company's effective tax rate and consequently its earnings.

A number of companies adopted ASU 2016–09 early, leading to large increases in earnings. The six biggest U.S. banks increased earnings by $1.4 billion, with Goldman Sachs leading the group with $475 million, followed by JP Morgan Chase with $373 million.[242]

In mid-2014, FASB modified the rule for stock-based compensation to address an oversight in FASB ASC 718. It pertains to stock compensation that allows employees to leave the company before the shares vest or before the performance targets are met. In that situation, the compensation costs are recognized in the reporting period in which it is probable that the performance target will be met. If it is probable that the target will be met before the employee leaves the company, any remaining compensation costs that have not been expensed by the company are recognized over the rest of the time the employee is with the company.

There does not appear to be any specific provisions in the FASB Codification or in other pronouncements governing the impact of stock options on foreign tax credit utilization that specifically impact GAAP tax expense. Further, prior to the enactment of the TCJA, which introduced the 245A 100 percent dividends-received deduction for foreign-source dividends, the U.S. federal tax benefit of stock options could be obtained indirectly upon dividend distributions of foreign subsidiaries.

---

[241] SFAS No. 123(R) (FASB ASC 718), Accounting for Stock-Based Compensation (2004).

[242] *See* Dakin Campbell and Felice Maranz, *Wall St banks reap $1.4bn gain as a tax rule plumps profit*, Gulf Times (April 22, 2017).

The principles of tax and financial accounting regarding non-qualified deferred compensation are straightforward and generally non-controversial, provided the compensation expense is not disallowed as a deduction (for example, due to the compensation being in excess of $1 million and payable to covered employees of publicly held companies). Nonetheless, there are tracking and classification issues that should be considered by those charged with responsibility for preparing financial statements.

ILLUSTRATION 7-23: A publicly traded corporation grants non-qualified stock options to its employee on March 15, 2019. The employee is immediately vested in the options. On the grant date, the fair market value of the stock is $40 with an exercise price of $40. On the exercise date of March 15, 2022, the stock is worth $60. The corporation, using the fair-value method to value the options, records a financial statement expense of $15 in the grant year 2019. When the employee exercises the stock option in 2022, the corporation is entitled to a $20 deduction ($60 value of stock minus $40 exercise price). The $15 stock option expense recorded on the financial statements in 2019 is a temporary difference that reverses in 2022, the year the corporation takes a tax deduction of $20. The $5 excess of the $20 tax deduction over the $15 financial statement expense is a permanent difference with the tax effect as an income tax benefit thereby reducing the company's effective tax rate in 2022.

Technical Tax Matters

When a corporation grants non-qualified stock options to its employees, there generally are no immediate tax consequences to either the corporation or the employees if the options do not have a readily ascertainable fair market value and the exercise price of the option is at least equal to the fair market value of the underlying option shares when the option is granted.[243] Since a significant amount of nonqualified stock options are granted to top executives, the tax benefit has been materially diluted due to the TCJA. As a result of the tax reform, no tax deduction is allowed for compensation expense that exceeds $1 million paid to both current and former "covered employees" of a publicly traded corporation.[244]

Generally, unless certain requirements set forth in IRC Section 409A are satisfied, amounts deferred under a nonqualified deferred compensation plan are currently includible in gross income to the extent not subject to a substantial risk of forfeiture[245] and not previously included in gross income. For this purpose, a "nonqualified deferred compensation plan" includes nonqualified stock options.[246] If the exercise price of a nonqualified option to purchase "service recipient stock" is (or could become) less than the fair market value[247] of the underlying option stock on the date the option is granted, then the option provides for the deferral of compensation and is thus subject to IRC Section 409A. "Service recipient stock" generally means a class of stock that qualifies as common stock (under IRC Section 305) of the corporation to whom the services are

---

[243] IRC Section 83(e)(3); IRC Section 409A.

[244] IRC Section 162(m).

[245] Thus, a grant of restricted property generally will not constitute a deferral of compensation for purposes of IRC Section 409A.

[246] Generally, a nondiscounted stock option issued with respect to the service recipient stock is not subject to IRC Section 409A, provided the terms of the stock option or stock appreciation right do not include any additional deferral feature.

[247] For this purpose, lapse restrictions as defined in Treas. Reg. § 1.83–3(i) are disregarded.

provided or generally of a corporation in a chain of organizations connected through a controlling interest which includes the service recipient corporation.[248] Conversely, an option to purchase service recipient stock does not provide for a deferral of compensation (and is not subject to IRC Section 409A) if (i) the option exercise price may never be less than the fair market value of the underlying stock (disregarding lapse restrictions as defined in Treas. Reg. § 1.83–3(i)) on the date the option is granted and the number of shares subject to the option is fixed on the original date of grant of the option; (ii) the transfer or exercise of the option is subject to taxation under IRC Section 83 and Treas. Reg. § 1.83–7; and (iii) the option does not include any feature for the deferral of compensation other than the deferral of recognition of income until the later of (1) the exercise or disposition of the option under Treas. Reg. § 1.83–7, or (2) the time the stock acquired pursuant to the exercise of the option first becomes substantially vested (as defined in Treas. Reg. § 1.83–3(b)).[249]

When an employee exercises a stock option, the employee has compensation income equal to the excess of the fair market value of the stock received on exercise less the exercise price.[250] The corporation is entitled to a deduction, unless limited by IRC Section 162(m), in the same year the employee has compensation income and the deduction is equal to the amount of compensation income included by the employee.[251]

The economic benefit enjoyed by employees who received share-based compensation and the company that received cash from the exercise of the stock options and the higher tax benefit from the compensation expense is offset by the lower share value of the existing shareholders of the company. The diminution in value is compounded at high-growth companies. For instance, since its founding in 1997, Amazon's stock price has appreciated nearly 160,000 percent by the end of 2021. While Amazon's shareholders are elated with their investment returns, one can challenge whether similar success could have been achieved with a properly structured cash incentive compensation plan.[252] The value created by stock options is mostly an illusion since it is simply a reallocation of the business's enterprise value from existing shareholders to the company's employees that were granted the stock options. The changes to the accounting rules partly disrupt the illusionary economic windfall with these economic realities. This revelation should not be misconstrued to mean that incentive compensation, whether in the form of cash or equity grants, do not benefit shareholders—they do in the majority of cases. It simply challenges the notion that share-based compensation, in some miraculous way, creates economic value that cannot be achieved with other forms of incentive compensation.

Financial Accounting for Income Taxes (FASB ASC 740) Recognition and Measurement of Deferred Taxes

In Illustration 7-23, the tax position should be certain and thus no recognition and measurement issues arise assuming full compliance with IRC Section 409A.

---

[248] Treas. Reg. § 1.409A–1(b)(5)(iii). In addition, the stock must not have any preferences as to distributions, other than distributions of service recipient stock and distributions in liquidation. Treas. Reg. § 1.409A–1(b)(5)(iii)(A).

[249] Treas. Reg. § 1.409A–1(b)(5)(i)(A).

[250] IRC Section 83(a).

[251] IRC Section 83(h).

[252] *See* Boris Ewenstein, Bryan Hancock and Asmus Komm, *Ahead of the Curve: The Future of Performance Management*, McKinsey Quarterly (May 16, 2016).

General Principles of Deferred Taxes

When a corporation grants stock options to its employees, for financial accounting purposes, it must determine the total compensation expense under the fair-value method.[253] It must then allocate the total compensation expense over the period in which the employees perform the service (i.e., the service period), which is generally the vesting period for the options.[254] For example, if the options vest over two years, the total compensation expense would be allocated over the two-year period. The offset to compensation expense is recorded as equity (i.e., additional paid-in capital) resulting in a deductible temporary difference. As a result, a deferred tax asset is recorded equal to the applicable tax rate multiplied by the deductible temporary difference. If the option is later exercised and the compensation deduction for tax purposes exceeds the compensation expense for financial accounting purposes, the tax effect of the excess is treated as income tax benefit.[255] If the compensation deduction is less than the compensation expense for financial accounting purposes, the tax effect of the difference is treated as income tax expense.[256]

The Treasury Stock Method is the approach used to determine the dilution to financial earnings from the grant of stock options and other contractual rights that could result in the issuance of equity.

The dilutive effect of employee stock options is calculated pursuant to the application of the Treasury Stock Method of Accounting, which is detailed in FASB ASC 260–10.[257] As now provided by FASB ASC 260–10, it is assumed that all options will be exercised at the beginning of the reporting period. In effect, the assumption that all options are exercised applies only to "in the money options," i.e., options whose exercise price is less than the current market price. The Treasury Stock Method assumes that the company will utilize the proceeds received from the employees related to the exercise of the options to repurchase its shares in the market at the average market price during the reporting period. Under ASU 2016–09, the Treasury Stock Method no longer assumes the tax benefits resulting from the exercise in excess of the tax benefit recognized at issuance are also utilized to purchase shares in the market at the average price during the reporting period in accordance with FASB ASC 260–10–45–29. The tax benefit will be lower post-TCJA since the tax rate is lower and compensation expense in excess of $1 million payable to covered employees of publicly held companies is no longer deductible. The excess of the number of shares subject to "in the money options" over the number of shares notionally repurchased in the market during the reporting period is the number of diluted shares that will be included in the denominator for purposes of computing diluted earnings per share.

While there are a number of interesting issues to be considered in applying the Treasury Stock Method (such as a decrease of stock price, a decrease of the average market value during the year, or an actual exercise of options during the year), there are

[253] FASB ASC 718–10–30–2.

[254] FASB ASC 718–10–30–25.

[255] FASB ASC 718–740–35–2.

[256] *Id.*

[257] FASB ASC 260–10–45–22; FASB ASC 260–10–45–23; FASB ASC 260–10–55–93; FASB ASC 260–10–55–94; FASB ASC 260–10–45–2; FASB ASC 260–10–45–28; FASB ASC 260–10–45–28; FASB ASC 260–10–45–29; FASB ASC 260–10–45–30; FASB ASC 260–10–45–31; FASB ASC 260–10–45–36; and FASB ASC 260–10–45–37.

two significant issues to be considered in determining the amount of tax benefit utilized in determining the hypothetical shares repurchased, which, therefore, reduces dilution. First, it is assumed that any incentive stock options exercised will be held by the employee for the requisite period and that no tax deduction is available to the employer because of a "disqualifying disposition."[258] An assumption of disqualifying disposition does not appear to be permitted even if based on significant historical experience. Second, and more importantly, computation of the tax benefit utilized for the offset apparently is not subject to the valuation allowance process of FASB ASC 740.[259] ASU No. 2016–09 eliminated the requirement that the company must reduce income tax payable before it can recognize the income tax benefit has been removed. ASU 2016–09 also amended the Treasury Stock Method to exclude the excess tax benefits or tax deficiencies in the diluted earnings computation.

SOX

On July 26, 2006, the SEC adopted amendments to the disclosure requirements for executive and director compensation, related party transactions, director independence and other corporate governance matters and security ownership of officers and directors.[260] The amendments are intended to make disclosures of executive compensation clearer and more complete. Compensation disclosure begins with a narrative Compensation Discussion and Analysis ("CD&A"). In the CD&A, companies will be called upon to answer questions regarding the timing of stock option grants, including:

- Whether a company has any program, plan or practice to time option grants to its executives in coordination with the release of material non-public information?
- What was the role of the compensation committee in approving and administering such a program, plan or practice? How did the board or compensation committee take such information into account when determining whether and in what amount to make those grants? Did the compensation committee delegate any aspect of the actual administration of a program, plan or practice to any other persons?
- What was the role of executive officers in the company's program, plan or practice of option timing?[261]

These corporate disclosures are being closely reviewed by SEC staff and could reveal material weaknesses. A major role of the board of directors is the consideration of executive compensation policies. The board can improve the tone-at-the-top by using forms of compensation that emphasize performance measures rather than stock prices.

Since the TCJA amended IRC Section 162(m) to disallow a deduction for compensation that exceeds $1 million to top executives, including those that are no

---

[258] IRC Section 421(b) (effect of a disqualifying disposition). FASB ASC 718–740–25–3 explicitly provides, in an analogous situation, that the tax effect of a disqualifying disposition shall be recognized only when it occurs.

[259] FASB ASC 718–740–30–2.

[260] *See* SEC Release No. 33–8732A.

[261] *See* SEC Release No. 33–8732A, § A.2.

longer employed by the company, both direct and indirect compensation, such as retirement payments, must be identified and tracked to the retired executives.

Chapter 8

ATTORNEY-CLIENT AND RELATED PRIVILEGES

Table of Sections

§ 8.01 Attorney-Client Privilege

[1] In General

Protecting tax analysis and advice—whether prepared internally or externally—from disclosure to taxing authorities is an important element of executing the tax planning policies of a business. Moreover, the implementation of the financial statement disclosure rules relating to uncertain tax positions may also highlight and provide the applicable tax authorities with a potential roadmap to a company's sensitive tax positions.

The purpose of this chapter is not to create experts who can master all of the many nuances of the various privilege protections but rather to sensitize readers to the general contours of the principles, the possibility of seemingly innocuous actions having dramatic consequences (e.g., waiver of a privilege), and potential outcomes to common situations. Indeed, the issues that can arise in connection with such privilege issues can be quite subtle, especially in the types of situations that frequently arise in tax planning and controversy situations.

> **ILLUSTRATION 8-1:** USCo is a U.S.-based manufacturer of cameras that has formed a wholly-owned corporate subsidiary (MafCo) in Mafonia for purposes of manufacturing a specific line of cameras. USCo has licensed certain manufacturing technology to MafCo, and MafCo sells the cameras to USCo for resale in the United States. MafCo has accumulated significant capital, largely as the result of transfer pricing policies that result in the bulk of the combined income being earned by MafCo, which enjoys a low tax rate as the result of a Mafonia exemption.
>
> When MafCo sells cameras to USCo, MafCo provides financing to USCo. The Service indicated that its examination will evaluate whether the income of MafCo should be treated as income under subpart F of the IRC and thus potentially taxable to USCo prior to repatriation of such income.
>
> Under IRC Section 956, certain U.S. shareholders are taxed currently on their share of undistributed earnings of a controlled foreign corporation (CFC),

like MafCo, that is made available to the U.S. shareholders, except in carefully defined circumstances.

USCo has reviewed the issue and discovered that there appear to be extreme departures from normal USCo internal guidelines that could have significant U.S. tax consequences under IRC Section 956. In addition, it appears that a series of backdated documents has been included in the USCo files for the possible purpose of camouflaging the actual facts.

Illustration 8-1 poses these issues in the context of an examination into the financial policies of MafCo that will reveal irregularity and efforts to cover up problems with backdated documents. The situation could be dangerous to MafCo, USCo, and all persons involved in the matters. In this connection, USCo inquires whether the information obtained in its internal investigation, and the conclusions reached as a result of it, will be protected by the attorney-client privilege.[1]

[2] Definition

The attorney-client privilege is a common law evidentiary matter[2] that protects confidential communications between a client and attorney made for the purpose of obtaining legal advice against disclosure to third parties.[3] U.S. courts have long recognized the privilege because of the perceived need to ensure the free flow of communication between client and attorney in order that the client have effective legal assistance and the belief that such a free flow will occur only if confidentiality is ensured.[4] This policy creates tension with the policy of full and complete disclosure of all relevant and material evidence in a judicial or administrative proceeding. In the context of federal tax investigations, these potentially conflicting policies must be balanced—the policy of the attorney-client privilege to foster full disclosure of facts and open communications between attorney and client and the policy of making all relevant facts available to the Service.[5]

Whether the privilege applies to a particular communication depends on the factual context in which the communication is made and the purposes served by the attorney's involvement in the communication process. The party asserting the privilege has the burden of establishing it.[6] Thus, in Illustration 8-1, if the Service seeks to obtain from USCo documents, studies, background data, notes, or related matters, USCo bears the

---

[1] Attorney-client protections from disclosure are not mutually exclusive of work-product protections from disclosure. *See* discussion at Section 8.02. These two protections often overlap.

[2] The privilege is recognized as applicable for evidentiary purposes in litigation by Federal Rules of Evidence 501. *See generally* Lebovitz & Loube, *The Attorney/Client Privilege in International Tax Practice*, 7 Int'l Tax Rep. 1 (Feb. 1996); McDermott, Hudspeth, Hoffman & Safer, *The Applicability of the Attorney-Client Privilege and the Work Product Doctrine in Transfer Pricing Examinations*, 4 Tax Mgmt. Transfer Pricing Rep. 860 (Mar. 29, 1995); Greenhouse & Malone, *Privilege in the IRS Audit Process—How and When Does It Apply?* 91 J. Tax'n 133 (Sept. 1999); *Kayle, The Tax Adviser's Privilege in Transactional Matters: A Synopsis and a Suggestion*, 54 Tax Law. 509 (2001).

[3] *See generally* 8 J. Wigmore, *Wigmore on Evidence* §§ 2292, 2311 (1961); Michael Saltzman and Leslie Book, *IRS Practice and Procedure* ¶ 13.11 (Thomson Reuters) [*IRS Practice and Procedure*].

[4] *Upjohn Co. v. United States*, 449 U.S. 383, 389 (1981). In contrast, many jurisdictions outside the U.S. do not provide protections against the disclosure of tax advice.

[5] Experience strongly suggests that waiver of attorney-client privilege (and other protections against disclosure) should be the exception rather than the rule, and that waiver should only occur after careful consideration and consultation with counsel. *See* Section 8.01[4][a].

[6] *Weil v. Investment/Indications, Research & Management, Inc.*, 647 F.2d 18, 25 (9th Cir. 1981); *United States v. Tratner*, 511 F.2d 248, 251 (7th Cir. 1975).

burden of establishing the privileged nature of communications reflected in the documents.

The privilege has been described in different ways, but the essentials are generally stated as follows:

(1) Where legal advice of any kind is sought,

(2) from a professional legal advisor in his capacity as such,

(3) the communications relating to that purpose,

(4) made in confidence,

(5) by the client,

(6) are at his insistence permanently protected,

(7) from disclosure by himself or by the legal advisor,

(8) except if the protection is waived.[7]

Although this description of the privilege concerns communications by the client to the attorney, it is also recognized that certain communications by the attorney to the client are privileged.[8] Legal advice or opinion from an attorney to a client, whether an individual or an entity, has consistently been recognized by the courts as within the protection of the privilege.[9]

Two primary reasons have been advanced for applying the privilege to communications from attorneys to clients. The first is that if such communications were revealed, they would expressly or by inference identify confidential information communicated by the client to the attorney.[10] The second is that legal advice given to the client should remain confidential,[11] without regard to whether it reveals information that was transmitted from the client to the attorney. Certain older cases apparently determined that only the first rationale justifies application of the privilege and have held that advice given by an attorney to a client is privileged only if the advice could reveal confidential information furnished by the client.[12] Most courts have taken the

---

[7] 8 J. Wigmore, *Wigmore on Evidence* § 2285 (1961). A test for application of the privilege was also succinctly formulated by Judge Wyzanski in *United States v. United Shoe Mach. Corp.*, 89 F. Supp. 357, 358–359 (D. Mass. 1950), as follows: "(1) The asserted holder of the privilege is, or sought to become, a client; (2) the person to whom the communication was made (a) is a member of a bar of a court, or his subordinate, and (b) in connection with this communication he is acting as a lawyer; (3) the communication relates to a fact of which the attorney was informed (a) by his client (b) without the presence of strangers (c) for the purpose of securing primarily either (i) an opinion on law or (ii) legal services or (iii) assistance in some legal proceeding, and not (d) for the purpose of committing a crime or tort; and (4) the privilege has been (a) claimed and (b) not waived by the client." Several other courts have adopted Judge Wyzanski's standard. *See, e.g., United States v. Kelly*, 569 F.2d 928, 938 (5th Cir.), *cert. denied*, 439 U.S. 829 (1978); *In re LTV Sec. Litig.*, 89 F.R.D. 595, 600 (N.D. Tex. 1981).

[8] "That the attorney's communications to the client are also within the privilege was assumed in the earlier cases and has seldom been brought into question." 8 J. Wigmore, *Wigmore on Evidence* § 2320 (1961).

[9] *United States v. Amerada Hess Corp.*, 619 F.2d 980, 986 (3d Cir. 1980); *Garner v. Wolfinbarqer*, 430 F.2d 1093, 1096 n.7 (5th Cir. 1970), *cert. denied sub. nom., Garner v. First Am. Life Ins. Co.*, 401 U.S. 974 (1971); *8 in 1 Pet Prods., Inc. v. Swift & Co.*, 218 F. Supp. 253 (S.D.N.Y. 1963).

[10] 8 J. Wigmore, *Wigmore on Evidence* § 2320; *Diversified Indus., Inc. v. Meredith*, 572 F.2d 596, 611 (8th Cir. 1977).

[11] *United States v. Amerada Hess Corp.*, 619 F.2d at 986.

[12] *See, e.g., Mead Data Cent., Inc. v. U.S. Dept. of Air Force*, 566 F.2d 242, 254 (DC Cir. 1977); *SCM Corp. v. Xerox Corp.*, 70 F.R.D. 508, 516 (D. Conn. 1975), *appeal dismissed*, 534 F.2d 1031 (2d Cir. 1976). *See also Radiant Burners, Inc. v. American Gas Ass'n*, 320 F.2d 314, 323 (7th Cir.), *cert. denied*, 375 U.S. 929 (1963)

view, however, that the second rationale also justifies application of the privilege. These courts have held that the privilege protects from disclosure communications from an attorney to the client without regard to whether the communications could reveal confidential information provided by the client.[13] Even if the more restrictive construction of the privilege is followed, the privilege will normally protect legal advice given by counsel to the client since disclosure of an attorney's advice to a client generally will reveal the substance of the confidential information previously communicated by the client to the attorney.[14]

[3] Requirements for Application

In order for a communication to be protected from disclosure by the attorney-client privilege, each of several requirements must be satisfied.

[a] Person Asserting Must Be a Client

The person asserting the privilege must be a client.[15] The attorney-client privilege is personal to the client, not the attorney. The privilege does not attach to communications by an attorney in the scope of employment with persons other than the client or the client's agent.[16] The apparent simplicity of this element is misleading. Although it may often be easy to determine who the client is when only a natural person is involved, the determination of whether the person who was a party to the communication for which the privilege is claimed is a client is less simple when the party employing the attorney is a corporation.

Prior to the Supreme Court's opinion in *Upjohn Co. v. United States*,[17] the courts recognized that the attorney-client privilege applied to corporate clients.[18] There was disagreement, however, as to the scope of the privilege in the corporate setting. One view of the privilege's scope was that the privilege applied to communications between counsel and only those employees within the corporation's "control group."[19] The control group was defined to include those employees "in a position to control or even to take a substantial part in a decision about any action which the corporation may take upon the advice of the attorney."[20] These persons were thought to personify the corporation and

(the privilege should be "strictly construed within the narrowest possible limits consistent with the logic of the principle").

[13] *Natta v. Hogan*, 392 F.2d 686, 692–693 (10th Cir. 1968); *Schwimmer v. United States*, 232 F.2d 855, 863 (8th Cir.), *cert. denied*, 352 U.S. 833 (1956); *In re LTV Sec. Litig.*, 89 F.R.D. at 602–603 (court reasoned that the free interchange of information between attorney and client is necessary in order for counsel to formulate sound legal advice, is fostered by a broad construction of the privilege, and would be chilled were clients or attorneys required to disclose advice of counsel not reflecting confidential information transmitted from the client).

[14] *In the Matter of Fischel v. United States*, 557 F.2d 209, 211 (9th Cir. 1977).

[15] This element does not require that a client formally engage the attorney. Instead it means that the putative client is seeking legal advice. *See* Section 8.01[3][b] and Section 8.01[3][c]. In any event, it is now clear that the overriding purpose of the attorney-client privilege is to encourage full and frank communications between attorneys and their clients to enable the provision of sound legal advice.

[16] *United States v. Goldfarb*, 328 F.2d 280, 282 (6th Cir.), *cert. denied*, 377 U.S. 976 (1964).

[17] 449 U.S. 383 (1981).

[18] *Radiant Burners, Inc. v. American Gas Ass'n*, 320 F.2d 314, 323 (7th Cir. 1963).

[19] *See, e.g., City of Philadelphia v. Westinghouse Elec. Corp.*, 210 F. Supp. 483 (E.D. Pa. 1962), *mandamus and prohibition denied sub nom., General Elec. Co. v. Kirkpatrick*, 312 F.2d 742 (3d Cir. 1962), *cert. denied*, 372 U.S. 943 (1963). *See also Natta v. Hogan*, 392 F.2d at 692.

[20] *City of Philadelphia v. Westinghouse Elec. Corp.*, 210 F. Supp. at 485 (E.D. Pa. 1962).

were therefore allowed to claim the privilege.[21] Other courts took a more expansive view of the privilege.[22]

The control group test was rejected by the Supreme Court in *Upjohn Co. v. United States*,[23] in which the Court held that the privilege protected from compelled disclosure information communicated by employees of the Upjohn Company (Upjohn) to inside and outside counsel. After members of senior management learned that one of Upjohn's subsidiaries had made payments to or for the benefit of foreign government officials in order to secure government business, it was decided that Upjohn's General Counsel should conduct an internal investigation. Questionnaires respecting such payments were sent to various corporate employees, who were instructed to return the questionnaires, as completed, to the General Counsel. The General Counsel and outside counsel also interviewed many Upjohn employees as part of the investigation. After Upjohn voluntarily submitted a report concerning the matter to the SEC and the Service, the Service issued a summons demanding that Upjohn produce questionnaires, memoranda, and notes respecting the investigation. Upjohn refused to produce these documents on the grounds that they were protected by the attorney-client privilege and that they were protected under the work-product doctrine because they constituted the work product prepared by attorneys in anticipation of litigation.[24]

The Sixth Circuit applied the control group test and held that the privilege did not apply to communications that were made by officers or employees not responsible for directing Upjohn's actions in response to legal advice.[25] The Supreme Court reversed, stating that "the narrow 'control group test' cannot . . . govern the development of the law in this area."[26] The Court recognized that the privilege protected both communications from clients to attorneys and communications from attorneys to clients.[27] Because the communications at issue were made by Upjohn employees to counsel, however, the Supreme Court focused on the application of the privilege to communications from employees and said little concerning the protection afforded by the privilege to communications from attorneys to clients.

In rejecting the control group test, the Supreme Court noted that the privilege protects information given to counsel by employees to enable counsel to give the corporate client "sound and informed advice."[28] Certain communications by middle-level and lower-level employees should also be protected by the privilege, the Court stated, because these employees may have information needed by counsel if counsel is to

---

[21] *Id.*

[22] *Harper & Row Publishers, Inc. v. Decker,* 423 F.2d 487 (7th Cir. 1970), *aff'd per curiam* by an equally divided court, 400 U.S. 348 (1971) (subject-matter test); *Diversified Indus., Inc. v. Meredith,* 572 F.2d 596, 609 (8th Cir. 1978) *(en banc)* ("modified subject matter" test, also termed the "Weinstein" test, required three prerequisites: (1) the communication must have been made for the purpose of securing legal advice, (2) a superior must have requested the communication so that the corporation could secure legal advice, and (3) the communication must not have been disseminated beyond those corporate personnel who needed to know its contents).

[23] 449 U.S. 383 (1981).

[24] *See* Section 8.02. This is an example of the overlap between the attorney-client privilege and work product protections against disclosure.

[25] *United States v. Upjohn Co.*, 600 F.2d 1223, 1225 (6th Cir. 1979).

[26] 449 U.S. at 397.

[27] *Id.* at 390.

[28] *Id.*

adequately advise the client respecting actual or potential legal difficulties.[29] The Court further noted that the control group test frustrated the purpose of the privilege by discouraging the communication of relevant information by employees of the corporate client to attorneys seeking to render legal advice to the client.[30] Because the control-group standard was nebulous and its application was unpredictable, it was rejected by the Court.[31]

The *Upjohn* Court did not enunciate any test to be applied generally in determining the application of the privilege in the case of corporate clients. The Court did state, however, that the communications that were protected from disclosure by the privilege in the case before it were made by Upjohn employees to counsel for Upjohn acting as such "at the direction of corporate superiors"[32] in order to secure legal advice from counsel. The Court further found that the legal counsel sought related to matters within the scope of the employees' corporate duties and were made by employees who were "sufficiently aware that they were being questioned in order that the corporation could obtain legal advice." The Court noted that the communications were considered highly confidential when made and were kept confidential thereafter by Upjohn.[33] The Court did not indicate whether all of these criteria had to be satisfied in each individual case involving a corporate client in order for the privilege to apply. Indeed, the Court stated that it was not drafting "a set of rules" to determine for all cases when the privilege would apply.[34]

Although *Upjohn* does not clearly identify the scope of the privilege within the corporate setting, it does indicate that the privilege reaches beyond communications involving the corporation's control group. Employees who act at the direction of corporate superiors in communicating with counsel regarding matters within the scope of their corporate duties in order for the corporation to obtain legal advice are generally covered by the privilege.[35]

Whether an employee communicates with counsel orally, rather than in writing, is irrelevant to the application of the privilege.[36] The privilege may extend not only to oral communications between an attorney and client, but may also, under proper circumstances, cover documentary material. In order for a particular document to be privileged, it must be shown that the client prepared it as a means of transmitting

---

[29] *Id.* at 391.

[30] *Id.* at 392.

[31] *Id.* at 393.

[32] The Court did not discuss the meaning of the term "at the direction of corporate superiors" but did note that the directive to the Upjohn employees was made by the Chairman of the Board of Upjohn. By using the term "corporate superiors," the Court probably meant that it was not a condition to the application of the privilege that the directive to an employee be made by one of the few individuals at the top of the corporation's organizational pyramid. Whether a directive to an employee from an immediate boss or superior would be sufficient to permit application of the privilege was not addressed.

[33] 449 U.S. at 394.

[34] *Id.* at 396.

[35] It should be noted that state courts are not required to follow the Federal Rules of Evidence and are not bound by *Upjohn*. *Compare Macey v. Rollins Envtl. Servs., Inc.*, 179 N.J. Super. 535, 432 A.2d 960, 963 (App. Div. 1981) (following Upjohn), *with Consolidation Coal Co. v. Bucyrus-Erie Co.*, 89 Ill. 2d 103, 116–120, 432 N.E.2d 250, 256–258 (1982) (rejecting the *Upjohn* test, adopting the control group test). Thus, a communication that is protected against disclosure by reason of the attorney-client privilege for federal law purposes may not necessarily be so protected for state law purposes.

[36] *Eglin Fed. Credit Union v. Cantor*, 91 F.R.D. 414, 418 (N.D. Ga. 1981).

confidential communications or that it was a record of some confidential matter prepared by the attorney.[37]

Application of the privilege to communications between counsel for a corporation and an employee of a parent, subsidiary, or affiliate corporation may be an important issue in many tax contexts. The authority indicates that a corporation and any parent, subsidiary, or affiliated corporation will be treated as constituent members of the "client" for purposes of applying the privilege. One case addressing this issue is *United States v. United Shoe Machinery Corp.*[38] In determining that the privilege applied to certain letters to or from members of independent law partnerships, the court recognized several related corporations as constituent members of the client: "[f]or present purposes the client is United Shoe Machinery Corporation and all its subsidiaries and affiliates considered collectively."[39]

[b] Counsel Must Be Acting as an Attorney

The second requirement focuses on whether counsel was retained to render legal advice or is engaged in another capacity. In order for the attorney-client privilege to be applicable, the parties to the communication in question must bear the relationship of attorney and client, and the attorney must have been engaged or consulted by the client for the purpose of obtaining legal services or advice.[40] Thus, a communication is not privileged simply because it is made by or to a person who happens to be an attorney.[41] The privilege may not apply, for example, where an attorney is hired to act solely as an accountant,[42] to act only as a negotiator or business agent,[43] to act merely as a scrivener,[44] or to give purely business advice.[45] As a general matter, however,

---

[37] *United States v. Merrell*, 303 F. Supp. 490 (N.D.N.Y. 1969).

[38] 89 F. Supp. 357 (D. Mass. 1950).

[39] *Id.* The court noted that all of these corporations used the same outside and inside counsel, the legal affairs of the corporations were "closely related," and, except for convenience in billing and formal accounting, there was no attempt to regard one particular corporation as "the client." *Id. See also United States v. American Tel. & Tel. Co.*, 86 F.R.D. 603, 616 (D.D.C. 1979) ("The cases clearly hold that a corporate 'client' includes not only the corporation by whom the attorney is employed or retained, but also parent, subsidiary, and affiliate corporations"). In adopting substantive and procedural guidelines relating to the law of privilege, the court recognized for purposes of applying the privilege in the case before it that the term "client" included "the named defendants (*American Telephone & Telegraph Co.*, *Western Electric Co.*, and *Bell Telephone Laboratories, Inc.*), the wholly-owned subsidiaries and majority-owned subsidiaries considered collectively, but not the minority-owned companies." (86 F.R.D. 616). But the court refused to recognize subsidiaries in which the parent had only a minority interest as constituent members of the "client"; the court also recognized that a communication involving unrelated corporations could be privileged if the advice or assistance was on a basis that was confidential among the clients and related "to a matter in which the clients have a substantial identity of legal interest." *Id.* at 616.

[40] *Diversified Indus., Inc. v. Meredith*, 572 F.2d at 602 (law firm conducting investigation held to be acting in legal capacity).

[41] *See Wells Fargo v. United States*, 09-CV-2764 (D. Minn. June 16, 2014): Communications that are circulated to in-house counsel for purposes other than obtaining legal advice are not privileged.

[42] *In re Coulton*, 201 F. Supp. 13, 16 (S.D.N.Y. 1961), *aff'd*, 306 F.2d 633 (2d Cir. 1962), *cert. denied*, 371 U.S. 951 (1963). This issue arises frequently with respect to when counsel becomes, directly or indirectly, an income tax return preparer.

[43] *JP Foley Co. v. Vanderbilt*, 65 F.R.D. 523, 526 (S.D.N.Y. 1974).

[44] *Canaday v. United States*, 354 F.2d 849, 857 (8th Cir. 1966).

[45] *Radiant Burners, Inc. v. American Gas Ass'n*, 320 F.2d at 324 ("it seems well settled that the requisite professional relationship is not established when the client seeks business or personal advice, as opposed to legal assistance"); *Cavallaro v. United States*, 284 F.3d 236 (1st Cir. 2002) (no privilege against recordkeeper summons for documents created by an accounting firm while working on estate and corporate merger matters with counsel, where not engaged by counsel); *United States v. Ackert*, 169 F.3d 136 (2d Cir. 1999) (no privilege for discussions between in-house counsel and promoter of investment challenged by the Service since the

communication with outside counsel is presumed to be made for purposes of obtaining legal advice.[46]

An attorney may be acting in the capacity of an attorney for purposes of the privilege even when he performs acts other than drafting legal documents or conducting legal research based on confidential information received from the client. As recognized by the Court in *Upjohn*, communications made by or to an attorney who makes a factual investigation for the purpose of obtaining information to enable him or her to render sound legal advice may be privileged.[47]

Upjohn and other cases also have made clear that it makes no difference to the application of the privilege whether the attorney at issue is the corporation's general counsel, a member of the general counsel's staff, or outside counsel. As long as the attorney in question is acting in the capacity of attorney, the privilege may apply.[48]

The fact that a corporation's management needs, in the normal course of business, information obtained in a factual investigation undertaken by attorneys to aid in furnishing legal advice does not preclude the operation of the privilege.[49] Management's choice to make other business use of information so obtained does not nullify the privilege, provided that the other use does not constitute a waiver of the privilege.[50]

In the corporate context, courts sometimes try to draw a distinction between legal advice from the legal department and tax advice provided by lawyers in the finance or tax department. Despite the confusion that can sometimes be found in case law, it is clear that tax advice is legal advice.[51] Thus, communications to and from an attorney in

---

communications were for the purpose of obtaining information not requesting legal advice; the court stated that privilege does not protect communications between counsel and third parties); *United States v. Frederick*, 182 F.3d 496 (7th Cir. 1999), *cert. denied*, 120 S. Ct. 1157 (2000) (no privilege or work-product doctrine protection when attorney and accountant were both engaged for the purpose of preparing a return; court held that a "dual-purpose document," intended for both preparing tax returns and preparing for litigation, is not privileged).

[46] *United States v. ChevronTexaco Corp.*, 241 F. Supp. 2d 1065, 1073 (N.D. Cal. 2002); *see also Boca Investerings Partnership v. United States*, 31 F. Supp. 2d 9, 99–1 USTC ¶ 50,182 (D.C. 1998). ("Because an in-house lawyer often has other functions in addition to providing legal advice, the lawyer's role on a particular occasion will not be self-evident as it usually is in the case of outside counsel. A court must examine the circumstances to determine whether the lawyer was acting as a lawyer rather than as a business advisor or management decision-maker.") Thus, although the privilege applies to communications between a corporation and its in-house counsel in the same manner and to the same degree as communications with outside counsel (*see United States v. Mobil Corp.*, 149 F.R.D. 533, 537 (N.D. Tex. 1993)), when the communication is with in-house counsel for a corporation, the corporation must clearly demonstrate that the advice to be protected was given in a professional legal capacity. This requirement prevents corporations from shielding their business transactions from discovery simply by funneling their conversations through a licensed attorney. *See Avianca, Inc. v. Corriea*, 705 F. Supp. 666, 676 (D.D.C. 1989).

[47] 449 U.S. at 390–391 ("the privilege exists to protect not only the giving of professional advice to those who can act on it but also the giving of information to the lawyer to enable him to give sound and informed advice . . . The first step in the resolution of any legal problem is ascertaining the factual background and sifting through the facts with an eye to the legally relevant").

[48] *Id.* at 395; *United States v. Mobil Corp.*, 93–1 USTC ¶ 50,335 (N.D. Tex. 1993); *In re LTV Sec. Litig.*, 89 F.R.D. at 601; *United States v. Lipsky*, 492 F. Supp. 35, 41 (N.D. Tex. 1979); *Burlington Indus., Inc. v. Exxon Corp.*, 65 F.R.D. 26, 36, 37 (D. Md. 1974).

[49] *In re LTV Sec. Litig.*, 89 F.R.D. at 600, 601.

[50] *Id.* at 601.

[51] *See, e.g., United States v. ChevronTexaco Corp.*, 241 F. Supp. 2d 1065, 1076 (N.D. Cal. 2002) (tax analysis of transaction is "rooted virtually entirely in the law"). While the overwhelming weight of authority is that legal advice regarding tax matters is privileged, in a recent case, *In re Grand Jury*, 13 F.4th 710 (9th Cir. 2021), 2021 U.S. App. LEXIS 27420, the Ninth Circuit stated "[w]e are aware, for example, that normal tax advice—even coming from lawyers—is generally not privileged, and courts should be careful to not

connection with receiving tax advice should also be privileged if it is not intended to be disclosed on a tax return.[52] One court has raised serious doubt as to whether the attorney-client privilege should apply to "boiler-plate templates that [were] almost, if not completely, identical" and "nothing more than an orchestrated extension of [the tax advisor's] marketing machine."[53] Nonetheless, the central question is whether a client was seeking legal—i.e., tax—advice, and if the answer is yes, privilege applies and can be invoked to protect against disclosure to the Service and other third parties.

[c] Communication Must Be Between Attorney and Client

In order for a communication to be privileged, it must be between the attorney and the client. As reflected in the *Upjohn* case, certain employees of a corporate client may not be recognized as "the client," and communications between them and counsel accordingly would not be subject to the privilege.[54]

Communication between in-house and outside counsel regarding legal advice to be given to the corporate client would generally be protected by the privilege.[55] If the intercounsel communication does not concern confidential information, however, the communication may not be within the scope of the privilege. Even so, if such communication or any other communication to which an attorney was a party was made in anticipation of litigation, the communication may still be protected from disclosure by the work-product doctrine even though the privilege does not apply.[56] Written statements, private memoranda, and personal recollections prepared or formed by counsel for a client in anticipation of litigation generally may not be discovered by a party adverse to the client.[57]

---

accidently create an accountant's privilege where none is supposed to exist." 2021 U.S. App. LEXIS 27420, *14, note 5 (emphasis added). This conclusion was quite shocking to the tax bar on a variety of fronts and, on January 27, 2022, the Ninth Circuit appropriately amended its opinion. The court removed its reference to "normal tax advice." In particular, the court changed the language in footnote 5 to "[w]e are aware, for example, that normal tax return preparation assistance—even coming from lawyers—is generally not privileged, and courts should be careful to not accidentally create an accountant's privilege where none is supposed to exist." *See* 2021 U.S. App. LEXIS 39178 (9th Cir., Jan. 27, 2022), at *14. This change is more in line with prior precedent which recognizes the significant difference between tax advice related to tax return preparation versus legal tax advice regarding the interpretation of cases, statutes and regulations. *See also* Section 8.01[3][d].

[52] *United States v. Abrahams*, 905 F. 2d 1276, 1284 (9th Cir. 1990) (overruled on other grounds, *United States v. Jose*, 131 F.3d 1325 (9th Cir. 1997)).

[53] *United States v. KPMG LLP*, 316 F. Supp. 2d 30, 40 (D.D.C. 2004); *compare United States v. BDO Seidman*, 2004 U.S. Dist. LEXIS 12145 *8 (June 29, 2004) (rejecting government's improper marketing-arrangement argument for lack of evidence.)

[54] *See* Section 8.01[3][a]. *See also United States v. Kovel*, 296 F.2d 918 (2d Cir. 1961), which held that the attorney-client privilege extends to certain confidential communications by an attorney or client to an accountant hired to assist the attorney in advising on legal matters. *See* discussion at Section 8.04[3].

[55] *See generally U.S. v. Sanmina Corp & Subsidiaries*, 115 AFTR 2d 2015–1882 (DC CA 2015): Attorney-client and work product privileges applied to two tax-advice memoranda supporting a $503 million worthless stock deduction, even though the memoranda were (i) prepared by in-house tax department lawyers discussing worthless stock deduction and the tax effect of related liquidation, (ii) distributed to the taxpayer's internal tax team and external accountants providing tax advice, and (iii) relied on by outside counsel's valuation report that was provided to the IRS; the memoranda were privileged communications that were not waived upon (a) distribution to taxpayer's accountants under the tax practitioner privilege in IRC Section 7525, or (b) providing the valuation report to the IRS since references to the memoranda therein did not disclose their content; furthermore, the memoranda met work product privilege as being created in anticipation of litigation.

[56] *Hickman v. Taylor*, 329 U.S. 495 (1947). *See* Section 8.02.

[57] *Hickman v. Taylor*, 329 U.S. at 511.

[d] Communication Must Be Made and Maintained in Confidence

In order for the privilege to attach to an attorney-client communication, the communication must have been made between privileged persons and maintained in confidence.[58] *In confidence* means the communicating person reasonably does not expect its contents to be disclosed to anyone outside the attorney-client relationship. Thus, the presence of a third party at an attorney-client meeting may destroy the privilege, which is something organizations should be vigilant about. There are exceptions, however, to the general rule that the presence of a third party destroys the privilege. For example, the presence of agents, such as legal secretaries and assistants, will not destroy the privilege. In some circumstances, an agent of the client, such as an insurance agent or accountant, may be present at meetings with the attorney if the agent's presence is needed to assist the attorney in providing legal advice.[59] The challenge of maintaining the confidentiality of an attorney-client communication is best met by sharing such communications on a "need-to-know" basis or with employees who are authorized to speak or act for the company.[60] To preserve the privilege, a company must also limit any further distribution of the documents or other communications in keeping with the claim of confidentiality[61] and otherwise take reasonable precautions to preserve the confidentiality of a communication in order to avoid a potential waiver as discussed in Section 8.01[4].

Certain types of information have been recognized as not protected by the privilege, however, even if they pass between the attorney and the client in confidence. For example, the privilege does not operate when an attorney is acting as a mere conduit of otherwise unprivileged information.[62] An attorney who has received an unprivileged communication from a person, such as an accountant, an appraiser, or a consultant, generally is not entitled to resist disclosure on the ground that he or she later conveyed such information to the client. Thus, if a report prepared by the accounting or finance department of a corporate client without direction from the attorney that would otherwise not be protected by the privilege was transmitted to the attorney and then retransmitted to management, the report may not be protected by the privilege.[63] This would be especially true if the report was prepared before the attorney became involved in the matter.[64] Documents prepared by an accountant and transmitted to an attorney and then on to the client have been recognized as privileged, however, when the accountant was employed by the attorney to assist the attorney in furnishing legal advice.[65]

The privilege does not protect the underlying facts of a communication against disclosure, because the protection of the privilege extends only to communications and not to facts. A fact is one thing and a communication concerning that fact is an entirely

---

[58] *Mead Data Cent., Inc. v. U.S. Dep't of Air Force*, 566 F.2d at 253.

[59] *Upjohn Co v. United States*, 449 U.S. 383, 389 (1981).

[60] *Miller v. Haulmark Transp. Sys.*, 104 F.R.D. 442, 445 (E.D. Pa. 1984).

[61] *Federal Trade Commission v. GlaxoSmithKline*, 294 F.3d 141, 147 (D.C. Cir. 2002).

[62] *Radiant Burners, Inc. v. American Gas Ass'n*, 320 F.2d at 324; *In re LTV Sec. Litig.*, 89 F.R.D. at 603.

[63] In this instance, the underlying document may not be privileged, though the communication or transmittal of that document to and from the attorney is likely privileged.

[64] *Bouschor v. United States*, 316 F.2d 451, 456 (8th Cir. 1963).

[65] *United States v. Clark*, 74–2 USTC ¶ 9562 (D. Idaho 1974). *See also United States v. Kovel*, 296 F.2d 918 (2d Cir. 1961), discussed at Section 8.04[3].

different thing. The client cannot be compelled to answer the question, "What did you say or write to the attorney?" However, the client may not refuse to disclose any relevant fact within her knowledge merely because she incorporated a statement of such fact into her communication to her attorney.[66]

The privilege does not encompass information concerning the nature of the attorney-client relationship. The terms and conditions of the attorney's employment, including the existence of a retainer and the amount of the attorney's fees, and the purpose for which the attorney has been engaged are outside the bounds of the privilege.[67] That being said, often attorney invoices contain the description of services rendered to a client, which constitutes privileged information. Thus, care should be taken when deciding whether to produce attorney invoices to the IRS. In many instances, the description of services rendered should be redacted due to privilege, especially when these descriptions are detailed. The Service often requests the invoices not to substantiate the amount paid to a law firm, but as a back-door way to determine the legal and factual issues that were the focus of the attorney's work. Experience shows that the Service will often protest these redactions, but it rarely does more than complain.[68]

The attorney-client privilege will not apply to a client's communications with an attorney " 'for the purpose of getting advice for the commission of a fraud' or crime."[69] The IRS and Department of Justice Tax Division have argued that certain aggressive tax shelter transactions are "suggestive" of civil tax fraud, and therefore, communications in furtherance of the alleged tax shelter should not be protected against disclosure by the attorney-client privilege.[70] Similarly, the IRS has argued that the "complexity" of certain transactions suggest tax fraud.[71] Courts have largely rebuffed these arguments for the basic reason that "the complexity of the transaction . . . [may] reflect[ ] creativity on the part of the [taxpayer's] attorney, but neither complexity nor the deep involvement of counsel are indicative of fraud."[72] Further, it is clear that communications made in the course of defending against charges of past misconduct are protectable, whereas communications made in the course of a continuing fraud are not protectable.[73]

---

[66] *City of Philadelphia v. Westinghouse Elec. Corp.*, 205 F. Supp. at 831, quoted in *Upjohn Co. v. United States*, 449 U.S. at 395, 396.

[67] *In re LTV Sec. Litig.*, 89 F.R.D. at 603; *Cohen v. Uniroyal, Inc.*, 80 F.R.D. 480, 483 (E.D. Pa. 1978). *See IRS Practice and Procedure* ¶ 12.05[12].

[68] One potential option to preserve the privilege is to prepare two separate billing statements that include a simple invoice to be submitted to the organization's accounting department and a detailed billing description of the services to the legal department. Further distribution of the detailed billing description should, of course, be limited.

[69] *United States v. Zolin*, 491 U.S. 554, 563 (1989), quoting *O'Rourke v. Darbishire*, 1920. A. C. 581, 604 (P. C.).

[70] *See* Memorandum of Law in Support of United States' Motion for Summary Enforcement of Summonses, *United States v. Jenkins & Gilchrist, P.C.*, docket No. 03-CV-5693 (N.D. Ill. March 5, 2004).

[71] *United States v. Windsor Capital Corp.*, 524 F. Supp. 2d 74, 77–78 (D. Mass 2007).

[72] *Id.*

[73] *Id.* A practical reality is that the strength of a privilege may be impacted by the context in which it is asserted. A fairly common issue deals with so-called IRS "John Doe" summons requests for the production of documentation that would reveal the identities of taxpayers who participated in tax shelters. Typically, such summonses are issued to banks or commercial couriers. *In Taylor Lohmeyer Law Firm P.L.L.C. v. United States*, 125 AFTR 2d 2020–1844 (957 F.3d 505) (5th Cir. 2020), such a summons was actually issued to a law firm. The summons arose out of an IRS investigation of an unnamed taxpayer who allegedly used the firm's services to establish foreign accounts and entities, avoiding over $2 million in U.S. income tax. The IRS then

[4] Waiver

Information that is otherwise within the attorney-client privilege may lose its protection from disclosure if the privilege is waived. The waiver may be expressed or implied. The privilege may be waived by full or partial disclosure of, or by making testimonial use of, the privileged subject matter. The rules surrounding waiver and its scope have long rested on fairness considerations,[74] but a party claiming the privilege must affirmatively demonstrate nonwaiver.[75]

Several federal courts have applied a two-part test in determining whether the privilege has been constructively waived. The first component is a subjective inquiry as to whether the holder intended to waive the privilege. The second part of the test is an objective inquiry as to whether it is fair and consistent with the assertion of the claim or defense being made to allow the privilege to be invoked. In evaluating whether the communication for which the privilege has been claimed satisfies this second part of the test, the principal issue is whether the holder of the privilege has delved so far into the privileged matter that fairness requires that the privilege be terminated notwithstanding the absence of an intent to waive it.[76]

In some instances, it is unclear whether communications were not intended to remain confidential and were therefore not privileged in the first instance, or whether there had been a waiver of privilege. This nuance often arises in the context of tax-return preparation. Therefore, particular care should be given to the information provided to the tax return preparer. In this area, seeking the advice from counsel experienced in making these nuanced judgment calls is critical. Although there are exceptions, the rule of thumb is that information provided to tax-return preparers that is used to prepare the return may not be privileged.

[a] Effect of Voluntary Disclosure

The voluntary disclosure of a part of the privileged information may result in a waiver as to all communications concerning the subject disclosed.[77] In other words, the courts have generally held that a waiver as to one document waives the privilege with respect to all documents concerning the same subject matter.[78] Although it can be harsh when the scope of its application is broad, the "subject-matter-waiver" rule is ultimately

---

sought the identities of other clients of the firm who may have similarly used its services. The law firm moved to quash the very broad summons and sought blanket protection from disclosure. It contended that the client identities were privileged because, although the identity of clients is generally not privileged, revealing the identities here would lead to the disclosure of confidential information. The Fifth Circuit held that the clients' identities were not privileged because the identities were not "connected inextricably with a privileged communication" and because the IRS agent's declaration supporting the summons did not state that the IRS knew the substance of the legal advice given to the clients. The law firm's petition for rehearing *en banc* was denied in a close, 9–8 poll, with the dissenting judges noting prior precedent that client identities are privileged where disclosure would reveal the client's confidential motive for retaining an attorney and voicing concerns about the viability of the system of justice at large due to direct pressure being placed on the attorney-client privilege by an executive power. The case is being appealed to the Supreme Court.

[74] *See generally* 8 J. Wigmore, *Wigmore on Evidence* § 2327 (1961).

[75] *United States v. Landof*, 591 F.2d 36, 38 (9th Cir. 1978).

[76] *Sedco Int'l, SA v. Cory*, 683 F.2d 1201, 1206 (8th Cir.), *cert. denied*, 459 U.S. 1017 (1982); *United States v. Woodall*, 438 F.2d 1317, 1324 (5th Cir. 1970), *cert. denied*, 403 U.S. 933 (1971); Harding, " 'Show and Tell': An Analysis of the Scope of the Attorney-Client Waiver Standards," 14 Rev. Litig. 367 (1995).

[77] *Weil v. Investment/Indications, Research & Management, Inc.*, 647 F.2d at 24; *United States v. Aronoff*, 466 F. Supp. 855, 862 (S.D.N.Y 1979).

[78] *Standard Chartered Bank v. Ayala Int'l Holdings Inc.*, 111 F.R.D. 76, 85 (S.D.N.Y. 1986).

based on fairness principles, since it prevents a party from using the attorney-client privilege as both a sword and a shield by selectively waiving privilege as to favorable communications but asserting privilege with respect to harmful ones.

In determining the scope of the subject-matter waiver, courts will consider whether the privilege holder is attempting to use the privilege offensively and the extent of the prejudice to the opposing party that results from the holder's selective disclosure.

In *Weil v. Investment/Indications, Research & Management*,[79] the Ninth Circuit addressed the question of whether a party may disclose a privileged communication about a matter relevant to issues in the case and then invoke the privilege to prevent disclosure of other communications about the same matter. The Ninth Circuit noted that it has been widely held that voluntary disclosure of the content of a privileged communication constitutes a waiver of privilege as to all other communications on the same subject.[80] Fairness requires that when a certain level of disclosure has been reached, the privilege ceases whether or not the privilege holder intended that result.[81] In *Weil*, the court held that there was a waiver of the attorney-client privilege, but because the disclosure occurred early in the proceedings and was made to opposing counsel rather than to the court, and the opposing party was not prejudiced, the privilege was waived only as to communications about the matter actually disclosed.[82]

Federal Rules of Evidence, Rule 502, imposes limits on the subject-matter waiver of attorney-client privilege and work product in a federal proceeding or to a federal agency. It was written largely in response to widespread complaints that litigation costs had become prohibitive in part due to excessive document review and production costs that were driven by litigants' fear of a potential subject-matter waiver as a result of a minor or innocent disclosure of privileged material. Rule 502(a) therefore provides that the subject-matter waiver only applies if the waiver is intentional, and fairness requires additional disclosure (e.g., selective and misleading presentation of evidence). Rule 502(b) provides that when an inadvertent disclosure is made in a federal proceeding or to a federal agency, the disclosure does not operate as a waiver in a federal or state proceeding if the party (1) took reasonable steps to prevent disclosure, and (2) promptly took reasonable steps to rectify the error.[83]

---

79 647 F.2d 18 (9th Cir. 1981).

80 *Id.* at 24.

81 *Id.* (quoting 8 J. Wigmore, *Wigmore on Evidence* § 636 (1961)).

82 *Weil*, 647 F.2d at 25. In *United States v. Bell*, 95–1 USTC ¶ 50,006 (N.D. Cal. 1994), the court found that *Weil* would not require the disclosure of documents prepared by an expert to assist the taxpayer with regular business activities, as to which privilege had initially been asserted. Other courts have applied a fairness test to determine the appropriate scope of the subject-matter waiver. *See Consol. Litig. Concerning Int'l Harvester's Disposition of Wisconsin Steel (II)*, 1987 U.S. Dist. LEXIS 10912, *15 (N.D. Ill. 1987) (the court did not impose the subject-matter waiver when disclosure was made to non-litigant because the adverse party was in no worse position); *United States v. Rockwell Int'l*, 897 F.2d 1255, 1265 (3d. Cir. 1990) (acknowledges disagreement as to the extent of waiver resulting from disclosure to auditor). The waiver may also be limited to documents contemporaneous to the subject transaction and not extend to legal advice rendered at a later date, such as a post-transaction evaluation. *In re Pioneer Hi-Bred Int'l, Inc.*, 238 F.3d 1370 (Fed. Cir. 2001); *Long-Term Capital Holdings v. United States*, 3:01 CV 1290, 2003 U.S. Dist. LEXIS 7826 (D. Conn. Feb. 14, 2003). The analysis to determine whether communications are under the same subject matter can be rather involved. *See Pennison v. United States*, 118 A.F.T.R.2d (RIA) 5964 (E.D. La. 2016), citing to *Hunter v. Copeland*, Civil Action No: 03–21584, 2004 U.S. Dist. LEXIS 22209 (E.D. La. Nov. 2, 2004) (identifying seven factors to be considered).

83 Even prior to Rule 502(b), an inadvertent disclosure of privileged documents did not always result in waiver if the privilege holder made efforts "reasonably designed" to protect and preserve the privilege. *See United States v. De La Jara*, 973 F.2d 746, 750 (9th Cir. 1992). Although courts will consider other factors in

It has long been a general rule that if a taxpayer waives the attorney-client privilege, the waiver is with respect to all adversaries, including parties in an unrelated action.[84] However, Rule 502(c) provides that when the disclosure is made in a state proceeding and is not the subject of a state-court order concerning waiver, the disclosure does not operate as a waiver in a federal proceeding if the disclosure (1) would not be a waiver under Rule 502 if it had been made in a federal proceeding; or (2) is not a waiver under the law of the state where the disclosure occurred. Finally, Rule 502(d) provides that a federal court may order that the privilege or protection is not waived by disclosure connected with the litigation pending before the court—in which event the disclosure is also not a waiver in any other federal or state proceeding.[85]

[b] Disclosure to Third Party

The courts have been in disagreement as to whether the disclosure of otherwise privileged information to a governmental agency constitutes a waiver of the privilege.[86] However, voluntary disclosure of otherwise privileged information to a non-government third party generally constitutes a waiver of the right to assert the privilege respecting all parties.[87] In particular, a corporation waives the privilege when it discloses information to an accountant, unless the accountant's services are a necessary aid to the rendering of effective legal services to the client.[88] Moreover, no accountant-client privilege is recognized under federal law.[89]

The privilege issues that may arise in connection with providing confidential information and documents to independent auditors are set forth in Illustration 8-2.

ILLUSTRATION 8-2: USCo is a U.S.-based entity operating a worldwide manufacturing, distribution, and servicing business. USCo invests heavily in

deciding whether inadvertent disclosure justifies waiver of the privilege, such as the scope of discovery and the time taken to rectify the error, the most important factor is the degree of care used to protect privileged documents. *See Baranski v. United States*, 116 A.F.T.R.2d (RIA) 5414 (E.D. Mo. 2015) (the manner in which the government produced documents weighed against a finding that the government took reasonable precautions against inadvertent waiver).

84 *See, e.g., United States v. Bergonzi*, 216 F.R.D. 487 (N.D. Cal. 2003); *McMorgan & Co. v. First Cal. Mortg. Co.*, 931 F. Supp. 703 (N.D. Cal. 1996).

85 An example of an application of Rule 502(d) involved Microsoft Corp. agreeing, pursuant to a stipulated motion, to allow the IRS to inspect certain documents for a limited time during a joint meeting for which Microsoft claimed privilege with the understanding that Microsoft, in permitting the IRS a "quick peek," did not waive its privilege claims. *United States v. Microsoft Corp.*, W.D. Wash., No. 2:15-cv-00102, motions filed 5/23/16. An agreement on the effect of disclosure in a federal proceeding is binding only on the parties to the agreement, unless it is incorporated into a court order. *See* Federal Rules of Evidence Rule 502(e).

86 *Compare Permian Corp. v. United States*, 665 F.2d 1214, 1222 (D.C. Cir. 1981) (waiver), *with Diversified Indus., Inc. v. Meredith*, 572 F.2d at 611 (limited waiver). *See also Johnston v. Commissioner*, 119 T.C. 27, 36 (2002) (attorney-client privilege is impliedly waived when a taxpayer affirmatively raises a claim that can only be effectively disproven through discovery of attorney-client communications); *In re G-1 Holdings, Inc.*, 92 A.F.T.R.2d 2003–6070 (D.N.J.) (privilege waived when taxpayers affirmatively used attorney advice as defense to accuracy related penalty). *See also* Federal Rules of Evidence Rule 502(a).

87 *But see Schaeffler v. U.S.*, 806 F.3d 34 (2d Cir. 2015) (common interest doctrine as an exception to waiver); *see* Section 8.05[5][b].

88 *United States v. Cote*, 456 F.2d 142, 144 (4th Cir. 1972). *In re John Doe Corp.*, 675 F.2d 482, 488, 489 (2d Cir. 1982); *United States v. El Paso Co.*, 682 F.2d 530, 539–541 (5th Cir. 1982). Other post-*Upjohn* decisions that have also recognized disclosures to non-government third parties as waivers of the privilege include *Eglin Fed. Credit Union v. Cantor*, 91 F.R.D. 414, 419 (N.D. Ga. 1981) and *SICPA N. Am., Inc. v. Donaldson Enters.*, 179 N.J. Super. 56, 430 A.2d 262, 266 (Law Div. 1981).

89 *Couch v. United States*, 409 U.S. 322, 335 (1973); *Matter of Newton*, 718 F.2d 1015, 1021 (11th Cir. 1983), *cert. denied, Trio Mfg. Co. v. United States*, 466 U.S. 904 (1984). *But see* Section 8.04[2] (IRC Section 7525).

> research and development (technology intangibles), as well as in brand and image advertising (marketing intangibles). These intangibles contribute a significant part of USCo's profitability. USCo has established wholly-owned subsidiaries in all foreign countries in which there is a significant potential market. USCo restructured its global business model, in part, by forming an international technology company to be responsible for developing product and marketing intangibles for USCo's products ("Int'lCo"). Int'lCo was formed in a country having a low effective tax rate ("ForCntry").
>
> In the first two years following the restructuring, a significant amount of the worldwide income of the USCo group is allocated to Int'lCo, through improper transfer pricing methodologies and otherwise. USCo did not obtain any opinions or other support for the U.S. and other-country tax results of the restructuring. Assume that USCo hires a new auditor to prepare its audit and audited financial statements (NewAuditor), which reviews the restructuring transaction and determines that there are significant U.S. tax risks resulting from the restructuring, including significant "intangible strip issues" in each of the foreign operating subsidiaries of USCo.
>
> NewAuditor determines that there are material weaknesses arising from its SOX Section 404 review which could have potentially draconian consequences. Accordingly, it seems reasonable that the USCo tax executives would provide all the support that exists with respect to the Material Weakness Analysis Project to be undertaken by NewAuditor.
>
> Assume that the General Counsel of USCo has engaged transfer pricing experts at the law firm of Honey & Jones to independently evaluate the restructuring and determine whether it could render all appropriate opinions meeting transfer pricing penalty and related requirements in the U.S. and all other pertinent countries. On reviewing the situation, Honey & Jones informally advised the General Counsel that there were material exposures in each country, including the United States, and that it could not render opinions defending the results of the restructuring because the restructuring was carried out on aggressive grounds that produced results that, in the experienced view of Honey & Jones, did not meet applicable arm's-length standards. Honey & Jones also advised that there were transfer pricing penalty exposures in the United States and some of the other countries.

Should the work product of Honey & Jones be turned over to NewAuditor in connection with its SOX Section 404 review? In this regard, the PCAOB has adopted Auditing Standard No. 3, which established new requirements for the scope of workpapers that the auditor must maintain. Further, during 2003, the AICPA amended its interpretation of auditing standard (AU) section 326, Evidential Matter, as it pertains to the effect of an inability to obtain evidential matter relating to income tax accruals. The revised interpretation, which has been included in the PCAOB's Reorganized Auditing Interpretations, states as follows:

> If the client's support for the tax accrual or matters affecting it, including tax contingencies, is based upon an opinion issued by an outside adviser with respect to a potentially material matter, the auditor should obtain access to the opinion, notwithstanding potential concerns regarding attorney-client or other forms of privilege. The audit documentation should include either the actual

> advice or opinions rendered by an outside adviser, or other sufficient documentation or abstracts supporting both the transactions or facts addressed as well as the analysis and conclusions reached by the client and adviser. Alternatives such as redacted or modified opinions may be considered, but must nonetheless include sufficient content to articulate and document the client's position so that the auditor can formulate his or her conclusion. Similarly, it may be possible to accept a client's analysis summarizing an outside adviser's opinion, but the client's analysis must provide sufficient competent evidential matter for the auditor to formulate his or her conclusion. In addition, client representations may be obtained stating that the client has not received any advice or opinions that are contradictory to the client's support for the tax accrual.[90]

If USCo provides the work product of Honey & Jones, whatever it may be, to NewAuditor, this may waive the attorney-client privilege.[91] Any workpapers provided to NewAuditor may provide an audit trail for the Service and other-country tax authority examiners.

[c] Disclosure to Employees

A disclosure of information by a corporation to employees other than those who need to know the information to assist counsel in furnishing legal advice raises questions of waiver. Generally, employees to whom disclosure could be made without waiving the privilege might include employees who (i) are in a position to add to, clarify, or correct information being supplied to counsel, (ii) are directly dealing with counsel on the matter in question, or (iii) may be required to make decisions on the basis of the legal advice provided.[92] For example, in *Upjohn*, certain employees received questionnaires and were told "to treat the investigation as 'highly confidential' and not to discuss it with anyone other than Upjohn employees who might be helpful in providing the requested information."[93] The Supreme Court noted that the responses to the questionnaires and the notes of the interviews had been treated as confidential and were not "disclosed to anyone except Upjohn's general counsel and outside counsel."[94] By these statements, the Court appeared to recognize with approval that Upjohn had maintained an appropriate level of confidentiality with regard to the information within the corporation.

[d] Disclosure Between Related Corporations

The communication of otherwise privileged information between related corporations generally does not constitute a waiver of the privilege regarding the

---

[90] AI 28: Evidential Matter Relating to Income Tax Accruals: Auditing Interpretations (AU section 9326, Evidential Matter: Auditing Interpretations of Section 326, paragraph 2.22). *See also* https://pcaobus.org/oversight/standards/archived-standards/pre-reorganized-auditing-standards-interpretations/details/AU9326.

[91] Although attorney-client privilege may be waived, work product protections may survive. *See* Section 8.02[3][a] and Section 8.05[5].

[92] *See* Sachs, *Implications of the Upjohn Decision for Tax Practitioners*, 40 NYU Inst. Fed. Tax'n ¶ 38.03[1] (1982). In some circumstances, an agent of the client, such as an insurance agent or accountant, may be present at meetings with the attorney if the agent's presence is needed to assist the attorney in providing legal advice. *See Miller v. Haulmark Transp. Sys.*, 104 F.R.D. 442, 445 (E.D. Pa. 1984).

[93] *Upjohn Co. v. United States*, 449 U.S. at 387.

[94] *Id.* at 395.

information. In *Duplan Corp. v. Deering Milliken, Inc.*,[95] the court considered the communication of information by a corporation to its parent, subsidiary, and affiliate corporations. Holding that the communication of otherwise privileged information by the corporation to a related corporation did not waive the confidentiality privilege, the court stated that "although an interest of a third party corporation from a commercial standpoint would not establish a sufficient community of interest, the fact that the communications are among formally different corporate entities which are under common ownership or control leads this court to treat such inter-related-corporate communications in the same manner as intra-corporate communications."[96] The *Duplan* court cited the leading case of *United States v. United Shoe Machinery Corp.*,[97] in which the court there stated that the client was United Shoe Machinery Corporation and all its subsidiaries and affiliates considered collectively. The *Duplan* court concluded:

> Thus, if a corporation with a legal interest in an attorney-client communication relays it to another related corporation, the attorney-client privilege is not thereby waived. If the communication were relayed to an unrelated third-party corporation, the privilege would be waived.
>
> If any communication is made among Chavanoz [a French corporation], its parent, affiliates, and/or subsidiaries for which an attorney-client privilege is claimed, there is no waiver of the privilege.[98]

The court in *Duplan* in fact went further and held that the privilege was not waived by the communication of otherwise privileged information between unrelated corporations that had a sufficient community of interest in the information. The court found that a corporation that was unrelated to the parent-client corporation had a community of interest with the parent because it had a duty to act through its patent department as a legal advisor to the parent-client corporation on patent matters. Finding this community of interest to be sufficient, the court held that there was no waiver of the privilege when confidential information was transferred from one of the corporations to the other.[99]

The commingling of otherwise privileged information with nonprivileged, nonconfidential information in a corporation's general files generally does not constitute a waiver of the privilege, although such a practice should be avoided.[100]

§ 8.02 Work-Product Doctrine

[1] Overview

Information that is not protected by the attorney-client privilege may still be protected from disclosure by the work-product doctrine, an independent source of protection against disclosure. The work-product doctrine was first enunciated in

---

95 397 F. Supp. 1146 (D.C.S.C. 1974).

96 *Id.* at 1184.

97 89 F. Supp. 357 (D. Mass. 1950).

98 *Duplan*, 397 F. Supp. at 1184–1185.

99 *Id.* at 1175, 1184. The court also stated that a community of interest exists among separate corporations where they have an identical legal interest with respect to the subject matter of a communication between and a client concerning legal advice. *Id.* at 1172.

100 *James Julian, Inc. v. Raytheon Co.*, 93 F.R.D. 138, 142 (D. Del. 1982).

Hickman v. Taylor[101] and has been held to apply to information sought via an IRS summons issued pursuant to IRC Section 7602.[102]

The *Hickman* Court provided that the work product privilege has two purposes. First, to "preserve a zone of privacy in which a lawyer can prepare and develop legal theories and strategy 'with an eye toward litigation' free from unnecessary intrusion by his adversaries"[103] who could effectively take a free ride. Second, the privilege further avoids the resulting deterrent to a lawyer's committing his thoughts to paper and the consequential inefficiencies that would arise.[104] The work-product doctrine thus serves to protect information assembled by an attorney (or prepared by the attorney's client or potentially a similarly aligned party, such as the client's independent auditor[105]) and the attorney's mental impressions, as well as the "legal theories and strategies he has pursued or adopted as derived from interviews, statements, memoranda, correspondence, briefs, legal and factual research, mental impressions, personal beliefs and other tangible and intangible means."[106] Work product represents the efforts expended by an attorney during the course of an attorney-client relationship; its attendant protection against disclosure belongs to and may be exercised by the attorney.[107]

The work-product doctrine protects a broader range of materials than the attorney-client privilege. Work-product protection applies to some information supplied to an attorney during preparation of a case, such as the impressions, observations, and opinions of a person hired by the attorney and acting under his supervision in preparation for litigation.[108] Work-product protection has been extended to a variety of different types of data, reflecting the various routes by which counsel may develop a matter. This has included notes, memos, and materials prepared by the attorney;[109] notes made by a party or witness at counsel's request;[110] conversations regarding a suit and how it should be handled;[111] materials used to choose a posture with respect to litigation prepared by client employees for review by counsel or senior executives;[112] and

---

[101] 329 U.S. 495 (1947).

[102] *See Upjohn v. United States*, 449 U.S. at 396–402 (protecting as work product attorney's notes and memoranda based on witnesses' oral statements to the extent they revealed the attorney's mental processes and holding that disclosure would not be required simply on a showing of substantial need and inability to obtain an equivalent without undue hardship).

[103] *Hickman*, 329 U.S. at 510–11.

[104] *Id.* at 511.

[105] In *United States v. Deloitte Touche LLP*, 610 F.3d 129 (D.C. Cir. 2010), the D.C. Circuit Court held that the work product privilege was available to a document created by the taxpayer's independent auditor prepared in connection with determining the appropriate tax reserve since the document contained legal advice of the taxpayer's legal counsel that was provided in anticipation of litigation). *See* Section 8.05[5][b].

[106] *State ex rel. Dudek v. Circuit Court for Milwaukee County*, 150 N.W.2d 387 (Wis. 1967).

[107] Ghent, *Development Since Hickman v. Taylor of Attorney's 'Work Product' Doctrine*, 35 ALR 3d 412, 423 (1971).

[108] *Scourtes v. Fred W. Albrecht Grocery Co.*, 15 F.R.D. 55 (D. Ill. 1959).

[109] *Hickman v. Taylor*, 329 U.S. 495 (1947).

[110] *Derderian v. Polaroid Corp.*, 121 F.R.D. 13 (D. Mass. 1988) (party seeking notes had access to persons actually involved in the notes); *S&A Painting Co. v. OWB Corp.*, 103 F.R.D. 407 (W.D. Pa. 1984).

[111] *Ceco Steel Prods. Corp. v. HK Porter Co.*, 31 F.R.D. 142 (N.D. Ill. 1962).

[112] *Hydramar, Inc. v. General Dynamics Corp.*, 119 F.R.D. 367, 370 (E.D. Pa. 1988) (found to be opinion work product in this situation).

computer printouts prepared for use of counsel (mental impressions and legal opinions included in program used to prepare the reports).[113]

It should also be noted that among the differences between the work-product doctrine and the attorney-client privilege is that the former provides only a qualified immunity from discovery while the latter is absolute. An adversary may obtain work-product if substantial need[114] for the information can be established and obtaining the information from other sources would result in undue hardship. Even if these factors are established by the adversary, however, the attorney's thoughts, mental impressions, conclusions, opinions, and legal theories are still protected from disclosure.[115]

[2] "Anticipation of Litigation"

For work-product protection against disclosure to apply, the work must have been performed "in anticipation of litigation."[116] Note that work-product protections are narrower than attorney-client privilege—work product requires "anticipation of litigation" while attorney-client privilege only requires that a client is seeking legal advice, regardless of whether litigation is anticipated. In many cases, work-product protections and attorney-client privilege provide overlapping protections against involuntary disclosure of information to third parties.

[3] Waiver

[a] General

The principles regarding waiver of the work-product doctrine have some differences from the attorney-client privilege. One basic difference is that unlike the attorney-client privilege, which belongs to the client, the work-product doctrine belongs to the attorney and may be waived by him. Another difference is that the work-product protection is not waived by disclosure to a third party as the attorney-client privilege generally is,[117] but, as with the attorney-client privilege, facts within work-product materials are subject to

---

[113] *Santiago v. Miles*, 121 F.R.D. 636 (W.D.N.Y. 1988). Interesting work product privilege issues arise in connection with awards paid to whistleblowers under IRC Section 7623, which permits the U.S. government to compensate whistleblowers who provide significant information that leads to the collection of taxes. *See generally*, Coder, *Law Firm Analyzes Unrecognized Tax Benefit Reserves Among Fortune 500*, Tax Analysts Doc. No. 2010–19374 (Sept. 2, 2010) (citing report from the Ferraro Law Firm that sets forth the FASB ASC 740–10 unrecognized tax benefit reserves of the Fortune 500 companies, and notes that the details in the tax accrual work papers often make for valuable tax whistleblower submissions).

[114] Substantial need sufficient to overcome a work product claim is generally limited to situations where there is no equivalent or alternative source, such as an interview memorandum for a witness who is dead or unavailable. *See, e.g., In re Grand Jury Investigation*, 599 F.2d 1224 (3d Cir. 1979). *See also Hartz Mountain Indus., Inc. v. Commissioner*, 93 T.C. 521, 527–28 (1989) (taxpayer ordered to produce work-product materials prepared by counsel during settlement negotiations in prior antitrust litigation, because (1) there was no substantial equivalent of the materials in showing the taxpayer's intent regarding the settlement, and (2) the work product was prepared a decade before in a different litigation); *Sterling Trading Opportunities, L.L.C. v. Commissioner*, T.C. Memo. 2007–339 (IRS allowed to obtain notes taken by the attorney and client in a meeting about alleged tax shelter transactions because the IRS had demonstrated substantial need and lack of other means for obtaining equivalent information).

[115] Federal Rules of Civil Procedure 26(b)(3). Mental impressions, conclusions, opinions or legal theories may be discoverable only upon a showing of "more than substantial need and undue hardship," a standard sometimes described as "between high and absolute." *See Upjohn Co. v. United States*, 449 U.S. 383, 400–02 (1981).

[116] This requirement is discussed more fully at Section 8.05[5].

[117] *In re Sealed Case*, 676 F.2d 793 (D.C. Cir. 1982). *See also Merrill Lynch & Co., Inc. v. Allegheny Energy, Inc.*, 229 F.R.D. 441 (S.D.N.Y. 2004) (work-product privilege not waived when disclosure is made to third party that shares common interest in controversy).

disclosure.[118] Work-product protection may be waived in two ways. First, it is waived if the attorney attempts to make testimonial use of the protected material.[119] It may also be waived by voluntary disclosure to an adversary.[120] The scope of waiver depends on considerations of fairness under the circumstances.[121] If there is no prejudice to the other party, a court may restrict waiver to the statement or information disclosed.[122]

The danger that information disclosed to an accountant for purposes other than aiding in the furnishing of legal advice may later be discoverable by the Service is demonstrated in *United States v. Arthur Young & Co.*,[123] in which Arthur Young & Co., a public accounting firm, was responsible for reviewing the financial statements of a publicly held client as required by the federal securities laws. In the course of its review, Arthur Young & Co. prepared tax accrual workpapers to verify the client's statement of its contingent tax liabilities. On auditing the client's returns, the Service learned that the client had made certain questionable payments from a special account. Thereafter, the Service instituted a criminal investigation of the client and issued an administrative summons to Arthur Young & Co. that required the accounting firm to make all of its files concerning the client available to the Service. When Arthur Young & Co. resisted the summons, the Service commenced an enforcement action.

The Second Circuit held that, in certain circumstances, a work-product immunity doctrine protected from disclosure tax-accrual workpapers prepared by independent accountants in the course of compliance with the federal securities laws and that the doctrine applied in this case. Reversing the Second Circuit's decision, the U.S. Supreme Court held that the tax-accrual workpapers were subject to disclosure under the pertinent criminal provisions of the Code,[124] and that there was no justification for the judicial creation of a work-product doctrine for tax-accrual workpapers.[125]

In *U.S. v. Deloitte*,[126] the D.C. Circuit held that the taxpayer did not waive the work product privilege with respect to documents prepared by the taxpayer or its counsel in anticipation of litigation, even though the taxpayer disclosed those documents to its independent auditors as part of the auditor's review of the adequacy of the taxpayer's tax reserve for book purposes. The court distinguished *Arthur Young* based on the fact that in *Deloitte* the government was not merely seeking discovery of the auditor's views on a company's financial statements, but rather an attorney's thoughts and mental impressions developed in anticipation of litigation. Citing from the concurring opinion

---

[118] *See, e.g., Admiral Ins. Co. v. United States District Court for the District of Ariz.*, 881 F.2d 1486 (9th Cir. 1989) (holding that the operation of an evidentiary privilege does not shield from discovery the underlying facts). *See also United States v. Deloitte & Touche LLP*, 610 F.3d 129 (D.C. Cir. 2010); *United States v. Textron*, 577 F.3d 21 (1st Cir. 2009) (*en banc*), discussed at Section 8.05[5].

[119] *United States v. Nobles*, 422 U.S. 225, 239–240 (1975). *See also Sporck v. Peil*, 759 F.2d 312, 317–19 (3d Cir. 1985); *Salem Financial, Inc. v. United States*, 102 Fed. Cl. 793 (2012) (the court held that the taxpayer waived work-product protection, attorney-client privilege, and tax practitioner privilege under IRC Section 7525 by putting the tax advisor's advice at issue in defense of penalties).

[120] *In re Subpoena*, 738 F.2d 1367 (D.C. Cir. 1982).

[121] 8 J. Wigmore, *Wigmore on Evidence* § 2321 (1961).

[122] *See, e.g., United States v. Nobles*, 422 U.S. 225 (1975) ("fishing expedition" not allowed; court could review materials in camera); *Weil v. Investment/Indications, Research & Management*, 647 F.2d 18 (9th Cir. 1981).

[123] 465 U.S. 805 (1984).

[124] IRC Section 7602.

[125] *United States v. Arthur Young & Co.*, 465 U.S. at 815.

[126] 610 F.3d 129 (D.C. Cir. 2010).

in *Hickman*, the *Deloitte* court held that allowing the discovery of taxpayer documents that were prepared in anticipation of litigation would "let the government litigate on wits borrowed from the adversary."

[b] Disclosure to Avoid Penalties

Taxpayers are permitted under certain circumstances to rely on tax advice to avoid tax penalties.[127] However, taxpayers need to be painfully aware that affirmative reliance on tax advice to avoid imposition of tax penalties may waive work product privilege that potentially protects against disclosure of such tax advice. For example, in *Salem Financial, Inc v. United States*,[128] the Service disallowed the taxpayer's reported foreign tax credits and related deductions. During the controversy, the Service sought certain documents prepared by the taxpayer's Big Four auditor that the taxpayer claimed were prepared in anticipation of litigation and thus subject to work product protection.[129] The IRS asserted, and the court agreed, that the taxpayer waived the work product privilege with respect those documents due to taxpayer's reliance on the documents in its reasonable cause defense to avoid IRC Section 6662 accuracy-related penalties. The court found that since "[s]ubject matter waiver precludes [taxpayer] from using [its auditor's] favorable advice as a defense to penalties while simultaneously shielding potentially unfavorable advice that appears to have influenced [taxpayer's] tax reserve position."[130] The court also held that the taxpayer cannot cherry pick selected parts of tax advice rendered to avoid penalties, but protect the remainder of the advice from the IRS. Thus, a taxpayer may face a difficult dilemma: whether to assert a reasonable reliance defense for tax penalties based on tax advice, or forgo such defense and seek to claim that such documents are subject to privilege.[131]

---

[127] *See, e.g.*, IRC Section 6662(c) (Section 6662(b)(1) negligence penalty may be avoided by taxpayer's reasonable reliance on advice of counsel or a qualified accountant); IRC Section 6664(c)(1) and Treas. Reg. § 1.6664–4(b)(1) (penalty does not apply to portion of underpayment if it is shown that taxpayer relied on professional advisor and such reliance was reasonable and in undertaken in good faith).

[128] 102 Fed. Cl. 793 (2012).

[129] *See generally* Section 8.02.

[130] *See also Evergreen Trading LLC v. United States*, 80 Fed. Cl. 122 (2007) (taxpayers required to produce tax documents unless they expressly disavow any reliance-upon-counsel defenses to the accuracy penalties at issue).

[131] There have been other cases along these lines. *Compare AD Investment 2000 Fund LLC v. Commissioner*, 142 T.C. 248 (2014) (court required disclosure to IRS of two tax opinions after taxpayers asserted the reasonable belief defense to IRC Section 6662 penalties under Treas. Reg. § 1.6662–4(g)(4), finding that the attorney-client privilege was forfeited with respect to the opinions as the taxpayers placed the partnerships' "legal knowledge and understanding into issue" to establish their reasonable legal beliefs and assert a good-faith and state-of-mind defense) and *Eaton Corporation & Subsidiaries v. Commissioner of Internal Revenue*, TC Order, Docket No. 5576-12 (2015) (Tax Court order concluded that assertion of a reasonable-cause/good-faith defense puts into issue otherwise privileged information that would reveal the experience and knowledge along with the subjective intent and state of mind of those who acted on behalf of the taxpayer regarding the taxpayer's good-faith efforts to comply with the tax law), *with U.S. v. Micro Cap KY Insurance Company*, 119 A.F.T.R.2d (RIA) 1279 (E.D. Ky. 2017) (concluding taxpayer email documents requested by the IRS in a captive insurance case were protected under the attorney-client privilege, even though the taxpayers asserted reliance on those documents as a reasonable cause defense to penalties in a different, but related, Tax Court case). *See also In re Pioneer Hi-Bred Int'l, Inc.*, 238 F.3d 1370, 1374–75 (Fed. Cir. 2001) (disclosure of and reliance on tax advice as to tax consequences of merger in a proxy statement "waived the attorney-client privilege with respect to all documents which formed the basis for that advice, all documents considered by counsel in rendering the advice, and all reasonably contemporaneous documents reflecting discussions by counsel or others considering that advice"). In the author's opinion, there is a substantial difference between disclosing the substance of tax advice and merely stating that tax advice was obtained, though the IRS will almost certainly challenge the assertion of privilege and work-product protections in such a scenario.

§ 8.03 Application in International Tax Matters

The extent of privilege and work-product protection in the context of international tax matters involves a variety of competing considerations. In the traditional litigation context, privilege and work-product matters arise as they have since the early days of the English common law.[132] There is nothing unique about international tax controversies in this respect.[133] This is also true of transfer pricing controversies prior to the effective date of the transfer pricing penalty.[134] In these situations, transfer pricing analyses enjoy the same protections as any other materials prepared by or for counsel.

The transfer pricing penalty of IRC Section 6662(e) and IRC Section 6662(h) has ushered in a new era. That penalty requires that the corporation prepare its transfer pricing documentation contemporaneous with the filing of its return, for which documentation must be provided to the Service within 30 days of request. As such, the transfer pricing documentation may be viewed as an element of the tax return itself, which would seriously complicate the analysis of privilege related matters, even if counsel renders the opinions in question.

§ 8.04 Extension of Privilege to Nonlawyers Authorized to Practice Before the Service

[1] In General

The availability of a confidentiality privilege for communications between taxpayers and their attorneys—but not between taxpayers and other professionals or persons authorized to practice before the Service—has been the source of significant controversy over the years. There are at least two elements to this issue. One is a marketing, or "fairness," issue. Nonlawyers argue that they suffer from a professional service marketing disadvantage when competing for significant consulting or controversy projects, because they cannot provide the same level of confidentiality enjoyed by "lawyers."

The second element arises from the expansion of accounting and consulting firms to include lawyers. In this sense, the individual has the same licensing and skills regardless of whether she practices in a law, accounting, or consulting firm. This has been a serious ambiguity. It has also led some bar groups to question whether such lawyers may be engaged in the unauthorized practice of law, in the sense that fees from legal services are shared with non-lawyers.[135]

The availability of a confidentiality privilege can be critical in the context of taxation practice and procedure, where the substantive issues are often unsettled and the amounts in controversy are frequently significant. Because planning for these transactions and developing strategies to resolve controversies often occur over a significant period, the availability of planning or preparation files to the Service could

---

[132] It is important to note that English common law does not extend to civil law countries, and consequently in these countries there may be little, no, or different protections for advice traditionally covered by privilege and work product in the United States.

[133] *See, e.g., United States v. Bell*, 95–1 USTC ¶ 50,006 (N.D. Cal. 1994).

[134] IRC Section 6662(e) and IRC Section 6662(h). Gottschalk, *Protecting Sensitive Transfer Pricing Documentation*, 5 Transfer Pricing 89 (June 4, 1997).

[135] *See* Dunn, *Tanner Would Extend Client Privilege to Accountants*, TNT 209–6 (Sept. 29, 1997). *See also Unauthorized Practice Complaint Against Arthur Andersen Dismissed*, 98 STN 158–18 (Aug. 17, 1998).

seriously jeopardize the position of the taxpayer. Indeed, in several recent IRS victories in international taxation controversies, the government's position has been strengthened by the availability of the records of the accountants who undertook the planning.[136]

[2] IRC Section 7525

The landscape in this area was altered in a dramatic and interesting fashion by Congress in the IRS Restructuring and Reform Act of 1998 (the IRS Restructuring Act).[137] While Congress statutorily extended, for federal income tax purposes, the attorney-client privilege to communications with certain authorized nonlawyer representatives, it did so in a way that provides stark restrictions on the scope of the privilege allowed. It also did not extend the work-product doctrine to such nonlawyer representatives,[138] and denied the privilege in the case of written communications with nonlawyers regarding certain corporate tax shelter matters. The latter exclusion is likely to cause even more confusion than existed prior to enactment of the IRS Restructuring Act.

In general, IRC Section 7525 as enacted by the IRS Restructuring Act provides that:

> [w]ith respect to any tax advice, the same common law protections of confidentiality which apply to a communication between a taxpayer and an attorney shall also apply to a communication between a taxpayer and any federally authorized tax practitioner to the extent the communication would be considered a privileged communication if it were between a taxpayer and an attorney.[139]

"Federally authorized tax practitioners" are (in addition to attorneys) certified public accountants, enrolled agents, and enrolled actuaries authorized to practice before the Service. A company's in-house tax advisor can also provide IRC Section 7525 privileged advice to the company.[140] The extended privilege granted by the provision may only be asserted in noncriminal tax proceedings before the Service, and in the federal courts with regard to such noncriminal tax proceedings brought by or against the United States.[141]

Moreover, the extension of confidentiality does not apply to written communications to a person relating to participation in a "corporate tax shelter." The specific language of the exclusion is that the confidentiality privilege shall not be applicable to:

---

[136] *See, e.g., Laidlaw Transp. v. Comm'r*, TC Memo 1998–232; *InverWorld v. Comm'r*, TC Memo 1996–301.

[137] The IRS Restructuring and Reform Act of 1998, Pub. L. No. 206, 105th Cong., 2d Sess. (July 22, 1998).

[138] Nonetheless, work-product protections may extend to materials prepared by non-attorneys, assuming that they were prepared in anticipation of litigation. *See, e.g., Schlicksup v. Caterpillar Inc.*, No. 09-CV-1208 (C.D. III. Aug. 19, 2011), citing *Caremark, Inc. v. Affiliated Computer Services, Inc.*, 195 F.R.D. 610, 615 (N.D. Ill. 2000). ("[W]hether a document is protected depends on the motivation behind its preparation, rather than on the person who prepares it.")

[139] IRC Section 7525(a)(1), added by IRS Restructuring Act § 3411(a). The extension of privilege to authorized federal tax practitioners is effective in the case of communications that occur on or after July 22, 1998. IRS Restructuring Act § 3411(c).

[140] *See United States v. Eaton Corp.*, 110 A.F.T.R.2d (RIA) 5638 (N.D. Ohio 2012).

[141] IRC Section 7525(a)(2). The provision does not, however, limit the present attorney-client privilege of confidentiality.

> any written communication which is—(1) between a federally authorized tax practitioner and (A) any person, (B) a director, officer, or employee, agent, or representative of the person, or (C) any other person holding a capital or profits interest in the person, and (2) in connection with the promotion of the direct or indirect participation of the person in any tax shelter (as defined in section 6662(d)(2)(C)(ii)).[142]

The cross-reference to the definition of "tax shelter," which includes any partnership, entity, plan, or arrangement "a significant purpose of which is the avoidance or evasion of income tax" is a very broad definition that could apply to many transactions not commonly thought of as abusive transactions.[143]

Congress has been concerned about so-called corporate tax shelters, and previously required registration of such shelters when provided in confidential form.[144] These actions have reflected congressional concern about the promotion of plans by taxpayer representatives that have a significant purpose of reducing federal tax liability (often colloquially referred to as "tax products"). Conference Report No. 105–599 (the Conference Report) explains the exclusion of corporate tax shelter communications from the extended privilege by noting that

> The Conferees do not understand the promotion of tax shelters to be part of the routine relationship between a tax practitioner and a client. Accordingly, the Conferees do not anticipate that the tax shelter limitation will adversely affect such routine relationships.[145]

The corporate tax shelter limitation is applicable only with respect to the extension of privilege to federally authorized practitioners, and does not include attorneys to whom the privilege was applicable prior to enactment of the IRS Restructuring Act of 1998. Stated differently, IRC Section 7525 does not limit the common-law attorney-client privilege, but it does limit the scope of privilege statutorily extended to non-attorneys.

As noted above, the extended privilege is not applicable in the case of criminal tax matters before the Service[146] or criminal tax proceedings in federal court brought by the United States[147] (which would presumably include any stage of such proceedings). In addition, because the privilege established by IRC Section 7525 applies only to the extent that communications would be privileged if they were between a taxpayer and an

---

[142] IRC Section 7525(b).

[143] *See* Conf. Rep. No. 599, 105th Cong., 2d Sess. 135 (June 24, 1998) (the 1998 Conference Report). *See also Valero Energy Corp. v. United States*, 569 F3d 626 (7th Cir. 2009) (defining promotion of a tax shelter broadly to mean furtherance or encouragement of a tax shelter and rejecting an interpretation that would limit the exception to prepackaged tax shelter products rather than an individualized tax reduction plan); *Countryside Ltd. Partnership v. Commissioner*, 132 T.C. 347 (2009) (holding that the exception for tax shelter promotion was ambiguous, and based on the legislative history, pronouncing the exception inapplicable to "routine relationships" between advisors and taxpayers and individualized tax advice). A case that has more recently caused some alarm regarding the application of IRC Section 7525 involved a summons enforcement dispute over documents related to a taxpayer's cost-sharing arrangement that the court found fell within the tax shelter exception of the rule. *See Order, United States v. Microsoft Corp.*, No. 15–102, at ECF No. 187 (W.D. Wash. Jan. 17, 2020). This conclusion is quite remarkable given that cost-sharing arrangements are a sort of safe-harbor and have been approved and regulated by Treasury, the OECD, and foreign governments for over 50 years. The decision has been heavily criticized and appears to be an outlier. *See* Johnson, Hildy & Horne, *Cost Sharing Is a Tax Shelter Now. Wait, What?* 168 Tax Notes Fed. 2193 (Sep. 21, 2020).

[144] IRC Section 6111(d).

[145] 1998 Conference Report 135.

[146] IRC Section 7525(a)(3)(A).

[147] IRC Section 7525(a)(3)(B).

attorney, the privilege itself is subject to all of the limitations of the attorney-client privilege, including waiver by disclosure.[148] The extension is applicable only for defined tax matters and is not applicable in the case of other federal or state proceedings.[149]

The extension to federally authorized practitioners is also limited in scope. By its terms, the extension applies to only "the same common law protections of confidentiality which apply to a communication between a taxpayer and an attorney."[150]

[3] Kovel Relationships

As noted, the attorney-client privilege applies only to specified communications between lawyer and client, and does not extend to communications between accountants and their clients.[151] However, In *United States v. Kovel*, the Second Circuit held that the privilege might apply in limited circumstances to communications made with an accountant hired by the attorney to assist the attorney in proving legal advice to the client.[152] The *Kovel* Court noted since "accounting concepts are a foreign language to some lawyers in almost all cases, and to almost all lawyers in some cases," the attorney-client privilege should protect communications made from a client to an accountant under the same circumstances under which the privilege would protect communications made in confidence to an interpreter of a foreign language. The Court cautioned, however, that the protection provided is limited,[153] and held that "what is vital to the privilege is that the communication be made in confidence for the purpose of obtaining legal advice from the lawyer. If what is sought is not legal advice but only accounting

[148] *See* Section 8.01[4].

[149] 1998 Conference Report 135 (such as proceedings before the SEC, or in dealings with nontax regulatory bodies in administrative or court proceedings). In a case involving tax shelter promotion matters alleged to have been undertaken by a public accounting firm, a federal district court, for the first time, upheld the privilege for authorized practitioners under IRC Section 7525. *See United States v. BDO Seidman*, 95 A.F.T.R.2d 2005–1725 (N.D. Ill. 2005).

[150] IRC Section 7525(a)(1).

[151] *See generally*, Section 8.01[2], *United States v. Arthur Young & Co.*, 465 U.S. 805 at 817 (1984).

[152] Independent of the so-called "Kovel privilege" and the protections provided by IRC Section 7525, certain documents prepared by an accountant may qualify for protection from discovery under the work product privilege, which protects documents prepared "in anticipation of litigation" from disclosure. *See, e.g., United States v. Deloitte Touche LLP*, 610 F.3d 129 (D.C. Cir. 2010); *United States v. Textron*, 577 F.3d 21 (1st Cir. 2009); *Wells Fargo & Co. v. United States*, No. 10–57 (D. Minn. 2013). *See* Section 8.02; Section 8.05[5].

[153] The "Kovel privilege" has been limited over the years. *See, e.g., Cavallaro v. United States*, 284 F.3d 236, 249 (1st Cir. 2002). In this case, the attorney failed to demonstrate that the hiring of an accountant by the attorney assisted the attorney in providing legal advice; involvement of accountant must be nearly indispensable or serve some specialized purpose in facilitating the attorney-client communications); the attorney also failed to prove that accountants were hired to assist lawyers in providing legal advice. *See also United States v. Adlman*, 68 F.3d 1495, 76 AFTR 2d 95–7188, 95–2 USTC ¶ 50579 (2d Cir. 1995) (memoranda prepared by an accounting firm at the request of an attorney, who was also company officer, addressing tax consequences of restructuring not protected by the attorney-client privilege; the memoranda were not prepared to assisting counsel in rendering legal advice to company based in part on (i) the accounting firm rendered extensive other services to the corporation but did not differentiate on its invoices the tax memoranda work from its other work for the corporation; (ii) no contemporaneous evidence, such as a separate retainer agreement, existed that supported the position that the accounting firm tax memoranda work was a different arrangement from its normal accounting work for the corporation; (iii) the attorney, who was also a corporate officer, did not have the tax expertise to assess the tax implications of the restructuring; and (iv) the accounting firm, rather than the attorney, prepared all the written analyses of the tax consequences and the accounting firm tax conclusions set directly to corporation); *United States v. Ackert*, 169 F3d 136, 138 (2d Cir. 1999) (communication between the corporate tax attorney and investment banker was not deemed privileged; "a communication between an attorney and a third party does not become shielded by the attorney-client privilege solely because the communication proves important to the attorney's ability to represent the client"); *Evergreen Trading LLC v. United States*, 80 Fed. Cl. 122 (2007) (no privilege where accountant was engaged by counsel to provide independent tax advice, rather than assist with accounting principles).

service, or if the advice sought is the accountant's rather than the lawyer's, no privilege exists."[154]

§ 8.05 Tax Accrual Workpapers

[1] In General

In ascertaining the correctness of any return or determining the tax liability of any person, IRC Section 7602(a) authorizes the Service to (i) examine any relevant or material books, records, and other material, (ii) issue an administrative summons to the taxpayer or any person having possession or custody of relevant data, and (iii) take the testimony of the recipient of the summons under oath.

In *United States v. Arthur Young & Co.*,[155] the U.S. Supreme Court held that tax accrual workpapers prepared by a taxpayer's outside auditors in the ordinary course of its audit to verify the taxpayer's statement of its contingent tax liabilities are "relevant" to an IRS audit, and not protected from disclosure under the work-product privilege.[156]

Although the decision in *United States v. Arthur Young & Co.* permitted the Service to request tax accrual workpapers as relevant to the Service's examination process, the Service has implemented a policy of requesting such workpapers only in unusual circumstances (the "policy of restraint").[157] As discussed below, however, in the case of certain potentially tax-motivated transactions, the Service exercises its right to request tax accrual workpapers. Further, whether the policy of restraint applies in the context of workpapers prepared in connection with financial statement disclosure of uncertain income tax positions pursuant to FASB requirements[158] remains an important and evolving issue confronting taxpayers and their advisors.[159]

[2] Tax Accrual and Audit Workpapers

In general, large public and non-public companies and their independent auditors prepare three different types of tax workpapers: (i) tax accrual workpapers, (ii) audit workpapers, and (iii) tax reconciliation workpapers. The Internal Revenue Manual ("IRM") sets forth different guidelines regarding a request by the Service to review these

---

[154] *Kovel*, 296 F.2d at 922.

[155] 465 U.S. 805 (1984).

[156] The Court in *Arthur Young & Co.* stated that "our complex and comprehensive system of federal taxation, relying as it does upon self-assessment and reporting, demands that all taxpayers be forthright in the disclosure of relevant information to the taxing authorities. Without such disclosure, and the concomitant power of the Government to compel disclosure, our national tax burden would not be fairly and equitably distributed. In order to encourage effective tax investigations, Congress has endowed the IRS with expansive information-gathering authority; § 7602 is the centerpiece of that congressional design." 465 U.S. 805, 815–16. *See also United States v. Bisceglia*, 420 U.S. 141, 145–46 (1975) (citing *United States v. Powell*, 379 U.S. 48 (1964), the Court stated that the powers granted to the Service by IRC Section 7602 to examine a taxpayer's books or other data which may be relevant and to issue summons in furtherance of that investigation "unquestionably involve some invasion of privacy, [but] they are essential to our self-reporting system. . . .").

[157] Subsequent to the U.S. Supreme Court decision in *Arthur Young & Co.*, the Service announced that it would continue its policy of not routinely requesting tax accrual workpapers during examinations. Announcement 84–46, 1984–18 I.R.B. 18.

[158] *See generally* Section 3.08 (discussing the financial statement disclosure requirements imposed by FASB ASC 740–10 on a company's uncertain income tax positions).

[159] *See* Section 8.05[6].

documents in connection with the audit of a taxpayer's tax return. These rules do not, however, apply to any criminal investigation by the Service.[160]

[a] Definition of Tax Accrual Workpapers

IRM Section 4.10.20.1.1(2) defines tax accrual workpapers as audit workpapers prepared by the taxpayer, the taxpayer's accountant or the taxpayer's independent auditor relating to the taxpayer's reserve for tax liabilities,[161] regardless of how that reserve might be reported on audited financial statements and to footnotes disclosing those tax reserves on audited financial statements. The tax accrual workpapers reflect an estimate of a company's tax liabilities.[162]

IRM Section 4.10.20.1.1(2)(a) states that the scope and quality of the tax accrual workpapers will vary, and typically include:

> determinations and related documentation of estimates of potential or contingent tax liabilities related to tax positions taken by the taxpayer on certain transactions. In addition, there may be an audit trail and/or complete explanation of the transactions. There may also be information on whether there was reliance on outside legal advice; an assessment of the taxpayer's position and potential for sustention; references to promotional materials; and comments on unwritten agreements, confidentiality agreements, restitution agreements, contingency fees, expectations, and other material facts surrounding the transactions.

Consistent with the policy of restraint, an IRS agent may not inquire about the existence or amount of a tax reserve established for any specific transaction since that typically amounts to an indirect request for a portion of the tax accrual workpapers relating to that specific transaction.[163] IRM Section 4.10.20.1.1(2)(b) notes, however, that a company's tax accrual workpapers do not include the total amount of the reserve established on a company's general ledger for all contingent tax liabilities applicable to a specific reporting period. Furthermore, any financial statement disclosure of a company's uncertain income tax positions as required by the FASB rules on accounting for uncertain tax positions and filed with the SEC is publicly available to the Service and not is covered by any form of Service restraint.[164]

[b] Audit Workpapers

As distinguished from tax accrual workpapers, audit workpapers are those workpapers created and retained by the independent auditor of a taxpayer that include information about the procedures and tests performed by the auditor, the information obtained, and the conclusions reached by the independent auditor's review of a

---

160 IRM Section 4.10.20.1(2) (05-04-2017).

161 These tax liabilities include current, deferred and potential or contingent tax liabilities. IRM Section 4.10.20.1.1(2) (07-12-2004).

162 The Internal Revenue Manual notes that in practice, tax accrual workpapers are alternatively referred to as the tax pool analysis, tax liability contingency analysis, tax cushion analysis, or tax contingency reserve analysis. The name given the workpapers by the taxpayer, the taxpayer's accountant, or the independent auditor is not determinative.

163 IRM Section 4.10.20.1.1(2)(c) (07-12-2004).

164 *See* Section 8.05[6], Section 3.08 and Section 3.09.

taxpayer's financial statements.[165] The audit workpapers, which may be shared with the taxpayer, may include work programs, analyses, memoranda, letters of confirmation and representation, abstracts of company documents, and schedules or commentaries prepared or obtained by the auditor. These workpapers provide important support for the independent auditor's opinion as to the fairness of the presentation of the financial statements, in conformity with generally accepted auditing standards and generally accepted accounting principles.

[c] Tax Reconciliation Workpapers

Tax reconciliation workpapers are those used in assembling financial data in preparation of the taxpayer's tax return, including final trial balances, adjusting entries and reconciliations of financial statements income to taxable income.[166] Significantly, tax reconciliation workpapers are not tax accrual workpapers even though they are used in the preparation of tax accrual workpapers.[167]

[3] Service Policy of Restraint for Tax Accrual Workpapers and Audit Workpapers

[a] Non-Listed Transactions

Under the policy of restraint, audit or tax accrual workpapers generally will be requested by the Service only in unusual situations.[168] As discussed below, this policy does not apply to certain so-called "listed transactions."[169] The policy of restraint also does not apply to tax reconciliation workpapers, which Service agents are advised to routinely request at the commencement of a tax audit.[170]

Despite the policy of restraint, a Service examiner may request audit or tax accrual workpapers under the following limited circumstances:

a. a specific issue has been identified by the Service examiner for which there exists a need for additional facts;

b. the examiner has sought from the taxpayer and available third parties all the facts known to them relating to the identified issue; and

c. the examiner has sought a supplementary analysis (not necessarily contained in the workpapers) of facts relating to the identified issue and the examiner has performed a reconciliation of the taxpayer's Schedule M-1 or M-3 as it pertains to the identified issue.[171]

---

[165] IRM Section 4.10.20.1.1(3) (07-12-2004). *See Regions Financial Corp. v. United States*, 101 A.F.T.R. 2d 2008–2179 (N.D. Ala. 2008) (tax accrual workpapers were protected by work protect doctrine and not waived by disclosure to auditors).

[166] IRM Section 4.10.20.1.1(1) (07-12-2004).

[167] Further, any preexisting documents that a taxpayer, its in-house accountant, or the taxpayer's outside auditor might rely upon to make evaluations or decisions regarding the tax reserves do not constitute tax accrual workpapers or audit workpapers. IRM Section 4.10.20.1.1(1) (07-12-2004).

[168] IRM Section 4.10.20.3 (12-08-2020).

[169] The policy of restraint does not apply to the Service's request for tax accrual workpapers involving listed transactions with respect to a return filed after February 28, 2000. A listed transaction means a transaction described in Treas. Reg. § 1.6011–4, and includes pursuant to Treas. Reg. § 1.6011–4(b)(2) transactions that are substantially similar to those specifically identified by the Service as listed transactions.

[170] IRM Section 4.10.20.2(1) (05-04-2017). *See also* Section 3.09.

[171] IRM Section 4.10.20.3.1(2) (07-20-2004).

IRM Section 4.10.20.3.1(1) cautions its examiners that a taxpayer's audit or tax accrual workpapers typically should be requested with discretion and then only when the factual data relating to the identified issue cannot be obtained from the taxpayer's records or from available third parties. Further, such request should only apply to the portion of the workpapers that is material and relevant to the tax audit.[172]

[b] Listed Transaction Exception

In 2002, the Service modified its policy of restraint in requesting tax accrual workpapers with respect to audits of tax returns in which the taxpayer obtains a benefit from one or more listed transactions.[173] The Service's policies governing requests for tax accrual workpapers in listed transactions apply only to returns filed after February 28, 2000, and vary according to when the tax return in question was filed.

Prior to requesting tax accrual workpapers under the modified policy relating to listed transactions, the Service examiner must first determine that there is a reasonable belief that the taxpayer has engaged in a listed transaction (including a transaction that is substantially similar to a listed transaction).[174] This belief may be based on, for example, (i) taxpayer disclosure filed with the Office of Tax Shelter Analysis, or (ii) other acknowledgement by the taxpayer that it engaged in a listed transaction.[175]

[i] Returns Filed After February 28, 2000 but Before July 1, 2002

For a return filed prior to July 1, 2002 and after February 28, 2000, that claims any tax benefit arising out of a listed transaction, the Service may in "appropriate circumstances"[176] request tax accrual workpapers pertaining to the listed transaction, if the taxpayer had an obligation to disclose the transaction under Treas. Reg. § 1.6011–4, and failed to do so.[177] Generally, the request will be limited to the tax accrual workpapers for the years under examination, although it may extend to other years that may be directly relevant to the examination years.

[ii] Returns Filed on or After July 1, 2002

With respect to the audit of a return filed on or after July 1, 2002 in which the benefit of a listed transaction was claimed, the IRM establishes the following standards concerning a request for tax accrual workpapers. If the return relates to only one listed transaction that was disclosed[178] under Treas. Reg. § 1.6011–4, the Service will generally

---

[172] IRM Section 4.10.20.3.1(1) (07-12-2004). The determination of what is material is based upon the examiner's judgment and an evaluation of the facts and circumstances of the audit.

[173] Announcement 2002–63, 2002–2 C.B. 72.

[174] *See* https://www.irs.gov/businesses/corporations/tax-accrual-workpapers-frequently-asked-questions.

[175] Examiners are advised to consult with the Field Counsel of the Service to determine if a taxpayer has engaged in a listed transaction (including a transaction that is substantially similar to a listed transaction).

[176] IRM Section 4.10.20.3.2.2(1)(a) (07-12-2004) states that "appropriate circumstances" exist when the situations for which the tax accrual workpaper request is justified, although the Service states that situations when a tax accrual workpaper request would not be appropriate would be rare.

[177] IRM Section 4.10.20.3.2.2(1)(c) (07-12-2004). The disclosure meets this requirement if it (i) is on the return; (ii) is made pursuant to Announcement 2002–2, 2002–1 C.B. 304; or (iii) complies with Rev. Proc. 94–69, 1994–2 C.B. 804, if applicable.

[178] Disclosure is satisfactory if it is disclosed on the return and complies with Treas. Reg. § 1.6011–4. IRM Section 4.10.20.3.2.3(1) (01-15-2005). Under certain circumstances, disclosure may also include a protective disclosure filed by the taxpayer. *See* Service Workpaper FAQ Q&A 2.

request the tax accrual workpapers applicable only to that transaction.[179] If, on the other hand, the listed transaction was not disclosed, then the Service will routinely request all tax accrual workpapers.[180]

Further, if a return is examined that claims the tax benefit of either (i) multiple listed transactions, or (ii) a properly disclosed listed transaction but "reported financial accounting irregularities" exist (such as restatement of earnings), the Service as a discretionary matter[181] will request all tax accrual workpapers for the year under examination.[182]

Service Workpaper FAQ Q&A 12 provided additional guidance concerning the meaning of "reported financial accounting irregularities"[183] and states that such term includes, but is not limited to, situations when a company restates earnings resulting from what may be (i) earnings manipulation (such as improper acceleration of revenue recognition or recognition of nonexistent revenue), (ii) expense manipulation, fraudulent accounting practices, corporate mismanagement, or (iii) any other improper activities. Service Workpaper FAQ Q&A 12 clarified that, although the listed transaction workpaper policy relating to reported financial irregularities applies when the taxpayer has a disclosed listed transaction, no requirement exists that the reported financial accounting irregularities be connected to the disclosed listed transaction before the examiner will request the tax accrual workpapers. In the event a company had reported financial accounting irregularities and had an undisclosed listed transaction, the Service will request all of the tax accrual workpapers for the tax year at issue. That request is made under the nondiscretionary undisclosed listed transaction standard of IRM 4.10.20.3.2(3) rather than the reported financial irregularities standard.

IRM Section 4.10.20.3.2(7) states that if a transaction becomes a listed transaction subsequent to the filing of a tax return, then upon audit of the return the Service will request the tax accrual workpapers, provided that at the time of the request the transaction is a listed transaction.

[4] IDRs and Summons Relating to Tax Accrual Workpapers

IRM Section 34.6.3.6.1.1(1) provides that the examiner will prepare an Information Document Request (IDR) when a request is made for audit or tax accrual workpapers. In practice, the IRS has several safeguards in place to ensure that tax accrual workpapers are requested only in limited situations, including (i) the availability of Service Field Counsel in drafting the IDR, and (ii) review of the IDRs by the Large and Midsize Business Division of the Service. IDRs relating to tax accrual workpapers are generally placed on an expedited timetable with the Service.

---

[179] IRM Section 4.10.20.3.2.3(1) (01-15-2005). In this situation, the Service may also request tax accrual workpapers of other years if directly relevant to the examination years. *See also* IRM 4.10.20.3.2(2) (12-08-2020) (accord).

[180] IRM Section 4.10.20.3.2.3(2) (01-15-2005). *See also* IRM Section 4.10.20.3.2(3) (12-08-2020).

[181] The phrase "discretionary matter" in this context means the exercise of prudence in executing policies, although the presumption is that the Service will request all tax accrual workpapers. In the rare event that the examiner believes that requesting all workpapers might not be appropriate, the examiner must obtain Service consent. *See* IRM Section 4.10.20.3.2(5)–(6) (12-08-2020).

[182] IRM Section 4.10.20.3.2(4) (12-08-2020).

[183] Service Workpaper FAQ Q&A 12 provides that the "reported financial irregularities" standard requires careful factual and legal analysis on a case-by-case basis.

In the event the requested tax accrual workpaper is not produced, the IDR will request a description of the document being withheld, including the number of pages contained in the document, and the specific reason why the document is not provided. If failure to produce the document is based on a claim of privilege, the taxpayer (or third party) should provide the examiner with a detailed privilege log.

Pursuant to IRM Section 34.6.3.6.1.2(1), if a recipient of an IDR fails to produce audit or tax accrual workpapers, the examiner must determine whether to issue a summons, based on whether the workpaper request (i) is made under the unusual circumstances standard of IRM Section 4.10.20.3(1) or (ii) involves a listed transaction. When the workpaper request is based on the unusual circumstances standard, the decision to issue a summons should be based on all the facts and circumstances surrounding the case, including whether compliance with the summons will be unreasonably onerous. The Internal Revenue Manual requires that the summons should provide a specific and unambiguous description of the records demanded so that the summoned party can reasonably be expected to identify the exact records sought.

IRM Section 34.6.3.6.1.2(3) states that when tax accrual workpapers involving listed transactions are not produced in response to an IDR, the summons should describe the records sought with "reasonable certainty." This standard is met if the description is specific and unambiguous, and the summoned party can reasonably be expected to identify the exact records sought.

[5] Application of Work-Product Doctrine to Tax Accrual Workpapers and Other Tax Documents

[a] Overview

Whether the work-product doctrine applies to preclude the government from obtaining tax accrual workpapers and similar confidential tax documents that are furnished to, or prepared by, the taxpayer's independent auditor was addressed by two federal circuits, the First Circuit in *United States v. Textron Inc.* and the District of Columbia Circuit in *United States v. Deloitte LLP.* These two circuits reached different conclusions. In June 2013, the U.S. District Court for the District of Minnesota in *Wells Fargo & Co. v. United States*[184] granted work product protection to tax accrual workpapers prepared to analyze the "recognition" step of FASB ASC 740–10.

In 2009, the First Circuit (*en banc*) in *Textron* denied the work product privilege, while the following year the District Court Circuit in *Deloitte* upheld the work product protection based on similar facts. Thereafter, the *Wells Fargo* court applied the work product privilege to tax accrual workpapers to the extent such documents related to legal analysis and related material to comply with the FASB ASC 740–10 "recognition step." Thus, the current state of the law with respect to the application of the work product doctrine to tax accrual workpapers unfortunately is far from settled. The conflicting decisions in *Textron* and *Deloitte* widened the split among the circuits regarding securing work product protection for tax accrual workpapers and similar tax documents prepared as part of an audit of the taxpayer's financial statements. The reach of the work product doctrine in tax controversies will continue to be a critical issue in those situation where the Service's policy of restraint does not apply (e.g., "listed" transactions and taxpayers

---

[184] No. 10–57 (D. Minn. 2013); 2013 TNT 110–21 (June 7, 2013).

with financial accounting irregularities). Further, work product disputes may increase as the Service audits the disclosures made on Schedule UTP, discussed below.[185]

[b] The "in Anticipation of Litigation" Standard

Before discussing the *Textron* and *Deloitte* decisions, it is important to review a critical requirement of the work product privilege, i.e., that work product be prepared "in anticipation of litigation." Two alternative standards have been developed by the Circuit Courts to establish if work product is prepared "in anticipation of litigation," which adds to the uncertainty in determining if the work product privilege is available with respect to the taxpayer documents. On the one hand, the majority of the circuits[186] apply the so-called "because of" litigation test, which is a broad standard that asks "whether, in light of the nature of the document and the factual situation in the particular case, the document can fairly be said to have been prepared or obtained because of the prospect of litigation."[187] In contrast, the Fifth Circuit in *United States v. El Paso Co.*[188] adopted a different standard, the "primary motivating purpose" test. That more narrow standard evaluates whether a document was prepared in anticipation of litigation by inquiring whether the primary motivating purpose behind its creation was to aid in future possible litigation.

Adlman. The "because of" standard was applied in *United States v. Adlman*,[189] where, in contemplation of a challenge by the Service, the taxpayer's tax advisor prepared a memorandum evaluating the merits of the tax issues relating to the tax treatment of the taxpayer's proposed merger. In response to the Service's summons to obtain the memorandum, the court held that "work-product protection should not be denied to a document that analyzes expected litigation merely because it is prepared to assist in a business decision [the proposed merger]."[190] The *Adlman* court provided as an example of a work product protected document, a memorandum prepared by the company's attorneys estimating the likelihood of success in litigation and an accompanying analysis of the company's legal strategies and options to assist it in

---

[185] *See* Section 8.05[6]. *See* Codification Of Statements On Auditing Standards, AU § 9326, para. 2.22 (AICPA 2003) ("If the client's support for the tax accrual or matters affecting it, including tax contingencies, is based upon an opinion issued by an outside adviser with respect to a potentially material matter, the auditor should obtain access to the opinion, notwithstanding potential concerns regarding attorney-client or other forms of privilege.").

[186] *See, e.g., U.S. v. Roxworthy*, 457 F.3d 590 (6th Cir. 2006) (adopting the "because of" test); *U.S. v. Adlman*, 134 F.3d 1194, 1197–1205 (2d Cir. 1998) (discussing the different approaches taken by courts here, and concluding that the "because of" standard is the appropriate one). Likewise, in addition to the Second and Sixth Circuits, the First, Third, Fourth, Seventh, Eighth, Ninth and the District of Columbia Circuits apply the "because of" test. *See, e.g., Maine v. U.S. Dept. of Interior*, 298 F.3d 60, 68 (1st Cir. 2002); *In re Grand Jury Proceedings*, 604 F.2d 798, 803 (3d Cir. 1979); *Nat'l Union Fire Ins. Co. v. Murray Sheet Metal Co.*, 967 F.2d 980, 984 (4th Cir. 1992); *Binks Mfg. Co. v. Nat'l Presto Indus., Inc.*, 709 F.2d 1109, 1119 (7th Cir. 1983); *Simon v. G.D. Searle & Co.*, 816 F.2d 397, 401 (8th Cir. 1987); *U.S. v. Torf (In re Grand Jury Subpoena)*, 357 F.3d 900, 907 (9th Cir. 2004); and *Senate of P.R. ex rel. Judiciary Comm. v. U.S. Dept. of Justice*, 823 F.2d 574, 587 (D.C. Cir. 1987). The Tenth, Eleventh, and Federal Circuits have not adopted any standard, although as discussed below, in *Regions Financial Corp. v. U.S.*, 101 A.F.T.R. 2d 2008-2179, 2183 (N.D. Ala. 2008), a district court in the Eleventh Circuit concluded in dicta that the Eleventh Circuit would use the "because of" test.

[187] *In re Sealed Case*, 146 F.3d 881, 884 (D.C. Cir. 1998).

[188] 682 F.2d 530, 542–543 (5th Cir. 1982) ("The primary motivating force behind the tax pool analysis . . . is not to ready El Paso for litigation over its tax returns. Rather, the primary motivation is to anticipate, for financial reporting purposes, what the impact of litigation might be on the company's tax liability."). *See also U.S. v. Davis*, 636 F.2d 1028, 1040 (5th Cir. 1982) (tax return workpapers prepared by attorney not protected).

[189] 134 F.3d 1194 (2d Cir. 1998).

[190] 134 F.3d at 1199.

estimating what should be reserved for litigation losses, which are requested by the company's auditors.

Schaeffler. The Second Circuit Court of Appeals in *Schaeffler v. U.S.*[191] unanimously reversed a district court's holding that (1) the taxpayer waived the attorney-client privilege relating to a tax memorandum prepared by Ernst & Young (EY) addressing the U.S. federal income tax consequences of the taxpayer's refinancing and restructuring transactions when the taxpayer shared the tax memorandum with its bank consortium, and (2) the work-product doctrine did not protect documents the taxpayer prepared in anticipation of IRS litigation. *Schaeffler* involved a complex debt refinancing and major corporate restructuring of the taxpayer (the Schaeffler Group). The taxpayer made a tender offer to acquire a minority stock interest in a target company. The taxpayer intended to finance the tender offer with proceeds of an 11 billion Euro loan agreement with a consortium of banks. During the term of the tender offer, the trading price of the target company's stock declined drastically (due in large part to the announcement of Lehman Brothers' bankruptcy), resulting in a significantly higher-than-expected number of shareholders who accepted the offer. Accordingly, the taxpayer was obligated to pay a substantially higher price for the tender offer than initially estimated, causing the taxpayer to refinance the acquisition debt facility with the bank consortium and restructure its corporate structure (collectively, the Transactions). The increased financing threatened the taxpayer's solvency and ability to repay its debt obligations. The taxpayer believed an IRS challenge to the taxpayer's tax positions regarding the Transactions was very likely, and so the taxpayer engaged EY to prepare an analysis (the Tax Memo) advising on the U.S. federal tax implications of the Transactions, including likely outcomes of potential arguments by the IRS. Because the banks had an interest in the outcome of any possible IRS challenge to the Transactions, the Schaeffler Group and the bank consortium signed an Attorney Client Privilege Agreement whereby the taxpayer agreed to share with the banks any privileged and confidential documents, including the Tax Memo, prepared by the taxpayer and its tax advisors in connection with the Transactions, with the understanding that the parties did not intend to waive any privilege. Thereafter, the taxpayer shared the Tax Memo and related documents with the bank consortium. During an audit of the taxpayer, the IRS issued a summons requesting the legal opinions and analysis related to the Transactions, which included the Tax Memo. The taxpayer sued to quash the summons arguing the requested documents were protected by the work-product doctrine and attorney-client privilege.[192]

At the District Court level, the taxpayer argued that the privilege relating to the Tax Memo was not waived when the document was shared with the bank consortium because (1) the taxpayer and the consortium had a common legal interest, and (2) the Tax Memo was prepared in "anticipation of litigation" as required by the work-product doctrine. The District Court disagreed. With respect to the work-product privilege, the lower court first found that such privilege was not waived based on sharing the Tax Memo with the consortium because the disclosure furthered the common commercial desire of the taxpayer and the bank consortium to avoid the taxpayer's loan default and insolvency. But the lower court determined that the work-product privilege was waived

---

[191] *Schaeffler v. United States of America*, 806 F.3d 34 (2d Cir. 2015), rev'g, 22 F. Supp. 3d 319 (DC NY 2014).

[192] On remand, the taxpayer's petition to quash various summons that IRS issued to the taxpayer's accounting firm seeking privileged information had become moot, *Schaeffler et al. v. U.S.*, 117 AFTR 2d 2016–2139 (DC NY 2016).

based on a finding that the Tax Memo was not prepared in anticipation of litigation. The District Court noted that the Tax Memo did not specifically refer to litigation and, given the size and complexity of the Transactions, the comprehensive tax analysis set forth in the Tax Memo would have been provided in similar form regardless of any anticipated tax audit or litigation.[193] Further, the lower court held that the taxpayer waived the attorney-client privilege when the Tax Memo was shared with the consortium because the requisite "common legal interest" was lacking between the taxpayer and the banks. The District Court concluded that because the bank consortium's interest was commercial and financial rather than legal, the "common interest" or "joint defense" exception to waiver of the privilege did not apply. The lower court also noted that the banks lacked a common legal stake in the taxpayer's possible tax litigation since they would not be named as a co-defendant in such litigation.

The Second Circuit reversed the District Court, clarifying both the meaning of "anticipation of litigation" in tax cases and the proper application of the common-legal-interest doctrine. Although the attorney-client privilege is generally waived by voluntary disclosure of the communication to another party, the Second Court held the privilege relating to the Tax Memo was not waived by disclosure to the banks since the banks were engaged in a "common legal enterprise" with the taxpayer with respect to the Transactions. Under the present facts, the Second Circuit found that the consortium's common interest with the taxpayer constituted a sufficient legal character to prevent a waiver upon providing the Tax Memo to the consortium. The threat of taxpayer's insolvency and default gave the taxpayer and the banks a strong common interest in obtaining particular tax treatment of the Transactions. The Second Circuit also held that the work-product doctrine to the Tax Memo was not waived since it contained legal analysis that fell squarely within the privilege's purpose as formulated by *Hickman*.[194] Relying on its decision in *Adlman*,[195] the appellate court held that the work-product doctrine protected the Tax Memo because such document was specifically intended to address tax issues that could arise in anticipated tax litigation. The appeals court also rejected the lower court's conclusion that the Tax Memo would have been prepared in the substantially the same form based on the tax ethical guidelines imposed on EY in rendering tax advice and found that no legal requirement existed that obligated the "highly detailed, litigation-focused analysis and advice" set forth in the Tax Memo.

The Second Circuit's decision in *Schaeffler* is significant since it broadly interpreted (1) the "in anticipation of litigation" standard of *Adlman,* and (2) the common interest/joint exception to privilege waiver. Although application of the work-product privilege continues to be important to protect disclosure of sensitive tax analysis to a taxpayer's independent auditor for financial statement tax reserve purposes,[196] under certain circumstances the common legal interest doctrine protects the privileged status of disclosure of such tax analysis to third parties (and their advisors) who share a common legal interest in the tax treatment of the taxpayer's transactions.

---

[193] The lower court also noted that Circular 230 (as it existed during 2009 and 2010, the years at issue) precluded a tax practitioner from considering the audit risk of a taxpayer's tax return when providing tax advice and thus concluded that Circular 230 required EY to consider fully the relevant legal issues of the restructuring and refinancing, regardless of whether EY anticipated litigation with the IRS. On appeal, the DOJ Tax Division did not even try to support this erroneous holding of the District Court.

[194] *Hickman v. Taylor*, 329 US 495 (1947).

[195] *United States v. Adlman*, 134 F.3d 1194 (2d Cir. 1998).

[196] *See, e.g., United* States *v. Deloitte*, 610 F.3d 129 (D.C. Cir. 2010).

Roxworthy. The "because of" test was also applied in *United States v. Roxworthy*,[197] where the Sixth Circuit Court of Appeals reversed a district court decision that required a taxpayer to provide the Service with tax opinions issued to the taxpayer by the taxpayer's accounting firm. The tax opinions at issue analyzed the tax consequences of certain transactions entered into by the taxpayer. The Service argued that the work-product doctrine did not apply because the memoranda had been prepared for penalty protection and not in anticipation of litigation. The appellate court in *Roxworthy* disagreed and held that the taxpayer did anticipate litigation "because a yearly Service audit of [taxpayer] was a certainty due to the company's size, the transaction at issue," and the accountants having advised taxpayer that the Service targeted the type of transaction in question.[198] The Sixth Circuit, which concluded that a document can be created both for use in the ordinary course of business (such as for penalty protection) and in anticipation of litigation without losing its work-product protection, adopted the "because of" test as the standard for determining whether documents were prepared in anticipation of litigation, which typically recognize both a subjective and objective element to the analysis. Under that analysis, a party must have had a subjective belief that litigation was a real possibility, and that belief must have been objectively reasonable, and the document for which the privilege is asserted cannot be one that would have been prepared in the normal course of business regardless of the anticipation of litigation.[199]

Regions Financial. Interestingly, the U.S. District Court in *Regions Financial Corp. v. United States*[200] held that opinions prepared by the taxpayer's outside tax advisors that analyzed the tax treatment of two listed transactions were protected by the work-product doctrine and therefore were not waived when those documents were furnished to the taxpayer's independent auditor. Although the Eleventh Circuit, the jurisdiction in which the *Regions* court resides, has not decided which of the two standards it follows, the *Regions* court concluded in dicta that the Eleventh Circuit would follow the "because of litigation" test. However, the court found that such determination was not necessary because its conclusion would be the same regardless of which test is applied. Although litigation was not certain at the time that the taxpayer requested the tax opinions, the court held that certainty is not required, citing *United States v. Davis*:[201] "Litigation need not necessarily be imminent, as some courts have suggested, as long as the primary motivating purpose behind the creation of the document was to aid in possible future litigation." *Regions* held that under both the "primary purpose" and the "because of" tests, the critical issue is the purpose for which the documents were created.[202]

In this regard, the First Circuit decision (*en banc*) in *Textron*[203] seems to have deviated from the "because of" work product standard used in the First Circuit by requiring the taxpayer to demonstrate that the document at issue actually would be used

---

[197] 457 F.3d 590 (6th Cir. 2006), *rev'g* No. 04-MC-18-C (W.D. Ky. 2005). The *Roxworthy* case, which did not involve tax accrual workpapers, presents a summary of case law relating to this issue.

[198] *Roxworthy*, 457 F.3d at 600.

[199] The Service has announced that it will not acquiesce in *Roxworthy*. Action on Decision (AOD) 2007–04 (Oct. 1, 2007).

[200] N.D. Ala., No. 2:06-CV-00895-RDP (May 8, 2008).

[201] *United States v. Davis*, 636 F.2d 1028 at 1040.

[202] The *Regions* court dismissed any notion that work-product doctrine only applies if the documents at issue served no use other than preparing for litigation.

[203] 577 F.3d 21 (1st Cir. 2009) (*en banc*) discussed at Section 8.05[3].

in litigation. The D.C. Circuit court in *Deloitte* observed: "Judge Torruella's dissenting opinion in *Textron* makes a strong argument that while the court said it was applying the 'because of' test, it actually asked whether the documents were 'prepared for use in possible litigation,' a much more exacting standard."[204]

[c] Textron: Denial of Work Product Privilege to Tax Accrual Workpapers

During 2009, the First Circuit Court of Appeals, in an *en banc* (all judges participating) opinion, reversed the prior decisions of the case[205] and denied work product protection to tax accrual work papers.[206] In *Textron*, the government issued a summons requesting the tax accrual workpapers of Textron Inc. and its subsidiaries (Textron) relating to various "sale-in, lease-out" (SILO) transactions that Textron entered into in 2001. These transactions occurred before the Service modified its policy on requesting workpapers for listed transactions in 2002 and prior to the Service designating SILO transactions as listed transactions (which occurred in 2005).[207] The "tax accrual workpapers" at issue consisted of a spreadsheet containing (i) a list of Textron's tax returns items that Textron's counsel believed might be challenged by the IRS due to uncertainty under the tax laws, (ii) estimates (expressed as percentages) by Textron's counsel of the probability of prevailing in litigation on those issues; and (iii) the dollar amounts of tax reserve reflecting the possibility that Textron might not prevail in litigation. The tax accrual workpapers also included backup workpapers reflecting notes and memoranda written by Textron's in-house tax attorneys revealing their opinions as to which items should be included on the spreadsheet and the hazard of litigation percentage that should apply to each item.

Textron asserted that the tax accrual workpapers were prepared to ensure that Textron was "adequately reserved with respect to any potential disputes or litigation that would happen in the future." Textron's independent auditor examined Textron's final tax accrual workpapers for 2001, the tax year at issue, in connection with its audit with the understanding that the information was confidential. The auditor expressly agreed not to disclose the workpaper information. The government alleged that the SILO transactions entered into by Textron constituted listed transactions described in Treasury Regulation § 1.6011–4(b)(2).[208]

---

[204] *Deloitte*, 610 F.3d at 138.

[205] Initially, in April 2006, U.S. District Court for the District of Rhode Island held that the work product doctrine applied to the tax accrual workpapers of the taxpayer, Textron, and that Textron did not waive that privilege by furnishing the workpapers to its auditors. Textron and Subsidiaries, No. 06 198 (D. R.I. Apr. 28, 2006). On appeal, a First Circuit panel affirmed the district court's holding that Textron's tax accrual workpapers were protected work product and that the privilege was not defeated by the business purpose for creating the documents. *United States v. Textron Inc.*, 553 F.3d 87 (1st Cir. 2009). However, on March 25, 2009, the First Circuit vacated its ruling and voted to rehear the case *en banc*. *United States v. Textron*, 560 F.3d 513 (1st Cir. 2009).

[206] *See United States v. Textron*, 577 F.3d 21 (1st Cir. 2009) (*en banc*), reprinted at Daily Tax Rep., at K-3, Aug. 13, 2009. *See generally First Circuit En Banc Textron Ruling*, Daily Tax Rep., at K-1 (Aug. 17, 2009); *En Banc First Circuit Reverses Course in Textron*, 2009 TNT 155–1.

[207] In Notice 2005–13, 2005–1 CB 630, the Service identified, as "listed transactions," situations where taxpayer enters into a purported sale-leaseback (also called "sale-in, lease-out") with a tax-indifferent person in which substantially all of tax-indifferent person's payment obligations are retracted, and where taxpayer's risk of loss or profit due to change in value of leased property, are limited.

[208] The government further argued that all of Textron's tax accrual workpapers for the year of the transactions should be disclosed, rather than only those workpapers related to the SILO transactions, because the company engaged in several listed transactions. Relying on Service Announcement 2002–63, 2002–2 CB

Speaking for the court, Judge Boudin noted that no one disputed that the immediate purpose of the workpapers was to support the tax reserve for financial accounting purposes. The court found that litigation was always a possibility and the analyses would not have been prepared "but for" the potentiality of litigation with the IRS over the tax shelter investment (the SILOs). The court then declared that, following its prior opinion enunciating the "because of" test, the Textron workpapers were independently required by statutory and audit requirements, and that the work product privilege does not apply due to the mere possibility that litigation might occur in the future. While declaring that it was following its prior "because of" opinion, the First Circuit, in essence, adopted an "immediate motive" test.

In support of this view, the court seems to have taken judicial notice of some hypothetical lawyers' experience. It said: "Every lawyer who tries cases knows the touch and feel of materials prepared for a current or possible (i.e., "in anticipation of") lawsuit. None with experience in lawsuits would talk about tax accrual work papers in those terms." This statement borders on the absurd, aside from the de novo determination of what "every lawyer" knows. In the context of the tax shelter situation involving the SILO transactions (listed transactions), controversy with the IRS was a virtual certainty. The analysis of the lawyers, accountants, or other experts whose advice was relied upon, internal or external, would be critical to an assessment of the likelihood of prevailing in the litigation. This information was appropriately considered with respect to the initial investment in the transactions, the reserves taken for preparing financial statements, and in preparing for the inevitable IRS controversy.

Perhaps, the judge has experience to lead to his judicial notice of what "every lawyer" knows, but the tax accrual workpapers are critical elements in preparing tax cases for controversy, whether for trial or for negotiation. The statement that the papers have no such feel to a trial lawyer is mystifying. The motivation of the court seems to be captured at the end of the opinion in the interesting explanation that "tax collection is not a game. Underpaying taxes threatens the essential public interest in revenue collection." Fortunately, there was a strong dissent from Judge Torruella, who appropriately quoted the famous statement of Justice Potter Stewart in *Jacobellis v. U.S.* about recognizing obscenity—"I know it when I see it"—to describe the new rule in the First Circuit. The "outcome determinative" posture of the majority opinion was said, appropriately, to be "not even a good rule."

[d] Deloitte: Application of Work Product Privilege to Tax Documents

After *Textron*, many worried that documents prepared to support the financial accounting treatment of tax reserves recorded on a taxpayer's books were entitled to little or no protection as privileged work product, even if those documents were prepared in anticipation of litigation and contained mental thoughts and opinions of counsel. Significantly, the 2010 decision by the U.S. Court of Appeals for the District of Columbia in *United States v. Deloitte & Touche LLP*[209] provides needed reassurance for taxpayers asserting the work product privilege in the continuing battles between taxpayers and the Service regarding disclosure of tax workpapers and related documents.

72, the Justice Department asserted that the government is entitled to seek all tax accrual workpapers if the taxpayer has engaged in two or more listed transactions.

[209] 610 F.3d 129 (D.C. Cir. 2010).

In *Deloitte*, the U.S. government challenged Dow Chemical's tax treatment of certain affiliated tax-shelter partnerships and subpoenaed Dow's outside auditor, Deloitte, to produce various documents related to Dow's tax position. The documents related to tax-shelter partnerships in which Dow was a partner that generated tax benefits. Deloitte objected and asserted work product protection. The documents at issue were (i) two documents that addressed the tax issues relating to partnerships in which Dow was a partner: (a) a 1998 analysis created by Dow's in-house counsel and (b) a 2005 tax opinion from Dow's outside counsel (collectively, the "Dow documents"), and (ii) a 1993 memorandum prepared by Deloitte based on a meeting with Dow and its outside counsel regarding possible litigation of the tax treatment of the Dow partnerships and the resulting accounting treatment (the "Deloitte memorandum"). The government argued that the Deloitte memorandum was not work product since it was prepared by an accounting firm, rather than the taxpayer (Dow) or its legal counsel, and further that it was prepared as part of the financial review of Dow's tax reserve, rather than in anticipation of litigation. The government also asserted that, although the Dow documents constituted work product, Dow waived the privilege when it disclosed those two documents to Deloitte.

In direct contrast to the *Textron* decision, *Deloitte* upheld Dow Chemical's claim of work product privilege regarding the documents that were used by Dow's outside auditor, Deloitte LLP, in connection with Deloitte's audit of Dow's financial statements. In rendering its decision, the *Deloitte* court sharply disagreed with analysis adopted by the First Circuit in *Textron* concerning when the work product privilege protects tax accrual workpapers and other documents prepared for, or disclosed to, financial auditors in connection with the auditor's review of financial statement reporting. Rather than concentrating on who prepared the document in question and whether the document was used for an ordinary business purpose, *Deloitte* focused on whether the content of the document contained legal opinions and analysis of counsel, which was what the work product doctrine intended to protect.[210] The court found that documents constituted attorney work product and the privilege was not waived by disclosing the documents to Deloitte in connection with Dow's audit.

The court acknowledged that the Deloitte memorandum was prepared in connection with Deloitte's routine financial audit process to support Dow's financial statements. But, it concluded that the document was prepared in anticipation of litigation and thus subject to the work product privilege, stressing the contents of the document, not its function, controls. The court found that a document prepared in anticipation of litigation may be used "for ordinary business purposes without losing its protected status."[211]

Although the government conceded that the Dow documents were work product, it contended that Dow waived the protection when those documents were furnished to Deloitte. Unlike the attorney-client privilege, the work product privilege is generally not waived unless disclosure of the subject matter enables an adversary to gain access to the

[210] The court emphasized that the only relevant inquiry to determine if the work product doctrine protects the document in question is "whether the document contains work product—the thoughts and opinions of counsel developed in anticipation of litigation." 610 F.3d at 136

[211] 610 F.3d at 138. The court emphasized that "[A] document can contain protected work-product material even though it serves multiple purposes, so long as the protected material was prepared because of the prospect of litigation." *Id.* The Circuit Court did, however, remand the case to the lower court to determine whether all of the Deloitte memorandum included Dow's counsel's mental impressions or whether a redacted version could be disclosed to the government without revealing the protected work product.

information. Thus, a document prepared in anticipation of litigation generally is not waived under the work product doctrine upon disclosure to an accountant.[212] The court found that Deloitte was not, and was not expected to be, an adverse party to Dow in the current tax controversy, and further that Deloitte was not a conduit to the adverse party (i.e., the Service). Thus, the court held that Dow did not waive the work product privilege upon disclosure of the Dow documents to its independent financial auditors, even though such disclosure was in connection with the auditor's review of Dow's tax reserve for book purposes.

Dow had a reasonable expectation that Deloitte would not disclose the Dow documents to the Service since the American Institute of Certified Public Accountants ("AICPA") Code of Professional Conduct imposes a duty of confidentiality on auditors. Further, the court noted that although it was theoretically possible that an independent auditor may be required to disclose confidential information obtained from a client, the government failed to demonstrate that such possibility existed under the facts before it.[213]

[e] Wells Fargo: Privilege Applies to Tax Accrual Workpaper Analysis, but Not to Listing and Identification Procedure of Uncertain Tax Positions

During June 2013, the U.S. District Court for the District of Minnesota in *Wells Fargo & Co. v. United States*[214] weighed in on the application of the work product privilege to tax accrual workpapers prepared to comply with FASB ASC 740–10 and held that identification by the taxpayer (Wells Fargo) of each of its uncertain tax positions is not entitled to work product protection. The court did, however, conclude that the analysis of the FASB ASC 740–10 "recognition and measurement" requirements is protected.

During an audit of Wells Fargo's 2007 and 2008 returns, the IRS issued multiple summonses seeking Wells Fargo's tax accrual workpapers,[215] as well as testimony describing Wells Fargo's processes for identifying uncertain tax positions.[216] Wells Fargo's tax accrual workpapers included document "narratives"[217] summarizing Wells

[212] *See, e.g., In re Grand Jury Subpoenas*, 561 F. Supp. 1247 at 1257 (E.D.N.Y. 1982) ("Disclosure of work product to a third party does not waive its protection unless it substantially increases the opportunity for potential adversaries to obtain the information.").

[213] The court noted that an independent auditor can fulfill its duties without "revealing every piece of information it reviews during the audit process." 610 F.3d at 143.

[214] No. 10-57 (D. Minn. 2013); 2013 TNT 110–21 (June 7, 2013) (hereafter "Wells Fargo").

[215] The summons defined "tax accrual workpapers" very broadly as: "all accrual and other financial workpapers or documents created or assembled by the Taxpayer, an accountant for the Taxpayer, or the Taxpayer's independent auditor relating to any tax reserve for current, deferred, and potential or contingent tax liabilities, however classified or reported on audited financial statements, and to any footnotes disclosing reserves or contingent liabilities on audited financial statements. They include, but are not limited to, any and all analyses, computations, opinions, notes, summaries, discussions, and other documents relating to such reserves and any footnotes. Such documents may also be referred to as the 'tax pool analysis,' 'tax liability contingency analysis,' 'tax contingency reserve analysis,' 'tax cushion analysis,' or any other similar name." *Id.* at para. 14.

[216] During the seven-year period ending 2003, Wells Fargo engaged in a number of so-called "Sale-in-Lease-Out" ("SILO") transactions, which since 2005 have been characterized by the IRS as "listed transactions." Subsequent to 2004, Wells Fargo filed refund claims alleging that it was entitled to the benefits of SILO transactions until an adverse court decision was rendered against it in 2011. The IRS concluded that, although Wells Fargo did not engage in listed transactions during the years under audit, the IRS' "policy of restraint" did not apply because Wells Fargo had engaged in multiple listed transactions in prior years.

[217] Wells Fargo's accountants primarily created these document narratives while contemporaneously consulting with Wells Fargo's attorneys. *Wells Fargo* at para. 65.

Fargo's FIN 48 analysis, which consisted of (i) a brief description of each uncertain tax position; (ii) the relevant taxing jurisdiction; (iii) the relevant tax year(s); (iv) the FIN 48 "unit of account"; (v) the gross tax benefit associated with the uncertain tax position; (vi) Wells Fargo's conclusion as to whether the uncertain tax position is more likely than not to be sustained in litigation under FIN 48's recognition step; and (vii) assuming the position meets the recognition threshold, Wells Fargo's conclusion as to the amount of benefit that is more likely than not to be achieved in settlement or litigation.[218] In addressing the court's first issue, whether the IRS' summonses were properly issued for a valid cause, the court had little problem concluding that the summons met the relatively low requisite standard for tax summons since the requested information assisted verifying that Wells Fargo's returns were substantially correct. In this regard, the court noted that in prior years, Wells Fargo claimed tax benefits from transactions that subsequently were characterized as listed transactions, and engaged in other questionable tax practices, including improperly claiming tax deductions from SILO transactions entered into in taxable years prior to the years in controversy. In response to Wells Fargo's argument that the IRS inappropriately violated the IRS' own policy of restraint since Wells Fargo had not claimed the benefits of any listed transactions "during the audit period," the court noted that such policy is not an interpretation of the law, and further that the IRS need not abide by its policy of restraint to sustain an otherwise valid summons.[219]

After upholding the validity of the IRS summons, the major issue addressed by the *Wells Fargo* court[220] was whether any of the summoned tax accrual workpapers[221] were protected by the work product doctrine. The court acknowledged that in the Eighth Circuit (the Circuit to which the *Wells Fargo* decision is appealable), material is "prepared in anticipation of litigation" and thus eligible for the work product privilege if created "because of" litigation.[222] The court noted that two types of work product exist (i)

---

[218] *Wells Fargo* at para. 63.

[219] The court noted that the IRS has changed its position numerous times regarding when it will request uncertain tax positions and tax accrual workpapers, including a decision in 2010 to implement a "Schedule UTP," on which certain corporations are required to report their uncertain tax positions as part of their tax return, citing Uncertain Tax Positions—Modified Policy of Restraint, Mar. 23, 2011, http://www.irs.gov/Businesses/Corporations/Uncertain-Tax-Positions-Modified-Policy-of-Restraint; Uncertain Tax Positions—Schedule UTP, http://www.irs.gov/Businesses/Corporations/Uncertain-Tax-Positions-Schedule-UTP. Consistent with prior changes in position, the IRS has recently proposed updates to Schedule UTP for the 2022 tax year. Notably, among the proposed changes is the requirement for corporate taxpayers to report incremental amounts associated with each uncertain tax position taken in the 2022 tax year and identify rulings or regulations adverse to their positions. Prior versions of Schedule UTP required taxpayers to report for each of their UTPs the primary sections of the Internal Revenue Code associated with it, whether the position was permanent or temporary (or both), the employer identification number of any passthrough entity involved, an indication of whether it was a major tax position, and its ranking by size. *See* Wallace, *IRS Updates Report for Uncertain Tax Positions*, 177 Tax Notes Fed. 443 (Oct. 17, 2022). *See* Section 3.11[3] for a general discussion of Schedule UTP.

[220] The court also held that (i) the attorney-client privilege protected the discovery of eight e-mails whereby Wells Fargo employees secured legal advice from Wells Fargo in-house lawyers, which correspondences had not been disclosed to KPMG or other third parties outside of Wells Fargo, and (ii) IRS failed to demonstrate the relevancy of its examination of Wells Fargo's federal tax returns, and thus denied access, to the requested tax accrual workpapers related to Wells Fargo's state and local uncertain tax positions.

[221] The court cited taxpayer's testimony that the phrase "tax accrual workpapers" is used to refer to documents generated to assist in the FIN 48 analysis, and that tax accrual workpapers are generally thought to include workpapers prepared by the taxpayer, the taxpayer's accountant or the taxpayer's independent auditor that relate to the computation of the taxpayer's tax reserve for financial reporting purposes. Wells Fargo at para. 55.

[222] *See generally*, Section 8.05[5][b].

"opinion" work product, which contains the mental impressions, conclusions, opinions, or legal theories of an attorney, and (ii) "ordinary" work product, which is any other work product, such as raw factual information strategically selected or organized by an attorney.[223] The court explained that if "ordinary" work product is prepared in anticipation of litigation, it is not discoverable unless the party seeking discovery has a substantial need for the material and cannot obtain the substantial equivalent through other means. Conversely, "opinion" work product enjoys a nearly absolute immunity and can be discovered only in very rare and extraordinary circumstances. Based on those standards, the court held that Wells Fargo's identification of uncertain tax positions and factual information related to those uncertain tax positions is not protected by the work product privilege because that information was created in the ordinary course of business (and not in anticipation of litigation).[224] Although Wells Fargo typically identified its uncertain tax positions at the time of entering into each transaction and involved its attorneys at that time to analyze the tax positions,[225] the mere identification of uncertain tax positions was not performed in anticipation of litigation. Rather, such identification occurred in the ordinary course of business since Wells Fargo's attorneys were acting more as business advisors helping to structure business transactions. The court admitted the difficulty in determining when a hypothetical possibility of litigation in the future constitutes "in anticipation of litigation" for purposes of the work product doctrine, but concluded that Wells Fargo has not met its burden of establishing that it was preparing for anticipated litigation when it identified its uncertain tax positions.[226]

Although Wells Fargo's tax accrual workpapers were found not to be prepared in anticipation of litigation, the *Wells Fargo* court held that the FASB ASC 740–10 "recognition and measurement" analysis did qualify for work product status since it involved legal analysis prepared in anticipation of litigation. The FIN 48 recognition analysis was "largely" performed for Wells Fargo by tax attorneys.[227] Interestingly, beginning with the preparation of its 2007 FIN 48 workpapers, Wells Fargo began attaching to each "document narrative" a one-page attorney memorandum signed by a Wells Fargo attorney in order to create "contemporary evidence" of the involvement of attorneys in the tax accrual workpapers, thus seeking to preserve the privileged status of those workpapers.[228] The court emphasized that Wells Fargo was actively participating in both litigation against the IRS and in disputes with IRS Appeals regarding many uncertain tax positions, and litigation appeared likely for other tax

[223] *See In re Murphy*, 560 F.2d 326, 329 n.1 (8th Cir. 1977).

[224] Based on Wells Fargo testimony that the company would not enter into a transaction unless there was at least a 70 percent chance of success in litigation, the court found it unlikely that the company anticipated that every uncertain tax position would be litigated.

[225] The involvement of Wells Fargo's attorneys with Wells Fargo's tax positions often began well before the FIN 48 analysis took place. *Wells Fargo* at para. 63.

[226] The court explained that even if Wells Fargo had identified its uncertain tax positions when its attorneys conducted the FIN 48 analysis, the identification process nevertheless would still not be protected since "ordinary" privileged materials must relate in some way to legal thinking connected to litigation and mere identification of FIN 48 positions is too far removed from any litigation to be protected work product or considered created "because of" litigation. Instead, the court found that Wells Fargo's listing of its uncertain tax positions was part of a regularly conducted business activity.

[227] *Wells Fargo* at para. 94.

[228] *Wells Fargo* at para. 66. Obviously, the role of the in-house tax attorneys in interacting with the company's accountants to apply FIN 48's recognition and measurement tests was crucial to preserve the protections of the work product doctrine.

positions.[229] The court found the FIN 48 recognition and measurement analysis appeared to have been created while Wells Fargo anticipated litigation since such analysis referred to challenges by the IRS and developments in possible litigation, along with settlement calculations, strengths and weaknesses of its position, and assessments of the chances of prevailing in litigation.[230] The court specifically warned, however, that its decision did not provide a blanket privilege for all tax accrual workpapers and cautioned that its decision is limited to the unique circumstances of Wells Fargo, which (i) substantially limited the number of tax positions requiring FIN 48 analysis, and (ii) specifically demonstrated that it anticipated litigation with regard to each of its uncertain tax positions when those uncertain tax positions were created.[231]

In addressing the last work product issue, the court found that KPMG's FIN 48 analysis contained in KPMG's tax accrual workpapers was protected by the work product doctrine to the same extent as Wells Fargo's tax accrual workpapers, even though KPMG are not attorneys. KPMG's FIN 48 recognition and measurement work was found to be closely tied to the FIN 48 analysis of Wells Fargo's attorneys.

[f] Comments on Deloitte, Textron and Wells Fargo

The D.C. Circuit's decision in *Deloitte* stands in stark contrast to the First Circuit's decision in *Textron*. In essence, *Textron* concluded that there is no work product doctrine protection for tax accrual workpapers. In the context of complying with the FASB rules on accounting for uncertain income tax positions under FASB ASC 740–10, this interpretation would mean that such workpapers would likely be available via Service subpoena if the policy of restraint is relaxed. Fortunately, the government defeat in *Deloitte* provides hope to taxpayers by adopting a more reasonable approach to the availability of the work product privilege, consistent with the underlying purpose of such doctrine (i.e., to protect work product prepared in connection with litigation). Because of the contrary conclusions reached by the First and D.C. Circuits, it presently is unclear what is protected in the FASB-mandated process outside of those two circuits.[232] The *Wells Fargo* court appears to focus on content of the tax accrual workpaper, rather than its function, to determine if work product privilege applies, even if such material is contained in documents prepared for business reasons. In this regard, *Wells Fargo* is inconsistent with the First Circuit's decision in *Textron*, which held that it is not enough that the materials were prepared by lawyers or represent legal thinking since it is only work done in anticipation of trial that is protected by the work product doctrine. It appears likely that the U.S. Supreme Court will need to address the issue, hopefully to file the First Circuit's decision in *Textron* where it belongs—in the ash heap of history. Until then, in our experience, knowledge of the FASB ASC 740–10 process will enable a taxpayer and its advisors, other than its auditor, to evaluate specific situations,

---

[229] The court contrasted disputes with IRS Appeals, and tax litigation, with an IRS examination, which the court noted is not, in and of itself, litigation and will not necessarily lead to litigation.

[230] The court stated that its conclusion is not affected by the fact that Wells Fargo's accounting group created many of the tax accrual workpapers.

[231] The court found Wells Fargo did not waive the work product protection by disclosing the workpapers to KPMG since KPMG was not adversarial to Wells Fargo. In this regard, KPMG took steps to protect the confidentiality of client information and did not disclose the workpapers to any third party. Although in some circumstances, KPMG might be required to disclose confidential client information to the Securities and Exchange Commission or the Public Company Accounting Oversight Board, such possibility was too remote.

[232] Based on *El Paso*, taxpayers in the Fifth Circuit may experience difficulty claiming work product privilege for certain tax accrual workpapers or similar tax documents provided to auditors as part of the auditor's financial statement review.

determine how to proceed in that process in light of the uncertain environment, and then defend its positions.

Because large companies are required to make detailed financial and tax disclosure (e.g., Schedule M-3, Schedule UTP, FASB ASC 740–10 financial statement disclosure of uncertain tax positions, etc.), maintaining the privileged status of legal and tax analysis and opinions of potential tax controversy issues continues to be important, especially in light of conflicting court decisions. Taxpayers should release to the Service only the requisite concise descriptions of sensitive tax issues, and avoid disclosing any legal analysis or opinions to the Service. If required, the taxpayer should only reference any legal analysis or opinions to the Service.

[6] Application to FASB ASC 740–10 Workpapers and Schedule UTP Documents

As discussed in detail in Chapter 3, the FASB ASC 740–10 process begins with an identification of a company's uncertain income tax positions. If the company determines that an uncertain tax position is more likely than not to be sustained based on the technical merits, then the income tax benefit must be measured, which includes assessing the amounts and probabilities of outcomes that could be realized from the tax position on settlement or other resolution.

Significantly, FASB ASC 740–10 contains detailed rules that require the financial statement disclosure of tax benefits that are not recognized (in whole or in part) for book purposes.[233] Although this disclosure generally is on an aggregate,[234] rather than an issue-by-issue, basis, FASB ASC 740–10 workpapers typically will include a separate analysis of each uncertain income tax position of the company.[235]

A controversial aspect of the FASB rules on accounting for uncertain tax positions is not only the "roadmap" that the requisite disclosure of the company's uncertain tax positions provides to the taxing authority, but also the possibility that the taxing authority will seek the company's related workpapers. The Service currently has a "policy of restraint" in place which places restrictions on an examiner's request of a

---

[233] To the extent possible, companies should take care regarding what FASB ASC 740–10 documents are provided to outside auditors since such information might not be protected by the work-product doctrine. In certain circumstances, it may be possible to protect FASB ASC 740–10 documents under the work-product doctrine if the taxpayer can demonstrate that the written communications were prepared by inside or outside legal counsel in anticipation of litigation. To preserve the attorney-client privilege with respect to legal advice rendered in connection with a specified tax position which it is anticipated may be litigated, such documents should be clearly designated as privileged, the reasons why it was prepared in anticipation of litigation should be stated, and it should not be provided to the FASB ASC 740–10 auditors (or other third parties). A company should obtain a clear understanding regarding those FASB ASC 740–10 documents that its outside auditors require to perform their FASB ASC 740–10 procedures prior to furnishing those documents (or portions thereof) to them.

[234] When it is reasonably possible that the total amounts of unrecognized tax benefits will significantly increase or decrease within twelve months of a company's reporting date, FASB ASC 740–10 requires that the company disclose the nature of the uncertainty, the nature of the event that could occur within twelve months to cause a change, and an estimate of the range of change or a statement that an estimate cannot be made. *See* Section 3.08.

[235] Pursuant to FASB ASC 740–10, a company is also required to monitor subsequent changes to its income tax positions, which could result in financial statement disclosure of revisions to a company's uncertain tax positions, including the disclosure of a position that previously was not required to be disclosed.

taxpayer's tax accrual workpapers, except in limited and unusual circumstances and in listed transactions.[236]

The FASB rules on accounting for uncertain tax positions bring a variety of additional considerations to the table, mainly the reality that the probability tables and resultant public disclosures are mandated for U.S. GAAP purposes. As such, a taxpayer's evaluation of its own exposure with respect to uncertain tax positions is extant and provided to everyone involved in the U.S. GAAP process, including external parties, which means at least the auditor.

The Service has issued a chief counsel memorandum[237] that concludes that workpapers that are prepared to support a company's compliance with the FASB rules on accounting for uncertain tax positions should constitute tax accrual workpapers that are subject to the IRS's policy of restraint as outlined in IRM Section 4.10.20.2(2), unless unusual circumstances exist or the workpapers are related to certain listed transactions.[238] The chief counsel memorandum reasons that FASB ASC 740–10 sets forth tax accounting and financial reporting guidelines, but neither FASB ASC 740–10 nor the other applicable FASB pronouncements impose documentation requirements or specific record keeping rules on a company or its auditors. Rather, those requirements and rules, which are established by the SEC, PCAOB, and the AICPA, have not changed since the issuance of FASB ASC 740–10. Accordingly, the Chief Counsel of the Service concludes that FASB ASC 740–10 has not modified whether a document is considered to be a tax accrual workpaper as defined by IRM Section 4.10.20.2(2).[239]

Of course, since this policy of restraint is self-imposed, there is no assurance that the Service will not change its policy.[240] Moreover, since the restraint policy does not apply to listed transactions, it is possible that a transaction that is not characterized as a listed transaction when entered into by a taxpayer loses its exempt status under the restraint policy because it is subsequently characterized as a listed transaction by the Service.[241]

The Chief Counsel of the Service initially announced that a company's reconciliation workpapers relating to its effective tax rate are neither tax accrual workpapers nor audit

---

[236] *See* Section 8.05[3].

[237] Chief Counsel Memorandum, AM 2007–0012 (Mar. 22, 2007), which was released June 8, 2007.

[238] The Service's policy of restraint does not apply to tax accrual workpapers relating to one or more listed transactions in the following circumstances: (i) if a listed transaction was properly disclosed by the taxpayer to the Service, the Service will request only those workpapers related to the specific listed transaction, (ii) if a listed transaction was not disclosed, the Service generally will request all tax accrual workpapers, (iii) if the taxpayer claims tax benefits on its return from multiple listed transactions, then the Service will request all workpapers, and (iv) if the Service examines a return that claims benefits from a disclosed listed transaction, but concurrent reported financial accounting irregularities exist, the Service likewise would request all workpapers. Announcement 2002–63, 2002–2 CB 72.

[239] It has been reported that the SEC's enforcement staff generally is expected to request workpapers that are subject to attorney-client privilege only on a case-by-case basis. 2007 FRW 123–19, *SEC Will Require Companies to Submit Privileged Workpapers on a Case-by-Case Basis, Says Official* (Tax Analysts, June 26, 2007).

[240] *See* Service Large and Mid-Size Business Division Memorandum (LMSB–04–0507–044, May 10, 2007) (acknowledging Chief Counsel advice that FASB ASC 740–10 workpapers are considered tax accrual workpapers that are subject to Service policy of restraint, but noting that LMSB is evaluating its tax accrual workpaper policy to ensure it remains appropriate and therefore that the policy is subject to change in the future regarding requests for tax accrual tax workpapers covered by FASB ASC 740–10).

[241] *See generally*, *Textron* at Section 8.05[5].

workpapers for purposes of the Service's policy of restraint.[242] The Service reached this conclusion since the effective tax rate reconciliation workpapers (i) are prepared by the taxpayer, rather than the company's auditor, (ii) are not prepared for the purpose of determining the proper amount of the reserve for contingent tax liabilities, and (iii) do not follow procedures used or tests performed by the auditor in reviewing a taxpayer's financial statements, and are not retained by the auditor to document the performance of an audit. The IRS subsequently reconsidered this position and concluded (without public explanation or analysis) that its restraint policy does apply to rate reconciliation workpapers.[243]

Further, any financial statement disclosure of a company's uncertain income tax positions as required by the FASB rules on accounting for uncertain tax positions[244] and filed with the SEC is publicly available to the Service and not is covered by any form of Service restraint. Further, the Service can be expected to routinely request workpapers for listed transactions that a company discloses on tax returns in accordance with Service Announcement 2002–63.[245]

FASB ASC 740–10 also raises important privilege issues with respect to tax advice that might be obtained by a company to support the company's conclusion that the position meets the more likely than not threshold. If such a tax opinion is included as part of the tax accrual workpapers provided to the company's auditor, the privilege might be lost. This issue has become more relevant in recent years as auditors increasingly are requesting more information and documents from companies, such as tax opinions and other potentially privileged tax analysis, as support for the tax reserve of the company's financial statements.[246]

FASB ASC 740–10 also has potentially adverse tax consequences to multinational companies. For example, if a foreign country requests FASB ASC 740–10 workpapers of a U.S. company pursuant to a treaty information exchange provision, will the Service exercise its policy of restraint and deny the request?[247]

The Service said in Announcement 2010–76[248] that it is expanding its policy of restraint in the context of an audit to apply to the disclosure of issues on the Schedule. The policy of restraint will apply to documents relating to uncertain tax positions and the workpapers that document the completion of Schedule UTP, Uncertain Tax Positions Statement,[249] to be filed by certain corporations. Announcement 2010–76 applies to documents otherwise satisfying the attorney-client privilege, the IRC Section 7525 tax advice privilege, or the work product doctrine, even though the taxpayer has disclosed

[242] Service Chief Counsel Notice (CC–2007–015) (June 20, 2007).

[243] IRS Chief Counsel Notice (CC–2008–008) (Dec. 31, 2007).

[244] *See* Section 3.08 and Section 3.09.

[245] 2002–2 CB 72.

[246] *See* Codification of Statements on Auditing Standards, AU § 9326, para. 2.22 (AICPA 2003) ("If the client's support for the tax accrual or matters affecting it, including tax contingencies, is based upon an opinion issued by an outside adviser with respect to a potentially material matter, the auditor should obtain access to the opinion, notwithstanding potential concerns regarding attorney-client or other forms of privilege.").

[247] *See generally*, reported statements of Service Large and Mid-Size Business Division senior adviser Robert Adams, Daily Tax Rept. No. 27 at G-1 (2/9/07) (Service considering changing its "policy of restraint" concerning the control of accrual working papers, specifically whether it would release disclosures required by FASB ASC 740–10 to requesting parties, such as foreign governments possessing information exchange treaties with the United States).

[248] Announcement 2010–76, 2010–41 IRB 1.

[249] *See* Section 3.11.

the document to a financial auditor as part of an audit of the taxpayer's financial statements.

Pursuant to Announcement 2010–76, the taxpayer is permitted during an examination to redact from tax reconciliation workpapers relating to the preparation of Schedule UTP (i) working drafts, revisions, or comments concerning the concise description of tax position reported on Schedule UTP; (ii) the amount of any reserve related to a tax position reported on Schedule UTP; and (iii) the amount of any reserve related to a tax position reported on Schedule UTP to the designation of a tax position as a major tax position. Announcement 2010–76 does not apply, however, if (i) the taxpayer has engaged in any activity or taken any action (other than that described in Announcement 2010–76) that would waive the attorney-client privilege, the IRC Section 7572 tax advice privilege, or the work product doctrine, or (ii) a request for tax accrual workpapers is made under IRM Section 4.10.20.3 because unusual circumstances exist or the taxpayer has claimed the benefits of one or more listed transactions.

As noted, the extension of the policy of restraint to Schedule UTP workpapers only applies "during an examination." If the controversy remains unresolved and is litigated, the policy of restraint no longer is effective, and the Service might seek the Schedule UTP workpapers during litigation. Thus, taxpayers should exercise caution in preparing the Schedule UTP supporting workpapers, and preserving any work product privilege relating to those workpapers by not disclosing such workpapers.[250] In that regard, during March 2011, the Service released Frequently Asked Questions (FAQ) on Schedule UTP and provided the following guidance with respect to the application of the policy of restraint.[251]

> Question # 5. Do the changes to the policy of restraint announced in Announcement 2010–76 apply to documents requested by IRS Appeals?
>
> Answer # 5. Yes. It would be very unusual for Appeals to conduct any substantive fact-finding during its case consideration. Nevertheless, the changes to the policy of restraint apply to any request for documents during the administrative process of determining the correct tax liability, which includes Appeals' consideration of proposed audit adjustments.
>
> Question # 6. Do the changes to the policy of restraint announced in Announcement 2010–76 apply to documents requested by IRS Counsel after the filing of a Tax Court petition?
>
> Answer # 6. In general, Counsel attorneys will not issue discovery requests for documents or information that the IRS would not seek under its policy of restraint. The application of the policy of restraint to actions taken by Counsel in Tax Court litigation will be addressed in a revision to the Chief Counsel Directives Manual.
>
> Question # 7. What is the effective date of the changes to the policy of restraint announced in Announcement 2010–76?

---

[250] It should be noted that the decisions in Textron and Deloitte may not be directly applicable to documents prepared for Schedule UTP disclosures to the extent that those documents do not contain the thoughts of an attorney developed in anticipation of litigation. It may be beneficial to engage an attorney to assist with that process to the extent that litigation with the Service is anticipated.

[251] Published at 2011 TNT 57–21.

Answer # 7. The changes announced in Announcement 2010–76 apply to any request for documents outstanding on or made after September 24, 2010, in any open examination.

Recently in *Wells Fargo,*[252] which addressed work product protection to tax accrual workpapers for tax years (2007 and 2008) prior to the effective date of Schedule UTP,[253] a federal district court in Minnesota held that the privilege applied to (i) the FASB ASC 740–10 analysis whether a tax benefit derived from a tax position more-likely-than-not will be sustained upon examination, (ii) measurement of the largest amount of tax benefit greater than 50 percent likely to be realized upon settlement, (iii) the monetary amount of a recorded reserve for a specific uncertain tax position, (iv) FASB ASC 740–10 "units of account" information, and (v) other materials containing legal analysis. It is interesting to note that the *Wells Fargo* decision found that the following information was not covered by the work product privilege, which information is generally consistent with the information required on Schedule UTP: (i) identification of uncertain tax positions, (ii) facts underlying the taxpayer's federal uncertain tax positions, (iii) the taxpayer's process for identifying its federal uncertain tax positions, and (iv) other opinions and materials prepared by the taxpayer's auditing firm relating to uncertain tax positions, unless closely tied to, and incorporating, the legal analysis of the taxpayer's attorneys.

---

[252] No. 10-57 (D. Minn. 2013); 2013 TNT 110–21 (June 7, 2013).

[253] *See* Section 8.05[5][e].

Chapter 9

TRANSFER PRICING AND PERMANENT ESTABLISHMENT MATTERS

Table of Sections

§ 9.01 Overview and Checklist

FASB ASC 740–10 prescribes a recognition threshold and measurement requirement to determine the financial statement treatment of a tax position taken (or expected to be taken) in a tax return. Evaluation of a tax position for financial statement purposes involves the following two-step process:

- Recognition: The company must determine if it is more likely than not that the tax position will be sustained upon examination, including resolution of any related appeals or litigation, based on existing tax authority. If the position does not satisfy the more likely than not standard, no benefit is booked, and the company records applicable interest and penalties for accounting purposes. If the position meets the more likely than not standard, the measurement provisions are applied.
- Measurement: A tax position that meets the more likely than not threshold based on the technical merits is measured under FASB ASC 740–10 to determine the amount of benefit that the company recognizes in its financial statements. A more likely than not tax position is measured at the largest amount of benefit that is greater than 50 percent likely of being realized upon settlement.

FASB ASC 740–10 also provides guidelines on derecognition of a previously recognized tax benefit, recognition of a tax position that initially did not meet the more likely than not standard, accounting treatment of interest and penalties, and financial statement disclosure of unrecognized tax benefits.[1]

FASB ASC 740–10 broadly applies to all US federal, state and local income tax positions, and also to foreign tax positions that are based on income.[2] In essence, material[3] income tax positions are broadly categorized for FASB ASC 740–10 purposes into positions that (i) are highly certain to be sustained, for which FASB ASC 740–10 permits full recognition and otherwise will not have much practical application, (ii) fail the more likely than not threshold, for which FASB ASC 740–10 precludes recording a financial benefit, and (iii) satisfy the recognition standard, but are not reasonably certain to be upheld, for which FASB ASC 740–10 will have the most application.

A tax position that specifically is subject to FASB ASC 740–10 includes (i) a decision not to file a tax return in a particular jurisdiction (for example, a company's determination that its activities in a foreign treaty country do not rise to the level of a permanent establishment requiring the filing of an income tax return in the foreign jurisdiction), (ii) an allocation or a shift of income between jurisdictions (for example, transfer pricing methodologies), and (iii) a characterization of income or a decision to exclude reporting taxable income in a tax return.[4]

Perhaps the most common—and material—international taxation issue to be addressed by taxpayers, tax administrations and auditors relates to the terms and conditions of transactions between related or affiliated parties involving whether the consideration paid by one party to the other for intercompany goods and services meets normal arm's length terms, commonly referred to as transfer pricing. Indeed, even with the recent spate of new tax legislation in the U.S. and abroad, transfer pricing issues continue to be a main focus of the taxing authorities.

Checklist of Potential Tax Issues or Positions

1. Do the Company and its Foreign Affiliates have appropriate transfer pricing documentation opinions for the current year and pertinent prior years?
2. What do the conclusions/opinion language in the transfer pricing opinions and studies obtained by the Company imply with respect to FASB ASC 740–10 and the measurement threshold?[5]
3. Have the Company and the Foreign Affiliates appropriately identified any transfer pricing exposure in each country?
4. Have there been arrangements put in place that could be deemed to involve the transfer (strip or migration) of intangibles from or to one of the Foreign Affiliates?
5. Could the Company transfer pricing arrangements result in the loss of any tax attributes in the United States or the countries where the Foreign Affiliates operate (net operating loss carryovers, or otherwise)?

---

1 *See* Section 9.04.

2 FIN 48, paragraph 3.

3 Following paragraph 24, FIN 48 stated that it does not apply to immaterial items.

4 FASB ASC 740–10–20.

5 *See* Section 9.03.

6. Do the transfer pricing arrangements of the Company Global Group create a permanent establishment ("PE") of the Company (or conceivably another member of the Company Global Group), in any of the countries where the Foreign Affiliates operate?[6]

7. If so, how is profit or loss to be allocated in the countries where the Foreign Affiliates operate?

8. Do the Group's transfer pricing arrangements meet the evolving international taxation requirements coming from a variety of directions,[7] including country-by-country reporting?[8]

§ 9.02 Illustration

ILLUSTRATION 9-1: USCo is a U.S.-based multinational enterprise (MNE) operating a world-wide manufacturing, distribution and servicing business relating to unique products (Unique Products). USCo provides to customers: (1) hardware, (2) software, and (3) installation services (which are provided with intangible property developed by USCo). USCo, and its global group (the USCo Global Group) are on a calendar year basis. USCo invests heavily in research and development (technology intangibles), as well as in brand and image advertising (marketing intangibles). These intangibles contribute a significant part of USCo's profitability. The Unique Products and associated services are provided on a similar basis in every commercially significant market of the world, with adaptations to the unique circumstances of specific markets. USCo has established wholly-owned subsidiaries in all foreign countries in which there is significant potential market for its goods and services. The function of the foreign affiliates is to provide resale of hardware and software, as well as installation services (the "Foreign Installation Affiliates" or FIAs).

The historic transfer pricing arrangement was that USCo sold the hardware and software to FIAs, using a resale price methodology designed to produce an arm's length rate of return in each of the FIAs. In some cases, the FIAs have been highly profitable; in others, losses have been incurred. Effective on January 1, Year 1, USCo restructured its global business model (the "Restructuring"). It formed an international technology company to be responsible for developing products and marketing intangibles for Unique Products in markets excluding the United States and Canada (Int'lCo). Int'lCo was formed in a country having a ten percent tax rate (FoRCntry). FoRCntry has a treaty with the United States following the U.S. Model. There were three steps in the Restructuring. First, USCo and Intl'Co entered a cost sharing arrangement,[9] pursuant to which Intl'Co made a buy-in payment for the arm's length value of the existing intangibles, acquiring the right to develop further the intangibles, and agreeing to bear an appropriate portion of future R&D costs. Second, USCo entered a supply agreement pursuant to which it agreed to supply hardware and software to Int'lCo using the comparable profit method

---

[6] *See* Section 9.12.

[7] *See* Section 1.03 and Section 9.10.

[8] *See* Section 9.10[2]

[9] *See* Cym Lowell & Mark Thomas, *U.S. International Transfer Pricing* ¶ 10.03 (Thomson Reuters) [*U.S. International Transfer Pricing*].

(CPM), with a profit level indicator of return on capital employed (ROCE). The ROCE was nine percent.[10] Third, USCo terminated its distribution agreements with the Foreign Installation Affiliates. Int'lCo then entered installation services agreements with each of the FIAs, which provided that the FIAs would provide installation services for Int'lCo. The transfer pricing methodology under the Agreement is the Cost Plus Method[11] with a mark-up of five percent. Prior to the Restructuring, the sales and operating income of USCo and the FIAs aggregated was as follows (averaged per year for three years; in $ millions):

	USCo	FIA
Net Sales	8,500	2,800
Operating Income	1,200	850
Operating Profit Margin	14%	30%

In the first two years following the Restructuring, the sales and operating income of USCo, the FIAs and Int'lCo aggregated were as follows (averaged per year for the two years; in $ millions):

	USCo	FIA	Int'lCo
Net Sales	7,500	1,400	3,000
Operating Income	825	70	1,690
Operating Profit Margin	11%	5%	56%

In connection with the Restructuring, USCo, the FIAs and Int'lCo received transfer pricing studies from the pertinent offices of Global Audit & Co. Each study provided a range of transfer prices for the three elements of the Restructuring, as well as noting the pertinent documentation requirements in each country. The conclusion of each study was as follows:

"Global Audit & Co. hopes that this study will be helpful in the transfer pricing work of USCo and its affiliates."

There is no other documentation, opinions or other support for the U.S. and other country tax results of the transactions relating to the Restructuring. Global Audit & Co. advised that these transfer pricing studies were all that was needed to be prepared for U.S. and pertinent other country purposes.

In Illustration 9-1, the Restructuring involved three elements: (i) USCo and Int'l Co entered a cost sharing arrangement; (ii) USCo entered a supply agreement pursuant to which it agreed to supply hardware and software to Int'lCo using the comparable profits method[12]; and (iii) USCo terminated its distribution agreements with the Foreign Installation Affiliates, and Int'lCo entered installation services agreements with each of the FIAs, with a transfer pricing methodology of cost plus with a mark-up of five percent.

[10] *See U.S. International Transfer Pricing* ¶ 4.10.

[11] *Id. at* ¶ 6.07.

[12] *See* Treas. Reg. § 1.482–5.

The net effect of the Restructuring after a three-year period was that Int'lCo was earning the bulk of the operating income of the global group.

Beyond the initial reporting of the transactions making up the Restructuring, there will inevitably be a range of further considerations that must be taken into account. For example in the situation of Illustration 9-1, there will likely be transfer pricing exposure in the countries in which the FIAs conduct business, which could lead to examination issues in the U.S. and the foreign countries, as well as potential correlative adjustments once such cases are resolved. These uncertain tax positions will need to be addressed via internal and external analysis, negotiation with the auditor,[13] disclosure pursuant to FASB and pertinent securities law requirements,[14] and preparation for tax authority examination.[15] Moreover, Illustration 9-1 presents numerous instances of Sarbanes-Oxley Corporate Fraud and Accountability Act (SOX) issues,[16] as well as a range of issues under the U.S. Treasury Circular 230 governing ethical considerations in issuing tax opinions generally.[17]

Illustration 9-1 presents a common situation in which tax authorities in pertinent countries could assert that there has been a movement of functional activities from the U.S. or other countries to Int'lCo, including a transfer of a wide range of intangibles. The principal transfer pricing issue between USCo and Int'lCo will be whether the arrangements pertinent to the Restructuring provide for arm's-length results to USCo, which will be determined under normal intangible transfer criteria.[18] The issue as between Int'lCo and the FIAs will be the arm's-length nature of the functions performed by the FIAs, including the restructuring of their functions and risks.

In the event that there are differences that arise in Illustration 9-1 that USCo desires to resolve, the Service has instituted a specific transfer pricing program to resolve such matters in advance (e.g., via an advance pricing agreement (APA) through the IRS's Advance Pricing and Mutual Agreement (APMA) Program).[19]

§ 9.03 Application of FASB ASC 740–10

Pursuant to the recognition requirement of FASB ASC 740–10,[20] a company recognizes the financial statement effects of a tax position when it is more likely than not that the position will be sustained upon examination by the taxing authority based on the applicable technical merits. For this purpose, the term "more likely than not" means a likelihood of more than 50 percent.[21] This analysis is made based on the company's good faith determination, assuming the position will not be offset against, or aggregated with, other tax positions in settlement negotiations with the tax authority.[22] As stated above, if the more likely than not threshold is not met with respect to an income tax position, none of the corresponding benefit is reflected in the financial statements.

---

13 *See* Section 9.03[6].

14 *See* Section 9.05.

15 *See* Section 9.09.

16 *See* Section 9.06.

17 *See* Section 9.07.

18 *See U.S. International Transfer Pricing* ¶ 5.05.

19 *See* Section 9.07; *U.S. International Transfer Pricing* ¶ 12.01.

20 A complete discussion of FASB ASC 740–10 is set out in Chapter 3.

21 FASB ASC 740–10–25–6.

22 FASB ASC 740–10–25–7.

If the position satisfies the more likely than not recognized threshold, then the company is permitted to record the benefit amount which, on a cumulative basis, has a greater than 50 percent chance of being sustained on settlement. Significantly, in applying the recognition standard, FASB does not permit a company to take into account that it might offset one tax position against another or negotiate with the tax authority different tax positions.[23] However, this principle should be limited in certain circumstances in the transfer pricing context, where tax authorities may apply aggregation and offset concepts to transfer pricing arrangements, as will be discussed below.[24]

Applying the FASB ASC 740–10 standards to the often intricate complexity of international taxation issues, where there are: (i) competing substantive and income allocation rules; (ii) two or more jurisdictions seeking to tax the same income (or shift the same loss elsewhere); and (iii) treaties to police conflicts between certain countries can be an interestingly challenging task, are discussed below.

An inevitable element of managing a multinational business concerns review and potential reassignment of research, manufacturing, or marketing functions within the group. Such reassignment may raise a series of transfer pricing issues. The essential questions will, typically, be whether the reassignment requires an adjustment of transfer pricing methods or a transfer of an intangible or other asset, as well as the nature of appropriate documentation.[25]

[1] Unit of Account for Transfer Pricing

To calculate the FASB ASC 740–10 financial benefit of a tax position, a company must first determine the appropriate "unit of account" relating to one or more tax positions.[26] The company thereafter applies the recognition analysis to each unit of account. FASB ASC 740–10 states that creating the proper unit of account is based in part on (i) how the company prepares and supports its income tax return, and (ii) how it expects to handle the tax issue or issues with the taxing authority during an examination.[27] Establishing the appropriate unit of account for a specific tax issue involves application of management's good faith judgment to the particular facts relating to the tax position,[28] and thus each company may establish different units of accounts based on similar facts.[29]

FASB ASC 740–10 actually provides little guidance as to how units of account are determined. In this regard, FASB explained the absence of greater specificity as follows:[30]

---

[23] FASB ASC 740–10–25–7. For example, in determining whether it is more likely than not that a company will prevail on one issue, the company is not permitted to consider that historically the tax authority has conceded that particular issue in exchange for the company conceding one or more other tax issues. Likewise, in evaluating the recognition of one tax position, management is not permitted to consider the possibility of aggregating another stronger position during audit negotiations and settle both positions on a combined basis.

[24] *See* Section 9.03[2].

[25] *See U.S. International Transfer Pricing* ¶ 10.02.

[26] FASB ASC 740–10–25–13.

[27] FASB ASC 740–10–25–13; FASB ASC 740–10–55–89.

[28] FASB ASC 740–10–25–13.

[29] A company's unit of account methodology generally must be applied consistently each year.

[30] FASB ASC 740–25–13.

Unit of Account

B13. The Exposure Draft indicated that the appropriate unit of account would be a matter of individual facts and circumstances evaluated in light of all available evidence. Respondents to the Exposure Draft requested that [FASB] provide additional guidance on the unit of account in the final [version of FIN 48]. [FASB] believes that it is not possible to provide definitive guidance that would address every circumstance on how to determine the unit of account. Because the individual facts and circumstances of a tax position and of an enterprise taking that position will determine the appropriate unit of account, [FASB] does not believe a single defined unit of account would be applicable to all situations.

B14. [FASB] decided to describe two factors that should affect the determination of the unit of account: the manner in which the enterprise prepares and supports its income tax returns and the approach the enterprise anticipates the taxing authority will take during an examination. Both factors would be expected to vary with the facts and circumstances of a tax position and of the enterprise taking that position. In addition, consistent with other presumptions in this Interpretation, the Board believes that the determination of the unit of account should presume that taxing authorities will evaluate the position and have full knowledge of all relevant information.

In the context of international transfer pricing issues, the determination of the appropriate unit of account is an interesting exercise. Tax preparation, support, and reporting with respect to international transfer pricing arrangements will be done on a separate country basis. In addition, transfer pricing results will generally be supported by contemporaneous documentation specific to such jurisdiction, and the results will be separately examined in each jurisdiction.[31]

Accordingly, it is convenient to think of the unit of account for transfer pricing purposes as being the transactions relating to each country. While such a separate country unit of account approach may be convenient for many issues, and perhaps for transfer pricing in some contexts, it is actually only the starting point of the analysis. These issues arise with respect to the movement of goods, intangibles, services, or capital between affiliated enterprises (related parties) and across international borders, where there is value or benefit on either side of the transaction. Controversies may arise if the price charged in the transactions is perceived by the tax authority on one side or the other of the transactions as not being "arm's length." In this regard, tax authorities apply the arm's length standard, and related theories such as so-called permanent establishment allocations,[32] to prevent tax base erosion. Examination of such positions will involve at least two countries, as demonstrated by considering any of the potential transfer pricing issues in Illustration 9-1. If one country, such as one of the tax authorities in an FIA country in Illustration 9-1, makes an adjustment, there may be a treaty between the countries in question that could alleviate or ameliorate any double taxation if the appropriate treaty mutual assistance provisions were followed.[33] There

---

[31] FASB ASC 740-10-25-13; FASB ASC 740-10-55-89. *See U.S. International Transfer Pricing* ¶ 10.02.

[32] *See* Section 9.12.

[33] *See* Cym Lowell & Mark Martin, *U.S. International Taxation: Practice & Procedure* ¶ 9.04 (Thomson Reuters) [*U.S. International Taxation: Practice & Procedure*].

may also be domestic correlative relief provisions in law or procedural policy that could eliminate some or all double taxation.[34]

Each of these possibilities must be taken into account. For example, in the transfer pricing context, the unit of account could be: (i) all transfer pricing on a global basis; (ii) one unit of account for the U.S. and another for global affiliates; (iii) one for the U.S., one for countries with transfer pricing documentation and/or treaty protection, and the rest of the world; and (iv) so on.

[2] Aggregation or Offsetting of Positions in Transfer Pricing

As noted above, in applying the recognition standard FASB ASC 740–10 does not permit a company to take into account that it might offset one tax position against another or negotiate with the tax authority different tax positions.[35] In general this policy makes sense, since it assures that the principles of FASB ASC 740–10 will be applied to the merits of individual tax positions. On the other hand, the principle makes little sense in the transfer pricing context, where a specific tax exposure may be subject to attack or offsetting adjustment in more than one country. In this connection, transfer pricing guidelines typically allow tax authorities to apply aggregation and offset concepts to transfer pricing arrangements on a single country basis,[36] as well as between countries where there are applicable treaty arrangements.[37]

When pertinent transfer pricing guidelines allow (or require) aggregation or offset of transfer pricing arrangements, such guidelines should apply, as it appears that FASB ASC 740–10 was not directed at such situations.

FASB prescribes a recognition threshold and measurement attribute for the financial statement treatment of a tax position taken or expected to be taken in a tax return.[38] Assume in Illustration 9-1 that the unit of account for purposes of the FASB ASC 740–10 analysis is the transfer pricing between USCo and Int'lCo. The first step in the FASB ASC 740–10 process is that USCo must determine whether it is more likely than not that its tax position as to its transfer pricing with Int'lCo will be sustained upon examination, including resolution of any related appeals or litigation processes, based on the technical merits of the position, assuming that the position will be examined by the appropriate taxing authority that has full knowledge of all relevant information. In Illustration 9-1, the pertinent tax authorities would be the United States (in the case of USCo) and FoRCntry. Assume that USCo has determined that it is more likely than not that its transfer pricing methodology meets the arm's length standard. Therefore, USCo will recognize in its financial statements the results of transfer pricing with Int'lCo.

The second step in the FASB ASC 740–10 analytical process is measurement. Specifically, a tax position that meets the more-likely-than-not recognition threshold is

---

[34] *See* Section 9.03[3] and *U.S. International Transfer Pricing* ¶ 3.09.

[35] FASB ASC 740–10–25–7. For example, in determining whether it is more likely than not that a company will prevail on one issue, the company is not permitted to consider that historically the tax authority has conceded that particular issue in exchange for the company conceding one or more other tax issues. Likewise, in evaluating the recognition of one tax position, management is not permitted to consider the possibility of aggregating another stronger position during audit negotiations and settle both positions on a combined basis.

[36] *See, e.g.*, Treas. Reg. § 1.482–1(g)(4)(i); *see also* 2022 OECD Guidelines ¶¶ 1.51–1.55, 1.134–1.138, and 3.9–3.12.

[37] *See* Section 9.03[3].

[38] *See* Section 3.04.

measured to determine the amount of benefit to recognize in the financial statements. The tax position is measured as the largest amount of benefit that has a greater than 50 percent likelihood of being realized upon settlement. For this purpose, FASB ASC 740–10 provides, in effect, a tax probability table to be used with respect to the measurement of each tax position.

In most such situations there will be a variety of transactions between USCo and Int'lCo. It may be that some of the transactions involve inadequate consideration to USCo, and that in others it receives excessive compensation. The U.S. transfer pricing regulations allow the offsetting of such excessive and inadequate transactions.[39] The same results should be applicable for purposes of accounting for uncertain income tax positions, since this is a simple recognition of application of underlying substantive tax principles which would be applied in the final resolution of a transfer pricing controversy with the IRS. These principles are applied in the same transfer pricing opinion for the context of Illustration 9-1.

[3] Application of Treaty Concepts

Similar considerations apply in the treaty context. In Illustration 9-1, because there is a tax treaty between the U.S. and FoRCntry, and the FoRCntry tax rate of ten percent is less than the U.S. tax rate of 21 percent, there should be no possibility of double taxation. In other words, if part of the profits of USCo is reallocated to Int'lCo based on a transfer pricing adjustment, then a correlative adjustment should be made to USCo pursuant to the tax treaty.[40] As a result, under the FASB rules on accounting for uncertain income tax positions, USCo would only need to evaluate its tax position for accrual of penalties and interest expense to FoRCntry.

In Illustration 9-1, if part of the profits of Int'lCo is reallocated to USCo based on a transfer pricing adjustment, then a correlative adjustment should be made to Int'lCo pursuant to the tax treaty.[41] Because the FoRCntry tax rate of ten percent is less than the U.S. tax rate of 21 percent, there will be an increased tax exposure to USCo of 11 percent.[42] As a result, under the FASB rules on accounting for uncertain income tax positions, USCo may need to prepare a FASB ASC 740–10 probability table for its increased tax exposure as well as evaluate its tax position for accrual of penalties and interest expense to the U.S.

[4] Application of FASB ASC 740–10 to Illustration 9-1

As noted above, FASB ASC 740–10 prescribes a *recognition threshold and measurement attribute* for financial statement treatment of a tax position taken or expected to be taken in a tax return. In the context of Illustration 9-1, the "tax position" in question is the financial reporting of the dramatically lower effective tax rate in 2006 versus 2005 due to the Restructuring. This could result in a permanent reduction of income taxes payable, a deferral of income taxes otherwise currently payable to future years, or a change in the expected realizability of deferred tax assets, depending upon how USCo approaches the matter.

---

[39] *U.S. International Transfer Pricing* ¶¶ 3.10 and 3.11.

[40] *See* U.S. Model Tax Treaty, art. 9(2).

[41] *Id.*

[42] *See, e.g.*, Rev. Rul. 92–75, 1992–2 C.B. 197; Rev. Rul. 80–231, 1980–2 C.B. 219.

[a] Recognition

The first step in the FASB ASC 740–10 process is that USCo must determine whether it is more-likely-than-not that this tax position will be sustained upon examination, including resolution of any related appeals or litigation processes, based on the technical merits of the position, assuming that the position will be examined by the appropriate taxing authority that has full knowledge of all relevant information. In Illustration 9-1, the pertinent tax authorities would be the United States (in the case of USCo) and foreign tax authorities in the case of the FIAs.

The advice that USCo has received is a very general statement in the transfer pricing study, namely, that "Global Audit & Co. hopes that this study will be helpful in the transfer pricing work of USCo and its affiliates."

Does this satisfy the "more-likely-than-not" threshold? Obviously not.

For convenience of discussion, let's assume that for a subsequent year, USCo obtained a "more-likely-than-not" opinion from Global Audit & Co.

[b] Measurement

The second step in the analytical process is measurement. Specifically, a tax position that meets the more-likely-than-not recognition threshold is measured to determine the amount of benefit to recognize in the financial statements. The tax position is measured at the largest amount of benefit that has a greater than 50 percent likelihood of being realized upon settlement.

For this purpose, FASB ASC 740–10 provides, in effect, a tax probability table to be used with respect to the measurement of each tax position. The table assumes, for example, that a tax position with a benefit of $100 qualifies for recognition under the FASB ASC 740–10 criteria. With respect to measurement, the enterprise has considered the amounts and probabilities of the possible estimated outcomes of the tax position as follows:

Possible Estimated Outcome	Individual Probability of Incurring (%)	Cumulative Probability of Occurring (%)
$100	5	5
80	25	30
60	25	55
50	20	75
40	10	85
20	10	95
0	5	100

Because the largest amount of benefit that is greater than 50 percent likely of being realized upon settlement or resolution (the minimum more-likely-than-not standard), the enterprise would recognize a tax benefit of $60 in the financial statements.[43] There would be a liability for unrecognized tax benefits of $40. The enterprise should also

[43] FASB ASC 740–10–55–103; FASB ASC 740–10–55–104.

evaluate the tax position for accrual of statutory penalties as well as interest expense on the difference between the amounts reported in the financial statements and the tax position taken on the tax return.[44]

The measurement concepts of FASB ASC 740–10, including the probability table, are nicely illuminated by considering Illustration 9-1. Under the original opinion from Global Audit & Co., which would not allow the tax position to meet the more-likely-than-not recognition threshold, USCo would not recognize any financial statement benefit related to the tax position.[45]

Under the subsequent year opinion, the more-likely-than-not recognition threshold is met. This simply gets the matter across the FASB ASC 740–10 threshold, so that a measurement can be undertaken. This measurement process must consider the amounts and probabilities of the outcomes that could be realized upon settlement using the facts, circumstances, and information available at the reporting date. This is the purpose of the probability table to be completed by management of USCO (the enterprise) with respect to the tax position (the benefit of the Int'lCo structure in year 1). Assume that this analysis produces the following results (assuming that "more-likely-than-not" means greater than 50 percent):

Possible Estimated Outcome	Individual Probability of Incurring (%)	Cumulative Probability of Occurring (%)
$591 (100%)	10	10
473 (80%)	25	35
354 (60%)	25	60

Because the largest amount of benefit from the USCo tax position that is greater than 50 percent likely of being realized upon settlement or resolution (the minimum more-likely-than-not standard), USCo would recognize a tax benefit of $354 in its financial statements. There would be a liability for unrecognized tax benefits of $237 ($591 less $354). USCo should also evaluate the tax position for accrual of statutory penalties as well as interest expense on the difference between the amounts reported in the financial statements and the tax position taken on the tax return.

[5] Transfer Pricing Opinions for FASB ASC 740–10

In short, even if the opinion of Global Audit & Co. in Illustration 9-1 meets the more-likely-than-not standard, this will not be sufficient to avoid provision in the financial statements. In the event that USCo in Illustration 9-1 would like to avoid any such provision, it appears that it would have to: (i) get an opinion stating, in essence, that 100 percent of the benefit of the tax position will be available; or (ii) obtain a ruling or other form of agreement with the IRS or other pertinent tax authority.

In this regard, the world of taxation opinions requires higher levels of certainty—at least "more-likely-than-not" or "should". Opinions using the traditional rubric of tax opinions—such as "reasonable basis," "substantial authority" and so on—will mean

[44] FASB ASC 740–10–55–112.

[45] FASB ASC 740–10–55–86.

nothing from a financial statement standpoint, regardless of whether the taxpayer is a public or private MNE.

One effect of FASB ASC 740–10 is to tighten up the opinion-writing process and to provide an even clearer incentive for MNEs to get uncertain tax positions resolved via rulings, APAs, pre-filing agreements (PFAs) or otherwise.

[6] Dealing with the Auditor

Once an opinion has been rendered, it may then be necessary to address the matter with the independent auditor who must review the matters in the context of their duties with respect to the financial statements of company.

§ 9.04 Subsequent Recognition, Derecognition and Measurement

A company's determination that an uncertain tax position either meets or fails the more likely than not recognition requirement may change as new information later becomes available. After a tax return position is reflected in a company's financial statements, management is required to reassess its FASB ASC 740–10 analysis for that position based on any new available information existing at each subsequent reporting date and re-examine whether that information causes (i) the company's previous recognized tax position to be "derecognized"[46] or re-measured, or (ii) the company's previous unrecognized tax position to be recognized and measured under FASB ASC 740–10.[47]

Thus, even though an uncertain tax position initially satisfies the FASB rules on accounting for uncertain income tax positions, and a financial statement benefit is properly recorded, as of each subsequent balance sheet date, management must reaffirm that the position continues to meet the recognition threshold and the recorded benefit is appropriate based on any new facts or circumstances. If a previously recognized position is no longer more likely than not to be sustained because of a change in facts or circumstances, the company must "derecognize" the position and eliminate any book benefit when that change in circumstance first occurs.[48] A revision to the recorded benefit of a recognized tax position might result, for example, from the issuance of an adverse legal decision, an amendment to the tax law, or the settlement by the company with the taxing authority.

Conversely, recognition of a previously unrecognized tax position occurs in the first financial reporting period in which the more-likely-than-not threshold is met for that position.[49] More specifically, if the recognition threshold is not initially satisfied, a company is permitted to recognize and measure the tax position benefit when one of the following conditions first exists:

- it is more likely than not that the position will be sustained;
- the position is "effectively settled;" or

---

[46] FASB ASC 740–10–40.

[47] FASB ASC 740–10–25–14.

[48] FASB ASC 740–10–40–2.

[49] FASB ASC 740–10–25–8. *See* Section 3.05.

- the applicable statute of limitations period to examine the tax position has expired.[50]

However, FASB ASC 740–10 precludes a company from reevaluating its FASB ASC 740–10 conclusion in subsequent reporting periods based merely on a new analysis of information that was available when the tax position was originally adopted.[51]

When FASB ASC 740–10 was first promulgated, it was not clear at what point an uncertain tax position was settled based on resolution of a tax audit, thus allowing a company to reflect the benefits of a settlement in its financial statements. For example, a question arose whether a tax position is settled for FASB ASC 740–10 purposes upon closing an audit if the statute of limitations for assessments remained open and the governmental agency had the right subsequently to reopen the audit. Also, it was uncertain whether a company could properly treat a tax issue for an unaudited year as, in essence, settled based on an actual settlement of the same issue in a different year that was audited.

FASB ASC 740–10–25–9 provides that a tax position could be effectively settled upon examination by a taxing authority, thereby permitting previously unrecognized tax benefits to be recognized for financial statement purposes. FASB ASC 740–10–25–10 states that an uncertain tax position is considered effectively settled through examination if:

- the taxing authority has completed all of its required or expected examination procedures (including appeals),
- the company does not intend to appeal or litigate the tax position, and
- it is "remote" that the taxing authority would reexamine the tax position.[52]

If a governmental agency concludes an audit for a given tax period, it is not necessary for the auditor to examine a specific tax position during the audit period for the position to be treated as effectively settled under FASB ASC 740–10–25–11. The FASB Standard clarifies, however, that closing an audit for a given year and settling all open issues does not result in effective settlement of identical or similar tax positions for periods that have not been examined.

Resolution of transfer pricing matters is a frequent element of reporting for periods subsequent to recording the tax position.[53] The net results of both the recording and resolution can be critical elements of the effective tax rate planning strategy of a MNE.

As noted, one of the requisite conditions to report a position as effectively settled is that reopening of the closed audit is remote based on the tax authority's policy regarding reopening of closed examinations. The IRS procedures for reopening an audit generally provide that the IRS will not reopen an audit absent (a) fraud, material factual

---

[50] FASB ASC 740–10–25–8.

[51] FASB ASC 740–10–25–14.

[52] FASB ASC 740–10–25–10.

[53] *See* Section 3.05[1]. *See, e.g.,* Parker, *In April 14 Companies Report Changes to Reserves from Transfer Pricing Cases,* 23 BNA Transfer Pricing Rep. 94 (May 15, 2014); Parker, *February Search for Transfer Pricing Issues in SEC Filings Reveals 60 Companies, 12 APAs,* 22 BNA Transfer Pricing Rep. 1318 (Mar. 6, 2014).

misrepresentation, or similar circumstances, (b) substantial inconsistency with an established IRS position; or (c) serious administrative omission.[54]

§ 9.05 Disclosure

FASB ASC 740–10–50–15A requires each public entity to disclose in its financial statements, at the end of each annual reporting period, a reconciliation of the total beginning and ending unrecognized tax benefits for the period.[55] Many have speculated as to whether these requirements provide the Service with a "roadmap" to a company's uncertain tax positions.[56]

The SEC, through its Form 10-K and 10-Q filings, makes public the manner in which public companies are complying with the disclosure rules.[57] Based on SEC filings made by public companies, FASB ASC 740–10 disclosures have been very general in nature. They have generally disclosed broadly described issues, such as describing transfer pricing positions without mention of the specific issue or foreign jurisdiction involved.[58]

It does not appear that the FASB ASC 740–10 disclosures to date have provided the taxing authorities with a clear roadmap.[59]

In the case of transfer pricing matters, the disclosure process is complex, reflecting the nature of FASB ASC 740–10 analyses of transfer pricing matters in general.

In the disclosure context, the question is how these analyses are to be translated into an appropriate format that meets FASB ASC 740–10 requirements without creating any more of a roadmap for tax authority evaluation than is inevitable from the FASB ASC 740–10 process.

The FASB ASC 740–10 disclosure provisions require that a public enterprise must disclose the following at the end of each annual reporting period presented,[60] which have been framed with specific regard to transfer pricing matters via brackets and italics:

1. A tabular reconciliation of the total amounts of unrecognized tax benefits at the beginning and end of the period *[relating to units of account for transfer pricing positions]*, which must include at a minimum:
    a. The gross amounts of the increases and decreases in unrecognized tax benefits as a result of *[transfer pricing]* . . . positions taken during a prior period.
    b. The gross amounts of increases and decreases in unrecognized tax benefits as a result of *[transfer pricing]* . . . positions taken during the current period.

---

[54] *See* Rev. Proc. 2005–32, 2005–32 IRB 1206.

[55] Details of the requirements appear in Chapter 3. *See* Section 3.10.

[56] *See U.S. International Transfer Pricing* ¶ 10.07[6][i][i].

[57] *See* Section 3.10[4].

[58] *See* Section 3.10[3][a]. *But see* Andrew Velarde, *Tech Giants Give First Glimpse of Altera's Financial Impact*, 95 Tax Notes Int'l 550 (Aug. 5, 2019).

[59] Studies on this issue are discussed in Chapter 3. *See* Section 3.08 and Section 3.10[3][a].

[60] *See* Section 3.08[1].

c. The amounts of decreases in the unrecognized tax benefits relating to settlements *[of transfer pricing positions]* with taxing authorities.

d. Reductions to unrecognized tax benefits as a result of a lapse of the applicable statute of limitations *[with respect to transfer pricing positions]*.

2. The total amount of unrecognized tax benefits *[with respect to transfer pricing positions]* that, if recognized, would affect the effective tax rate.

3. The total amounts of interest and penalties recognized in the statement of operations and the total amounts of interest and penalties recognized in the statement of financial position *[with respect to such transfer pricing positions]*.

4. For *[transfer pricing]* positions for which it is reasonably possible that the total amounts of unrecognized tax benefits will significantly increase or decrease within twelve months of the reporting date:

   a. The nature of the uncertainty.

   b. The nature of the event that could occur in the next twelve months that would cause the change.

   c. An estimate of the range of the reasonably possible change or a statement that an estimate of the range cannot be made.

5. A description of tax years that remain subject to examination by major tax jurisdictions [*with respect to transfer pricing positions*].

While the nature of a specific disclosure will, needless to say, depend on the specific facts, circumstances and conclusions reached with respect to the situation in question, it is possible to discern the approach to disclosure that can be expected in the future, based on how initial disclosures were made for the first effective year of FASB ASC 740–10 with respect to which any increase or decrease in unrecognized tax benefits was recorded as an adjustment to retained earnings. In the future, the adjustment will be to earnings, which increases the stakes for all concerned. A MNE that increased its liability for unrecognized tax benefits when FASB ASC 740–10 became effective and that expects to reduce a portion of its FASB ASC 740–10 liability thereafter will need to determine the amount of impact (if any) that each later annual reconciliation has on the MNE, to then be disclosed appropriately.

There is a rather extensive body of disclosures from the first effective year of FASB ASC 740–10 with respect to transfer pricing matters which may assist other taxpayers to identify the critical elements to be taken into account in making a disclosure.[61]

The FASB ASC 740–10 disclosures made in the first effective year related to the initial round of reporting with adjustments being taken in retained earnings and without current reported earnings impact.

Analysis of these disclosures is interesting. The nature of each disclosure varies, of course, with the situation in each company, given its international operations, nature of

---

[61] *See Quarterly FIN 48 Disclosures Continue to Report Transfer Pricing Uncertainties, Encompass Many Sectors,* 16 BNA Transfer Pricing Rep. 548 (Nov. 15, 2007) (which summarizes disclosures by 55 major MNEs in various industries and with a wide range of specific issues).

transfer pricing issues and examinations, Competent Authority proceedings, unit of account determinations and so on. Nonetheless, it is certainly possible to draw some general conclusions about the disclosure process. Not surprisingly, the disclosures fall into a pattern based on the nature of the items that are disclosed. In some cases, the disclosures are extremely general in nature. In others, they are specific. A summary of the issues almost universally addressed follows:

1. Determination of the appropriate unit of account. A critical issue in the FASB ASC 740–10 context generally, in the transfer pricing context, this is also a complex matter, since there will be issues in the dealings of each affiliate with each of its related parties. In some cases, the unit of account may be: (a) all transfer pricing matters (b) issues arising with affiliates located in a country with which the U.S. (or other pertinent country has a treaty); (c) affiliates that have transfer pricing documentation; (d) items (b) and (c) together; (e) matters arising with affiliates in other countries; or (f) otherwise as suits the situation in question.
2. Net increase or decrease in its tax liability for unrecognized tax benefits, and the extent to which such items would have an impact on effective tax rate. These are usually stated in gross figures, without any indication of specific issues.
3. The amount of accrued liability for penalties and interest.
4. Existence of material examinations. In a few situations, there is disclosure of the country and the amount of the potential exposure. For the most part, the disclosure is ambiguous on any details, or it is ambiguous on crucial details.
5. Posture of the MNE with respect to pending controversies, with the language typically that the reporting company will "vigorously defend" the matters in question, which are not expected to have a material adverse effect on the company's consolidated financial position.
6. Extent to which the amount of unrecognized tax benefits will significantly increase or decrease within the next 12 months, via expiration of statute of limitations, receipt of ruling or APA, resolution of controversies or otherwise.
7. Availability of offsets, such as correlative adjustments from transfer pricing controversy resolution, foreign tax credits or otherwise.

An illustration of such a disclosure, in the context of the factual situation noted in Illustration 9-1, could be roughly as follows:

> Effective [date], we adopted FIN 48 (later FASB ASC 740–10) which prescribes a more-likely-than-not threshold for financial statement recognition and measurement of a tax position taken or expected to be taken in a tax return. This interpretation also provides guidance on derecognition of income tax assets and liabilities, classification of current and deferred income tax assets and liabilities, accounting for interest and penalties associated with tax positions and income tax disclosures. The cumulative effects of applying this interpretation have been recorded as a decrease of $ ___ million to beginning retained earnings.

> As of [date], the total amount of unrecognized tax benefits was $ million, of which $ million would benefit the effective tax rate, if recognized. The total amount of unrecognized tax benefits anticipated to result in a net decrease of unrecognized tax benefits within 12 months of [date], for all open tax years, is currently estimated to be between $ ___ and $ ___ million. The net estimated decrease is primarily due to anticipated audit closures and lapses in statutes of limitations.
>
> We are currently under examination by a number of tax authorities, which have proposed adjustments to tax for issues such as transfer pricing, certain tax credits and the deductibility of certain expenses.
>
> It is reasonably possible that the total amount of unrecognized tax benefits will decrease in the range of approximately $_million to $ ___ million in the next twelve months as a result of the settlement of certain tax examinations.
>
> Tax authorities in the following jurisdictions may assert additional taxes against us based on tax years currently under examination and subsequent years that will likely be audited:
>
> - United States, [date range]
> - FoRCntry [date range]

One of the areas of anxiety of MNEs concerning this disclosure process has been the extent to which the disclosures will provide a road map for tax examiners. The format of disclosure presented above, which contains slightly more information than normal, certainly with respect to transfer pricing matters, is hardly likely, standing alone, to provide much of a roadmap in the absence of the workpapers.

The anxiety about road maps is genuine and understandable. On the other hand, the information presented above is hardly more than is readily available via perusal by international examiners of public information. Certainly a few Information Document Requests in an IRS examination could obtain far more information without coming close to FASB ASC 740–10 workpaper issues.

In any event, this fascinating process continues to evolve.

§ 9.06 SOX Section 404 Considerations (Assessment and Certification of Internal Controls)

In 2002, the U.S. Congress reacted to the financial scandals of Enron, WorldCom, Tyco et al. by enacting the Sarbanes-Oxley Act (SOX).[62] Among the impositions of SOX was the requirement in Section 404 that requires a company to establish that it has controls in place to ensure accurate financial reporting, and further requires a company's auditor to attest to the auditor's assessment of those internal controls.

SOX Section 404 requires that: (i) a company establish that it has controls in place to ensure accurate financial reporting; and (ii) its auditor attest to the effectiveness of the company's internal controls. Specifically, Section 404 provides as follows:

> Annual reports filed with the SEC must be accompanied by a statement by the management of its responsibility for creating and maintaining adequate

[62] *See* Chapter 5.

> internal controls. Management must also present its assessment of the effectiveness of those controls. In addition, the company's auditor must report on and attest to management's assessment of the company's internal controls. Such attestation shall not be the subject of a separate engagement [from the audit itself].

The legislative history of SOX highlighted the importance placed upon this financial control certification: "the auditor's assessment of the issuer's system of internal controls should be considered to be a core responsibility of the auditor and an integral part of the audit report."[63] Such a strong declaration of responsibility for the auditor not only signals the seriousness of the U.S. Congress, it may also establish a standard that will be critical in future financial scandal litigation (both for executives as well as the auditor).

The SOX Section 404 requirements raise genuinely interesting and trouble-some issues from a transfer pricing standpoint. These requirements did not become effective, for accelerated filers, until fiscal years ending after 15 November 2004.

On its face, the control issues might not seem to be so significant. After all, presumably all well-managed companies' international taxation groups at this point have assured that each company has appropriate transfer pricing policies and contemporaneous documentation requirements in all pertinent countries. These requirements have evolved over the years to the point that penalty compliance arrangements have become routine for many companies. While the Service has only recently reinvigorated its examination of such documentation,[64] it is consistently reported in surveys of international tax executives that transfer pricing is the number one issue of concern. Why? Because of compliance burdens and exposure from examination by tax authorities on all sides of a company's business and planning paradigms.

If a company has adopted appropriate transfer pricing policies and complied with contemporaneous documentation requirements, should this not mean that meeting the control requirements of SOX 404 is an *a fortiori* matter? It seems apparent that the answer is not so simple. Even at this early level of experience with the SOX Section 404 requirements, it is apparent that there are serious issues to be taken into account, including, at least, the following:

1. Are the transfer pricing policies of the MNE actually followed in the routine transactional experience of the company (so-called "Discrepancy Issues")?
2. If there are Discrepancy Issues, do they constitute material weakness?
3. Are there non-routine transactions, restructurings or other events that could independently constitute material issues?
4. If the auditor determines it appropriate to examine specific matters, how much information is it appropriate for the MNE to provide?

---

[63] *See* S. Rep. No. 107–205, 107th Cong., 2d Sess. 31 (2002).

[64] *See U.S. International Taxation: Practice & Procedure* ¶ 5.03. Taxing authorities are also burdened by the complexities of many of the new taxation measures and appear to be reflexively leaning on transfer pricing issues due to their familiarity and consistency as a source of revenue.

5. Are there attorney-client privilege issues to be addressed in such situations?
6. As we now seem to be living in an increasingly transparent world from the standpoint of provision of information on planning and tax exposure matters to tax authority examiners and auditors, how should a MNE conduct serious transfer pricing analyses in such a transparent world?

We will address each of these issues in turn.

[1] Do Discrepancy Issues Exist?

This is the initial area of focus for the auditor's SOX Section 404 control assessment. Specifically, are the transfer pricing policies of the company actually followed for book and tax purposes? For example, in Illustration 9-1, the USCo group has established transfer pricing methodologies ("TPMs") for cost sharing buy-in payments by Int'lCo, as well as various service provider arrangements between Int'lCo and the FIAs. The auditor will seek to determine that these TPMs are actually followed down through the organization. In the event that there are failures, then the auditor will seek to determine the materiality of such failure.

Experience in related contexts suggests that it should not be surprising if there are Discrepancy Issues in the financial systems of the company. For example, in the Service's APA Program the Annual Program Report each year identifies the additional adjustments that are made by the APA Program based on the taxpayer annual reports, often indicating a failure to accurately apply the TPMs agreed upon.[65]

In situations where there are Discrepancy Issues, it is often a result of: (i) the TPMs being administered by the pertinent financial personnel of the company, often in disparate divisions or geographic units, who do not fully understand details of the TPMs (and do not direct questions to the Tax Department); or (ii) the integration of financial accounting and reporting systems up, down and across a major company can have serious inter-face or other limitations; or (iii) other matters that have nothing to do with an intentional failure to follow the TPMs or game the system. Our experience in obtaining such information in connection with Service examinations, other country tax authority examinations, APA annual reports or renewals, and so on, indicates that such issues are reasonably common. It should not be surprising if the SOX auditor, indeed, discovered such Discrepancy Issues. To the extent there are such issues, they should be routine in most situations, in the sense that they can be readily addressed and resolved for financial accounting and tax purposes.

[2] Do Discrepancy Issues Constitute Material Weaknesses?

In situations where there are Discrepancy Issues, the next question is whether they indicate the presence of material weakness in the financial statements (tax reserve or otherwise). In this regard, the answer may be different depending upon the nature of the company and the country in question. For example, in the context of a U.S.-based company, the issues may be eliminated on a global consolidated basis for book purposes. The situation for a U.S.-based subsidiary consolidated group of a non-U.S.-based company may have entirely different issues (as well as existing controversy surrounding application of SOX to such companies).

---

[65] *See U.S. International Transfer Pricing* ¶ 12.02.

On the other hand, regardless of consolidation results, Discrepancy Issues could pose tax issues in the U.S. and other countries, which may need to be taken into account. These issues could, depending on the situation at hand, include at least the following: net operating losses and other tax attributes, earnings and profits, foreign tax credit determination, availability of double taxation relief under the Competent Authority provisions of pertinent treaties, taxpayer-initiated adjustments having tax impact in multiple countries, exposure to transfer pricing penalties in the U.S. or other countries, and so on.

[3] Might Other Events Independently Constitute Material Weaknesses?

The answer will, needless to say, depend upon the types of transactions undertaken by the MNE in question, the nature of positions taken for respective country tax liability, support for the positions taken, and so on.

> The type of problems that will arise in some circumstances is indicated by considering, again, Illustration 9-1. It will be recalled that USCo and Int'lCo entered into a cost sharing agreement and completely restructured the operations of the global business, with the net result that after the first two years of the post-restructured arrangement Int'lCo, a new company, had earned a significant portion of the operating income of the group (56 percent in the two years following the Restructuring). The Auditor of the USCo received transfer pricing studies for each element of the restructuring, that concluded as follows:

"Global Audit & Co. hopes that this study will be helpful in the transfer pricing work of USCo and its affiliates."

The SOX Section 404 question in this situation of Illustration 9-1 is whether the tax reserve of USCo is sufficient to cover any financial exposures with respect to the Restructuring, both in the year the Restructuring was completed and in the current year. The net result of the Restructuring was the earning of a significant part of the group operating income in the friendly tax environs of Int'lCo, as opposed to USCo or the FIAs. If the full benefit of the lower effective tax rates in FoRCntry (the location of Int'lCo) is taken in the USCo financial statements without any reserve, the auditor will have to determine whether there is an appropriate basis for this position.

When the auditor looks into the back-up for this no-reserve position, what will it find: the transfer pricing studies, which actually provide no opinion of any kind, just a compilation of information.

Let us assume, for the sake of discussion, that in the current year USCo hired a new auditor for the purpose of preparing its audit and audited financial statements ("NewAuditor"). When NewAuditor reviews the matter, it is reasonable to anticipate that it will have serious concerns about the no-reserve position. There is no other documentation, opinions or other support for the U.S. and other country tax results of the transactions relating to the Restructuring. Global Audit & Co. had advised that these transfer pricing studies were all that needed to be prepared for U.S. and pertinent other country purposes.

Assume further that when NewAuditor's transfer pricing experts examined the situation, they determine that there are significant U.S. risks for U.S. tax purposes due to the terms of cost sharing agreement and the movement of such significant intangible assets to Int'lCo for what is, in NewAuditor's determination, marginal compensation.[66] In addition, NewAuditor believes that there are significant "intangible strip issues" in each of the FIA countries.[67]

In light of such conclusions, there is likely to be a material weakness perceived by NewAuditor, which will have to be addressed before the financial statements can be issued. We will refer to this below as the "Material Weakness Analysis Project."

[4] How Much Information Is Appropriate for the Company to Provide?

The consequences of the auditor determining that there are material weaknesses arising from its SOX Section 404 review has potentially draconian consequences for a company, such as USCo in Illustration 9-1. Accordingly, it seems reasonable that the USCo tax executives would provide all support that exists with respect to the Material Weakness Analysis Project to be undertaken by NewAuditor.

Let's assume further that the General Counsel of USCo has engaged transfer pricing experts at the law firm of Honey & Jones to independently evaluate the Restructuring and determine whether it could render all appropriate opinions meeting transfer pricing penalty and related requirements in the U.S. and all other pertinent countries. Upon reviewing the situation, Honey & Jones has informally advised the General Counsel that there are material exposures in each country, including the United States, and that it could not render opinions defending the results of the Restructuring. Why? Because the Restructuring was carried out on aggressive grounds, that produced results that, in the experienced view of Honey & Jones, do not meet applicable arm's length standards. Honey & Jones has also advised that there are transfer pricing penalty exposures in the United States and certain of the FIA countries.

Should the work product of Honey & Jones be turned over to NewAuditor in connection with its SOX Section 404 review? This is an interesting question. In this regard, we note that the Oversight Board has adopted Auditing Standard No. 3 (AS 1215), which established requirements for the scope of work papers that the auditor must maintain. In addition, FASB ASC 450 clarifies that recognition of a tax return benefit must be "probable" of being sustained before being recognized in financial statements.[68] Since the term "probably" is not a customary term for tax opinion purposes, we wonder: it is the same as a "should" level of opinion but less than a "more likely than not" level of opinion? Or does it indicate some other level of opinion?

Finally, on April 9, 2003, the American Institute of Certified Public Accountants ("AICPA") amended its interpretation of auditing standard AU section 9326, Evidential Matter, as it pertains to the effect of an inability to obtain evidential matter relating to income tax accruals. The AICPA's revised interpretation, which has been included in the PCAOB's Reorganized Auditing Interpretations, states as follows:

> If the client's support for the tax accrual or matters affecting it, including tax contingencies, is based upon an opinion issued by an outside adviser with

---

[66] *See U.S. International Transfer Pricing* ¶ 5.08[10][g].

[67] *See International Transfer Pricing* ¶ 5.09.

[68] *See* Burgess J.W. Raby & William L. Raby, *Painting the Accounting Practitioner Into a Tax Practice Corner,* 2005 TNT 178–4 (Sept. 15, 2005).

> respect to a potentially material matter, the auditor should obtain access to the opinion, notwithstanding potential concerns regarding attorney-client or other forms of privilege. The audit documentation should include either the actual advice or opinions rendered by an outside adviser, or other sufficient documentation or abstracts supporting both the transactions or facts addressed as well as the analysis and conclusions reached by the client and adviser. Alternatives such as redacted or modified opinions may be considered, but must nonetheless include sufficient content to articulate and document the client's position so that the auditor can formulate his or her conclusion. Similarly, it may be possible to accept a client's analysis summarizing an outside adviser's opinion, but the client's analysis must provide sufficient competent evidential matter for the auditor to formulate his or her conclusion. In addition, client representations may be obtained stating that the client has not received any advice or opinions that are contradictory to the client's support for the tax accrual.[69]

In response to the revised interpretation, there has apparently been a dramatic increase in requests for privileged materials, particularly legal opinions and litigation assessments relied upon by companies in formulating contingency reserves and for oral assessments of loss contingency ranges and other client confidences.

These queries are viewed by the American Bar Association as being at odds with the standards developed by the ABA and the AICPA thirty years ago and embodied in ABA Statement of Policy Regarding Lawyers' Response to Auditors' Requests for Information (December 1975). That policy was aimed at providing clients with appropriate advice concerning public disclosures on contingencies and providing responses to auditors in a form intended to preserve the client's ability to assert applicable privileges with respect to both communications with counsel and advice received concerning those communications. Until recently, that policy formed the basis of practice for both accountants and lawyers with respect to responses to auditors' letters.

In evaluating these types of requirements, it will also be appropriate to consider the updated requirements of Circular 230, addressing the ethical obligations of practitioners, including lawyers and accountants, before the U.S. Treasury.

It seems likely that the appropriate means of handling the situation relating to the Material Weakness Analysis Project is for USCo to use other professional advisors, such as Honey & Jones, to address the situation in a spirit that will produce a result that does meet an arm's length, or other applicable, standard in a process that be cooperative and collegial as opposed to a contentious squabble between NewAuditor, USCo and Honey & Jones.

[5] Are There Attorney-Client Privilege Issues to Be Addressed?

It is certainly possible that the nature of the situation may raise questions as to whether the attorney-client privilege that may attach to material turned over to the

[69] AI 28: Evidential Matter Relating to Income Tax Accruals: Auditing Interpretations (AU section 9326, Evidential Matter: Auditing Interpretations of Section 326, paragraph 2.22). *See also* https://pcaobus.org/oversight/standards/archived-standards/pre-reorganized-auditing-standards-interpretations/details/AU9326.

auditor has been waived.[70] For example, in Illustration 9-1, NewAuditor is undertaking its Material Weakness Analysis Project. Should USCo provide its attorney's work product, whatever it may be, to NewAuditor, this may waive the attorney-client privilege with respect to that work product and may provide a through audit trail for the Service and other country tax authority examiners.

[6] Given Increasing Transparency, How Can a Company Undertake Serious Transfer Pricing Planning?

There are, indeed, many elements of an increasingly transparent world, from the standpoint of tax authority information relating to a company, within which international transfer pricing and overall planning must be undertaken. The list of transparency imperatives includes, among other things

- SOX,
- declarations by the Oversight Board and the FASB,
- transfer pricing penalties and documentation requirements in the U.S. and 90-plus other countries,
- likely weakening of attorney-client privilege (discussed below),
- transparency of information exchange agreements between developed countries and low-tax jurisdictions,
- anti-tax shelter and other anti-abuse initiatives of the Service and other tax authorities, and
- militancy by the OECD and other organizations (such as the European Union) to police what are perceived as harmful tax practices.

In view of the many transparency elements now extant and applicable to transfer pricing and international taxation practice, our suggestion is generally that transfer pricing planning should be undertaken on as global a basis as possible, with appropriate units (business lines or otherwise). Furthermore, companies such as USCo in Illustration 9-1 should consider undertaking their planning assuming that the results will be reviewed by the Service and many other country tax authorities. This is an important assumption, because, once it is made, the company will: (i) evaluate a transaction on the basis of how defensible it is in the pertinent countries; and (ii) document the transaction with one eye on such future examinations, as well as the now-customary penalty provisions (transfer pricing and other penalties). The net result of the planning should be to produce appropriate tax reserve information, which can be reviewed by the auditor in the SOX Section 404 context.

Once such a process has been undertaken, it seems appropriate for the company to consider obtaining tax authority confirmation of the tax matters in question, even if confirmation is obtained for only one tax authority (say the Service). This could be via binding rulings, APAs or other arrangements in specific countries.[71]

---

[70] *See* Chapter 8.

[71] *See* Section 9.11[1].

§ 9.07 Circular 230 and Transfer Pricing Opinions

The regulations under Section 6662(e) and (h) provide an exclusion to the transfer pricing penalty for reasonable documentation.[72] In colloquial expression, it is common to refer to the transfer pricing documentation provided by outside advisors (lawyers, accountants, economic consulting firms, or otherwise) as involving an "opinion."

The SOX requirements discussed above impose strict requirements on the internal financial controls that a company must have in place to assure conformity of policy to practice. In the transfer pricing context, a failure of a company's internal controls that creates a material exposure for financial accounting purposes could cause the auditor to fail to issue its opinion, which would itself have a material impact upon the company and its officers.

The U.S. Treasury maintains its own ethical requirements for practice before itself and the Service which are set out in the so-called Circular 230 issued by the Treasury,[73] which were materially revised in 2014.

The new standards provide that a practitioner "may give written advice (including by means of electronic communication) concerning one or more Federal tax matters" if such advice meets the following requirements. It must:

1. Be based on reasonable factual and legal assumptions (including assumptions as to future events);
2. Reasonably consider all relevant facts and circumstances that the practitioner knows or reasonably should know;
3. Reasonable efforts are made to identify and ascertain the facts relevant to written advice on each Federal tax matter;
4. Not rely upon representations, statements, findings, or agreements (including projections, financial forecasts, or appraisals) of the taxpayer or any other person if reliance on them would be unreasonable;
5. Relate applicable law and authorities to facts;[74] and
6. Does not take into account the possibility that a tax return will not be audited or that a matter will not be raised on audit.

In evaluating whether these requirements are met, the Service will apply a "reasonable practitioner standard," considering all facts and circumstances, including, but not limited to, the scope of the engagement and the type and specificity of the advice sought by the client.[75] Where the advice will be used by a person other than the practitioner (or a member of the practitioner's firm) in promoting, marketing, or recommending an arrangement a significant purpose of which is the avoidance or evasion of any tax, the

[72] *See U.S. International Transfer Pricing* ¶ 10.04.

[73] Section 822 of the American Jobs Creation Act of 2004, P.L. 108–357, added 31 USC § 330(d), which grants the U.S. Treasury Department the authority to impose standards for written advice relating to a matter that is identified as having a potential for Federal tax avoidance or evasion, and authorizes the Service to censure and impose monetary penalties on an advisor who violates any provision of Circular 230.

[74] While Circular 230 does not impose a specific requirement to include in the written advice itself any particular piece of information or analysis, the preamble notes encouragement to practitioners to describe all relevant facts, law, analysis, and assumptions in appropriate circumstances. In essence, whether such analysis is actually included in the advice, it would at least need to be reflected in file memoranda of the practitioner.

[75] Circular 230 § 10.37(c)(1).

standard will give emphasis to the additional risk caused by the practitioner's lack of knowledge of the particular circumstances of the target of the advice.[76]

[1] Transfer Pricing Opinions and Circular 230—Potential Sanctions and Costs

Shortly after release of the 2004 version of Circular 230, Treasury officials were quoted as saying that it is "unlikely that transfer pricing documentation would be a covered transaction."[77] This seems over-reaching, or, more likely, reflects a lack of understanding of the significance of the issues addressed in transfer pricing opinions, in general, and "transfer pricing documentation," in particular. In any event, in the context of the 2014 revision of Circular 230 it is apparent that its requirements will define due diligence in this area in the future.

For example, let's consider the situation in Illustration 9-1. USCo and Int'lCo entered a cost sharing agreement and completely restructured the operations of the global business, with the net result that after the first two years of the post-restructured arrangement Int'lCo, a new company, had earned a significant portion of the operating income of the group (56 percent in the two years following the restructuring). The Auditor of the USCo provided transfer pricing studies for each element of the restructuring, concluding as follows:

> "Global Audit & Co. hopes that this study will be helpful in the transfer pricing work of USCo and its affiliates."

We noted above that such an "opinion" would almost certainly pose serious problems from a SOX Section 404 standpoint (see Section 9.06 above). How would it fare under the Circular 230 requirements?

There are three essential U.S. transfer pricing issues in this context. The first is that the opinion is plainly "advice" subject to the 2014 version of Circular 230. Second is whether the requirements noted above are satisfied. The study in Illustration 11.1 appears to provide no opinion of any kind. It merely provides some economic data along with a declaration of hope that it will be helpful in the transfer pricing of USCo and its affiliates.

It seems apparent that such an approach would, at least, not meet the requirements of relating applicable law and authorities to facts (item number 5, above).

The third issue concerns the status of the auditor's study conclusion for purposes of the reasonable documentation exclusion from the transfer pricing penalty—the subject addressed by the Treasury officials quoted above. Would this study provide reasonable documentation? In this regard, it is appropriate to consider the actual requirements of the transfer pricing penalty with respect to the nature of the conduct that will satisfy the exclusion. Treas. Reg. § 1.6662–6(d)(2)(iii) provides the essential requirement of the documentation:

> The documentation . . . establish[es] that the taxpayer *reasonably concluded* that, given available data and the applicable pricing methods, the method (and

[76] Circular 230 § 10.37(c)(2).

[77] *See Official Says Transfer Pricing Documentation Unlikely Circular 230 Covered Opinion,* Daily Tax Rep., at J-1 (July 6, 2005).

its application of that method) provided the most accurate measure of an arm's length result under the best method rule. . . . (emphasis supplied)[78]

Does the study of Global Audit & Co. meet this standard, assuming it is the "documentation" for USCo transfer pricing penalty purposes? Since the study, frankly, seems to be simply a compilation of data, without an analysis of the various alternative of means of evaluating the cost sharing and related transactions and expresses no conclusion, there seems to be little basis for having any confidence that it would be viewed as providing a basis for USCo to have *reasonably concluded* that it had chosen, and applied, the most accurate measure of arm's length results.

Similarly, it seems doubtful that the study could be viewed to meet the due diligence requirements of Circular 230.[79] In this regard, it may be appropriate in many circumstances involving potentially material issues—such as the issues in Illustration 9-1—to view the Circular 230 guidelines as a definition of the steps that should be taken by practitioners to be in a position to reasonably *conclude* that arm's length methods have been chosen and applied.

Furthermore, it seems likely that the Service Examination Teams will utilize Circular 230 standards as a further guideline for what must be included in an opinion that can reasonably be relied upon. Interestingly in this regard, the Circular 230 due diligence requirements when applied in the cost sharing context are quite similar, for example, to the Large and Mid-Sized Business (LMSB) cost sharing examination checklist released in 2005.[80]

The regulations under Sections 6662(e) and (h) certainly do not refer to the Circular 230 standards. However, this would seem unnecessary, since Circular 230 applies to all persons practicing before the Service.

A critical element about transfer pricing documentation in this context is that the documentation should address the material transfer pricing issues that are pertinent for the tax return in question. As noted, the penalty regulations require documentation that the method selected "and its application" meet the pertinent reasonableness standard. For example, in Illustration 9-1, the contemporaneous documentation for USCo, for U.S. transfer pricing reasonable documentation exclusion purposes, should address the current year cost sharing buy-in payments, the sale of tangible goods, provision of inbound or outbound services and so on. These can be seriously material issues from a tax, or tax provision standpoint—especially in light of the apparent shift of income to Int'lCo.

In short, the Circular 230 requirements impose upon practitioners essentially the same ethical standards with respect to rendering written tax advice as SOX Section 404 imposes on multi-national entities for purposes of determining, and controlling, material tax exposures.

---

[78] Treas. Reg. § 1.6662–6(d)(2)(iii).

[79] The potential treatment of an opinion such as the one discussed in text is reflected in the Tax Court opinion in *Canal Corp. v. Commissioner*, 135 T.C. 199 (2010), in which the court rejected an auditing firm tax opinion for purposes of penalty protection because the opinion appeared to have been purchased for a fixed fee without any apparent technical analysis being undertaken (the opinion in question was also a draft). It also seems apparent that the Circular 230 standards were not followed in preparing the opinion.

[80] *See Checklist for Cost Sharing Arrangements,* Daily Tax Rep., at L-10 (Aug. 8, 2005). In 2011, the IRS updated its operational division to focus on large company and international matters; accordingly, the Large and Medium Size Business unit was reorganized as the Large Business and International ("LB&I") unit.

Will these requirements change the means of rendering transfer pricing advice? Based on our experience, transfer pricing advice often seems to be essentially in the format of the study in Illustration 9-1. This is certainly not universally the case. It seems that these issues are often framed in terms of the cost of preparing such advice. Frankly speaking, preparation of opinions for transfer pricing advice or documentation, like other tax opinions, by responsible professional practitioners should involve all of the steps of due diligence set out in Circular 230, as well as the reasonable documentation exclusion. Such due diligence should also have produced an opinion that would pass muster under SOX Section 404.

Accordingly, a cynical person might respond to a suggestion that the cost of preparing advice or opinions that meet all of the requirements, SOX Section 404, Circular 230 and so on, is greater than the cost incurred to provide some existing form of advice, such as the study in Illustration 9-1, by noting that such prior advice probably would not have met the reasonable documentation standard of the transfer pricing penalty to start with, much less the standards of SOX Section 404 or Circular 230.

Our experience is that these incremental requirements have not caused a material increase in the cost of preparing an outside opinion for transfer pricing purposes, as such an opinion should involve all of the steps of factual and legal due diligence required by SOX Section 404 and Circular 230.

§ 9.08 Arm's Length Price Compared to "Fair Value"

International Financial Reporting Standards (IFRS) allows all stakeholders in a company to receive comparable financial information. The IFRS accounting standards have been created to give a fair view of the value of a company. Intercompany transactions do not create any value for the company as a whole. Rather, they shift value between one part of a company and another part of the same company, hence there is no income recognition on a consolidated basis. The treatment of intercompany transactions is not defined in IFRS.

"Fair value" is defined in IFRS 13 as "the amount for which an asset could be exchanged, or a liability settled, between knowledgeable, willing parties in an arm's length transaction." IFRS 13 (effective for annual periods beginning on or after January 1, 2013), adopts a slightly modified definition: "fair value is the price that would be received to sell an asset or paid to transfer a liability in an orderly transaction between market participants at the measurement date (i.e., an exit price)."

Intercompany transactions are critical elements of the global operations of multinational companies. Transfer pricing is also critical for determining the effective tax rate of the group.[81] The arm's-length principle of transfer pricing defines value based on analysis of pricing in comparable transactions between two or more unrelated parties dealing at arm's length. In contrast to financial accounting, for income tax purposes, the fact that an inter-company transaction has not led to a realization of income from non-group sources is of limited relevance.

Due to the material profits (or losses) potentially triggered from inter-company transactions, transfer pricing may have a material impact on the tax positions of both companies and countries. In both areas, it is important to consider whether the arm's

[81] *See* Section 9.04.

length standard used for transfer pricing is consistent with the accounting principles under IFRS.

From an initial view, it may seem that the arm's length and fair value are similar, as both focus on the price that would be agreed to between independent parties. Closer examination reveals that this is certainly not the case. The following table provides a detailed comparison of the arm's length principle and fair value:

Comparison of Arm's Length Principle and Fair Value

	Arm's Length Principle	Fair Value
Controlled Transaction	Recognized as Actually Structured	Recognized as Actually Structured
Reference Transaction	Independence requirement Comparability requirement –Actual object –Actual transaction –Actual participants –Actual market	Independence requirement Comparability requirement –Actual object –Hypothetical transaction –Hypothetical participants –Hypothetical market
Valuation	Dual perspective Aggregation of multiple transactions, broad commercial criterion Arm's length range Best method rule Profit maximization Motive immaterial	One-sided perspective Aggregation of multiple transactions, narrow technical criterion Highest and best use principle Best method rule Profit maximization Motive immaterial
End Result	Subjective, entity-specific value	Objective, market-based value

In other words, "arm's length" and "fair" value provide distinct valuation standards that diverge in significant respects. The arm's length value requires a subjective, entity-specific valuation, whereas fair value requires an objective, market-based valuation. Accordingly, valuations performed under the two standards will not necessarily match, as the standards have different objectives. The aim of the arm's length principle is to prevent income shifting, tax base erosion, and double taxation, while the fair value concept is intended to inform readers of financial statements about the fair value of the booked assets and liabilities.

A major difference is that the arm's length principle is always applied to actual transactions, whereas fair value is often used in the absence of an actual transaction that may dictate the outline of the reference transaction.[82]

§ 9.09 Transparency, Transfer Pricing, and the Examination Process

[1] Background

The analyses under the FASB rules on accounting for uncertain income tax positions, like the results of the auditor's review of SOX section 404, will certainly provide the Service with an interesting roadmap for conducting examinations in the future, obviously facilitating the examination process. In 2006, senior IRS officials indicated that there would be a "revolution" in large corporate audits with new reporting and filing requirements, faster cycle times, and more disclosure.[83] This revolution coincided with the change in how significant tax issues are being examined by financial accounting auditors, often on a real-time basis, arising from the SOX. This has been highlighted by the requirements of FASB ASC 740–10 for disclosing uncertain tax positions.

These examination and reporting initiatives impact how companies prepare for IRS examinations, as they directly impact the information that will be available for the tax authorities to review. Because of SOX and FASB ASC 740–10, there is an increased emphasis on identifying and disclosing areas of financial risk arising from tax positions. As such, auditors must review and evaluate more information related to such tax positions. This review often extends to opinion materials and other work product that jeopardizes the ability to subsequently assert that such materials are privileged.

The IRS has long recognized that tax workpapers utilized in connection with the audit of financial statements can serve as a useful tool for IRS examining agents, but the IRS has voluntarily exercised restraint in requesting such workpapers.[84] The IRS has also extended this policy of restraint to FASB ASC 740–10 workpapers. However, the IRS has periodically reviewed its policy of restraint on requesting such workpapers.[85]

An additional element of transparency relates to the evolution of Schedule M-3, which requires corporations with $10 million or more in assets to make expanded disclosure of book-tax accounting matters. Schedule M-3 is designed to improve the IRS's ability to evaluate compliance risk quickly; identify emerging issues and trends; select its workload (based on risk); and reduce the time it takes to complete an examination.[86] Thus, Schedule M-3 is intended to expand the roadmap for IRS examination teams to find critical issues, all supported, of course, by potentially significant penalties.

---

[82] For a detailed explanation of the relationship of fair value, arm's-length value, and other value determinations in the transfer pricing context, *see U.S. International Transfer Pricing* ¶ 5.09.

[83] *See Korb Predicts "Revolution" in Audits of Biggest Corporate Taxpayers,* BNA Daily Tax Rep., at G-1 (Jan. 25, 2006); and *Korb Discusses "Coming Revolution" in Large Corporate Exams,* Tax Analysts Doc. No. 2006–1408 (Jan. 24, 2006).

[84] *See* Section 3.08[2].

[85] *Id.*

[86] *See Korb Discusses "Coming Revolution" in Large Corporate Exams,* Tax Analysts Doc. No. 2006–1408 (Jan. 24, 2006).

SOX, FASB ASC 740–10 and related IRS initiatives have created an increasingly transparent environment vis-á-vis the provision of information on planning and tax exposure matters to auditors and, subsequently, tax authority examiners. By the time the IRS commences the examination of a corporation, the auditor will have conducted its own extensive examination, as required by SOX and FASB ASC 740–10. This will need to be taken into account by MNEs in preparing support for its tax positions and the inevitable examination of such positions.

In essence, the evolution[87] in the handling of large corporate audits is being fueled by SOX and FASB ASC 740–10.[88] In addition, the evolution of Schedule M-3 and the implementation of electronic tax return filing are also allowing the IRS to quickly identify examination issues.[89]

[2] IRS Request for FASB ASC 740–10 Materials

In any event, one of the issues that will inevitably arise is whether the Service will seek the FASB ASC 740–10 materials in future examinations. Service officials are routinely quoted as indicating that they are discussing internally whether the Service will exercise restraint on demands for FASB ASC 740–10 materials, similar to the longstanding policy on tax accrual workpapers, as noted above. The "restraint" policy of the IRS is based on considerations of sound tax administration, as opposed to the case law (which may provide privilege under certain circumstances).

The coldly practical advice is that the documentation should be prepared assuming that it may be requested by the IRS, and foreign tax authorities. After all, there may be little protection for such information, except in unusual situations.

Interestingly, Service officials plainly reflect ambivalence on this issue. Needless to say, there is a built-in conflict between the understandable desire of tax administrators for taxpayer self-evaluation data and respect for the privacy of internal deliberations.

Specifically, a senior LMSB official has indicated that it might inquire about FASB ASC 740–10 analysis more often than has been the past practice, including re-examination of previously examined years in special circumstances. While Service policy has long been to not conduct second exams, and they are rare, the official speculated that the transparency in FASB ASC 740–10 disclosures could cause an increase in second examinations when they are appropriate because the required special circumstances for reopening an exam may be signaled in published financial statements.

Similarly, with respect to the Service's traditional policy of restraint in requesting tax accrual workpapers, the official clarified that while FASB ASC 740–10 is designed to communicate more transparency about tax risks to financial statement readers, the

---

[87] *See Korb Predicts "Revolution" in Audits of Biggest Corporate Taxpayers,* BNA Daily Tax Rep., at G-1 (Jan. 25, 2006); *Korb Discusses "Coming Revolution" in Large Corporate Exams,* Tax Analyst Doc. No. 2006–1408 (Jan. 24, 2006).

[88] *See Cost of Certainty Is Transparency, IRS Says,* Tax Analysts Doc. No. 2007–9509 (April 13, 2007); *Korb Discusses "Coming Revolution" in Large Corporate Exams,* Tax Analyst Doc. No. 2006–1408 (Jan. 24, 2006).

[89] *See Cost of Certainty Is Transparency, IRS Says,* Tax Analysts Doc. No. 2007–9509 (April 13, 2007).

IRS has always used public information to more efficiently manage its compliance enforcement activities.[90]

In this regard, it is interesting that the U.S. Competent Authority advises that the Service does not contemplate disclosing such information to foreign officials, and if there is such disclosure it will be only after careful consideration.[91]

Finally, we note that in this new world MNEs seem increasingly to disclose the presence of APAs on transfer pricing issues, which should eliminate the FASB ASC 740–10 process for covered transactions.

§ 9.10 Base Erosion and Profit Shifting

Following prominent media reports, and internal tax authority analyses, the G-8 and G-20 countries made the political decision in 2012 that the effective tax rate planning strategies of some MNEs inappropriately denuded the tax base of countries. Accordingly, the G-8 and G-20 directed the OECD to undertake to develop recommendations to address "Base Erosion and Profit Shifting" ("BEPS").[92] This BEPS project includes transfer pricing, compliance, treaty mechanisms, and so on. The work was intended to address so-called double non-taxation (otherwise known as homeless income). A cynic could have noted at the time that the project appeared to be a re-tooling of other work by the OECD over the years, though it is certainly a high-profile project.[93] There will be inevitable evolutions in the current OECD/UN model income tax treaties, which date in their present form to the immediate post-World War I period of the 1920s, as well as information sharing, simultaneous examinations, and transfer pricing methodologies.

The BEPS project was divided between fifteen Action Plans to address tax planning strategies perceived to have been developed to exploit gaps or mismatches in tax rules allowing income to be earned in locations where tax rates are low or non-existent.[94] With respect to transfer pricing, the initial broad commitment of countries was to implement so-called country-by-country reporting, which will entail, in essence, a EU-style master file with separate country-by-country files,[95] as discussed below.[96] The U.S. has adopted its own template in final regulations, also discussed below.[97]

The Action Plans were finalized in late 2015.[98] The substantive and procedural principles presently evolving will inevitably provide further fuel for conflict between countries over which country has the right to tax income of business. As such disputes arise, business is typically in the posture of a stakeholder (it is the taxpayer) and it is

---

[90] *See* Daily Tax Rep., at G-1 (Feb. 9, 2007). In 2011, the IRS updated its operational division to focus on large company and international matters; accordingly, the Large and Medium Size Business unit was reorganized as the Large Business and International ("LB&I") unit.

[91] *See* Daily Tax Rep., at I-1 (Feb. 7, 2007).

[92] *See* Section 1.01[1][b].

[93] *See* Cym Lowell, Mark Thomas & Mark Levey, *International Transfer Pricing OECD Guidelines* ¶ 2.06[4] [*OECD Transfer Pricing*]. A "BEPS 2.0" project is currently underway and could have even more far-reaching ramifications for MNEs. *See OECD Transfer Pricing* ¶ 9.08[1][b][iv].

[94] A complete discussion of BEPS and related matters is set out in *OECD Transfer Pricing* ¶ 2.08.

[95] Country-by-country reporting is addressed in detail in *OECD Transfer Pricing* ¶ 10.02[3].

[96] *See* Section 9.10[2].

[97] *See* Section 9.10[2].

[98] A detailed explanation of all BEPS Actions is set out in *OECD Transfer Pricing* ¶ 2.08[2][c].

the business that is at risk of double taxation if the controversy is not successfully resolved by all parties.

BEPS is one on a lengthy list of evolutions underway in the world of international taxation that will inevitably expand the range of transfer pricing and related controversies. In the present context, the critical element is to take into account the checklists of items to be addressed whenever there is evolution in the functions and risks of a global business.

[1] Checklist of BEPS Considerations

Below is a checklist of potential issues to be addressed by MNEs forming their working groups to address BEPS considerations:[99]

[ ] Overview:

- Treaty and transfer pricing historical evolution
- Effective tax rate (ETR) planning for MNEs
- BEPS focus of G-20 and OECD, emblematic of specific country considerations
- Role of UN, IMF, World Bank, NGOs, and others

[ ] Designing MNE planning models:

- Developing Country-by-country (CbC) global template:[100] master file, country files, CbC file
- Anticipating tax base defense models for countries
- Addressing BEPS action items pertinent on a subject or country adaptation basis
- Tax consequences of evolutions from existing effective tax rate (ETR) models: (1) technical analysis format; (2) attorney-client protection; (3) business restructuring implications of evolutions (the full range of supply-chain rationalization matters, including exit taxes in countries like Germany, India, and China); (4) issues with specific countries
- Economic modeling of potential evolutionary scenarios: (1) software design, (2) integration of modeling with ETR plan, (3) Evaluation and review process
- Review of tax treaty elements (BEPS or otherwise): (1) residence (and fiscally transparent entities); (2) transfer pricing (Associated Enterprises article (Article 9) from the U.S. Model Income Tax Convention); (3) business profits; (4) permanent establishments (PEs);[101] (5) electronic, digital, cloud, and future commerce (not really

[99] A similar check list for the specific country-by-country reporting provisions is set out at Section 9.10[2][d]. For a detailed post-BEPS planning discussion, with checklists, *see OECD Transfer Pricing* Chapter 13A.

[100] *See* Section 9.10[2].

[101] *See* Section 9.12.

categorized separately for treaty purposes; including transfer pricing, withholding taxes depending on characterization, value added tax (VAT), and so on); (6) mutual agreement (Competent Authority); (7) dispute resolution; (8) update modeling as appropriate

- State and local tax considerations
- VAT, customs, or other considerations
- Anticipation of financial auditor review: (1) SOX, (2) FIN 48 (FASB ASC 740–10), (3) prior reserve positions, (4) other as appropriate
- Update modeling
- Internal management review and approval
- Implementation: (1) legal agreement updating, (2) documentation updating, (3) adaptation of any APAs or other tax authority agreements, (4) specific country ruling updating, (5) preparation for auditor review

[2] Country-by-Country Reporting

In the BEPS process, Action 13 of the OECD/G20 Base Erosion and Profit Shifting Project resulted in the development of standardized transfer pricing (TP) documentation requirements for OECD member and other countries.[102] The specific documents include a master file, local file, and country-by-country report (the CbC report; all three reports are collectively referred to as the CbC package). These documents may need to be filed, in whole or in part, with local tax authorities for taxable periods commencing in 2016. In the case of the U.S., final regulations adopting the U.S. version of CbC were finalized in June 2016.[103] The U.S. requirements are generally consistent with the OECD framework.

The critical consequence of the CbC process, as well as many of the other BEPS reports, will be an inevitably heightened focus of tax authorities on testing locally reported TP results on a profit split basis. We have found that such a focus does not, itself, provide any basis for concern.[104] Many MNEs have developed means of testing reported TP results on such a basis (e.g., as elements of APA or Competent Authority processes), although typically these are not included in local documentation.

We note below the requirements of the CbC package and suggest a process for MNEs to develop compliance and planning processes, including an agenda/checklist.[105] In view of the fact that TP documentation in all countries can be expected to evolve to the BEPS

[102] *See* OECD/G20 Base Erosion and Profit Shifting Project, *Action 13: Guidance on the Implementation of Transfer Pricing Documentation and Country-by-Country Reporting*, 2015.

[103] *See* Internal Revenue Bulletin 2016–29, TD 9773, *Country-by-Country Reporting* (June 20, 2016); Form 8975; Rev. Proc. 2017–23. *See also* https://www.irs.gov/businesses/international-businesses/country-by-country-reporting-guidance.

[104] *See* Furuya, Ueda, Fujita, and Lowell, *International Tax Disputes: A Ray of Hope from Japanese Experience*, International Transfer Pricing Journal, 15 IBFD (Vol. 23, No. 1, Jan./Feb. 2016).

[105] For a detailed explanation of the CbC process, *see OECD Transfer Pricing* ¶ 10.02[2].

CbC standards, we suggest that it is at least appropriate for all MNEs to commence preparing their documentation in the CbC format for 2016.[106]

[a] OECD Guidelines

The final report on Action 13 was issued on October 5, 2015 (OECD 2015 Guidance).[107] It replaces the 2010 TP Guideline (Chapter V) provisions dealing with documentation, and also replaces the Annexes providing guidance for preparation of CbC packages. It also includes a CbC implementation package (designed for use by countries to enact supporting legislation). All of this is discussed below.

The OECD 2015 Guidance recommends that the first CbC packages be filed for MNE fiscal years beginning on or after January 1, 2016,[108] in the case of groups with revenue more than 750 million Euros.[109]

1. In General

The OECD 2015 Guidance provide guidelines for tax administrations to take into account in developing rules and/or procedures on documentation to be obtained from MNEs in connection with a TP inquiry or risk assessment. It also provides guidance for pinpointing documentation that would be most helpful in identifying transactions that satisfy arm's-length principles and hence in facilitating tax examinations and resolution of TP issues.[110] The hope is that clear and widely adopted documentation rules can reduce compliance costs that could otherwise arise in a TP dispute.[111]

The documentation guidelines have three principal objectives (the Objectives):[112]

- Ensure that taxpayers give appropriate consideration to TP requirements in establishing prices and other conditions for transactions between their controlled entities, and reporting the income derived from such transactions in respective tax returns;
- Provide tax administrations with the information necessary to conduct an informed TP risk assessment; and
- Provide tax administrations with useful information to employ in conducting an appropriately thorough audit of the TP practices of entities subject to tax in their jurisdiction, although it may be necessary to supplement the documentation with additional information as the audit progresses.

---

106 A form of CbC documentation is set out in Cym Lowell & Mark Martin, *U.S. International Taxation: Agreements, Checklists & Commentary* Form 2.11 (Thomson Reuters).

107 *See* OECD/G20 Base Erosion and Profit Shifting Project, "Action 13: Guidance on the Implementation of Transfer Pricing Documentation and Country-by-Country Reporting," 2015.

108 *See* OECD 2015 Guidance, ¶ 50. However, it is recognized that some countries may need time to pursue domestic legislative authorization processes.

109 *See* OECD 2015 Guidance ¶ 52. The Guidelines advise that this threshold will exclude approximately 85 to 90 percent of MNE groups from the CbC package filing requirement, although the remaining filers will account for about 90 percent of global corporate revenues. *See* ¶ 53 of the Guidance.

110 *See* OECD 2015 Guidance, ¶ 1.

111 *Id.* at ¶ 4.

112 *Id.* at ¶ 5.

2. Three Tiers of Documentation

In order to achieve the Objectives, countries should adopt a standardized approach to TP documentation, consisting of (i) a master file containing standardized information relevant for all MNE group members; (ii) a local file referring specifically to material transactions of the local taxpayer; and (iii) a CbC report containing certain information relating to the global allocation of the MNE's income and taxes paid together with certain indicators of the location of economic activity within the MNE group.[113]

This will provide tax administrations with relevant and reliable information to perform an appropriate risk assessment. It will also provide MNEs with "a means and an incentive to meaningfully consider and describe their compliance with the arm's length principle in material transactions."[114]

a. Master File

The master file should provide a high-level overview of the MNE group business, including the nature of its global business operations, its overall TP policies, and its global allocation of income and economic activity in order to assist tax administrations in evaluating the presence of significant TP risk. The master file should include lists of important agreements, intangibles, and transactions. Taxpayers should use prudent business judgment to determine the appropriate level of detail for the information supplied. The requirements could be satisfied by specific cross-references to other existing documents.[115]

The master file information is to provide a "blueprint" of the MNE group.[116] The information can be grouped in five categories: (i) organizational structure, (ii) description of business, (iii) intangibles, (iv) intercompany financial activities, and (v) the MNE's financial and tax positions.[117]

b. Local File

The local file provides more detailed information regarding the material intercompany transactions relating to the local affiliate and associated enterprises in other countries. Such information includes relevant financial data for those specific transactions, a comparability analysis, and selection of the most appropriate TP method.[118]

c. CbC Report

The purpose of the CbC report is to provide data for high-level TP risk assessment by pertinent tax authorities. The report should set out global income among the controlled group members, taxes paid, and certain indicators of economic activity among the pertinent countries in which the MNE group operates. There should also be a listing of all group members, including the jurisdiction of incorporation (if different from jurisdiction of residence) and nature of its main business activities.[119]

---

[113] *Id.* at ¶ 16.

[114] *Id.* at ¶ 17.

[115] *Id.* at ¶ 18.

[116] The information can be presented on a line-of-business basis. *See* 2015 Guidelines ¶ 20.

[117] *Id.* at ¶ 19.

[118] *Id.* at ¶ 22.

[119] *Id.* at ¶ 24. Information to be included in the CbC report is set out in Annex III to Chapter V of the Guidelines. It is suggested that the CbC report include all countries in which the MNE group has "an entity

The CbC Report format requires a breadth of information that is far beyond what has traditionally been included in TP documentation in most countries. The OECD report includes two model tables that reflect the nature of the CbC data being sought, which are on pages 29 and 30 of the OECD 2015 Guidance.

3. Use of the CbC Packages

According to the OECD 2015 Guidance, the countries participating in the BEPS Project agree that use of the CbC packages will be subject to the following conditions: (i) confidentiality,[120] consistency in application of requirements to domestic and foreign groups,[121] appropriate utilization in conducting examinations and making proposed adjustments,[122] and a framework for the exchange of the CbC packages consistent with the implementation package developed in the BEPS process.[123]

[b] Implementation and Planning

The CbC elements of the OECD 2015 Guidance reflect agreement of participants in the BEPS process. These elements will need to be approved in appropriate manners on an individual country basis[124] unless a multilateral agreement can be developed on a broad basis (which is well underway). All such processes are subject to a variety of limitations and hurdles.[125] Accordingly, the future of the formal CbC requirements remains to be determined.

On the other hand, the CbC requirements reflect a broad consensus among countries with respect to the information necessary for conducting TP examinations of MNE groups when there are material cross-border flows and the potential for concern about the overall TP strategy of the group. The CbC data will facilitate risk assessment and tax base protection as it provides a global data template that will enable tax authorities to see the overall picture and proceed with examinations and adjustments accordingly.[126]

It will be appropriate for many MNEs immediately to consider integrating the CbC elements into their standard TP documentation processes. The master and local reports may not pose serious hurdles for many groups, but the CbC report may pose serious obstacles for those groups that have not undertaken system or profit split formats for prior examination, APA, or Competent Authority purposes (due to systems limitations, accounting differences, false assumptions, country-specific issues, and so on). Our

---

resident for tax purposes, regardless of the size of business operations in that tax jurisdiction." *See* OECD 2015 Guidance, ¶ 34.

[120] *Id.* at ¶ 57. The confidentiality protections should be equivalent to the protections under the Multilateral Convention on Mutual Administrative Assistance in Tax Matters, a Tax Information Exchange Agreement, or a tax treaty meeting the internationally agreed standard of information upon request.

[121] *Id.* at ¶ 58.

[122] *Id.* at ¶ 59.

[123] *Id.* at ¶¶ 60–61 and Annex IV.

[124] *Id.* at ¶¶ 48–50.

[125] For example, the CbC Guidelines address a variety of largely administrative matters that will depend on local or treaty law evolution.

[126] Such processes have also been a fact of life for at least 25 years in a variety of countries. The nature of the examinations and the means of resolving any disputes have evolved over this period. For example, the Japan-U.S. relationship, which has evolved from a contentious process to a smooth and harmonious competent authority relationship (as exists in other contexts as well).

experience is that there are inevitably surprises when a robust system profit analysis is undertaken.

In some cases, it may be appropriate to commence the process of preparing the CbC package but not include it in formal documentation until applicable local law or the multilateral agreement processes are clarified.

[c] Concerns About CbC

Not surprisingly, the dramatic evolution in TP documentation reflected in the CbC proposals has generated a variety of concerns, including the following:

- Do these evolutions apply to our group?
- Will compliance with the CbC requirements pose risks to our global effective tax rate strategy?
- When should we commence the CbC process (most MNE groups began in 2016 or 2017)?
- If our home country does not require a CbC package, does this exempt us from the CbC requirements in countries in which we do business?[127]
- Does it matter if our home country has a treaty with these local countries?
- How can we maintain consistency in data reported in respective country forms?
- Will tax authorities request a broad range of such reports seeking to establish inconsistency?
- What will happen if (when?) foreign countries publish the CbC package?
- How will the CbC package data be kept confidential to the tax administration?[128]
- Will CbC data lead to expanded use of profit split or formulary apportionment methodologies in examinations or otherwise?
- Other issues will inevitably arise as the CbC process commences for each MNE given its specific situational parameters.

[d] Checklist for CbC Implementation Processes

A checklist can be helpful in evaluating potential CbC implications.

Formation of Working Group:

[ ] Compose the working group to address the matters noted below

---

[127] Under the OECD Guidelines, a foreign subsidiary of a MNE could be deemed a "constituent" or "surrogate parent" entity with a local CbC package filing obligation if the MNE's home country did not require such reporting, if reports are not shared, or if there are repeated failures to share the reports (which OECD principles would typically require local legislative or regulatory action to become binding), as discussed below.

[128] This will certainly not be possible. An additional element of the BEPS process is the automatic exchange of information among tax authorities. At the present time, a wide range of countries are entering, or modifying, the exchange of information agreements to facilitate the exchange of CbC reports. *See OECD Transfer Pricing* ¶ 12.01[6] and *U.S. International Taxation: Practice & Procedure* ¶ 9.03. There are also other information sharing regimes intended to facilitate transparency, including the U.S. and international agreements relating to the exchange of financial information.

[ ] Determine the role of attorney-client privilege if necessary

[ ] The working group could be composed of experts from the following:

- Internal departments: tax (domestic and international); transfer pricing (if separate); CFO (financial accounting); information technology; supply chain; legal
- External international tax technical advisor
- External transfer pricing advisor, including software used for documentation (there are today a variety of providers offering software solutions for CbC; some can be useful as elements of working group evolution)
- Financial auditor (as appropriate in terms of independence and related matters pertaining to auditor)

Current Global Effective Tax Rate (ETR) Planning:[129]

[ ] Refresh and confirm the building blocks of the existing ETR plan

[ ] Implementation mechanics

[ ] Structural aspects

[ ] TP building blocks:

- functional analysis
- TP performed on a one-sided basis
- integration with non-TP building blocks

[ ] Allocation of taxable income by country

[ ] Formulation of global results on a system-profit or profit-split basis (a two-sided TP basis)[130]

CbC Formulation for Global Documentation:

[ ] Complete a draft of the documentation (local, master, and CbC)

[ ] Evaluate local reports

[ ] From the standpoint of each local tax authority

[ ] From the standpoint of the home or other pertinent country tax authority

[ ] Prepare a risk assessment for each building block of the global ETR strategy

[ ] Prepare a synthesis of likely tax authority evaluations (which will be instructive in the process of re-evaluating the ETR strategy, restructure as appropriate, and prepare for controversy, as noted below)

---

[129] For a detailed discussion of effective tax rate planning, *see OECD Transfer Pricing* Chapter 13A.

[130] If the MNE has utilized profit-split methodologies for TP documentation, examination, dispute resolution, or otherwise, this experience will be invaluable in adapting to the CbC world.

Reevaluate the Global ETR Plan:

[ ] Revisit the building blocks of the ETR plan—evaluate in view of the CbC analysis above

[ ] Determine whether you need to change the building blocks

[ ] Determine whether you need to update the ETR plan

[ ] Consider restructuring options

Impact of Potential Restructuring:

[ ] Income tax

[ ] TP

[ ] Exit or restructuring taxes

[ ] Existing examinations or pending disputes

[ ] Consumption taxes

[ ] Financial accounting

[ ] Financial reporting

[ ] Other as appropriate

Preparing for Controversy:

[ ] Categorize building blocks of existing global ETR plan

[ ] Model:

- Risk of tax authority challenge (for example, where some of the building blocks are specifically mentioned in the BEPS final reports)
- Potential impact of successful challenge on global ETR
- Likelihood of successfully being able to defend a challenge
- Cost-benefit analysis of defending tax authority challenges

[ ] Decide which building blocks will be proactively amended

[ ] For those building blocks that the group decides will not be amended:

- Proactively prepare responses to possible tax authority enquiries
- Gather and organize existing data and other materials supporting group's position

[ ] For building blocks that the group will be amending, are currently under audit, or are being challenged:

- Articulate controversy positions in relation to each building block
- Consider impact of restructuring on tax authority perception of existing building blocks

Agenda for Proceeding (including tax authority outreach)

[e] Concluding Statement

In short, the evolution of CbC packages has the potential to impact significantly the effective tax rate planning of all MNEs, which will, in turn, impact the financial accounting and reporting issues addressed in this text.[131]

§ 9.11 Dealing with Transparency in Transfer Pricing Matters—a Suggested Approach

As fully discussed above, there are many elements contributing to increased transparency with respect to a MNE's international transfer pricing and overall tax planning. It is predictable that there will be ongoing debates between the various parties to these issues as to how transparent the system should or can be. One's point of view, needless to say, will depend upon the place occupied in the debate—a member of the Oversight Board, an auditor, an outside lawyer or accountant, a plaintiff's lawyer, and so on. The collegial, academic, theoretical and practical debates between all of these folks can certainly provide interesting theatre sometimes, as those seated around this particular table jockey for their respective positions. The tax executives of the MNE in question are in the middle.

The issue, then, is to find a practical solution to address these elements of transparency and to achieve the objectives that we identified in discussing Illustration 9-1:

1. Achieve the global effective tax rate objectives of the MNE;
2. Coordinate with the global cost efficiency models being implemented by the MNE;
3. Meet the transfer pricing compliance and documentation requirements in each country, including avoidance of any penalties;
4. Prepare for the inevitable transfer pricing examinations in the countries of USCo and the FIAs, where income has been reduced as it has been increased in Int'lCo as a result of the Restructuring;
5. Avoid any reallocation of income to USCo or the FIAs, which would have the effect of materially altering the effective tax rate of USCo, which has been duly taken into account in the market capitalization of USCo;
6. Satisfy the control requirements of SOX;
7. Avoid any difficulties from having utilized its auditor—Global Audit & Co.—for the various transfer pricing opinions relating to the Restructuring, which had followed a pattern that the auditor had installed with many of its clients;
8. Avoid having the auditor grossly increasing the transfer pricing documentation fees to comply with SOX or Circular 230 requirements; and
9. Not have to disclose, and maintain privilege with respect to, the analysis of the Restructuring undertaken by USCo's outside tax counsel.

---

131 *See* Section 3.08[3].

In order to achieve these objectives, our experience indicates that it may be appropriate for the company to embrace a planning and confirmation process that would have several elements that have been used for many years in many contexts, and which can certainly be adapted to achieve objectives such as those noted above.

[1] Elements of the Global Planning Process

In our experience, it has been possible for many years to patiently develop a long-term, global effective tax rate model of a company that would have the following elements:[132]

1. Develop a clear understanding of the risk and functional relationships between the related parties in each material business a unit or product line;
2. Identify an appropriate arrangement of such risks and functions that in the idiosyncratic situation of this company will:
   a. Coordinate with operational efficiency plans of the group; and
   b. Achieve the overall effective tax rate that is the target of the group.
3. Determine an incremental implementation plan to move from the current situation to the contemplated situation and consistently apply the plan;
4. Avoid utilization of "products" sold and implemented by external consultants (as in the context of Illustration 9-1);
5. Obtain confirmation of the arm's length nature of these arrangements for purposes of each critical country, which confirmation can be evolved into appropriate global transfer pricing documentation; and
6. Obtaining tax authority confirmation of the principal matters in question, even if confirmation is obtained for only one tax authority (say, the Service). This could be via binding rulings, APAs, PFAs or other arrangements in specific countries.

The net result of such a process is that transparency is welcomed, not feared.

[2] Addressing a Currently Problematic Situation

How would these elements be adapted to a situation in which there are current problems? This is, of course, the situation in Illustration 9-1. USCo and its affiliates adopted a transfer pricing arrangement that feels like a common method utilized by many companies in recent years, triggering a range of concerns in tax authorities and the OECD itself. Assume that the analysis of Honey & Jones is accurate and there are exposures to USCo and its affiliates in various countries.

Our suggestion in such a situation would be to follow the same type of approach noted above, simply taking the current situation with its extant exposures and planning forward. The steps should be essentially the same.

---

132 *See OECD Transfer Pricing* Chapter 13A.

§ 9.12 Permanent Establishment Matters

A common tax planning issue with U.S. multinational companies, as well certainly as foreign-based groups, is for an affiliate located in one foreign jurisdiction (the home country) to perform various activities in another foreign jurisdiction (the host country). If a tax return is not filed in the host country where the activities are undertaken, the applicable foreign tax authority may assert that the affiliate is subject to tax in that jurisdiction based on the argument that such activities to rise to the level of a taxable presence in the host country. Absent a treaty, the significant risk is that the income generated by the activities in the host country will be subjected to double tax. In the treaty context, the taxable presence issue is referred to as a "permanent establishment" (PE). In the current world of international taxation, these PE issues have become endemic as tax administrations seek to expand their domestic tax bases, or prevent their diminution via international tax planning.

The concept of a PE is critical to the application of many important treaty provisions.[133] For example, the existence of a PE in a contracting state is necessary for the taxation by that state of the business profits of a resident of the other state. When business is conducted in a treaty country through a PE, the state in which the PE is located may tax the enterprise on a net basis on the income that is attributable to the permanent establishment. The PE concept is relevant in determining which contracting state may tax certain gains or "other income."

The term PE is defined, for example, in Article 5 of the 2006 U.S. Model Treaty. A PE is a "fixed place of business through which the business of an enterprise is wholly or partly carried on."[134] Under this definition, the place of business must be "fixed" in the sense that a particular building or physical location is used by the enterprise for the conduct of its business. It must also be foreseeable that the enterprise's use of the building or other physical location will be more than temporary. To this general definition, the Model Treaty, like most U.S. treaties, adds a list of specific facilities that are presumptively treated as permanent establishments.[135] This list is illustrative and not exclusive.

A corporation looking to enter a foreign market frequently will conduct some aspect of its operations in that market through agents. For tax purposes, a question arises whether the activity or place of business of the agent may be attributed to the foreign principal, causing the principal to have a PE in the foreign country that would subject it to tax there. If the agent is a broker, general commission agent, or any other agent of an independent status, who is acting in the ordinary course of his or her business as an independent agent, then the activity of the agent will not result in the foreign principal having a PE.[136] There are two conditions that must be satisfied to rely on this provision: (1) the agent must be both legally and economically independent of the principal; and (2)

---

[133] *See OECD Transfer Pricing* ¶ 12.02 and *U.S. International Practice and Procedure* ¶ 9.01[2][b]). Currently, the critical PE issue relates to the principles to be formulated relating to digital commerce, which could ultimately cause material change in applicable transfer pricing and PE standards. *See OECD Transfer Pricing* ¶ 12.02[2] and *U.S. International Transfer Pricing* ¶ 9.06.

[134] U.S. Model Tax Treaty, art. 5(1).

[135] U.S. Model Tax treaty, art. 5(2).

[136] U.S. Model Tax Treaty, art. 5(6).

the agent must be acting in the ordinary course of its business in carrying out activities on behalf of the principal.

If the local agent is not an independent agent, then the activities undertaken by the agent for the foreign principal will constitute a PE of the principal if the agent has and habitually exercises in the country an authority to conclude contracts that are binding on the principal.[137] The type of contracts that the agent has authority to conclude must be those relating to the essential business operations of the principal, rather than ancillary activities. The activities of the agent must also be of a type that if exercised through a fixed place of business by the principal would constitute a PE. Thus, if the agent's activities are limited to those activities of a preparatory or auxiliary character, the agent cannot be a PE of the principal even if it has the authority to conclude contracts.[138]

The evolution of multinational business has placed increasing strain on traditional PE and transfer pricing concepts.[139] Such evolution includes electronic commerce, global financial dealing, service-provider, and related arrangements.

Correlative or Other Offsets. Frequently, the transfer pricing and PE exposure in one foreign country could lead to a correlative adjustment in a different country.[140] Assuming the tax rates are comparable, or that an analysis of the potential correlative adjustments and Competent Authority procedures indicates that there will not be double taxation, this may prevent the need for a deferred tax liability for a specific transfer pricing exposure. There may also be direct or indirect foreign tax credits or deductions available. Therefore, even in the event of a transfer pricing adjustment without relief from double taxation, there could be a mechanism for avoiding an uncertain-income-tax-position liability. Consequently, in many instances the ultimate tax exposure related to double taxation resulting from transfer pricing adjustments would be dependent on tax rate differentials and other factors, as discussed in Illustration 9-2:

ILLUSTRATION 9-2: The situation is the same as in Illustration 9-1.

> From a transfer pricing perspective, USCo sells hardware and software to FIAs, using a resale price methodology designed to produce an arm's length rate of return in each of the FIAs. For all of its open tax years, the USCo has been a profitable enterprise, earning operating margins between 12 to 16 percent. The results for the FIAs have been more variable, but overall the FIAs have earned operating margins for the same period in the range of five to nine percent.

In Illustration 9-2, the initial inquiry in the FASB ASC 740–10 context would be identifying the appropriate unit of account. As discussed above, this can be done on a country-by-country basis. From the U.S. perspective, the first question would be whether USCo's transfer pricing positions met the more-likely-than-not recognition threshold for the year in question. This may require a determination regarding whether USCo's transfer pricing documentation satisfies this criterion, as also discussed above.

137 U.S. Model Tax Treaty, art. 5(5).

138 *Id.*

139 *See U.S. International Transfer Pricing* ¶ 11.01.

140 *See* Section 9.03[2].

Assuming the recognition threshold is satisfied, the FASB ASC 740–10 measurement process must take into account the amounts and probabilities of the outcomes that could be realized upon effective settlement using the facts, circumstances, and information available at the reporting date. This is the purpose of the probability tables to be completed by the management of USCo with respect to its transfer pricing tax positions.

One approach that could be taken in the case of Illustration 9-2 is to treat the total tax benefit as the U.S. tax on the difference between the actual operating income of the FIAs and the operating income which would result from the most aggressive position that could be taken by the IRS,[141] as the IRS could assert that such income should be included in the U.S. tax base. For example, the IRS could assert that the FIAs should only be earning an overall operating margin of three percent, reflecting the IRS view that the FIAs are merely distributors for USCo. The tax on the difference between this amount and the actual operating income of the FIAs is the maximum tax benefit with respect to the transfer pricing arrangements of USCo. Essentially, the tax benefit is having no additional income allocated to the United States and having USCo's position sustained without adjustment.

Permanent Establishment. If USCo has PE exposure in the foreign jurisdiction, for example, a similar analysis would apply. However, the most aggressive position that would apply in the foreign jurisdiction would require an analysis of the portion of USCo's income that could be allocated to such potential PE.

Possible Estimated Outcome	Individual Probability of Incurring (%)	Cumulative Probability of Occurring (%)
$350,000	30	30
270,000	50	80
200,000	15	95
	5	100

The probability table would start with the benefit at the top. The probability analysis would then take into account the amounts and probabilities of the alternative outcomes that might be realized in resolving the position, considering examination, domestic appeals, litigation, Competent Authority or otherwise. Note that in the case of international tax positions involving affiliates that are entitled to the benefits of bilateral tax treaties (i.e., Competent Authority), it is necessary to evaluate both sides of the transaction. If a treaty is applicable, and its terms are met, there should be no double taxation as a result of an adjustment. But this needs to be evaluated, as the Competent Authority is a theoretical proposition in many countries, regardless of whether the other country is an experienced Competent Authority country such as the United States or other OECD Member countries. This is another reason that a country-by-country unit of account analysis is helpful.

Assuming each country where the FIAs operate is treated as a unit of account and the recognition criteria are satisfied, through an opinion, documentation or otherwise,

[141] We have used operating income in this example to simplify the analysis. The use of operating income may be appropriate in certain circumstances, although it may be appropriate to apply a more transactional analysis to determine the most aggressive position that could be asserted by the tax authority.

the measurement process would be the converse of the analysis conducted for the U.S. The total tax benefit would be the tax (calculated at the appropriate rate) associated with the difference between the actual operating results USCo and the operating income which would result from the most aggressive position that could be taken by the pertinent foreign country ("Foronia"), as the Foronia tax authority could assert that such income should be included in the Foronia tax base. In this case, the Foronia tax authority could take the position that USCo should only be earning an operating margin of seven percent on sales of Unique Products to Foronia, reflecting Foronia's belief that USCo should only earn contract manufacturing type returns on sales of Unique Products. The tax on the difference between this amount and the actual operating income of USCo on such related party transactions is the maximum tax benefit with respect to the transfer pricing of the Foronia FIA. The probability analysis would then take into account the amounts and probabilities of the alternative outcomes that might be realized in resolving the position, as was the case in analyzing the US unit of account.

The FASB ASC 740–10 issues that might arise in connection with a PE are illustrated below.

> **ILLUSTRATION 9-3:** The situation is the same as in Illustration 9-2. USCo is a U.S.-based MNE operating a worldwide manufacturing, distribution, and servicing business. USCo provides to customers (1) hardware; (2) software; and (3) installation services (which are provided with intangible property developed by USCo).
>
> In Dominia, which has a ten percent tax rate, USCo has a wholly-owned Dominia subsidiary that operates a call center (DomCo). Dominia and the United States have a treaty based on the U.S. Model Tax Treaty. DomCo has received an economic incentive from national and local government units, as well as a preferential income tax regime. DomCo and USCo have entered a "Call Center Services Agreement," pursuant to which DomCo will provide call center services for USCo and its international affiliates. The transfer pricing methodology under the agreement is the cost-plus method with a mark-up of 5 percent.
>
> The Call Center Services Agreement provides that USCo will provide to DomCo all intangible property (software and written) relating to the conduct of the call center operations with respect to USCo products and procedures, as well as all customer referrals. In other words, DomCo will not be responsible for developing the DomCo protocols or seeking customers. Rather, its function is limited to operating the call center pursuant to the policies and procedures, and to the customers, provided by USCo.
>
> USCo has considered whether DomCo's activities constitute a dependent agent PE of USCo in Dominia, such that an allocation of a portion of the profits or losses of USCo should be made for Dominia tax purposes. USCo has determined that DomCo is a not a dependent agent PE of USCo and therefore USCo does not have a PE in Dominia.

PE issues in foreign countries pose interesting issues under FASB ASC 740–10, due to the aggressive stance of some tax authorities with respect to PE and PE allocation matters. Even though the US company may believe its tax position is certain (e.g., there is no PE in the foreign country), the foreign taxing authority may assert a novel and/or radical PE theory. Even though, viewed objectively, there should be no chance of double taxation, under FASB ASC 740–10 the actual prospects for success must be taken into account.

The first step in the FASB ASC 740–10 process is that USCo must determine whether it is more likely than not that its tax position of no PE in Dominia will be sustained upon examination, including resolution of any related appeals or litigation processes, based on the technical merits of the position, assuming that the position will be examined by the appropriate taxing authority that has full knowledge of all relevant information.[142] In Illustration 9-3, the pertinent tax authorities would be the United States (in the case of USCo) and the Dominia tax authority in the case of DomCo. Assume that USCo has determined that it is more likely than not that it does not have a PE in Dominia, and therefore it owes no taxes to Dominia due to the presence of a treaty between the United States and Dominia.

The second step in the FASB ASC 740–10 analytical process is measurement. Specifically, a tax position that meets the more-likely-than-not recognition threshold is measured to determine the amount of benefit to recognize in the financial statements. The tax position is measured as the largest amount of benefit that has a greater than 50 percent likelihood of being realized upon settlement.[143] In Illustration 9-3, because there is a tax treaty between the U.S. and Dominia, and the Dominia tax rate of 10 percent percent is less than the U.S. tax rate of 21 percent, there should be little possibility of double taxation. In other words, if USCo is later determined to a have a PE in Dominia and part of its income is attributed to the Dominia PE, then the taxes paid to Dominia should be credited against USCo's U.S. tax liability to eliminate any possibility of double taxation. As a result, under FASB ASC 740–10, USCo should only need to evaluate its tax position for accrual of penalties and interest expense to Dominia.

It is possible that any taxes that USCo pays to Dominia may be treated as a voluntary tax. Such a circumstance may arise, for example, if USCo does not pursue the Competent Authority process, but instead litigates and losses the PE case in Dominia. If so, then USCo may be denied a foreign tax credit. In such case, double taxation will arise and USCo will need to prepare a FASB ASC 740–10 probability table.

§ 9.13 Advance Resolution Programs

The IRS has a number of advance ruling programs (or, in effect, quasi-advance ruling programs) that allow taxpayers to resolve uncertain tax positions prior to such issues being raised by the IRS in examination.[144] Such programs include the private letter ruling (PLR) process,[145] the APA process,[146] the pre-filing agreement (PFA)

---

[142] *See* Section 3.04[2].

[143] *See* Section 3.04[3].

[144] *See U.S. International Taxation: Practice and Procedure* Chapters 10, 11, and 12; *see also* Michael Saltzman and Leslie Book, IRS Practice and Procedure ¶ 3.05 and ¶ 9.04 (Thomson Reuters) [*IRS Practice and Procedure*].

[145] *See IRS Practice and Procedure* ¶ 3.05.

[146] *See U.S. International Taxation: Practice and Procedure* Chapter 9.

program, and the compliance assurance process (CAP).[147] Other countries have similar programs.

In most cases, once the taxpayer completes a PLR, an APA, a PFA, or other advance ruling with a tax administration (an Advance Ruling), the agreement represents a binding agreement between the taxpayer and the tax administration(s). Therefore, an Advance Ruling will generally eliminate uncertainty with respect to the company's tax positions covered by such Advance Ruling. This advantage of an Advance Ruling is even more important after the promulgation of FIN 48 (FASB ASC 740–10), as an Advance Ruling will eliminate tax uncertainty.[148] A related benefit is that a company's external auditor may allow a company not to book a tax expense when a favorable ruling is likely—in other words, a "pass adjustment" to avoid booking a tax expense in one reporting period and reversing it in a subsequent reporting period. This has been achieved in a variety of situations.

As transfer pricing issues are often the most significant and prevalent tax issue faced by an MNE, APAs are a critical tool to be considered in managing tax uncertainty. Since 1991, the IRS has offered taxpayers the opportunity to reach an agreement in advance of filing a tax return on transfer pricing issues.

Procedures for obtaining, processing and administering an APA are currently found in Revenue Procedure 2015–41.[149] The APA Program has jurisdiction to resolve transfer pricing issues under Section 482 of the Code, the income tax regulations under Section 482, and relevant income tax treaties to which the United States is a party. One of the innovative features of the early APA program was the ability to resolve issues that are not, strictly speaking, transfer pricing issues but nonetheless intimately connected with the transfer pricing transactions covered by the APA. For example, it may be possible in certain situations to address U.S. trade or business/permanent establishment, expense allocation, sourcing, subpart F, or related issues as part of the APA. Such issues could be dealt with as critical assumptions, or in other appropriate manners depending on the nature of the issues and specific circumstances. In prior revenue procedures, such issues were referred to as "collateral." In Revenue Procedure 2015–41, they are referred to as interrelated issues. The ability to resolve such collateral or interrelated issues is an important element of the flexibility offered by the APA program.

An APA resolves transfer pricing issues on a prospective basis via a collaborative process between taxpayers and the IRS. A "bilateral" APA is an agreement between the IRS and a taxpayer on specified related party transactions coupled with an agreement between the United States and a treaty partner that the transfer pricing methods in such transactions are correct. Although the IRS encourages taxpayer to seek bilateral APAs, the IRS may execute an APA with a taxpayer without reaching agreement with a foreign tax authority (i.e., a "unilateral" APA). A unilateral APA binds the taxpayer and the IRS, but does not prevent foreign tax administrations from taking different positions on the appropriate transfer pricing method for a transaction. A unilateral APA may also preclude mutual agreement procedure (Competent Authority) consideration.

---

[147] Announcement 2005–87, 2005–2 CB 1144; *see* Trivedi & Elliott, *LB&I Expands, Makes Permanent CAP Real-Time Audit Program,* Tax Analyst Doc. 2011–6831 (Apr. 1, 2011). *See also* https://www.irs.gov/businesses/corporations/compliance-assurance-process.

[148] *See* Chapter 3.

[149] 2015–35 IRB 263 (Aug. 31, 2015). Revenue Procedure 2015–41 is currently in the process of being updated and revised.

For multinational enterprises, a common arrangement is to obtain a bilateral APA with an established treaty partner of the United States, such as the U.K., and a unilateral APA for all other countries. Using this approach, there is certainty with respect to the U.S.–U.K. arrangements and no potential adjustments by the IRS on arrangements with other countries. Also, if there is a proposed adjustment by another country, the U.S. negotiating position with respect to such country will be established, and the precedent of the U.S.–U.K. bilateral APA will likely be persuasive to such other country.

Because an APA resolves issues prospectively, the filing an APA request does not completely suspend any examination or other enforcement proceedings. However, in appropriate cases, a transfer pricing method agreed to in an APA may be applied to tax years prior to those covered by the APA (a so-called "rollback" of the transfer pricing method). In this context, IRS Examination has jurisdiction to determine whether the rollback will be applied. Similarly, if a rollback is requested in connection with a bilateral APA, the rollback will be handled in the Competent Authority process.[150]

While an APA can require a significant investment in time, company resources, and professional fees that may give some MNEs pause, the reality is that even the smoothest transfer pricing examination can require at least a commensurate expenditure of these items. Avoiding a transfer pricing examination in the first place is a huge advantage of an APA as such examinations are inherently costly and can be difficult to resolve on a basis that is acceptable to the MNE—not to mention that large penalties are increasingly being threatened in the United States and asserted in other countries even though documentation is present.

If the issue cannot be resolved at the examination level, taking a significant transfer pricing case through an administrative Appeals or litigation process is a risky matter in the United States, and often an un-winnable situation in foreign countries. Litigation is typically extremely time-consuming and expensive, and it is increasingly public. In our experience, it would typically cost many times more to take a complicated transfer pricing case from examination through the litigation process than it would to negotiate an APA. When one considers that litigation is a one-off solution that may only address two or three years of adjustments, the cost-benefit scale tips heavily in favor of an APA, particularly when APA renewals can generally be easily obtained so long as the underlying facts of the covered transactions remain materially the same. Moreover, in bilateral matters, the failure to achieve a 100 percent victory in litigation will likely create double taxation. Also, most APAs are completed in three to four years (and even more quickly in the case of renewals of bilateral matters and for unilateral APAs), whereas the examination process followed by administrative appeals and litigation can easily take three to ten years or longer. As litigation cannot definitively protect the taxpayer from double taxation in a bilateral case, it should generally be considered as a last resort for a transfer pricing controversy. Instead, to achieve such protection from double taxation, the taxpayer must pursue a resolution in Competent Authority, where such treaty assistance is available.

[150] The Competent Authority process is a treaty-based tax dispute resolution procedure, which allows taxpayers to resolve tax controversies arising from cross-border business and financial arrangements. The Competent Authority procedures are set forth in Revenue Procedure 2015–40, 2015–35 IRB 236 (Aug. 31, 2015).

Many considerations go into whether an APA should be pursued, and ample due diligence as to the likely outcomes (and to gather the facts necessary to support such outcomes) must be undertaken. The MNE must also be prepared to engage in a transparent and collaborative process with the taxing administration(s)—something that some MNEs find easier to contemplate than others. (Of course, in fairness to such reticent taxpayers, some taxing administrations are certainly easier to deal with than others.) The MNE may also desire a total victory that only litigation can provide; in such a case, an APA may not be the right choice as they generally do not produce such a resolution. Nevertheless, we have often found that cases may be resolved through an APA in a manner that is more favorable than the taxpayer originally envisioned and also is acceptable to the tax administration(s).

Table of Cases

Table of Statutes

Table of Regulations

Table of Rules

Index

References are to Pages